Proceedings

8th Euromicro Workshop on Parallel and Distributed Processing

EURO-PDP 2000

Proceedings

8th Euromicro Workshop on Parallel and Distributed Processing

January 19 – 21, 2000

Rhodos, Greece

IEEE COMPUTER SOCIETY

Los Alamitos, California

Washington • Brussels • Tokyo

IEEE Computer Society Order Number PR00500
ISBN 0-7695-0500-7
ISBN 0-7695-0501-5 (case)
ISBN 0-7695-0502-3 (microfiche)
ISSN Number 1066-6192

Additional copies may be ordered from:

IEEE Computer Society
Customer Service Center
10662 Los Vaqueros Circle
P.O. Box 3014
Los Alamitos, CA 90720-1314
Tel: + 1-714-821-8380
Fax: + 1-714-821-4641
E-mail: cs.books@computer.org

IEEE Service Center
445 Hoes Lane
P.O. Box 1331
Piscataway, NJ 08855-1331
Tel: + 1-732-981-0060
Fax: + 1-732-981-9667
mis.custserv@computer.org

IEEE Computer Society
Asia/Pacific Office
Watanabe Bldg., 1-4-2
Minami-Aoyama
Minato-ku, Tokyo 107-0062
JAPAN
Tel: + 81-3-3408-3118
Fax: + 81-3-3408-3553
tokyo.ofc@computer.org

Editorial production by Bob Werner
Cover art production by Joe Daigle/Studio Productions
Printed in the United States of America by The Printing House

IEEE
COMPUTER
SOCIETY

Table of Contents

8th Euromicro Workshop on Parallel and Distributed Processing — EURO-PDP 2000

Program Chair's Message ... xi

Program and Organizing Committee ... xii

Reviewers ... xiii

Keynote Address
Chair: P. Kacsuk

The Grid: Where We've Been, Where We Are, and Where We're Going
C. Kesselmann

Session 1: Distributed and I/O Systems
Chair: C. Kesselmann

ViMPIOS, a "Truly" Portable MPI-IO Implementation ... 4
K. Stockinger, E. Schikuta

Specification-driven Monitoring of TCP/IP ... 10
R. Hofmann, F. Lemmen

A QoS Performance Measure Framework for Distributed Heterogeneous Networks ... 18
J. Kim, D. Hensgen, T. Kidd, H. Siegel, D. St. John, C. Irvine, T. Levin, N. Porter, V. Prasanna, R. Freund

Communication Support for Distributed Multimedia Components ... 28
A. Saleh, G. Justo

Short Presentations 1: Applications
Chair: V. Getov

Parallelizing a Global Optimization Method in a Distributed-Memory Environment ... 38
Z. Szczerbiński, S. Kowalik

Fast Parallel Algorithms for 3D Reconstruction of Angiographic Images ... 43
R. Rivas, M. Ibáñez

A Robust Multigrid Solver on Parallel Computers ... 48
R. Montero, M. Prieto, I. Llorente, F. Tirado

Finite Element Computations on Cluster of PC's and Workstations ... 56
A. Spyropoulos, J. Palyvos, A. Boudouvis

Distributed and Randomized Enumeration ... 62
P. Dembiński

Heterogeneous Client-Server Architecture for a Virtual Meeting Environment ... 67
M. Masoodian, S. Luz

Session 2: Web Based Computing I
Chair: K. Klöckner

Introduction 76

Replicating the R in URL 77
C. Allison, M. Bramley, J. Serrano, D. McKechan

Security Mechanisms for the MAP Agent System 84
A. Puliafito, O. Tomarchio

Implementation of an Annotation Service on the WWW — Virtual Notes 92
S. Koch, G. Schneider

Session 3: Performance Analysis
Chair: P. Cremonesi

Introduction 100

FINESSE: A Prototype Feedback-guided Performance Enhancement System 101
N. Mukherjee, G. Riley, J. Gurd

Performance and Transparency of Message Passing and DSM Services within the GENESIS Operating System for Managing Parallelism on COWs 110
A. Goscinski, M. Hobbs, J. Silcock

Predictability of Bulk Synchronous Programs using MPI 118
A. Zavanella, A. Milazzo

Session 4: Web Based Computing II
Chair: K. Klöckner

Gypsy: A Component-based Mobile Agent System 126
M. Jazayeri, W. Lugmayr

Towards Reference Architectures for Distributed Groupware Applications 135
K. Sandkuhl, B. Messer

ENTER: The Personalisation and Contextualisation of 3-Dimensional Worlds 142
T. Guinan, G. O'Hare, N. Doikov

Session 5: Computer Architectures
Chair: F. Tirado

Tailoring a Self-Distributing Architecture to a Cluster Computer Environment 150
R. Moore, B. Klauer, K. Waldschmidt

A Framework for Process Migration in Software DSM Environments 158
I. Zoraja, A. Bode, V. Sunderam

PQE_HPF — A Library for Exploiting the Capabilities of a PQE-1 Heterogeneous Parallel Architecture 166
R. Baraglia, R. Ferrini, D. Laforenza, P. Palmerini, R. Perego

A Case Study of Trace-driven Simulation for Analyzing Interconnection Networks: cc-NUMAs with ILP Processors 174
V. Puente, J. Prellezo, C. Izu, J. Gregorio, R. Beivide

Short Presentations 2: Models and Languages
Chair: Yanis Ioannidis

Scalability Analysis of Parallel Systems with Multiple Components of Work 182
E. Tambouris, P. Van Santen

Specification for Reactive Bulk-Synchronous Programming 190
Y. Chen

First Steps in Metacomputing with Amica 197
T. Fink, S. Kindermann

Parallel Programming with Data Driven Model 205
V. Tran, L. Hluchý, G. Nguyen

A Knowledge-based Approach to Scheduling Jobs in Metacomputer Environment 212
J. Nabrzyski, J. Pukacki, M. Stroiński

Consistency Requirements of Distributed Shared Memory for Lamport's Bakery Algorithm for Mutual Exclusion 220
J. Brzeziński, D. Wawrzyniak

Session 6: Scheduling and Mapping
Chair: A. Antola

Introduction 228

Modelling Message-Passing Programs for Static Mapping 229
C. Roig, A. Ripoll, M. Senar, F. Guirado, E. Luque

Optimal Scheduling for UET-UCT Grids into Fixed Number of Processors 237
T. Andronikos, N. Koziris, G. Papakonstantinou, P. Tsanakas

Groups in Bulk Synchronous Parallel Computing 244
J. Gonzalez, C. Leon, F. Piccoli, M. Printista, J. Roda, C. Rodriguez, F. Sande

Panel on Metacomputing
Moderator: F. Vajda
Panelists: P. Kacsuk, K. Klöckner, C. Kesselman, V. Getov, D. Laforenza

Panel Statement 254

Keynote Address
Chair: Y. Cotronis

Databases and the Web: An Oxymoron or a Pleonasm?
Y. Ioannidis

Session 7: Languages and Compilers
Chair: F. Vajda

Introduction 258

CELLAR: A High Level Cellular Programming Language with Regions 259
G. Folino, G. Spezzano

Generating Structured Program Instances with a High Degree of Locality 267
C. Leopold

Asynchronous Progressive Irregular Prefix Operation in HPF2 275
F. Brégier, M-C. Counilh, J. Roman

The Parallel Cellular Programming Model 283
P-C. Cagnard

Short Presentations 3: Distributed Shared Memory Systems
Chair: D. Laforenza

Introduction 292

Self-Similarity in SPLASH-2 Workloads on Shared Memory Multiprocessors Systems 293
J. Sahuquillo, T. Nachiondo, J. Cano, J. Gil, A. Pont

Two Management Approaches of the Split Data Cache in Multiprocessor Systems 301
J. Sahuquillo, A. Pont

Evaluation of a Virtual Shared Memory Machine by the Compilation of Data Parallel Loops 309
F. Baiardi, D. Guerri, P. Mori, L. Ricci

Using Agent Wills to Provide Fault-Tolerance in Distributed Shared Memory Systems 317
A. Rowstron

The TIRAN Approach to Reusing Software Implemented Fault Tolerance 325
O. Botti, V. De Florio, G. Deconinck, R. Lauwereins, F. Cassinari, S. Donatelli, A. Bobbio, A. Klein, H. Kufner, E. Thurner, E. Verhulst

Combining Low-Latency Communication Protocols with Multithreading for High Performance DSM Systems on Clusters 333
L. Lefèvre, O. Reymann

Session 8: Applications
Chair: S. Smith

Introduction 342

Parallel Simulated Annealing for the Set-Partitioning Problem 343
Z. Czech

2-D Wavelet Packet Decomposition on Multicomputers 351
M. Feil, A. Uhl

Towards Efficient BSP Implementations of BSR Programs for Some Computational Geometry Problems 357
C. Cérin

Short Presentations 4: Tools and Environments

Chair: J. Bass

Introduction 366

A Performance Simulation Technique for Distributed Programs: Application to an SOR Iterative Solver 368
R. Aversa, B. Di Martino, N. Mazzocca, U. Villano

Monitoring and Debugging Message Passing Applications with MPVisualizer 376
A. Cláudio, J. Cunha, M. Carmo

Pipelining-based Tradeoffs for Hardware/Software Codesign of Multimedia Systems 383
J. Castellano, D. Sánchez, O. Cazorla, Á. Suárez

PVM Application-Level Tuning over ATM 391
C. Di Napoli, M. Giordano, M. Furnari, F. Vitobello

Reusable Message Passing Components 398
J. Cotronis

An Efficient Algorithm for the Physical Mapping of Clustered Task Graphs onto Multiprocessor Architectures 406
N. Koziris, M. Romesis, P. Tsanakas, G. Papakonstantinou

Index of Authors 415

Program Chair's Message

Welcome to the 8th Euromicro Workshop on Parallel and Distributed Processing! This series of workshops started in 1993 and since that time it has been successfully organized every year. It has been recognized as one of the main events in Europe in the field of parallel and distributed systems, where Europe's leading experts can meet regularly and exchange ideas. Thanks to the enthusiastic European community that regularly visits these workshops a high standard of quality is maintained year by year. Besides the Europeans a significant number of participants arrive from all over the world each year, ensuring an even wider perspective of discussions during the workshops.

I am lucky to have managed to attend all the workshops of the series so far and could follow its history, so I felt especially honored when I was elected as program chair for the 8th Workshop. It is always a great challenge to organize a big event like Euromicro PDP but it seemed to be even more challenging this year with all the dramatic changes we have witnessed in the field of parallel and distributed computing. These are: the crisis of supercomputers on the one hand, and, the rise of cluster computing and metacomputing on the other, along with the rapid spread of web computing.

As the program chair I felt that we have to react to these new emerging directions of parallel and distributed systems and I tried to shift the character of the technical program from the traditional fields towards these new areas. Accordingly, I invited Carl Kesselmann to give a keynote talk generally on metacomputing, and specifically on the Globus system he developed with Ian Foster and other researchers in the United States. The other invited speaker is Yannis Ioannidis, who will address distributed database issues. I also invited Ferenc Vajda to organise a panel discussion on metacomputing. In addition to these arrangements Konrad Klöckner has successfully organized two special sessions on web computing, demonstrating the increasing interest of the community in the new research fields.

Finally, the workshop includes two keynote sessions, eight sessions of full paper presentations and four sessions of short presentations. These sessions cover the following topics: distributed and I/O systems, performance analysis, web computing, computer architectures, distributed shared-memory systems, computational models, languages and compilers, tools and environments, and applications of parallel and distributed systems. Additionally, the program includes a panel on metacomputing with panelists Carl Kesselmann, Domenico Laforenza, Konrad Klöckner, Peter Kacsuk and Vladimir Getov.

The increasing number of submitted papers shows the growing research potential of the community. I believe shifting the character of the workshop towards the new fields mentioned above will result in more and more submitted papers in the coming years. The review procedure also demonstrates the strength of the Euromicro PDP community. A board of highly qualified reviewers, including many prestigious experts both from Europe and the US participated in the review process that resulted in the selection of 27 papers for full presentation and 24 papers for short presentation.

At this point I would like to thank all the authors for their work; without them there would be no workshop. I would like to acknowledge the excellent work of the reviewers and the members of the Program Committee. I am particularly grateful to Konrad Klöckner, who organized special sessions on web computing. I owe special thanks to Yiannis Cotronis for his outstanding organization at the local level. I am particularly indebted to Chiquita Snippe-Marlisa, Euromicro's administrative manager, who guided us in the organization of the workshop. Thanks are due to Deborah Plummer and Bob Werner at the IEEE Computer Society for their great efforts in preparing the proceedings.

Above all, I would like to thank my deputy program chair Norbert Podhorszki, and his deputy Zsolt Nemeth, for their outstanding job in organizing the review process, maintaining the Euromicro PDP web page and supporting me in the construction of the workshop proceedings.

The Euromicro PDP workshop has a nice tradition: it is not just work, it is also fun. This time participants can enjoy both the pleasant environment of the picturesque island of Rhodes and the workshop's high-quality technical program, as well as the friendly atmosphere of a close community of computer professionals. I hope that you will find both the technical program and the workshop venue stimulating and you will spend a very pleasant and useful time in Rhodes.

Enjoy the workshop!

Peter Kacsuk, Program Chair
MTA SZTAKI
Hungarian Academy of Sciences

Program and Organizing Committee

Program Chair
Peter Kacsuk
Norbert Podhorszki (Deputy)

Organizing Chair
Yiannis Cotronis

Local Organizing Committee
Yiannis Cotronis
Konstantinos Tsolakidis
Zacharias Tsiatsoulis

Program Committee

A. Antola (I)
J. Bass (UK)
P. Bonnin (F)
L. Brunie (F)
B. Chapman (UK)
A. Clematis (I)
Y. Cotronis (GR)
P. Cremonesi (I)
J. Cunha (P)
M. Dal Cin (DE)
B. Di Martino (I)
J. Dongarra (USA)
T. Fahringer (A)
M. Gerndt (DE)
A. Gonzalez (E)
A.M. Goscinski (AU)
W. Gentzsch (DE)
G. Haring (A)
L. Hluchy (SK)
W. Hohl (D)
A. Hurson (USA)
G. Ianello (I)
K. Klöckner (DE)
H. Kosch (A)
R. Lins (BR)
I. LLorente (E)
E. Luque (E)
P. Milligan (UK)
J. Myoupo (F)
E. Pissaloux (F)
P. Sage (UK)
N. Scarabottolo (I)
J. Silva (P)
S. Smith (UK)
V. Sunderam (USA)
F. Tirado (E)
R. Trobec (SLO)
M. Tudruj (PL)
A. Tyrrell (UK)
M. Vajtersic (SK)
M. Valero (E)
S. Winter (UK)
R. Wismueller (DE)
F. Zambonelli (I)
E. Zapata (E)

Reviewers

Franck Amiot
Anna Antola
Rafael Asenjo
Jan Astalos
Gerardo Bandera
Julian Bass
Rudolf Berrendorf
Patrick Bonnin
Lionel Brunie
Ramon Canal
Roberto Canonico
Barbara Chapman
Andrea Clematis
Domenico Cotroneo
Yannis Cotronis
Paolo Cremonesi
Jose Lorenzo Cruz
Jose C. Cunha
Mario Dal Cin
Beniamino Di Martino
Miroslav Dobrucky
Patricio Domingues
Jack Dongarra
David Espadas-Valladares
Thomas Fahringer
Martin Furer
Wolfgang Gentzsch
Michael Gerndt
Vladimir Getov
Antonio Gonzalez
Andrzej M. Goscinski
Tom Gross
Karl-Erwin Grosspietsch
Gopal Gupta
Robinson Guy
Guenter Haring
Ladislav Hluchy
Wolfgang Hohl
Ali R. Hurson
Giulio Iannello
Peter Kacsuk
Konrad Klöckner
Harald Kosch
Rafael Lins
Ignacio M. LLorente
Juan Lopez
Thomas Ludwig
Peter Luksch
Emilio Luque
Pedro Marcuello
Pedro Medeiros
Panagiotis Melas
John Metzner
Peter Milligan
Bernd Mohr
Carlos Molina
Jean-Frederic Myoupo
Vijaykrishnan Narayanan
Zsolt Nemeth
Friedrich Neumann
Luis Pinuel
Edwige Pissaloux
Oscar Plata
Norbert Podhorszki
Manuel Prieto
David Pritchard
Larry Pritchet
Goncalo Quadros
Luis Felipe Romero
Gudula Ruenger
Paul Sage
Jesus Sanchez
Nello Scarabottolo
Volkmar Sieh
Joao Gabriel Silva
Stephen L. Smith
Vaidy Sunderam
Francisco Tirado
D. Viet Tran
Roman Trobec
Oliver Tschche
Jordi Tubella
Marek Tudruj
Andy Tyrrell
Ferenc Vajda
Marian Vajtersic
Mateo Valero
Narayanan Vijaykrishna
Stephen Winter
Roland Wismueller
Wouter van Oortmerssen
Franco Zambonelli
Emilio Zapata
Mario Zenha-Rela

Keynote Address

Session 1:
Distributed and I/O Systems

ViMPIOS, a "Truly" Portable MPI-IO Implementation*

Kurt Stockinger[†] Erich Schikuta
Institute for Applied Computer Science and Information Systems
Department of Data Engineering, University of Vienna,
Rathausstr. 19/4, A-1010 Vienna, Austria

Abstract

We present ViMPIOS, a novel MPI-IO implementation based on ViPIOS, the Vienna Parallel Input Output System. ViMPIOS inherits the defining characteristics of ViPIOS, which makes it a client-server based system focusing on cluster architectures. ViMPIOS stands out from all other MPI-IO implementations by its "truly" portable design, which allows not only applications to be transferred between parallel architectures easily but also to keep their original performance characteristics on the new platform as far as possible. This is kept by the "smart" AI-Blackboard module of ViPIOS, which is responsible for an appropriate data layout. Specifically in this paper we concentrate on the algorithm, which maps MPI-IO data structures on respective ViPIOS structures, and thus allows to exploit the ViPIOS properties.

1 Introduction

Over the last few years the so-called I/O bottleneck turned out as the limiting factor in high-performance computing. Thus, the performance of parallel systems in many applications is not bound by the number of available processors, but by the bandwidth of the I/O subsystem.

Therefore, the research on parallel I/O turned out as an important area in the high performance computing community. An important contribution is MPI-IO as part of the MPI standard [4], which supports parallel file accesses analogously to the MPI message passing scheme. It allows non-contiguous file access patterns and supports collective disk operations.

At the moment four different MPI-IO implementations are available, namely ROMIO [7], PMPIO [2], HPSS [9], and MPI-IO/PIOFS - an MPI-IO implementation by IBM Watson Research Center specific for the IBM SP-2 architecture. The predominant MPI-IO implementation is ROMIO, which is also part of the MPICH library, the most popular MPI implementation available for the widest spectrum of parallel systems.

One design goal of MPI (and thus MPI-IO) was portability, which allows the migration of applications from one parallel architecture to another one without loosing performance drastically.

However, hereby all available systems show a general weakness. They can not guarantee portability in the sense of the above definition. They allow the migration of applications between different systems, but they can not guarantee the same performance characteristics.

In this paper we present a novel MPI-IO implementation, ViMPIOS (Vienna Message Passing/Parallel Input Output System), a portable, client-server based MPI-IO implementation, which tackles the performance problem of the other systems.

ViMPIOS is based on ViPIOS, a fully-fledged parallel I/O runtime system, which was developed focusing on cluster systems. The main characteristics of ViPIOS are its client-server architecture and a smart AI-based file distribution mechanism.

The data layout defined by the programmer is used to determine a near optimal disk layout specific for the underlying I/O architecture. This allows high performance not only in dynamically changing environments, e.g. multi-user and multi-tasking situations typical in cluster systems, but also for the migration of applications form one system to another one with different I/O architectures.

This is reached in ViPIOS by the introduction of an additional data abstraction layer. Conventionally, the physical data layout on disk is defined by the programmer via MPI-IO data types in the application program. It can be further be tuned by specific hints, which try to catch the underlying storage architecture. However, if the application is used on other hardware systems, it has to be ported by hand specifically according to differentiating I/O characteristics (as number of disks, disk characteristics, bus systems etc.) to guarantee the expected performance. Here ViMPIOS shows its strength. Due to the smart AI layout apparatus in ViPIOS the adaptation to a new system is auto-

*This work was carried out as part of the research project "Language, Compiler, and Advanced Data Structure Support for Parallel I/O Operations" supported by the Austrian Science Foundation (FWF Grant P11006-MAT)

†Now at IT Division, CERN, CH-1211 Geneva 23, Switzerland. Email: Kurt.Stockinger@cern.ch

matically done within the ViPIOS system transparently to the programmer. Therefore, ViMPIOS, the MPI-IO layer of ViPIOS, is the only MPI-IO implementation so far, which provides full portability from one system to another one without additional program modifications and without loosing performance.

In the first section of the paper the data abstraction mechanism in ViPIOS is described. The second section gives with a short description of MPI-IO and what is actually realized in ViMPIOS. Later, we elaborate on the design and implementation of advanced derived data types which are typical for MPI-IO. We point out the extended flexibility of ViPIOS' internal representation of derived data types and we also show that besides standard MPI-IO data types even more complex description mechanism are possible. To round up our approach we describe a typical MPI-IO application program and justify our approach by a performance comparison to ROMIO.

2 Data Abstraction in ViPIOS

Generally speaking the distribution of the data in focus of a high-performance application is defined by the high level distribution mechanism of high-performance languages or library interfaces. In most systems which support parallel I/O this data distribution information builds the basis for the physical data layout on disks. This approach is found in all conventional MPI-IO implementations, which endangers the portability principle of high-performance applications. Such an effect is a result to different I/O characteristics, e.g. number and performance of disks, bus systems and many more, and situations with changing and/or not foreseeable system characteristics, e.g. the workload in multitasking environments (typical for cluster systems). In order to characterize parallel I/O efficiently, we define two issues which have to be addressed: *static fit property* and *dynamic fit property*.

The static fit property tries to adapt the disk access profile of the program according to the necessities of the problem specification or the programming paradigm (typical for the Single Program Multiple Data, SPMD, approach). This can be realized by the programmer or the compiler. For example, a specific distribution of the application is resembled by a corresponding data layout on disks.

The dynamic fit property denotes the adaptability of the I/O runtime subsystem to application's and/or environment's characteristics which could not be foreseen at compile time.

We see a solution to this problem in a combination of both approaches, which is a dedicated, smart, concurrent executing runtime system, gathering all available information on the application process both during compilation and the runtime execution.

This approach is followed in ViPIOS, the Vienna Parallel Input Output System [5]. ViPIOS is an I/O runtime system which provides efficient access to files by optimizing the data layout on the disks and allowing parallel read/write operations. ViPIOS is based on a database approach and supports high-performance languages (as HPF [3] and the VFC [1]), standard interfaces (MPI-IO) and persistent files.

The data administration approach in ViPIOS follows the data independence principle known from database systems. Adapted to a parallel I/O system this means that the physical data layout on disk is not defined by the problem layout of the application program and the programmer's hints alone.

Central part of ViPIOS is the *Fragmenter* [8], a kernel module, which is responsible for data layout decisions and the dynamic data distribution of the application data to the disks. The Fragmenter is based on a mathematical cost model describing the performance profile of the underlying hardware and applies a combination of an A^* algorithm and AI-blackboard system, which represents the expert knowledge about data layout, message passing, and buffer management. This approach is comparable to the way followed in the Panda system [6], where also unconventional methods (neural networks, fuzzy sets, genetic algorithms and simulated annealing) are applied to deal with uncertain or incomplete knowledge.

Generally two independent data layers exist, the logical or *Problem* layer and the physical or *Disk layer*:

- The Problem layer defines the problem specific data distribution among the cooperating parallel processes.
- The Data layer defines the physical data distribution among the available disks.

These layers are separated conceptually from each other. The distribution of the data in the problem layer is defined by the programmer by the data distribution mechanism of his programming paradigm, e.g. the data type structures in MPI. The Fragmenter defines the data layout in the Data Layer and provides also the mapping functions between the Problem and the Data Layer. The concept is depicted in Fig. 1.

This functionality in ViPIOS allows a totally new approach to the development of a dynamically adapting MPI-IO implementation. Basis for this approach is an algorithm which maps the MPI data structures to the proprietary ViPIOS structure. This algorithm is defined in the following sections.

3 Derived Data Types in MPI-IO

In this section we give a short overview of MPI-IO derived data types. However, rather than giving detailed information of the MPI-IO syntax, we will elaborate on a formalized description of a typical MPI-IO application which

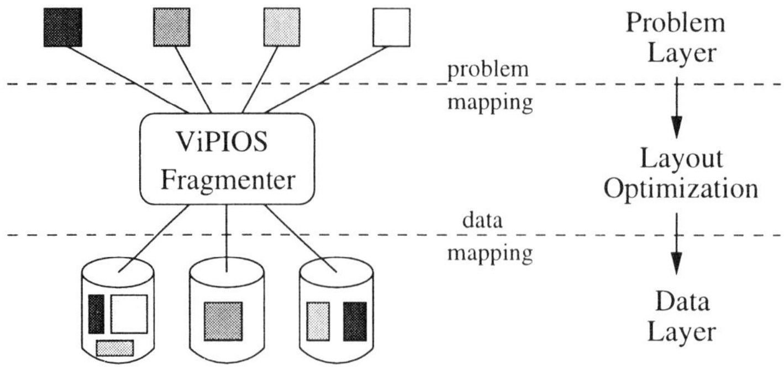

Figure 1. Data abstraction.

we will use as the basis for our further analysis throughout the rest of this paper. Later on we will present the ViPIOS Distribution-Mapping-Algorithm which, on the one hand, accomplishes the implementation of MPI-IO derived data type features, and, on the other hand, formalizes the mapping mechanism to the underlying ViPIOS, the actual "brain" of ViMPIOS.

We start with a short algorithm on a typical MPI-IO program with a file view based on a derived data type. The single steps are:

- Step 1: Specification of the data file to be accessed, e.g. 2-dimensional file array with 6x4 elements.
- Step 2: Specification of the distribution and the corresponding distribution arguments, e.g. CYCLIC(2), CYCLIC(1).
- Step 3: Creation of the processor grid, i.e. number of processors of each dimension of the data file, e.g. 2x2 (2 processors per dimension).
- Step 4: Integration into the derived data type, e.g. MPI_Type_create_darray.
- Step 5: application of the newly created data type in the file view.

The whole algorithm is summarized graphically in Fig. 2.

4 ViMPIOS Distribution-Mapping Algorithm

On giving a formalized specification of an MPI-IO program, we can now deduce an algorithm which describes the distribution and the mapping of data onto the ViPIOS internal data structures. Again, we will choose a graphical approach to discuss how the MPI-IO features are implemented in ViPIOS such that the strength of ViPIOS, namely portability and dynamic user-independent optimized data distribution are still exploited.

The ViMPIOS Distribution-Mapping Algorithm consists of the following four basic phases:

- Phase 1: Distribution Analysis
  - Simple Case
  - Complex Case
- Phase 2: Projection
- Phase 3: Integration
- Phase 4: Mapping onto ViPIOS

Let us now briefly describe each step of the algorithm. First, in the *Distribution phase*, the data file which is to accessed has to be analyzed. Thus, assume a one-dimensional file of 4 elements and a processor grid with 2 processors. Further assume a CYCLIC(2) data distribution, which means that each processor gets 2 elements. We call this a *simple case* since each processor has the same workload. In contrast, the so-called *complex case* is considered as the case where at least 2 processors have a different workload. This is true, for example, if the file consists of 6 elements rather than 4. Thus, processor 0 would get 4 elements whereas processor 1 merely gets 2.

This distribution analysis has to be done for each dimension of the file. We refer to this step as the *Projection phase*. Taking a look at the introductory example yields a complex case for the dimension 0 - since 6 elements are distributed onto 2 processors according to CYCLIC(2) - and a simple case for the dimension 1 (since 4 elements must be distributed onto 2 processors).

During the *Integration phase*, the results from the projection of each dimension must be combined into one derived data type.

Let us apply this algorithm to processor 0. The graphical analysis is given in Fig. 3.

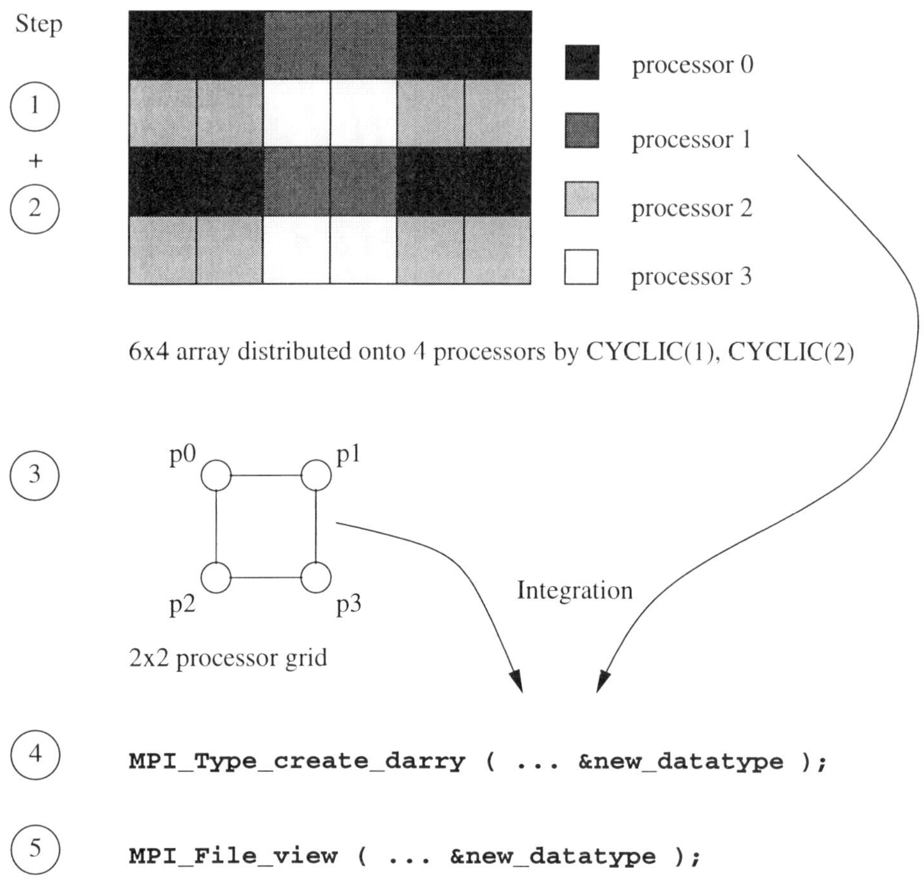

Figure 2. Formalized description of an MPI-IO program.

During the analysis and the projection phase of dimension 0, the results can be used directly. In other words, the array consists of 6 elements whereas 4 elements are to be accessed by processor 0. However, there is a stride of 2 elements between the second and the third basic block (see Fig. 3, Dim 0).

According to the next projection step, the access pattern of dimension 1 consists of 2 elements with a stride of one in between them (see Fig. 3, Dim 1). However, since the previous dimension (dimension 0) has to be considered as well, each basic block does not consists of only one data element but each basic block is made up by the access pattern defined by dimension 0. Even the stride between the two basic blocks is defined by the extent of the access pattern of dimension 0. Thus, although the number of elements of dimension 1 is merely 2 (two basic blocks), the number of elements actually accessed is 8 since each basic block consists of 4 elements (see Fig. 3, Result)

Finally, in the *Mapping phase*, the information yielded from the Integration phase must be mapped to the ViPIOS' internal data structure. We will not go into detail but merely describe the basic approach by means of a simple example. Again, a graphical analysis (see Fig. 4) shall motivate our approach.

According to Fig. 4 (part a) the access pattern of a single data block can be implemented by a simple MPI data type, e.g. MPI_INT. A contiguous access pattern (Fig. 4, part b) is then described by the derived data type MPI_Type_contiguous. A simple case access pattern (Fig. 4 part c) is implemented by means of MPI_Type_vector. Any other more complex access pattern can be realized by means of MPI_Type_struct, which allows defining data blocks of variable lengths. The access pattern depicted in Fig. 4, (part d) can be regarded as a typical complex case, since the workloads of processor 0 and processor 1 are different. However, internally the complex case for processor 1 is interpreted as a simple case (2 blocks of 2 elements) and a further simple case, namely one additional element. These two *simple cases* are combined by means of MPI_Type_struct to be treated as a complex case.

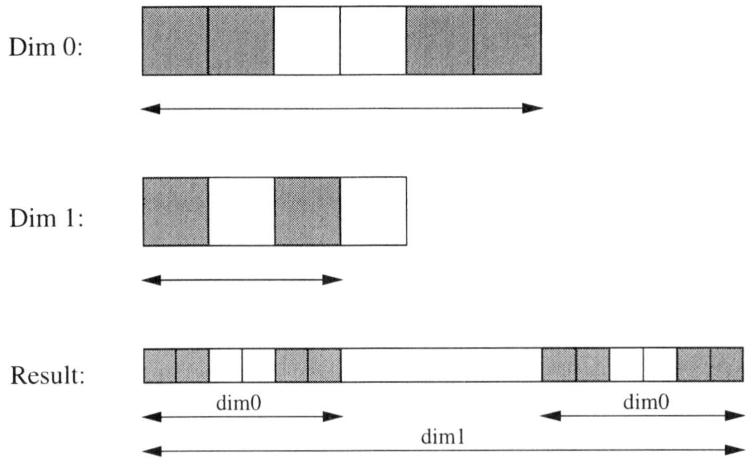

Figure 3. ViMPIOS distribution mapping.

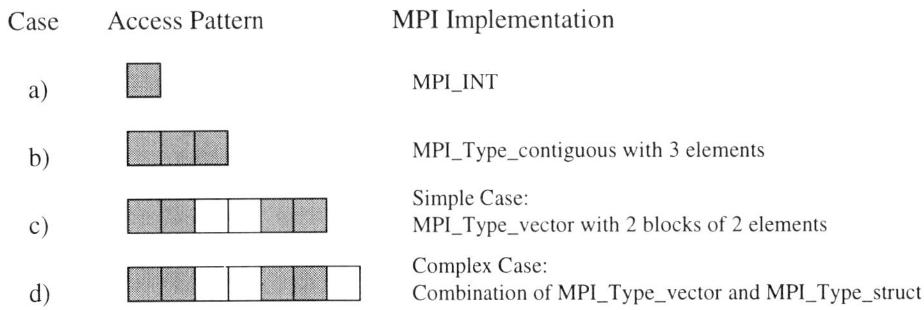

Figure 4. Mapping mechanism onto MPI data types.

5 ViPIOS Access Descriptor

On analyzing the access pattern and expressing it in terms of MPI derived data types, we can now map this information to the ViPIOS internal Access Descriptor. In particular, each value of the derived data type, which can be any complex combination of simple data types and derived data types, must be stored into the ViPIOS Access Descriptor. By means of defining offsets and strides, the access pattern of each processor as well as complex data types, which are not directly supported by MPI-IO derived data types, can be specified. Thus, the ViPIOS Access Descriptor can be used for mapping all MPI-IO derived data types and even more complex nested access patterns.

6 Analysis and Justification

A justification of our approach can easily be derived by a quite simple MPI-IO application. To show the advantage of our approach we used the program "simple.c", which is part of the test suite of the ROMIO package. It writes to separate files and reads the data back afterwards. Each MPI-IO process creates its own file which is distinguished by appending the process rank to the file name.

Our test environment consists of two available cluster systems. One cluster consists of Sun workstations connected by a conventional 10 Mbit Ethernet, the other is a Linux cluster with a 100 Mbit Fast-Ethernet interconnect.

First, we executed the MPI-IO program on the Sun cluster with 4 processors creating files of 4 MB size each. In the default installation of ROMIO the program creates its files locally in the ROMIO installation directory which is in a cluster environment by default linked via NFS to all cooperating processors. Thus, all 4 files are created on the same disk which leads to a sequential disk access scheme. The same program executed in the ViMPIOS environment creates automatically, totally transparently to the programmer, the files on the local disks of the respective processors. This is a result of the Fragmenter, the AI-based automatic data distribution module of the ViPIOS layer. The difference is about a factor of 5 in the execution times. The performance values are given in seconds in Tab. 1.

	ROMIO (default)	ROMIO (adapted)	ViMPIOS
Sun Cluster	27	5	5.5
Linux Cluster	15.1	2.5	2.9

Table 1. Performance comparison of ROMIO to ViMPIOS (time in sec.)

This can be corrected in ROMIO by the programmer choosing the respective local file system by changing the program code (which was not necessary in ViMPIOS). The respective results are comparative, even slightly better, to the ViMPIOS implementation[1].

Using the program on the Linux cluster delivers in the ViMPIOS environment a similar performance behaviour, but the ROMIO implementation need additional code adaptation to the MPI-IO program to direct the file accesses to the local files again. The difference in the absolute values between the Sun and Linux cluster is a result of the slower network interconnect.

Thus, it is easy to show that true portability (program migration without performance tradeoff) could only be reached by ViMPIOS. The ROMIO implementation needs additional programmers efforts.

7 Conclusion and Future Work

We presented ViMPIOS, a novel MPI-IO implementation based on ViPIOS, which adapts the problem specific data layout transparently to the user guaranteeing performance in changing I/O environments. Specifically, we described an algorithm to map MPI-IO data structures to corresponding ViPIOS structures. At the moment extensive performance tests are on the way, whereas the first results are very promising.

ViPIOS provides a wide spectrum of application interfaces, which spans from an I/O library to an independent data server system. In the near future the work will progress by the integration of an advanced buffer management module, the realization of a parallel file system implementation, and a Java interface.

References

[1] B.M. Chapman et al., *Vienna FORTRAN compilation system*, User's Guide, Vienna, 1994.

[2] Samuel A. Fineberg, Parkson Wong, Bill Nitzberg, and Chris Kuszmaul, *PMPIO— a portable implementation of MPI-IO*, Proceedings of the Sixth Symposium on the Frontiers of Massively Parallel Computation, IEEE Computer Society Press, October 1996, pp. 188–195.

[1]The slight performance advantage of ROMIO can be explained by the prototype implementation of ViMPIOS

[3] High Performance FORTRAN Forum, *High performance fortran language specification, version 1.1*, 1994.

[4] Message-Passing Interface Forum, *MPI-2.0: Extensions to the message-passing interface*, ch. 9, MPI Forum, June 1997.

[5] Erich Schikuta, Thomas Fuerle, and Helmut Wanek, *Vipios: The vienna parallel input/output system*, Euro-Par'98 (Southampton, England), Springer-Verlag, September 1998.

[6] K. E. Seamons, Y. Chen, P. Jones, J. Jozwiak, and M. Winslett, *Server-directed collective I/O in Panda*, Proceedings of Supercomputing '95 (San Diego, CA), IEEE Computer Society Press, December 1995.

[7] Rajeev Thakur, Ewing Lusk, and William Gropp, *Users guide for ROMIO: A high-performance, portable MPI-IO implementation*, Tech. Report ANL/MCS-TM-234, Mathematics and Computer Science Division, Argonne National Laboratory, October 1997.

[8] Helmut Wanek and Erich Schikuta, *A blackboard approach for the automatic optimization of parallel I/O operations*, PaCT'99 (St. Petersburg, Russia), Springer-Verlag, September 1999.

[9] Richard W. Watson and Robert A. Coyne, *The parallel I/O architecture of the high-performance storage system (HPSS)*, Proceedings of the Fourteenth IEEE Symposium on Mass Storage Systems, IEEE Computer Society Press, September 1995, pp. 27–44.

Specification-driven Monitoring of TCP/IP

Richard Hofmann
Lehrstuhl Informatik 7
University of Erlangen-Nürnberg
Martensstraße 3, D-91058 Erlangen
phone: ++49-9131-85-27026
fax: ++49-9131-85-27409
Email:rhofmann@informatik.uni-erlangen.de

Frank Lemmen
FLI3, Lucent Technologies
Bell Labs Innovations
Thurn-und-Taxis-Str. 10, D-90410 Nürnberg
++49-911-526-2102
++49-911-526-3183
flemmen@lucent.com

Abstract

Specification-driven monitoring is a novel technique for systematically analyzing the functional and temporal behavior of a system starting from specification to the implementation with the help of monitoring. This paper briefly shows the method and the tools belonging to it. The main part comprises a measurement study of a TCP/IP protocol stack fully specified in SDL. This study shows, how the TCP protocol stack was analyzed and improved in terms of correctness and performance. After correcting a difficult error in the runtime system, the throughput of the system improved by a factor of 10.

1 Introduction

The application of telecommunication systems is growing at an exponential pace without a foreseeable end. Examples are the Internet, but also end devices and the infrastructure for mobile communication. In order to handle the ever reducing product cycles in an industrial measure, formal methods are used for the design of communication systems, e.g. the specification languages SDL [SDL88] and MSC [MSC92], standardized by the ITU.

Formal design methods on the one hand side allow the checking of important system properties in early design phases, e.g. lifeness or reachability of certain system states. On the other hand side, the tool support helps the designer to synthesize the source code directly from the specification. Using such a methodology, functionally correct systems can be generated very efficiently

All currently known design environments supporting the formal design of parallel an distributed systems lack a universal capability for specifying and implementing non-functional requirements, especially timing requirements. In the research area approaches for extending specification languages with such aspects, e.g. SDL* [SSD97] and PMSC [FLM+97]. These approaches allow the specification of non-functional properties, like time restrictions, resource usage, cost and the like. The goal is a general methodology and tools for the design of parallel and distributed systems, that care of all these issues from the starting point of the design on.

Even systems that have generally been designed under consideration of non-functional, especially temporal aspects may exhibit errors in their functional or temporal behavior. To find such errors is the task of empiric system analysis using monitoring techniques. In the remainder of this work we shall present in the following section the *specification-driven monitoring*, that starts at specification level and move the designer into a position to search for functional and temporal errors at that level he is familiar with.

By that, the method to a large extent automatically takes care of the configuration of the evaluation tools and the evaluation of the measured data. The usability and the usefulness of specification-driven monitoring will be dealt with in the third section, where it was used for analyzing a TCP/IP protocol that was fully specified in SDL for finding and eliminating functional errors and a performance bottleneck.

2 Specification-driven Monitoring

The starting point of specification-driven monitoring is the use of a formal specification, from that all information necessary for monitoring will be derived. From that procedure results an abstraction of the object system to those

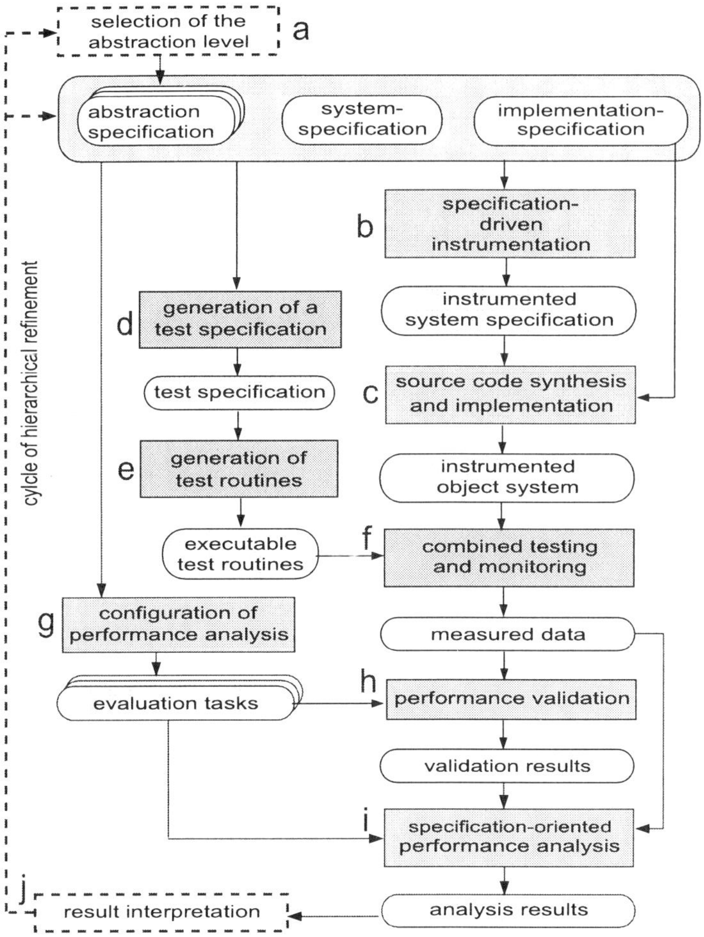

Figure 1: The method of specification-driven monitoring

activities that are really relevant for performance analysis. In addition, this allows an automatic, model-driven instrumentation of the object system, based on that a largely automatic measurement and evaluation can be carried out.

An essential prerequisite for carrying out specification-driven monitoring is that the system to be analyzed, i.e. the *object system* has to be fully specified in a formal language, e.g. SDL and that additional abstraction specifications, e.g. MSC-diagrams, exist that provide different abstract views on the object system. In the following, we shall describe the components that comprise specification-driven monitoring in a general way.

2.1 Abstraction Specification and System Specification

The method starts with the selection of an appropriate abstraction level (Figure 1a) on that the performance evaluation has to be carried out. With MSCs as the abstraction specification this happens by selecting an appropriate scenario that shows the interaction of relevant processes. This action is shown in Figure 1 as a stroked line because it has to be done by the user.

2.1.1 Integration of Specification and Instrumentation

On the way to connecting abstraction specification with system specification, the objects comprising the abstraction specification are mapped to corresponding objects of the system specification. The objects identified by this procedure are then instrumented within the system specification. As this step leads to an instrumented system specification, we call it *specification-driven instrumentation* (Figure 1b).

2.1.2 Source Code Synthesis and Implementation

Subsequent to instrumentation, the synthesis tool automatically generates instrumented program code in a high level language from the system specification (Figure 1c). This synthesis step necessitates an *implementation specification* that contains non-functional aspects of the system design, e.g. the configuration of the source code generator.

As the instrumentation instructions are defined syntactically correct in the respective specification language and no special annotations for instrumentation are used, arbitrary source code generators can be applied. The free choice of a source code generator is a big advantage, because there are many different factors that can lead to the selection of source code generator within one particular project. These factors especially comprise the efficiency and the amount of the source code generated, the programming language of the source code, the structure and readability of the source code, and to what extent the specification language is supported by the source code generator. Based on the instrumented program code, derived from the system specification and the abstraction specification, we are now in a state where an instrumented object system can be implemented.

2.1.3 Combined Testing and Monitoring

After implementing the instrumented object system, the actual performance measurement can be carried out by monitoring the dynamic behavior of the object system, which in turn leads to event traces (Figure 1f). The performance measurement is carried out within the conformance test methodology as designed and standardized by the ITU, because only by that, a reactive object system can be forced to carry out the desired order of events in accordance with good engineering practice.

So to speak, the conformance of an instrumented object system will be tested, so that during the test, the actual measurement data are generated. Note that the conformance test based on the system specification can be controlled via the same abstraction specification as the monitoring, because it is possible to largely automatically generate a test specification from a formal system specification and formally specified test cases (Figure 1d), from that again executable test routines can be generated (Figure 1e). The test routines stimulate the object system in order to behave exactly as specified in the abstraction specification. It is this behavior that has to be monitored during the performance measurement.

2.1.4 Performance Validation and Analysis

When controlling monitoring by abstraction specifications that define performance requirements in addition to the mere functional behavior, then the actual performance analysis can be preceded by a *performance validation* (Figure 1h) that automatically checks, if the requested performance is obtainable. Typically, a *performance analysis* Figure 1i) only has to be carried out for those cases, where the system lacks the specified performance for discovering the reason. Thereby, the performance validation not only decides about the necessity of a performance analysis, but it can especially be used for focussing the performance analysis on the relevant orders of events in the system to be analyzed.

For carrying out the evaluation of the event traces monitored in a specification-driven manner, the evaluation environment has to be configurable, too. Such a configurable evaluation environment is e.g. SIMPLE [Klar95] that therefore is well-suited for a use in specification-driven monitoring, and it will be used here for implementing it. All object system specific information, necessary for the evaluation, are derived from the abstraction specification and the system specification, i.e. the evaluation is configured specification-driven (Figure 1g).

2.1.5 Result Interpretation

During a *result interpretation* (Figure 1j), the analysis results can now offer hints, why the object system did not provide the specified performance. If the desired insight into the system's behavior could not be achieved yet, or there are other aspects to analyze, the specification-driven monitoring can be restarted from that point. Thus, it is possible to change the abstraction level of the performance measurement or to use an alternative abstraction specification on the same abstraction level. In particular, the system specification can be improved before restarting the monitoring, if the analysis results recommend that.

3 Specification-driven Monitoring of an SDL-specified TCP/IP-protocol

The usefulness and the applicability of the specification-driven monitoring will be demonstrated with the help of a measurement study that was performed with this method on an SDL-specified TCP/IP protocol. Therefore, in section 3.1 we describe the object system for the measurement study by its SDL specification, its implementation details, and its configuration. Section 3.2 demonstrates the hierarchical search for a performance bottleneck, within that additional performance relevant specification errors could be identified and corrected.

3.1 The Object System

Our object system consists of an SDL specification of a TCP/IP protocol that was originally designed with the goal of performance simulation in mind [Rüh95,Wes97]. We have extended this specification in a way that it could automatically be synthesized by the code generator of Tau [Tel98].

Figure 2 shows the system diagram of the protocol stack, which mainly reflects TCP/IP's structure. The transport layer and the Internet layer appear as individual blocks named *TCPLayer* and *IPLayer*, that are able to communicate via defined channels with other layers. The application layer is divided into the blocks *SocketLayer* and *Application*, where the former one contains a simplified specification of the socket application programming interface to TCP/IP and the latter one to a great extent simplified versions of the programs *Telnet* and *FTP*, which can for example generate interactive and block-oriented traffic to TCP/IP.

The network layer does not exist as an SDL specification, because it has to directly interact with the serial port of the host computer. Therefore, it was implemented in C and integrated into the environment of the SDL system in order to provide a network access layer via the channel *IP_ch* for the SDL-specified IP-layer.

The SDL specification includes the complete functionality of the TCP protocol stack, and it was designed based on state diagram of TCP, that was published in the TCP standard [Pos81] and improved in the host requirements RFC [Bra89]. The IP protocol was specified only rudimentarily and it includes the packaging of TCP segments into IP packets, their forwarding to the network access layer and their delivery to the TCP layer. Other functions of the IP layer, especially those for routing and segmentation, have not been specified.

The SDL system from Figure 2 was implemented with the help of the design environment SDT by generating C-Code from the SDL specification, that was compiled and linked to an autonomous program. This implementation model is called *light integration* in [Tel98]; where the SDL system communicates with hardware and other resources

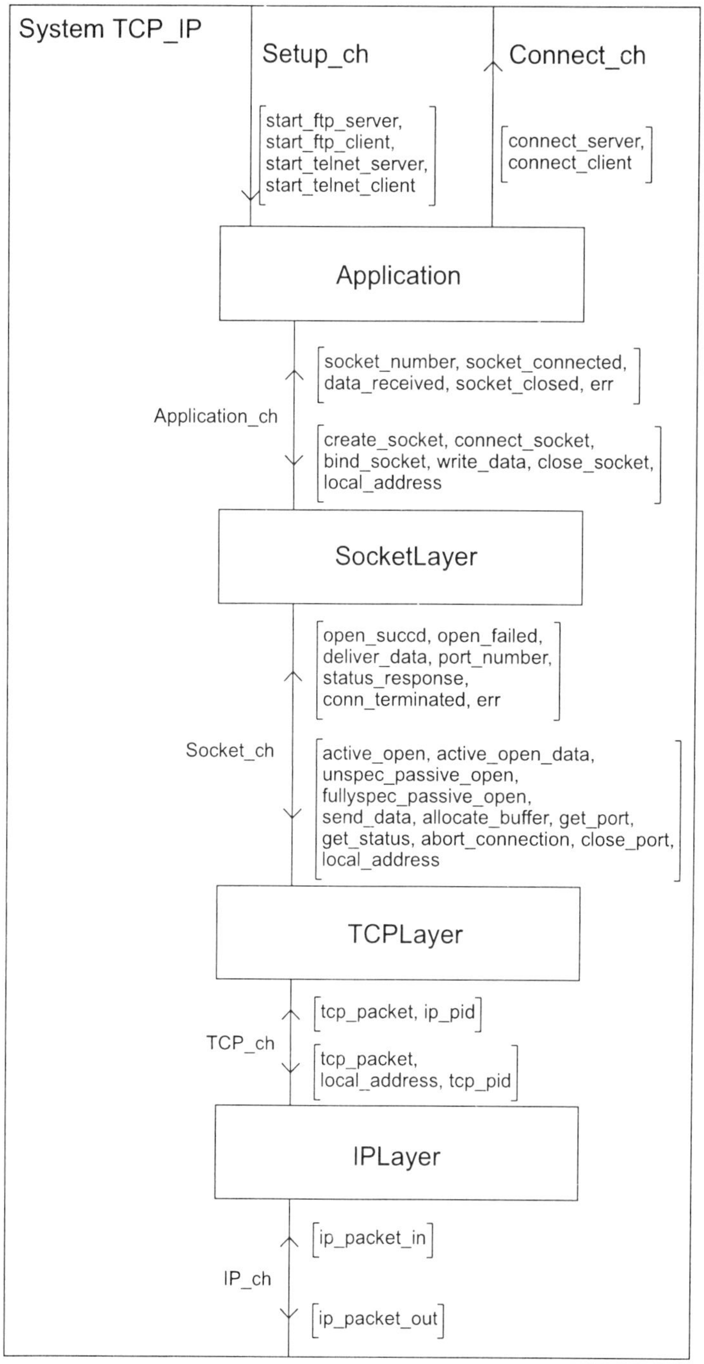

Figure 2: System diagram of the SDL specification

controlled by the operation system by calls to environment functions provided by the tool vendor.

The network access layer of the TCP/IP protocol stack that contains both the software and the hardware components of the physical interface to the network was crafted on top of an RS232 interface. We chose *Serial Line Internet Protocol* (SLIP) as the protocol for the network access layer [Rom88] that offers a very simple mechanism for a TCP/IP communication over serial point to point connections. This method introduced in 1984 now is an official Internet standard and is used especially for connecting PCs over the serial port, a modem and the telephone line to the Internet access point of a provider.

For carrying out a distributed measurement the SDT-generated application of the TCP/IP protocol stack was run on two independent Sun workstations that were interconnected by a serial RS232 connection. One of the systems was configured as client and the other as server, where a transmission of 10 messages with 1024 bytes of user data was used for functional analysis of the essential protocol paths. Applying a data transfer of medium length, 100 messages at 1024 bytes of user data, the performance relevant protocol mechanisms, like e.g. timer and acknowledgement mechanisms, have been investigated. For collecting statistical data about the execution times of procedures and transitions a longer data transfer of 1000 messages was applied.

3.2 Measurement Study

A performance test preceding the specification-driven monitoring resulted in the conclusion, that the TCP/IP system is far from reaching the specified performance. As the serial port was configured for 19200 bps, a raw data rate of 1600 byte/s could be achieved. Taking into consideration protocol overhead, during the performance test, a throughput of roughly 1000 byte/s should be achieved. The transmission of a single TCP segment with 1024 bytes of user data should take place within one second under these circumstances. In reality, the transmission of 100 messages at 1024 bytes each took about 1100 seconds, which corresponds to a throughput of 93 byte/s.

3.2.1 Analysis of the SDL System on the Block Level

In order to search for the reasons of this insufficient performance, the specification-driven monitoring starts with an analysis of the end to end transmission times between corresponding protocol layers and the packet delay time through the TCP layers on sender and receiver side. This is equivalent to an analysis of the SDL system on the block level, where the

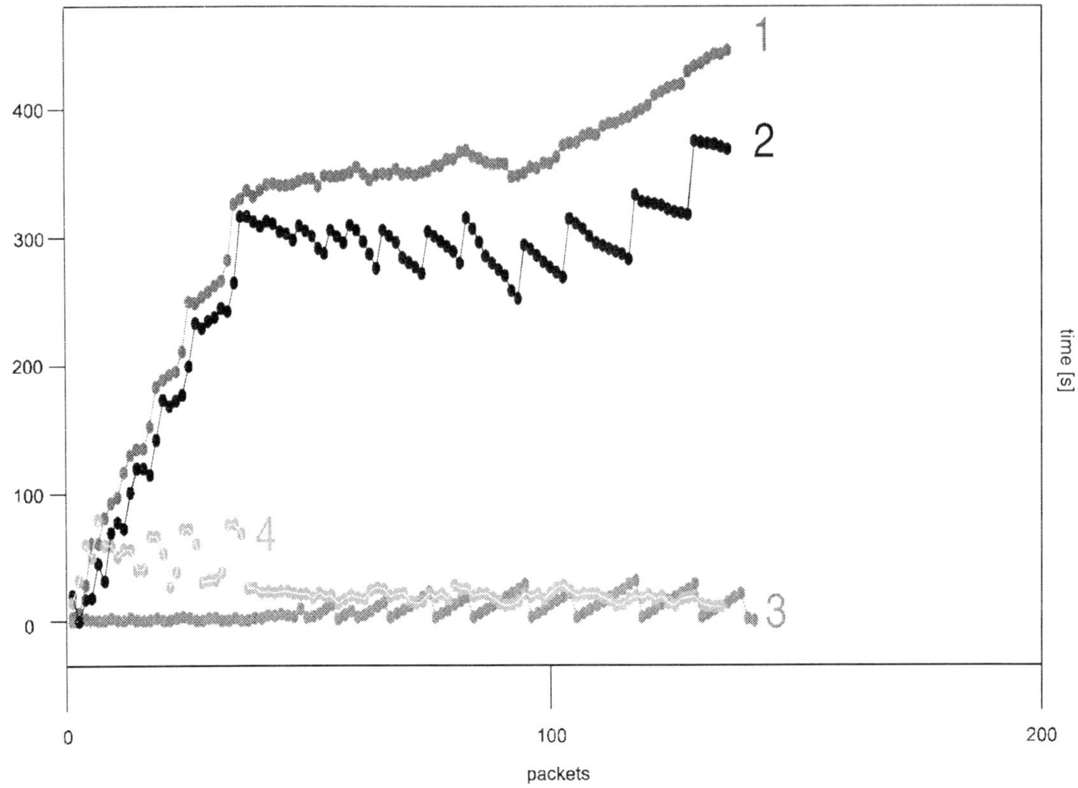

Figure 3: transmission times and delay times of 1024 byte packets of an FTP-transmission of 100 Kbyte

signal transfers between blocks are monitored. As an abstraction specification for controlling a measurement of that kind, an MSC that describes the communication of the SDL system on block level is the favorite choice.

The TRCSTAT diagram[1] in Figure 3 visualizes the result of this measurement. Line 1, describing the packet delay times between the upper service access point of the TCP layers (channel *Socket_ch* in Figure 2), confirms the result of the performance test. The transmission times start in the expected range of one second, but rise with increasing number of packets rapidly to 350 seconds and reach values of 450 seconds until the end of the transmission.

These enormous packet delay times come about, because data leave the protocol stack on the sender side in bursts and will be transferred upward the same way at the receiver side. Therefore, using a different scheduling policy, we forced a more regular data transmission. Though this resulted in a reduction of the end to end delays to 50 seconds per packet, it could the reduce the total delay only to 800 s. Note that, although this change in the scheduling policy could not eliminate the bottleneck, it resulted in a performance improvement of about 23 percent.

As the packet delay times between the upper service access points of the IP layer (channel *TCP_ch* in Figure 2), represented by line 3 are responsible for only a small fraction of the total transmission time, it can be inferred, that the performance bottleneck is within the TCP layers. Line 2, describing the delay time of the packets through the TCP layer of the sender, confirms this assumption, because these delay times are in relative proximity to the end to end delays of the TCP packets.

The rapid increase of the delay times allows to infer that the TCP layer on the sender side is increasingly flooded with data, arriving much faster then they can be sent. The sawtooth shape of line 2 indicates that the acknowledgements from the receiver side arrive very slowly at the sender side, so that every acknowledgement acknowledges

[1] TRCSTAT is a tool within the SIMPLE environment that computes elementary trace statistics, e.g. event frequencies, event distances and durations.

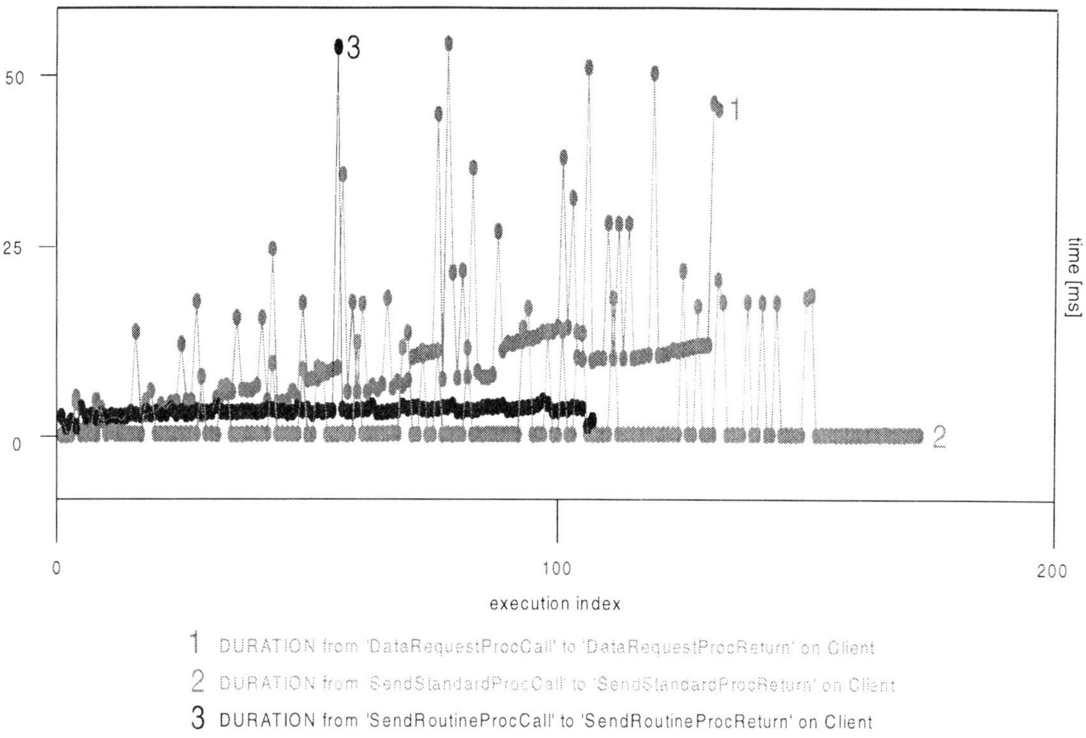

Figure 4: Execution times of essential procedures for the data transfer

a number of data packets. Every time an acknowledgement arrives, the sender is able to transmit a burst of data packets until the sending window is closed again and he has to wait for the next acknowledgement.

Packets through the TCP layer of the receiver, represented by line 4, start with strongly fluctuating delay times, but later they swing to fairly low value. So, the performance analysis could be reduced to the TCP layer, where from the multitude of potential causes for the performance bottleneck initially the possibility was chosen, that functional errors in performance relevant parts of the TCP protocol, e.g. timer or retransmission mechanisms, lead to the temporal misbehavior. This investigation revealed an error in the specification of the timer mechanism that actually paralyzed it, which can under no circumstances be tolerated. As a reason for the bottleneck, this issue did not come into consideration.

3.2.2 Analysis of the SDL System on the Transition Level

The preceding measurements indicate, that the detected performance bottleneck mainly concerns the data transmission phase. This recommends to restrict the analysis of transition execution times to those transitions that are crucial for the data transfer. On the basis of the structural construction of the SDL specification, a large fraction of the protocol activities takes place within a hierarchy of procedures, that are called during transition executions. The TRCSTAT diagram in Figure 4 shows the execution times of these procedures, that admittedly reach maximum values of 50 milliseconds but typically amount to less than 10 milliseconds.

Consequently, the immense time that messages need for passing the TCP layer of the client can not be caused by the protocol activities and the corresponding protocol mechanisms. Further analysis will therefore deal with the interaction of the protocol layers and the processes specified within them, especially regarding the exchange of messages.

The TRCSTAT diagram in Figure 5 shows the signal transmission times between processes. As a comparison with the procedure execution times in Figure 4 shows, the signal transmission times stand in a crass disproportion to the execution time of the actual protocol activities. While the maximum values for the procedure execution times remain in the range of 50 milliseconds, the signal transmissions take at least one second.

A closer look to the signal transmission times depicted in Figure 5 shows partly arbitrary but also regular fluctuations of the values between one and eight seconds. Actually, most of the transmission times are integer multiples of

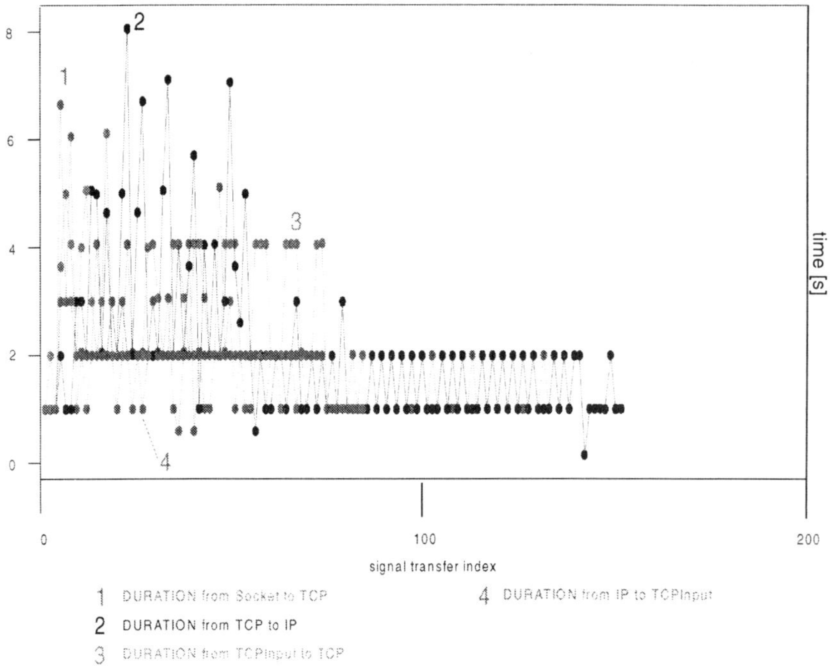

Figure 5: Signal transfer times between SDL processes

1 second. It is particularly interesting, that no coherence between the amount of transferred data and the transmission time, i.e. large data packets and small control packets show the same temporal behavior.

3.2.3 Localization and Fix of the Performance Bottleneck Within the Runtime System

This observation allows to conclude, that the performance bottleneck is located within the runtime system, because that is mainly responsible for the signal transfers. The analysis of this system is not yet suited for specification-driven monitoring, because it is not specified formally. This means, that at this place neither event selection nor instrumentation can be done specification-driven. This problem can be remedied by specification-driven control of the monitoring of the runtime system, which is part of our future work.

Finally, we could locate the performance bottleneck within the operating system driver for the RS232 interface. This driver was configured to busy-wait at each read request at most one second for receiving data. As a consequence, the solution of this problem was to delegate the monitoring of the RS232 interface to the operating system, so that the receipt of data will be indicated by an interrupt. That way, the waiting times for incoming messages could be reduced to zero.

The TRCSTAT diagram in Figure 6 shows the transmission times of the particular messages between the service access points after fixing the RS232 driver. The transmission times between the upper service access points of the TCP layer, represented by line 1, and the transmission times between the upper service access points of the IP layer, represented by line 3, settled in to a mean value of 600 milliseconds. The delay times of the messages through the TCP layer, represented by line 2 and line 4, whose values were in the range of 300 seconds in Figure 3, now are irrelevant.

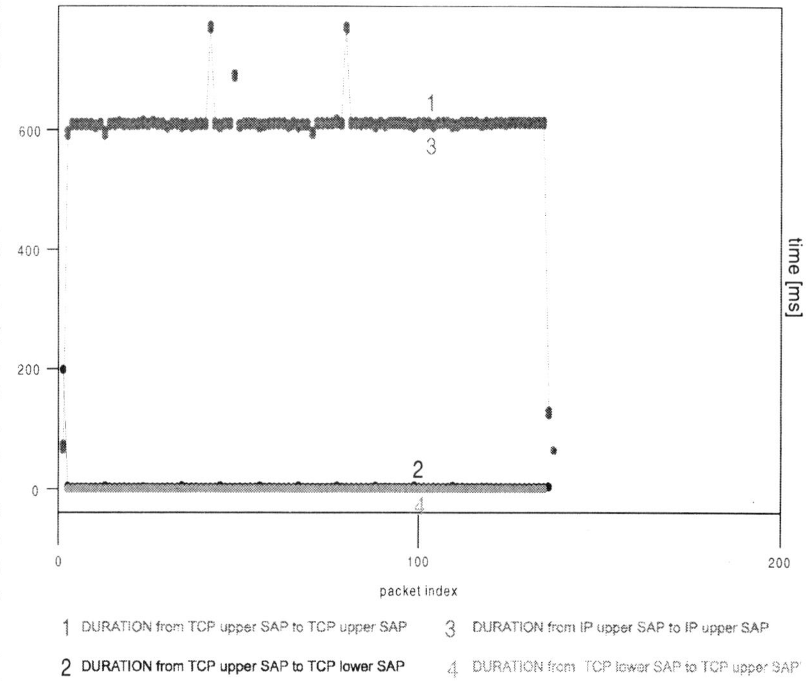

Figure 6: Transmission times and delay times of 1024 byte packets of an FTP transfer of 100 Kbytes after fixing the performance bottleneck

4 Conclusion

During the preceding analyses in search for a performance bottleneck in the SDL specification of the TCP/IP protocol and its implementation, several modifications and corrections have been provided before the actual performance bottleneck in the runtime system could be located and fixed. The measurement study particularly revealed, how a performance bottleneck, initially detected within a performance test, could be pursued step by step and then eventually identified.

The monitoring on block level (sec. 3.2.1) first confirmed the results of the performance test and restricted the main part of the problem to the TCP layer. After fixing functional errors within the SDL specification of the TCP protocol that may result in an insufficient performance, the analysis of the TCP protocol on the transition level showed that all protocol activities were performing temporally correct. As a result of extremely high signal transmission times between the particular SDL processes, the performance bottleneck could first be restricted to the runtime system and finally be located and fixed within that (sec. 3.2.3).

Backward looking, it would have been noticeable to start searching for the performance bottleneck within the runtime system, because the investigated SDL system had already shown adequate performance during a simulative performance analysis [HW97]. As the simulated and the implemented SDL system mainly differ by the runtime system, the probability for finding the problem there would have been very high. On the other hand side, proceeding like that would not have discovered the functional errors of the SDL specification, that definitely can cause bad performance.

The measurement study of an SDL-specified TCP/IP protocol presented in this work has shown by example, that with monitoring on the specification level, performance evaluation of real communication systems can be carried out adequately. The analysis results from SDL-driven monitoring not only enabled to restrict the performance bottleneck to the runtime system, but also they additionally identified functional errors in the system specification that caused erroneous protocol behavior. Of course, not all possible performance bottlenecks can be identified on the specification level, but they can be recognized on that level and they can be restricted to parts of the specification or the runtime system.

This work also has shown that a measurement-based approach for system analysis only on the specification level not always suffices, because the underlying mechanisms, e.g. the runtime system in the current work or the underlying operating system, are excluded from the considerations. Future work will consequently deal with extending the runtime system with dynamic instrumentation points, so that it can be integrated into a dynamic specification-driven monitoring. This way, those activities within the runtime system or the operating system could be monitored specification-driven, that are candidates for a performance bottleneck detected on the specification level.

References

Bra89 Braden, R.T. (Hrsg.): *Requirements for Internet Hosts – Communication Layers.* RFC 1122, 1989

FLM+97 Faltin, N; Lambert, L; Mitschele-Thiel, A; Slomka, F.: An annotational Extension of Message Sequence Charts to Support Performance Engineering. In Cavalli, A; Sarma, A. (eds.): *SDL'97: Time for Testing — SDL, MSC and Trends.* Elsevier, 1997.

HW97 Hintelmann, J.; Westerfeld, R.: Performance Analysis of TCP's Flow Control Mechanisms using Queueing SDL. In Cavalli, A; Sarma, A. (eds.): *Proc. of the Eighth SDL Forum*, Evry, France, 23-26 September 1997

Klar95 Klar, R. et al.: *Monitoring and Modeling of parallel Systems (in German).* Teubner. Stuttgart, 1995.

Kra99 Kraus, F.: *Implementation and Performance Analysis of a TCP/IP Stack, Implemented in SDL (in German).* Masters Thesis, IMMD7, University Erlangen-Nürnberg, January 1999.

MSC92 CCITT: *Recommendation Z.120, Message Sequence Charts (MSC).* Genf 1992

Pos81 Postel, J.B. (Hrsg.): *Transmission Control Protocol.* RFC 793, 1981

Rom88 Romkey, J.: *A nonstandard for transmission of IP datagrams over serial lines: SLIP.* RFC 1055, 1988

Rüh95 Rühl, J.: *SDL-basierte Modelle zur Leistungsbewertung von TCP: Systemmodellierung Memo.* 15 Fachbereich 6 / Informatik Universität GH Essen, Juli 1995, zugleich Diplomarbeit, Wirtschaftsinformatik DII Universität GH Essen, 1995.

SDL88 CCITT: *Recommendation Z.100, Specification and Description Language, SDL.* Blue Book, 1988.

SSD97 Spitz, S.; Slomka, F.; Dörfel, M.: SDL* — An Annotated Specification Language for Engineering Multimedia Communication Systems. In *6th Open Workshop for High Speed Networks.* Institut für Nachrichtenvermittlung und Datenverarbeitung (IND), Universität Stuttgart, Oktober 1997.

Tel98 Telelogic: *Telelogic Tau 3.3 Documentation.* Telelogic AB, Malmö (Sweden), 1991-1998.

Wes97 Westerfeld, R.: *Spezifikation und Analyse von zukünftigen TCP-Varianten mit Hilfe von SDL-Werkzeugen.* Diplomarbeit, Wirtschaftsinformatik, DII Universität GH Essen, 1996/97.

A QoS Performance Measure Framework for Distributed Heterogeneous Networks

Jong-Kook Kim[1], *Debra A. Hensgen*[2],
Taylor Kidd[2], *Howard Jay Siegel*[1], *David St. John*[3], *Cynthia Irvine*[2],
Tim Levin[3], *N. Wayne Porter*[2], *Viktor K. Prasanna*[4], and *Richard F. Freund*[5]

[1]Purdue University
ECE School
West Lafayette, IN 47907-1285, USA
{kim42, hj}@purdue.edu

[2]Naval Postgraduate School
CS and ECE Departments
Monterey, CA 93943, USA
{irvine, nwporter}@cs.nps.navy.mil
{hensgen, kidd}@acm.org

[3]Anteon Corporation
2600 Garden Rd., Ste. 220A
Monterey, CA 93940, USA
{stjohn, levin}@cs.nps.navy.mil

[4]University of Southern California
Department of EE-Systems
Los Angeles, CA 90089, USA
prasanna@ganges.usc.edu

[5]NOEMIX Inc.
1425 Russ Blvd., Ste. T-110
San Diego, CA 92101 USA
rffreund@noemix.com

Abstract

In a distributed heterogeneous computing environment, users' tasks are allocated resources to simultaneously satisfy, to varying degrees, the tasks' different, and possibly conflicting, quality of service (QoS) requirements. When the total demand placed on system resources by the tasks, for a given interval of time, exceeds the resources available, some tasks will receive degraded service or no service at all. One part of a measure to quantify the success of a resource management system (RMS) in such a distributed environment is the collective value of the tasks completed during an interval of time, as perceived by the user, application, or policy maker. The Flexible Integrated System Capability (FISC) ratio introduced here is a measure for quantifying this collective value. The FISC ratio is a multi-dimensional measure, and may include priorities, versions of a task or data, deadlines, situational mode, security, application- and domain-specific QoS, and dependencies. In addition to being used for evaluating and comparing RMSs, the FISC ratio can be incorporated as part of the objective function in a system's scheduling heuristics.

This research is supported by the DARPA/ITO Quorum Program, by the DARPA/ISO BADD Program and the Office of Naval Research under ONR grant number N00014-97-1-0804, and by the DARPA/ITO AICE Program under contract number DABT63-99-C-0010.

1. Introduction

In many distributed environments, the tasks that are executing have different quality of service (QoS) requirements. These different QoS requirements impose different machine and resource requirements. Furthermore, these tasks may require input data from a variety of distributed sources. Mixed-machine heterogeneous computing (HC) environments provide a distributed suite of different types of machines, connected by diverse types of networks, to meet the varied computational and input requirements of such task mixtures (e.g., [4, 8, 18]). The goals of a resource management system (RMS) in an HC environment are to assign communication, computation, and other resources in an attempt to satisfy users' requests, which may require different types and levels of QoS. Due to limitations on resource availability in certain situations, some tasks will receive degraded service or none at all. A performance measure is needed to quantify the collective value of the tasks completed during an interval of time, as perceived by the user, application, or policy maker. This measure can be a part of a metric to assess the success of an RMS (other parts may include execution time, ability to work with different operating systems, and user interface). This research describes attributes that can be combined to derive such a performance measure, and provides a way to combine them.

The Flexible Integrated System Capability (FISC) ratio is introduced in this research. It is a multi-dimensional performance measure, and may include priorities, versions of a task or data, deadlines, situational mode, security, application- and domain-specific QoS, and task dependencies. This FISC performance measure combines these attributes to determine the collective value of the tasks completed during an interval of time on a distributed computing system.

The FISC ratio can be used for the postmortem analysis of a system to determine the best scheduling heuristic for a given environment. It can also compare, via experimentation or simulation, the effectiveness of changing the resources available in a given distributed system. Furthermore, the FISC ratio can be incorporated as part of the objective function in a system's scheduling heuristics.

This research is part of three related DARPA activities: the DARPA Quorum-sponsored Management System for Heterogeneous Networks (MSHN) project [10], the DARPA Battlefield Awareness and Data Dissemination (BADD) program [22, 7], and the Agile Information Control Environment (AICE) program [1]. The goal of the Quorum MSHN project is to design, prototype, and refine a distributed RMS that leverages the heterogeneity of resources and tasks to deliver the requested QoS. In the Quorum environment, it is sometimes the case that not all tasks requested can achieve their most preferred QoS. Thus, there must be a performance measure that can determine a collective value of the set of tasks that were completed in a given time interval by a particular resource management strategy.

One aspect of the BADD and AICE programs involves designing a scheduling system for forwarding (staging) data items prior to their use as inputs to a local application in a wide area network (WAN) distributed computing environment. The BADD and AICE systems are similar to the Quorum environment in that, in some situations, not all data requests will be satisfied with their most preferred QoS by their deadline. Thus, the goal of the scheduler is to satisfy a set of requests in a way that has the greatest collective perceived value.

The performance measure described in this research is used to evaluate, for a given interval of time, the total value of tasks completed in the MSHN project and the total value of data received in the BADD and AICE programs. In this sense, the set of completed tasks for the MSHN project is equivalent to the set of satisfied data item requests for the BADD and AICE programs. A major difference between MSHN and BADD/AICE is that in MSHN tasks are assigned to resources by the RMS. In the BADD/AICE project, task assignments are given and fixed *a priori*, but the movement of data to the tasks must be scheduled. Throughout the rest of this paper, task will be used to represent a user's process execution in the Quorum MSHN context, and a user's request for a data item in the BADD/AICE context. While this research is motivated by military applications, the FISC ratio can be adapted for other environments, such as industrial intra-nets, government agency intra-nets (e.g., NASA), and computational grids [9].

The next section provides a brief overview of some of the literature related to this work. In Section 3, several examples of individual QoS requirements are presented. These requirements may be considered when formulating the performance measure to be used in building and assessing RMSs. Section 4 shows how all the example QoS attributes can be combined into a single measure. This section also presents a baseline for that measure and discusses a generalized form of the performance measure. An example of how this measure would be instantiated in a military C4I (command, control, communications, computers and intelligence) environment is provided in Section 5. The last section presents a brief summary of this research.

2. Related Work

The FISC performance measure discussed here embodies parameters that are considered important in scheduling tasks and communications on a distributed computing system. There is much literature on scheduling and mapping of tasks, messages, and data items; in this section, some of the literature is described.

An optimistic priority-based concurrency control protocol that schedules active transactions with firm-deadline in real-time database systems is described in [12]. This protocol combines forward and backward validation processes to control more effectively concurrent transactions with different priorities. The protocol is designed such that deadlines of higher priority transactions have a greater probability of being met than those of lower priority transactions. While this is also the case for MSHN and BADD/AICE, the research presented here includes other attributes that are important in evaluating the overall value of the tasks completed.

In [17], priority is used for the mapping, adjustment, and dropping of messages. The priority of a task is adjusted by the length of time it was blocked by a higher priority message and tardy messages that already missed their deadlines are dropped. This Least-Laxity-First priority mapping gives an improved missed deadline ratio, which is the rate of messages missing their deadlines. In [17], priority and deadline is used as measures of performance but the research effort does not consider other QoS attributes used in heterogeneous distributed networks.

An algorithm that allows transmission of messages belonging to several classes of situational mode is presented in [20]. The algorithm takes into account the actual priority of a message in a given class. This algorithm rejects packets with deadlines shorter than a minimum acceptance deadline defined for a particular class. There can be more than one simple deadline. This and other important QoS attributes are discussed in detail.

Data staging, an important data management problem for a distributed heterogeneous networking environment, is discussed in [28]. This was done under the assumption that each requested data item is associated with a specific deadline and priority. The research presented here generalizes part of the objective function used in [28] to include more types of deadlines and other QoS attributes.

From the works mentioned, parameters such as task priority and deadline appear to be important attributes for making scheduling decisions regarding tasks, messages, or data items. A measure of the overall value is needed that can be used in an objective function to compare and analyze the algorithms, protocols, and heuristics while incorporating all the QoS parameters used. The works mentioned above consider only a few of the QoS parameters that are being used in a distributed system. Other parameters, e.g., accuracy, precision, and security, that are QoS requirements and part of the users' requests, must be included in the performance analysis. These and other QoS parameters that affect the overall value of requests satisfied are discussed in this research.

The research on a performance measure presented here builds on and extends a body of earlier work in this field. Some examples are mentioned here.

The ERDoS project [5] describes an objective function for optimizing the effectiveness of its QoS scheduling mechanisms in meeting clients' needs. This function reflects the benefit received by the user and a weight assigned to each user application. An approach where requested QoS is taken into account when scheduling computational resources in a network is presented in [19]. The model proposed a benefit function that uses application deadlines and application priorities as metrics in maximizing the total benefit for the applications. Multiple versions of a task in addition to priorities and deadlines in the objective function are described in [14]. The FISC performance measure presented in this paper serves a purpose similar to the ones in [5, 19, 14]. However, the research presented here provides a more detailed description of a measure using more parameters, so that it can be used to find the performance of an effective schedule in the Quorum MSHN and BADD/AICE environments. Furthermore, the QoS input specification for ERDoS [24] accounts for only two specific security parameters (confidentiality and integrity), whereas the security component of the performance measure in this research can describe an arbitrarily complex set of security features.

The FISC ratio is similar to the utility function described in [31] in that both measure the system value. The utility function in [31] calculates the system value by summing the value of resources allocated and resources reserved depending on the duration of a job, the deadline of a job, and the price of allocated time slots. The FISC ratio uses a conceptually similar calculation, but formulates it differently and includes priorities and other QoS measures to calculate the collective value of task completed.

A security policy that allows a percentage of packets authenticated to vary with network load is described in [25]. This type of policy can be accommodated with the variant components included in the FISC security vector (see Subsection 3.5). While the FISC security vector contains a set of Boolean security policy statements, it does not specify a general-purpose language for these statements. Related work on network security policy specification languages can be found in [2, 3], and works in progress [6, 23]. A framework for quantifying the strength of a set of security mechanisms is described in [30], where high-level static security properties can be decomposed hierarchically. However, in [30] the approach cannot accommodate the measurement of how well an executed task meets the security requirements of its environment. Nor does [30] account for variant security policies or mechanisms.

The FISC ratio measures the effectiveness of a schedule in terms of tasks completed and percentage of their requirements satisfied. In [26], other types of attributes for evaluating different QoS and RMS services in distributed real-time systems are investigated. Some examples include survivability (fault-tolerance), openness (open architecture), and testability (easily testable and verifiable). These are outside the scope of the FISC performance measure, which focuses on the collective worth of the completed tasks.

3. Example QoS Attributes

3.1. Overview

Examples of attributes that need to be considered in the FISC performance measure will be described in this section. The attributes discussed include user-based and application-based priority levels, user preferences for different versions of a task, deadlines, security, other application- and domain-specific QoS attributes, and task dependencies. The attributes used in any given situation must have interpretations that are meaningful to the users, policy makers, and the RMS. A method of determining the weightings, worths, functions, and factors are described in this section.

3.2. Priorities

Policy makers determine the number of priority levels and assign some semantic meaning to each priority level, such that each level qualitatively reflects the relative importance (e.g., high, medium, and low). The policy makers may be the commanders in a military environment or executives in a corporation. Policy makers may assign different users, or classes of users, restricted ranges of priority levels that can be assigned to their tasks. Alternatively, a task itself could have an immutable priority level assigned to it by the policy makers. Each priority level will then be given a weight that can be calculated by a priority weight function, which is pre-determined by policy makers, described later in this section.

Priority levels with relative, quantitative weightings should be incorporated in scheduling systems so that a task with a higher importance will have a higher probability of meeting its QoS requirements. Application users and system builders often assign an arbitrary numbering scheme to priority levels that does not meaningfully quantify the relative importance of one priority level to another. Such a scheme, therefore, cannot be used alone in the measure. A more meaningful weight must instead be assigned to each priority level so that the relative importance can be reflected in the performance measure.

The relative importance (weighting) of priority levels may vary depending upon the situational mode. For example, there may be military modes of peace and war. In the peace mode, it might be just as important to complete ten low priority level tasks as to complete one high priority level task. However, in the war mode, one high priority level task might be more important than 1000 medium priority level tasks. This dependency can be indicated in the performance measure by expressing the weight of all priority levels as a function of the situational mode.

It is assumed that the FISC ratio is being used to compute the value of a subset of tasks successfully completed, during some time interval, from a set of t tasks that have been requested. Let the priority level (e.g., high, medium, low) of task j ($0 \leq j < t$) be p_j, and let m be the situational mode. The priority weight function $\pi(p_j, m)$ calculates the weight of p_j given m. The weight assigned to a priority level may be considered to be the maximum value of completing the corresponding task, if all of the task's specified QoS requirements are completely satisfied.

3.3. Versions

A task may exist in different versions, each with its own resource requirements. Because available resources will vary dynamically, it may not be possible to complete the most desired version of a task. For example, a user requesting a map application may most desire a 24-bit color, three-dimensional topographical map. However, if this cannot be given to the user due to limited resources, the user would rather have a black and white, two-dimensional map than nothing at all. When a user's first choice of a task version cannot be completed, a method for choosing an alternative version is needed. Having multiple versions of a task is related to the precision and accuracy parameters discussed in [24], in the sense that each version of a task may have different accuracy and precision.

For each version of a given task, in a given situational mode, a worth (preference) relative to the other versions will be indicated by the application developer, the user, and/or the policy makers. In the above example, the black and white version may only be worth 75% of the color version to the user. When selecting a version of a task to execute, an RMS's scheduling algorithms must consider this worth and the task's resource requirements as well as the availability of these resources. For example, one version may not be viable because its bandwidth requirement is too high.

	worth			normalized worth		
Task \ version	0	1	2	0	1	2
0	1	1	8	.125	.125	1
1	25	35	40	.625	.875	1
2	.2	.3	.5	.4	.6	1
3	.1	.2	.7	.143	.286	1

Table 1: Worths and normalized worths that indicate preference for each version of a task.

The worths assigned to different versions of a task must be normalized so that there is a consistent scheme for evaluating worths across tasks and versions. For example, assume that all factors except version worths are equal across a set of tasks. The user can specify any number for the worth of a version as shown in Table 1. Therefore without a normalization procedure, a version with the smallest worth of a certain task can always be chosen for processing ahead of other tasks for no logical reason. For example, the version 0 of task 1 that is the version with the lowest worth of task 1 would be chosen over the version 2 of task 0 that is the version with the highest worth for task 0. In extreme cases, worths that are not normalized could make the priority irrelevant depending on how priorities and worths of version interact.

To avoid this type of anomalous behavior, worths are normalized as follows. Assume there are $\underline{I_j}$ number of versions for each task j. Let $\underline{v_{ij}}$ be the $\underline{i}$-th ($0 \leq i < I_j$) version of task j. Let $\underline{w_{ij}(m)}$ be the worth the user assigns to i-th version of task j given m, the situational mode. Example $w_{ij}(m)$ values are provided in Table 1. One approach to the normalization problem is to divide each indicated worth of a task version by the largest worth for that task, resulting in the normalized worth as shown in Table 1. The normalized worth ($\underline{\eta_{ij}}$) of $w_{ij}(m)$ is then given by

$$\eta_{ij} = w_{ij}(m) \,/ \max_{0 \leq a < I_j} w_{aj}(m). \tag{1}$$

As shown in Table 1, all worths for all versions of each task are normalized by the version with the largest worth. Therefore, the version with the largest worth of each task will have a normalized worth of 1 and the rest of the versions will have normalized worths that are relative to the version with the largest worth. This is the reason why the indicated worths for each task need not sum to one.

Another approach to the normalization would be to divide each version's worth by the total sum of the version worths of the task. This would not guarantee equal value for the most preferred version of each task. Furthermore, this approach would allow a greedy person to obtain a higher value for his/her preference for the version with the largest worth. For example, consider task 0 and task 1 in Table 1. If this alternative approach is used, the normalized worth for task 0 would be .1, .1, and .8, while for task 1 it would be .25, .35, and .4. This means that, even if task 0 and task 1 have the same priority, the largest worth version of task 0 is worth more than the largest worth version of task 1, which should not be the case. In extreme cases, priorities may be irrelevant depending on how priorities and worth of versions interact.

3.4. Deadlines

Many tasks in typical heterogeneous computing environments have deadlines associated with them. Frequently, due to limited resources and the multiplicity of tasks sharing these resources, not every task can be completed by its deadline. Three types of deadlines will be considered for the i-th version of task j: earliest ($\underline{e_{ij}^{d}}$), soft ($\underline{s_{ij}^{d}}$), and firm ($\underline{f_{ij}^{d}}$). These three deadlines are illustrated by example in Figure 1. The deadline attribute discussed here is related to the timeliness parameter in [24].

The earliest deadline (e_{ij}^{d}) is the time when the system is ready to complete a task, based upon, for example, the availability of the required input data. Therefore, if a task completes before the earliest deadline the task has 0 value.

The soft deadline (s_{ij}^{d}) is the time by which a task must complete to be of full value to the user [27]. If a task is completed between the earliest deadline and the soft deadline, then the task will have its maximum value.

A task that is completed after its firm deadline (f_{ij}^{d}) will have 0 value, because the task will be of no use after that deadline [15, 27]. For example, if a task that shows a map of an area completes after a mission is finished, then it will have no value. If a task completes between its soft and firm deadline, then it will have some fraction of its maximum possible value. For each task, the fraction of total value for each point between the soft and firm deadlines, and the time between the soft and the firm deadlines, may be a function of the situational mode. For example, during war mode, the soft and firm deadlines may be identical.

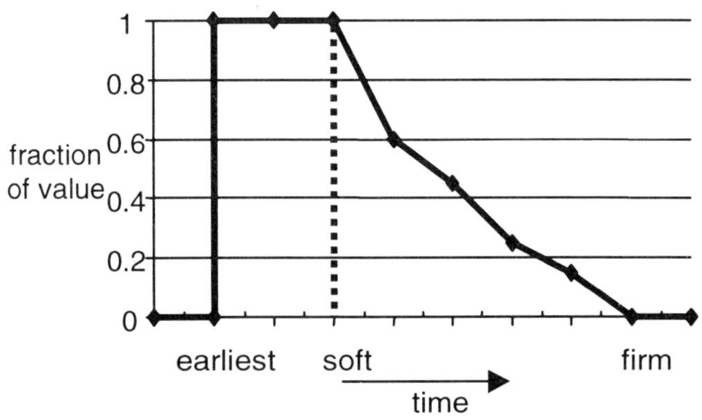

Figure 1: The deadline coefficient graph (non-increasing) shows the variation in the value of a task with various deadlines.

Let $\underline{\tau_{ij}}$ be the time that the i-th version of task j actually completes. The deadline function $\underline{\delta_{ij}(\tau_{ij}, m)}$ assigns a fraction of the maximum value of the i-th version of task j based on m, τ_{ij}, e_{ij}^{d}, s_{ij}^{d}, and f_{ij}^{d}, where $0 \leq \delta_{ij}(\tau_{ij}, m) \leq 1$. If no version of a task is completed, $\delta_{ij}(\tau_{ij}, m) = 0$ for all versions of the task. The deadlines may be the same for all versions of a certain task.

3.5. Security

User and task security requirements are met by "security services." Overall network security can be viewed as a multi-dimensional space of security services. This multi-dimensional space can be represented with a vector ($\underline{S}$) of security components, where the functional requirement for each component is specified by a Boolean statement for each given situational mode. Both resources and tasks may have multiple security components [11].

The instantiation of a network task either meets, or does not meet, each component's requirement. For example, consider the i-th version of task j. Let $\underline{R}_{ij}$ be an ordered set of resources utilized by v_{ij} and let $\underline{S}_{ij}$ be a sub-vector of vector S. A component $\underline{c}$ in S is in S_{ij} if and only if c depends on v_{ij} or on an element of R_{ij}, and is denoted $\underline{S_{ij}.c}$. Let $\underline{Z}_{ij}$ be 1 if the instantiated Boolean value of all c in S_{ij} is true and 0 otherwise. Z_{ij} corresponds to the required security attributes. This means that if minimum security requirements are not met, then no benefit is accrued from executing v_{ij}.

Additionally, some security components of a task can be variant in that they allow a range of behavior with respect to a requirement (e.g., length of cryptography key may vary between 40 and 256). For variant components, the user may request a particular value or permit a choice from a component's defined range. The RMS must select a specific value within the user's range while considering resource availability, for the completed task to have a non-zero value. The measure will give only partial credit for a task completed with less than the most secure value in the defined range. Thus, additional benefit is accrued if increased security is selected within the range.

The desire to provide *adaptable* security motivates the inclusion of variant security components in the system [16]. Thus, security affects the performance measure when components are variant. For example, assume the percentage of authenticated packets can range between 50% and 90% in increments of 10%. The increment quantizes the range. Let $[\underline{S_{ij}.c}]$ be the number of quanta in $S_{ij}.c$ (in the above case this is five) and $\underline{g_{ij}.c}$ be the fraction of c in S_{ij} satisfied. If a task achieves the third quantum (70%), then $g_{ij}.c$ is $3/[S_{ij}.c] = 3/5 = 0.6$. Suppose $\underline{n}$ is the number of security components in S_{ij}. To quantify the effectiveness of the RMS in providing variant security, let $\underline{A}_{ij}$ be the sum of all $g_{ij}.c$ divided by n as shown in Equation 2.

$$A_{ij} = \Big(\sum_{c \in S_{ij}} g_{ij}.c\Big)/n \qquad (2)$$

The above is just one possible way to combine the values of these security components. For example, the $g_{ij}.c$ values in A_{ij} equation can have relative weightings for given m. Thus, if the military situation changes from peace to war, encryption rate would be considered relatively more important and might be given a high relative weighting.

The overall security factor is defined as: $\underline{\sigma}_{ij} = A_{ij} \times Z_{ij}$, where $0 \leq \sigma_{ij} \leq 1$. It indicates how the value of a task may be degraded due to lack of its most desirable security services.

3.6. Other Application- & Domain-Specific QoS

There is a multi-dimensional space of application- and domain-specific QoS attributes (e.g., jitter level, frame rate, bit error rate) that can also be represented by a vector. There will be zero or more such components per task or data set. These components can be specified in the same way that security was represented. The FISC ratio will use $\underline{\alpha}_{ij}$ to denote such QoS components, analogous to the security factor σ_{ij} [13].

3.7. Dependencies

There are many possible types of inter-task dependencies, e.g., for the MSHN environment, consider a task whose only function is to generate data for other tasks (descendants). There may be an inter-related set of such tasks. If there is a descendant along a path of tasks that does more than just generate data for a subsequent task and if this descendant completes its execution, then the tasks that did nothing more than generate data for this particular task will have value, otherwise they will not. This is because the end user that submitted a task for completion will acknowledge the task to be finished only when the actual results can be determined. If there is no descendant task that produces a result important to a user, all predecessors are worthless to the user.

The first task in a path that does more than generate data for a subsequent task will be known as a required associate of all of its predecessors. This is one way of determining the value of ascendants that only generate data for subsequent tasks. The variable ρ_{ij} will be used to represent whether a required associate of a given task completes. That is, if at least one required associate of a given task completes, then $\rho_{ij} = 1$, otherwise $\rho_{ij} = 0$. For the BADD/AICE environment, a similar definition of required associates can be established based on the set of data requested by a given application.

4. Performance Measure

4.1. FISC Ratio

The question of what it means to "provide good QoS" to a mixture of applications in a distributed system is considered in this section. In general, it is a difficult problem to determine whether a distributed system has delivered good service to a mixture of applications with different priorities, receiving different degraded level of QoS etc. A meaningful way to combine the QoS attributes previously discussed is motivated and proposed in this section.

First, consider a set of tasks, possibly with different priorities and different deadlines, where the firm and soft deadlines are identical. Assume also that each task only has a single version. Therefore, the initiators of a task need not specify a preference for a version. It is obvious that a system with sufficient resources will complete all tasks by their deadlines. However, if resources are insufficient and tasks cannot complete by their deadlines, then the RMS will complete the tasks with the higher priorities by their deadline. Such an RMS maximizes

$$\sum_{j=0}^{t-1} \pi(p_j, m) \times \delta_j(\tau_j, m), \tag{3}$$

where $\delta_j(\tau_j, m)$ is 1 if the task is completed by its deadline and 0 otherwise. Even when the deadline is more general, as described in Subsection 3.4, it is easy to see that the same criterion should be maximized.

Now consider the same situation, except with tasks having multiple versions. Again, if there are sufficient resources to complete the most preferred versions of each task, then an RMS will allocate resources and initiate those most preferred versions. However, if resources are insufficient for completing the most preferred versions of all tasks, the RMS must consider using less preferred versions for some tasks. Typically, this will result in a reduction of both the value of completing the task and the amount of the resource consumed. Thus, for the resources available the RMS should maximize

$$\sum_{j=0}^{t-1} \pi(p_j, m) \times [\max_{0 \leq i < I_i} \delta_{ij}(\tau_{ij}, m) \times \eta_{ij})]. \tag{4}$$

If only one version of a task is completed, δ_{ij} for all other versions would be 0. Therefore, the max function would be used to indicate whether a version of a task is completed within its deadline.

Similarly, the RMS must consider any reductions in value of a task's completion that is a result of not receiving all required and desired security, and other application- and domain-specific QoS requirements. Furthermore, any dependencies must be obeyed for a task's completion to have any value. One way to accomplish this is to multiply Equation 4 by ρ_{ij}, σ_{ij}, and α_{ij}:

$$\sum_{j=0}^{t-1} \pi(p_j, m) \times [\max_{0 \leq i < I_i} [\eta_{ij} \times \rho_{ij} \times \delta_{ij}(\tau_{ij}, m) \times \sigma_{ij} \times \alpha_{ij}]]. \tag{5}$$

However, the measure shown above makes it difficult to compare one RMS, operating within one distributed system, to another RMS operating in a different distributed system. To allow this kind of comparison, the equation

$$\frac{\sum_{j=0}^{t-1} \pi(p_j, m) \times [\max_{0 \leq i < I_i} [\eta_{ij} \times \rho_{ij} \times \delta_{ij}(\tau_{ij}, m) \times \sigma_{ij} \times \alpha_{ij}]]}{\text{baseline}} \tag{6}$$

normalizes the collective value of the completed tasks by the results from some baseline, which depends on the tasks and underlying distributed system. This will be discussed further in Subsection 4.2.

Recall the goal of the FISC measure is to determine the performance of a schedule (mapping) for tasks in an oversubscribed distributed system by calculating the collective value of the tasks completed. This measure can also be used as a critical part of an objective function of a scheduling heuristic. Components in addition to the FISC measure may be useful in the determining of the objective function. For example, in [29] the objective function that is used includes expected time between when the data request will be satisfied and its deadline (i.e., urgency).

4.2. Baseline

This section provides a baseline for the FISC ratio. The purpose of the baseline in the FISC ratio is to determine how an RMS performs compared to another RMS in a given environment. If the RMS cannot perform much better than this baseline, then a naive algorithm for resource assignment would perform almost as well as the RMS. The baseline builds upon and extends the example given by [29]. The algorithm used to compute the baseline uses the concept of perfect completion. A task is said to achieve perfect completion if there exists available resources, to which it can be assigned, that would allow it to complete with $\eta_{ij} = \delta_{j} = \sigma_{ij} = \alpha_{ij} = 100\%$ and $\rho = 1$.

A simple algorithm, which assumes knowledge of the expected resources needed by a task to complete, can be used to obtain a baseline. For the results of the obtained baseline to be reproducible within a certain tolerance, an ordering of the tasks is needed.

The algorithm is shown in Figure 2 and it proceeds as follows. First, it assigns an ordering to the tasks according to their priorities, deadlines, and expected execution times where the above criteria are considered in the aforementioned order. For the tasks with the same priority level, the deadline would be used as a tiebreaker. If tasks have same priority level and deadline, the expected execution time would serve as a tiebreaker. Only if tasks have the same priority, deadline, and expected execution time would the ordering be random. Alternatively, additional characteristics of the task could be used for finer ordering. In other problem domains, other parameters could be more appropriate for ordering the tasks. After the ordering, the algorithm determines whether the first task (according to the ordering) can be expected to achieve perfect completion using the available resources. If so, it computes the expected availability of resources after that task has completed, under the assumption that the task uses the first such available resources. It also adds the weighted priority of this task to the baseline, which was initialized to 0. If a task cannot achieve perfect completion, nothing is added to the baseline and the task is not considered again. The same process is repeated for each task, considering them according to the ordering.

```
order tasks by priority, deadline, and expected
execution time
if all are equal, order is random

if task can get η_ij = δ_ij = α_ij = σ_ij = 100%
and ρ_ij = 1
    schedule
    add π(p_j, m)
    update status of resources
else
    no value added
    no resources consumed
```

Figure 2: Baseline algorithm.

4.3. Generalization

The previous subsection describes one instantiation of the FISC ratio. It can be generalized such that the numerator is any function of $\pi(p_j, m)$, η_{ij}, ρ_{ij}, $\delta_j(\tau_{ij}, m)$, σ_{ij}, and α_{ij} (or other factors), and each of these primary factors can be any function of secondary factors (e.g., primary factor σ_{ij} includes an average of $g_{ij}.c$ secondary factors in the security context described in Subsection 3.5). Let P_r be a primary factor where there can be u number of primary factors ($0 \leq r \leq u-1$) and s_e be a secondary factor where there can be v_r number of secondary factors ($0 \leq e \leq v_r - 1$). The generalization of FISC ratio can be represented as

$$FISC = \text{f}(P_0, P_1, \ldots, P_{u-1}) / \text{ baseline and} \qquad (7)$$

$$P_r = \text{f}_r(s_0, s_1, \ldots, s_{v_r - 1}),$$

where each s_e is a secondary factor for P_r. Linear or nonlinear weightings of each factor, depending on the importance of the factor considered in a given environment, may be included in all the functions of primary and secondary factors.

The baseline described is one method of normalizing the numerator of the FISC ratio. Other methods for normalizing could be incorporated to compare the performance of different RMSs in a given environment.

5. Examples of FISC Ratio Use

As an example of how the FISC ratio might be applied in practice, consider the following scenario. The Joint Force Air Component Commander (JFACC) staff are preparing an Air Tasking Order (ATO). As the ATO develops, one tool available to the JFACC staff for its evaluation is the Extended Air Defense Simulation (EADSIM) system from US Army Space and Missile Defense Command. EADSIM is a warfare modeling application offering great flexibility in the areas modeled, the capabilities of the platforms simulated, and the method of simulation (deterministic or stochastic) [21].

EADSIM utilizes a wide range of computing resources, depending on the features enabled. For example, the stochastic mode may use approximately 20 times the computing resources as the deterministic mode (based on the number of runs required to obtain a statistically significant number of samples). Of course, results obtained in stochastic mode are likely to be more reliable.

The JFACC planners select two versions of EADSIM, the stochastic mode and the deterministic mode, and submit them, with different preferences, to their RMS for execution. Because this information is urgently needed for combat mission planning, the priority of this request is seven on a scale of ten (ten being highest). The deadline is firm, with the simulation results required within an hour. If received within an hour the results will achieve some fraction of their maximum worth. After that time, they receive 0 value. The stochastic version is preferred because it will produce higher confidence results, but the deterministic simulation may also be useful. The stochastic version is assigned a preference of eight, on a scale of ten, while the deterministic version is assigned a preference of five. Security level in this case is binary. The information must be sent over a secure link. If it is, a version is assigned a security value of 1, if not, it is assigned a security value of 0. If only one of the two versions can be completed, and these are the only ones to choose from, then the stochastic version will be completed because it will give a higher value than the deterministic version. This is a simple case; usually other factors have to be considered (e.g., expected execution time) when scheduling tasks.

An RMS such as MSHN would evaluate the expected resource requirements of each version as well as the ability to complete each version based on the current resource availability. Using this information, the RMS could make a wise decision by maximizing an objective function where the FISC ratio would be a major component. While this example is from a military environment, the FISC ratio can be adapted for other environments as well.

6. Summary and Future Work

The FISC ratio provides a way to quantify the value of the performance received by a set of applications in a distributed system. Thus, it can be used to evaluate the effectiveness of the mapping of a collection of requests to resources done by a scheduler. In addition, it may be used in a simulation mode to analyze the impact of proposed changes to the distributed system. Therefore, the FISC performance measure presented here will help the distributed computing community in the implementation of resource management systems and the analysis and comparison of such systems. Furthermore, the FISC ratio may be used as a critical part of a scheduling heuristic's objective function. A generalization of the ratio is also discussed in this research. Additional issues that may be considered in future research include weighting the relative importance of the π, η, ρ, δ, σ, and α factors, using a non-linear combination of task values to compute the overall measure, and using of negative fractions in the deadline function in case of catastrophic results from a missed deadline could be incorporated.

Acknowledgments: The authors thank B. Beaton, G. Koob, J. Rockmore, E. Chong, M. Jurczyk, I-J. Wang, S. Jones, T. D. Braun, N. Beck, S. Ali, S. Chatterjea, A. Naik, P. Dharwadkar, J. Kresho, and N. Rowe for their valuable comments.

References

[1] Agile Information Control Environment Proposers Information Package, BAA 98-26, http://web-ext2.darpa.mil /iso/aice/aicepip.htm, Sep. 1998.

[2] L. Badger, D. F. Stern, D. L. Sherman, K. M. Walker, and S. A. Haghighat, "Practical domain and type enforcement for Unix," *1995 IEEE Symp. Security and Privacy*, May 1995, pp. 66-77.

[3] M. Blaze, J. Feigenbaum, and J. Lacy, "Decentralized trust management," *1996 IEEE Symp. Security and Privacy*, May 1996, pp. 164-173.

[4] T. D. Braun, H. J. Siegel, N. Beck, L. L. Boloni, M. Maheswaran, A. I. Reuther, J. P. Robertson, M. D. Theys, and B. Yao, "A taxonomy for describing matching and scheduling heuristics for mixed-machine heterogeneous computing systems," *17th IEEE Symp. on Reliable Distributed Systems*, Oct. 1998, pp. 330-335.

[5] S. Chatterjee, B. Sabata, and J. Sydir, *ERDoS QoS Architecture*, ITAD-1667-TR-98-075, SRI, Menlo Park, CA, May 1998.

[6] M. Condell, C. Lynn, and J. Zao, "Security policy specification language," *INTERNET-DRAFT*, Network Working Group, Oct. 1998, ftp://ftp.ietf.org/internetdrafts/ draft-ietf-ipsec-spsl-00.txt.

[7] DARPA, Battlefield Awareness and Data Disse-mination, Apr. 1999, www.darpa.mil/iso/ badd/.

[8] M. M. Eshaghian, ed., *Heterogeneous Computing*, ArTech House, Norwood, MA, 1996.

[9] I. Foster and C. Kesselman ed., *The Grid: Blueprint for a New Computing Infrastructure*, Morgan Kaufmann, San Francisco, CA, 1999.

[10] D. A. Hensgen, T. Kidd, D. St. John, M. C. Schnaidt, H. J. Siegel, T. D. Braun, M. Maheswaran, S. Ali, J. Kim, C. Irvine, T. Levin, R. F. Freund, M. Kussow, M. Godfrey A. Duman, P. Carff, S. Kidd, V. Prasanna, P. Bhat, and A. Alhusaini, "An overview of MSHN: the Management System for Heterogeneous Networks," *8th Heterogeneous Computing Workshop (HCW '99)*, Apr. 1999, pp. 184-198.

[11] C. E. Irvine and T. Levin, "Toward a taxonomy and costing method for security services," *15th Annual Computer Security Applications Conf. (ACSAC '99)*, Dec. 1999, to appear.

[12] J. H. Kim and H. S. Shin, "Optimistic priority-based concurrency control protocol for firm real-time database systems," *Information & Software Technology*, Vol. 36, No. 12, Dec. 1994, pp. 707-715.

[13] J. K. Kim, D. A. Hensgen, T. Kidd, H. J. Siegel, D. St. John, C. Irvine, T. Levin, N. W. Porter, V. K. Prasanna, and R. F. Freund, *A Multi-Dimensional QoS Performance Measure for Distributed Heterogeneous Networks*, ECE School, Purdue, technical report in preparation.

[14] J. P. Kresho, *Quality Network Load Information Improves Performance of Adaptive Applications*, Master's Thesis, Dept. of Computer Science, Naval Postgraduate School, Monterey, CA, Sep. 1997 (D. A. Hensgen, advisor).

[15] C. G. Lee, Y. K. Kim, S. H. Son, S. L. Min, and C. S. Kim, "Efficiently supporting hard/soft deadline transactions in real-time database systems," *3rd Int'l Workshop on Real-Time Computing Systems and Applications*, Oct./Nov. 1996, pp. 74-80.

[16] T. Levin and C. Irvine, *Quality of Security Service in a Resource Management System Benefit Function*, Technical Report, Computer Science Dept., Naval Postgraduate School, to appear.

[17] J. P. Li and M. W. Mutka, "Priority based real-time communication for large scale wormhole networks," *8th Int'l Parallel Processing Symp.*, Apr. 1994, pp. 433-438.

[18] M. Maheswaran, T. D. Braun, and H. J. Siegel, "High-performance mixed-machine heterogeneous computing," *6th Euromicro Workshop on Parallel and Distributed Processing*, Jan. 1998, pp. 3-9.

[19] M. Maheswaran, "Quality of service driven resource management algorithms for network computing," *Int'l Conf. on Parallel and Distributed Processing Techniques and Applications* (*PDPTA'99*), June/July 1999, pp. 1090-1096.

[20] D. C. Marinescu, "A protocol for multiple access communication with real-time delivery constraints," *IEEE INFOCOM '90*, June 1990, pp. 1119-1126.

[21] N. W. Porter, *Resources Required for Adaptive C4I Models in a Heterogeneous Computing Environment*, Master's Thesis, Dept. of CS, Naval Postgraduate School, Monterey, CA, to appear (D. A. Hensgen, advisor).

[22] A. J. Rockmore, *BADD Functional Description*, Internal DARPA Memo, Feb. 1996.

[23] T. Ryutov and C. Neuman, "Access control framework for distributed applications," *INTERNET-DRAFT*, CAT Working Group, Nov. 1998, ftp://ftp.ietf.org/internet-drafts/draft-ietf-cat-acc-cntrl-frmw-01.txt.

[24] B. Sabata, S. Chatterjee, M. Davis, J. Sydir, and T. Lawrence, "Taxonomy for QoS specifications," *3rd Int'l Workshop on Object-Oriented Real-Time Dependable Systems* (*WORDS '97*), Feb. 1997, pp. 100-107.

[25] P. A. Schneck and K. Schwan, "Dynamic authentication for high-performance networked applications," *6th Int'l Workshop on Quality of Service* (*IWQoS '98*), May 1998, pp. 127-136.

[26] B. Shirazi, L. Welch, B. Ravindran, C. Cavanaugh, B. Yanamula, R. Brucks, E. Huh, "DynBench: a dynamic benchmark suite for distributed real-time systems," in *Parallel and Distributed Processing: IPPS/SPDP Workshops*, J. Rolim et al., eds., Springer, Berlin, Apr. 1999, pp. 1335-1349.

[27] J. A. Stankovic, M. Supri, K. Ramamritham, and G. C. Buttazzo, *Deadline Scheduling for Real-Time Systems*, Kluwer Academic Publishers, Norwell MA, 1998, pp. 13-22.

[28] M. Tan, M. D. Theys, H. J. Siegel, N. B. Beck, and M. Jurczyk, "A mathematical model, heuristic, and simulation study for a basic data staging problem in a heterogeneous networking environment," *7th Heterogeneous Computing Workshop* (*HCW '98*), Mar. 1998, pp. 115-129.

[29] M. D. Theys, M. Tan, N. B. Beck, H. J. Siegel, and M. Jurczyk, *Heuristics and a Mathematical Framework for Scheduling Data Requests in a Distributed Communication Network*, TR-ECE 99-2, ECE School, Purdue, Jan. 1999, 58 pp.

[30] C. Wang and W. A. Wulf, "A framework for security measurement," *The Nat'l Information Systems Security Conf.*, Oct. 1997, pp. 522-533.

[31] W.E. Walsh, M. P. Wellman, P. R. Wurman, and J. K. Mackie-Mason, "Some economics of market-based distributed scheduling," *18th Int'l Conf. on Distributed Computer Systems*, May 1998, PP. 612-621.

Communication Support for Distributed Multimedia Components

Ahmed Saleh
Centre for Parallel Computing
University of Westminster
115 New Cavendish St.,
London W1M 8JS, UK.
ahmeds4@cpc.wmin.ac.uk

George R.R. Justo
Centre for Parallel Computing
University of Westminster
115 New Cavendish St.,
London W1M 8JS, UK.
justog@wmin.ac.uk

Abstract

The development of distributed multimedia applications has always been a challenge for both expert and non-expert developers. Middlewares and supporting frameworks have emerged to simplify this process by providing reusable components that can be plugged together in many configurations to help application developers building up their applications. In distributed multimedia, the adoption of such frameworks allows the exchange of media (i.e. audio, video, etc.) and configuration data (i.e. where, how, etc.) transparently through the network. Application developers do not have to deal with details related to the location of data sources and destinations, network protocols used, or even the Quality of Service (QoS) requirements at the network level. Most framework designers tend to concentrate on the aspect of generalising and enhancing the functionality of the framework components and leave the communication between these components to be managed by one of the standard distributed object platforms such as CORBA, DCOM or JavaRMI. This paper describes research undertaken to tackle the problems of designing and managing communication between distributed multimedia components. The design of a supporting framework will be explained with emphasis on the communicational aspect of its components. The paper also includes a case study which illustrate the use of the framework.

1. Introduction

Multimedia systems have a specific nature, which differentiate them from other information or data systems. Unlike most other systems, multimedia systems encompass a large variety of integrated technologies that interact at real time. Multimedia systems, such as video games, teleconferencing, the Internet, and multimedia presentations require the use of different data types that should be dynamically handled and integrated in such a way to produce a complete and efficient system that does not require much involvement from the user.

When distribution starts to be a requirement, which nowadays always is, every system divides its components according to its real life nature in order to produce an open scaleable system. Generally, distributed computing networks link a variety of platforms with different operating systems, variant data formats and many applications that must interact to provide the appropriate services (i.e. storage, compression, transformation, decoding, etc.) needed for an efficient delivery of the system to the user's workstation without any interference from the user.

One of the key principles of distributed systems is that processing does not have to be performed locally but on the most appropriate machine available. Many multimedia system designers are trying to embody this principle in their systems, as most multimedia systems are distributed in nature in that the components of the system may be from sources distributed on various nodes of a corporate network. The introduction of distribution in multimedia systems has presented new challenges for many software and hardware designers.

Most frameworks that provide support for multimedia applications are composed of a number of distributed components each of which has a specific interface that allows other components to access its services. These components interact and co-operate to generate, render and exchange multimedia sessions, using real-time and or pre-recorded media. Communication between distributed components involves the exchange and manipulation of two different types of data, configuration data and media data. Configuration data is the type of data used to locate services over the network, contact specific components, specify media types and QoS, or even to specialise a general-purpose component to perform a specific task. This type of data is considered as non-real time data that has to be accurate regardless of the time taken to send/receive it, so it can be transmitted directly over a TCP/IP network or through a middleware/framework for distributed computing implemented over TCP/IP. On the other hand, the media data (or real-time data) is the encoded media itself which need to be transmitted with the least possible delay and it is subject to different QoS requirements. This type of data can be delivered directly using network protocols like DTP available at sub-layers (i.e. ATM), or through special middleware platform that allows full transparency for components location and remote communication.

The aim of this paper is to explain how distributed multimedia components can be located over the network and how they can communicate and exchange different configuration data. Furthermore, the design of a supporting framework for developing distributed multimedia applications will be briefly explained and how it can be extended/modified by application developers. Finally, an example of a video-on-demand application based on the framework is presented to illustrate its use.

2. A Framework for Configurable distributed multimedia applications

An *object-oriented framework* is a set of abstract classes that creates a reusable design for a specific software family or domain, providing an infrastructure needed to develop an application [15]. However, the design of frameworks should not concentrate only on describing a set of classes and relations between them but they should provide additional built-in functionalities and a group of default implementations that can ease the job of application developers to develop their applications.

Efficient frameworks should allow different instantiation of the entire framework while being flexible enough to be customised to a particular application [11]. Frameworks should provide a clear abstraction that can be used in different contexts (flexible), platform-independent implementation to make it easier to be ported (portable), clear derivation and modification methods for application developers to add/modify functionalities (flexible), and finally a well defined interface that can allow application developers to understand and use such frameworks (understandable).

The scope of our framework is to concentrate on the requirements for developing distributed multimedia applications and the run-time support for such applications. The key approach of the framework described here is to provide application developers with a collection of distributed components that enables them to develop their own applications according to their architectural view of the system. In other words, the framework does not impose any constraints on application developers to follow a specific architectural style to build up their application, however it may dynamically reconfigure itself during run time to improve the application performance/QoS, or it may suggest some changes (e.g. addition of supporting components) to optimise the application functionality.

The framework depicted in this paper is a multilayerd framework (Fig. 1), composed of a collection of distributed components (independent software objects that performs specific operations regardless to their location or environment) and connectors (intermediate objects that provide communication for distributed components to exchange services) that interact and communicate through remote method invocation to form a framework of reusable components that can be tailored to develop a specific multimedia application.

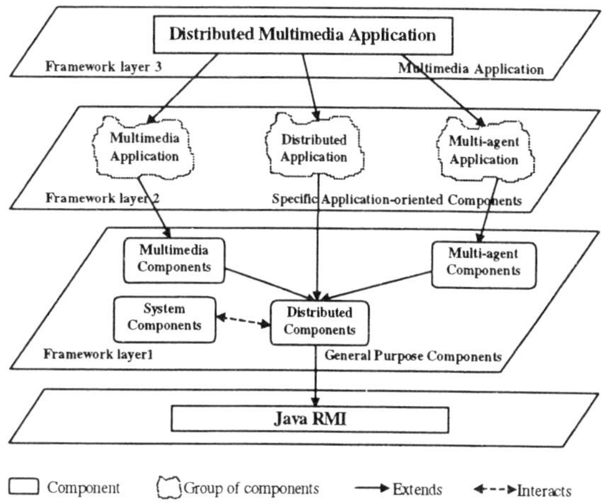

Figure 1. Framework Layers.

The main idea behind using multiple layers is to simplify the management and integration of different distributed components from one layer to another. Hence, allowing multimedia application developers to navigate between the framework layers and customise its components according to their application needs and development skills.

The framework comprises three main layers i) General-purpose layer ii) Specific application-oriented layer iii) Application layer. The components of each layer extends (i.e. instantiates the main functionality and properties of) the components of the corresponding lower layer and add more features to them in order to tailor the components of the topmost layer to support the development of a specific multimedia application.

3. The Architecture of the Framework

In order to create a framework of reusable components, it is very important to specify the operations and methods of interaction between component. The careful specification of such entities will ease the job of application developers in extending and modifying the framework components. In our framework, the interface of each component has been clearly defined in such way that the input and output of each component is well known to other components. Also, the functionality and properties of each component is described carefully in the form of records kept in a general file that can be accessed by any component of the framework.

The framework also introduces a configurable approach [7] that separates the concerns or paradigms of a distributed multimedia application into a set of reusable components that can be upgraded, shared, connected or substituted by components from other systems. This approach can lead to the construction of well-structured distributed multimedia applications that can be easily modified, extended and most importantly can be integrated with other systems. All the framework components are implemented in Java and communicate through JavaRMI (Remote Method Invocation) and also use Java reflection (to dynamically change classes structure during run time, by adding new methods and redirecting method invocations). In the next section, we outline the main components of each layer of the framework.

3.1. General purpose Layer

The components of this layer defines the basic requirements for building any distributed multimedia application. They are divided into four main categories (Fig. 2) according to their functionality: distributed components (a set of components that provides the basic functionality for any components to communicate), system components (a collection of general foundation components for managing and controlling the system resource), multimedia components (components that can create and handle media objects) and multi-agent components (a group of components that co-operates together to monitor/optimise the framework performance).

❑ **Distributed Components:** These are the core components of the framework, as all other components should be derived from one of these components in order to ensure openness and full distribution of the final application. Distributed components comprise a *Communication Manager, Main Component* and *Main Connector*. The *Communication Manager* is the central component responsible for activating other components and connectors, managing the communication between components, searching for local components and locating remote components through contacting other *Communication Mangers*. The *Main Component* and *Main Connector* are the basic components that support the software architectural concepts [14] of this framework. The *Main Component* comprises the basic services required for creating a distributed component that can be dynamically activated, easily located on the network, exchange messages, and register itself with the system once it starts running. The *Main Connector* is an intermediate basic component used by any two components to communicate. It can forward messages between distributed components and in many cases, it can be used to enhance or alter the content of the forwarded message/data before forwarding it. At any level of the framework, components does not need to know any information about connectors, they can simply request services of other components and the *Communication Manager* takes full responsibility for locating/creating the appropriate connector to connect them.

❑ **System Components:** The current prototype of the framework has only one system component, which is the *System Manager*. This component is responsible for starting up and tracking all *Communication Managers* distributed over the network. It can also check the availability of application components located on different machines upon a request from any *Communication Manager*.

❑ **Multimedia Components:** The management and co-ordination of media resources within our framework is achieved by a collection of multimedia components. This collection comprises a *Media Control Manager*, an *Event Handler*, an *Interface* and a *Media Handler*. The *Media Control Manager* provides the fundamental services for generating, playing, rendering and converting any type of media. The *Event Handler* listens and reacts to different types of run-time events while presenting a certain type of media. The *Interface* is basically a collection of GUI (Graphical User Interface) classes that creates and manages the framework user interface. Application developers can use this component to create their own user interface. Also, the *Interface* component can collaborate with the *Media Handler* component to produce an appropriate user interface for playing different media types.

❑ **Multi-agent Components:** This group of components is responsible for monitoring the framework performance (e.g. while playing media or transmitting data) and carrying out changes needed to optimise the performance or to recover from failures that might happen during the applications execution. The main components of this group are; *Agent Structure* (which specifies the responsibilities and functionality of each agent), *Agent Type* (which specifies the constraints and privileges of each agent) and the *Agent Communication* (which provides the communication support for all agents). These components are responsible for observing, gathering and formulating general information about the system either from a series of users' actions or from previous system faults/reactions. They can also allow the system to imitate, predict or suggest the appropriate upcoming reaction when the user faces a problem.

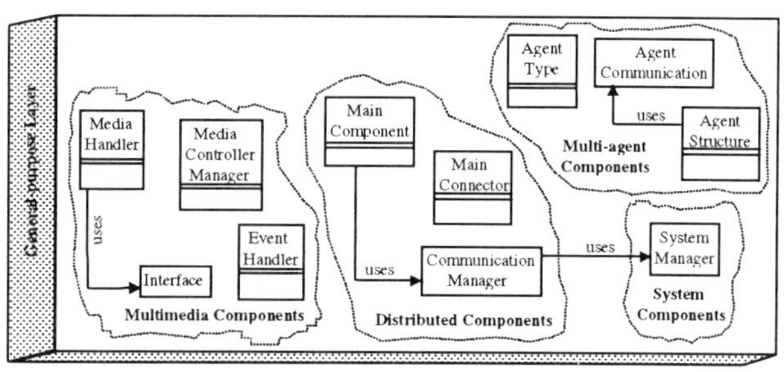

Figure 2. Framework General-purpose layer.

3.2. Specific application-oriented layer

The components of this layer are more concerned with the features intended specifically to support the needs of distributed multimedia applications. At this layer, the interface of each component is well defined, each component is allocated a unique reference by which it can be contacted. Components are split into three categories: *Provider, Requester* and *Connector*. Also, the communication protocol between components is defined at this layer, as components will start to interact and acquire data/support from each other. The components of this layer include *Media* (a component that gathers all the essential functionality to build up a media component. Any media component such as *Text, Video, Audio, etc.* has to be derived from this component), *Media Controller* (responsible for controlling the presentation and transformation of media objects, and *Streams* (a special type of connectors that can send/receive and synchronise between sending/receiving different types of real time media).

3.3. Application Layer

At this layer, application developers can create their own new components or extend/modify the framework components to build up their applications. Although all components are equally accessible by application developers regardless their location at the framework (i.e. layer location), components at the application layer are built in such a way that developers can understand/modify them much easier than components of lower layers. In addition, components of this layer can be used directly by developers without any modification, they just need to be plugged in together to form their desired application. An example of a simple video-on-demand application that has been built on top of this framework is illustrated in section 5.

4. Managing Communication between Distributed Components

One of the important characteristics of a software component is that it cannot do everything by itself, it can only carry out its tasks once it has been provoked by another component and provided with the right data. Therefore frameworks has been designed in such a way that they can allow several components to interact and collaborate in order to perform a specific task. But how can a component contact another component without knowing what kind of data it requires, where it is located or even if it is running or not?

As we have already mentioned, the *Communication Manager* is the core component responsible for identifying and locating components in our framework. An instance of the *Communication Manager* is kept on each machine within the network. Each *Communication Manager* maintains a registration system by which each component located on the same machine has to register itself once it starts up. This registration procedure requires each component to inform the *Communication Manager* with the type of service it provides, the data it requires and the connectors it is connected to (if any). This registration has to be performed by the component in both cases whether the component has been explicitly activated by the application developer or implicitly activated by the *Communication Manager*. Accordingly, each *Communication Manager* has to register with the *System Manager*, which is the first component of the framework that has to be started.

The location of the *System Manager* can either be static, (i.e. previously known to all *Communication Managers*), or it can change according to the performance of the framework and in this case *Communication Managers* has to search for it. The main idea of creating such registration hierarchy is to allow the *System Manager* to track *Communication Managers* distributed over the network, even more it allows the *Communication Managers* to track their local components. Therefore, distributed components can be easily located and relevant information about any component can be easily retrieved once its service is required.

One of the novel properties introduced by our framework is to allow distributed components to request the service of other components without knowing whether these components are currently running or not. This facility is supported by the *Communication Manager* which can dynamically activate any component during run time as long as its service is required. Each component extends the *Main Component* has a special method called "StartUp" that has to be invoked either by the component itself (in case it is created by the application developer) or by the *Communication Manager* (in case it is dynamically activated at run time). This feature provides great flexibility for the framework and eases the job of non-expert application developers while using the framework. The System Manger, *Communication Manager*, components and connectors communicate with each other according to a well-defined protocol and a sequence of steps (Fig. 3) that has to be followed:

I) Once the *System Manager* has started, other components within the framework can start up. Since every component has to register with its local *Communication Manager* once it starts up, it has to contact the *Communication Manager* to perform such registration (step 2) before doing anything else. If the local *Communication Manager* for this component is not available, the component has to contact the *System Manager* to activate the *Communication Manager* on that machine. The Communication Manager then registers with *the System Manager* (step 1) after it starts up.

II) When a component requires the service of another component, it has to send a connection request (step 3) to the component via the *Communication Manager*, which checks its registry to find whether the required component is running locally or not. If the component is located, the *Communication Manager* checks again whether it is connected to a connector (any two components communicate through a connector) and whether this connector is compatible with the service required by the requesting component. Then if all these checks are passed, the ID of the connector will be returned (step 10)

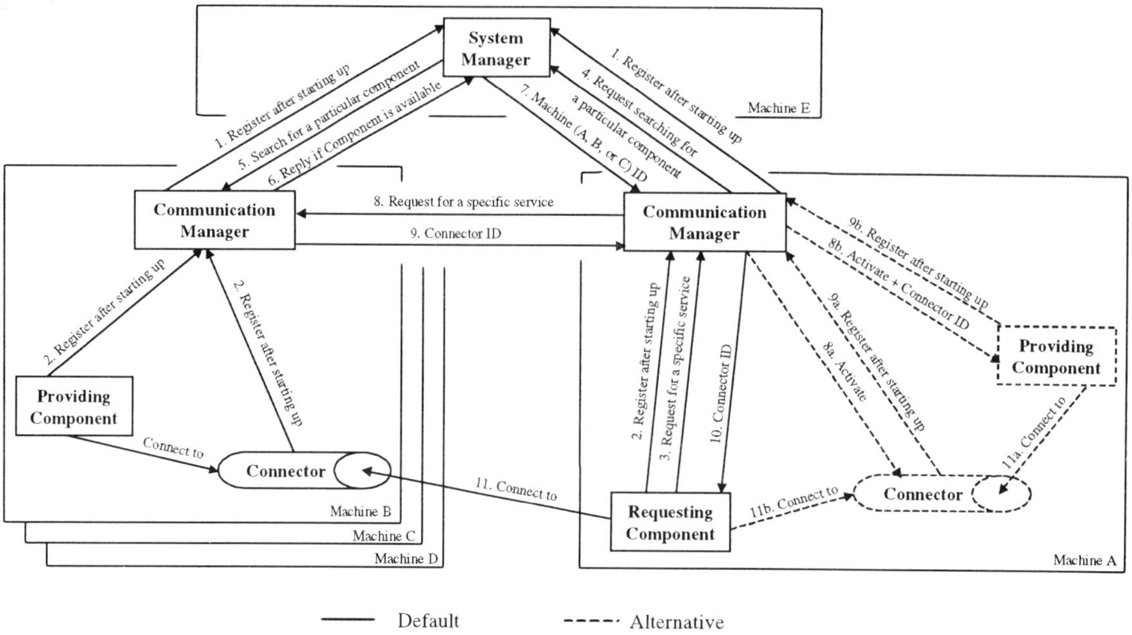

Figure 3. Components communication protocol.

to the requesting component, which will be used to establish the connection (step 11).

III) If the required component is not running locally, the *Communication Manager* contacts the *System Manager* (step 4) which checks if the component is running on another machine (step 5, 6) and returns the ID of the machine (step 7) where it finds the component to the *Communication Manager*. The *Communication Manager* will use this ID to contact the *Communication Manager* of the other machine (step 8) to check whether the component is already connected to a connector that can forward the service required by the requesting component. If so, it returns the ID of that connector (step 9) to the *Communication Manager* which forwards it to the requesting component (step 10).

IV) Finally, if the required component is not found neither remotely nor locally, then the *Communication Manager* has to activate/create an instance of that component (step 8b, 9b) on the local machine and connects it to the appropriate connector (step 11a). Similarly, if the connector supporting the service required is not available, the *Communication Manager* has to create it (step 8a, 9a) and pass its ID to both components (step 8b, 10) to establish the connection between them (step 11a, 11b). In the case of creating or activating a component by the *Communication Manager*, the checking for availability of the connector has to be done first (so it can be created if it is not available) and its ID can be passed automatically to that activated component (step 8b), which will be used to establish a connection with the connector once the component starts up (step 11a).

The Communication between components is based on Java RMI [8] and in many cases we use the Java reflection mechanism [2] to overcome the restrictions imposed by RMI to specify the name and destination of the servers before establishing any kind of communication between clients and servers. For example, in the case of a component requesting the service of another component, it does not know the name or type of service this component provide. Therefore, reflection can be used to determine the class name and methods used by this component.

5. Case Study: A Video-on-demand application.

With the continuous development of distributed multimedia applications, telecommunications and media capturing and playing devices, distance learning has become one of the leading areas to take advantage of this development. Distance learning students can access lectures either on-line (i.e. live at the same time the lecture is running) or in a pre-recorded form. In this example we are focusing on the latter, where students are located in a remote place (i.e. home or other university) and trying to use their computers to watch some lectures that has been recorded previously and saved on files at the university machines. Students can acquire the file names either from the lecturer (e.g. by E-mail), or they can search through the lectures directories using a menu interface that can show them a list of files, from which they can select the file they want.

Students should not have any restrictions on the number of files they can access, but each student can only watch one lecture at a time. Also, they have the ability to control the playback of the lectures through their own machines.

We assume that the university machine should be capable of dealing effectively with all students without affecting the quality of the service provided for each student. This can be implemented by constructing the system in such a way that it can handle each user separately until it reaches a certain limit, then it can replicates itself and allow its new copy to deal with new requests.

5.1. Architectural description of the Video-on-demand system

One of the most important things that have to be considered while designing a framework is how to support its customisation. Customisation can be difficult to implement when you want to provide a flexible and general framework, but you also want to maintain the focus of the framework and minimise the complexity of reusing it.

The approach we have followed in the design of our framework to help communicate how to use the framework was the separation of concerns and modularity [6]. Application developers can directly use some of the components without any modification, they can also extend some of the specific application-oriented components by deriving new classes that can specialise, add or override selected operations, while keeping other standard operations unchanged. Furthermore, some components can be specialised by parameterisation. All these specialised components can then be combined in a variety of ways to produce the desired application system quickly and efficiently.

Bearing in mind the above considerations, a prototype of a video-on-demand system has been built (Fig. 4) using five main components.

- *Video Provider*: A component that uses the *Media* component to generate media streams and send them to *Video Players*.
- *Video Provider Factory*: A component that extends the *Media Provider* component and is used to create and manage *Video Provider* components.
- *Video Player*: A component that extends the *Media Player* component and uses the *Media* component to acquire video streams and play them. Note that the *Media Controller* component has to be parameterised by the type of service required (i.e. play, transform, etc.) to create the *Media Player* component. The *Media Player* extends the functionality of the *Main Component* and provides additional operations to support the service required.
- *Video Stream Connector*: A component that forwards video streams from *Video Provider(s)* to *Video Player(s)*.
- *Video Connector Factory*: A component that extends the *Media Connector* and is used to create and manage *Video Stream Connectors*.

In order to maintain a suitable QoS level and to enhance the scaleability to the system. The system deals with each student separately through configuring the *Sound Provider* and *Sound Stream Connector* to spawn separate

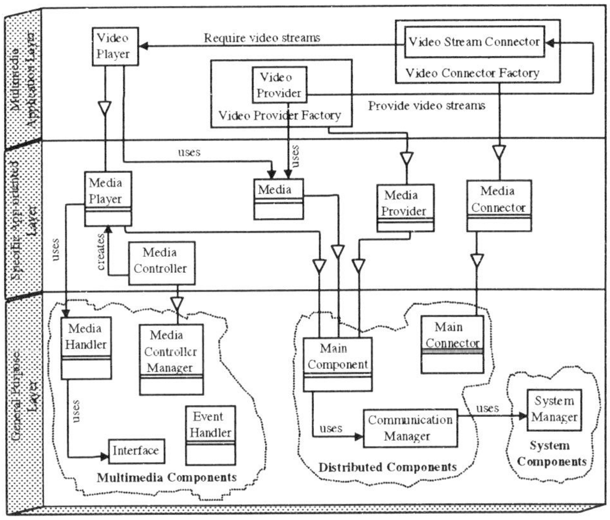

Figure 4. OMT-like description of the architecture of a video-on-demand system.

threads to handle requests coming from different studdents. Accordingly, each *Sound Provider* (and *Sound Stream Connector*) maintains a limited number of threads (i.e. number of students) by which the system can keep its QoS unaffected. If the number of students exceeds this limit, new *Sound Provider(s)* and *Sound Stream Connector(s)* has to be dynamically created to service these students.

Sound Providers and *Sound Stream Connectors* have to inform their local *Communication Manager* with the current number of *Sound Player(s)* (students) using their services. This information is used by the *Communication Manager* when it receives a new service request to decide whether to allow this *Sound Provider/Sound Stream Connector* to accept new connections (i.e. service new students) or to start up a new *Sound Provider/Sound Stream Connector* to handle those new requests.

Components of this application can locate each other and communicate using the protocol explained in section 4, and they can be reconfigured by the application developer using some of the specialisation methods mentioned before to provide and play different types of media.

6. Related work and Conclusion

Reconfigurable distributed systems have been an active research area for more than a decade, many researchers have investigated and proposed developing authoring and run time presentation support for multimedia applications in a distributed context.

For example, Djinn [10] is one of the frameworks that have been constructed to support the development of multimedia groupware applications. It is based on a collection of components (active objects) which produce/consume different media types and events through ports. Also, it supports a specific type of connectors and composite components that allow arbitrarily complex structures to be encapsulated and manipulated as a single object. Although the Djinn connectors and ports support event and stream communication, they hide all the details of networks and communication protocols from the application developer. Djinn is mainly concerned with real time support for groupware applications and their related issues of quality of service. In addition, most of its implementation details are hidden and its dynamic reconfiguration is quite limited.

Bates [1] has based his research on the abstraction of some generic requirements from current and emerging multimedia applications. Using these requirements it is possible to formulate an approach to authoring which can be used to build a wide range of multimedia applications. His approach masks the environment complexities from the user and generally specifies all presentation functions, device access methods and event handling. This makes the construction of multimedia applications much easier, and enables applications portability and maintainability in the future. However, Bates' approach of hiding most of the environment complexities from the application developer restricts the developer's freedom to upgrade or extend the framework components to support new applications.

Another approach was proposed by Will [16]. His research goes further by providing a set of object classes (Hyperform platform) that allows hypermedia services to be tailored to particular requirements and facilities to integrate external tools into the system, which provides scope for the development of a wide range of hypermedia functionality. Hyperform provides an open development environment based on an extended client-server architecture that supports its extensibility. The integration facilities provided by this platform suggests that inter-operations between Hyperform platforms located on separate nodes on the network can be possible, but this is not explicitly supported. Also, it is based on extended client-server architecture, which prevents the developers from implementing different architectural styles, and it does not assist application developers in any way to build up their multimedia applications.

C++CL [7] was a first attempt to create an object-oriented framework for developing distributed software architectures. However, it does not support the development of distributed multimedia applications in particular. Although existing support platforms simplify the presentation of complex distributed multimedia applications, they do not assist the development of the application itself. Also, the hidden management of links, and lack of modularity have made these platforms too generic and difficult to apply by non-expert developers.

Current supporting frameworks now incorporates the requirements needed to support the integration and presentation of multimedia applications. Most of these frameworks concentrate on a particular aspect of the application development life cycle (i.e. presentation, QoS, communication or integration) but none of them have considered an architectural approach of developing such applications.

In this paper we have shown that the combination of software architectural concepts with object-oriented frameworks can lead to the development of a new generation of well designed multimedia applications that can be easily reconfigured to suit different architectural styles and different working environments. The framework outlined in this paper has introduced a new approach that separates the concerns of a distributed multimedia application into a set of reusable components that can be extended, modified and dynamically activated at run time. This approach allows application developers to access the basic components of the system, creating a new generation of distributed multimedia applications that can be easily maintained, extended and integrated with other systems. Also, the clear definition of component names, functionality, interface and methods of reuse improves the understanding and reuse the framework components.

7. Future work

Our framework is still under construction and additional features will be added to improve its components' functionality and performance (e.g. QoS is one of the areas that still needs a lot of attention in our framework). We intend to validate the framework with the development of a large distributed multimedia application. Finally, the overall performance and behaviour of the framework will be enhanced by a group of intelligent agents.

8. References

1. Bates, J.: Presentation Support for Distributed Multimedia Applications. University of Cambridge. PhD thesis, 1994.
2. Brose, G.: Reflection in Java, CORBA and JacORB. Berlin Free University, Institute of Information, Takustrabe 9, D-14195 Berlin, Germany. Lecture Notes in Computer Science, Springer 1998.
3. Fayed, M. and Schmidt, D.: Object-Oriented Application Frameworks, Communication of the ACM, Vol. 40, No. 10, Oct. 1997, PP. 32 - 38.
4. Garrido, A. and Rossi, G.: A Framework For Extending Object-Oriented Applications With Hypermedia Functionality, New Review of Hypermedia and Multimedia, Vol. 2, 1996.
5. Goose, S., Dale, J., Hill, G., De Roure, D. and Hall, W.: An Open Framework for Integrating Widely Distributed Hypermedia Resources. University of Southampton, Jun.1996, http://www.ecs.soton.ac.uk/~jd94r.
6. Jacobson, I., Griss, M. and Jonsson, P.: Software Reuse – Architecture, Process and Organisation for Business Success. New York, ACM Press, 1997.
7. Justo, G. R. R. and Cunha P.R.F.: An Architectural Application Framework for Evolving Distributed Systems, Journal of Systems Architecture: Special Issues on New Trends in Programming and Execution Models for Parallel Architectures, Heterogeneously Distributed Systems

and Mobile Computing. Vol. 45, No. 15, Sep. 1999, PP. 1375 – 1384.
8. Little, M. C. and Wheater, S. M.: Building Configurable Applications in Java. Department of Computer Science, Newcastle University, Newcastle upon Tyne, UK. CDS, 1998.
9. Malcom, K., Poltrok, S. and Schuler, D.: Industrial Strength Hypermedia: Requirements For a Large Engineering Enterprise, In Proceeding of Third ACM Conference on Hypermedia '91, ACM Press, 1991.
10. Mitchel, S.: DJINN: A Programming Framework for Distributed Multimedia GroupWare Applications. Department of Computer Science, Queen Mary and Westfield College, University of London. Technical report, July 1996.
11. Mulhauser, M. and Gecsei, J.: Services, Frameworks, and Paradigms for Distributed Multimedia Applications, IEEE Software, Fall 1996, PP. 48 - 61.
12. Osterbye, K. and Will: The Flag Taxonomy of Open Hypermedia Systems, In Proceeding of Hypertext '96, U.K., ACM Press, 1996.
13. Sanchez, J., Leggett, J. and Schnase, J.: HypeActive: Extending An Open Hypermedia Architecture To Support Agency. Texas A&M University and Washington University. ACM Transactions on Computer-Human Interaction, Vol. 1, No. 4, Dec. 1994, PP. 357 - 382.
14. Shaw, M. and Garlan, D.: Software Architecture: Perspectives on an Emerging Discipline, Prentice-Hall, 1997.
15. Tepfenhart, W. and Cusick, J.: A Unified Object Topology, AT&T. IEEE Software, Jan. 1997, PP. 31 - 35.
16. Will, U. and Leggett, J.: HyperForm: A Hypermedia System Development Environment. Texas A&M University. ACM Transactions and Information Systems, Vol. 15, Jan.1997, PP. 1 - 31.

Short Presentations 1: Applications

Parallelizing a Global Optimization Method in a Distributed-Memory Environment

Zdzisław Szczerbiński
Polish Academy of Sciences
Institute for Theoretical and Applied Computer Science
Bałtycka 5, 44-100 Gliwice, Poland
zdzich@hotmail.com

Stanisław Kowalik
Silesian Technical University
Faculty of Mining and Geology
Institute for Management and Restructuring in Mining
Akademicka 2, 44-100 Gliwice, Poland
stan@boss.gorn.polsl.gliwice.pl

Abstract

We present research into parallelizing the zone-parallel method of global optimization. The method belongs to the class of genetic algorithms and is briefly described in the paper. Upon introduction to genetic algorithms, parallelization models for genetic algorithms are presented. The subsequent part of the paper is devoted to the global optimization problem of finding sources of tremors in coal mines. First, a short description of the S-P method for localizing hypocenters of tremors is given; the method requires minimizing the error function for hypocenter location. Next, a practical coal-mining example is given where data on a tremor are collected by seismometers and the location of the hypocenter is found by employing the zone parallel method. Experimental results are presented which were obtained from implementing both the sequential and parallel versions of the zone-parallel method in a local area network of Sun Ultra workstations. The results show suitability of the island model of parallelization for this optimization method, as well as disproving usefulness of the master-slave model.

1. Introduction

The *global optimization* problem occurs very often in various areas of science and technology. It consists in finding, for a nonlinear multivariable function which may have many local maxima/minima, the optimum with the highest/lowest function value. We may denote it as

$$max_{(x_1,x_2,\ldots,x_m)\in D} f : R^m \to R$$

and

$$min_{(x_1,x_2,\ldots,x_m)\in D} f : R^m \to R$$

where D is some closed region in R^m. It is often assumed that the region D is specified by a set of lower and upper bounds on the variables x_i, $i = 1, 2, \ldots, m$. The global optimization problem is generally difficult to solve. Firstly, it is difficult to specify simple and deterministic mathematical rules upon which to base reliable and effective algorithms. Secondly, obtaining accurate solutions for practical optimization problems usually requires huge amounts of computations. For these reasons, for many years the pace of research in this area was fairly slow. Only in recent years has it accelerated thanks to advances in both optimization algorithms and computer technology.

Global optimization methods utilized today are very diverse. Many approaches address only cases where the optimized function has special mathematical properties, e.g. concavity. Of more importance, however, are the more general cases. Here, there have been developed trajectory methods [1], deflation and tunneling methods [9], interval arithmetic methods [4] and the simulated annealing method [7]; for a comprehensive survey see [6]. In recent years there has been much research into methods which employ genetic algorithms. One of them, called the zone-parallel method of global optimization, has been described in [8]. In this paper, we present our research into parallelizing this method. Our theoretical considerations are accompanied by experimental results obtained from implementation of two parallelization models in a distributed-memory environment.

The paper is organized as follows. In section 2, general principles of genetic algorithms are presented. Next, the zone-parallel method of global optimization is briefly described. Section 3 gives a short description of possible models for parallel genetic algorithms. In section 4, we describe practical results obtained from implementing the zone-parallel method, in both its sequential and parallel versions, on Sun Ultra workstations working in a local area

1066-6192/99 $10.00 © 1999 IEEE

network. The above implementation was used in solving a typical mining industry problem of localizing the hypocenter of tremors. Concluding remarks and directions for future research are contained in section 5.

2. Global optimization with genetic algorithms

2.1. Genetic algorithms

A *genetic algorithm* is a computational model of biological evolution. It is based on natural laws of genetics. Its first step is random generation of a population of individuals. The next step, called selection, consists in making copies of "better" individuals and deleting "worse" ones. In order to cathegorize individuals, for each of them there is computed the value of some cost function ("fitness"). Copying is not exact. With some probability, there is crossover (partial exchange of genetic material between two individuals) and mutation (random change of an elementary piece of an individual's genetic code). As a result, a new population is created. The process of selection, with its associated crossover and mutation, is next iteratively repeated. After a sufficiently large number of iterations the resulting population consists of much "better" individuals than the initial ones.

In order to perform crossover and mutation, it is necessary to decode the genetic material of individuals. In the simplest case, each individual is represented by a string of bits; this corresponds to a combination of genes in a chromosome. Crossover then indicates swapping a group of bits between strings, and mutation — a single bit flip. The above, simple model of binary representation is due to Holland [5]. In recent years, genetic algorithms have taken many forms and their relation to Holland's model is sometimes fairly distant. The literature is ripe with experiments involving various types of individuals' representations. Also, the operations of crossover and mutation take many forms; sometimes, thoroughly new genetic operations are introduced. Hence, some authors reserve the term "genetic algorithm" to Holland's model (with certain extensions) only; the remaining, "akin" types of algorithms form two classes, called *evolutionary programming* and *evolution strategies*. All the above types of algorithms are collectively called *evolutionary algorithms* [10, 12].

Genetic algorithms, in their many forms, are extensively applied to solving problems in many areas of science and technology. Their most common application is, presumably, in global optimization of multivariable functions. Here, they are particularly useful in cases where

- the optimized function is very complicated,
- the exact value of the global optimum is not required and its approximation is sufficient.

In genetic algorithms applied to global optimization, the population of individuals is a set of points in region D (see section 1) which are potential solutions to the optimization problem. In the course of population evolution, better solutions have a greater chance of survival and remain in the population whereas worse ones are eliminated. As a result of genetic operations, in each generation there appear, with some probability, solutions which are better than the ones obtained so far. Consequently, the search process is guided towards the global optimum. For a given problem, the optimum may never be achieved; however, after a sufficiently large computation time the obtained solution (the point for which the function value is highest/lowest) is in the proximity of the optimum which is satisfactory enough to accept the solution as optimal.

Genetic algorithms are employed to optimize multivariable functions in, for example, aircraft design and image processing. This paper describes a genetic algorithm applied to global optimization in geology and mining. An individual (point in the region of potential solutions) is represented by its coordinates which are floating-point real numbers. The algorithm's characteristic features are absence of crossover and replacement of eliminated individuals by new ones which are randomly generated. Its short description is given in the next subsection.

2.2. The zone-parallel method of global optimization

There is given a function $f(x_1, x_2, \ldots, x_m)$ defined on some region D in m-dimensional space. The region D is specified by bounds: lower xl_i and upper xu_i for each variable x_i, $i = 1, 2, \ldots, m$. We assume that the function $f(x_1, x_2, \ldots, x_m)$ may have local optima. The objective is to find the global optimum i.e. the point in region D for which the value of $f(x_1, x_2, \ldots, x_m)$ is, depending on the type of optimization, either highest or lowest.

The initial step of the algorithm is random selection of n points in region D; each point is assigned a consecutive integer index. Let us denote the i-th coordinate of the point with index j by $x_{i,j}$, $i = 1, 2, \ldots, m$, $j = 1, 2, \ldots, n$. The following steps are executed iteratively a declared number of times:

1. sorting n points
   - for finding the maximum — in descending order,
   - for finding the minimum — in ascending order,

   with respect to the value of $f(x_1, x_2, \ldots, x_m)$; new assignment of indices to points is done according to the order of points after sorting;

2. grouping the points, beginning from point with index 1, into 3 adjacent subsets Z_1, Z_2 and Z_3 with respective populations n_1, n_2 and n_3, specified as follows:
   - $n_1 = n_2 = \lfloor \frac{n}{3} \rfloor$,
   - $n_3 = n - 2n_1$;
3. generating a new set of n points as follows:
   - subset Z_1 remains unchanged,
   - subset Z_2 is eliminated and replaced by n_1 points randomly selected from the neighborhood of n_1 points in Z_1:

     $x_{i,j} := x_{i,j-n_1} + (\alpha_{ij} - \frac{1}{2}) \sqrt[m]{\frac{\prod_{i=1}^{m}(xu_i - xl_i)}{n}}$,
     $i = 1, 2, \ldots, m$, $j = n_1 + 1, n_1 + 2, \ldots, 2n_1$,
     α_{ij} — random number from interval [0; 1],
   - subset Z_3 is eliminated and replaced by n_3 points randomly selected from region D;
4. return to step 1.

After a declared number of iterations, point 1 has the value of $f(x_1, x_2, \ldots, x_m)$

- for finding the maximum — highest,
- for finding the minimum — lowest

in region D. A detailed description of the zone-parallel method, including motivation for its steps, has been given in [8].

3. Parallelization of genetic algorithms

There are, basically, three approaches to parallelizing genetic algorithms.

In the *master-slave model* of parallelization, the algorithm is restructured so that fitness evaluation for individuals is performed on different processing units, e.g. processors in a multiprocessor system or computers in a workstation cluster. This requires a master unit executing the basic algorithm and other units computing the cost function. If the number of individuals does not exceed the number of processing units, each unit computes a value for one individual. Otherwise (the most common case) each unit computes values for a number of individuals. This is done in a sequential manner unless system architecture and software mechanisms provide for another level of parallelism, as in the case of a multiprocessor workstation in a parallel distributed environment. The master slave model is ideal for applications where fitness evaluation is the most time-consuming part of a genetic algorithm. An algorithm parallelized according to this approach is sometimes called *micro-grained*.

The *island model* of parallelization is designed for *coarse-grained* parallel and distributed systems. The initial population of individuals is divided into partitions. Next, each partition is assigned to a separate processing unit. Each unit then runs its own copy of the unchanged, sequential genetic algorithm on its partition of individuals. Two models of communication between processing units are possible here. In the *isolated* island approach, all processing units work in a perfectly parallel manner, without communicating one another except at the final stage of computations where the best individuals from all units must be compared so as to select the "globally" best one. In the *connected* island model, the units occasionally communicate one another in order to exchange individuals between populations. A widely adopted technique is to periodically broadcast one's best individual to other units and thus guide them towards a possibly better direction in evolution of their populations. Another approach is to exchange individuals with other populations within a predefined neighborhood.

In the *cellular model* of parallelization, each individual is assigned to a separate processing unit. For each unit there is defined a neighborhood within which communication with other units is possible. Selection, crossover and mutation are applied within the neighborhood only. This model is adequate for *fine-grained* parallel systems, especially the massively parallel processors (MPPs).

4. A practical application of global optimization: finding sources of tremors in coal mines

4.1. Localizing the hypocenter of a tremor with the S-P method

The method S-P [8] utilizes differences between occurrences of the transverse (S) and longitudinal (P) seismic waves following a tremor. Let us assume that s seismometers collect data on these waves. Denoting by V_S and V_P the velocities of waves S and P, respectively, we may characterize the tremor with the following set of equations

$$(x-x_i)^2+(y-y_i)^2+(z-z_i)^2 = k^2\tau_i^2, i = 1, 2, \ldots, s \quad (1)$$

where

x, y, z — coordinates of the tremor's hypocenter,

x_i, y_i, z_i — coordinates of seismometer i,

τ_i — difference between times of occurrences of related waves S and P at seismometer i,

$k = \frac{V_P V_S}{V_P - V_S}$ — characteristic parameter for the (geological) area surrounding the tremor's hypocenter.

i	x_i [m]	y_i [m]	z_i [m]	τ_i [s]
1	0	0	0	0.2461
2	0	0	1000	0.2192
3	2000	0	0	0.2432
4	2000	0	1000	0.1863
5	0	2000	0	0.3210
6	0	2000	1000	0.3346
7	2000	2000	0	0.3037
8	2000	2000	1000	0.3046
9	0	1000	0	0.2191
10	1000	1000	0	0.1115
11	0	1000	1000	0.2253
12	1000	1000	1000	0.0717

Table 1. Seismometer measurements of time intervals between waves S and P caused by a tremor.

The system of equations (1) has 4 unknown variables: x, y, z and k. Its numerical solution may be obtained with the method of nonlinear smoothing [11]. (1) may be written as

$$\tau_i = \frac{\sqrt{(x-x_i)^2 + (y-y_i)^2 + (z-z_i)^2}}{k}, i = 1, 2, \ldots, s$$

The error function for hypocenter location is then

$$B(x, y, z, k) = \sum_{i=1}^{s} (\tau_i - \frac{\sqrt{(x-x_i)^2 + (y-y_i)^2 + (z-z_i)^2}}{k})^2$$

Coordinates x, y, z and k of the global minimum of function $B(x, y, z, k)$ are the solution of the system of equations (1). It can be seen that the problem of localizing the hypocenter has become an optimization one. Below we show its solution, with the zone-parallel method, for an example tremor.

4.2. Applying the zone-parallel method to the analysis of an example tremor

In a coal mine, 12 seismometers have been mounted. Eight of them are at the vertices of a cubicoid of size 2 km $\times$ 2 km $\times$ 1 km. The remaining four seismometers are on the cubicoid's two selected, opposite faces. Table 1 contains data gathered by the seismometers after a tremor typical for the mining region of Upper Silesia (Poland).

The tremor's hypocenter was found with the S-P method. As shown above, this involved optimizing function $B(x, y, z, k)$; the optimization was done with the zone-parallel method. First, the sequential version of this method (as described in section 2.2) was implemented in Fortran 90 and run on a Sun Ultra workstation. The number of points was $n = 20$ and the declared number of iterations 300. The bounds for variables x, y and z were the cubicoid's edges; the lower and upper bounds for k were 5500 m/s and 6500 m/s, respectively (the range usually adopted for tremors in Upper Silesia). After the computation time of 0.3 s the global minimum was found at the point with coordinates (in meters) $x = 1063.1$, $y = 665.6$, $z = 599.0$. The value of parameter k was 5687.2 m/s. The value of function $B(x, y, z, k)$ at this point was 0.00278.

Next, two models of parallelization for the method were implemented in a distributed-memory environment. The hardware platform of the environment consisted of four Sun Ultra workstations working in a local area network with the TCP/IP transport protocol. The distributed-memory model of parallel computation was provided by `mpich` [3], a public-domain implementation of the MPI message-passing standard. The method was implemented in High Performance Fortran (HPF) and transformed into Single Program Multiple Data (SPMD) executables by ADAPTOR, a public-domain HPF compilation system [2]. Two versions of the HPF program were developed, for the master-slave and island model, respectively.

In the master-slave model implementation, 5 points of the total $n = 20$ were assigned to each of four computers for parallel evaluation of the function $B(x, y, z, k)$ in these points. However, the computation time was an order of magnitude larger in comparison with the sequential version. The reason were very time-consuming data transmissions between computers, especially during the process of sorting all n points (step 1 in section 2.2).

The island model implementation proved far more successful. We have chosen the isolated island model. The region D was partitioned as follows. Four equal parts were cut, along two symmetry axes, from the rectangle formed in a two-dimensional coordinate system by the lower and upper bounds for x and y, and the whole range of z and k was associated with each such "subrectangle". Thus, each computer executed the sequential algorithm in a subregion whose volume was equal to a quarter of the volume of D. This enabled a more accurate search of the region D for the best solution (there were now 20 points in each subregion rather than in the whole region). As a result, after 300 iterations the obtained solution was better than the one provided by the sequential version: the value of function $B(x, y, z, k)$ was 0.00268. The coordinates of the global minimum were (in meters) $x = 1088.7$, $y = 611.8$, $z = 597.4$; the value of parameter k was 5771.7 m/s. The computation time was 0.5 s, larger than for the sequential version. This was due to time-consuming transfers of final results from computers with logical numbers 2, 3 and 4 to computer 1 whose additional task was to select the best result from the global minima obtained for the four subregions.

5. Conclusions

We have described our research into practical parallelization of a genetic algorithm for global optimization. The obtained experimental results prove usefulness of the isolated island model of parallel computation in a distributed-memory environment. After distributing the region of possible solutions among four locally networked workstations, we found a solution which was better than the one provided by the sequential algorithm executed on a single workstation. Our research into utilizing the master-slave model has shown that this approach is not applicable to distributed-memory systems if frequent communication is necessary between slave units.

Our planned future research in this area concerns parallelizing the zone-parallel as well as other global optimization methods in a distributed-memory supercomputer environment.

References

[1] F. Aluffi-Pentini, V. Parisi, and F. Zirilli. A global optimization algorithm using stochastic differential equations. *ACM Transactions on Mathematical Software*, 14:345–365, 1988.

[2] T. Brandes. *ADAPTOR Users Guide (Version 4.0)*. GMD (German National Research Center for Information Technology), Schloss Birlinghoven, Germany, 1996.

[3] W. Gropp, E. Lusk, N. Doss, and A. Skjellum. A high-performance, portable implementation of the MPI message passing interface standard. *Parallel Computing*, 22(6):789–828, September 1996.

[4] E. R. Hansen. Global optimization using interval analysis – the multidimensional case. *Numerical Mathematics*, 34:247–270, 1980.

[5] J. H. Holland. *Adaptation in Natural and Artificial Systems*. The University of Michigan Press, Ann Arbor, MI, 1975.

[6] R. Horst and H. Tuy. *Global Optimization, Deterministic Approaches*. Springer Verlag, Berlin, 1992.

[7] S. Kirkpatrick, C. D. Gelatt, Jr., and M. P. Vecchi. Optimization by simulated annealing. *Science*, 220(4598):671–680, May 1983.

[8] S. Kowalik. The zone-parallel method of multivariable function optimization and its application to localizing the hypocenter of tremors. *Archives of Theoretical and Applied Computer Science*, 10(1–2):71–91, 1998 (in Polish).

[9] A. V. Levy and A. Montalvo. The tunneling algorithm for the global minimizer of functions. *SIAM Journal on Scientific and Statistical Computing*, 6:15–29, 1985.

[10] Z. Michalewicz. *Genetic Algorithms + Data Structures = Evolution Programs* 3rd ed. Springer Verlag, Berlin, 1996.

[11] J. Stoer. *Einfuehrung in die Numerische Mathematik I*. Springer Verlag, Berlin, 1976.

[12] X. Yao. Global optimisation by evolutionary algorithms. In N. Mirenkov, Q.-P. Gu, S. Peng, and S. Sedukhin, editors, *Proceedings of the Second Aizu International Symposium on Parallel Algorithms/Architecture Synthesis*, pages 282–291, Aizu-Wakamatsu, Fukushima, Japan, March 1997.

Fast Parallel Algorithms for 3D Reconstruction of Angiographic Images

R. Rivas
Facultad de Ciencias.
Escuela de Computación.
Universidad Central de Venezuela.
Apartado 47002, Caracas 1041-A,
Venezuela
rrivas@strix.ciens.ucv.ve

M. B. Ibáñez
Departamento de Computación y
Tecnología de la Información
Universidad Simón Bolívar,
Apartado 89000, Caracas 1080–A,
Venezuela
ibanez@ldc.usb.ve

Abstract

The reconstruction of angiographic images can be seen as a discrete optimization problem where a blind search is not suitable. A Branch-and-Bound algorithm can be used to explore the space state using a-priori information.

The critical issue in parallel search algorithms is the distribution of the search space among the processors. We work with two control schemes: centralized and distributed. According to the data distribution we propose three different mappings: static, semistatic and iterative. We achieve good load balance and a nearly optimum speedup.

1. Introduction

Angiographic images are bidimensional representations of coronaries [5]. Tridimensional reconstruction is based on two (or more) bidimensional images taken and projected onto the 3D-space. An automatic algorithm [4] has several steps. The first one is *image formation*, that involves taking the image, correcting distortions, preprocessing and modeling the projections mathematically; the second one is *segmentation* in which the 2D images are divided into parts called arterial segments; the next step is *reconstruction* which consists on the object's position valuation at the 3D space from these segments, and finally *visualization* which allows to see the structures just reconstructed in the space. The reconstruction step is the object of this work.

Reconstruction is a problem with a non-unique solution where additional constraints or *a-priori* information is necessary. We use the *a-priori* information stated by P. Windyga [9]. The process starts by matching of image structures (arterial segments) which includes the right solution and many others and the goal is to find *the* real solution.

The reconstruction of angiographic images can be seen as a discrete optimization problem where a blind search is not suitable. A Branch-and-Bound algorithm can be used to explore the space state using *a-priori* information given by the filters. The critical issue in parallel search algorithms is the distribution of the search space among processors [3], [2]. The workload for a search into the search space or a piece of it cannot be estimated before hand, thus it is necessary to do dynamic load balancing. We propose different alternatives to follow the methodology stated at [12] and [8] where a dynamic load balancing strategy follows a load evaluation phase in order to estimate the computer's load. Then, load balancing must be done if the cost of imbalance exceeds the cost of load balancing. Finally a sub space is selected and migrated.

In this paper we present one sequential algorithm and six parallel ones which are classified upon the control scheme as *centralized* or *distributed* and the data distribution as *static*, *semistatic* or *iterative mapping*. The sequential algorithm is presented at the next section together with an analysis of the amount of time and space required by the method. In Section 3, we show the schemes with centralized control. In Section 4 we describe two distributed algorithms. Discussion of the load balancing of the parallel algorithms are also included. Finally, in Section 5, we analyze the different schemes given in this work.

2. Computational Aspects

Tridimensional reconstruction of angiographic images based on 2D images, is a multiple solution problem. A matching of the image structures (arterial segments) is given, this matching includes the right solution. ANIA [1], a tool developed at the Universidad Simón Bolívar by Dr. P. Windyga's group [4] provides the 3D-search space for our work. In order to discriminate among the wrong so-

[1] A tool for ANgiographic Image Analysis and study

lutions, a set of filters have been developed by P. Windyga [9], this include 2D properties (object projection properties) such as *superposition* and *completion conditions*; 3D properties (object properties) such as *verticality* and *traversing conditions*, and knowledge about structural properties of the coronary arteries such as the *ramification condition*. The description of these filters is presented below.

Ramification Condition: RC The only ramification allowed is bifurcation. Cycles are forbidden.

Superposition Condition: SC The visual superposition of two segment projections onto any of the 2D plans must be small, in practice it can not exceed 18 mm.

Completion Condition: CC Every segment at the 2D projections must have an image into the 3D-image reconstruction.

Verticality Condition: VC The segments must have vertical orientation, that is they must go down from the main artery to the heart's lower extreme.

No Traversing Condition (or Vectorial Projection): VP The arteries can not either traverse the heart, or go in opposite direction to the blood flow.

In order to find the right solutions, we developed a sequential algorithm that works in two phases: the preprocessing phase and the combining phase. Preprocessing takes a **D**irected **G**raph (**DG**) which is a representation of the 3D-search space and it is transformed into a **T**otal **S**olution **T**ree (**TST**) by applying the *Verticality Condition* to its segments. Then, each possible path from the TST's root to the end-points whose edges satisfy the *Vectorial Projection*, is identified as an **U**nitary **T**hread (**UT**). The input to the combining phase is a set of **UT**s. A first set of solutions is built with every possible combination of two UTs which satisfy the **SC** and **RC** filters. Then, a new set of solutions with three UTs is built by joining every 2UT-solution to the remaining UTs and testing the validity of the **SC** and **RC** conditions. This process continues until no more UTs can be joined to any previous nUT-solution. This process can be formally stated as follows.

1. $Solutions \longleftarrow \{\}$
   $\forall < u_1, u_2 > \ \in UT \times UT$
   if valid(u_1, u_2, SC, RC) then
   $Solutions \longleftarrow Solutions \bigcup \{< u_1, u_2 >\}$
2. $S \longleftarrow \{\}$
   $\forall\, s =< u_1, \ldots, u_n > \ \in Solutions$
   $\forall\, u_i \in UT - \{u_1, \ldots, u_n\}$
   $\forall\, u_j \in \{u_1, \ldots, u_n\} \mid valid(u_i, u_j, SC, RC)$
   $S \longleftarrow S \bigcup \{< u_1, \ldots, u_n, u_i >\}$
   if $S = \{\}$ then
   exit
   else
   $Solutions \longleftarrow S$

This sequential algorithm is similar to the Agrawal's combinatorial algorithm [1] used for Data Mining in Large Databases. In our case, the association rules are the filtering conditions and the process ends when all the solutions that fit the conditions are obtained.

The **D**irected **G**raph used for our experiments was obtained from real data provided by the Milwakee County Medical Center [6]. It has 248 segments, and we start the combining phase of the algorithm with 261 unitary threads. Thus the maximum number of possible solutions is 2^{261}, this quantity can be achieved if filtering conditions are not used. When filtering conditions are used, the search space grows while the algorithm combines 2,3,...,8 unitary threads, then the search space decreases up to the combination of 12 unitary threads. At this point, a small group of possible real Solutions are produced and they can then be examined by a physician. At its maximum point, the search space has around 54190 possible Solutions and it needs at least 1.3 Mega Bytes to be stored. The runtime of the sequential algorithm over a Transputer T805 is 1 hour, 22 minutes and 53 seconds.

2.1. General Framework

We examined the performance of our application using up to eight nodes on our Parsytec MultiCluster-3 platform. Each processor node (Transputer T805) has 4 Mbytes of RAM memory, and works at 30 MHz.

For our experience, we report the following times:

Computing Time. It is the total processing time. It does not include the data structure handling for communications.

Overhead. It is the time used preparing data for communications.

Idle Time. We classified it into two categories:

Communication Waiting Time. It is the time spent waiting for communication while processing.

Rebalance Time. It is the time a processor spends after finishing its work and just before total computation is over.

The load balancing strategies that we present have a coarse granularity. Thus, the communication time is not significant and we do not show it.

An important aspect to be considered in parallel algorithms is the platform constraints. In our case, we have very strong memory limitations, that is why we developed a packing method (see [6]) which allows us to save storage space with a low communication time but increasing the data handling overhead.

3. Centralized Control Schemes

The simplest parallel solution we propose is called *Centralized Control-Static Mapping* (CC-SM). It has a *master* processor and $n-1$ *slave* processors, the *master* does the preprocessing phase and the step 1 from the combining phase, then it distributes the search space by sending $|Solutions|/(n-1)$ (the Solutions with two unitary threads) to the $slave_1$, the second $|Solutions|/(n-1)$ to the $slave_2$ and so on. The *slaves* also compute the Solutions with two unitary threads, then they expand the search space assigned by executing the second step from the combining phase. Finally, the *slaves* send the *master* the Solutions found.

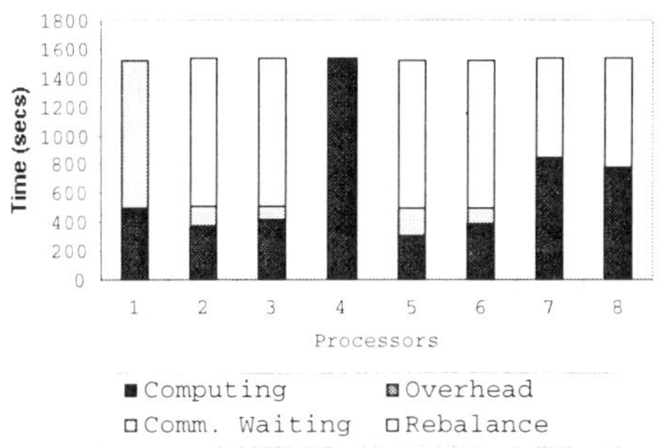

Figure 1. CC-SM Algorithm

Every processor tries to find the Solutions independently inside the search space assigned. In Fig. 1 we can see that processor 4 has the largest search space, it spent more time than the others in computing and preparing Solutions to be sent to the *master* processor. Processors 2, 3, 5 and 6 are idle for up to 75% of their time. Thus this scheme has a severe load imbalance.

In order to solve the load imbalance problem, we propose the *Centralized Control-Iterative Mapping Algorithm* (CC-IM) which distributes the work dynamically among the processors. The *master* sends the Solutions with two unitary threads to the *slaves* as before. The *slaves* receive their search space, they execute an iteration of the second step from the combining phase, and send the Solutions found to the *master*. Then, the *master* distributes equal number of Solutions previously found among the *slaves* and restarts the process.

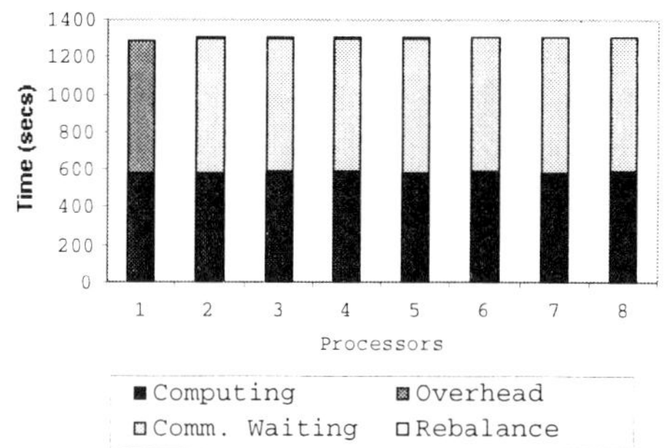

Figure 2. CC-IM Algorithm

Fig. 2 shows a better load balance, in fact, almost every processor finishes at the same time. However, due to the way the workload is distributed, there is a bottleneck at the *master* processor (see communication overhead in Fig. 2). Although the dynamic distribution of work results in communication overhead, this scheme is worthwhile because the program runtime goes from 1511 secs. at the CC-SM scheme to 1310 secs. at the CC-IM one.

In order to minimize the amount of communications, the CC-IM algorithm is improved in two different ways as follows. The *slave* processes send the amount of Solutions found to the *master* at every iteration. The *master* coordinates the transfer of Solutions from the busy *slaves* to the ones with low workload. Let $S_1, \ldots, S_n$ be a *slave's* Solutions to divide up, and let $p+1$ be the number of processes. Fig. 3 shows the algorithm CC-IMa where the splitting strategy is that every *slave* process sends its solutions to the other processes as follows, $[S_1, \ldots, S_{n/p}], \ldots, [S_{((p-1)n/p)+1}, \ldots, S_n]$. Fig. 4 shows the splitting strategy (CC-IMb) where the Solutions are divided in the following way, $[S_1, S_n, S_{2n}, \ldots], [S_2, S_{n+1}, S_{2n+1}, \ldots]$

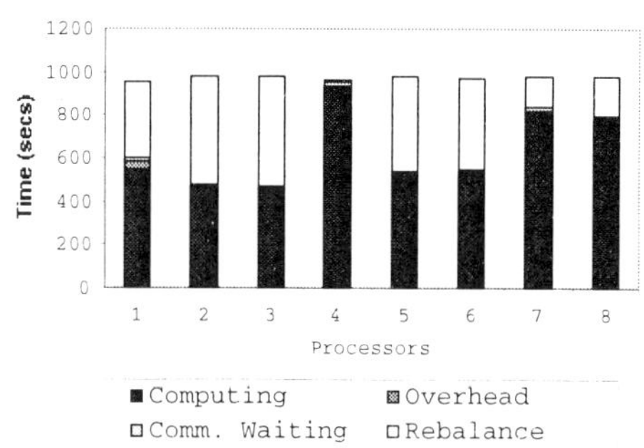

Figure 3. CC-IMa Algorithm

Now, all the processors spend more time doing extra

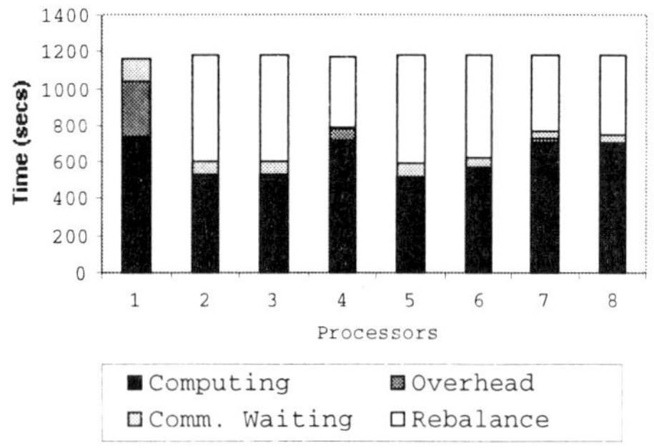

Figure 4. CC-IMb Algorithm

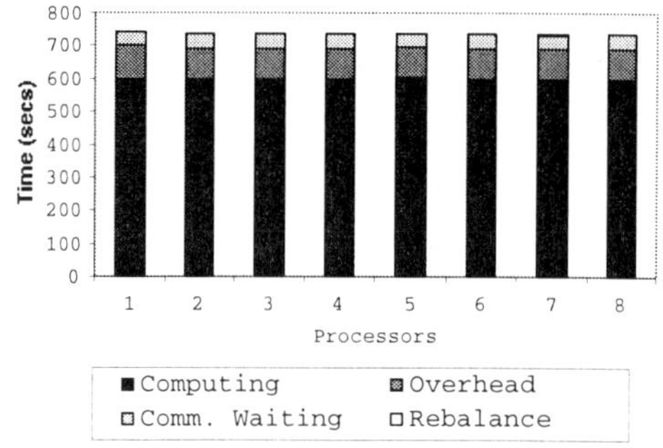

Figure 5. DC-IM Algorithm

computation than in the former methods, this is especially noticeable at the CC-IMb strategy. The CC-IMa algorithm reports a smaller runtime (980 secs) than the CC-IMb scheme (1184 secs.) and it has a better load balance. Both schemes improve the algorithm performance, by minimizing the amount of information exchanged among the processors. However, they have a load imbalance problem, the maximum differences of termination time are 514 and 592 seconds respectively.

4. Distributed Control Schemes

The next two algorithms change the schedule policy from centralized to distributed. We call the first method *Distributed Control-Iterative Mapping* (DC-IM), and it works as follows. The processors take disjoint parts of the search space represented by the Solutions with two unitary threads. After each iteration, each processor distributes the Solutions achieved equally among its partners. Fig. 5 shows how this method achieves a good load balance and improves the runtime (753 secs). The sum of the entire extra computing times is 747.56 secs, almost the same as in CC-IM algorithm (758.45 secs.) but now it is distributed among all the processors, avoiding the bottleneck at the *master* processor. The sum of the load balancing times in this scheme is 18.93 secs., we can hardly improve it, however, the speedup is 6.6 over 8 processors.

The latest method is lightly modified by interchanging the Solutions among the processors after a fixed number of iterations, we call this algorithm *Distributed Control-Semistatic Mapping* (DC-SM), and we found experimentally that 3 times gives the best performance. The results are shown in Fig. 6.

This method has a runtime of 720 secs., and it presents the best speedup (6.9 over 8 processors). It shows a better sum of load balancing times (14.08 secs.) and a better extra-computing time (264.73 secs.), most of it while doing synchronization.

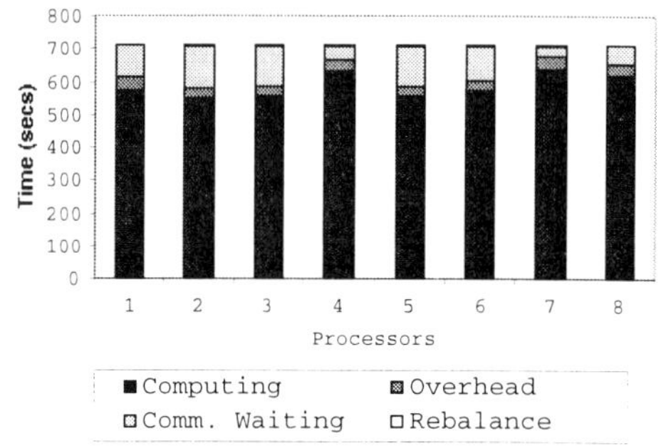

Figure 6. DC-SM Algorithm

5. Conclusions

We presented several load-balancing schemes to solve the problem of 3D-reconstruction of angiographic images from 2D-images. The schemes were classified as *centralized* and *distributed*. In our experiments, the centralized techniques show either a severe load imbalance or a high overhead due to the bottleneck at the master process, while the distributed schemes have a better runtime and avoid the bottleneck.

Among the centralized schemes, we found that the CC-SM algorithm has a poor load balance due to the non uniform amount of work given to the slaves by the master process. The other three centralized algorithms improve the load balance by redistributing the partial solutions at each step of the algorithms. Nevertheless, these schemes have a high overhead.

The distributed algorithms do not have a bottleneck and to avoid the imbalance problem they share the search space periodically. When the search space redistribution is made too often, the overhead is high. Experimentally we found that the best performance is achieved when the search space is redistributed every three iterations.

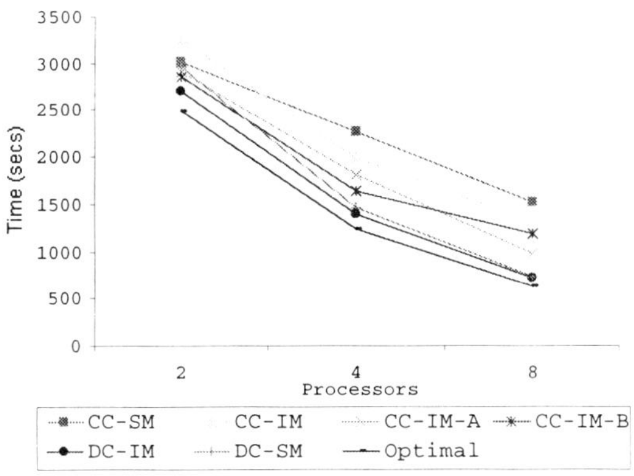

Figure 7. Runtime of the schemes with 2,4 and 8 processors

Fig. 7 summarizes the different run times obtained for each algorithm. Speedup is nearly optimum, and the difference is mainly due to the necessary overhead used to handle the data structures for communication processes. Further work must improve the data compression and transfer algorithms to reduce this overhead.

References

[1] R. Agrawal, T. Imielinski, and A. Swami. Mining association rules between sets of items in large databases. In *ACM SIGMOD Conference*, Washington, D.C., May 1993. ACM.

[2] G. Fox, R. Williams, and P. Messina. *Parallel Computing Works!* Morgan Kaufmann Publishers, Inc., 1994.

[3] V. Kumar, A. Grama, A. Gupta, and G. Karypis. *Introduction to parallel computing. Design and analysis of algorithms.* The Benjamin/Cummings, 1994.

[4] A. La Cruz, G. Morinelli, P. Windyga, G. Bevilacqua, and J. Silva. ANIA: A tool for angiographic image analysis and study. In *XVII IEEE-EMBC Conference*, pages 381–382, Montreal, Canada, 1995. IEEE.

[5] G. Passariello and F. Mora. *Imagenología Médica*. Equinoccio, 1995.

[6] R. Rivas. *Paralelizacion del proceso de reconstruccion tri-dimensional de imagenes cardiovasculares por particion longitudinal del dominio.* Master Thesis, Univ. Simon Bolivar Venezuela, 1999.

[7] R. Rivas, M. Ibáñez, Y. Cardinale, and P. Windyga. A Parallel Algorithm for 3D Reconstruction of Angiographic Images. In P. S. M. B. A. H. B. Hertzberger, editor, *High-Performance Computing and Networking*, pages 168–177. Springer, April 1999.

[8] J. Watts and S. Taylor. A Practical Approach to Dynamic Load Balancing. *IEEE Transactions on parallel and distributed systems*, 9(3):235–248, March 1998.

[9] P. Windyga. *Evaluation et modelisation de connaissances pour la reconstruction tridimensional du reseau vasculaire cardiaque en angiographie biplan.* PhD Thesis, Univ. Rennes France, 1994.

[10] P. Windyga, I. López, G. Bevilacqua, M. Garreau, and J. Coatrieux. Utility of 2D properties in the reconstruction of coronary arteries from biplane angiographic images. In *XVII IEEE-EMBC Conference*.

[11] P. Windyga, G. M., S. M., C. J.L., and L. H. Three-dimensional reconstruction of the coronary arteries using a priori knowledge. In *Medical and Biological Engineering and Computing*, pages 158–164. 36, 1998.

[12] C. Xu and F. Lau. *Load balancing in parallel computers. Theory and Practice.* Kluwer Academic Publishers, 1997.

A Robust Multigrid Solver on Parallel Computers *

R.S. Montero M. Prieto I.M. Llorente
F. Tirado
Departamento de Arquitectura de Computadores y Automatica
Facultad de Ciencias Fisicas
Universidad Complutense, 28040 Madrid, Spain
(rubensm,mpmatias,llorente,ptirado)@dacya.ucm.es

Abstract

In this paper two well-known robust multigrid solvers for anisotropic operators on structured grids are compared: alternating-plane smoothers with full coarsening and plane smoothers combined with semicoarsening. The study takes into account not only numerical properties but also architectural ones, focusing on cache memory exploitation and parallel characteristics. Experimental results for the sequencial algorithms have been obtained on two different systems based on the MIPS R10000 processor but with different L2 cache sizes (an SGI O2 workstation and an SGI Origin 2000 system). Two different parallel implementations for the latter robust approach have been considered. The first one has optimal parallel characteristics but due to deterioration of the convergence properties its realistic efficiency is not satisfactory. In the second one, some processors remain idle during a short period of time on every multigrid cycle, however the algorithm is more efficient since it preserves the numerical properties of the sequencial version. Parallel experiments have also been taken on a Cray T3E system.

1 Introduction

Several methods have been proposed in multigrid literature to solve anisotropic operators and achieve robustness when the coefficients of a discrete operator can vary throughout the computational domain (due to grid stretching or variable coefficients):

- Alternating-direction plane smoothers in combination with full coarsening [1, 10]
- Block smoothing in combination with semi-coarsening [2]
- Recombination of the corrections of more than one semi-coarsening grid (multiple semi-coarsening)[12]
- Standard coarsening combined with a semi-coarsened smoother (flexible multiple semi-coarsening)[16]
- Point-wise smoothing combined with a fully adaptative coarsening process (Algebraic Multigrid)[15]

Single-block grids are widely used in the numerical simulation of many Physical systems. Single-block algorithms are very efficient (especially for structured grids with stretching) due to their relatively easy implementation (on both sequential and parallel computers) and good architectural properties (parallelism and cache memory exploitation). Moreover, single-block grids are used as building blocks for multi-block grids that are needed to deal with complex geometries or to facilitate parallel processing.

In this paper we compare two common approaches to achieve robustness on single-block structured grids: alternating-plane smoothers combined with standard coarsening and plane smoothers combined with semi-coarsening. We study the numerical and architectural properties of both approaches for the solution of a 3D discrete anisotropic elliptic model problem on stretched cell-centered grids.

This paper is organized as follows. The numerical scheme used by our simulations is described in section 2. The numerical results (convergence factor) obtained for different anisotropic problems are found in section 3. Architectural properties (memory hierarchy use and parallel efficiency) are presented in sections 4 and 5 respectively. The paper ends with some conclusions.

*This work has been supported by the Spanish research grants TIC 96-1071 and TIC IN96-0510 and the Human Mobility Network CHRX-CT94-0459. We would like to thank Ciemat and CSC (Centro de Supercomputacion Complutense) for providing access to the systems that have been used in this research.

1066-6192/99 $10.00 © 1999 IEEE

2 The Numerical Problem

2.1 Mathematical Model and Discretization

As a test problem, we have consider the general diffusion equation:

$$\frac{\partial}{\partial x}\left(\alpha\frac{\partial\phi}{\partial x}\right)+\frac{\partial}{\partial y}\left(\beta\frac{\partial\phi}{\partial y}\right)+\frac{\partial}{\partial z}\left(\gamma\frac{\partial\phi}{\partial z}\right)=S_\phi(x,y,z) \tag{1}$$

along with some suitable boundary conditions. Discretization of equation (1) over a 3D computational grid by means of a finite volume technique leads to the discrete operator:

$$\begin{aligned} & \frac{2\alpha}{\Delta x}(X_p\phi_{i+1jk}-(X_p+X)\phi_{ijk}+X\phi_{i-1jk}) \\ + & \frac{2\beta}{\Delta y}(Y_p\phi_{ij+1k}-(Y_p+Y)\phi_{ijk}+Y\phi_{ij-1k}) \\ + & \frac{2\gamma}{\Delta z}(Z_p\phi_{ijk+1}-(Z_p+Z)\phi_{ijk}+Z\phi_{ijk-1}) \\ = & S_{\phi_{ijk}} \end{aligned} \tag{2}$$

Where, in order to get a less cumbersome expression we have defined the discrete coefficients:

$$\begin{aligned} X &= \frac{1}{x_{i+1jk}-x_{i-1jk}}; X_p = \frac{1}{x_{i+2jk}-x_{ijk}} \\ Y &= \frac{1}{y_{ij+1k}-y_{ij-1k}}; Y_p = \frac{1}{y_{ij+2k}-y_{ijk}} \\ Z &= \frac{1}{z_{ijk+1}-z_{ijk-1}}; Z_p = \frac{1}{z_{ijk+2}-z_{ijk}} \end{aligned}$$

2.2 Introduction to Multigrid Methods

There are several methods to solve a system of linear equations like the one defined by (2). In this paper we have studied some relevant properties of one of the most popular, known as multigrid. It is based on two fundamental principles, relaxation and coarse grid correction. The relaxation procedure is based on a standard iterative method, called a smoother in multigrid literature. It is only used to damp high frequency or oscillatory components of the error, since it fails in attenuating low-frequency components. To solve this, a coarser grid correction is used, because on a suitably coarser grid, low-frequency components appear more oscillatory, and so that the smoother can be applied effectively. These operators, i.e. smoother and transfer grid operators, have to be carefully chosen since the overall performance of the algorithm can decrease dramatically.

With multigrid based on standard coarsening (doubling the mesh size in all coordinate directions) and point relaxation as smoother, the above problem is solved properly when anisotropy does not exist. However, if the problem is solved on a stretched grid or the equation coefficients differ with each other throughout the domain (computational and physical anisotropy respectively) the multigrid fails to smooth error components.

2.3 Robust Algorithms

Regular multigrid is not suitable for a general anisotropic problem. In order to solve such a problem, we have to change either the relaxation method or the coarsening procedure. Several ways have been proposed in literature to make multigrid a robust solver so that it can deal with a wide range of problems (a more precise definition of a robust solver can be found in [17]).

Now, we will focus on the two alternatives under study in this paper:

Alternating Plane Smoothers: A general rule in multigrid is to solve simultaneously those variables which are strongly coupled by means of plane or line relaxation [1]. In a general situation the nature of the anisotropy is not known beforehand, so there is no way to know which variables are coupled. One solution consists in exploring all the possibilities, i.e. to use plane relaxation in the three possible coordinate directions.

Semi-coarsening: Several robust methods have been proposed based on changing the coarsening strategy. Among them, we have considered the multigrid scheme presented in [2]. For a 2D problem, the basic idea is simply to use x-line relaxation and y-semicoarsening (doubling the mesh size only in the y-direction) together, or in the same way, to use both y-line relaxation and x-semicoarsening. This approach extends naturally to 3-D in the form of xy-plane relaxation (xz-plane, yz-plane) and z-semicoarsening (y-semicoarsening, x-semicoarsening). The prolongation operator implemented in this study uses full-weighted interpolation.

2.4 The code

The test code has been developed in C. The system of equations is solved by the full approximation scheme (FAS). This multigrid method is more involved than the simpler correction scheme but can be applied to solve non-linear equations. Both approaches (alternating plane and semi-coarsening) have been implemented in an "all-multigrid" way. The block smoother (2D-solver) is a robust 2D multigrid algorithm based on full coarsening and alternating line smoothers. The Thomas' algorithm or 1D Multigrid is used to solve the lines.

Lexicographic Gauss-Seidel relaxation is always used in the following experiments. Test cases have been performed on a 64x64x64 grid and a general (1,1) V-cycle is used whenever multigrid is applied. To reduce roundoff errors, we have fixed the right-hand side of equation (1) and the appropriate Dirichlet boundary conditions such that its solution is zero. Thus, asymptotic convergence factors can be accurately measured.

3 Convergence rate

In order to compare the robustness of both approaches we consider a 3D Cartesian grid with exponential stretching in the three dimensions (see figure 1). Robustness is absolutely necessary in this example since the anisotropy varies throughout the whole domain. Although anisotropy sources can be either physical (diffusion coefficients) or computational (grid stretching), the example is general since the effect on the system of equations is equivalent for both sources.

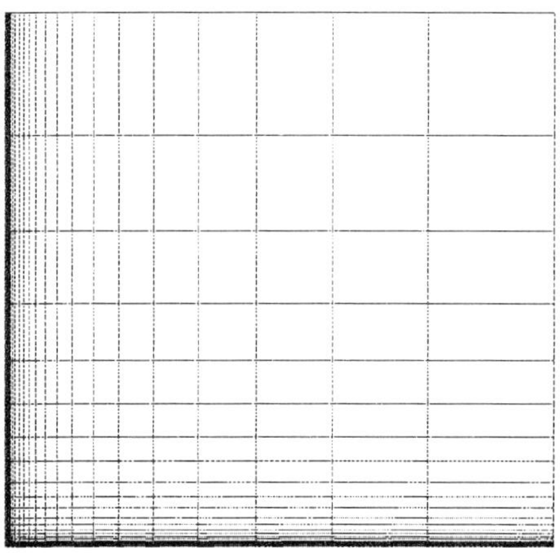

Figure 1. 64x64 grid with exponential stretching factor of 1.3

As figure 2 (top chart) shows, both methods solve the problem effectively. For the semi-coarsening approach, each coarsening direction exhibits the same performance since a dominant direction does not exist. The alternating plane smoother improves its convergence factor as the anisotropy grows (as was shown in [10]).

On the other hand, when the anisotropy is located on one plane the best coarsening procedure is the one that maintains coupling of strongly connected unknowns. For example if we make the coefficients grow in the xy-plane (see figure 2, bottom chart), z-coarsening gets a better convergence factor because the smoother becomes an exact solver for high anisotropies. Alternating plane smoothers presents a similar behaviour, it becomes a direct solver when the unknowns are strongly coupled, i.e. the better the plane is solved the better obtained convergence.

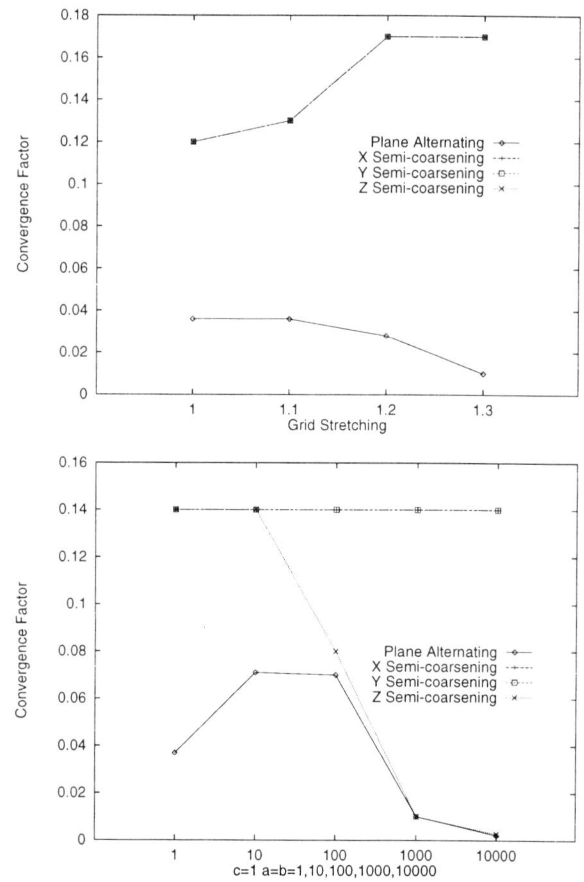

Figure 2. Convergence factor for the isotropic equation and different grid stretching factors (top chart), and anisotropic equation on an uniform grid ($au_{xx}+bu_{yy}+cu_{zz}=0$) for several coefficient sets (bottom chart)

The behaviour exhibited by the convergence rate of the alternating plane approach can be explained in terms of the smoothing factor of the three alternating sweeps. If the problem is essentially isotropic, then each of the three alternating sweeps contributes to the smoothing factor. In problems with a moderate anisotropy in the xy-plane, the high-frequency error is reduced mainly in the z-direction sweep. In strongly anisotropic problems the z-direction sweep reduces the smooth error components as well, actually solving the problem rather than just smoothing the error.

In conclusion, we can state that the alternating plane smoother approach exhibits a better convergence factor than the semi-coarsening one. However, we should note that the operation count per multigrid cycle is higher and so the convergence per work unit must be used as a definitive metric to compare both approaches.

4 Memory Hierarchy Exploitation

When we are trying to compare two different algorithms, one has to take into account not only their numerical efficiency, but also their architectural properties. It is well known that the better a program exploits the spatial and temporal locality the less time it takes. Indeed, the maximum performance that can be obtained in current microprocessors is limited by the memory access time. The latency of memory access in terms of processor performance grows by a factor of 2-3 every three years and this situation seems likely to continue over the next few years [18].

Using the SGI perfex profiling tool, we have measured that the number of L1 and L2 cache misses of the alternating plane smoother are in general greater than the semi-coarsening. Although not all misses incur the same timing penalties in current microprocessors, they can be used for evaluating how the algorithms exploit the memory hierarchy. The measurements have been taken on two different systems with the same R10000 processor running at 250 MHz, an O2 Workstation and one processor of an Origin 2000 system (O2K). This processor has a 32 KB primary data cache, but the external L2 cache size varies: 1MB on the O2 and 4MB on the O2K. We should also note that the code has been compiled using different optimization options on both systems: Ofast=ip32_10k on the O2 and Ofast=ip27 on the O2K. As expected, the x and y-semicoarsening algorithms produce less misses due to the memory organisation of the 3D data structures. These algorithms exhibit more spatial locality that the z-semicoarsenig and the alternating approach.

For a 32x32x32 problem size, the number of L1 misses (around the same on both systems) of x-semicoarsening approach are about 12% and 50% fewer than those obtained for the y-semicoarsening and the alternating approach, respectively. These differences grow slightly for the 64x64x64 problem size.

Figure 3 shows the number of L2 cache misses on both systems for 32x32x32 and 64x64x64 problem sizes. It is interesting to note that the alternating approach and the z-semicoarsenig have around 1.75 and 2.5 times more misses than the x-semicoarsening on the O2 system for both problem sizes. However, on the O2K system, where the large second level cache allows a better exploitation of the temporal locality, the differences grow with the problem size

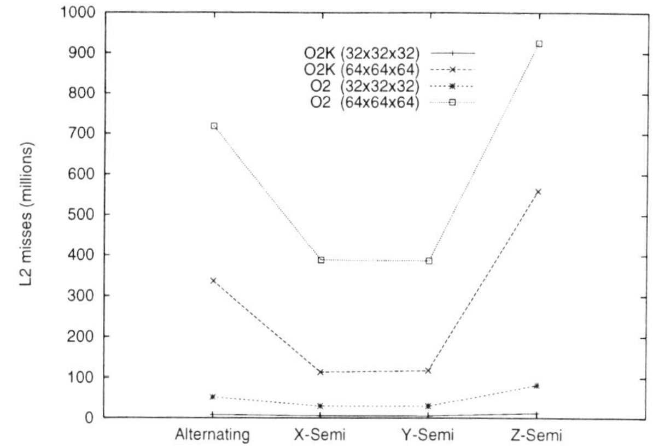

Figure 3. Millions of L2 cache misses for the 64x64x64 and 32x32x32 problem sizes on an O2000 system and O2 workstation

since, for smaller problems, the spatial locality has less impact on the number of cache misses. The greatest differences between both systems are obtained for the x and y-semicoarsening (around 3.4 times more misses on the O2 system) due to temporal locality effects, which are lower on the alternating an z-semicoarsenig approaches where the spatial locality has more influence.

Therefore, in order to make a more realistic comparison between the two methods and the different semi-coarsening directions, we have to measure the convergence factor per work unit (WU) (the WU has been defined as the execution time needed for evaluating the equation metrics on the finest grid). As figure 4 shows the alternating plane smoother has a better behaviour than the semi-coarsening, i.e. it reduces the same error in less time.

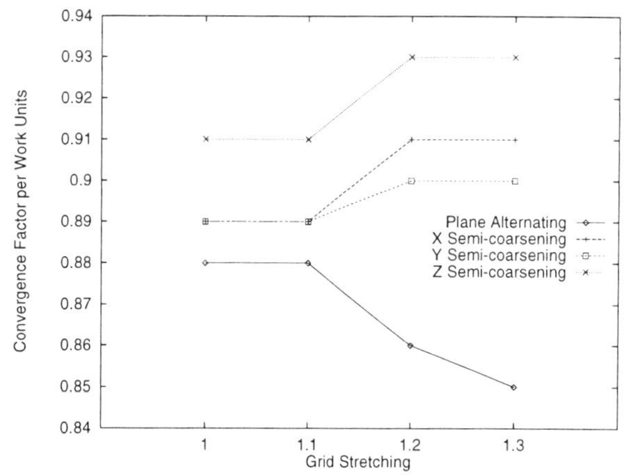

Figure 4. Convergence factor per Work unit (WU) in the 64x64x64 stretched grid.

We should also note, that the memory requirements of the semi-coarsening approach are about twice as large as the alternating-plane one (see figure 5).

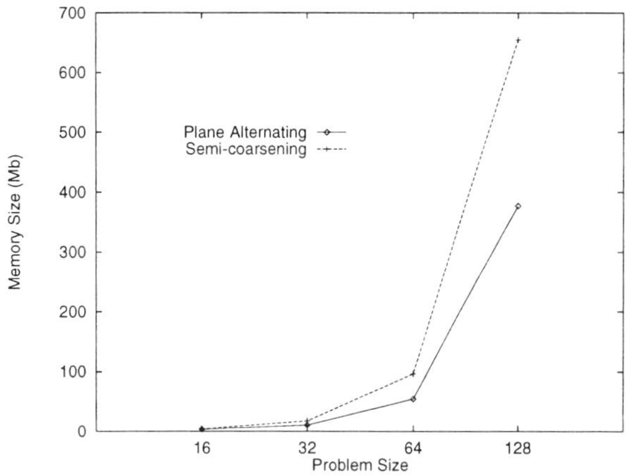

Figure 5. Amount of memory required by our code on an SGI Origin 2000 for 16x16x16, 32x32x32, 64x64x64 and 128x128x128 grid sizes.

5 Parallel Properties

5.1 Outline

To get a parallel implementation of a multigrid method, one can adopt one of the following strategies (see, e.g., [11]).

1. Domain decomposition: domain decomposition is applied first. Then, a multigrid method is used to solve problems inside each block.
2. Grid partitioning: domain decomposition is applied on each level.

Domain decomposition methods are often considered with finite element discretizations on parallel computers. They are easier to implement and imply fewer communications since they are only required on the finest grid. Additionally, they can be applied to general multi-block grids. However, the decomposition methods lead to algorithms which are numerically different from the sequential version and they have a negative impact on the convergence rate.

Grid partitioning retains the convergence rate of the sequential algorithm. However it implies more communication overheads since exchange of data are required on each grid level. In addition, it should be noted that due to the lack of definition of global planes and lines, grid partitioning is not viable in general multi-block grids. An hybrid approach that applies the V-cycle on the entire multi-block domain while the smoothers are performed inside each block (domain decomposition for the smoother) has been proposed in [9].

Alternating-plane presents worse parallel properties than the other robust approach analyzed since, regardless of the data partitioning applied, it requires the solution of tridiagonal systems of equations distributed among the processors. The parallel solution of this kind of systems has been widely studied, see for example [3, 6, 7, 8]. A specific solution for 2D alternating-line problems based on a pipeline Thomas's algorithm that could be extended for our 3D problem has been analyzed on [5, 4]. The parallel efficiency of this algorithm obtained on a Cray T3E using MPI for problem sizes range from 256x256 to 1024x1024 cells varies between 0.6 to 0.8 respectively. However, current memory limits do not allow us to solve 3D problems where their corresponding 2D planes are big enough to obtain satisfactory efficiencies on medium-sized parallel computers.

Since the semi-coarsening approach does not need the alternating plane smoothers, an appropriate 1D data decomposition and plane-smoother combination can be chosen so that a parallel tridiagonal solver is not needed. Thus, for instance, an x-direction partitioning is suitable for x-semicoarsening combined with yz-plane smoothers.

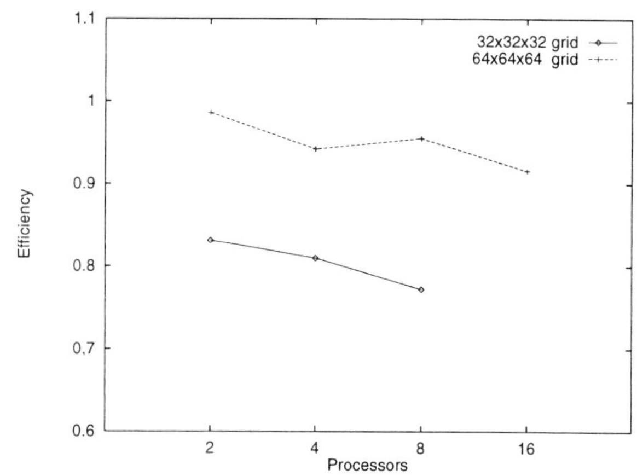

Figure 6. Parallel efficiency obtained on a Cray T3E using 64x64x64 and 32x32x32 grid sizes for up to sixteen processors with an U-cycle method.

5.2 Experimental results

The parallel code has been developed using native MPI versions. The compiler options have been set to -O3 on the Cray T3E (for the O2K see the previous section).

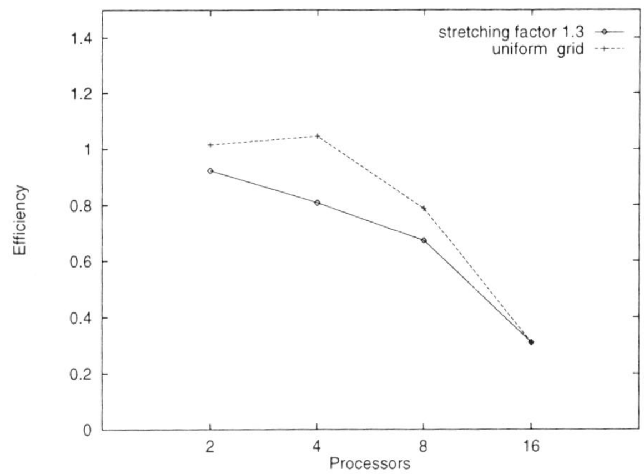

Figure 7. Realistic parallel efficiency obtained on a Cray T3E using 64x64x64 grid size for up to sixteen processors (x-semicoarsening with an U-cycle method).

Common grid transfer operators such as bilinear (2D) or trilinear (3D) interpolation and full weighted restrictors are parallel by nature. Hence, they do not suffer any change on the parallel code. However, the lexicographic Gauss-Seidel smoothers employed in the previous sections can no longer be applied, consequently they have been replaced by plane relaxation in a red-black zebra order of planes. This variation introduces a slightly change on the numerical properties of our parallel code [10].

Since the linear system of equation has to be solved "exactly" on the coarsest grid (by means of an iterative solver), it is usually chosen as coarse as possible to reduce the computational cost. However, from a parallel point of view, this decision may cause some processors to remain idle on the coarsest grids, reducing the parallel efficiency of the multigrid algorithm.

Our first algorithm avoids idle processors using an approach known as the parallel U-Cycle method [19] where the number of grid levels has been fixed so that the coarsest grid employed on each processor has one plane (this will be refered hereafter as critical level). Figure 6 presents the parallel efficiency obtained on the T3E using five iterations of the smoother on the coarsest grid. The efficiency has been measured using the time spent on a multigrid cycle.

As we have explained before, if a dominant direction does not exist, y-semicoarsenig and x-semicoarsening are more efficient from an architectural point of view, since they exhibit a better spatial locality. For the same reasons, they are also the best choice from a message passing point of view, since message passing performance also depends on the spatial locality of the messages [14]. Using the Apprentice profiling tool, we have measured that the time spent

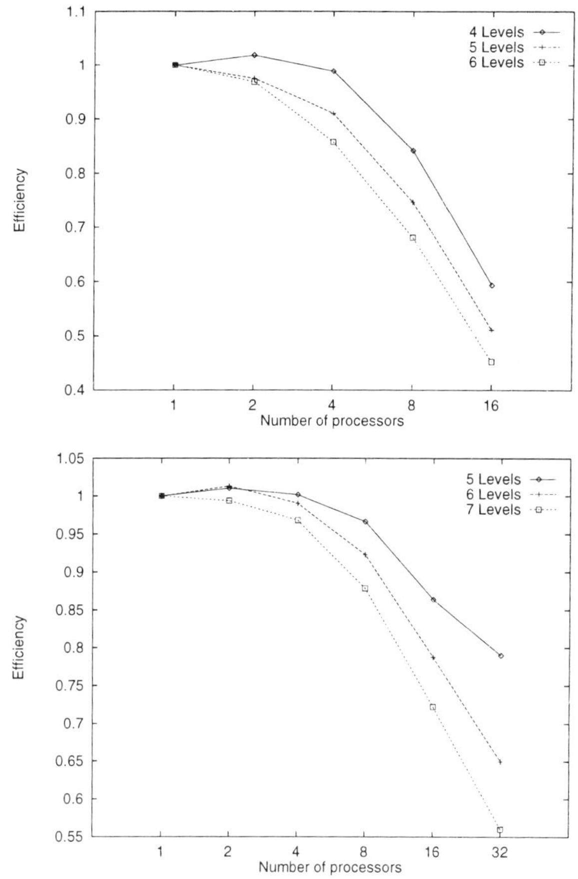

Figure 8. Parallel efficiency obtained in a Cray T3E using a 32x32x32 problem size (top chart) and 64x64x64 (bottom chart).

performing data cache operations on a two processor simulation using z-partitioning, i.e. using z-semicoarsening, is about 17% larger than in the x-partitioning for a 64x64x64 problem size. This difference is lower that in the SGI systems analysed above due to better behaviour of the T3E memory hierarchy when spatial locality does not exist [13].

However, in this approach, the number of iterations needed to solve the system of equations on the coarsest problem grows with its size and five iterations may not be enough for obtaining the exact solution. So, parallel efficiency has to be expressed using the execution time needed for solving the whole problem, i.e. reaching a certain residual norm (we have chosen 10^{-12}). Figure 7 shows the results using this realistic efficiency on a Cray T3E. It is satisfactory using up to eight processors. However, in the sixteen processor simulation the efficiency decreases since the iterative method used for solving the equation on the coarsest level needs to converge a number of iterations that grow with the system size. Isotropic simulation have better

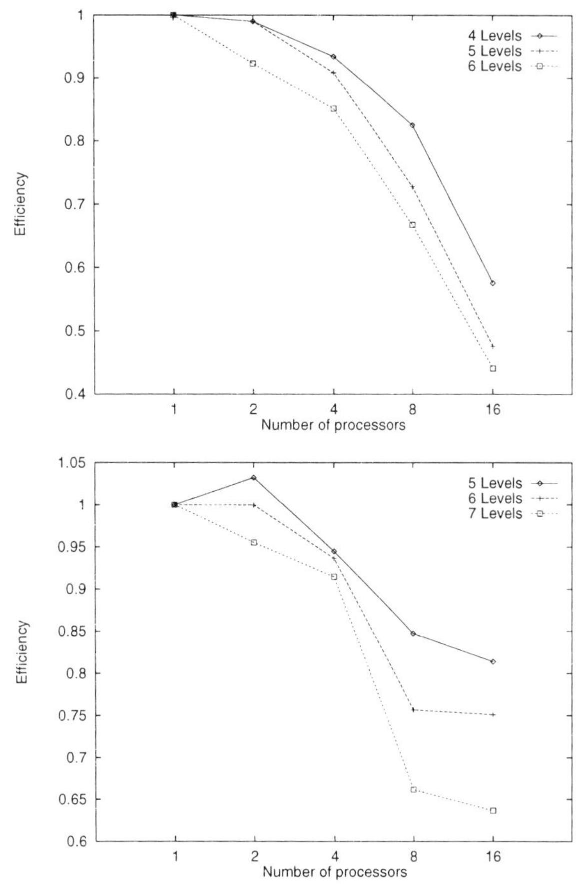

Figure 9. Parallel efficiency obtained in a SGI O2K using a 32x32x32 problem size (top chart) and 64x64x64 (bottom chart).

parallel efficiencies than the anisotropic cases due to convergence properties.

Our second approach implements a true V-cycle method. Thus, as we go down below the critical level we have to dynamically rearrange the comunication patterns and grid distribution. Note that the number of idle processors is doubled on every level below the critical one. In order to improve the algorithm below the critical level a damped Jacobi smoother has been employed, since it has better parallel properties [10]. This change has no important effect on the convergence factor as well as the weight is choosen properly [10].

As figures 8 and 9 show, the parallel efficiency dramatically improved with respect to the first approach. Although results going down to the coarsest level are presented, obviously it is not neccesary to reach it, since the system can be solved on a previous grid without the numerical properties worsening.

It is interesting to note that the sixteen processor simulation for the 64x64x64 problem size on the O2K does not decrease the parallel efficiency. A better memory hierarchy exploitation is the reason for this fact, since in this case the local problem sizes (around 6MB) are similar to the L2 cache size (4MB). Note that on the Cray T3E the L2 cache size is not large enough (96KB) to store all the local data, and so this behaviour is not exhibited.

Similar results have been obtained for stretched grids since the algorithm preserves the numerical properties of the sequential version.

6 Conclusions

Two common multigrid robust approaches for anisotropic operators have been compared taking into account both numerical and architectural properties:

- Both alternatives present similar convergence rates for low anisotropies. However, the alternating-plane smoothing process becomes an exact solver for high anisotropies and so, the convergence factor tends to zero with an increasing anisotropy. This optimal behaviour is not shown by semi-coarsening approach when all the strongly connected unknowns (coordinates with relative larger coefficients) are not relaxed simultaneously.

- With regard to the cost-per-cycle, the alternating-plane approach is about a 38% more expensive. This difference depends not only on the number of operations (by means of the SGI perfex profiling tool, we have found that the number of floating-point operations used on the alternating-plane algorithm is a 26% larger than on the semi-coarsening one) but also, on the memory hierarchy use. Among the three possibilities that can be employed on the semi-coarsening approach, yz-plane relaxation and x-coarsening is the best choice because it exhibits a better spatial locality (the code is written in C). This fact is also important in the parallel setting because communication costs depend also on the spatial locality of the messages.

- The memory requirements of the semi-coarsening approach are about twice larger than the alternating-plane one.

- Parallel implementation of the alternating-plane approach involve the solution of distributed planes and lines that make them complicated. These difficulties can be avoided by the semi-coarsening approach and a proper linear decomposition. However, using an U-Cycle technique in order to avoid idle processors, the parallel efficiency obtained is not satisfactory due to the number of iterations required for solving the system on the coarsest grid. Thus, a trade-off between numerical and parallel properties has to be considered, and a true V-cycle seems to be the better choice despite some processors remain idle during a short period of time on every multigrid cycle.

References

[1] A. Brandt. Multigrid techniques: 1984 guide with applications to fluid dynamics. Technical Report GMD-Studien 85, May 1984.

[2] J. E. Dendy, S. F. McCormick, J. Ruge, T. Russell, and S. Schaffer. Multigrid methods for three-dimensional petroleum reservoir simulation. In *Tenth SPE Symposium on Reservoir Simulation*, february 1989.

[3] C. C. Douglas, S. Malhotra, and M. H. Schultz. Transpose free alternating direction smoothers for serial and parallel methods. MGNET at http://www.mgnet.org/, 1997.

[4] D. Espadas, M. Prieto, I. Llorente, and F. Tirado. Solution of alternating-line processes on modern parallel computers. In *Proceedings of the 28th International Conference on Parallel Processing (ICPP '99)*, September 1999.

[5] D. Espadas, M. Prieto, I. M. Llorente, and F. Tirado. Parallel resolution of alternating-line processes by means of pipelined techniques. In *Proceedings of the 7th. Euromicro Workshop on Parallel and Distributed Systems*, pages 289–296. IEEE Computer Society Press, Febraury 1999.

[6] J. C. Agüi and J. Jimenez. A binary tree implementation of a parallel distributed tridiagonal solver. *Parallel Comput.*, 21:233–241, 1995.

[7] J. López, O. Platas, F. Argüello, and E. L. Zapata. Unified framework for the parallelization of divide and conquer based tridiagonal systems. *Parallel Comput.*, 23:667–686, 1997.

[8] Krechel, Plum, and Stüben. Parallelization and vectorization aspects of the solution of tridiagonal linear systems. *Parallel Comput.*, 14:31–49, 1990.

[9] I. M. Llorente, B. Diskin, and N. D. Melson. Smoothing properties of plane smoothers for multiblock grids. In *Proceedings of the Ninth Copper Mountain Conference on Multigrid Methods*, 1999.

[10] I. M. Llorente and N. D. Melson. Robust multigrid smoothers for three dimensional elliptic equations with strong anisotropies. Technical Report 98-37, ICASE, 1998.

[11] I. M. Llorente and F. Tirado. Relationships between efficiency and execution time of full multigrid methods on parallel computers. *IEEE Trans. on Parallel and Distributed Systems*, 8:562–573, June 1997.

[12] A. Overman and J. V. Rosendale. Mapping robust parallel multigrid algorithms to scalable memory architectures. In *Proceedings of the Sixth Copper Mountain Conference on Multigrid Methods*, 1993.

[13] M. Prieto, D. Espadas, I. Llorente, and F.Tirado. Message passing evaluation and analysis on cray t3e and sgi origin 2000 systems. In *Proceedings of the 4th Euro-Par Conference (Euro-Par '99)*, August 1999.

[14] M. Prieto, I. Llorente, and F. Tirado. Partitioning regular domains on modern parallel computers. In J. M. L. M. Palma, J. Dongarra, and V. Hernández, editors, *Proceedings of the 3th International Meeting on Vector and Parallel Processing*, pages 411–424, 1999.

[15] J. Ruge and K. Stüben. Algebraic multigrid (AMG). In S. McCormick, editor, *Multigrid methods*, volume 5 of *Frontier in Applied Mathematics*. SIAM, 1986.

[16] T. Washio and K. Oosterlee. An evaluation of parallel multigrid as a solver and a preconditioner for singularly perturbed problems, Part II: Flexible 2D and 3D multiple semicoarsening. Technical Report 1012, GMD, 1996 (to appear in SIAM J. Sci. Comp.).

[17] P. Wesseling. *An Introduction to Multigrid Methods*. John Wiley & Sons, New York, 1992.

[18] W. A. Wulf and S. A. McKee. Hitting the memory wall: Implications of the obvious. *Comp. Arch. News, Assoc. for Computer Machinery*, March 1995.

[19] D. Xie and L. R. Scott. The parallel u-cycle multigrid method. In *Proceedings of the 8th Copper Mountain Conference on Multigrid Methods*, 1996.

Finite Element Computations on Cluster of PC's and Workstations

A. N. Spyropoulos, J. A. Palyvos and A. G. Boudouvis*
Department of Chemical Engineering
National Technical University of Athens
Zografou Campus, Athens 15780, Greece
*boudouvi@chemeng.ntua.gr

Abstract

In the last decade distributed processing on cluster of PC's and workstations became a popular alternative way for parallel computations due to their low cost compared with the cost of parallel supercomputers. The most important factor that limits the parallel efficiency of an algorithm running on a cluster is the low bandwidth and high latency of the network that interconnects the computers. Specially designed parallel algorithms must be applied that have low communication overhead. A parallel method on Galerkin/finite element computations on cluster of PC's and workstations is presented. This method is based on a parallel preconditioned Krylov-type iterative solver for the solution of large, sparse and non-symmetric equation systems. Two important aspects of the method are addressed: the storage of the coefficient matrix of the system and of the preconditioning matrix, and the performance of the preconditioner. The matrix storage affects the parallel efficiency of the matrix vector product. The preconditioner contributes to the parallel efficiency and is of critical importance for the convergence rate of the iterative method. The performance of the method is analyzed in terms of parallel speedup, storage efficiency and convergence rate.

1. Introduction

The restarted Generalized Minimum Residual (GMRES(m), [6]) method, is the Krylov-type method of preference for the solution of large, sparse and non-symmetric linear systems, such as those arising from the discretization of partial differential equations with the Galerkin/finite element method. The combination of the GMRES(m) method and good preconditioning is the state-of-the-art in the iterative solution of large algebraic equation systems. Classical parallel preconditioners based on ILU (Incomplete LU) variants [7] do not exhibit high parallel efficiency due to high communication load between the processors that is required for their construction. This is an extra limiting factor for their implementation on a cluster of PC's and workstations. The low bandwidth and the high latency of an ethernet network - commonly used in clusters – make performance worse, compared with the supercomputer high speed networks. Moreover, preconditioning must be performed several times when parameter continuation or eigenvalue computations are needed [8].

Besides the preconditioner, the parallel efficiency of the preconditioned GMRES(m) is strongly affected by the original finite element matrix storage format. It is also affected by the domain decomposition method, especially when the finite element grid is unstructured. In this paper only structured grids are used. Thus the interest is on the choice of the preconditioner so that the communication overhead is lowered and the convergence of the GMRES(m) solver is improved. The preconditioned version of the GMRES(m) is based on a deflation technique [3], which removes the smallest eigenvalues of the original matrix that slow down the convergence rate [4], [9]. Resulting from the domain decomposition method, three communication modes between the processors are addressed, namely no communication, global communication and neighboring communication. The parallel implementation of the preconditioned GMRES(m) by deflation basic operations, vector updates, inner products, matrix-vector products, is described and the required communication is analyzed. The efficiency of the preconditioned GMRES(m) is analyzed in terms of the convergence rate, parallel speedup and storage requirements. The proposed parallel method has small memory requirements and high parallel efficiency when it is used on a cluster.

In section 2 an outline is given of the restarted GMRES with right preconditioner based on a deflation technique. The domain decomposition method associated with the finite element tessellation is described in section 3. In section 4 are presented the basic operations of the preconditioned GMRES(m) with their parallel implementations. Results are in section 5 and they include the achieved speedup and the convergence performance of the deflated preconditioner.

2. Preconditioned GMRES(m)

The GMRES method solves a linear system

$$Ax = b \quad (1)$$

where x, b $\in \mathbf{R}^N$ and A $\in \mathbf{R}^{N \times N}$, iteratively. Starting from an initial guess x_o of the solution of (1), it constructs an orthonormal basis V_m of the m-dimensional Krylov subspace

$$\boldsymbol{K}_m(A,u) \equiv \text{span}\{u, Au, A^2u, \ldots, A^{m-1}u\},$$
$$u = r_o/\beta,\ r_o = b - Ax_o, \text{ and } \beta = \|r_o\|_2$$

and finds an approximate solution of (1)

$$x_m = x_o + V_m y_m \quad (2)$$

such that x_m minimizes $\|b - Ax_m\|_2$ or, equivalently,

$$y_m = \min_y \|\beta e_1 - \overline{H}_m y\|_2,\ y \in \mathbf{R}^N \quad (3)$$

where $\overline{H}_m$ is a ((m+1) x m) Hessenberg matrix whose non-zero entries were generated by the Arnoldi-Modified Gram-Schmidt process [6]; $e_1 \equiv (1, 0, \ldots, 0)^T$. The standard way of solving the least-squares minimization problem (3) is by QR-factorizing $\overline{H}_m$ using plane rotations.

As m increases, the computational cost of the Arnoldi process increases at least as $O(m^2)n$ and the memory requirements increase as O(mn) [7]. Therefore, when m is large, the GMRES algorithm becomes impractical, and a GMRES variant, the so-called restarted GMRES, or GMRES(m), is used instead; (m) implies that the algorithm restarts when the dimension of the Krylov subspace reaches m, using the last approximation x_m as a new initial guess. However, this restarting makes the GMRES(m) to converge slowly or to diverge for small values of m, because at each restart useful information about the previously built Krylov subspace is lost.

Preconditioning is the key to get fast convergence for the restarted GMRES algorithm. A linear system can be preconditioned either at left or right, which amounts to solving,

$$M^{-1}Ax = M^{-1}b \quad \text{or} \quad AM^{-1}(Mx) = b \quad (4a, b)$$

respectively; M is the preconditioning matrix. Each one of the iterations between two successive restarts is called inner iteration; an outer iteration is the set of the inner iterations between two successive restarts.

The preconditioner chosen here is described in details by Erel et al [3]. It is a right preconditioner based on a deflation technique:

$$M^{-1} = I_n + U(|\lambda_n|T^{-1} - I_r)U^T \quad (5)$$

I_n and I_r are unitary matrices of size (n x n) and (r x r), respectively. U is a (n x r) matrix, the columns of which form an orthonormal basis of the invariant r-dimensional eigen-subspace, call it P_r, corresponding to the smallest r eigenvalues of A; λ_n is the largest eigenvalue of A. T is the (r x r) matrix

$$T = U^T A U \quad (6)$$

The eigenvalues and the corresponding eigenvectors of A needed in (5) are approximated by those of the (m x m) Hessenberg matrix H_m, obtained from $\overline{H}_m$ by deleting its last row; $H_m \equiv V_m^T A V_m$.

The preconditioner is kept fixed during an outer iteration. Between restarts, however, the preconditioner is updated: The orthonormal basis of P_r is enriched by k additional eigenvectors of A (that are approximated by those of H_m); k is the increment of r and it is usually taken k = 1. It is the update of the preconditioner that requires the usage of right preconditioning, so that the residual norm, $\|b - Ax_m\|_2$, is non-increasing [3].

3. Domain decomposition

The original domain, tessellated by the finite element method, is divided into subdomains by a structured grid. A subdomain is defined as a separate group of elements and it is assigned to a processor. The subdomain nodes are called local nodes and they are numbered locally on each processor.

Let x^o be the N vector, which corresponds to the nodes of the original domain. These nodes are called global nodes. By x is denoted the local representative of the vector x^o on the processor p and its size is N_{local}. Any vector of nodal values is distributed in the same manner among the processors, meaning that the indices of the components of any vector, x, that are mapped to a given processor are the same; i.e., $[x(j)\ j = 1, \ldots, N_{local}]$.

The subdomain nodes, or local nodes, are either inner or communication nodes. The communication nodes are shared with other processors whereas the inner nodes are not shared with any other processor. Resulting from the local nodes distinction, two sets are defined on each processor. The set IN_p, the elements of which are the inner nodes on processor p; and the set COM_p, the elements of which are the communication nodes on processor p. The set $TOT_p \equiv IN_p \cup COM_p$ includes the local nodes on processor p and the set Ω includes the global nodes of the original domain. Moreover, a function, $f^p : TOT_p \to \Omega$, is defined on each processor p, which maps a local node to the corresponding global node.

Also on each processor p, a Local - to - Global Compatibility (LGC) condition is defined,

$$x(i) = x^o(f^p(i)), \forall i \in TOT_p \tag{7}$$

The LGC condition sets the equality between each local vector components and the corresponding global vector components. Each operation, of the parallel preconditioned GMRES(m) algorithm, is completed when the resulting vector satisfies the LGC condition.

4. Parallel implementation

The basic operations of the GMRES method are: (i) Vector updates, (ii) inner products, (iii) matrix-vector products. Moreover, preconditioning operations are needed for the preconditioned GMRES(m). These operations depend on the choice of the preconditioner. The deflation preconditioning technique can be analyzed in the same basic operations as the GMRES method.

4.1. Vector updates

Operations of the form $z^o = x^o + \gamma y^o$, where x^o, y^o, $z^o \in \mathbf{R}^n$ and $\gamma \in \mathbf{R}$, can be done for all (inner and communication) nodes that are local to a processor in parallel as follows:

```
DO i = 1, N_local
z(i) = x(i) + γ*y(i)
ENDDO
```

If the vectors x^o and y^o satisfy the LGC condition then, after the above do-loop, the resulting vector z^o will satisfy the LGC condition too. Thus, no communication between the processors is required.

4.2. Inner products

For the computation of an inner product $\gamma = (x^o, y^o)$ of two vectors x^o and y^o, each processor computes a local inner product γ_p, as follows:

```
DO i = 1, N_local
γp = γp + in(i)*x(i)*y(i)
ENDDO
```

The assisting vector [in(i) i = 1, . . . , N_{local}] marks the nodes with 0 or 1. Inner nodes are marked with 1. Among communication nodes, all but one are marked with 0; thus, the contribution from each communication node to the inner product is accounted for only once. The local inner products are summed up to the inner product through a global communication between the processors. The final global inner product is available on each processor.

4.3. Matrix-vector product

The (N x N) matrix A of the linear system (1) is stored partially in each processor in the Compressed Sparse Row (CSR) format described in [7]. Let A^p_{local} be the (N_{local} x N_{local}) matrix local to a processor, i.e., that part of A consisting of the rows and columns associated with the nodes that are local to the processor. A real vector AA is built which contains only the non-zero values of A^p_{local} stored row by row, from 1 to N_{local}. Let Nz be the length of AA; two integer vectors, [JA(j) j = 1,..., Nz] and [IA(i) i = 1,...,N_{local}+1], are constructed: JA(j) is the column number of the j-th element of AA at its original location in matrix A^p_{local}. IA(i), i = 1,. . . ,N_{local}, gives the position in the vector AA of the first non-zero element of the i-th row of matrix A^p_{local}; IA(N_{local}+1) ≡ IA(1)+Nz. Thus, the contributions from the processors to a matrix-vector product, $y^o = Ax^o$, can be computed in parallel as follows:

```
DO i =1, N_local
 k1 = IA(i)
 k2 = IA(i + 1) - 1
  DO j = k1, k2
  y(i) = y(i) + AA(j)*x(JA(j))
  ENDDO
ENDDO
```

If the vector x^o satisfies the LGC condition, then the resulting vector will satisfy the LGC condition only for the inner nodes and not for the communication nodes on each processor p:

$$y(i) = y^o(f^p(i)) \ \forall i \in IN_p \quad \text{and}$$

$$y(i) \neq y^o(f^p(i)) \ \forall i \in COM_p$$

This happens because the local matrices A^p_{local} includes only the nodal contributions of the assigned subdomain on each processor. Therefore, a communication is required between each processor and its neighbors.

4.4. Preconditioning operations

The preconditioning operations need a matrix vector product of the form

$$y^o = M^{-1}x^o \tag{8}$$

where M^{-1} is the preconditioning matrix defined in eqs. (5) and (6). The elements of the preconditioner matrix are not computed explicitly and so are not stored. In addition, the expression of the preconditioner eq. (5) is used to perform the matrix-vector product (8):

$$y^o = \left[I_n + U(|\lambda_n| T^{-1} - I_r) U^T \right] x^o \tag{9}$$

The columns of the (N x r) matrix U are distributed among the processors, i.e., each processor stores r vectors of length N_{local}. The (r x r) matrix T of eq. (6) is computed in two steps and is stored in each processor; this requires r parallel matrix-vector products

$$s^o_j = Au^o_j \ (j = 1, \ldots, r) \tag{10a}$$

where u^o_j is the j-th column of U, followed by r^2 parallel inner products

$$T = [t_{ij}] = (s^o_j, u^o_i) \ (i, j = 1, \ldots r) \tag{10b}$$

Then, the (r x 1) vector w is computed by r parallel inner products

$$w = U^T x^o \Leftrightarrow w(i) = (x^o, u^o_i) \ (i = 1, \ldots, r) \tag{11}$$

The matrix T and the vector w are the results of parallel inner products and thus are available on each processor. Therefore the computation of the (r x 1) vectors z and f can be done locally on each processor by solving the small linear system (12b) and by the vector update (13) respectively:

$$z = T^{-1}w, \quad \text{i.e., } Tz = w \tag{12a, b}$$

$$f = |\lambda_n| z - w \tag{13}$$

$$g^o = Uf \Leftrightarrow g^o = g^o + f(i)u^o_i \ (i = 1, \ldots, r) \tag{14}$$

The (n x 1) vector g^o in (14) can be computed by r parallel vector updates. Finally, a parallel vector update is performed to calculate the vector y^o:

$$y^o = x^o + g^o \tag{15}$$

5. Results and discussion

The described parallel preconditioned GMRES(m) by deflation has been applied on the solution of linearized equation sets, by Newton's method, resulting from the discretization by the Galerkin/finite element method of a three-dimensional, nonlinear and free boundary problem of interfacial magntohydrostatics. More details about the case study are given in [1], [5]. The computations where done on a heterogeneous cluster of PC's and workstations at the Computer Center of the Department of Chemical Engineering of the National Technical University of Athens. This cluster consists of 14 Linux PC's (10 Pentium Celeron, 4 Pentium Cyrix) and 2 Silicon Graphics workstations (R5000, R4600) interconnected with the Ethernet network at 10 Mbps. The message passing protocol PVM 3.4 was used and the parallel programming model is the SPMD (Single Program Multiple Data).

In the algorithm presented in this work, the processor communication load comes from the matrix-vector and the inner product operations. The serial computation time is consumed mainly at three steps of the algorithm: (a) Solution of the least-squares problem (3), (b) solution of the eigenvalue problem for the Hessenberg matrix H_m and (c) solution of the linear system (9b). Increasing m enhances the convergence of the GMRES(m) but increases the computational cost in stages (a) and (b) and the storage requirements. The serial computation time, as well as the storage requirements, of the preconditioner depend on r, the dimension of the invariant subspace P_r, which increases continuously with the outer iterations. An upper limit, r_{max}, on r is set; when it is reached, the update of the preconditioner stops and the outer iterations continue, until convergence, with the same preconditioner.

The parallel efficiency of the method is measured by the parallel speedup [2]. In parallel computations the speedup is limited by the serial computations and by the communication between the processors. The parallel speedup of the preconditioned GMRES(m) and the non-preconditioned GMRES(m) are compared in fig. 1; m = 20 and r_{max} = 10.

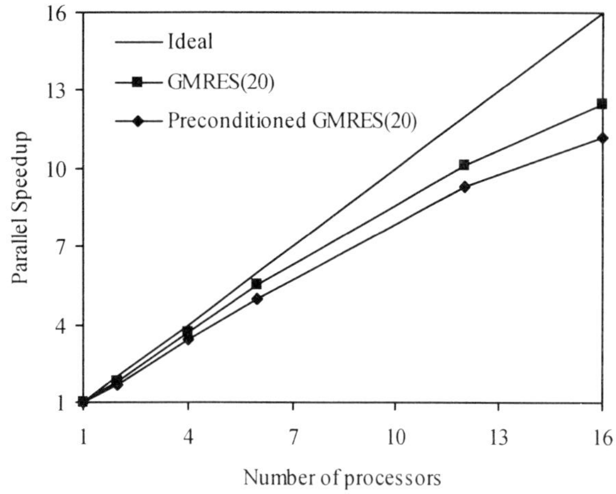

Figure 1. Parallel speedup of the GMRES(20) and the preconditioned GMRES(20); N=136851.

The comparison shows that the serial computations at the steps (b) and (c) and the additional communication load in the preconditioning, have no appreciable effect on the speedup. A significant advantage of the chosen preconditioner on an ILU-type preconditioner.

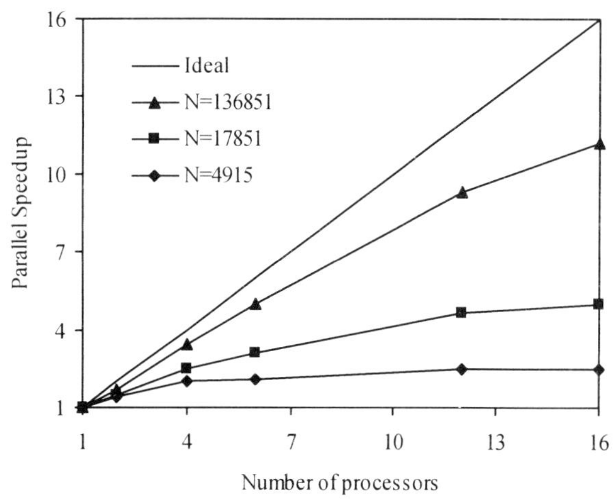

Figure 2. Parallel speedup of GMRES(20) preconditioned by deflation.

The scalability of the preconditioned GMRES(m) by deflation is shown in fig. 2. Increasing the number of processors the achieved speedup increases significantly faster in big problems than in smaller ones, because the computational time in the described parallel algorithm increases faster than the communication time when moving from a small problem size to a bigger one.

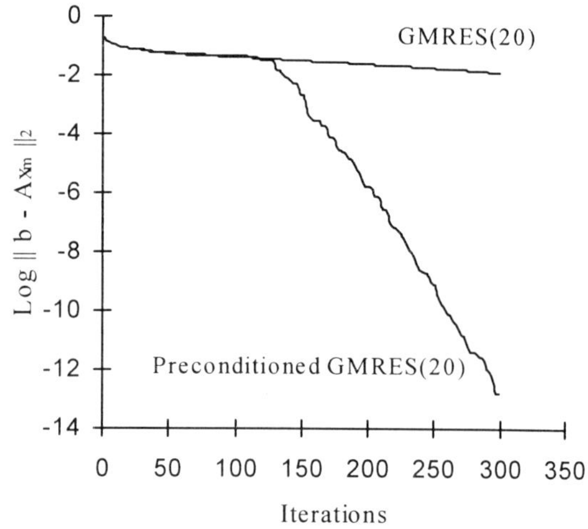

Figure 3. Convergence of GMRES(20) with preconditioning by deflation and without; N =136851.

The convergence rate of the preconditioned GMRES(20) against the non-preconditioned GMRES(20) is shown in fig. 3. The two algorithms exhibit the same convergence rate up to 129 iterations; this is due to the fact that the smallest eigenvalues of the Hessenberg matrix is not yet accurate approximations of the smallest eigenvalues of the matrix A. In the following iterations these eigenvalues became improved approximations and the preconditioned version converges faster than the non-preconditioned one. Moreover, the preconditioned GMRES(m) by deflation is found to converge fast even for nearly singular systems [8].

Acknowledgement. A. N. Spyropoulos is thankful to Edinburgh Parallel Computing Center for providing special training on high performance computing, through the TRACS program.

References

[1] A. G. Boudouvis, J. L. Puchalla, L. E. Scriven and R. E. Rosensweig, Normal field instability and patterns in pools of ferrofluid, *J. Magn. Magn. Mat.*, 65: 307 – 310, 1987.

[2] K. Dowd and C. Severance, *High Performance Computing*, O' Reilly, Sebastopol, 1998.

[3] J. Erhel, K. Burrage and B. Pohl, Restarted GMRES preconditioned by deflation, *J. Comp. Appl. Math.*, 69: 303 – 318, 1996.

[4] W. Joubert, On the convergence behavior of the restarted GMRES algorithm for solving nonsymmetric linear systems, *J. Numer. Linear Algebra Appl.*, 1: 427 – 447, 1994.

[5] A. G. Papathanasiou and A. G. Boudouvis, Three-dimensional instabilities of ferromagnetic liquid bridges, *Comp. Mech.*, 21: 403 – 408, 1998.

[6] Y. Saad and M. H. Schultz, GMRES: a generalized minimal residual algorithm for solving nonsymmetric linear systems, *SIAM J. Sci. Stat. Comp.*, 7: 856 – 869, 1986.

[7] Y. Saad, *Iterative Methods for Sparse Linear Systems*, PWS Publishing Company, Boston, 1996.

[8] A. N. Spyropoulos, J. A. Palyvos and A. G. Boudouvis, *Parallel Iterative Computations Near Singularities*, In proceedings of the 3rd National Congress on Computational Mechanics, pp. 673-680, N. Aravas and J. T. Katsikadelis, Eds., Volos, Greece, June 1999 (University of Thessaly Press, Volos, Greece, 1999).

[9] H.A. Van der Vorst and C. Vuik, "The superlinear convergence behaviour of GMRES", *J. Comp. Appl. Math.*, 48: 327 – 341, 1993.

Distributed and Randomized Enumeration

Piotr Dembiński[1]
Institute of Computer Science
Polish Academy of Sciences
ul. Ordona 21, 01-237 Warsaw, Poland

Abstract

The paper describes a randomized, distributed enumeration algorithm which (in contrast to deterministic solutions) works for all network topologies and with fully asynchronous communication. The algorithm's correctness and efficiency are argued. The expectation value of its execution time is of the order of the time needed for a broadcast.

Key words: *distributed algorithms; analysis of algorithms; interconnection networks.*

1. Introduction

Distributed algorithms (protocols) aim at solving a global network problem by local means, that is, by computations of network nodes that depend solely on the nodes' local states and exchange of messages between nodes. When the algorithm terminates the global result is known to all participating nodes.

Leader election or *nodes enumeration* are good examples of global problems for which known distributed solutions exhibit most of the typical design difficulties. Both problems require that no component is privileged and, therefore, each node performs exactly the same algorithm. Such distributed algorithms (protocols) are called sometimes *symmetric*. Let us formulate more precisely the enumeration problem which is the subject of interest in this paper.

Assume we have a *network of processes* P_1, P_2, ... , P_N the graph of which is finite, connected and without self-loops. Nodes of the graph correspond to the network processes and the graph edges represent the bi-directional communication links between them (unidirectional case can be also considered, but additional graph assumptions are needed). Each process (node) can perform some local computations (changing its local state) and it can exchange messages with *neighbor processes* (nodes), i.e., those directly linked to it by a communication channel (graph edge). Local computations are completely independent and inter-process communication is asynchronous.

The *enumeration problem* for a network of N nodes consists in finding a distributed algorithm (i.e., an algorithm that is performed independently by each node in the network) that:

- terminates with all nodes of the network (graph) *properly enumerated*, i.e., each node gets a unique label from the set {1, 2, ... , N},
- the final distribution of labels is known to all participating nodes,
- none of the nodes is privileged by the algorithm, i.e., each of them has equal chance to get anyone of the labels.

It is important to stress that the only global information, i.e., known to all nodes at the beginning, is the network size (number N).

One can immediately see that a solution to the enumeration problem is also a solution to the leader election problem. It is enough to agree that the node labeled by a selected label (e.g., 1 or N) is the leader. It is also true that a leader election algorithm may serve as a basis for solving the enumeration problem [10].

Considering only networks with asynchronous communication and deterministic protocols, it is known that the existence of solutions to both problems depends on the network topology represented by its graph. It is known that for some graphs - so called *ambiguous graphs* - there are no deterministic solutions. A recent and elegant characteristics of such graphs and impossibility of enumeration can be found in [8]. Other impossibility results are described, e.g., in [2] and [7]. Roughly speaking, in an ambiguous graph it is impossible to distinguish, by local means, some of its

[1] Partially supported by the Esprit Project 20288 CRIT-2 and INCO-Copernicus Project 977124 IDECOMP

subgraphs or, in other words, the graph can be "folded" to a smaller graph by a mapping that preserves the graph relation (i.e., a morphism) and is bijective if restricted to the neighborhood of any of the graph nodes. An example of a simple ambiguous graph structure is a ring (with at least six nodes) - the structure very often chosen for a network organization.

The situation changes when randomized protocols are considered, i.e., protocols in which each process can draw a random number to determine its next step. This fact has been recognized earlier, especially in works on fault-tolerant computations where randomized solutions to the Byzantine Agreement Problem (introduced first in [9]) have been studied as, e.g., in [1].

This short paper presents a simple randomized enumeration protocol that works efficiently for any network graph. A comparable result was independently proposed in [10] where iterated leader election (randomized) algorithm enumerates network nodes. Some randomized elements were also introduced in a version of the otherwise deterministic solution studied in [5].

We start this paper with some simplifying assumptions that are formulated in Section 2. Section 3 describes the protocol in detail. A sketch of the protocol correctness and an estimation of its performance are given in Section 4. Details on the estimation can be found in Appendix. (It is worth to point out that both the correctness and efficiency analysis are much easier to treat in randomized case if compared to a deterministic solution.) Concluding remarks (Section 5) end the presentation.

The algorithm has been implemented [4] in Estelle [6] and extensively simulated by the EDT simulator [3]. The simulation fully confirmed the obtained performance results.

2. Broadcasting assumptions

Consider a network of N nodes $x_1, x_2, \ldots, x_N$. Assume that each node x_k in the network receiving a message from a neighbor x_j, performs the following:

> **if** the message has been already received,
> i.e., it is already stored in the x_k memory
> **then** the message is discarded
> **else** the message is stored by x_k and it is
> forwarded to all x_k's neighbors but x_j.

Assume now that a message m is created by the node x_i, stored in the node local memory, and then sent to all the node neighbors. It seems obvious, in view of the above, that:

Fact 2.1. The procedure of forwarding the message m in the network eventually terminates and m is known to each node of the network i.e., it is received and stored by each node.

Due to the Fact 2.1 we can assume that a message sent by a node is received after certain delay by each other node in the network as if all nodes were directly connected. For example, if a network forms a unidirectional ring, then the maximal delay is proportional to the ring size. Therefore, further on we are not considering the problem of how the messages are broadcast. On the other hand, this problem is explicitly treated in the algorithm implementation in Estelle as specified in [4].

3. Randomized enumeration algorithm

As in previous sections, we consider a N-node network. The algorithm is performed in a (finite) number of rounds (DrawingRound procedure given in four steps below) and it can be described very shortly as follows (*active nodes* in a round are those not enumerated in previous rounds):

> In the current (first) drawing round, each active node independently draws a random number and broadcasts it (Step 1). Then it collects those numbers from all other active nodes (Step 2). Those active nodes whose random numbers are not repeated in other active nodes are separated and sorted (Step 3). The separated nodes are then enumerated by the order of their random values (Step 4). The remaining active nodes (if any), and only these nodes, are going to compete in the next round for labels greater than those assigned in the current (first) attempt. The whole algorithm terminates if there are no more nodes to be enumerated in the next round.

Let us specify the above idea in details. A message m is a triple m = (x, r, R), where x is a node (name) in the set of node (names) X, r denotes a round number and R is a (random) number, from a given interval, selected by the node x. Each node uses the following internal variables:

r	integer variable storing the current round number of the algorithm; initially r=0;
K	set of messages collected during the current drawing round; initially K=∅;
K1	subset of messages in K that identify nodes properly enumerated in the current round; initially K1=∅;

E	properly enumerated nodes until the current round, i.e., a set of pairs: a node and its assigned label (number) by the enumeration algorithm; initially E=∅;
s	size of the enumeration problem in the current drawing round; initially s=N;

The algorithm, for each node in the network, is defined by the following repeat-until construct:

```
repeat
   DrawingRound
until ( |E| = N ).
```

(|E| denotes the cardinality of the set E).

With the above definition of E, the DrawingRound procedure is performed until all N nodes in X are properly enumerated.

DrawingRound procedure, for each node x in X:

Step 1: r := r+1;
if x is not enumerated yet, i.e., (x, j) is not in E, for some j,
then create the message m = (x, r, R), with R a randomly selected number;
add m into the set K;
broadcast m;
fi;

Step 2 : collect and add into K all arriving messages that have different nodes and the round number that equals r - there is s or s-1 such messages depending on whether x hasn't or has been enumerated in previous rounds (i.e., whether the "if" condition from Step 1 was or was not satisfied, respectively);

Step 3 : K1 := {(y, r, P) ∈ K: there is no message (y', r, P') ∈ K with y≠y' and P=P' };
if K1 ≠ ∅
then sort K1 with respect to the third (random) value of its messages
fi;

Step 4 : **for** all messages (y, r, P) in K1 **do**
if (y, r, P) is k-th in the order created by sorting K1 in Step 3
then insert the pair (y, N-s+k) into the set E
fi;
s := |K-K1|; K := ∅; K1:= ∅;

It is worth to note that, with the assumption that a message broadcast (Step 1) by a node eventually reaches all other nodes in the network (Step 2), the DrawingRound procedure always terminates.

4. Analysis of the algorithm

In this section we formulate some simple facts about the randomized enumeration algorithm defined in the previous section. These facts prove that the algorithm always properly terminates (i.e., it terminates achieving a proper enumeration). An estimation of the algorithm efficiency is also discussed.

Let $E|_1$ ($E|_2$) denotes the set of first (second) elements of pairs in the set E, i.e., $E|_1$ is the set of nodes already enumerated and $E|_2$ is the set of their enumeration labels. Assume also in the formulation of (a)-(e) below, that if E and s denote the values of these variables when entering the DrawingRound procedure, then E' and s' will denote their values after the DrawingRound termination.

Directly from the definition of the DrawingRound steps, we have the following simple properties:

(a) $E \subseteq E'$;
(one can only add elements to the set)

(b) $E|_1 \subseteq E'|_1 \subseteq X$;
(labels are only assigned to nodes of the considered network)

(c) $E|_2 = \{1, 2, \ldots, N\text{-}s\}$;
(labels are properly chosen)

(d) $E'|_2 = E|_2 \cup \{N\text{-}s\text{+}1, \ldots, N\text{-}s\text{+}(s\text{-}s')\} = \{1, 2, \ldots, N\text{-}s'\}$;
(labels cannot be repeated in two different rounds)

(e) $N\text{-}|E| = s \geq s' = N\text{-}|E'|$.

From the properties (a)-(d) above, we have a general invariant property

(f) $|E| = |E|_1| = |E|_2|$

which says that for every two pairs (x, l) and (x', l') in E, both x ≠ x' and l ≠ l'.

Let us recall, that a finite set of nodes X is properly enumerated if to each element x ∈ X a unique label l(x) ⊂ {1, 2,..., |X|} is assigned. From (a)-(d) and (f) above, we can conclude

Fact 4.1. The set E defines a proper enumeration of all nodes in $E|_1$.

Fact 4.2. Each time, entering the DrawingRound procedure, the value of the variable E is the same for all nodes of the enumerated network (each node has the same "enumeration knowledge").

The termination condition of the enumeration algorithm (repeat loop condition) together with Facts 4.1 an 4.2 result in

Fact 4.3. If the algorithm terminates, then the final value of E in each node defines the same proper enumeration of the network (it means also that computations in all nodes terminate by the same round, even though the nodes may be enumerated in different rounds).

Let [1 : M] be an integer interval from which a random numbers are selected and M >> N. With this assumption and the property (e) above one can prove the following (details can be found in the Appendix):

Fact 4.4. The probability that the value of s is the same in the next round as it was in the previous one is M^{-s+1}.

The probability that the first (k-th) computation round is the last one is non-zero and grows while the value s decreases (see property (e) above and Appendix). Therefore, the probability that the whole enumeration algorithm never terminates, i.e., that it may have infinite number of rounds, equals 0.

Fact 4.5. The enumeration algorithm always terminates.

Fact 4.6. The expected number of rounds to terminate the enumeration algorithm is bounded by M/(M-N(N-1)).

The last result says that, with M >> N, it is almost certain that the algorithm terminates just in one round. For instance, if N=100 and M = 100000, then the above bound equals 10/9. All simulation experiments confirmed this "one round" result. In practice, it means that the time that is needed to reach the enumeration agreement is proportional to time necessary to spread a message in the network. In simulation, the random numbers were generated by a simple linear congruential method. The same method was used in all nodes. Each node generator had a different starting value assigned while initialized.

At last, we need not to add that, due to the probabilistic arguments, each node has equal chance to get anyone of the labels, i.e., none of the nodes is privileged by the algorithm.

5. Conclusions

A simple randomized enumeration algorithm has been presented. The power of the randomized approach (at least in this case) is in that information created (random number) locally by each node of a network needs only to be broadcast to all other nodes. No synchronization is required even if reduced to neighbor nodes as it is the case in [8]. The result is that the algorithm is truly distributed and works for all network configurations (graphs) and not only for a selected class of them (unambiguous graphs). It seems that the randomized approach leads usually to algorithms that are much simpler, easier to verify and, last but not least, much more efficient. Finally, it is worth to stress, that enumeration problem is a basis for many other distributed algorithm (one can say the same about the leader election algorithm) therefore its efficiency and feasibility is of great importance.

References

[1] M. Ben-Or, Randomized Agreement Protocols, *Lecture Notes in Com. Sci.* 448, 72-83 (1989)

[2] L. Bougé, On the Existance of Symmetric Algorithms to Find Leaders in Networks of Communicating Sequential Processes, *Acta Informatica* 25, 179-201 (1988)

[3] S. Budkowski, Estelle Development Toolset, *J. of Computer Networks and ISDN Systems*, vol. 25, No.1 (1992)

[4] P. Dembiński, Randomized Enumeration, Report 848, Institute of Computer Science of PAS (1998)

[5] P. Dembiński, Enumeration protocol in Estelle: an exercise in stepwise development, in S. Budkowski, A. Cavalli, E. Najm eds., Formal Description Techniques and Protocol Specification, Testing and Verification, Kluwer Academic Publishers, 147-162 (1998)

[6] ISO 9074, Information processing systems - Open Systems Interconnection - Estelle - A formal description technique based on an extended state transition model (1989)

[7] I.Litovsky, Y. Métivier, W. Zielonka, The power and limitations of local computations on graphs and networks, *Lecture Notes in Com. Sci.* 657, 333-345 (1993)

[8] A. Mazurkiewicz, Distributed Enumeration, *Information Processing Letters* 61, 233-239 (1997)

[9] M. Pease, R.Shostak, L. Lamport, Reaching Agreement in the Presence of Faults, *JACM 27*, 228-234 (1980)

[10] F. Vernadat, P. Azema, K. Drida, Distributed Coin Tossing, Proc. of the 14th Intern. Conference on Distributed Systems, IEEE Computer Society Press, 244-249 (1994)

Appendix

Drawing N numbers with replacement, one after another, from the set of M numbers, where M >> N, is called an *experiment*. A *successful experiment* is the one which results in all different N numbers. Because there are:

- M^N of N-element sequences from the set of M numbers, and
- M(M-1) ... (M-N+1) of N-element sequences in which every number is different,

then

$$pse = M(M-1) \ldots (M-N+1)\, M^{-N} = M!/((M-N)!M^N) \quad (1)$$

is the probability of performing a successful experiment.

Consider now a sequence of single experiments in the above sense. The task is to estimate the expected number of experiments needed to achieve a successful one. It is easy to show that this expected number equals 1/pse (in fact, it is the expected value of the geometric distribution). We are going to show that

$$1/pse < M/(M-N(N-1)) \text{ or, equivalently,}$$

$$pse > 1 - N(N-1)/M. \quad (2)$$

Assuming M > N(N-1) we directly have

$$M(M-1) \ldots (M-N+1) > (M-(N-1))^N \quad (3)$$

Let us prove, by induction with respect to k, the following, general inequality:

$$(m-a)^k > m^k - akm^{k-1} \quad (4)$$

for all k=2,3,..., with m>a (by (3) and substituting m=M, a=N-1 and k=N, we obtain (2)). We can write (4) in yet another, equivalent form

$$(m-a)^k = m^k - akm^{k-1} + b_{a,m,k}, \quad (5)$$

$$k=2,3,\ldots, b_{a,m,k} > 0$$

For k=2, (5) obviously holds. Assume now, that (5) holds for some k>2. We have:

$$(m-a)^{k+1} = (m-a)\,(m^k - akm^{k-1} + b_{a,m,k})$$

$$= m^{k+1} - akm^k - am^k + a^2km^{k-1} + (m-a)b_{a,m,k}$$

$$= m^{k+1} - am^k(k+1) + b_{a,m,k+1},$$

$$\text{where } b_{a,m,k+1} = a^2km^{k-1} + (m-a)b_{a,m,k} > 0.$$

Hence, by inductive argument, (5) holds. Therefore, by the above reasoning, we obtained (2).

Heterogeneous Client-Server Architecture for a Virtual Meeting Environment

Masood Masoodian, Saturnino Luz
Natural Interactive Systems Laboratory
Odense University
5230 Odense M, Denmark
{masood, luz}@nis.sdu.dk

Abstract

Magic Lounge is a shared virtual meeting environment which has been designed to support meetings between physically remote people who would like to interact with each other using any one of a number of heterogeneous communication devices. This paper describes the heterogeneous client-server architecture of the Magic Lounge which supports communication between PCs, PDAs, palmtops, and mobile telephones. This architecture combines a number of different technologies, including CORBA and MBone, to provide the necessary means of audio and textual communication between the users of different devices. This paper also discusses the various requirements of this type of meeting environment, as well as describing some of the Magic Lounge software tools and components which have been developed to provide intelligent communication services to its users.

1. Introduction

The widespread interest shown by ordinary people in the use of Internet-based communication tools and meeting environments has encouraged commercial companies as well as researchers to put considerable amount of effort into development of a wide range of such tools. Currently there are various virtual meeting environments [4, 13, 12, 18] which support communication and interaction between physically remote people using specific computer technology, which are often desktop personal computers with multimedia capabilities.

However, as mobile computing and communication devices, with accessibility to the Internet, are gradually becoming more available to the public, it is becoming necessary to develop systems that support the use of such devices for accessing Internet-based collaborative virtual meeting environments. Furthermore, due to the diversity and range of such portable devices in terms of their input and output capabilities, there is a need for systems that allow interaction between people using different types of technology, for instance someone with a mobile telephone interacting with someone with a PDA.

The objective of the Magic Lounge[1] project [1, 3] is to design and develop a virtual meeting environment which provides the necessary tools for communication and interaction needs of geographically separated individuals. These individuals may use any one of a number of heterogeneous devices (including PCs, PDAs, palmtops, and mobile telephones) to collaborate with one another.

The Magic Lounge system is also going to offer a range of advanced communication and collaboration services to facilitate the interaction between its meeting participants. Some of these services can be briefly described as:

- Intelligent multi-party communication management allowing recording and retrieving of the meeting communication history in a multimedia fashion.
- Content-based media conversion techniques coping with heterogeneous communication devices. These techniques will be used for converting text to speech, and speech to text.
- Speech-operated information retrieval for embedding third-party information services, such as those provided on the Internet.
- Speech and gesture-based interrogation and navigation of information spaces.

Although there are several systems and tools currently available which fully or partially provide some of these services and functionalities. Magic Lounge, however, is aiming to:

[1] The Magic Lounge project web site is located at: http://www.dfki.de/imedia/mlounge/

- Combine all of these functionalities into a single integrated system which is easy to use by ordinary people, who want to perform a range of non-specific ordinary tasks and activities [10].
- Provide all or at least a basic range of these intelligent communication services to people who may be using mobile devices rather than multimedia PC workstations.

To achieve these objectives, it has been necessary to develop a heterogeneous client-server architecture which adopts and extends a set of existing technologies to provide a framework for integrating some of the available human-to-human communication and interaction tools to create the Magic Lounge virtual meeting environment. This paper outlines and discusses the architecture of the Magic Lounge system. It also gives a brief description of some of the components of the Magic Lounge software. These components have been designed and developed to provide the type of services which are not currently supported by other virtual meeting environments.

2. Background

As mentioned earlier, there are several existing systems which offer, at least partially, some of the services proposed by the Magic Lounge. In some cases these systems can be easily adopted and changed, so that they can be included in other systems. Magic Lounge attempts to utilise, whenever possible, these types of systems to provide a few of its required functionalities.

Magic Lounge also relies on other types of technologies which can be used as a basis for its development and integration with other systems. There are in particular two types of technologies which are of extreme importance to the development of the Magic Lounge. These, which can be referred to as distributed and communication technologies, will be briefly described in the next two sections.

2.1. Distributed technology

A substantial amount of the Magic Lounge development effort has to be dedicated to the integration of all its software components. These components include not only the new parts, which have to be completely developed, but also those parts which have already been developed elsewhere but require modification and integration with the other existing parts. To simplify this process of integration, there are several important issues which have to be addressed.

The various components of the Magic Lounge are not only supposed to be able to run on different types of heterogeneous devices, but they are also supposed to be able to communicate with one another. This means that for instance a Magic Lounge client running on a palmtop device with limited capabilities should in fact be able to interact with a more powerful client running on a PC or a Unix workstation.

Besides this issue of platform heterogeneity, there is also the problem of using different programming languages. Although it was decided to implement all the new components of the Magic Lounge using the Java programming language, the already existing components have been implemented in different programming languages. There is also the problem of developing software components for some of the mobile devices for which there are no Java Run-Time Environments available. This means that adopting a simple Java-based client-server technology wouldn't solve the problem of integrating these components.

After considering various options for developing the Magic Lounge distributed system, it was decided to use the CORBA (Common Object Request Broker Architecture) technology [17]. The use of CORBA satisfies the requirements of the Magic Lounge for two reasons.

Firstly, CORBA allows different components of a software system to treat all the other components of the system in the same way, regardless of whether they are local or remote. This means that different parts of the Magic Lounge software can be developed to run of different types of devices, or that the components can be easily moved from one platform to another, without affecting the behaviour of the system.

Secondly, in CORBA a component's behaviour in relation to the other components is defined using a standard interface definition language (IDL). This definition describes the operations a component is prepared to perform, the input and output parameters it requires, and the type of errors which might occur during interaction with it. This means that the implementation of a component can be changed without changing its interaction with the others. It also means that the implementation can in fact be in any programming language, so long as CORBA supports that particular language (almost all the popular programming languages, including C, C++, Java, and Smalltalk are supported).

2.2. Communication technology

One of the main objectives of the Magic Lounge is to provide multi-party multimedia communication facilities to support interaction between users of devices with different limitations and capabilities in terms of their input and output. Although there are a number of systems which provide audio, video, and data conferencing, the majority of these have been developed for a particular platform, which are in many cases also tied to particular interface design assumptions and constraints.

The main focus of the Magic Lounge has not been on the development of communication tools or network infrastructure *per se*. Rather, the project has sought to focus on the issue of how existing tools and infrastructure can be integrated and used in support of a user group interacting in scenarios very close to their every-day life [10], many of these scenarios requiring the users to interact with others while they may be travelling and do not have access to their standard desktop computers. The dependency of the existing software tools on platforms, environments, devices, and other such requirements makes them unsuitable for the Magic Lounge users.

Given the nature of the targeted user group, as well as the need for supporting heterogeneous devices, the challenge faced by the Magic Lounge is to provide its users with an environment in which both synchronous and asynchronous interaction can take place.

The interaction in Magic Lounge has to be natural enough to avoid disrupting the essential patterns of synchronous communication, while at the same time supporting visualisation and access to the meeting content for those who are not able to interact in the synchronous mode.

Inability to take part in synchronous communication might arise due to time constraints (i.e. not being able to attend a meeting when it is in progress) or media constraints (i.e. not having access to a device with full multimedia capabilities). The former issue is addressed through structuring and storing the meeting contents in a central memory component [14]. The latter is addressed by an interface component designed to improve feedback and access to meeting memory in a way which is naturally generalisable across media-poor and media-rich devices (see Sections 4 and 5).

The infrastructure chosen to enable meeting the basic requirements of the Magic Lounge system, as sketched above, is based on IP multicasting, more specifically on the emerging MBone technology (virtual Multicast Backbone On the interNEt). The MBone [8] is a virtual network built on top of the existing Internet infrastructure. One of the advantages of the MBone is that it can be used for developing conferencing tools which can interact with one another regardless of the type of platform on which they operate.

IP multicasting [8] is a technology which allows isochronous media, such as real-time audio and video, which require delivery from source to destination within a certain bounded time, to be transferred in a large-scale manner over the Internet. In addition to scalability and cross-platform operability, one of the reasons for choosing to use the MBone, is the fact that there are numerous freely available audio and video conferencing tools which rely on it[2].

3. Architecture of the Magic Lounge

The current architecture of the Magic Lounge software has been designed based on the experiences gained through the design and implementation of an earlier version of the Magic Lounge software prototype. The previous architecture, which has been described elsewhere [11], was based on the Habanero collaborative framework [2]. However, since (i) the Habanero framework does not support construction of asynchronous collaborative software and (ii) there is no Habanero support for mobile devices, it was decided to design a new architecture for Magic Lounge which did not rely on the use of the Habanero framework (for further details see [11]).

Besides removing the Habanero framework from the previous architecture, there was also a need to modify this architecture to allow inclusion of new components. In particular, the new architecture was required to include support for audio conferencing functionality which was not a part of the first Magic Lounge prototype.

Figure 1 shows the architecture of the current Magic Lounge software prototype. As with the previous architecture, the current architecture is also based on a client-server model. In this model a central CORBA server is used to facilitate the interaction between a number of clients and tools. The Magic Lounge clients and tools are assumed to be heterogeneous, in the sense that different versions of the same tool or client will be developed for each particular communication device supported by the Magic Lounge. These tools will be tailored to cope with the input and output limitations and capabilities of the device for which they have been designed, while at the same time providing a set of functionalities which they will have in common with similar tools developed for the other devices.

The new Magic Lounge architecture supports inclusion of both synchronous and asynchronous types of collaborative tools. Tools from different Magic Lounge clients can interact with each other in real-time through the Magic Lounge CORBA Server, thus, allowing collaboration in synchronous mode. They can also interact in an asynchronous mode by allowing the exchange of persistent information via the central Magic Lounge Memory Sever.

---

[2]For a list of tools visit: http://www.mbone.com/

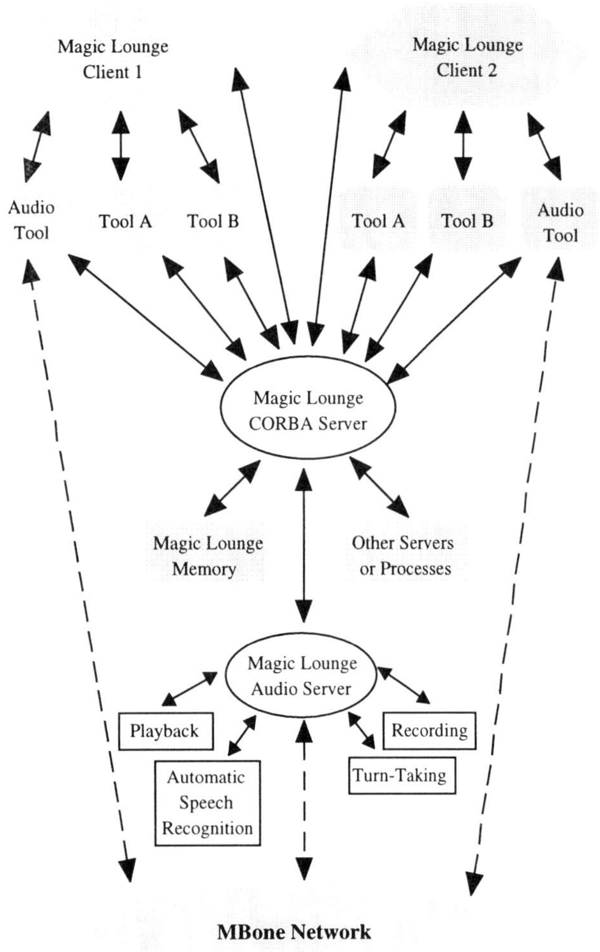

Figure 1. The Magic Lounge architecture

Magic Lounge architecture also includes a mechanism for adding external servers to provide the intelligent communication services described earlier. These servers which can be central or local to a particular type of device can register themselves with the Magic Lounge CORBA Server in a fashion similar to the Magic Lounge clients. Among these servers are the internal Magic Lounge Memory Server, and the Magic Lounge Audio Server.

The Magic Lounge Memory Server, to put it briefly, creates a structured history of the audio and textual conversations carried out during the Magic Lounge meetings [14]. This memory can be queried by the users to find out a range of information about the past and present meetings.

The Magic Lounge Audio Server, on the other hand, facilitates the audio conferencing aspect of the Magic Lounge meeting environment [9]. This server consists of two main components:

- A daemon based on a standard MBone audio tool which records the audio data exchanged during a meeting, plus a set of control-data similar to those displayed by standard client-side audio tools.
- A set of *plug-ins* which process the recorded audio data, and for instance play it back on demand. It is envisaged that the audio server will be improved to include the ability to query the audio database by topic, speaker, entity and so on. These functionalities will build upon existing automatic speech recognition, topic detection [19], and information extraction [5] technologies.

The underlying network structure assumed by the audio server and its corresponding audio client tool is the MBone. The basic client-side tools are adapted from the existing MBone audio tools which are based on IETF (Internet Engineering Task Force) standards and allow both point-to-point and multicast communication modes.

An overview of the architecture of the Magic Lounge Audio Server is shown in Figure 2.

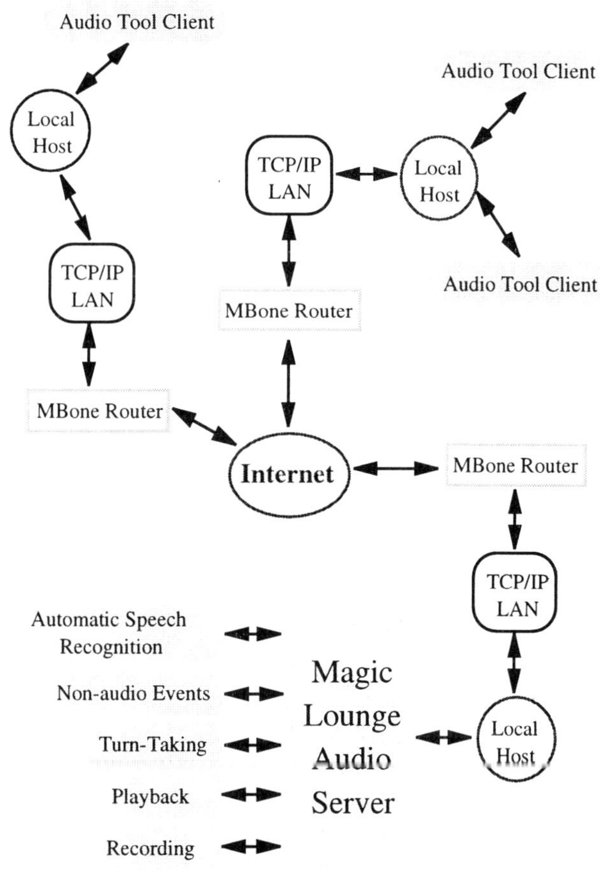

Figure 2. Magic Lounge Audio Server

The general setting adopted by the Magic Lounge audio conferencing system involves traditional per-to-per MBone communication. The Magic Lounge Audio Server itself can be regarded as an audio conference participant which does not register itself, but nevertheless "listens" and records all the audio exchanges. Events initiated by the other Magic Lounge components (such as the Magic Lounge Memory Sever) can, however, request services from the Audio Server in a standard client-server fashion through the Magic Lounge CORBA Server. The Audio Sever itself can in turn ask any of its plug-ins to provide the services requested by the other Magic Lounge components.

4. Magic Lounge prototype

Based on the architecture described above, a software prototype is currently under development. So far, the CORBA client-server communication infrastructure has been implemented, and a number of tools are being developed. Among these tools are: a textual chat tool with intelligent functions for tagging communicative acts, a memory tool for accessing and interrogating the internal Magic Lounge meeting memory [14], and an audio conferencing tool with a score-line graphical user interface for viewing the meeting history [9, 15].

The graphical user interface has been built on top of one of the standard MBone audio tools, called RAT [6]. The GUI component of the Magic Lounge Audio tool displays information about the audio conference, most of which are already provided by Real-Time Protocol (RTP) on which many MBone applications are based [16]. This set of information includes the following:

1. Identification of the meeting
2. Identification of each of the meeting participants
3. Description of the type of object (payload) carried by each contribution, for instance whether it is streaming audio, chat text, or hyperlink document
4. Start time
5. End time

The first two items of information can be extracted directly from the underlying transport protocol (RTP) and respective control data (RTCP). The third item is only partially supported in the core definition of RTP. However, since the protocol allows for the definition of extensions to its profile, future accommodation of non-audio data should be manageable within RTP itself. The forth and fifth items, on the other hand, require special post-transmission processing. The data for these items are extracted from sets of RTP packets, and simultaneously stored in the session database at the server side. They are then displayed incrementally at each client.

Figure 3 shows a screenshot of the first prototype of the audio meeting browser, displaying the audio contributions of each of the participants of a meeting as time bars.

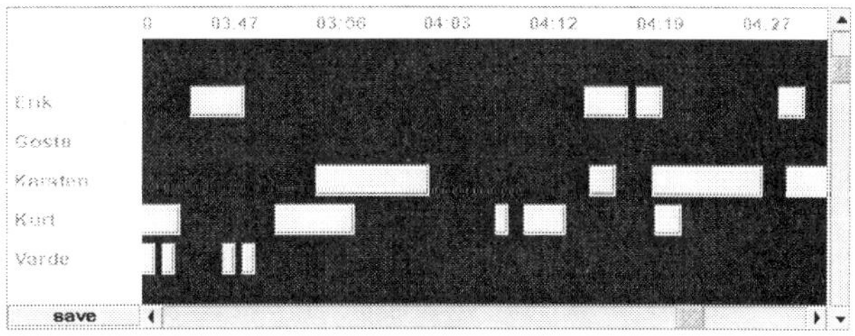

Figure 3. The Meeting Browser

Although the interface shown here is simple enough to allow a trimmed-down version to be implemented for mobile devices with limited display capabilities, it can be enriched with, for instance, textual tags which will increase its usefulness in accessing and retrieving audio contents of meetings. Currently there is also a more advanced version of this prototype under development. The new prototype combines the display of audio exchange information with other meeting events recorded in the Magic Lounge Memory (such as the information about the participants' login and logout times, and the textual contributions made through the chat tool).

As it was mentioned earlier, due to the different limitations that each of the various devices have, in terms of their input and output capabilities, it is necessary to develop different versions of each of the Magic Lounge tools for each of the supported communication devices. It is also clear that not all the tools can be supported by every device. For instance, it is not possible to develop a version of the audio tool for the PDAs. However, in such instances where the physical limitations of a particular device don't allow development of a tool for that device, another tool is created to provide a similar and perhaps somewhat a limited functionality.

At present several tools are being developed and evaluated to support the essential services of the Magic Lounge meeting environment for users of PC workstations, PDAs, palmtops, and mobile telephones.

5. Discussion

Although the architecture which has been described here provides a practical model for the development of the Magic Lounge software, there are a number of research challenges which still need to be overcome. One of these is related to combining audio and textual information in a meeting in which different users are accessing the meeting through different types of devices. For instance in such a meeting, a person with a mobile telephone can send and receive only audio messages, while at the same time another person with a PDA will be able to send and receive only textual messages. Therefore a system such as the Magic Lounge, which allows interaction between these types of technologies, has to be able to:

- Record the communication history in a heterogeneous form, to include both textual and audio contributions.
- Convert and present the communication history in a form which is suitable for the requirements of each particular device.

Internet-based textual chat systems, which allow recording of the communication history, have become widely available. There are also several MBone tools for recording audio conferences. Magic Lounge, on the other hand, attempts to combine both textual and audio-based communication, which is not supported by any of the existing systems. To illustrate this difference an example is given below.

Figure 4 depicts the communication history of a meeting between three people where *person A* has an audio connection, *person B* has an audio as well as a text-based connection, and *person C* has a text-based connection. Using conventional audio and textual communication systems, there wouldn't be any connection between *A* and *C* in this meeting, unless *person B* was facilitating the interaction between the other two participants.

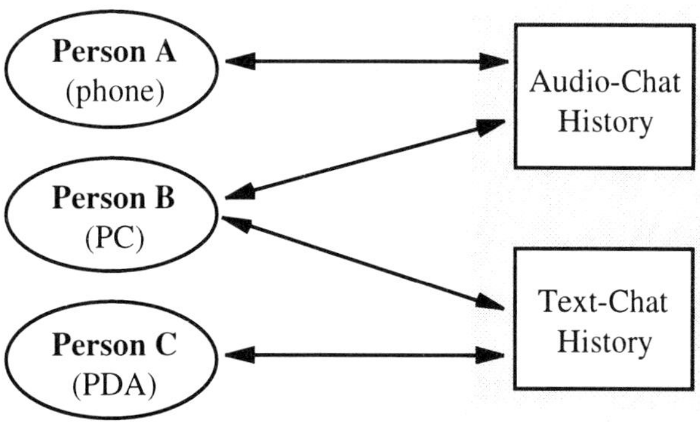

Figure 4. Separate audio and textual communication history

A possible solution to this problem is to combine the audio and textual communication history. Therefore, rather than recording the whole audio and textual contents of a meeting as two separate entities, the individual inputs of the participants, regardless of whether they are textual or audio, are recorded separately. In this way, the history is viewed as a sequential collection of audio and textual utterances of the meeting participants. This however, does not mean that at the physical storage level audio or textual conversation history has to be divided and stored as individual utterances. So long as the sequential time-based relationship between the audio and textual utterances is preserved, individual utterances can be accessed as if they were stored individually. Figure 5 depicts a combined audio-textual communication history.

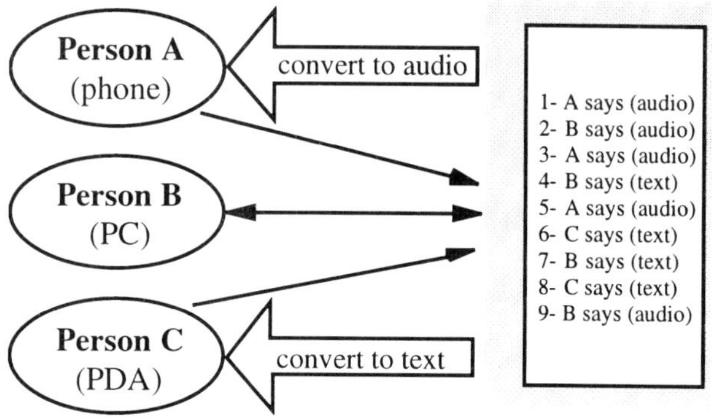

Figure 5. Combined audio and textual communication history

As Figure 5 shows, in a meeting with a combined audio and textual communication history participants receive the contributions of the others in a form which is suitable for their own communication device. This means that for instance all the textual messages are converted to audio format for a person with a mobile telephone, while the audio messages are converted to textual format for someone with a PDA. A person with a multimedia PC, on the other hand, can interact with the others using either text or audio (or both).

Although conceptually speaking, the idea of combined history is a possible solution to the problem of communication modality differences between the users of various devices, in reality, there are a few development-related obstacles which need to be overcome. One of these is due to the fact that the audio quality of the Internet-based telephony is not very high. This means that the currently available speech recognisers are not that effective with this type of audio input.

There are also problems associated with the physical limitations of the small portable devices [7]. For instance, PDAs and palmtops have limited input and output capabilities, which limit the amount of information that can be exchanged between such devices and PCs. Similarly, accessing a large amount of history information using a mobile telephone is not really practical. Therefore in the Magic Lounge environment, after converting the chat messages to device specific modes, it is necessary to summarise and present them in different ways to suit the users of different devices. However, the technology required for performing this type of information summarisation and presentation still needs to be developed.

6. Conclusions

This paper described a heterogeneous client-server architecture which has been designed and used for the development of the Magic Lounge virtual meeting environment. This architecture which relies on some of the capabilities of the CORBA and MBone technologies provides the necessary components for creating real-time collaborative environments for heterogeneous devices. It also provides a mechanism for inclusion of external servers which might be added in the future to extend the intelligent services which a collaborative work environment such as Magic Lounge offers.

This work is also identifying interesting research challenges related to conversion of audio and textual media, as well as presentation of information on different types of devices.

Although at present some of the limitations of the existing technologies, in particular mobile devices, restrict the type of functionality they offer, rapid technological developments will allow more extensive use of such devices in group communication and collaborative work in the near future. Therefore, further research in some of the areas identified in this paper will be of real benefit to the development of collaborative software for future mobile devices.

7. Acknowledgements

Magic Lounge is an ESPRIT long-term research project (No. 25458), funded under the European Network of Intelligent Information Interfaces (i^3) initiative. The Magic Lounge architecture and its software components have been designed and implemented collaboratively by all the members of this research project. The authors, therefore, would like to acknowledge the contributions of all the other project partners.

8. References

[1] N. O. Bernsen, T. Rist, J.-C. Martin, C. Hauck, D. Boullier, X. Briffault, L. Dybkjaer, C. Henry, M. Masoodian, F. Neel, H.-J. Profitlich, E. Andre, J. Schweitzer, and J. Vapillon. Magic Lounge: A Thematic Inhabited Information Space with "Intelligent" Communication Services. *Conference Proceedings of NIMES '98*, 188-192, 1998.

[2] A. Chabert, E. Grossman, L. Jackson, S. Pietrowicz, and C. Seguin. Java Object-Sharing in Habanero. *Communications of the ACM*, 41 (6), 69-76, 1998.

[3] B. Cleal, M. Masoodian, N. O. Bernsen, and L. Dybkjaer. Meeting in the Magic Lounge. *Conference Proceedings of INTERACT '99*, 2, 73-74, 1999.

[4] G. Fitzpatrick, W. Tolone, and S. Kaplan. Work, Locales and Distributed Social Worlds. *Conference Proceedings of ECSCW '95*, 1-16, 1995.

[5] R. Grishman. Information Extraction: Techniques and Challenges. *Lecture Notes in Computer Science*, 1299, 1997.

[6] O. Hodson, S. Varakliotis, and V. Hardman. A Software Platform for Multi-way Audio Distribution over the Internet. *Audio and Music Technology: The Challenge of Creative DSP, IEE Colloquium*, 1998.

[7] K. Kawachiya, H. Ishikawa. NaviPoint: An Input Device for Mobile Information Browsing. Conference *Proceedings of CHI '98*, 1-8, 1998.

[8] V. Kumar. *MBone: Interactive Multimedia on the Internet.* New Riders, 1996.

[9] S. Luz, and D. M. Roy. Meeting Browser: A System for Visualising and Accessing Audio in Multicast Meetings. *Proceedings of the International Workshop on Multimedia Signal Processing*, 587-592, 1999.

[10] M. Masoodian, and B. Cleal. User-Centred Design of a Virtual Meeting Environment for Ordinary People. *Conference Proceedings of HCI International '99*, 2, 528-532, 1999.

[11] M. Masoodian, and S. Luz. Architecture of the Magic Lounge Virtual Meeting Environment. *Conference Proceedings of Concurrent Engineering '99*, 216-222, 1999.

[12] T. Nishida. Facilitating Community Knowledge Evolution by Talking Virtualized Egos. *Conference Proceedings of HCI International '99*, 2, 437-441, 1999.

[13] M. Roseman, and S. Greenberg. TeamRooms: Network Places for Collaboration. *Conference Proceedings of CSCW '96*, 325-333, 1996.

[14] T. Rist, J.-C. Martin, F. D. Neel, and J. Vapillon. On the Design of Intelligent Memory Functions for Virtual Meeting Places: Examining Potential Benefits and Requirements. *Journal Le Travail Humain*, in print, 1999.

[15] D. M. Roy, and S. Luz. Audio Meeting History Tool: Interactive Graphical User-Support for Virtual Audio Meetings. *Proceedings of ESCA Workshop on Accessing Information in Spoken Audio*, 107-110, 1999.

[16] H. Schulzrine, S. Casner, R. Frederick, and V. Jacobson. RTP: A Transport Protocol for Real-Time Applications. *IETF Internet Draft draft-ietf-avt-new-04*, 1999.

[17] J. Siegel. OMG Overview: CORBA and the OMA in Enterprise Computing. *Communications of the ACM*, 41 (10), 37-43, 1998.

[18] P. J. Spellman, J. N. Mosier, L. M. Deus, and J. A. Carlso. Collaborative virtual workspace. *Conference Proceedings of GROUP '97*, 197-203, 1997.

[19] C. L. Wayne. Topic Detection and Tracking (TDT): Overview and Perspectives. *Proceedings of DARPA Broadcast News Transcription and Understanding Workshop*, 1998.

Session 2:
Web Based Computing I

Session 2 and 4: Web Computing

Session Chair: Konrad Klöckner

Communication facilities on the World Wide Web play a key role in the design and implementation of distributed systems for cooperation purposes. Interprocess communication facilities allow processes to be spread over the Web to communicate and to access remote resources. Performance of the whole distributed system, in particular a distributed workflow and communication system, depends on this facility.It was the development of efficient and cost effective interconnection structures on the one hand and the price performance evolution in microelectronics on the other hand which were prerequisites for the development of distributed communication applications. A general trend for introducing computing systems into almost every business oriented or leisure oriented activity, as well as computing system interfaces appeared. One of those new application areas is computer supported cooperative work. (CSCW). In its most general form, CSCW examines the possibilities and effects of technological support in distributed collaborative group communications and work processes. As local and wide-area networking technologies become more sophisticated, distributed group working is a well-suited scenario for computer use and presents theoretical and practical problems that have not been thoroughly addressed in computer science research. This session aims to bring together experts from academia and industry who share an interest in the study and design of effective Web computing solutions as well as approaches and methodologies. It focuses on understanding the impact of Web computing environments in order to facilitate the design of complex cooperation systems. This session is an opportunity for designers and researchers to discuss their experiences with implementing cooperative systems on the Web in large organisations such as industry, government and academia. It is open for sharing information about new Web technologies and practices.

In this session we have six papers dealing with the various aspects of Web computing. The first paper "Replicating the R in URL" is by C. Allison, M. Bramley, J. Serrano and D. McKechan. The paper details a design for resource management that supports arbitrary resource types, replicated instances of a given resource type, and multiple cooperating servers. It is based on experiences of the authors in the context of distributed learning environments.

The second paper is entitled "Security mechanisms for the MAP agent system" and it is written by A. Puliafito and O. Tomarchio. The authors propose a security schema for mobile agents and describe its implementation inside the reference platform. Some experimental results are also provided to evaluate the overhead introduced from the adoption of the proposed security mechanism.

The third paper "Implementation of an Annotation Service on the WWW – Virtual Notes" is by Stefan Koch and Georg Schneider. In the paper an annotation service is presented using only standard internet technology and can be widely used without further need for preparation by the prospective user.

The forth paper "Gypsy: A Component-based Mobile Agent System" is by Mehdi Jazayeri and Wolfgang Lugmayr. Gypsy is a component based, dynamically extensible environment for mobile agent systems. The paper gives an overview of the Gypsy project, the current system architecture and the design of the important components of the Gypsy system. The basic component of the system is a mobile agent from which both the system components and user agents are built. The Gypsy component model imposes a uniform architecture for all components.

The fifth paper is entitled "Towards Reference Architectures for Distributed Groupware Applications" and is written by Burkhard Messer and Kurt Sandkuhl. The presented approach describes a bunch of support components for software development projects like a reference architecture for groupware applications, reusable components and services and design and architecture patterns. The paper presents a view concept for software architectures, a global reference architecture for groupware applications and an example from the application field of web publishing.

The last paper "ENTER: The Personalisation and Contextualistion of 3-Dimensional worlds" is by Tom Guinan, G.M.P. O'Hare and N. Doikiv. The paper presents and investigates an immersive multi-user 3-dimensional system environment. The described system has been cast from the domain of virtual shopping malls but this is only one potential application domain. It offers user immersion in both a virtual world and that of a virtual community and it offers this through the judicious use of agent oriented techniques.

Overall, the Web technologies promise a better support of human communication across wider distances than was previously possible. Yet, if this vision is to be realised, many difficult problems remain to be solved and are the future challenges.

1066-6192/99 $10.00 © 1999 IEEE

Replicating the R in URL

Colin Allison, Martin Bramley, Jose Serrano, David McKechan
{ca,mntb,serrano,dm}@dcs.st-and.ac.uk
Division of Computer Science,
University of St Andrews,
Scotland

Abstract

The Web supports access to a very wide variety of services and objects via the simple naming mechanism provided by the Uniform Resource Locator or URL. When resources are read-only entities, which is still the common case, there is little problem in returning their output to clients in the face of multiple concurrent accesses. However, the Web is increasingly being adopted as the front-end for distributed multi-user applications, in which case resources must be maintained in an environment characterised by multiple concurrent reads and writes, and dynamic access control. This engenders basic needs for concurrency control and dynamic configuration in the single server scenario. Highly interactive Web environments, which do not benefit from caching, cause sufficient extra server load to necessitate the use of multiple servers. Replication is necessary when caching fails. The moderate complexity of single server resource management is then compounded. This report details a design for resource management that supports arbitrary resource types, replicated instances of a given resource type, and multiple co-operating servers. It is based on our experiences of coping with complexity in the context of Distributed Learning Environments.

1 Introduction

Distributed Learning Environments (DLEs) represent the hope that communications and information technology can improve and widen access to education while maintaining and improving its quality. Such multi–user environments typically consist of web-oriented networked applications and services. In contrast to earlier modes of Computer Based Learning where a student would work in isolation on a computer, DLEs have the potential to support teamwork and introduce real world input into the study environment. For example Finesse (Finance Education in a Scalable Software Environment) provides a group-oriented portfolio management facility which uses real time data from the London Stock Exchange [1]. In addition DLEs can support distance learning, anytime, anywhere, across a wide area network. DLEs consist of subject-specific resources and generic facilities. Desirable generic facilities for a DLE include:

- flexibility
- responsiveness
- availability
- coherence
- dynamic group configuration
- monitoring

Flexibility refers to the capability for integrating the diverse range of subject-specific resources into a DLE. Responsiveness is a function of server load. Availability depends on the ability to cope with server or network failure. A single server is particularly vulnerable to both high load degradation [2] and single point-of-failure. The adoption of multiple servers can be used to address these problems but demands a management facility for all aspects of resources – from replication coherence to dynamic group access control. Finally, monitoring is needed to provide feedback on resource usage. This typically takes the form of a tutor querying the system for information about a particular student, group, or resource.

Our experience with building the Finesse DLE has lead to a design for TAGS (Tutor and Group Support), an experimental framework for DLEs, which aims to support the generic facilities listed above. Before describing TAGS in more detail we review its genesis in the Finesse DLE.

2 The Finesse DLE

The Finesse project addressed problems associated with the teaching of finance courses in the UK Higher Education sector by constructing a networked, computer-based portfolio management facility. Finesse is currently used at the Universities of Dundee, Glasgow Caledonian, St Andrews, and Strathclyde for both undergraduate and post-graduate teaching.

1066-6192/99 $10.00 © 1999 IEEE

There are currently three resources available in Finesse: (i) a management facility for portfolios of stocks and shares which functions in a highly realistic trading environment (this is the only subject-specific resource) (ii) a lightweight groupware tool, the Notebook, and (iii) arbitrary URLs[1].

The portfolio management facility allows the management of a portfolio by a student group. The group maintains their portfolio by buying and selling shares chosen from a database of live data for approximately 1100 companies quoted on the London Stock Exchange (LSE). Monthly summary information dating back to 1990 is also provided for sector analysis. There are three main components to the Portfolio Management Facility. First, there is the real time data interface which reads share prices and other information from LSE data sources and writes it to the Finesse database. Second, there is the software which provides the interface between the database file of stock market information and the web-server. Finally, there is the web-server which provides the interface between the user and the programs which search and sort the database file. Tutors and students see a uniform integrated environment.

Groups in Finesse are allocated a Portfolio and a Notebook. At the start of the teaching period they are also allocated a nominal £100 million. They can inspect changes and historic data in a range of companies, buy and sell shares, look at the portfolio profit and loss, and follow links to other sources of market information. Groups are encouraged to use their Notebooks to communicate with each other and their tutors concerning their investment decisions.

Tutors monitor students by (i) examining the archive of intra-group communication provided in the Notebook, and (ii) querying the general activity records and portfolio history logs.

2.1 Drawbacks with Finesse

Finesse has met its educational goals and is highly valued by its users [3]. As with many long running software developments, the Finesse project suffered from ever expanding features. The users, groups and resources management subsystem grew in an ad hoc fashion. Each new resource type or modification to a template for an existing resource required the underlying system to be modified. With the exception of arbitrary URLs only CGI implementations of resources in UNIX environments could be incorporated. It also became apparent that there was a need to support a number of different resource types, which had to be located on different servers due to (i) technical reasons such as resources being architecture dependant, or (ii) administrative reasons such as organisational boundaries.

Additional monitoring facilities needed by tutors became increasingly awkward to implement and their growth in sophistication suggested the need for a uniform event reporting system.

Further drawbacks of Finesse included all the weaknesses of a single server system.

2.2 TAGS: A framework for users, groups and resources

The lessons learned from Finesse have informed the design of TAGS, which aims to provide a DLE for any cognate discipline. The management issues that appeared in Finesse – new resources, different roles, allocation of resources to users, monitoring – were identified as generic facilities that would arise in the development of any DLE, for any subject area. TAGS was accordingly conceived as a framework for users, groups and resources, and the relationships between them. DLEs will use TAGS as a generic framework, so that resource developers will be able to concentrate on the actual content they want to offer to students.

From the end user view i.e. tutors and students, TAGS hides all the system architecture aspects, providing tutors and students with a simple model based on pedagogical needs (see Figure 1).

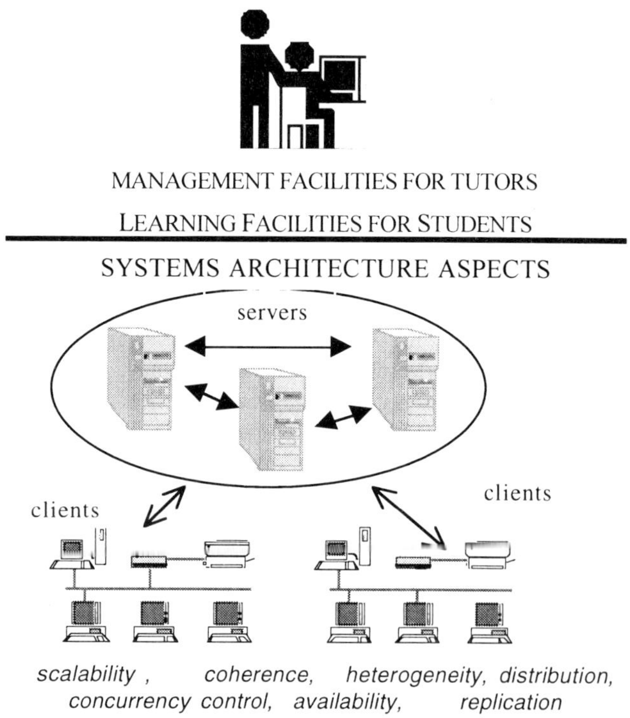

Figure 1: TAGS Design

[1] We distinguish between the use of a URL as a resource in itself, and its use as a path to a resource.

Students will use learning resources and co-operate with each other, while tutors will be able to track the activity of their tutees, manage them in groups and allocate them the appropriate resources they need.

3 TAGS Overview

TAGS has been designed as a modular and generic framework capable of supporting arbitrary relationships between tutors, students and learning resources. There are four basic entities in TAGS: users, groups, resources and events. Users, groups and resources are unique by name and type. Events are unique by timestamps, type and origin.

Groups form the basis of privileges and access, and also act as a dissemination channel. The system is primed with three groups: tutors, students and sys-admin. Tutors can:

- Create, edit and delete users, groups and resources. Tutors can only remove or edit entities which they have created.
- Organise students into groups.
- Allocate resources to groups.
- Monitor students' activities.

There is no restriction on the nature of a resource. It can be a simple timetable, an automated assessment exercise or an interactive multi-user simulation. All a users allocated resources appear on their "home page". This means that at a very basic level TAGS offers facilities for simple yet powerful web-site construction and organisation.

Access rights can be specified when a resource is allocated to a group. A resource may simply be distinguished as Read-only or Read-Write, or it may export a more subtle set of access methods. Figure 2 illustrates an example set of relationships between users, groups and resources.

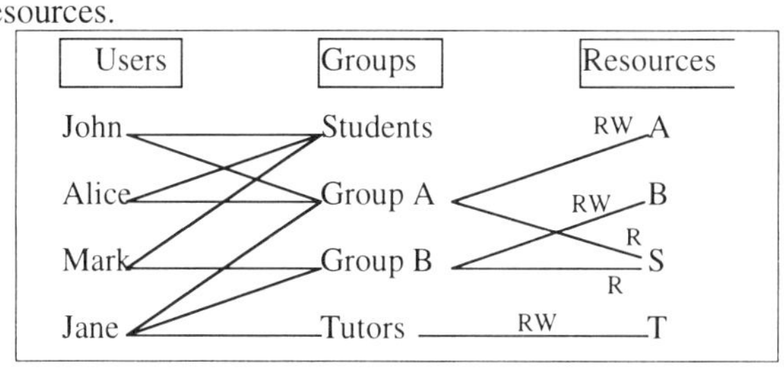

Figure 2: Basic Entity Relations

John, Alice and Mark are members of the Student group. There are no resources shown allocated to the Student group. Jane is a Tutor and has created Groups A and B. John, Alice and Jane are in Group A and have Resources A and S allocated. S is allocated on a Read-only basis, whereas A is Read-Write. Mark and Jane are in Group B which allows resource B as Read-Write and S as Read-only.

Monitoring is both direct and automatic. All users generate an activity record. Events underpin the monitoring system. Each users activity record consists of resource-specific and generic events. In addition, resources may maintain their own logs, which can be used for undoing state changes or resolving concurrency conflicts. Supervisors can directly inspect records through filters, or set conditions of interest and actions to be taken when these conditions are met. Predicate-based monitoring supports arbitrary interactive queries, and automatic detection of pre-set conditions of interest. The general form is: `<predicate> | <action list>`. For example, a student or group who have not completed an assignment by a certain date may trigger a system-generated report to be sent to their tutor via e-mail (see Fig. 3); alternatively the event may simply be logged for future reference. More subtle conditions can be set. A student may have failed to carry out a recommended sequence of steps in the right order. The tutor is notified automatically and may intervene to "undo" or correct the student's actions.

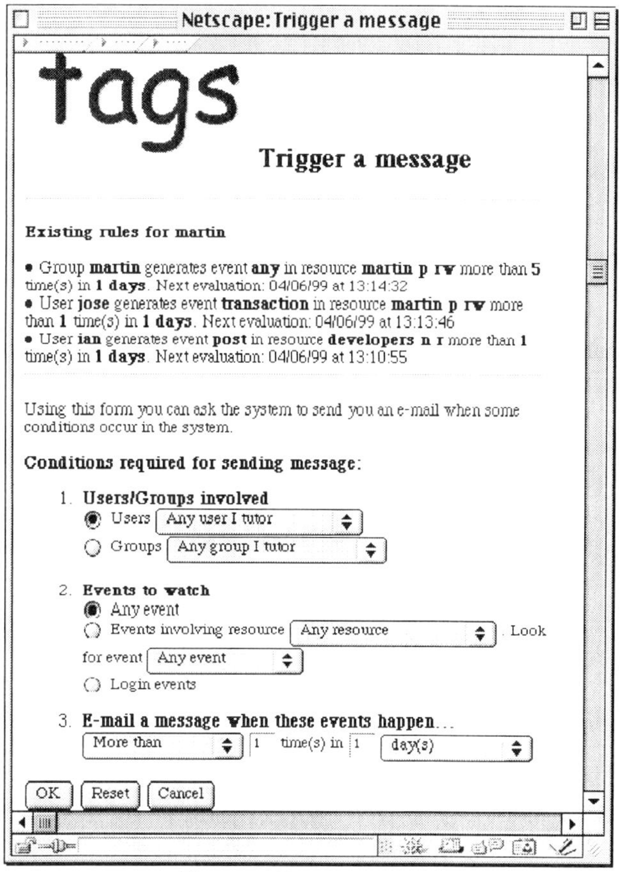

Figure 3: Event Watching

In a distributed environment the event format must support both wall clock time and detection of causal relationships across system boundaries.

4 Managing Resources in TAGS

Resources provide the content of a DLE. TAGS must be able to register and handle arbitrary resources. For TAGS to provide a facility for creating instances of a resource that can be assigned to groups it must know how to create an instance of a resource. This means that a standard resource description format is necessary. The current resource description format includes information on:

- how to create/delete instances of a resource
- degree of replication
- locations of instances
- replication coherence model
- types of events generated
- entry point for operations/methods

Figure 4 illustrates the current web interface to adding a new resource.

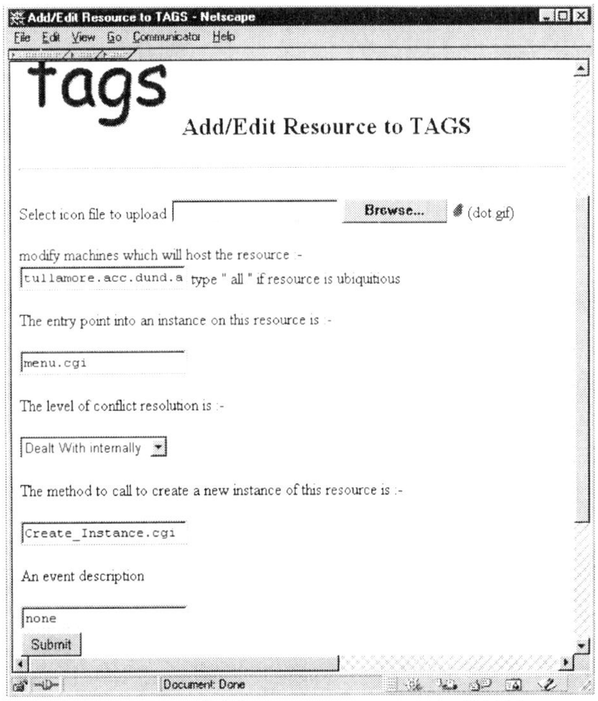

Figure 4: Adding a new resource to TAGS

Section 4.1 The GRM API

The Group and Resource Meta-data held by the system is referred to as the GRM, which is itself a resource. The GRM may be replicated but is currently restricted to only existing as a single instance. Each Resource must provide methods to create and delete instances of itself. The only exception to this is when a URL is a resource in itself (see footnote 1).

A Resource may need to continually query the GRM about its environment. For example, it may need to repeatedly verify that a user is allowed access. Continual verification is necessary when an administrator wants modifications to take place while users are active. Similarly, a resource may wish to query the GRM about other users within the system. The current API is shown in Table 1.

GRM → Resource	
Create_Instance(name)	*Create instance of this resource*
Delete_Instance(name)	*Delete instance of this resource*
Resource → GRM	
may_access(user, resource, instance)	*validates a users use of an instance*
get_groups(resource, instance)	*returns all groups which may access resource*
get_email(user)	*returns e-mail address of user*
get_users(group)	*returns all members of group*
alert_all(instance, message)	*sends alert to all accessors of inst*
alert_tutor(user, message)	*send message to users tutor*
get_replicas(instance)	*returns list of machines on which instance in replicated*

Table 1: The GRM API

Section 4.2 Event Logging Service

Events underpin the monitoring system. The predicate engine must have some prior knowledge of each possible event within each type of resource. This is part of the registration process. All possible events the resource may log are described. These definitions allow predicates to be built by tutors. At present each possible event in the TAGS environment must have a unique ID to facilitate searching and logging. When an instance of a resource wishes to log an event it must be as concise as possible and be non-blocking to avoid unnecessary delays. The API call is:

log_event(eventID,user,instance,otherdata)

4.3 Resource Synchronisation

Figure 5 illustrates the roles of Resource Handlers and Coherence Servers in the TAGS systems architecture. Five physical nodes are shown. For simplicity we have omitted web servers and resource handlers from nodes 2-5, although they would typically co-exist as shown on node 1.

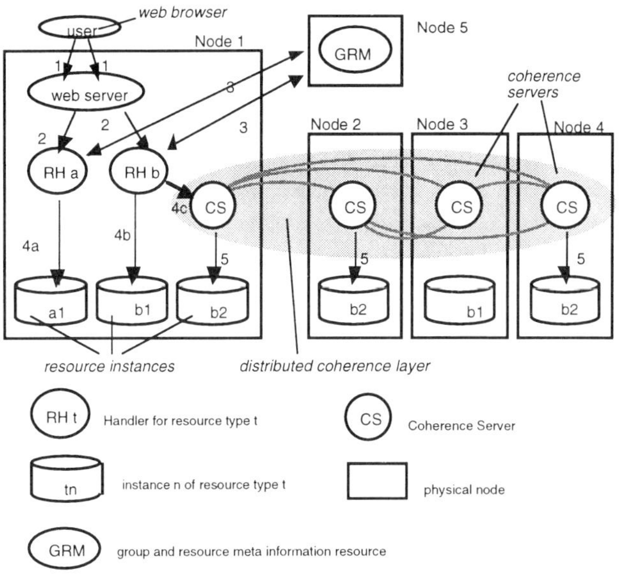

Figure 5: Synchronised Replication

The progress of a user's request is illustrated in the diagram by stages 1 - 5.

1) The user sends a request to a resource by following the URL of the appropriate resource handler.
2) The web server receives the HTTP request and invokes the resource handler, passing along all the information provided by the user in the CGI parameters (instance, user, command, etc.)
3) The resource handler asks the GRM whether the user is allowed to access the requested instance and whether it is replicated or not.
4a) If the instance is not replicated the resource handler accesses it immediately, modifies the state according to the request, and sends an appropriate response to the user.
4b) If the instance of the resource is replicated and the request is a read, then there is no need to broadcast the request, as it will not change the global state of any of the replicas of the instance. So, the resource handler can just read its local copy and return the result to the user.
4c) If the instance is replicated, and the request is a write, the resource handler sends the request to its local coherence server. This server will send the request to other coherence servers on other nodes to keep the different replicas consistent across the distributed system.
5) When all the coherence servers receive the request and it meets the coherence requirements, each node will execute it and update its local replica of the instance accordingly. An update can be blocking or non-blocking, depending on the coherence model.

Note that GRM system meta-information on resources, users and groups is itself a resource which may be replicated.

4.4 Coherence Models

When a resource is registered in TAGS, the developer can specify if it can be replicated or not. If replication is desired, a model of coherence must be chosen. We differentiate the following types of ordering for *reliably* communicated requests:

Eventual All coherence servers eventually deliver all requests, but order is not important.

Source Ordered All requests from the same source are applied at replicas in the order in which they were sent. This does not guarantee that *all updates* will applied in the same order at each replica.

Causal All coherence servers deliver causally related requests in the same (causal) order to each replica of a resource instance. Causal ordering is defined by Lamport [4]. It allows concurrent requests to be applied in any order.

Total All coherence servers deliver the same sequence of requests to each replica of a resource instance. This masks concurrency and imposes a total ordering on all requests in the system. This in itself does not guarantee either source-ordered or causal coherence.

Source Ordered & Total This imposes a total ordering on all requests and respects source ordering.

Causal &Total All coherence servers deliver the same sequence of requests to each replica of a resource instance. The sequence respects causal relations.

Implementation techniques for protocols which support different coherence models are known [5,6,7]. Preliminary experiments with the scalability of this approach are reported in [8]. The system also allows for a basic non-reliable delivery option. It may be inappropriate to retransmit a packet in a continuous media stream for example.

4.5 The Replication API

For a resource to be replicated, each replica must understand requests coming from its local coherence server. Moreover, resource handlers must know how to ask the coherence server to forward a request to all the replicas. This is achieved by the API between the Resource Handler and the Coherence Server (steps 4b, 4c in figure 3):

Resource Handler → Coherence Server	
send_request(instance, command, user, parameters)	*returns request id.*
wait_response(request id)	*blocks and returns result.*
send_and_wait(instance, command, user, parameters)	*blocks and returns result.*
is_busy(instance)	*returns list of pending requests for that instance*

The delivery of requests from the coherence server to the Resource Handler (step 5 in Figure 5):

Coherence Server → Resource Handler	
execute_request (instance, command, user, parameters)	returns success (and state of instance if read)

The API is implemented as a library that is dynamically linked to the resource handler and the coherence server. Once a resource is registered and its coherence model is specified, instances can be created. When creating instances of a replicated resource, each resource handler can specify where replicas of each instance should be located. The coherence server guarantees that requests will reach all replicas of a resource instance in the order specified by its coherence model.

4.6 Java Applets as Resource Instances

So far we have considered resources as data accessed by resource handlers, which are CGI scripts. It is also possible to have non-CGI components such as Java applets which executed on the user's machine. According to the sandbox security model of applets, they can only communicate with their home host. This can be a source of problems, as the applet needs to talk to the GRM, but the GRM may reside on another host. To overcome this, two options are available: a) the use of signed applets to allow applets to talk to other hosts or b) to use RMI and servlets so that applets can spawn a process in their home host that will make requests of the GRM on its behalf.

5 Related Work

With respect to the upper layers of TAGS we share some aims with BSCW and Web-CT. With respect to replication of resources we share some ground with the Warp and Globe projects.

BSCW (Basic Support for Cooperative Work) has been developed by GMD FIT, the German National Research Centre for Information Technology. BSCW extends the collaboration capabilities of e-mail and FTP by supporting information sharing in addition to traditional information exchange. A BSCW server communicates with a Web server by the CGI and contains a number of "workspaces". These consist of several shared information objects such as documents, links and folders. BSCW incorporates awareness mechanisms that allow every member of the group to know the state of the workspace at the current moment [9]. A group access control model proposed for BSCW is described in [10]. BSCW is aimed at a more general audience than TAGS, and primarily focuses on shared resources in the form of documents.

WebCT (World Wide Web Course Tools) has been produced by the University of British Columbia [11]. A tutor can design an interface for a particular course by using icons/buttons and an editing suite. The choice of tools includes exercises, e-mail, chat and a conference system. Tutors can track student progress, and the system can maintain grades. Though group project organisation is a feature it is not obvious to what extent groups can share the development of work.

The key aim of the Globe [12] project is to provide a worldwide framework for shared distributed objects, including web-based materials. Replication is key to the Globe strategy for providing scalability and plans have been outlined in [13,14]. In [13] a variety of *object* coherence models are discussed and these are complimented by a variety of *client* coherence options.

The Wide Area Resource Program (WARP) uses short-lived replication referred to as *cloning* [15]. It provides a global atomic total ordering on object updates and is very much a "one size fits all" approach. This contrasts with TAGS, which aims to exploit the higher-level semantics of a shared resource in order to provide the most effective replication strategies and concurrency control mechanisms.

6 Conclusions and Future Work

Distributed Learning Environments must provide a demanding combination of facilities for resource development and service provision: flexibility, responsiveness, availability, coherence, dynamic group and resource configuration and monitoring. Standard web caching does not improve performance in the highly interactive scenarios found in DLEs. We have accordingly adopted a replica-based approach. This raises problems in terms of coherence and flexibility and we have described how TAGS tackles these complexities while keeping the user interface simple for its user population of tutors and students.

Our design so far has not directly addressed the issues of load balancing [16], fault detection or transparency. One approach to load balancing is to dynamically monitor load distribution through calculating the outputs of *loadometers* executing on each server node [17], and allocate requests to appropriate cluster nodes via a front-end server. Reliable fault detection can be achieved by the careful use of failure suspectors [18]. Transparency – the automatic redirection of a requests between a client browser and destination server – is difficult to achieve in that it requires changes to the basic behaviour of a browser. One approach is to interpose a Java applet between all browser requests and the network [19].

Future work will investigate solutions to these issues and continue with the implementation and testing of the design outlined in this paper. To that end we will be using a testbed in the form of a 64-node Pentium/Linux cluster which allows use of either ATM or ethernet communication links. ATM links are of particular interest as a deployment of multiple servers in a DLE is likely to take the form of a wide-area cluster, a situation in which ATM is uniquely capable of providing useful Quality-of-Service guarantees [20] for co-operating nodes.

7 References

[1] D.M. POWER, R. MICHAELSON, C. ALLISON. "The Finesse Portfolio Management Facility", in Proc. of CTI-Accountancy, Finance and Management Conference, York, April 1998.

[2] ALLISON, C, BRAMLEY, M, SERRANO, J, "The World Wide Wait: Where Does the Time Go?" in Proc. Euromicro 98 Conference, *Engineering Systems and Software for the Next Decade*, pp 932-940, IEEE Press, Aug. 1998.

[3] C.V. HELLIAR, R. MICHAELSON. "Evaluating Finesse: experiences from the first year", the Scottish Meeting of the British Accounting Association, University of Stirling, September 1998.

[4] LAMPORT, L, "Time, clocks, and the ordering of events in a distributed system", Commun. ACM, Vol. 21, no. 7, pp. 558–565, 1978.

[5] BIRMAN, K., A. Schiper, P. Stephenson, "Lightweight causal and atomic group broadcast", ACM TOCS, Vol. 9, no. 3, pp. 272-314, 1991.

[6] ALLISON C. Developing Distributed Group Communication in pSR, *Proc. 4th Euromicro Workshop on Parallel and Distributed Processing* IEEE Press, Braga, January 1996.

[7] HADZILACOS V. & TOUEG S., Fault Tolerant Broadcasts and Related Problems in *Distributed Systems*, ed. Mullender,, Addison-Wesley (1993) 97-145.

[8] ALLISON, C, BRAMLEY, M, SERRANO, J, "A Replicated Resource Architecture for High Performance Network Service", in Proc. Euromicro PDP'99, Workshop on Parallel and Distributed Processing IEEE Press, February 1999.

[9] GMD FIT, Institute for Applied Information Technology. "BSCW". Software, 1998. see also http://orgwis.gmd.de/projects/BSCW/.

[10] SIKKEL, K., A Group-based Authorization Model for Cooperative Systems, in Proceedings of the European Conference on Computer Supported Cooperative Work (ECSCW'97), Lancaster, Sept. 1997, Kluwer.

[11] Internet Reference: <http://homebrew.cs.ubc.ca/webct/webct.html>

[12] Maarten van Steen, Philip Homburg, and Andrew S. Tanenbaum, Globe: A Wide-Area Distributed System, IEEE Concurrency, Vol. 7, No. 1, March 1999

[13] A.M. KERMARREC, I. KUZ, M. VAN STEEN, AND A.S. TANENBAUM. "A Framework for Consistent Replicated Web Objects." Proc. 18th Int'l. Conf. on Distributed Computing Systems, Amsterdam, May 1998.

[14] I. KUZ, A.M. KERMARREC, M. VAN STEEN, AND H.J. SIPS. "Replicated Web Objects: Design and Implementation." Proc. Fourth Annual ASCI Conf., Lommel, Belgium, June 1998.

[15] ALLISON C, HARRINGTON P, HUANG F, & LIVESEY M.J, A Global Atomicity Primitive, in IWOOOS'96, IEEE Press, Seattle, October 1996.

[16] CARDELLINI V, COLAJANNI, W AND YU, P.S., Dynamic Load Balancing on Web-server Systems, IEEE Internet Computing, Vol. 3, No. 3, June 1999.

[17] ALLISON C, HARRINGTON P, HUANG F, & LIVESEY M.J., Scalable Services for Resource Management in Distributed and Networked Environments in SDNE'96, pp98-105, IEEE Press, Macau, June 1996.

[18]. O. BABAOGLU, R. DAVOLI, A. MONTRESOR AND R. SEGALA. SYSTEM SUPPORT FOR PARTITION-AWARE APPLICATIONS. Proc. 18th Int'l. Conf. on Distributed Computing Systems, Amsterdam, PAGES 184-191, May 1998.

[19] YOSHIKAWA et. al., Using Smart Clients to Build Scalable Services, in Proc. Usenix 1997, Usenix Association, Jan 1997.

[20] ALLISON C, "Quality of Service for Wide Area Clusters", in Support for Composing Distributed Applications, (Proc. of the 8th ACM SIGOPS workshop), pp.126 - 130, Sintra, Sept. 1998.

Security mechanisms for the MAP agent system

Antonio Puliafito
Dipartimento di Matematica
Università di Messina
Salita Sperone, 98166 Messina - Italy
E-mail: *apulia@ingegneria.unime.it*

Orazio Tomarchio
Istituto di Informatica e Telecomunicazioni
Università di Catania
Viale A. Doria 6, 95125 Catania - Italy
E-mail: *tomarchio@iit.unict.it*

Abstract

Mobile agents represent a new communication paradigm which has recently obtained a great attention from researcher and practitioners. Interesting applications exist in the fields of distributed systems management, mobility and information retrieval. But, although widely recognized as a crucial point to be addressed, security has not been pursued in a satisfactory way yet. Most of all the existing software environment for agent programming do not offer security features or provide only partial implementations. In this paper we propose a security schema for mobile agent and describe its implementation inside the MAP platform. Some experimental results are also provide to evaluate the overhead introduced from the adoption of the proposed security mechanism.

Keywords: mobile agents, security, Java, distributed computing.

1 Introduction

The possibility to access many resources from a computer connected to a communication network has lead to new users' needs and to the development of new advanced services. On one hand, the large supply of information and, on the other hand, the rising number of users are continually causing problems of traffic congestion. The constant improvement in infrastructures should be followed by new techniques for programming distributed systems; such techniques should optimize the exploitation of the available bandwidth. The client-server approach, which has been usually used as the communication paradigm for distributed systems, has been recently extended by techniques based on the use of mobile code [8, 17, 11, 13]. In particular, we think that the mobile agent model can overcome some limits of the client-server one, since each agent can dynamically play the role of either client or server. There is some disagreement in literature about the way of defining a mobile agent [13, 7, 4]; we can consider an agent as an active object that can independently move in the network for completing its task, by interacting (if necessary) with other agents in the system.

This programming model leads to an increased flexibility in the design and creation of several distributed applications. Network management [3, 5, 18], distributed information retrieval, distributed computing [1, 4], are typical fields for agent-based applications [9].

The use of this model implies the creation of an infrastructure for supporting the execution of agents. This is possible in a local organization with almost no problem, but in a global scenario we need to assure that a generic computer can accept the execution of an agent coming from outside. In order to make such operations acceptable, we need to avoid that the execution of an agent coming from outside damages the local machine, and to assure the possibility of identifying the person who triggered and/or produced the agent. We therefore need to develop an adequate security model adapted to the specific issues of the agents; this model will have to assure an high level of protection to the agents and the hosts, so that the hosts can be protected from the attacks of unsafe agents, and the agents can run on the hosts of the network without being damaged [12, 6, 20]. The wide interest that agent technology is receiving, has produced the development of some software environment which allow agent programming, execution and mobility [15, 2, 16, 22, 19]. Although security issues are considered as a crucial goal which, if not addressed, can strongly delay or even stop the adoption of the agent programming paradigm, very limited effort has been devoted to such issues.

In this paper we present the security model for the MAP [1] agent platform [19], which has been developed at the University of Catania. This model is based on the encryption and authentication mechanisms present in Java 2 [10]. The rest of this paper is organized as follows. In Sec

[1]MAP is available at the following site: http://sun195.iit.unict.it/MAP

1066-6192/99 $10.00 © 1999 IEEE

tion 2 we present the specific security issues for the agent systems. In Section 3 we briefly describe the architecture of the MAP platform, while in section 4 we present the architecture of the security model implemented and provide some experimental results. Finally, in Section 5 we conclude, making some remarks about our work, and about any future work.

2 Agents security

The mobile agent systems have several features that make them suitable for the creation of applications in a distributed field. However, such systems cause new *security* issues that have to be adequately dealt with, in order to benefit from the features described, and to develop some applications that can be used on a large scale [20].

Even if strong security models have been studied and developed for the traditional distributed systems [21], agents cause new issues in this scenario. In traditional client-server systems, the active entities run under the control of the operating system of the machine in which they are running; the user who triggers an application is appropriately identified before accessing his/her account, and is consequently assigned some authorizations. At this point the operating system assures the protection of the critical resources of the system. The agent paradigm changes the terms of the security issue; a host may not "recognize" the user on behalf of whom an agent is running, or may not rely on what the agent might do when running locally.

The main issue is that the state of the agent, while crossing several more or less *trusted* hosts, may be modified in such a way that it changes its behaviour, and causes negative effects.

Several security purposes are desirable for an agent system. Most of these issues concern the interaction between the agent and the host on which it runs. The user on behalf of whom the agent runs wishes to be protected from malicious interpreters and from the intermediate hosts involved in the migration of its agent. Conversely, an interpreter and the host in which it runs need to be protected from the agents whose behaviour is wrong.

Since in several applications (where agents are used) different organizations provide services to many users, many of the parts involved do not trust on each other. A server might be interested in changing the state of an agent in order to benefit from this situation. Conversely, a malicious agent might have been created in order to search for some information that it is not allowed to obtain, thus taking illegal advantages from it.

In a few words, the specific points for an agent system are the following [14, 20]:

- protection of a host from the agents that reach it and run on it;
- protection of an agent from other agents;
- protection of an agent from the host where it runs;
- protection of an agent from the outside environment (for example, against the network attacks during the migration);

None of the existing agent systems can provide a security model that could deal with and solve any issue. Some of the requirements for developing a general security model are not practicable, according to what has been said in [6]. For example, the issues listed below do not seem to be completely practicable:

- verifying that an interpreter has not been changed;
- verifying that an interpreter runs an agent correctly;
- verifying that an interpreter runs an agent until its completion;
- verifying that a host sends an agent as required;
- keeping the data and the code of an agent private;
- communicating with a wide group of agent servers privately;
- distinguishing an agent from a clone.

Conversely, what seems to be practicable is the protection of a host from the actions of an agent, thanks to the use of authentication techniques and access control mechanisms. In this area, the issue is finding a responsibility for the agent's actions. We therefore need to make a distinction between the author of the agent's code and the user who uses it by triggering its execution. Besides (in order to avoid causing other problems in the host accepting an agent), we need to make sure that during the agent's migration there has been no attack on the communication channel, which in general has to be considered unsafe.

Similar techniques need to be used for protecting an agent from other agents. In general, an agent has to obtain specific authorizations in order to interact with other agents of the system.

3 MAP architecture

The MAP platform [19] allows the development of mobile agents applications by providing all the basic primitives needed for their creation, execution, communication, migration, etc. It has been entirely developed in Java, and this guarantees its portability on different hardware and software architectures. The migration implemented in MAP is a *weak migration*: the agents are able to carry the data-state of data with them, but not the execution-state. Besides, it integrates the paradigms of *remote execution* and *code on demand* [8], thanks to the exploitation of dynamic loading of classes, a mechanism present in Java. A graphic interface manages the agents in execution. This interface (shown in Figure 1) allows to verify which agents are active in the local server, and which ones are present in remote servers. Besides, through this interface we can trigger the execution of any agent present in the system, independently of its code location.

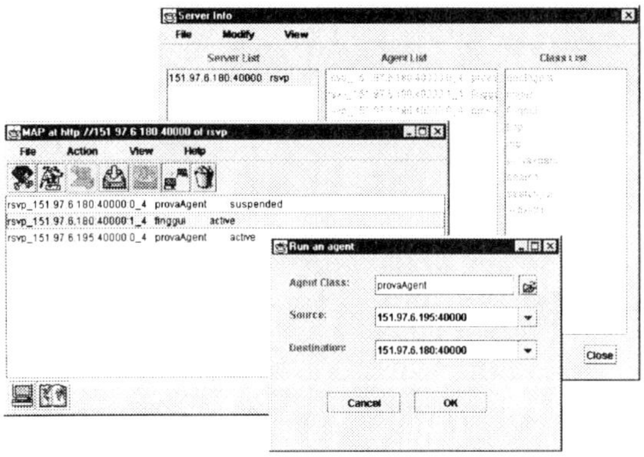

Figure 1. MAP graphical interface

The architecture of a generic MAP server is shown in Figure 2: it consists of an object called Server that contains all the entities needed for the operation of the platform itself. In a host there can be more than one Server, each identified by the host address and by the TCP port number on which the server is listening for accepting agents or messages coming from the network. The presence of a Server on a node characterizes it as belonging to the platform and enables it to accept and run agents coming from the network, as well as to activate other agents locally.

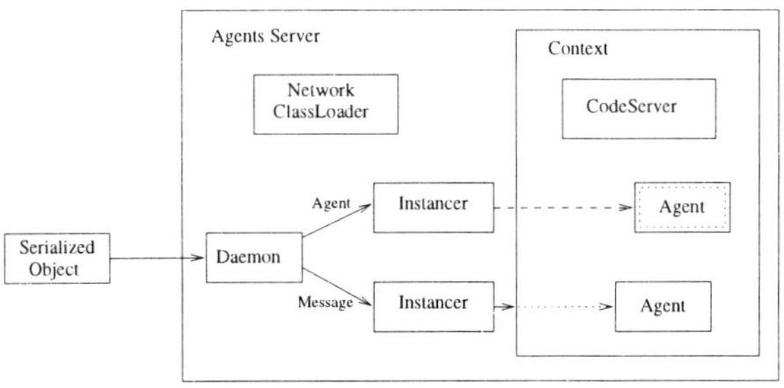

Figure 2. MAP server architecture

The Daemon is the entity of the MAP that listens on a certain port, waiting for agents coming from other nodes and for messages to be delivered to local agents. Both messages and agents travel in a serialized form. Each time a stream arrives from the network, the Daemon creates a specific entity called Instancer, whose task is to instance the serialized object, both if it is an agent and a message. In both cases, the object, once it is instanced, is passed to the Context, whose task will be to make it run (if it is an agent), or to send it to the receiver agent (if it is a message). The Context is one of the basic objects in a MAP server. In fact, it knows all the agents present on the server and gives the user all the functionalities needed for their management. It puts some methods at disposal, which enable to create an agent, to make it run, even on a server in which its code is not present, to suspend it, to deactivate it, to resume its execution, and even to kill it, if necessary. Each object coming from the network in serialized form, is passed to the Context, after having been instanced by the Instancer. If such object is an agent, the Context initializes it, by giving it a reference to the Context, and later, starts its execution, and consequently updates the list of local agents. Conversely, if the object is a message, the Context makes sure to deliver it to the receiver agent, of course after checking the agent's availability to receive such message, or of its actual presence on the server.

The NetworkClassLoader and the CodeServer are used to retrieve remote classes, enabling the agents to run on a specific MAP server, even when their class is not present there. In order to permit this, each time a specific object reaches a new server, the corresponding Daemon loads a new Instancer object with a NetworkClassLoader that deals with the loading of such classes. If one of the classes to which the agent or the message refers is not actually present locally, the NetworkClassLoader will search for it in the network, in a list of MAP servers fixed within the Context. Once the class is found, it is loaded from the remote site and saved in a cache memory managed by the Context, so that it can be accessed and used, if necessary, also by of the other agents of the server.

3.1 Agents' Structure

As we have already said before, agents represent the entities of the platform MAP that can move in the network for carrying out a task assigned by the user who created them.

Within our platform, an agent is able to:

- suspend itself and another agent: to suspend an agent means to stop its execution temporarily, by keeping all the references to the agent active;
- resume a suspended agent: to wake up an agent means to resume its execution from the point where it had been suspended before;
- deactivate itself and deactivate another agent: to deactivate an agent means to stop its execution, by down-

loading the agent to a disk in a serialized form, and by deleting all the references to it;

- reactivate an agent: it means to deserialize an agent that had been deactivated before, by giving all references back to it and restarting its execution from the beginning;

- create a new agent: to create an agent means to instance a new Agent object and to make it run;

- kill an agent: it means to stop the execution of an agent, by deleting all its references and cancelling its entry from the list of the agents in the server;

- migrate to a new server: to migrate an agent means to move it to another node, where it will start its execution from the beginning;

- communicate with other agent, through messages, both in a synchronous and in an asynchronous way.

From an implementation point of view, an agent is an object obtained by instancing a class deriving from the Agent class supplied by the platform. This enables the agent to take advantage from the methods put at our disposal by such class.

4 Security model in MAP

4.1 General architecture

The security model developed for MAP considers the issues of authentication and authorization, in order to protect- on one hand- the hosts from the agents, and- on the other hand- the agents from the other agents and from the attacks coming from the network. Some rules, which are called *security policies*, are defined. With these rules we specify the conditions according to which the agents can access host resources; we also specify the authentication needed for the entities for performing some operations, and the level of security in the communication among the agents on different hosts. The techniques used are based on public key encryption, in which each user has a pair of public and private keys, with which he/she can prove his/her identity.

For the purposes of the security model developed, the whole set of hosts in which a MAP server runs is divided into *domains* (see Figure 3).

As we will see below, several policies are adopted for agents belonging to the same domain or to different domains. Several hosts in a domain may therefore be grouped either physically (the hosts belonging to a specific subnet) or logically (hosts of the same organization, hosts belonging to a specific working group, etc). In each domain a trusted

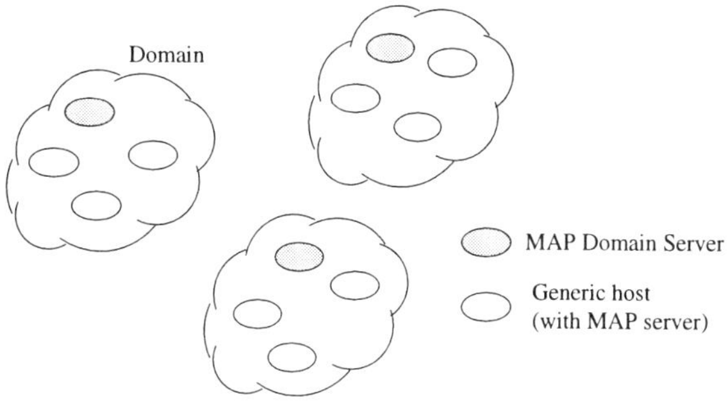

Figure 3. Domains and hosts in the MAP environment

host (*MapDS* - Map Domain Server) is located where a *domain administrator* operates. Its task is the definition of a security policy for the domain, concerning the accesses and the migrations of agents to and from other domains. The same way, a *host administrator* can be identified for each host, which takes care of defining a security policy for the host. The system developed forces the agents to follow the security policy of the host and of the domain where they run.

In fact, when the agent reaches a host, it is confined in a so-called *protection domain* where it can operate within fixed limits. For doing so, we need to find the origin of the agent, so to determine the set of *authorizations* to be given for the local execution of the agent. In fact, an agent is allowed to access the critical resources of a host only if the *Access Control List* (ACL) contains the appropriate authorizations.

Two entities are involved in the authentication of an agent: the author of the agent (the person who has written the code, and/or the company that has put it on the market) and the user who has started the execution of the agent.

In fact, in our opinion, both entities have to be involved for assigning specific authorizations to the agent. For example, if a reliable user uses an agent whose code has been created by an unknown person or even by an unreliable one, the set of authorizations to be assigned to the agent should be restricted.

The information concerning the author of the agent is kept in the so-called *credentials of the author*. They contain:

- the ID of the author of the code

- the public key certificate of the author

- the digital signature of the code

Conversely, the information concerning each user of the system is kept in the so-called *credentials of the agent*, which are associated to each agent triggered by the user. Such credentials are created each time the user triggers a new agent, and contain:

- the user's ID
- the digital signature of the agent
- the credentials of the author of the code

The credentials of the agent are inserted in it, and follow it during its migrations. In section 4.2 we will show how the information contained in the credentials is used for confining an agent in a specific protection domain.

As we said before, two security policies are defined concerning the single host and the domain. For the agents coming from nodes within the domain, the system authenticates the user that has triggered the agent: the authorizations to be associated to each agent are therefore associated to the single users. Conversely, when an agent comes from a different domain, the authorizations are associated to the domain: there is no longer the visibility of the single user. This choice has been made considering that, if the agent model is extended to a large number of users, the ACL present in each host might excessively grow, thus making the performances of the system slower. Therefore, when an agent has to be sent out of its domain, it will transit on the MapDS, where the domain administrator will take care of sending it.

4.2 Implementation details

The model described has been implemented by using the security features present in Java 2 [10]. In the latest version, considerable changes and improvements have been made to the Java security model, which was incomplete in some of its functionalities. In fact, in version 1.1 digital signature mechanisms had been introduced, but their only task was that of considering whether a class was trusted or not: a signed remote class could be considered equivalent to a local code, or confined in the sandbox (where it cannot access the local resources). Conversely, the model of Java 2 allows to provide some mechanisms of fine grain access control, which allow specifying the actions that a remote class can do within the local environment. This mechanism of access control can be extended, thus enabling the protection of new resources that have been dynamically added to the system. In this context, the term resource takes the widest meaning, since it can represent a file, a network connection, the access to the graphical system, or a logical resource. Another improvement is the possibility of an easy definition of the customized security policies.

The model of protection adopted in our agent system makes use of *"capability list"*: each protection domain (where the agents are confined when they reach each host) is associated with a list containing all the access rights (authorizations) that will be acquired by the agents. Each authorization consists of two parts: the resource for which the authorization specifies the access (for example a file), and the type of access that is allowed on that resource (for example, writing).

Below we will describe the actions performed by the system for sending and receiving an agent. When a server is activated, the host gets to know the domain to which it belongs, the other hosts belonging to the same domain, and the MapDS of its domain.

Activating and sending an agent

The system follows these steps for sending an agent:

- Loading the class
  The class of the agent is first searched in the local "cache", and then (if not found) in the local file system. The class may be present in the cache, if the agent has already been executed, or received from another node. Both the bytecode of the class and the credentials of the author associated to it are stored in the local cache.
- Verification of the class integrity
  Once the class has been loaded, its integrity has to be verified. If it is loaded from the cache, the credentials of the author present in it will be used for the verification. The integrity of the class may not be verified if someone (through an attack) managed to change either the credentials or the bytecode of the class within the cache: in this case we try to reload the class and the credential of the author from the file system, and will repeat the verification process. If the integrity is verified the subsequent step is started, otherwise a security warning will be notified to the user.
- Determination and confining in the protection domain
  In this phase, we determine the protection domain associated to the user who is preparing to trigger the agent. The class is therefore confined in this domain, since the user might decide to run the agent locally.
- Generation of the agent's credentials
  The user signs the agent with his/her own private key, thus generating the agent's credentials. If the agent has to be sent to a host belonging to the same domain, then the system serializes the state of the agent, signs it (by using the user's key), and then sends it through the network.

Receiving an agent

When receiving an agent that has to be executed, the system makes the following steps:

- Verification of the agent's state
  Once an agent has been received, a verification must be done of the integrity of the state. The key of the latest user who has put his/her signature on the state of the agent is loaded and used for this verification. If no problem is found, we can go to the subsequent step; otherwise, the agent is not executed, and the user who sent the agent is notified about this situation.

- Verification of the integrity of the agent's class
  In order to verify the integrity of the class that implements the agent, the credentials of the user who triggered it are used. If this verification is not successful, we need to determine if this is due to a change in the agent's attributes or of the bytecode of the class (wherever it has been found). At this point, several cases are possible, according to where the credentials of the author are, and where the class is (in the cache, in the local file system, or in other remote hosts). If after such verifications we cannot verify the agent's integrity, the user who sent the agent is notified about this situation.

- Confinement in the protection domain
  Once we have verified the integrity of the class and, at the same time, the identity of the user who sent the agent, it is confined in a protection domain, and obtains the corresponding authorizations.

Sending and receiving an agent out of its domain

If an agent has to be sent to a host outside its domain, it first reaches its MapDS. The administrator verifies that the user is enabled to send agents to other domains, and then verifies the integrity of the agent's class. If such verifications are successful, the domain administrator redefines the credentials by putting his/her signature. In fact, the host that will receive the agent will autenthicate only the domain, and the agent will then be confined to the appropriate protection domain accordingly.

4.3 Performance

In order to evaluate the overhead caused by the security mechanisms introduced in MAP, we have carried out some tests. The purpose was to evaluate the behaviour in the different operating situations in which the system can be. Three different cases have been considered:

1. migration from a host to another one located in the same domain
2. migration among three hosts in the same domain
3. migration from a host to another one located in a different domain

These tests have been carried out in machines with AMD K6 at 300 MHz processors and equipped with Windows 98, connected to a 10-Mbit Ethernet. Below we show the migration times obtained in each of the tests, both activating and deactivating the security mechanisms. The signature algorithm used is the DSA/SHA-1 present in the standard distribution of Java 2. The length of the key is 1024 bit and the size of the agent used for tests is 1 Kbyte.

The results for the first set of experiments are shown in Table 1. An agent is triggered by a host and migrates to another one, belonging to the same domain. These are the operations made by the host A: verifying the integrity of the class, generating the credentials, signing the state of the agent, and then sending it. Conversely, the host B verifies the integrity of the state, verifies the credentials, and then the agent is instanced. Each row of the tables represents a different situation in which the hosts can be. The agent's class could be already in the cache or should be loaded from the local file system or retrieved from the network. The first test is the worst of the cases: the host A has to load the class from the local file system, while B has to retrieve it through the network. The second test is an intermediate situation, since in both hosts the code of the agent is already present in the local file system. The third test is the best of the cases, and occurs when both hosts have the class of the agent in their cache, since they have previously executed a different instance of the agent. As can be observed the overhead introduced from the adoption of security mechanisms is in the range 1-1.5 seconds. In percentage, this will be less evident when the size of the agent will be higher than the hypotized value of 1KB.

In the second set of experiments we have tested the migration in the same domain between three hosts. In this case, the hosts make the following operations: host A generates the credentials of the agent, then signs the state and sends it to B. The host B verifies the integrity of the state and of the credentials, and executes the agent, whose only task is migrating to the host C. Before being sent to C, its state is signed by B. Finally, C verifies the integrity of the state and of credentials, and executes the agent. The tests carried out in this case (see Table 2) show the results according to the variation of the presence (in the cache or in the file system) of the class that implements the agent. As can be observed, the total migration times are slightly shorter than the double of the previous case, since the host B does not have to generate the credentials, but only needs to sign the state of the agent again (of course, after doing all the verifications).

In the third set of tests (see Table 3) we have tested the communication between two hosts (A and C) belonging to different domains. This implies (for what is provided by the security model) the transit through the host manager for the domain (B). We therefore have the additional cost of a migration and of a generation of credentials on the host B. The

Agent class location		Time (ms)	
Host A	Host B	With security	Without security
File system	Network	1980	660
File system	File system	1380	330
Cache	Cache	1040	160

Table 1. Migration overhead between two host belonging to the same domain

Agent class location			Time (ms)	
Host A	Host B	Host C	With security	Without security
File system	Network	Network	3880	1100
File system	File system	File system	2140	500
Cache	Cache	Cache	1740	300

Table 2. Migration overhead between three host belonging to the same domain

resulting times are therefore slightly higher than the ones corresponding to the previous case. Conversely, in case the security mechanisms are not enabled, the times result shorter, since the agent is not executed in the host B, but is sent to C as soon as it is received.

5 Conclusions

Mobile agents represent a very promising paradigm with challenging applications in system management, user mobility, services provisioning. As a consequence of code mobility, security is an essential requisite. In this paper we have discussed about security and agents, and we have proposed a security infrastructure for mobile agent systems. Implementation issues have been presented and experimental results obtained from the MAP agent platform have been provided.

Acknowledgments: this work has been carried out under the financial support of the Italian Ministero dell'Universitá e della Ricerca Scientifica e Tecnologica (MURST) in the framework of the MOSAICO (Design Methodologies and Tools of High Performance Systems for Distributed Applications) Project.

References

[1] L. Bic, M. Fukuda, and M. Dillencourt. Distributed Computing Using Autonomous Objects. *IEEE Computer*, 29(8):55–61, Aug. 1996.

[2] M. Breugst, I. Busse, S. Covaci, and T. Magedanz. Grasshopper - A Mobile Agent Platform for IN Based Service Environments. In *IEEE IN Workshop 1998*, Bordeaux, France, May 1998.

[3] M. Breugst and T. Magedanz. Mobile Agents - Enabling Technology for Active Intelligent Network Implementation. *IEEE Network*, 12(3):53–60, May/June 1998.

[4] D. Chess, C. Harrison, and A. Kershenbaum. Mobile Agents: Are they a Good Idea? Technical Report RC19887, IBM T.J. Watson Research Center, Mar. 1995.

[5] H. de Meer, A. Puliafito, J. Richter, and O. Tomarchio. Tunnel Agents for Enhanced Internet QoS. *IEEE Concurrency*, 6(2):30–39, April-June 1998.

[6] W. Farmer, J. Guttman, and V. Swarup. Security for Mobile Agents: Issues and Requirements. In *Proc. of the 19th National Information Systems Security Conf. (NISSC96)*, 1996.

[7] S. Franklin and A. Graesser. Is it an Agent or Just a program? A Taxonomy for Autonomous agents. *Intelligent Agents III: Agent Theories, Architectures and Languages*, 1997.

[8] A. Fuggetta, G. Picco, and G. Vigna. Understanding Code Mobility. *IEEE Transaction on Software Engineering*, 24, 1998.

[9] M. Genesereth and S. Ketchpel. Software Agents. *Communications of the ACM*, 37(7):48–53, July 1994.

[10] L. Gong. Java Security: Present and Near Future. *IEEE Micro*, 17(3):14–19, May 1997.

[11] R. Gray, D. Kotz, S. Nog, D. Rus, and G. Cybenko. Mobile agents: the next generation in distributed computing. In *Proc. of the Second Aizu Int. Symp. on Parallel Algorithms/Architecture Synthesis (pAs97)*, Fukushima, Japan, Mar. 1997.

[12] M. Greenberg, J. Byington, and T. Holding. Mobile Agents and Security. *IEEE Communications Magazine*, pages 76–85, July 1998.

[13] K. Rothermel and R.Popescu-Zeletin Eds.,. Mobile Agents. *Lecture Notes in Comp. Science*, LNCS1219, 1997.

[14] G. Karjoth, D. Lange, and M. Oshima. A Security Model for Aglets. *IEEE Internet Computing*, 4(1):68–77, July-August 1997.

[15] J. Kiniry and D. Simmermann. A hands-on look at Java Mobile Agents. *IEEE Internet Computing*, 1(4):49–52, July 1997.

Agent class location			Time (ms)	
Host A	Host B	Host C	With security	Without security
File system	Network	Network	5440	880
File system	File system	File system	3936	490
Cache	Cache	Cache	2530	270

Table 3. Migration overhead between two host belonging to different domains

[16] D. Lange and M. Oshima. Programming Mobile Agents in Java with the Java Aglet API. Technical report, IBM Tokyo Research Division, 1997.

[17] V. A. Phan and A. Karmouch. Mobile Software Agents: An Overview. *IEEE Communication Magazine*, 31(7):26–37, July 1998.

[18] A. Puliafito and O. Tomarchio. Using Mobile Agents to implement flexible Management strategies. *Computer Communication Journal*. to be published.

[19] A. Puliafito, O. Tomarchio, and L. Vita. MAP: Design and Implementation of a Mobile Agent Platform. *Journal of System Architecture*, 46(2):145–162, 2000.

[20] K. Schelderup and J. Olnes. Mobile Agent Security: Issues and Directions. In *IS&N'99*, volume LNCS1597, Mar. 1999.

[21] W. Stalling. *Network and Internetwork Security Principles and Practice*. Prentice Hall, 1995.

[22] M. Strasser, J. Baumann, and F. Hohl. MOLE - A Java Based Mobile Agent System. In *Proceedings of the 2nd ECOOP Workshop on Mobile Object Systems*, July 1996.

Implementation of an Annotation Service on the WWW - Virtual Notes

Stefan Koch and Georg Schneider
Department of Applied Computer Science
Vienna University of Economics and Business Administration
Augasse 2-6, A-1090 Wien, Austria
{Stefan.Koch,Georg.Schneider}@wu-wien.ac.at

Abstract

In this paper we present the implementation of Virtual Notes[1]*, an annotation service on the World Wide Web using only standard internet technology. Therefore Virtual Notes are immediately usable by anyone on the WWW without preparation. This makes the solution especially suited for environments lacking a coherent workgroup, e.g. teaching or research. Also described are the user interface, several use cases and the administrative side of the annotation service, where the overhead for employing Virtual Notes has been minimized.*

1. Introduction

The World Wide Web (WWW) has emerged as an important infrastructure for cooperative work, especially if undertaken by participants located in different places or maybe even distributed around the world. Reports and other documents are presented on the WWW and communication is facilitated by e-mail. The idea to also use this infrastructure as a basis for annotation services has only been the next logical step to further increase the possible level of cooperation.

Prior approaches to the application of WWW-technology to annotation services depend upon proprietary technology or make extensive use of non-standard applications or programming languages and thus require additional effort by every prospective user of the system.

One example is ComMentor [6, 7] that uses a remodeled browser with the annotations stored on a separate server. Both group and private annotations are possible in addition to public ones. Small icons mark the placement of annotations in the text to convey positional information. However, this browser needs of course to be installed and used by each prospective user of the annotation service.

GrAnT [8] uses a specialized proxy that merges document, annotations and a toolbar. This solution is browser-independent and includes in-place and group annotations. But it still requires that the user changes the configuration of his browser to use such a proxy.

Another solution is GroupWeb [4], a groupware Web browser implemented in GroupKit that incorporates annotations to any page. Only one annotation per page is possible that is not anchored to a specific place, but can be seen and edited by other users in a separate window. Telepointers used to implement gesturing are displayed over the same text in the windows of all participants regardless of settings. This solution of course requires access to the GroupWeb browser.

Also the Mosaic Web browser has been modified to fetch and display both group and public annotations from separate servers [5]. The information concerning which public annotation server(s) to contact for annotations is provided by the modified HTTP server supplying the base document, while any group annotation servers to be queried are configured with the client, i.e. the Mosaic browser.

A system primarly supporting discussions is HyperNews [5, 8]. The system allows the creation of base articles (or forums) for which annotations can be given. These annotations are presented in the form of a threaded discussion at the end of the HTML page. This page is dynamically combined from the base article and any existing annotations, both of which are stored within the HyperNews system. Interested users can receive notification by e-mail if any new comments are added to a document.

Commercially available solutions always have the problem of assuring the availability of the product for all users, especially in a heterogenous environment. Adobe Acrobat Exchange for example stores annotations (depicted as small stick-on notes) with the respective document. The user therefore needs writing privileges on the document to add annotations. This is a problem when being used collaboratively that can only be solved using additional soft-

[1]For a guided tour and examples, see http://lux6.wu-wien.ac.at/~robots/notes/doku/.

ware (e.g. PDF inFusion from ITM Associates with Lotus Notes). Additionally Lotus Smartsuite-based solutions can incorporate annotations, but again the product needs to be available to any prospective user.

Third Voice [11] is a product from Third Voice Inc. that modifies the Web browser of the user to connect to an annotation server and retrieve any annotations for the page currently visited. Public, group and private annotations are supported that are anchored to the text selected by the user that placed the note. Access to most of this functionality is provided by a toolbar incorporated in the Web browser.

Another tool that relies on browser modifications to provide some functionality for cooperation is Gooey from hypernix. Gooey supports the forming of online communities by providing means for chatting with any other Gooey users on the same Web page. This communication takes place in separate windows. Of course, for the browser modification to be realized, the product needs to be downloaded and installed.

This paper describes Virtual Notes, a solution that uses standard WWW technology in the form of Java, Javascript and HTML only. In addition, annotations are stored on a separate server and do not result in modifications to the document. In spite of this, the annotations can be placed anywhere on the page and stay at the same position regardless of the browser settings of any further users. This positioning of annotations delivers important contextual information, for example in correcting spelling errors.

Therefore Virtual Notes can be used by anyone with a Java- and Javascript-enabled browser without any special settings or installation. As surveys suggest, this requirement is met by most WWW-users [2]. The proposed solution is therefore applicable for cooperation among almost all users on the WWW and is not restricted to coherent workgroups. This seems especially important for interaction in an education or research environment, where heterogenous users need to cooperate effectively.

The overhead for employing this solution has been minimized as far as possible using different techniques described in this paper. Several possible applications for Virtual Notes are also detailed.

2. The Virtual Notes approach

2.1. Architecture

The proposed solution realizes an architecture based on distributed computing. On the uppermost level three components interact:

- the client (browser) of the user
- the server that supplies the base document (in HTML) and
- the annotation server.

The base document has to be prepared to manage annotations by including a few lines of Javascript-Code. This task is assisted by a CGI-form that returns any given page with the necessary modifications by e-mail. Additionally a macro automates this task for LaTeX2html generated documents.

This code causes the client to execute a query to the annotation server when the base document is requested and retrieves any annotations associated with the page. These annotations are then placed on the page and the result is displayed by the browser. The manipulation of an annotation (commenting on it or creating a new one) results in an insert operation at the annotation server and a reload to update the page presented to the user.

The server has been realized using a mixture of different technologies, including Perl, C++, Java and Linda [1] to store the annotations.

For any page containing annotations, the URL and the relative position in the page for every annotation are stored in addition to the annotation-text itself. To counter the problems resulting from different URLs associated with a given page (e.g. because of generation with LaTeX2html) the Linda-Server stores a list of known synonyms for every page containing annotations. These synonyms for pages are detected by a rule-based agent that tries several approaches to find other URLs that might reference the same page, tests these for identity and adds them to the Linda-Server if applicable.

For the management of the annotations by the owner of a page, a separate CGI-based interface has been provided. To authenticate the owner, an ID that has to be supplied on any enabled page has to be retrieved before using Virtual Notes. By using this ID and the given password, annotations can be removed one by one, for entire pages or for all pages associated with the user. The deletion of Virtual Notes is therefore only allowed for the owner of the page where the annotation is located.

This architecture described above allows for several Linda-Servers to be operated simultaneously with only minor changes to the system. In fact, only the Javascript-Code to be included in each Web page has to be changed in order to incorporate the new server. As the insertion of this code is assisted by a CGI-form or a macro for LaTeX2html, this change can easily be managed. The new server then acts as annotation server for this particular page (and any others that reference the same server). Therefore the load can be distributed among several Linda-Servers by assigning different pages to them. The annotations are of course still available to any user of the Web without any changes or preparations. Therefore this architecture allows for several servers operated all around the world, thus serving any pages from nearby and offering a completely scalable solution.

2.2. Technical realization

When a page containing one or more annotations is retrieved by a user, the following steps are performed (see Fig. 1):

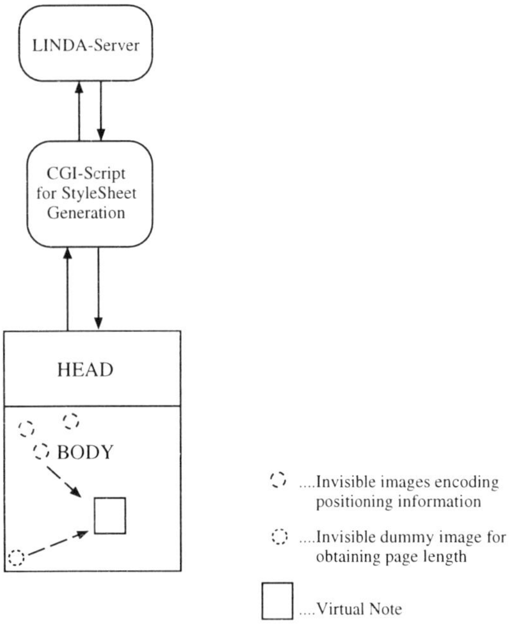

Figure 1. The process of positioning Virtual Notes on a HTML page

1. After the HEAD section of the base document has been loaded, Javascript-Code writes out a dynamically generated LINK tag which references a Style-Sheet.

2. Instead of being static, this Style-Sheet is generated by a CGI-Script. The above mentioned Javascript-Code appends the URL of the document to the query-part of the CGI-Call, thus enabling the CGI-Script to correctly identify the page. The Style-Sheet approach has been chosen as a means of retrieving dynamic information for an otherwise static page.

3. The CGI-Script will then try to find Virtual Notes for the given page on the annotation server. In order to be able to locate the database on any server a realization using an implementation of a Linda-Server [9] was chosen. Since a single page may be referenced by more than one URL (e.g. Web servers are often configured in a way that when presented with an URL which does not specify a concrete document, index.html or welcome.html is returned) a rule-based agent will test the retrieved documents from several URLs for identity the first time a page is accessed. In the case of a match an alias is inserted into the Linda-Server thus relieving subsequent requests from this task which downgrades performance. New rules for the discovery of possibly identical pages can easily be added.

4. The generated Style-Sheet contains encoded information about the number and position of notes on the page. Using a CGI-Script makes it possible to retrieve that information from any server on the Internet, otherwise security limitations would only permit connections to the host of origin.

5. Encoding of relevant information is achieved by defining absolute positions for named DIV tags.

6. Since it is not possible to directly access style information about a tag that does not exist in the document, it is necessary to generate HTML tags which position invisible images according to the dynamically loaded Style-Sheet.

7. In that way the position of the invisible images can be retrieved and used to dynamically position Java-Applets which implement the actual functionality of Virtual Notes.

8. Care has to be taken about the fact that the position of a certain note depends heavily upon user settings such as window size or the type of font being used. In order to approximate the initial position of the note a non-visible dummy-image is placed at the end of the page thus making it possible to retrieve the page-length in pixel. Since the position of a Virtual Note is transferred from the server in the form of percentages, multiplying the two figures will give a fairly good estimate for the absolute position of the note.

9. The Java-Applets open a connection to the Linda-Server mentioned above and retrieve their pertaining text.

10. Further functionality for different styles in displaying the Virtual Notes (see the section on the user interface) and commenting on existing annotations is also managed by these Java-Applets. If any new text is entered for an annotation, it is transferred to the Linda-Server and stored. In addition, each Virtual Note provides the means to delete it, which is only allowed for the owner of the page, who needs to provide his User-ID (see the section on the administration).

In order to create a new annotation on a page that has been enabled to accept them, the process is as follows (see Fig. 2):

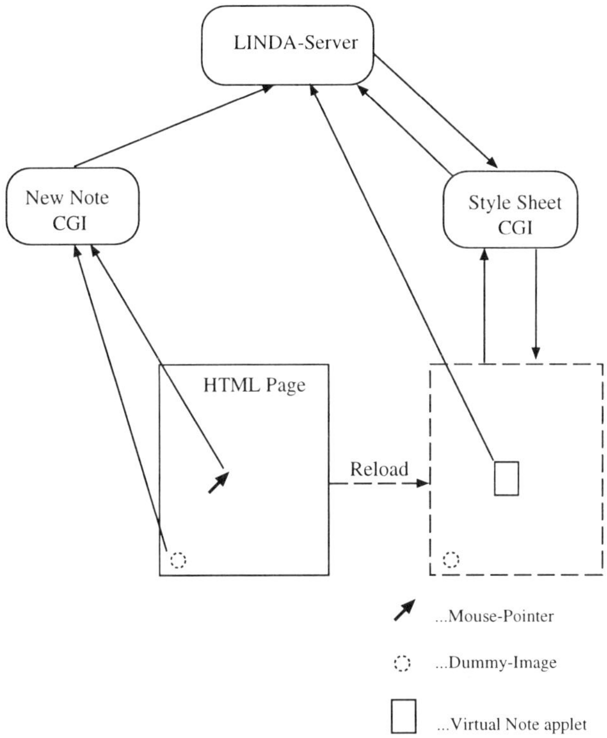

Figure 2. The process of adding a new Virtual Note to a HTML page

1. When a user clicks on a part of the document while holding down special keys (see the section on the user interface), the position of the mouse is recorded. This is managed by the Javascript-Code that has been included in the page.

2. By dividing this absolute position by the page length obtained from the dummy-image mentioned above an approximation for the relative position can be calculated[2]. Nevertheless this approach has certain advantages since it is for example possible to place a Virtual Note over a specific part of an image.

3. By calling a CGI-Script the information is then transferred to a server. The CGI-Script then opens a connection to the Linda-Server and updates Note-placement information for the given page. Special care has to be taken since in a Web-environment multiple users could be placing or deleting Virtual Notes at the same time. This is accomplished using a locking mechanism.

4. A reload-event is triggered in order to update the number of annotations on the current page making it possible for the user to enter text into the newly created Virtual Note, which is then transferred to the Linda-Server. This is managed by the Java-Applet implementing the Virtual Note, analogous to commenting on an existing annotation.

5. Finally, an e-mail message is sent to the owner of the page containing the text of the Virtual Note and the corresponding URL.

[2] It is not possible to calculate this position exactly, since text or images might be broken into the next line when a window is resized.

2.3. User interface

In order to accomplish the different interactions with the proposed annotation service the user interface has to be simple and intuitive to avoid additional mental load. The main task is still browsing and the annotation of pages needs to be smoothly integrated in this activity.

Therefore an annotation can be created by pointing the cursor at the chosen area of the page and clicking there while pressing the CTRL- and the ALT-Button (which is necessary because other combinations are in use by different window managers). This provides an intuitive way to select the portion of the HTML page the annotation refers to [8]. To keep as much of the page visible as possible the annotations are displayed as small icons depicting little stick-on-notes (see Fig. 3). This metaphor is already widely used for similar applications and should help novice users understand the functionality of Virtual Notes.

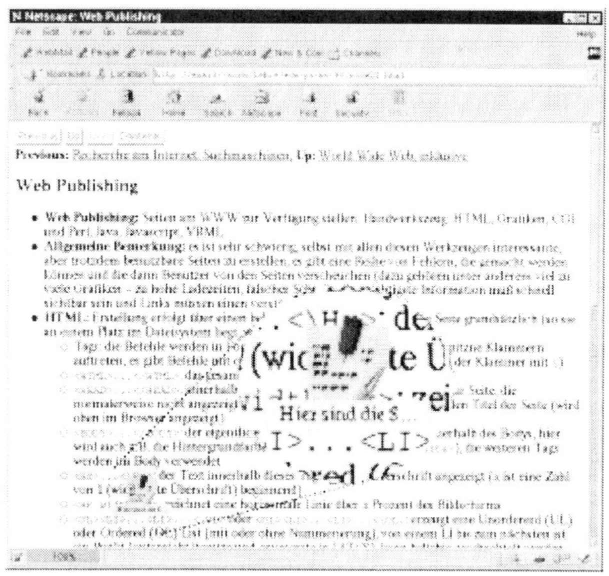

Figure 3. Screenshot of a Virtual Note (original size and magnified)

If the cursor is over one of them, the note expands to show it's text. If clicked upon, it stays in this form even if the cursor leaves, until the EXIT-Button is clicked. The note in full form contains, below the text (that is displayed in a form suggesting a conversation) a button to add text to this note (i.e. a new statement in the conversation, see Fig. 4).

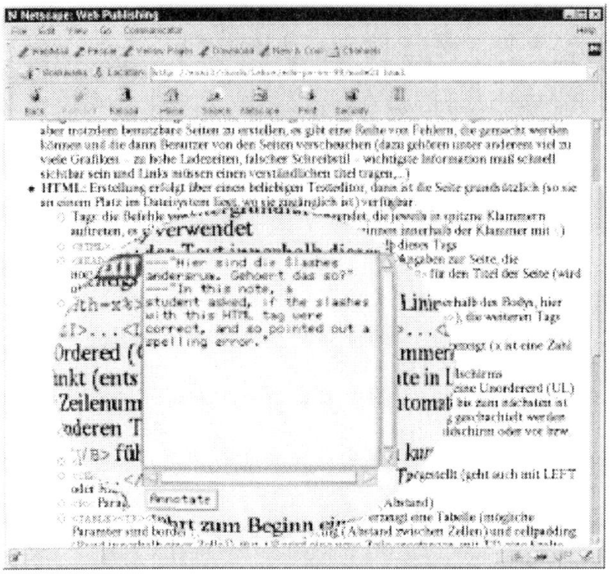

Figure 4. Screenshot of an opened Virtual Note (magnified)

In order to view the whole page without even the small icons of annotations displayed, the buttons CTRL and SHIFT can be pressed simultaneously while clicking anywhere on the page. The same operation makes all Virtual Notes visible again.

For convenience a banner can be added to denote a page as enabled for Virtual Notes. In addition, the banner links to a short description of Virtual Notes and their usage to help novice users or people who want to use the annotation service for their own Web pages. The banner also denotes the status of the annotation server, i.e. if the server is down, in order not to confuse users when Virtual Notes known to exist are not displayed.

2.4. Administration

The administrative part of the service contains three tasks that are accessible by CGI-forms:

1. In order to enable pages to accept annotations an User-ID has to be obtained. For this purpose a Web-based interface was created which generates unique User-ID/Password combinations after being provided with user data such as the e-mail address, which is necessary to implement notification functionality.
2. The User-ID identifies the owner of a page enabled for Virtual Notes. Therefore some mechanism has to be devised to integrate the User-ID with the necessary Javascript-Code in the page. Three approaches have been adopted:
   (a) Page-by-page over CGI-Interface: This Web-based interface lets the user submit an URL (where the page to be modified resides) together with a valid User-ID. The CGI-Script retrieves the Web page, inserts the necessary Javascript-Code and returns it to the user, who can save it.
   (b) Automatic LaTeX2html generation: A macro for the LaTeX2html translator was devised which automatically inserts the necessary code into all pages resulting from the translation. The User-ID is provided within the LaTeX-File.
   (c) Manual modification by user: Of course, the necessary Javascript-Code is also available for any user who wants to modify his Web pages manually, e.g. using some text editor. This code provided has only to be changed to incorporate the correct User-ID.
3. Finally a Web-based administration interface was added which allows users to selectively delete Virtual Notes placed on their pages. The above mentioned User-ID/Password combination is used to grant access to this feature. The deletion of a single annotation is also supplied by each Virtual Note, i.e. the corresponding Java-Applet.

A further service to facilitate the usage of the proposed annotation service is an automatic e-mail-notification of the user a page belongs to when a note is placed on it or commented upon (complete with the text of the annotation) to cancel the need to scan one's pages regularly. This also allows for quick disposal of any unwanted annotations, for example containing rude language or similar content.

2.5. Use cases

There are several use cases for this kind of service some of which are detailed below.

Collaborative writing includes the design and possible evaluation of WWW-sites by experts dispersed all over the world and an international project team composing a document. As annotations can be placed on any Web material, even graphics like mind maps, VLSI circuit layouts or construction plans can be annotated.

Distance editing includes the reviewing of scientific papers where the annotation service can insure the correct placement of feedback and the timeliness of its arrival.

Another use case for this application of Virtual Notes is the communication between tutor and student concerning a master thesis written while studying abroad. Also other documents written by students like seminar papers are often submitted using HTML and can thus profit from timely and correctly placed feedback from the teacher provided by Virtual Notes.

The proposed annotation service is already in use for the gathering of feedback from students participating in a course on Computer Science in order to raise the quality of the course in the next term based on this term's student's comments [3]. For example, one student wrote a memo for remembering a login procedure not explained in the course script. This kind of public memo, although intended primarily for private use, can give the teacher important hints on content missing from the course materials. Other students provided explicit feedback by using Virtual Notes to highlight spelling errors found.

Other uses include triggering online discussions, counselling of students, as blackboards for brainstorming or the coordination of meetings.

3. Conclusion

The proposed annotation service is based, as has been described, on standard internet technology, so it can be widely used without further need for preparation by the prospective user. It is therefore especially appropriate for situations without a coherent workgroup. Comparing this approach to existing systems, this also seems the most important advantage.

Other important features include the ability to position the annotations anywhere on the screen, thus conveying important contextual information, the storage of annotations on one or several separate servers and the provision of e-mail-notification for the owner of a Web page.

It has also been tried to facilitate the actual usage and the administration as much as possible, resulting in two ways of displaying annotations, the ability to make all notes on a page invisible and several tools to automatically enable pages for Virtual Notes.

Some of these features have already been realized with other annotation services described (like for example ComMentor [6, 7]), but only by requiring sometimes extensive changes to the system of any prospective user and therefore limiting the possible user base. As the benefit for each participant is directly related to the number of other participants, the notion of network externalities [10] does apply very well to annotation services. Therefore the possibility for all users of the Web to participate in the proposed system without costs incurred for installing or setting up some sort of client software can easily justify the effort on the side of an author to enable his pages.

Another difference to most of the annotation services presented is that the control about which Web pages are enabled to accept annotations and which annotations reside on a page is limited to the author (or owner) of the page. Several of the systems described (like for example Third Voice [11]) allow annotations to be placed on all Web pages, thus making unwanted comments on any page possible without providing for deletion by the owner of this page. The approach presented in this paper, by requesting a small modification to enable a Web page for annotations, leaves the decision whether any page should accept annotations or not to the author. In addition, the e-mail-notification reports the text and location of any Virtual Notes placed on the enabled Web pages without delay, therefore allowing for immediate deletion of any unwanted annotations (of course only if e-mail is checked regularly).

Possible enhancements (several of which have already been realized with other annotation services) include voice annotations, Virtual Notes not visible to all users like group or private annotations and the possibility for users to subscribe to a notification service. These users are subsequently informed of any new comments or the deletion of the Virtual Notes they indicated interest in. Also, different icons could be used for the representation of Virtual Notes, hinting at the creator or the type of content of the annotation like for example comment, report of spelling error or question.

References

[1] N. Carriero and D. Gelernter. Linda in context. *Communications of the ACM*, 32(4):444–458, Apr. 1989.

[2] Georgia Tech Graphics, Visualization & Usability Center. GVU's 10th WWW User Survey Results. http://www.gvu.gatech.edu/user_surveys/survey-1998-10/, 1998.

[3] A. Geyer-Schulz, S. Koch, and G. Schneider. Virtual Notes: Annotations on the WWW for learning environments. In *Proceedings of the Fifth Americas Conference on Information Systems (AMCIS 1999)*, pages 136–138, Milwaukee, WI, 1999.

[4] S. Greenberg. Collaborative interfaces for the web. In C. Forsythe, E. Grose, and J. Ratner, editors, *Human Factors and Web Development*. LEA Press, Mahwah, NJ, 1997.

[5] D. LaLiberte and A. Braverman. A protocol for scalable group and public annotations. *Computer Networks and ISDN Systems*, 27(6):911–918, Apr. 1995.

[6] M. Röscheisen, C. Mogensen, and T. Winograd. Shared web annotations as a platform for third-party value-added information providers: Architecture, protocols, and usage examples. Technical Report STAN-CS-TR-97-1583, Computer Science Department, Stanford University, Nov. 1994.

[7] M. Röscheisen, C. Mogensen, and T. Winograd. Beyond browsing: shared comments, soaps, trails, and online communities. *Computer Networks and ISDN Systems*, 27(6):739–749, Apr. 1995.

[8] M. A. Schickler, M. S. Mazer, and C. Brooks. Pan-browser support for annotations and other meta-information on the world wide web. *Computer Networks and ISDN Systems*, 28(7-11):1063–1074, May 1996.

[9] W. J. Schönfeldinger. *Kooperation und Kommunikation in heterogenen Rechner- und Sprachumgebungen mit Perl-Linda*. PhD thesis, Wirtschaftsuniversität Wien, Abteilung für Angewandte Informatik, 1996.

[10] C. Shapiro and H. R. Varian. *Information Rules: A Strategic Guide to the Network Economy*. Harvard Business School Press, Boston, 1998.

[11] A. Zeichick. Third voice: Extending the interpersonal communications potential of the world wide web. White Paper, http://www.thirdvoice.com/about/WhitePaperPage1.htm, Third Voice Inc., 1999.

Session 3:
Performance Analysis

Session 3. Performance analysis

Chairperson: Paolo Cremonesi

In parallel computing systems, the concept of quality is strictly connect with the performance of the systems. In fact, the execution of large scale computing applications in the shortest amount of time is one of the main factors motivating the usage of parallel systems (comprising both multiprocessor machines and networks of computers). The performance of a parallel program strictly depends on the characteristic of the target architecture (e.g., distributed or shared memory, communication latency and bandwidth, processor peak performance, I/O parallelism), on the scheduling discipline adopted (e.g., monoprogrammed vs. multi-programmed, one task per processor vs. many task per processor) and on the structure of the application being executed (e.g., application task graph, amount of data transmitted among processes, load balance). The plethora of the available systems as well as their inherent complexity make performance evaluation of such systems a very challenging problem. The papers presented in this session focus on the role of performance evaluation methodologies for the design, analysis, and prediction of performance of parallel applications.

The first paper, "*FINESSE: A Prototype Feedback-guided Performance Enhancement System*", introduces FINESSE, an environment which provides semi-automatic support for analysis of parallel program performance and for the application of transformations that are expected to reduce execution time. The environment is specifically targeted for use on single-address-space architectures. The performance improvement process involves repeated analysis of a series of implementations of the program, guided by feedback information based on both the program structure and run-time execution data. Performance is interpreted in terms of overheads, including: unparallelised code cost, load imbalance cost, memory access cost, scheduling cost. Use of the environment is iterative. In each cycle, the version which has just been produced in the development process is considered to be the current version, and the following steps are performed: static analysis, instrumentation and multiple executions, analysis of run-time behaviour, semi-automatic selection of suitable transformation aimed at reducing the time associated with the major performance problems, application of the selected transformation.

The second paper, "*Performance and Transparency of Message Passing and DSM Services Within the GENESIS Operating System for Managing Parallelism on COWs*", introduces GENESIS, a distributed operating system aimed at supporting parallel computing on Cluster of Workstations (COWs). GENESIS supports both Message Passing (MP) and Distributed Shared Memory (DSM). The paper focuses on the performance evaluation of a number of common parallel applications, employing both message passing and distribute shared memory, in order to show how much the execution performance deteriorates when DSM is employed in comparison with message passing. The implementation of the GENESIS uses the RHODOS microkernel and some basic servers. The RHODOS microkernel provides the bare minimum set of services to form a basic virtual machine.

The third paper, "*Predictability of Bulk Synchronous Programs Using MPI*", explores the predictability of Bulk Synchronous Programs (BSP) implemented with the Message Passing Interface. The Bulk-Synchronisation Parallel (BSP) model consists of three components: a collection of processors each with its own local memory, a communication network that can deliver messages point to point among processors, and a mechanism for efficient barrier synchronisation of all the processors. Two classic computational geometry problems (the Convex Hull and the Lower Envelope) are implemented as BSP algorithms and executed on three different parallel architectures: a Fujitsu AP1000, a CRAY T3E and a cluster of PCs. The paper compares the degree of predictability on these architectures analyzing the main sources of error.

FINESSE: A Prototype Feedback-guided Performance Enhancement System

N. Mukherjee, G.D. Riley and J.R. Gurd
Centre for Novel Computing,
Department of Computer Science,
University of Manchester,
Oxford Road,
Manchester, UK.
email:[nandini,griley,john]@cs.man.ac.uk

Abstract

FINESSE *is a prototype environment designed to support rapid development of parallel programs for single-address-space computers by both expert and non-expert programmers. The environment provides semi-automatic support for systematic, feedback-based reduction of the various classes of* overhead *associated with parallel execution. The characterisation of parallel performance by overhead analysis is first reviewed, and then the functionality provided by* FINESSE *is described. The utility of this environment is demonstrated by using it to develop parallel implementations, for an SGI Origin 2000 platform, of* Tred2, *a well-known benchmark for automatic parallelising compilers.*

1. Introduction

Parallel computers which share a common address space are generally acknowledged to be easier to program than those which have multiple address spaces and communicate via message-passing. However, once an application has been implemented on a single-address-space system, the reasons underlying poor performance can be difficult to diagnose. This paper introduces FINESSE, an environment which provides semi-automatic support for analysis of parallel program performance and for the application of transformations that are expected to reduce execution time. The environment is specifically targeted for use on single-address-space architectures.

Considerable prior research has been directed at performance analysis for parallel systems, resulting in a large number of research tools and several commercial products. However, the bulk of this work has been targeted at message-passing environments. The recent trend towards scalable, distributed shared memory architectures has highlighted a need for equivalent tools in the shared memory, single-address-space environment.

The approach supported by FINESSE differs from existing approaches in that it seeks to explain the performance behaviour of each parallel program *relative to* the performance of a serial reference version of the program, rather than simply monitoring performance data for the parallel program in isolation. The execution time *overhead*, O_p, of a parallel program executing on p processors is defined as being equal to $T_p - T_s/p$, where T_p is the execution time of the parallel program on p processors, while T_s is the execution time of the reference serial version of the program. A plot of $1/T_p$ versus p is known as a *performance curve*, which is usually plotted along with p/T_s versus p in order to illustrate the magnitude of the overhead and the way in which it varies with p. Performance improvement is achieved by reducing the overhead, thereby reducing execution time.

FINESSE also seeks to present performance data at the *program level*, rather than at the hardware level. While hardware performance data is easier to collect, it is seldom meaningful to a programmer, especially a non-expert. Moreover, many tools focus on one particular aspect of performance, for example communication or load balance, whereas FINESSE includes all sources of performance loss in a unified framework. By providing program-based analyses, the system is easy-to-use and is readily accommodated by non-experts.

For each *program unit*, FINESSE reports the total overhead resulting in that unit, and is able to display a breakdown of the overheads into an orthogonal set of structured categories. The user is thus able rapidly to both identify the nature of any performance problems, and to locate the point in the source-code where they are induced. Following this phase of *overhead analysis*, FINESSE provides semi-automatic support for the application of performance enhancing transformations. The case study reported in [20] illustrates the utility of this approach. Currently the target language is FORTRAN 77, but the techniques can be easily extended to handle FORTRAN 90, C and C++.

This paper describes the FINESSE environment and demonstrates its utility by describing the parallelisation of a well-known auto-parallelisation benchmark code, Tred2. The issues for parallelisation of this code are well-understood [12] and comparison with the parallelisation routes suggested by FINESSE are given.

The paper is organised as follows. Section 2 describes the requirements for, and design of, the FINESSE environment. Section 3 presents the Tred2 code and describes its structure; a brief overview of the nature of parallelism in the code is included. Section 4 describes the parallelisation of Tred2 using FINESSE; this illustrates the features of the environment and compares the parallelisation effort resulting from its use with that required for the known 'best' implementation. Section 5 presents related research, and Section 6 concludes.

2. The FINESSE Environment

This section describes the requirements and design of FINESSE, an environment providing semi-automatic support to a user attempting to improve the performance of a parallel program executing on a single-address-space, non-uniform memory access (NUMA) computer, such as the SGI Origin 2000. The performance improvement process involves repeated analysis of a *series of* implementations of the program, guided by feedback information based on both the program structure and run-time execution data.

Performance is interpreted in terms of the extra execution time associated with a small number of categories of parallel overhead including:

- **version cost:** the cost of any serial changes to a program to enable parallelism to be exploited;
- **unparallelised code cost:** the overhead associated with the serial fraction;
- **load imbalance cost:** due to uneven distribution of work to processors;
- **memory access cost:** both within local cache hierarchies and to memory in remote processors;
- **scheduling cost:** for example, the cost of parallel management code;
- **unexplained cost:** which accounts for any observed but unexplained overhead apart from the above.

There is a close relationship between the overhead categories used to characterise performance on a particular computer and the execution monitoring data which it is possible (directly or indirectly) to measure on that system. Improvements in performance are evaluated objectively, *relative to* either a base reference implementation (often the *best serial* implementation) or a previous version in the performance improvement history. Iteration of this process results in a semi-automatic, incremental development of implementations with increasingly better performance.

The FINESSE environment supports:

- management of versions of the program developed during the process.
- an objective judgement of the performance of each version.
- feedback-guided, semi-automatic performance improvement.
- the ability to *backtrack* in order to investigate a different development path.

Use of the environment typically begins with a (tuned) serial version of a program. Two phases can then be identified: in the initial phase, the (serial) code is executed in order to gather profile information, in particular to determine T_s. The second phase is then iterative; in each cycle, the version which has just been produced in the development process is considered to be the *current version*, and the following steps are performed:

- static analysis of the *current version* code, in order to create dependence and flow graphs;
- instrumentation and (possibly multiple) execution of the *current version*; [1]
- analysis of run-time behaviour of the *current version*, to identify performance problems;
- semi-automatic selection of suitable transformation(s) aimed at reducing the time associated with the major performance problem;
- application of the selected transformation(s) to the *current version*, thereby producing (a) *new version(s)* for subsequent analysis.

The run-time behaviour of the current version is reported by overhead category. During each iteration of the second phase, the objective embodied in FINESSE is to reduce the *maximum* cost associated with any overhead category. Suitable transformations to achieve this objective are suggested and, by default, applied. If the system is unable to determine a set of suitable transformations, the user's assistance

[1] For example, on SGI systems there is a limit to the number of hardware counters which can be monitored during an execution.

is sought. The system and/or user may find more than one set of transformations which are appropriate for tackling a particular performance problem; application of each set generates a new implementation, thus creating multiple new versions to be analysed. If the performance of a new version is poor, it may be discarded.

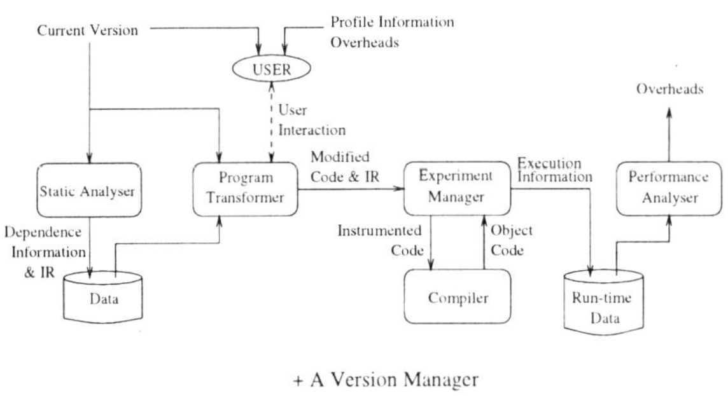

Figure 1. Overview of FINESSE.

The FINESSE environment is depicted in Figure 1; it consists of the following major components:

- A **version manager**, which keeps track of the status of each version (not shown in Figure 1).
- A **static analyser**, which converts a program into an intermediate representation (based on the abstract syntax tree) and calculates dependence information. This data is used to support the experiment manager and the program transformer (see below). [2]
- An **experiment manager**, which, in consultation with the version manager, the static analyser and the user, determines the exact set of experiments that need to be performed in order to gather the necessary run-time monitor information.
- A **database**, in which data from the static analyser and data collected during experiments is kept for each program version.
- A **performance analyser**, which analyses data from the database, and produces summaries of the performance in terms of the overhead categories. The analysed data is presented to the user and is also passed to the program transformer.
- A **program transformer**, which supports the selection and, ultimately, automatic application of program transformations to improve parallel performance. [3]

[2]Currently, FINESSE utilises the *Polaris* scanner [18] to support parsing of the source code and *Petit* [13] for dependence analysis.

[3]The prototype system does not implement automatic application of transformations; these are currently performed by hand.

3. The Tred2 Benchmark Code

Tred2 is a 110 line routine in the FORTRAN eigenvalue solver package, Eispack [27]. It reduces a symmetric matrix to symmetric tri-diagonal form using accumulating orthogonal similarity transformations.

The original Tred2 code contains imperfectly nested loops, `IF` statements and `GOTO`s. The version used as the initial serial implementation in this paper was produced by preprocessing the original using control-flow normalisation and variable substitution.

Tred2 contains no subprograms; there are two outer loops, both of which warrant being restructured in order to expose parallelism. At the next level, the majority of the work (99%) is performed by three loop nests. These loop nests access two 2-dimensional (size $N \times N$) and three 1-dimensional (size N) arrays as a whole. There are 23 loops in total.

3.1. Manual and Automatic Parallelisation

Manual and automatic parallelisations of the serial Tred2 source-code have been reported in [10]; this subsection summarises these results. Three auto-parallelising source-to-source compilers were used: *PFA* [17], *Polaris* (Pol) [18] and *Parafrase* (Pfr) [15]. The manual parallelisation (Man) followed the scheme presented in [20]. Each version was executed on a 4-processor SGI Challenge and on a 16-processor SGI Origin 2000. The dataset size used was $N = 512$ on the Challenge and $N = 800$ on the Origin 2000. Figure 2 shows the performance curves obtained for the four parallel versions; the *Ideal* curve is a plot of p/T_s versus p.

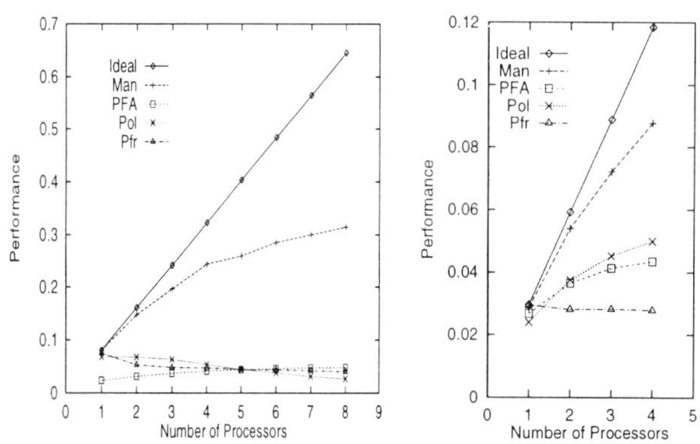

Figure 2. Performance curves for Tred2 on SGI Origin 2000 (left, for $N = 800$) and Challenge (right, for $N = 512$) systems.

Each of the three critical loops is parallelised in the *Manual* (Man) version, and performance improves significantly as p increases. The automatic compilers all parallelise a number of insignificant loops, but each of them *either* fails to detect parallelism in the expensive loops (due to conservative analysis), *or* applies ineffective transformations which result in parallel performance that is worse than for serial execution.

When targeted for the SGI Challenge platform, one of the three expensive loops is efficiently parallelised by the *PFA* and *Polaris* compilers, and their parallel codes perform better than the *Parafrase* version. However, on the Origin 2000, the performance of all three versions is equally poor. Although the *PFA* version exhibits some speedup when it runs on multiple processors, its $p = 1$ execution time is almost 3.5 times that of the serial code, and this disadvantage is not even recovered when $p = 8$. This is caused by additional overhead incurred due to the application of inefficient transformations, for example increasing access strides in loops by interchanging the array indices.

4. Using FINESSE to Improve Performance

This section describes the development, using FINESSE, of a parallel implementation of Tred2, for up to $p = 4$ on the SGI Origin 2000 platform. For the most part, the development follows paths which require minimal user intervention. The performance of the final version reached in this way is compared with that of a known "best" implementation found by an expert programmer.

Initially, the serial version of Tred2, as described in Section 3, is registered with FINESSE; this forms **Version 0** of the code development. The system then undertakes an initial analysis, generating an intermediate representation of the program, similar to an abstract syntax tree (AST), and a standard set of monitoring experiments is devised and executed in order to gather initial timing and frequency information. Analyses of this data are available to the user via the *initial window*, as shown in Figure 3. Here the user has selected node 1-39 in the AST representation, causing the associated source-code to be displayed, along with its cumulative execution time, a count of the number of times the node has been invoked (in this case, the number of iterations of the associated loop), and data dependence information from the static analyser. Note that each AST node is identified by a combination of program unit number and internal node number, as determined by FINESSE during analysis; the selected node is number 39 in program unit 1. The type of each node is given inside the corresponding square brackets; node 1-39 represents a loop.

When requested, overheads are displayed in tabular or graphical form (see Figures 7 and 8 for examples of the latter). A list of the loop nodes that are responsible for major performance problems, together with recommendations for reducing the associated overheads, is also produced. For example, if *unparallelised code cost* dominates the overhead, a list of the loop nodes is presented, in order of cumulative execution time, and *parallelisation* of these loops is recommended as the transformation to apply. This situation is shown in Figure 4, which is presented after the initial analysis of Version 0 of Tred2. The listed nodes are all loop nodes and the recommendation in each case is to parallelise the associated loop, if possible.

By selecting a node in the list, the user is informed whether-or-not parallelisation is legal and, if not, is shown the dependences which are inhibiting parallelisation. In general, the user can then either (1) request that the recommended transformations be applied, (2) make changes to the source code to remove inhibiting dependences, or (3) define further experiments to be conducted on selected nodes in order to obtain additional overhead data. Where parallelisation of unparallelised loop is the sole recommendation (the situation depicted in Figure 4), option (3) is not valid.

In Figure 4, the first two loop nodes in the list, 1-48 and 1-53, have been selected for investigation by the user. Apparently neither can be parallelised immediately, due to the dependences identified in the sub-window. The most expensive loop recommended for parallelisation is node 1-48 (remember that the list is in order of cumulative execution time). FINESSE reports that parallelisation of this loop is prohibited and gives information on which data items are responsible. User scrutiny of the associated code, using the *SourcePane* window, shows that it is an outer loop which has a complex structure; reorganising it to expose parallelism would require major effort. This loop is therefore left for the moment, and attention turns to the next most significant loop, node 1-53. This is an inner loop of 1-48 whose parallelisation is being inhibited by the shown dependences. However, inspection of the loop code tells the user that one of the reported dependences is a *dead* dependence and that the other can be overcome by *privatisation* of a scalar variable. [4] The user chooses, therefore, to parallelise this loop.

The next steps are not illustrated here, but they follow the same pattern as the foregoing. The third most expensive loop, node 1-12, also has a complex structure, and the user decides to leave it as it is. The *tree structure* window (Figure 3) reveals that the next two nodes in the list, 1-55 and 1-57, are contained within node 1-53 (they are nested loops), and have thus been dealt with already.

The remaining significant listed loops are nodes 1-39 and 1-27, which both lie inside node 1-12, plus nodes 1-40 and 1-30, which are contained within nodes 1-39 and 1-27, respectively. Parallelisation of node 1-39 is reported to be inhibited by an anti-dependence, but this can be removed

[4] The user would need to be fairly experienced to detect this, but both of these dependences could have been determined automatically by a more sophisticated static analyser than is available in the prototype; this will be implemented in a future version of the system.

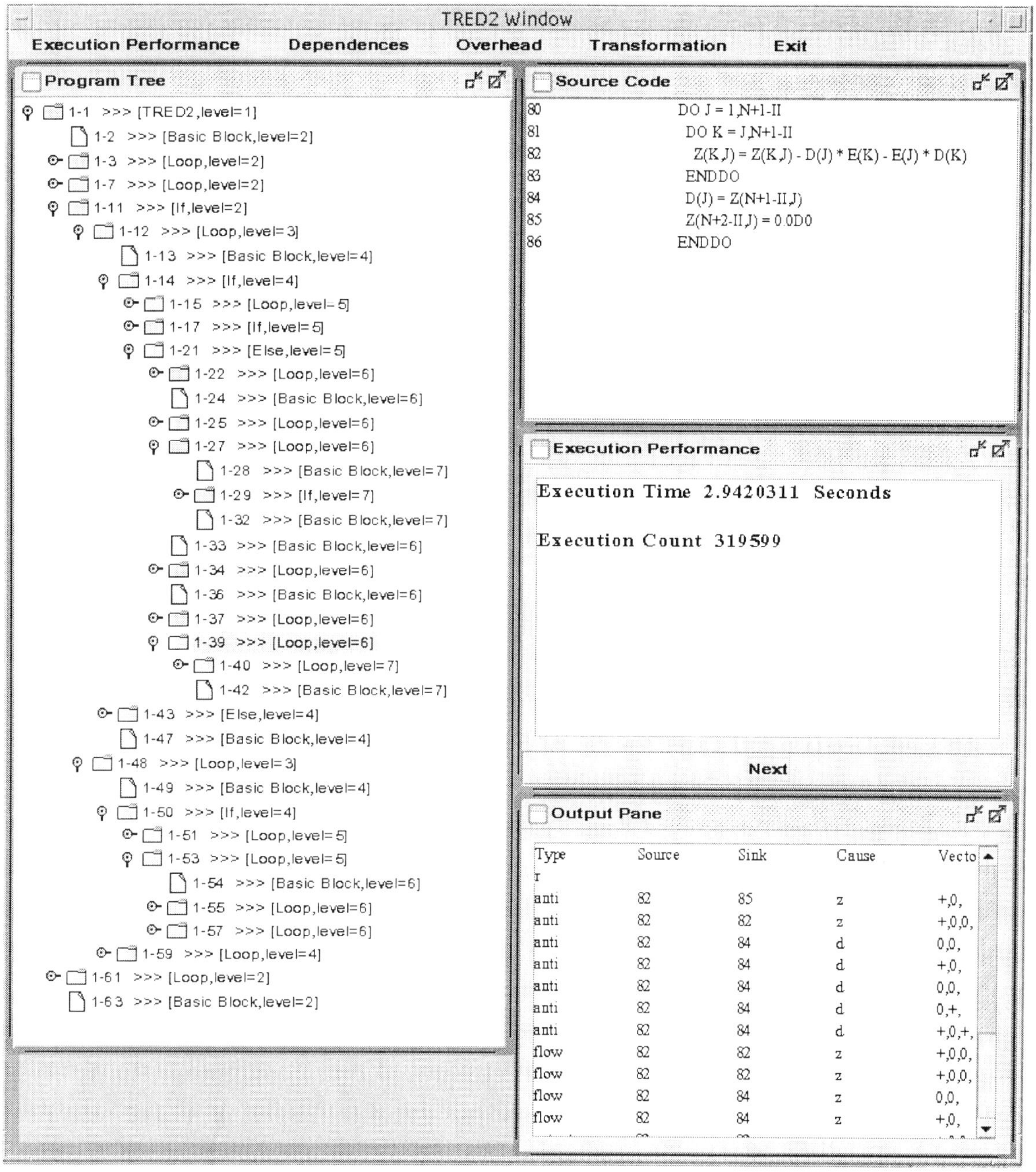

Figure 3. The initial window for Version 0 of Tred2.

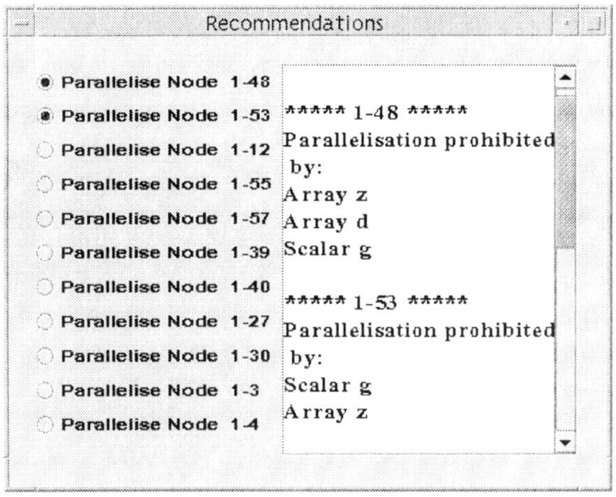

Figure 4. Recommendations for improving performance after initial analysis of Version 0 of Tred2.

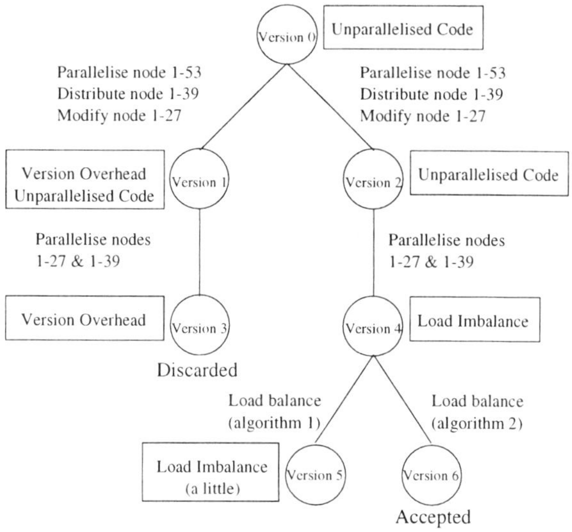

Figure 5. The complete version tree for parallelisation of Tred2.

by applying loop distribution.[5]

Finally, the user determines that there are two potentially effective ways (not described here) to restructure the code for loop 1-27 to expose parallelism and, therefore, decides to create the following two *new versions*:

- **Version 1:** in which node 1-27 is restructured one way, node 1-53 is parallelised and loop 1-39 is distributed.
- **Version 2:** in which node 1-27 is restructured the other way, and nodes 1-53 and 1-39 are dealt with as in Version 1.

FINESSE is now instructed to create these two new versions by applying the selected transformations and incorporating any user-altered code. The newly created versions are then processed similarly, creating additional new versions in a tree-like fashion. For reference, the complete version tree constructed during the parallelisation of Tred2 using FINESSE is shown in Figure 5. New sets of experiments are automatically devised and executed for each version, and the results of these analyses are made available to the user as before.

For Version 1, FINESSE reports that the major performance shortfall is still due to *unparallelised code cost* and that there is a large *version cost* overhead causing an increase in execution time over Version 0. After being instructed to execute an extra set of experiments and processing their results, FINESSE indicates that this overhead is mainly due to increased primary cache misses in node 1-27. This analysis supports the observation made by the expert programmer in [12]: the transformed loop 1-27 makes non-unit stride access through an array. Nevertheless, at this stage, the user decides not to discard Version 1, but to reduce the reported *unparallelised code cost* overhead by parallelising the restructured nodes 1-27 and 1-39, now possible automatically. This creates **Version 3**, containing three parallel loops.

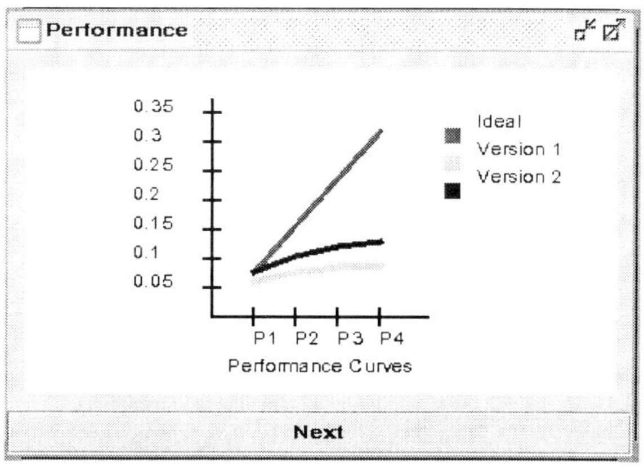

Figure 6. Performance curves for Versions 1 and 2 of Tred2.

Analysis of Version 2 shows that its performance is better than that of Version 1 (see Figure 6) and that, once again, the dominant overhead is *unparallelised code cost* (see Figure 7). FINESSE recommends the parallelisation of nodes 1-48, 1-12, 1-39 and 1-27, in that order. As with Version 0, parallelisation of nodes 1-48 and 1-12 is not attempted, due

[5] Currently this is also a user decision and action, but in a future version of the system these options will be reported by the static analyser and implemented by the program transformer.

to their complex structure. But automatic parallelisation of the other nodes is now possible, so the user confirms that this is required and FINESSE creates **Version 4**, again containing three parallelised loops.

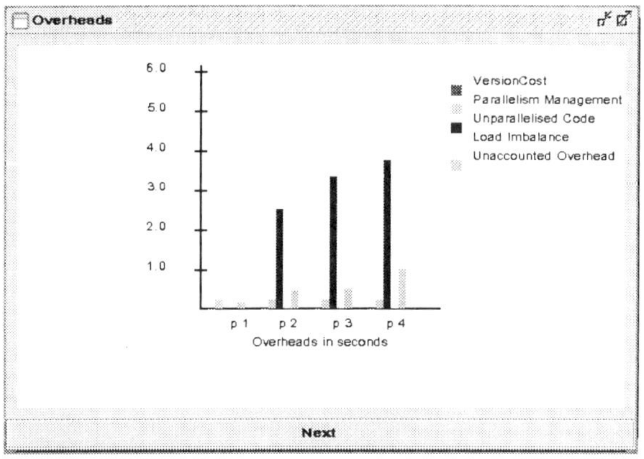

Figure 7. Overheads reported for Version 2.

FINESSE is now instructed to process these two new versions. It devises and executes another set of experiments and performs the associated analysis. The user now sees that the *unparallelised code cost* overhead in Version 3 has been reduced, resulting in better performance than Version 1. However, the *version cost* overhead inherited from Version 1 causes performance to be worse than for Version 2. Inspection of overhead data for nodes 1-27 and 1-39 shows that loops in these nodes suffer from *load imbalance cost* overhead. At this point, the user thus decides to discard Version 3.

Version 4 exhibits the best performance so far. The dominant overhead is *load imbalance cost* in nodes 1-27 (see Figure 8) and 1-39, plus a small amount of *memory access cost* and *unexplained cost*.

Inspection of the code for loop nodes 1-27 and 1-39 reveals that they both cover a *triangular* iteration space. In Version 4, the default strategy of FINESSE is to apply a simple *block partitioning* scheme. The user determines that this is the cause of the *load imbalance cost* and thus chooses to implement two different algorithms that are expected to reduce this overhead. The first implements a *cyclic partitioning* scheme, leading to **Version 5** of the code. The second uses an algorithm proposed by Sakellariou [21], and leads to **Version 6**.

The *load imbalance cost* decreases in both Version 5 and Version 6; both versions perform better than Version 4. However, for $p = 4$, a small amount of *load imbalance cost* is observed in Version 5 (see Figure 9). This does not happen in Version 6 (Figure 10), which thus outperforms Version 5. Indeed, Version 6 exhibits only small amounts

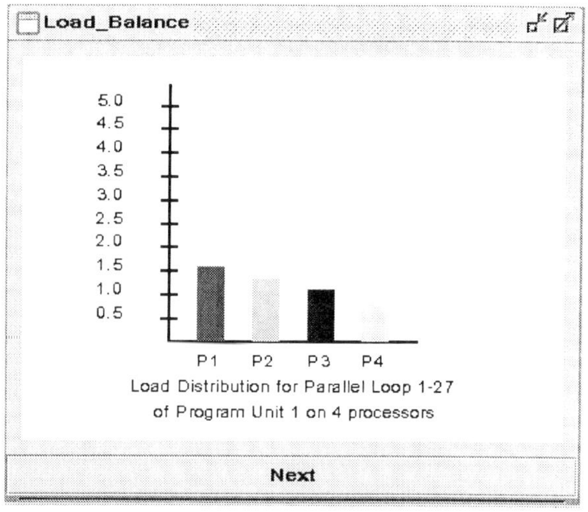

Figure 8. Load imbalance in Version 4.

of *memory access cost* and *unexplained cost*. The user decides that these overheads do not warrant futher effort and decides to accept Version 6 as an 'acceptable' parallel implementation. Development of the code ceases.

In Figure 11, performance curves for up to $p = 8$ on the Origin 2000 are shown for Version 6 and the best-known manual version of Tred2 [10]. Version 6 closely matches the performance of the best known version and is significantly better than Version 5. The effort required to reach this point using FINESSE is considerably less than that reported in [12].

5. Related Work

The large majority of existing tools for parallel performance analysis are aimed at the message-passing programming paradigm. Space does not permit an exhaustive list

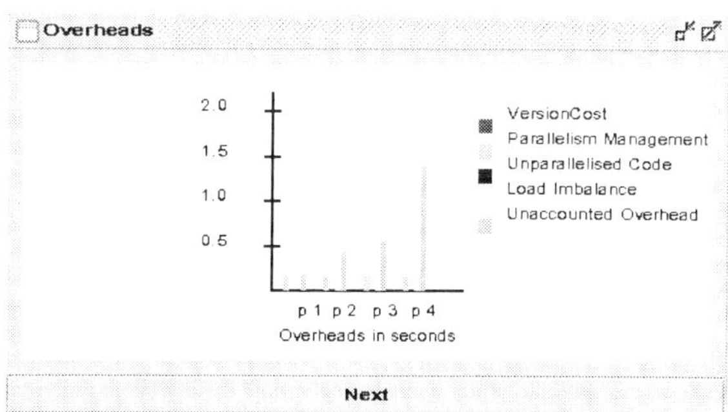

Figure 9. Overheads in Version 5.

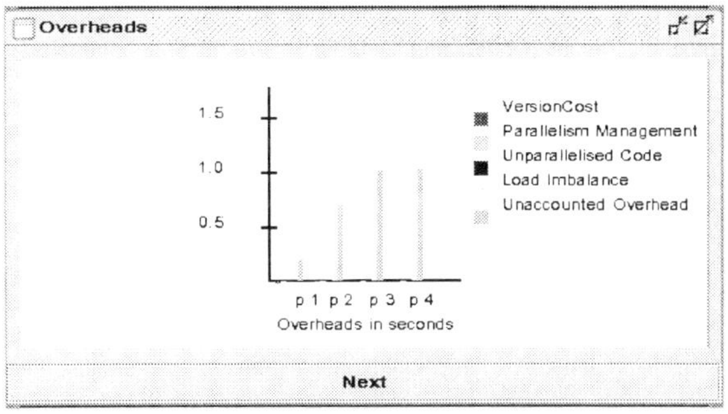

Figure 10. Overheads in Version 6.

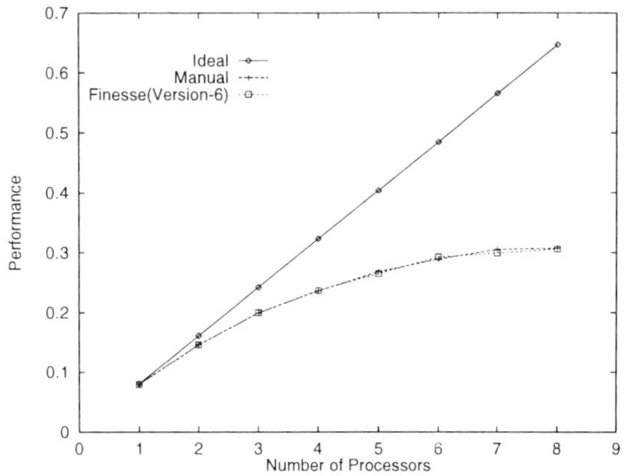

Figure 11. Final performance curves.

of these tools, but, restricting attention to tools which support FORTRAN or C, significant research efforts in this area include Paragraph [5], Pablo [16], AIMS [26], Paradyn [9], PMA [23] and XPVM [4]. Commercial systems include Vampir [11], MPP-Apprentice [24], Nupshot [25] and VT [2].

Tools for shared memory systems have received less attention, possibly due to the lack of a widely accepted standard for the associated programming paradigm, and because of the need for hardware support to monitor the memory system (the advent of OpenMP [14] seems likely to ease the former situation, while the PerfAPI [3] standards initiative will ameliorate the latter). A number of systems support visualisation of events occurring in threads libraries. Falcon [6] offers real-time event monitoring of thread activity as part of a larger computational steering package. PARADE [22] is a visualisation and animation suite which includes support for both threads and message-passing libraries.

Carnival [8] supports *waiting time analysis* for both message-passing and shared memory systems. This is the nearest to full overheads profiling that any other tool achieves; however, important overhead categories, such as memory accesses, are excluded, and no reference code is used to give an unbiased basis for comparison.

In the Blizzard software VSM system, Paradyn [9] has been adapted to monitor memory accesses and memory-sharing behaviour. SVMview [1] is another tool designed for a software VSM system (FORTRAN-S); however techniques for monitoring software systems do not transfer readily to hardware-supported virtual shared memory.

Commercial systems include ATExpert [7] (a precursor to MPP-Apprentice), for Cray vector SMPs, and Codevision, for Silicon Graphics shared memory machines, including the Origin 2000. Codevision is a profiling tool, allowing profiles of not only the program counter, but also the hardware performance counters available on the Origin 2000. It also features an experiment management framework.

6. Conclusions

This paper has presented FINESSE, a prototype environment designed to support performance improvement by means of systematic exploration of the parallel implementation space, guided by an overhead-oriented interpretation of performance loss *relative to* the performance of a reference (serial) implementation.

The environment provides automatic support for static analysis of an implementation, for generation of a set of experiments that gather appropriate execution-time data, and for the processing and presentation of overhead information based on this data.

FINESSE recommends courses of action and provides for automated application of transformations to expose and exploit parallelism based on its analyses. Manual intervention, through direct editing of source-code files, is also possible. This mixture of manual and automated techniques is attractive to users of all capabilities.

The utility of FINESSE has been illustrated through the exploration of a minimum-effort parallelisation of Tred2, a widely studied research code. Performance of the resulting implementation compares well with that of an implementation that was produced by an expert programmer using a time-consuming, fully manual parallelisation procedure.

The system is at an early stage of development, and many enhancements are envisaged. The environment will be ported to a number of other single-address-space platforms, including multiprocessor PCs. This will enable the relationship between the requirements of overhead analysis and the performance monitoring facilities provided on different platforms to be explored. Currently, FORTRAN 77 is the supported language, but extensions to C and C++ appear straightforward.

FINESSE supports a particular methodology for the development of parallel programs [19]. It would be interesting to compare the methodologies employed by users of tools to support the development of message-passing applications.

The level of automated analysis and the presentation of information and guidance and options presented to the user need to be exposed to a wider user-base.

Presently, the transformation system and recommendation mechanism are at an early stage of development. They can be improved further by enhancing the analysing power of the environment and incorporating the heuristics that are commonly used by expert programmers. An environment enhanced in this way will not only save effort during expert code development, but will also help the non-expert to develop a reasonably efficient parallel implementation of a given code.

Acknowledgements

The authors wish to thank their colleagues in the Centre for Novel Computing for their many contributions to the work presented in this paper. Nandini Mukherjee (Mukhopadhyay) has been funded by an award from the Commonwealth Scholarship Commission, whose support is gratefully acknowledged.

References

[1] D. Badouel, T. Priol and L. Renambot, *SVMview: a Performance Tuning Tool for DSM-based Parallel Computers*, Tech. Rep. PI-966, IRISA Rennes, Nov. 1995.

[2] J.D. Bucher and K.L. Beck, *Profiling on a Massively Parallel Computer*, Lect. Notes in Comp. Sci. **634**, 97–102, 1992.

[3] J. Dongarra, *Performance Data Standard and API*, available at: http://www.cs.utk.edu/ mucci/pdsa/perfapi/index.htm

[4] G.A. Geist, J. Kohl and P. Papadopoulos, *Visualization, Debugging and Performance in PVM*, Proc. Visualization and Debugging Workshop, Oct. 1994.

[5] I. Glendinning, V.S. Getov, A. Hellberg, R.W. Hockney and D.J. Pritchard, *Performance Visualisation in a Portable Parallel Programming Environment*, Proc. Workshop on Monitoring and Visualization of Parallel Processing Systems, Moravany, CSFR, Oct. 1992,

[6] W. Gu, G. Eisenhauer, K. Schwan, J. Vetter, *Falcon: On-line Monitoring and Steering of Parallel Programs*, available at: http://www.cc.gatech.edu/systems/papers/weiming98.ps

[7] J. Kohn and W. Williams, *ATExpert*, J. Par. and Dist. Comp. **18**, 205–222, 1993.

[8] W. Meira Jr., T.J. LeBlanc and A. Poulos, *Waiting Time Analysis and Performance Visualization in Carnival*, ACM SIGMETRICS Symp. on Par. and Dist. Tools, 1–10, May 1996.

[9] B.P. Miller, M.D. Callaghan, J.M. Cargille, J.K. Hollingsworth, R.B. Irvin, K.L. Karavanic, K. Kunchithapadam and T. Newhall, *The Paradyn Parallel Performance Measurement Tools*, IEEE Computer **28**(11), 37–46, 1995.

[10] N. Mukherjee and J.R. Gurd, *A comparative analysis of four parallelisation schemes*, Proc. 13th ACM Intl. Conf. on Supercomputing, ACM Press, 278–285, June 1999.

[11] W.E. Nagel, A. Arnold, M. Weber, H.-Ch. Hoppe and K. Solchenbach, *VAMPIR: Visualization and Analysis of MPI Resources*, available at: http://www.kfa-juelich.de/zam/PTdocs/vampir/vampir.html

[12] M.F.P. O'Boyle and J.M. Bull, *Expert Programmer versus Parallelizing Compiler: A Comparative Study of Two Approaches for Distributed Shared Memory*, Sci. Prog. **5**(1), 63–88, 1996.

[13] The omega project: Frameworks and algorithms for the analysis and transformation of scientific programs, available at: http://www.cs.umd.edu/projects/omega

[14] OpenMP Architecture Review Board, *OpenMP* FORTRAN *Application Interface*, available at: http://www.openmp.org/openmp/mp-documents/fspec.A4.ps

[15] Parafrase-2, A Vectorizing/Parallelizing Compiler, available at: http://www.csrd.uiuc.edu/parafrase2

[16] D.A. Reed, *Experimental Analysis of Parallel Systems: Techniques and Open Problems*, Lect. Notes in Comp. Sci. **794**, 25–51, 1994.

[17] *POWER* FORTRAN *Accelerator User's Guide*.

[18] Polaris, Automatic Parallelization of Conventional FORTRAN Programs, available at: http://polaris.cs.uiuc.edu/polaris/polaris.html

[19] G.D. Riley, *Techniques for Improving the Performance of Parallel Computations*, M.Sc. Thesis, Univ. Manchester, Oct. 1996.

[20] G.D. Riley, J.M. Bull and J.R. Gurd, *Performance Improvement Through Overhead Analysis: A Case Study in Molecular Dynamics*, Proc. 11th ACM Intl. Conf. on Supercomputing, ACM Press, 36–43, July 1997.

[21] R. Sakellariou and J.R. Gurd, *Compile-Time Minimisation of Load Imbalance in Loop Nests*, Proc. 11th ACM Intl. Conf. on Supercomputing, ACM Press, 277–284, July 1997.

[22] J.T. Stasko, *The PARADE Environment for Visualizing Parallel Program Executions: A Progress Report*, Tech. Rep. GIT-GVU-95-03, Graphics, Visualization, and Usability Center, Georgia Institute of Technology, Atlanta GA, Jan. 1995.

[23] B.J.N. Wiley and A. Endo, *Annai/PMA Performance Monitor and Analyzer*, Proc. 4th Intl. Workshop on Modeling, Analysis and Simulation of Comp. and Telecom. Systems (MASCOTS'96), IEEE Comp. Soc. Press, 186–191, Feb. 1996.

[24] W. Williams, T. Hoel and D. Pase, *The MPP Apprentice Performance Tool: Delivering the Performance of the Cray T3D*, **in**: K.M. Decker et al. (eds.), *Programming Environments for Massively Parallel Distributed Systems*, Birkhauser Verlag, 333–345, 1994.

[25] C.E. Wu, H. Franke and Y-H. Liu, *A unified trace environment for IBM SP systems*, IEEE Par. and Dist. Tech. **4**(6), 89–93, 1996.

[26] J.C. Yan, *Performance Tuning with AIMS- An Automated Instrumentation and Monitoring System for Multicomputers*, Proc. 27th Hawaii Intl. Conf. on System Sciences **II**, IEEE Comp. Soc. Press, 625–633, Jan. 1994.

[27] B.T. Smith, J.M. Boyle, J.J. Dongarra, B.S. Garbow, Y. Ikebe, V.C. Klema and C.B. Moler. *Matrix eigensystem routines - eispack guide*, Lect. Notes in Comp. Sci. **6**, 1976 (2nd edn.).

Performance and Transparency of Message Passing and DSM Services Within the GENESIS Operating System for Managing Parallelism on COWs

A. Goscinski, M. Hobbs and J. Silcock
School of Computing and Mathematics
Deakin University, Victoria 3217, Australia
{ang, mick, jackie}@deakin.edu.au

Abstract*

The primary paradigm for building parallel applications for execution on Clusters of Workstations (COWs) can be generalised into Message Passing (MP) and Distributed Shared Memory (DSM). Unfortunately, the currently available run-time environments and operating systems do not provide satisfactory levels of transparency, management support, and only support either MP or DSM. We propose a unique and novel approach where the MP and DSM services are provided to the application programmer as a cohesive and comprehensive set of parallel processing servers that are integral components of an operating system. The performance of a number of common parallel applications, employing both MP (raw and PVM based) and DSM, demonstrate the high quality of the proposed approach.

***Keywords**: Parallel Processing on COWs, Parallelism Management, Message Passing, Distributed Shared Memory, Performance Evaluation.*

1. Introduction

A problem exists with COWs as parallel platforms in that their resources (computational, memory and peripheral) are distributed over the set of workstations. Parallel processing requires the harnessing and the synchronised access to these distributed resources from the execution and communication points of view. Traditionally, this problem has been left to the application programmer to solve as little (to no) parallelism execution and communication management support has been provided by the underlying operating systems.

The physical distribution of memory requires that any parallel application executed on a COW employs either MP or DSM for communication between parallel processes executing on separate workstations. Parallel application programmers have been forced to use different environments depending on the communication paradigm used.

There are three goals of this paper. The first goal is to detail the important features of the GENESIS system which provides operating system support for message passing and shared memory based parallel applications to be executed on a COW. The second goal is to show how much the execution performance deteriorates when DSM is employed in comparison with MP. The third goal is to present the benefits, in particular ease of programming, use and transparency, of implementing these services, for managing parallelism, within the kernel of an operating system when compared to traditional solutions built outside the kernel. Thus, emphasis is placed on the programmability and performance of the system; with evidence provided in the form of a set of experimental results.

2. The GENESIS Parallelism Management Operating System

A parallel program can be divided into three distinct phases, the initialisation, execution and termination phases. The initialisation phase involves the instantiation of a set of child processes and, in the case of MP, the distribution of the data (work) to each of these child processes. The next phase involves each of the processes executing in parallel. It is during the execution phase that the actual work on the problem data is performed, and increasing the number of child processes executing in parallel on the problem data can improve the overall execution time. In the termination phase each process completes the work and, in the case of MP, returns the result back to the parent process before exiting. Communication between processes is required at the parallel execution phase whether performed explicitly by the user processes using MP or implicitly through shared memory, while parallelism management services are required at the initialisation and termination phases. This operation should be performed in a transparent manner.

2.1 Parallelism Management System Requirements

A system that is to support parallel processing on COWs efficiently and effectively must provide both the communication and execution services. When designing this system a number of important requirements must be met:

- Ease of Programming — the programmer should be provided with the option of the communication paradigm to be employed in their parallel application. The chosen method should also be clean and free of syntax and semantic complexities.
- Ease of Use — programmers should be provided a par-

* This work was partly supported by the ARC Grant 0504003157.

allel application environment that relieves them from being involved in many time consuming and error prone activities associated with the creation, placement and communication of processes.

- Transparency — the programmers must be unaware of the location on which there parallel applications are executed, and therefore unaware of the actual location of communicating parallel processes (using MP or DSM).
- Performance — the user must not experience poor performance from the system.

As stated in the introduction, the system should not be biased towards one particular communication paradigm and therefore must provide both MP and DSM services. The parallelism management services are required to simplify and improve performance of the instantiation of the child parallel processes. In addition, in order to also improve performance, the system must map the parallel processes to idle or lightly loaded workstations and maintain a balanced load over the COW. The access and management of workstations within the COW should not involve the user, and also must be provided dynamically.

2.2 Architecture of the GENESIS System

The GENESIS system is a newly designed operating system that supports parallel processing on COWs. It is a microkernel and client-server based system that employs the MP (basic and PVM) and DSM services. The approach taken with this environment has been to build the communication and execution services as an integral part of the operating system itself. Other approaches have followed a line where similar services have been implemented outside the operating system and form a clearly separated environment. A number of serious problems exist with the latter approach:

- most of the solutions used for DSM and PVM are performance driven and little work has been done on making them programmer friendly;
- they suffer from poor performance because of the duplication of services between PVM or DSM software and the operating system;
- they require programmers to be involved in many time consuming and error prone activities associated with the creation and placement of process on underutilised workstations; and
- they lack transparency and increase overheads due to the limitations placed on these systems by the operating systems on which they are built.

Although building a parallelism management environment on top of an existing operating system increases the portability of such systems, we claim here that it is because the underlying operating systems were not specifically designed and built to support parallel processing on COWs that these problems have developed. An operating system that is capable of managing parallelism for applications executing on COWs should [1]:

- possess the features of a distributed operating system in order to deal with distributed resources and their management, and hide distribution (distributed operating systems by their very nature provide a virtual machine, presenting a unified processing environment instead of a collection of individual workstations connected by a communication subsystem [2]); and
- provide efficient services which allow the transparent and dynamic establishment of a virtual parallel computer, instantiation of parallel child processes, distribution of data and co-ordination of execution.

Logically the GENESIS system is made up of an enhanced subset of a distributed operating system, a parallelism management system, and a programming and execution environment. The parallelism management system supports the management of parallel processes and the resources of the COW and the programming and execution environment, as shown in Figure 1.

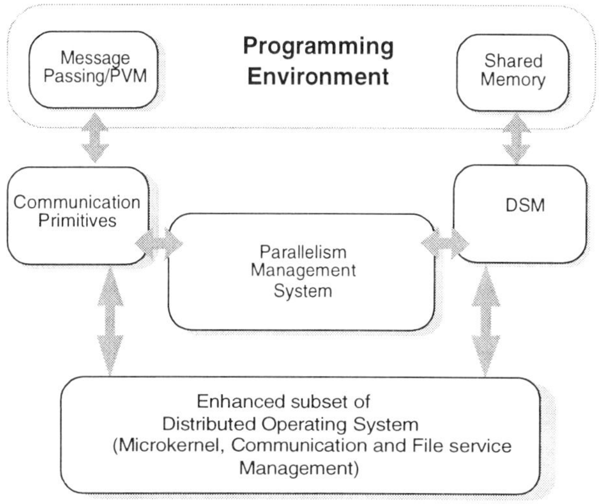

Figure 1: Logical Structure of GENESIS

The implementation of the GENESIS system (Figure 2) has been accelerated by the lessons learned from the development of the RHODOS distributed operating system [3]. Furthermore, GENESIS uses the RHODOS microkernel and some basic servers. The RHODOS microkernel provides the bare minimum set of services to form a basic virtual machine, by providing support for local interprocess communication, context switching and interrupt handling. The basic servers borrowed from RHODOS (because they satisfy the requirements of the parallelism management system) are kernel servers that provide remote communication, file support and process management.

The GENESIS Parallelism Management System was designed to provide the services of:

- Instantiation of Parallel Processes — responsible for

bringing new processes into existence and initiating their execution (such as process creation).

- Mapping of Parallel Processes to Workstations — responsible for maintaining a COW wide balanced load. Mapping decisions must be made both at the instantiation of the process (process allocation) and also during the execution phase (dynamic load balancing).
- Migration of Processes — responsible for moving processes from heavily to lightly loaded/idle workstations.
- Distribution of Initial Data — responsible for workload allocation to the child processes of a parallel application.
- Coordination of Parallel Processes — responsible for synchronisation between parent and child processes.

The distribution of data and coordination services are provided as inherent features of the GENESIS system. They are supported by the MP component of GENESIS. This service provides transparent communication between processes, regardless of their location within the COW. Processes which exist on the same workstation communicate using the identical mechanisms as when the processes exist on different workstations. GENESIS also supports the movement of processes between workstations with no disruption to the interprocess communication. Furthermore, the GENESIS system exploits a group communication service, that allows the programmer/system to set up a group, change or close the group; and to deliver, using different semantics, a message to the members of a group. All remote communication services are supported by the Network Manager, that employs, among other protocols, the Reliable Datagram Protocol (RRDP).

The process instantiation and process mapping services are implemented as individual servers within the GENESIS Parallelism Management System with the core of GENESIS being composed of the RHODOS microkernel code and the set of kernel server processes. The process instantiation and mapping services of the Parallelism Management Systems are provided by specialised kernel servers including the Process Execution; and Global Scheduling and Process Migration Managers, respectively. The local and remote communication services, i.e., the MP services are provided by the Inter-Process Communications (IPC) Manager and by the local IPC component of the microkernel. The DSM service is provided by the DSM system that is part of the Space (Memory) Manager. Furthermore, these services are provided transparently to the user allowing the full computational and memory resources of a COW to be utilised in an efficient manner.

One of the most important features of the GENESIS system is its user friendliness. GENESIS provides a complete environment for programmers that allows them to use MP either in its raw, basic form or through PVM or to use shared memory through the use of DSM, all within a single programming and execution environment.

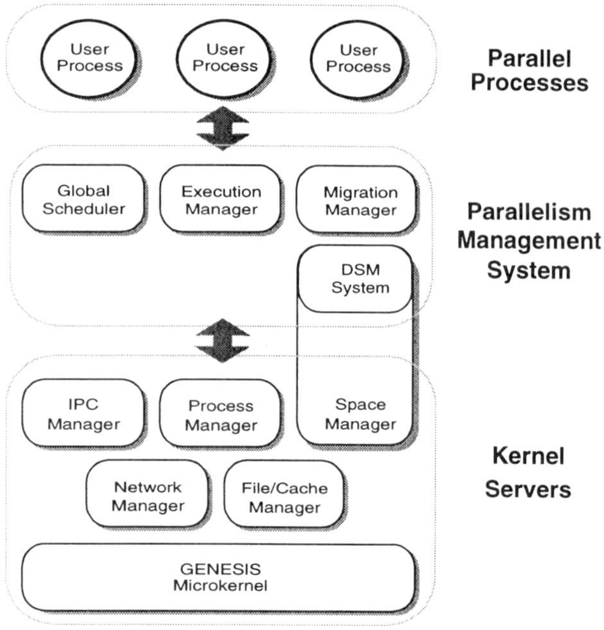

Figure 2: GENESIS Parallelism Management System

3. The GENESIS Programming Interface and Architecture

This section shows the interfaces the programmer has with the standard MP, PVM and DSM based services and their implementation within the GENESIS framework.

3.1 GENESIS Message Passing

GENESIS provides transparent communication services of standard MP and DSM as its integral components. The PVM communication is transparently provided by a service that is only a mapping of the standard PVM services onto the GENESIS communication services and benefits from additional services which are not provided by operating systems such as Unix or Windows.

Standard Message Passing. In order to hide distribution and make remote interprocess communication look identical to communication between local processes, we decided to build the whole operating system services of GENESIS around the interprocess communication facility. The standard MP service within the GENESIS parallel execution environment is provided by the Local IPC component of the microkernel, IPC Manager and Network Manager. These combine to provide a transparent local and remote MP service, which supports both the various qualities of service and group communication mechanisms.

GENESIS PVM. To deal with the weaknesses of the original PVM working in a Unix environment, we decided to move PVM into a operating system environment managing parallelism [4]. For GENESIS this involved the provision of transparency between local and remote operations for

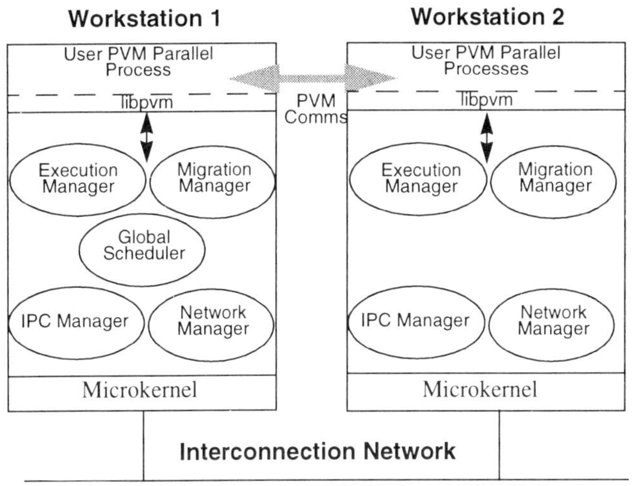

Figure 3: Architecture of PVM on GENESIS

IPC and management of processes and other resources. The architecture of GENESIS PVM is presented in Figure 3.

In this PVM server-free environment, PVM processes communicate directly with each other, significantly improving the performance of IPC. Processes are managed across the entire COW, with newly booted workstations automatically exploited and heavy loaded workstations being removed from the virtual machine. This is much better than Unix PVM where the user is responsible selecting individual workstations that make up the virtual machine.

Removing the server from the PVM model also improves the reliability of PVM applications. Under Unix PVM, each process depends on the local server for all interactions with other processes. If a server were to crash, the processes under its control do not have the ability to continue execution independently. Under GENESIS PVM, this dependency does not exist. This vulnerability in Unix PVM is extended further in that if a slave server loses contact with the master server, it will shut down, terminating all of the processes under its control. This event cannot occur in GENESIS PVM. Hence the reliability of PVM applications running under GENESIS PVM is improved.

3.2 Distributed Shared Memory

We decided to embody DSM within an operating system in order to create a transparent, easy to program and use environment and achieve high execution performance of parallel applications. Since shared memory can be viewed as a resource which requires management, we decided that the DSM system should be integrated into the Space Manager, as shown in Figure 4.

The placement of DSM in GENESIS' Space Manager has enabled several design requirements to be met [5]. Firstly, the programmer is able to use the shared memory as though it were physically shared, hence, the transparency requirement is met. Secondly, because the DSM system is

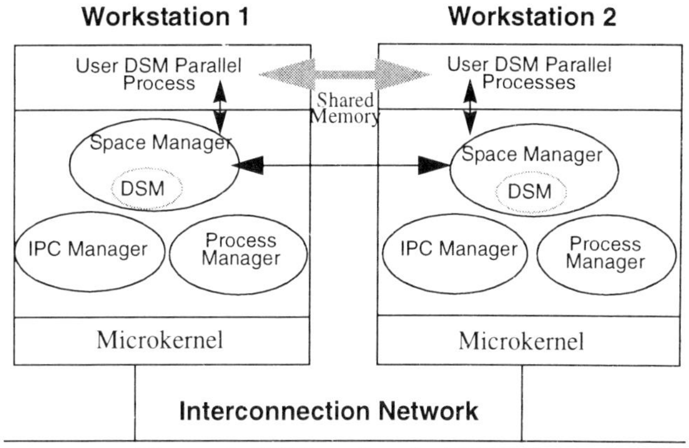

Figure 4: DSM system in GENESIS

in the operating system itself and is able to use its low level functions the efficiency requirements is met.

The GENESIS DSM system employs two consistency models: sequential and release. In the sequential consistency model, write operations are visible to all processes in the same sequence in which they occur. In the release consistency model, the weakest consistency model, the memory is made consistent only when a critical region is exited.

In GENESIS DSM synchronisation of processes sharing memory takes the form of semaphore type synchronisation for mutual exclusion. Barriers are used in GENESIS to co-ordinate executing processes. Processes block at a barrier until all processes have reached the same barrier; the processes then all continue execution.

3.3 Communication and Execution Primitives

The communication service primitives for the MP, PVM and DSM based programs are listed in Table 1. It can be seen that only two basic MP primitives are provided, those which allow a message to be sent and received. Similar primitives are provided in the PVM oriented services with the addition of buffer management primitives which allow messages to be packed and unpacked as required. Both MP and PVM, provide the barrier() primitive. The DSM based primitives, due to the shared memory model of communication, only require read, write and synchronisation primitives, such as wait(), signal(), and barrier().

Message Passing	PVM	DSM
send()	pvm_send()	read access
recv()	pvm_recv()	write access
barrier()	pvm_pkbuf()	wait()
	pvm_unpkbuf()	signal()
	pvm_barrier()	barrier()

Table 1: GENESIS Communication Primitives

The base send() and recv() primitives are provided as

system calls into the GENESIS microkernel, whereas every other primitive presented in this table is implemented as library call which basically is mapped onto the GENESIS send() and recv() calls.

Message Passing	PVM	DSM
proc_ncreate()	pvm_spawn()	proc_ncreate()
proc_exit()	pvm_exit()	proc_exit()

Table 2: GENESIS Execution Primitives

Table 2 lists the execution primitives used by the MP, PVM and DSM based programs. In general, only parallelism management services to support the instantiation and termination of parallel processes are required. For the MP and DSM based programs, the same primitives are used and include proc_ncreate() which allows a set of 'n' child processes to be created concurrently from an executable image (on disk); and proc_exit() which allows a process to terminate its execution.These primitives are provided as GENESIS library routines that are mapped to send() and recv() calls to the Execution Manager. The PVM primitives are implemented as library calls which are mapped onto the base proc_ncreate() and proc_exit() primitives [6].

4. Performance of Parallel Applications

The implemented GENESIS system was tested on a COW that is composed of 13 Sun 3/50 workstations interconnected by a shared 10 Mbps switched ethernet network. One of the workstations within the COW acts as a dedicated File Server and the remaining 12 workstations are used for normal user computation.

The experiments were performed with the number of workstations within the COW being varied from 1 to a total of 12. The number of child processes involved in the experiments were equal to the number of workstations (1:1 ratio). Each experiment was performed 20 times and the average result presented. The MP, PVM and DSM based programs detailed in the following sections were used by [7] and [8] and were adapted for execution on GENESIS.

4.1 Successive Over Relaxation (SOR)

The Red/Black SOR algorithm is used to solve partial differential equations. It uses a two dimensional array logically divided into a checker board pattern with each square being alternatively painted red and black. Calculating each row in succession, each element is computed as the average value of its four surrounding elements (above, left, bottom and right); a red element is calculated as the average of the sum of the four surrounding black elements; the black elements are calculated from the average of the surrounding four red elements. A number of iterations are performed to calculate the final array values.

Parallelism can be achieved by dividing the array into equally sized blocks of rows and performing the calculations on each block concurrently by separate child processes, following the SPMD model. Boundary rows must be shared between child processes and once calculated must be exchanged with their neighbouring processes. The programs that employ MP and PVM based communication services must exchange data between processes using messages, whereas with the DSM based program communication is implicit through the shared memory regions.

The performance, in the form of speed-up values, of the SOR parallel MP, PVM and DSM programs executed within the GENESIS environment is shown in Figure 5. The experiments were performed on an array size of 128 × 128 elements with 10 iterations to calculate the resultant array. It is evident from these results the MP version provides considerable performance improvements over the PVM and DSM versions.

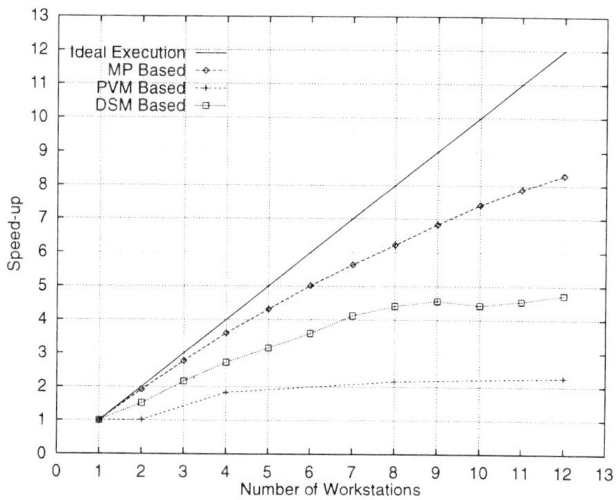

Figure 5: SOR Speed-up Results

4.2 Quicksort (QS)

The QS algorithm sorts an array of numbers into ascending (or descending) order. The algorithm is based on the recursive partitioning of an unsorted list into unsorted sub-lists such that all elements in the first sub-list are less than all the elements in the second sub-list. The recursive production of sublists continues until the size of the sublist reaches a threshold value (1024 in this case), at which point the sublist is sorted sequentially using the bubblesort.

Parallelism can be achieved by having multiple processes performing the partitioning and eventually the bubblesort on separate sections of the array of integers following the SPMD model. The interaction between the processes is either explicit using messages (MP and PVM) or implicit using shared memory (DSM).

The performance results for these experiments were obtained from executing QS on an array size of 128K integers. The performance results of the MP, PVM and DSM

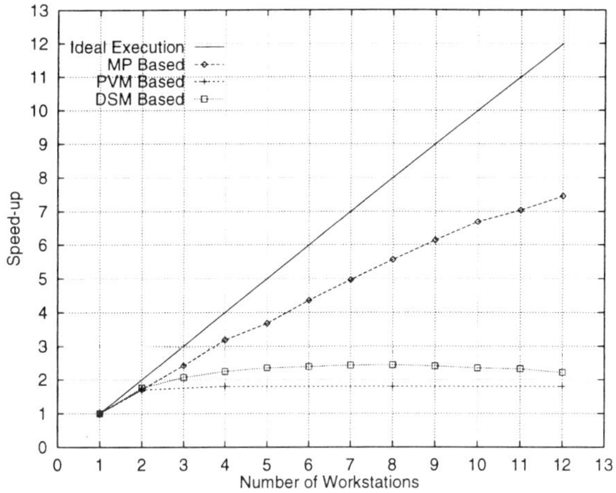

Figure 6: QS Speed-up Results

based QS parallel programs executed in the GENESIS environment, in the form of speed-up values, are presented in Figure 6. It is observed from these results that the QS program supported by MP provides better speed-up performance than those supported by PVM and DSM.

4.3 Travelling Salesman Problem (TSP)

The TSP exists when the minimum distance, or tour, is required to be found between all cities with specified distances between them. A city is selected as the starting city and all other cities must be visited exactly once. The basic algorithm used to solve this problem is based on an exhaustive search of all possible tours, where potential tours are solved until they exceed the current minimum tour length when the search of that particular tour is aborted. In this program a queue of partially solved tours (ordered by tour length) is maintained and the tours are solved recursively by the parallel processes.

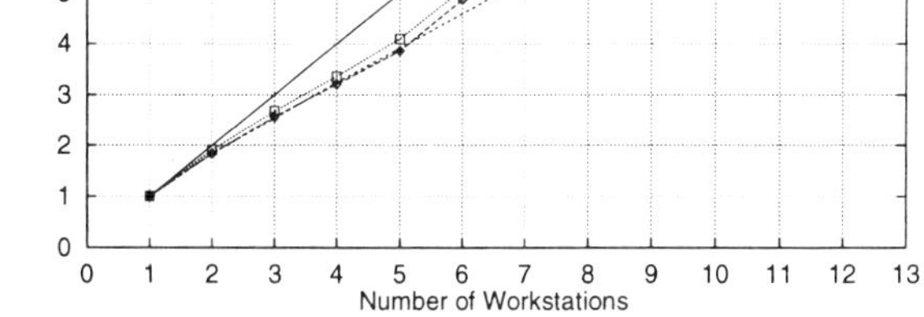

Figure 7: TSP Speed-up Results

The performance of the parallel MP, PVM and DSM program executed within the GENESIS environment are presented in Figure 7. The experiments were performed on 18 city tour, with the minimum threshold set to 13 cities. It is observed from these results that the TSP program employing DSM provides slightly better speed-up performance to those of the MP and PVM based programs. The reasons for these unexpected results are being studied now.

5. Easy-to-use and Program Environment

The GENESIS Parallelism Management System automatically provides the concurrent process creation service in a transparent manner and relieves the programmer from activities such as: the selection of workstations for the execution of their parallel programs; mapping processes to a virtual computer; process creation; and load balancing at process instantiation and execution.

The SOR, QS and TSP parallel applications only required one primitive to create and execute a set of parallel processes, where each creation request involves a sequence of operations. Until now the programming of this sequence and its operations have been the responsibility of the programmer. The operation and interaction between the kernel servers used to implement the concurrent creation service in a transparent manner is presented in Figure 8.

```
parent_code() {
    Issue call to Execution to create the child processes
    process_create( GROUP_CREATE, n, "child_prog" )
}
```

Request to group create multiple processes received by the Execution Manager through the **par_initialise**() call:

* The parent Execution Man which received the request contacts the Global Scheduler to select the set of workstations $W=\{w_1..w_m\}$ to be used and the number of child processes $N=\{n_1..n_m\}$ to be created on each workstation, where $m \leq n$ and $n = \sum n_j$, {j=1..m}
* The parent Execution Manager forwards on a request to create the respective number of child processes n_j to each of the Execution Managers on w_j using group communication
* For each workstation w_j $\{j=1..m\}$ in the workstation set W:
  — the Execution Manager contacts the Process Manager to allocate n_j new processes
  — the Execution Manager contacts the Space Manager to create memory for one child process
* The parent Execution Manager contacts the File Server to request the image of the child process be sent to the group of Execution Managers
* On each w_j the Execution Manager receives the child process executable image and populates the memory of the first child
  — the Execution Manager contacts the Space Manager to duplicate n_j-1 copies of the memory for of the children.
  — if w_j is remote then the Execution Manager returns to the Execution Manager on the parent workstation the names and details of the n_j children created on workstation w_j
* The parent Execution Manager contacts the Process Manager to link the n newly created children to the list of children instantiated by the parent

Figure 8: Group Process Creation Service

Figure 8 clearly shows that the underlying services required to complete the concurrent process creation are completely transparent to the parent process and thus to the programmer. The high level of transparency presented in this system considerably simplifies the writing of parallel programs for execution on COWs, thus relieving the programmer of time consuming and error prone activities.

6. Related Systems

Message Passing Based Systems. A number of systems have been developed to support the execution of parallel applications on Clusters of Workstations. Process instantiation in PVM is [9] based on a single creation mechanisms, therefore the total instantiation time is linearly related to the number of child processes to be created. This method of instantiation experiences serious scalability problems, as the number of workstations and child processes increases.

The approach taken with PVM has been to build an environment on top of existing network operating systems. This approach allows these environments to use the services of the underlying operating system, which improves the portability of these environments to different architectures. A major disadvantage is that these environments must use the higher level services provided by these network operating systems, which may not provide the desired functionality. As a results, the environments running as server and library code may have to both provide similar code to achieve the desired functionality and compete with other processes, which leads to increased overheads, duplication of services and poor execution performance.

Distributed Shared Memory. Much of the effort in DSM research has concentrated on improving performance of the systems, rather than reaching a more integrated DSM design [10]. Munin and Treadmarks are the best known DSM systems. Munin is a DSM system which uses multiple consistency protocols and runs on top of the V operating system. The initialisation stage of an application using Munin requires the application programmer to define the number of workstations to be used. The names of the workstations are then read from a file containing a list of workstations which has been created by the application programmer. Having identified the workstations on which the application will run, the programmer on each workstation must create a thread, initialise the shared data and create the synchronisation barriers [11].

TreadMarks is implemented on top of Unix. As in Munin, the application programmer is required to have substantial input into the initialisation of DSM processes by either entering the number of workstations required to execute an application and their names as command line arguments or creating a workstation list file which contains a list of the workstations that comprise the COW [12].

Execution Environments. An improvement to the common approach of the PVM system executing on top of an existing operating system is through the extension and enhancement of the underlying operating system to provide services and features supporting parallel processing.

The Beowulf system exploits distributed process space (BPROC) [13] in order to manage parallel processes. There are two basic issues of BPROC supporting distributed processes, ghost processes that represent remote processes on remote computers, and the method of starting processes. Processes can be started on remote computers if the logon operation into that remote computer was completed successfully. Starting processes in Beowulf is only done via *rsh*, sequentially, although these two features are hidden from the user by PVM. Another weakness of Beowulf is that BPROC does not address resource allocation or load balancing. The project does not attempt, at this stage, to provide transparent process migration.

The NOW system is based on the Solaris operating system from Sun Microsystems and combines specialised libraries and servers with enhancements to the kernel itself in the form of the scheduling and communication kernel modules. The enhancements to the operating system have been in the form of a global operating system layer (GLUnix) to provide network wide process, file and virtual memory management [14]. The limitations of running the system in user mode relate to the loss of transparency introduced when executing processes remotely.

The MOSIX system provides enhanced and transparent communication and scheduling services within the kernel, and also employs PVM to provide the high level parallelism support. MOSIX is based on the Unique Home-Node (UHN) model [15], where all of users processes appear to be run on the local workstation, but due to load imbalances, process migration may transparently migrate processes to a remote workstation. Once migrated, the process is divided into two, the deputy component which remains on the local workstations or UHN, and a remote component which encapsulates the running process on the remote workstation. The deputy component provides a method of handling all UHN dependent functions such as communication, signals and site dependent system calls.

A common and serious problem exists with the PVM, Beowulf, NOW and MOSIX systems, which is amplified when they attempt to support parallel processing. Each of these systems only supports the creation of single processes. Although the primitives provided by each of these systems enable the user to request multiple processes to be created, internally they are only created one at a time. This problem is the result of the reliance each of these systems have on the underlying network operating systems, which were designed and implemented to only support the creation of single processes. Another major problem of these systems is that they do not provide complete transparency with the exception of MOSIX, and a virtual machine is not set up automatically and dynamically.

7. Conclusions

GENESIS is a comprehensive system that provides programmers with an environment which allows them to use two forms of interprocess communication services: message passing or shared memory; within a single programming and execution environment. MP can be used either as raw MP or through PVM and shared memory is used through the DSM system. These services are integrated into the GENESIS operating and resource management system which has been built from scratch. The DSM system has been incorporated into the memory management system making it an integral feature of the operating system. The GENESIS system includes PVM which runs on top of the operating system to add an easy-to-use message passing mechanism to the programming environment.

The performance results indicate that the MP and PVM versions on QS and SOR are better than the DSM version. We believe however, that the ease of use provided by allowing programmers to use the shared memory paradigm in this environment outweighs the performance loss of DSM. Novice programmers will be furnished with an environment in which they can carry out parallel programming without having to write and debug unfamiliar message passing programs. In the case of TSP very little performance difference is exhibited by the three paradigms, the reasons for these results are being investigated. PVM shows slightly worse performance than MP but the advantage of providing this well known environment within GENESIS outweighs the lack of performance. The GENESIS system allows programmers to use the paradigm with which they are most comfortable and still achieve performance improvements over sequential execution.

8. References

[1] A. Goscinski. *"Towards and Operating System Managing Parallelism of Computing on Clusters of Workstations"*. (Submitted) Future Generation Computer Systems, 1999.

[2] A. Goscinski. "Distributed Operating Systems: The Logical Design". Addison-Wesley, 1991.

[3] D. De Paoli, A. Goscinski, M. Hobbs and G. Wickham. *"The RHODOS Microkernel, Kernel Servers and Their Cooperation"*. Proceedings of The IEEE First International Conference on Algorithms and Architectures for Parallel Processing (ICA3PP-95). pp. 345-354, Brisbane, April, 1995.

[4] J. Rough, A. Goscinski, and D. De Paoli, *"PVM on the RHODOS Distributed Operating System"*, Proc. of the 4th European PVM/MPI Users' Group Meeting, *Recent Advances in Parallel Virtual Machine and Message Passing Interface*, pp. 208-215, Cracow, Poland, November 3-5, 1997.

[5] J. Silcock and A. Goscinski. *The RHODOS DSM System*. Microprocessor and Microsystems, **22**(3-4), pp. 183-196, 1998.

[6] M. Hobbs and A. Goscinski. *"The RHODOS Remote Process Creation Facility Supporting Parallel Execution on Distributed Systems"*. J. of High Performance Computing. **3**(1), pp. 23-30. December 1996.

[7] H. Lu. *Message Passing Versus Distributed Shared Memory on Networks of Workstations*. Ph.D. Thesis, Rice University, May 1995.

[8] P. Keleher, Private Communication, April 1996.

[9] D. Beguelin, J. Dongarra, A. Giest, R. Manchek, S. Otto and J. Walpole. *"PVM: Experiences, Current Status and Future Directions"*. Oregon Graduate Institute of Science and Technology. Tech. Rep. CSE-94-015. April 1994.

[10] L. Iftode and J. P. Singh, *Shared Virtual Memory: Progress and Challenges*, Tech. Rep. TR-552-97, Dept. of Computer Science, Princeton University, October 1997.

[11] J. Carter, *Efficient Distributed Shared Memory Based on Multi-Protocol Release Consistency*, Ph.D. Thesis, Rice University, September 1993.

[12] *Concurrent Programming with TreadMarks*, ParallelTools, L.L.C. 1994.

[13] E. Hendriks, 'BPROC: Beowulf Distributed Process Space', Web Address, *http://www.beowulf.org/software/bproc.html*, April 1999.

[14] P. Ghormley, D. Petrou, S. Rodrigues, A. Vahdat and T. Anderson, 'GLUnix: a Global Layer for a Network of Workstations', *Software—Practice and Experience*, **28**(9), pp. 929-961, 1998.

[15] A. Barak, O. La'adan and A. Shiloh, 'Scalable Cluster Computing with MOSIX for LINUX', *Proc. Linux Expo '99*, pp. 95-100, Raleigh, N.C., May 1999.

Predictability of Bulk Synchronous Programs Using MPI

Andrea Zavanella
Dipartimento di Informatica
Universitá di Pisa Italy
mail zavanell@di.unipi.it

Alessandro Milazzo
Dipartimento di Informatica
Universitá di Pisa Italy
milazzo@cli.di.unipi.it

Abstract

The BSP cost model provides a general framework to design efficient and portable data-parallel algorithms. Execution costs of BSP programs are predicted combining a limited number of program and machine dependent parameters. BSP programs can be written using several programming tools. In this work we explore the predictability of Bulk Synchronous programs implemented with the Message Passing Interface. Two classic computational geometry problems: the Convex Hull (CH) and the Lower Envelope (LE) are considered as cases of study. Efficient BSP algorithms have been implemented using MPI and executed on three different parallel architectures: a Fujitsu AP1000 (distributed memory), a CRAY T3E (distributed shared memory) and a cluster of PCs (Backus). The paper compares the degree of predictability on these architectures analysing the main sources of error.

1. Introduction

The Bulk Synchronous Parallelism (BSP) is a "bridge" model for parallel computing developed to overcome the dependence from architecture when designing efficient parallel algorithms [13]. A BSP computer is a collection of p pairs of processor-memory nodes, a communication network and a synchronisation facility. A BSP program is a sequence of supersteps divided by global synchronisations. Each superstep includes three phases in which each processor executes: (i) *local computation*, (ii) *send or receive messages*, (iii) *global synchronisation*. The structure of a BSP computer and of a BSP superstep are shown in fig. 1. A touple (p, g, L, s) characterises the performance of a BSP computer. The g parameter, named *network permeability*, is the number of time steps employed to send a one-word message in the case of continuous traffic. A time step is the time needed to perform an elementary local operation (such as a FP operation). The parameter s (speed) is the number of time steps per second executed by each processor. A communication pattern where each node sends or receives at most h words is known as h-relation. The main assumption of the BSP model is that delivering a h-relations costs $(h \cdot g)$ time steps. The parameter L which is the *synchronisation periodicity* is the number of time steps required to perform a global synchronisation and for the theoretical bound on g to be realizable. Assuming that $w(i)$ is the number of time steps for the processor i local computation, a formal definition for the *work* W parameter is given in Eq. 1. The h parameter can be defined in different ways, in this work we made the assumption that $h = Max(h_r, h_s)$ where h_r and h_s are the maximum number of messages received or sent by any processor.

$$W = max_{(0 \leq i \leq p)} w(i) \tag{1}$$

There are several possibilities for the definition of the superstep cost, which generally differ for some constant factor, in this work, according to [12] we assume that:

$$T_{sstep} = W + h \cdot g + L \tag{2}$$

Assuming that W^j and h^j are the W and the h parameters for superstep j, the cost of a m supersteps program is:

$$T_{prog} = \sum_{j=0}^{m} W^j + h^j g + L \tag{3}$$

Designing parallel programs using BSP means finding a good balance between local computation (to minimise waste of CPU time) and communication (to minimise h). In other other cost models different trade-off are suggested: PRAM [4] does not account for communication, LogP [3] provides a model for point-to-point communications while CGM [2] charges a fixed cost for each communication round. An extension of BSP which accounts for unbalanced communication patterns, the E-BSP, is described in [8]. Juurlink and Wijshoff show how to improve BSP

[0]This Work has been partially supported by the italian M.U.R.S.T. (Project MOSAICO), Andrea Zavanella is partially supported by a TM-R grant

1066-6192/99 $10.00 © 1999 IEEE

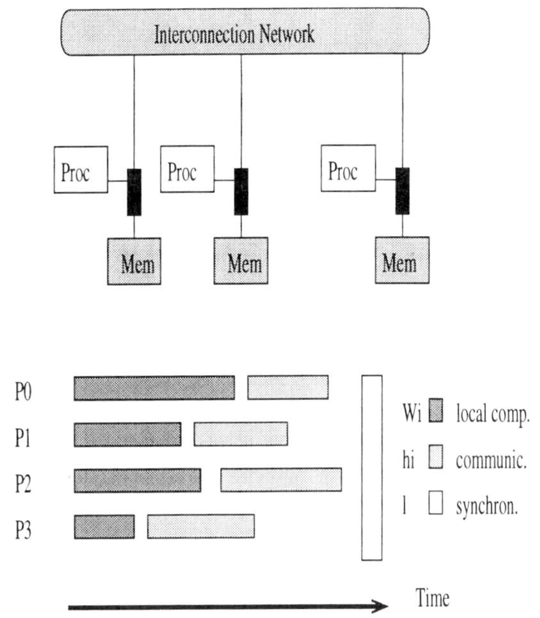

Figure 1. A BSP computer and a BSP superstep.

predictability by extending the model with a further parameter g' which is defined as the *permeability* in the case of a sparse h-relation (i.e. a scatter operation). The aim of E-BSP is differentiates between communication patterns that are insensitive to the bisection bandwidth and those that are not. Data parallel computations can be easily expressed in a BSP style using severals message passing tools particularly those with a SPMD[1] style like MPI [9] or the ad hoc designed BSP-lib [7]. Theoretically, once the BSP parameters of a given machine are known, programs can be designed in a BSP style to optimise communications and load balancing. The first goal of this work is exploring the BSP predictability when bulk synchronous programs are written using MPI. The main problems using MPI come from that synchronisations and "bulk" communications within supersteps are not optimised: messages are not combined and destinations are not randomized. The stability of the g parameter for modern parallel computer has been addressed in [6]. Skillicorn et al. in [12] has proposed an asymptotic value for g to modulate the effect of the start-up time according to the message size. Finally Gerbassiotis and Petrini have proposed different guidelines on the assessment of real computers values for BSP parameters [5]. Their results seem to support the idea of a more complex model to deal with both balanced and unbalanced communication patterns in some way supporting the idea behind the E-BSP model.

[1]Single Program Multiple Data

In order to evaluate the BSP predictability of MPI programs we have selected two computational geometry problems: the Convex Hull problem and the Lower Edge as cases of study. The BSP algorithms are briefly described in Sec. 2. In Sec. 4 the performance of a MPI version of CH and LE is compared to the prediction of the BSP model on a Fujitsu AP1000 [1] architecture. In Sec. 5-6 the results for the CH on a CRAY T3E [10] and on a cluster of PCs (Backus) are presented. Sec. 7 summarises the results of our experiments and present our conclusions.

2. The Cases of Study: CH and LE BSP Algorithms

CH algorithm : the algorithm adopted for the Convex Hull(CH) problem only uses two supersteps and the amount of data communicated is extremely small and balanced. In the first superstep each processor computes the Upper Hull(UH) and the Lower Hull(LH) of the local chunk of points using $2(n/p)log(n/p)$ operations. Each processor, can now computes and exchanges the average slope m_u and m_l of UH and LH with neighbours processors. The overall cost of the first superstep is then $2(n/p)log(n/p) + 2n/p + 4g + L$. In the second superstep each processor filters UH and LH using the information received by the neighbours to compute its portion of the global UH and LH. The upper bound for this operation, which can be unbalanced, is just $2(n/p)$. A scheme of the algorithm to compute the UH of a given set of points S is given in figure 2. The BSP cost to compute the CH of n points on p processors is given by Eq. 4.

$$T_{ch}^{bsp}(n,p) = T_{ss1} + T_{ss2} \tag{4}$$

A bound is given by Eq. 5:

$$T_{ss1} = (2(n/p)log(n/p) + 2(n/p) + 4g + L) \tag{5}$$

$$T_{ss2} = 2(n/p) + 4g + L) + (2(n/p) + L) \tag{6}$$

then:

$$T_{ch}^{bsp}(n,p) < 2(n/p)(log(n/p) + 2) + 4g + 2L \tag{7}$$

LE algorithm : the algorithm employed for the LE problem has a possibly unbalanced computational phase and a not completely predictable communication step. It uses three supersteps, the first one computes the LE on the local portion of the set and then all processors exchange the positions of the rightmost vertical lines. The cost of this step is $(n/p)log(n) + 2pg + L$. The second step computes the group of segments crossing each of the lines l_j received and

```
INPUT:
S set of points distribut-
ed over processors
OUTPUT:
 UH(S) distributed over processors
begin
 forall i do

  ss1:
   sequential algorithm to com-
pute UH(i)
   computes mu=average x/y ra-
tio in UH(i)
   exchanges m with processors i-
1 and i+1

  ss2:
   with t=(p1,p2) and m(t)=dx/dy in UH(i)
   if mu(i+1)>m(t) then eliminate p2
   if mu(i-1)>m(t) then eliminate p1

end
```

Figure 2. UH algorithm

```
INPUT:
S set of segments distribut-
ed over processors
OUTPUT:
LE(S) distributed over processors
begin
 forall i do
  ss1:

   computes sequentially LE(i)
   computes l(i) and broadcasts it

  ss2:
   computes Seg(j) set of seg-
ments crossing l(j)
      forall j
       send Seg(j) to proc j
       receive Seg from j
       Q=LE(i)- Seg(j)+Seg

  ss3:
   computes LE(Q)
end
```

Figure 3. LE algorithm

it sends them to the processor j. In this superstep h and W can only be bounded by n and n/p respectively. Thus the superstep costs $(n/p) + ng + L$. In the third superstep the segments left and those received are merged to build the set Q. Finally the local portion of LE is computed on Q. To assign a cost to the third superstep we assume that the number of segments in Q still remains n/p and then we have that the cost is $(n/p)log(n) + L$. A scheme of the algorithm is given in figure 3. The BSP cost to compute the LE of n segments is given by Eq. 8.

$$T_{le}^{bsp}(n,p) = T_{ss1} + T_{ss2} + T_{ss3} \tag{8}$$

$$T_{ss1} = (n/p)log(n) + 2pg + L \tag{9}$$

$$T_{ss2} = (n/p) + ng + L \tag{10}$$

$$T_{ss3} = (n/p)log(n) + L \tag{11}$$

A bound is given by Eq. 12:

$$T_{le}^{bsp}(n,p) < (n/p)(2log(n)+1) + (2p+n)g + 3L \tag{12}$$

3. Experiments

The experiments have been realized using the same programs and recompiling with the local CC compiler (using the `-O3` option). The values produced are averages on 100 experiments and the times have been measured using the `MPI_WTime` function. The data set size for all the experiments varies from 2000 to 20000 elements. A MPI probe program has been developed to compute the BSP communication parameters following the guidelines of the *bsp_probe* program included in the latest version of the bsp_lib. The program computes an average value for the parameters on a set of microbenchmarks (i.e. shift and total-exchange for communications). The evaluation of the speed parameter s simply execute an average on the execution of a F-P multiplication. The errors are evaluated using the following method: let T_m be the measured time and T_t the time predicted by the model, then the error is given by: $|T_m - T_t|/min(T_m, T_t)$.

4. Fujitsu AP1000

The first set of experiments are made on a Fujitsu AP1000 architecture [1] using a native implementation of MPI [11]. The AP1000 employed has 128 processing nodes. Each node includes a SPARC processor with 25Mhz clock and 16Mb RAM memory and 128Kb of cache memory. The interconnection network (T-NET) is a bidimensional torus with 25Mb/s bandwidth per link. The results reported for CH and LE are for execution with 64 and 128 processors. The comparison of predicted and measured times in Fig. 4 underlines that the model is extremely pessimistic for this architecture. The predicted times is in average 65% off the measured times for the CH processors and 20% off for the LE. In the case of CH the problem is partially due to the estimation of the number of points to be eliminated in the second superstep which is just an upper bound. However a certain difficulty is also related to the evaluation of the s parameter since not all of the FP operations involved in CH are multiplications. The model works better for the LE where the number of operations can be estimated with a larger degree of accuracy. It is worth to notice that, in this case, the second communication phase is difficult to cost due to the variable number of segments to be communicated. Furthermore here communication is not negligible and communication pattern is not perfectly balanced.

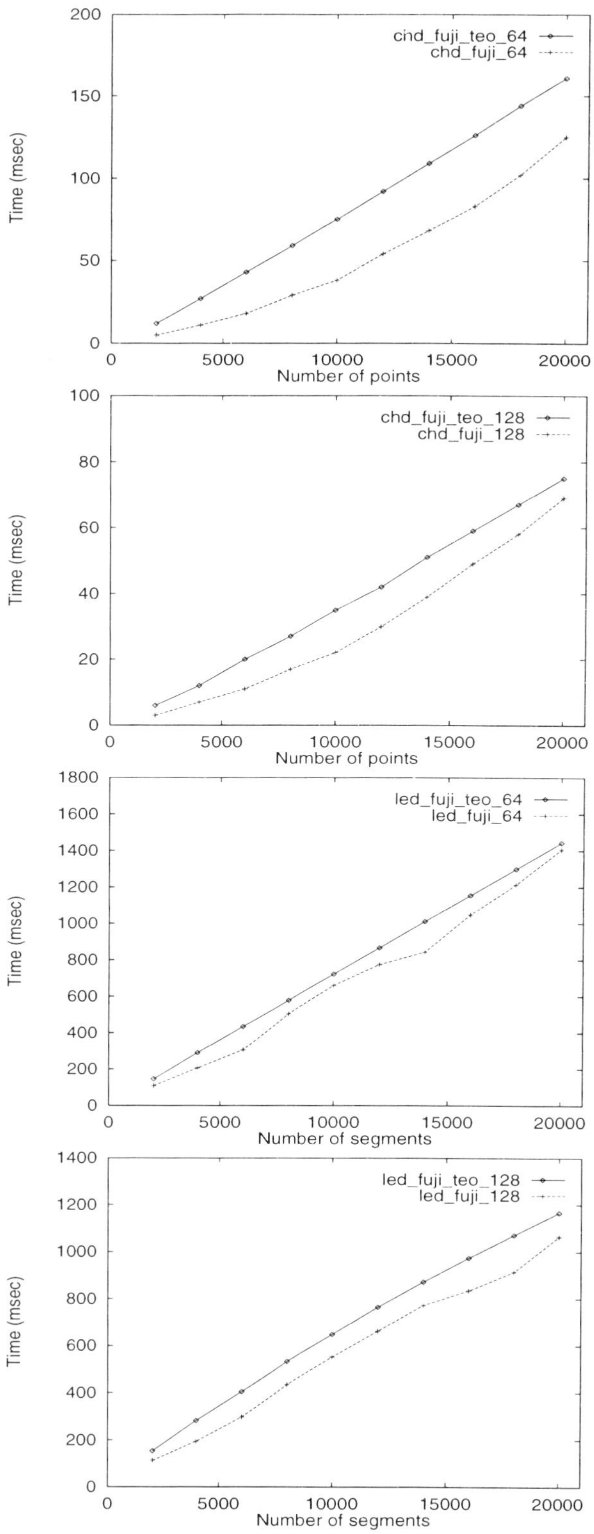

Figure 4. Predicted and measured times of CH and LE on Fuji AP1000

5. Cray T3E

The second set of experiments has been performed on a CRAY T3E computer [10]. The computer used has 256 nodes Alpha DEC 21164 clocked at 600Mhz with peak performance of 1200 MFLOPS. Each node has a 128 or 256 Mbytes of RAM and the 3-dimensional torus has a 480 Mbytes/sec of peak bandwidth for each of the six directions. The MPI version adopted is the one included in the MPT 1.2. The experiments have been executed using 4,8,16 and 32 processors. The curves in Fig. 5 show that predicted and measured times are in average 18% off which is probably due to a better estimation of the s parameter.

6. Backus a cluster of PCs

The third set of experiments has been performed on Backus: a cluster of 10+1 PCs running Linux. Each node has a Pentium II CPU clocked at 266Mhz with 128Mb of S-DRAM. PCs in Backus are connected by a Fast-Ethernet network with a bi-directional 100Mbit switch. The MPI version available on Backus was MPICH 1.1.1. The experiments have been executed using the cluster as single user and therefore times are not affected by external contention. The experiments in Fig. 6 show that the measured times are in average 29% off the predicted. We also observe that accuracy decreases as the number of processors increases. Moreover the experiments with larger data set have also larger errors.

7. Conclusions and Related Works

We have only explored a limited range of data parallel applications in which communication and computation are

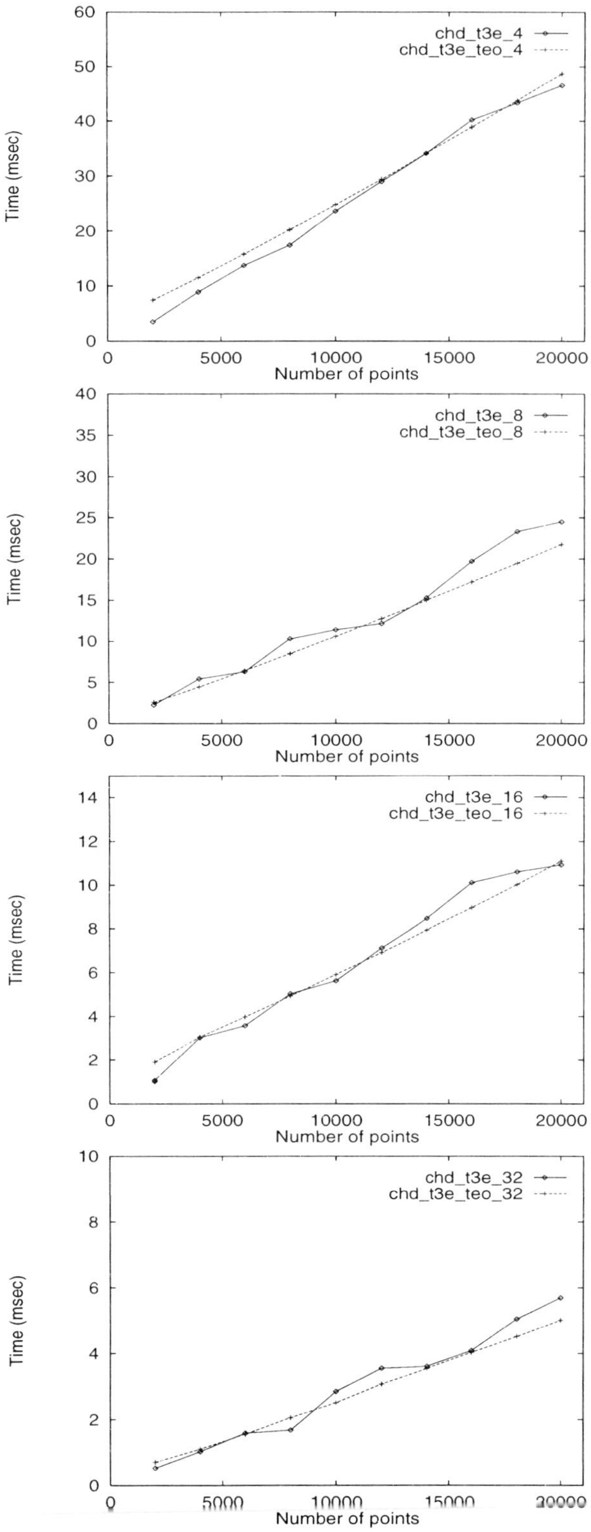

Figure 5. Predicted and measured times of CH on CRAY T3E

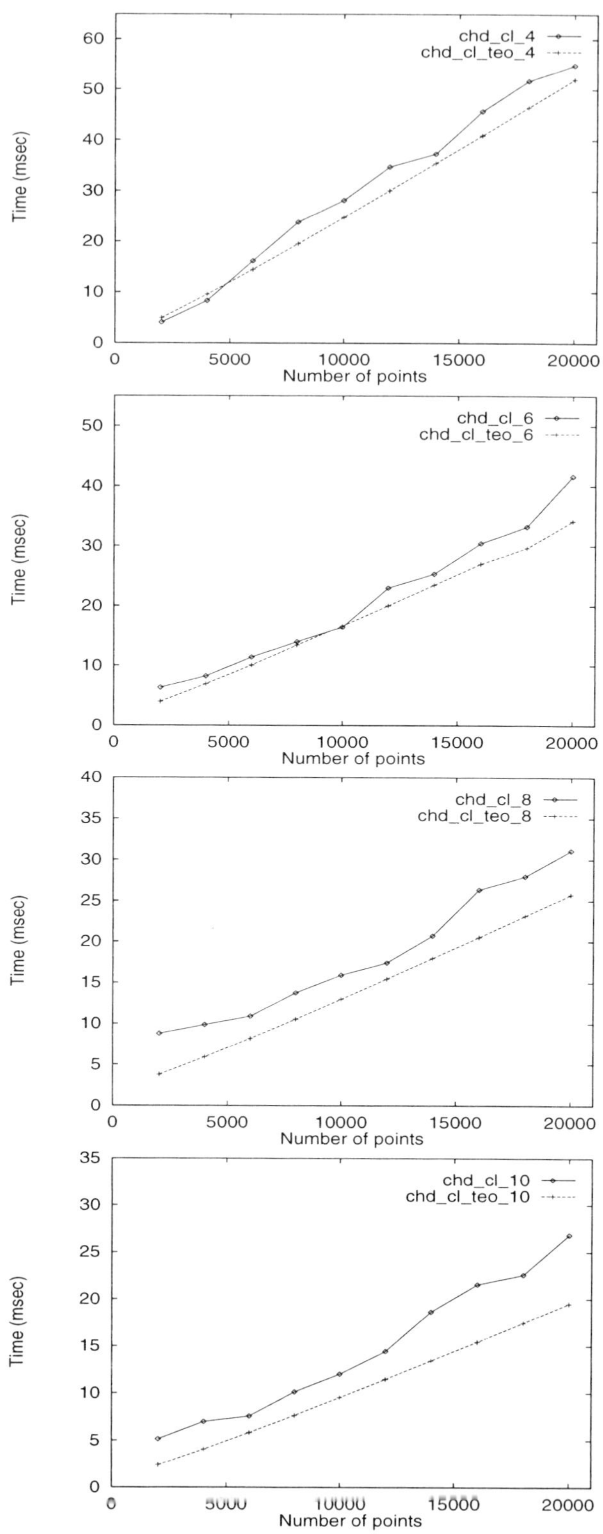

Figure 6. Predicted and measured times of CH on Backus

not completely oblivious. We met the conclusion that a reliable costs prediction of bulk programs written in MPI is still a difficult goal to achieve. The experiments on three different architectures have a minimun of 19% to maximun of 65%. Other works have investigated the weakness of the BSP model in presence of unbalanced communication patterns [8, 5] and in absence of a specific support to combine and randomize messages. Since communication in CH is almost negligible, and MPI has no specific support for BSP communications these results can only explain some of the results of LE in the Fujitsu AP1000. In the other experiments with CH we see that another difficult aspect of evaluate is computation. Since the predicted values are computed over upper bound on the number of operations the results in Sec. 6 are due to an overestimation of the s parameter. In synthesis, the problems of the BSP model to predict the performance of bulk programs written in MPI are:

- estimate g in the case of unbalanced communication pattern;
- derive exact h and w for each superstep;
- account for the end-point contention;
- estimate s in a machine independent way;

The last of these points is strictly connected to sequential model which is, at the end, the von Neumann model. In other words, we claim that in addition to the communication aspects, to achieve predictability of parallel programs, we should describe modern uniprocessors with more than a single scalar.

References

[1] Australian National University. *The Fujitsu AP1000.*

[2] E. Caceres, F. Dehne, A. Ferreira, and P. Flocchini. Efficient parallel graph algorithms for coarse grained multicomputers and BSP. *Lecture Notes in Computer Science*, 1256:390–406, 1997.

[3] D. Culler, R. Karp, D. Patterson, A. Sahay, K. Schauser, E. Santos, R. Subramonian, and von T. Eicken. Logp: Towards a Realistic Model of Parallel Computation. In *Proceedings of the 4th ACM SIGPLAN*, May 1993.

[4] S. Fortune and J. Wyllie. Parallelism in random access machines. In *Conference Record of the Tenth Annual ACM Symposium on Theory of Computing*, pages 114–118, San Diego, California, 1–3 May 1978.

[5] A. Gerbessiotis and F. Petrini. Network performance assessment under the bsp model. In S. Gorlatch, editor, *CMPP98 First International Workshop on Constructive Methods for Parallel Programming*, number 9805 in MPI. Universitat Passau, May 1998.

[6] J. Hill, S. Donaldson, and D. Skillicorn. Stability of communication performance in practice: from the cray t3e to networks of workstations. Technical Report PRG-TR-33-97, Programming Research Group, Oxford University Computing Laboratory, October 1997.

[7] J. Hill, B. McColl, D. Stefanescu, M. Goudreau, K. Lang, S. Rao, T. Suel, T. Tsantilas, and R. Bisseling. Bsplib: The bsp programming library. Technical Report May, Oxford University Computing Laboratory, 1997.

[8] B. H. H. Juurlink and H. A. G. Wijshoff. A quantitative comparison of parallel computation models. *ACM Transactions on Computer Systems*, 16(3):271–318, Aug. 1998.

[9] Message Passing Interface Forum. MPI: A message-passing interface standard. *International Journal of Supercomputer Applications*, 8(3/4), 1994. Also available as Technical Report CS-94-230, Computer Science Dept., University of Tennessee, Knoxville, TN, 1994.

[10] S. L. Scott. Synchronization and communication in the t3e multiprocessor. In *Proc. ASPLOS VII*, Cambridge, MA, Octobe 1996.

[11] D. Sitsky, D. Walsh, and C. Johnson. An efficient implementation of the Message Passing Interface (MPI) on the Fujitsu AP1000. Technical report, Department of Computer Science, Australian National University, Canberra, Australia, Oct. 1994.

[12] D. Skillicorn, J. Hill, and B. McColl. Questions and answers about bsp. *Scientific Programming*, 6(3):249–274, Fall 1997.

[13] L. G. Valiant. A bridging model for parallel computation. *Communications of the ACM*, 33(8):103, August 1990.

Session 4:
Web Based Computing II

Gypsy: A Component-based Mobile Agent System

Mehdi Jazayeri and Wolfgang Lugmayr
Distributed Systems Group
Technical University of Vienna, Austria
{jazayeri,lugmayr}@infosys.tuwien.ac.at

Abstract

Gypsy is a component-based, dynamically extensible environment for mobile agent systems. The runtime environment consists of lightweight servers that provide a distributed execution environment for agents, and a remote administration tool that supports the set-up and shutdown of servers and agents. A server hosts a number of places to which agents may move to execute their functions. Each place is specialized to support a particular service. A supervisor agent may contain several worker agents that may execute concurrently. A supervisor agent travels from place to place according to its itinerary and launches its workers at appropriate places. A mobile agent is the basic abstraction from which all other components, including servers and supervisor agents, are constructed. The primary goal of the Gypsy project is to build a multi-language, extensible environment for experimenting with mobile agents as a programming paradigm. The environment is implemented in Java and currently supports agents written in the Java or Python programming languages. This paper presents an overview of the Gypsy project, the current system architecture and the design of the important components of the Gypsy system.

1 Introduction

Mobile agents are programs with persistent identity which move around a network on their own volition and can communicate with their environment and with other agents. These systems use specialized servers to interpret the agent's behavior and communicate with other servers. Mobile agents may execute on any machine in a network without the necessity of having the agent code pre-installed on every machine the agent could visit. Mobile agents represent a new model in the evolution of executable content on the Internet, introducing program code that can be transported along with state information. White [23] provided much of the original inspiration for including mobility support in programming languages. The paper [3] compares different approaches to distributed computation including client-server, remote evaluation, and mobile code. The paper [10] compares mobile agents and push systems. The paper [17] describes a fine-grained approach to mobility, where individual program statements are mobile rather than classes.

This new concept for network computing has gained increasing interest, especially in the network management and mobile computing areas. Numerous software platforms for mobile agents have appeared and are still appearing: Aglets [15], D'Agents (formerly called Agent Tcl) [7], ARA [20], Grasshopper [22], Mole [21], and Voyager [19]. Most agent systems such as Aglets, Mole or Gypsy use Java and the Java virtual machine as mobile code system, where classes can be loaded at runtime over the network. Each of these platforms places emphasis on different aspects of mobile agents: Aglets on security, D'Agents and ARA on multi-language support, and Voyager on integration of an ORB. Currently, most agent systems do not interoperate with each other. Instead, most of these systems, such as Grasshopper, plan to implement the CORBA Mobile Agent System Interoperability Facility (MASIF) [18] for agent system interoperability.

Many issues on mobile agents are still subject of discussion [9], as can be seen from the various different implementation approaches. The main concerns involve tradeoffs between the degree of functional complexity, maintainability, and scalability of agent systems to wide-scale usage.

The Gypsy project has the following goals:

1. Implementation of a flexible and dynamically extensible environment for experimenting with mobile agent programming.

2. Investigation of mobile agents as a programming paradigm.

3. Discovery of mobile agent design patterns.

4. Support for mobile and detached computing.

5. Multi-language support based on language implementations in the Java programming language.

6. Effective security implementation for use in large networks.

7. Interoperability with other agent systems.

The current implementation supports goals 1, 4, and 5, and provides the platform for goals 2 and 3. Goal 6 is only minimally supported by extending the standard Java security mechanisms. Goal 7 is still not supported.

Gypsy uses a component-based approach for dynamically configuring servers, communicators and places through the use of mobile agents as a programming paradigm. The environment is implemented in the Java programming language and supports Python and Java scripting. The current status is described in its web site `http://www.infosys.tuwien.ac.at/Gypsy/` where the current implementation is available for download.

The rest of the paper is structured as follows: Section 2 gives an overview on the interaction details of the system. Section 3 describes the system architecture of Gypsy, featuring agents and servers. The following sections discuss our approach to mobility and security. The paper closes with a comparison with related work, current status and future work in the Gypsy project.

2 Gypsy Scenario

This section presents a scenario that we use as a driving use-case for Gypsy applications. This section will first give a user view of the problem and then the Gypsy system's view. The purpose of this section is to introduce Gypsy's terminology and components at a high level. The following sections will provide the details.

A user wants to fly to London the next weekend and wants to find the lowest-cost flight available. Rather than performing the search himself, he launches his mobile agent to do the work for him and report the results when they are available. The agent is launched from the user's portable device (telephone, laptop, appliance, etc.) which runs the Gypsy user interface. The agent may be specialized by the user for this particular task or it may take default values from the user's predefined profile. Once the agent is launched, the user may disconnect his portable device. The user has a permanent *user place* on a *home server* where his agents report to and wait on their return. The user may at any time connect to his home server place and inquire about his various agents. Besides user places, Gypsy servers may house a number of other *places* specialized for particular services. For example, a flight reservation place provides flight reservation services. A place registry provides information on all available places.

To construct an agent in this case, the person chooses a *flight search task* from a task list and fills out the relevant forms, e.g., travel date, deadline (need the information the next day), reporting period (send status message every 5 hops), and query properties. These properties enable the agent to ask a *place registry* for URIs of useful places to visit. A list of properties would be, in this case, *London, Heathrow, Gatwick*. The task also has, by default, a list of predefined properties such as *flight, airline, travel agency* which may also be edited by the user. Then the user adds a starting place, e.g., his favorite travel agency, to the route of the agent and launches it. If no starting URI is given, the agent will be launched to the home server to query the local place registry.

The agent arrives at the starting place and queries the local database for inexpensive flights. Then it queries the local place registry through the place interface for additional interesting places to visit. When the agent has reached its maximum reporting period, it sends a status message with its current results back to the owner by email or to the home server by a *status messenger* agent. When the agent has queried enough servers or the deadline has arrived, the agent returns to the user place on the home server. This place receives the agent and, depending on the notification strategy, informs the user by email or SMS message that the agent has returned.

The user asks the home server to forward the waiting agent(s) to his user interface. The returning agent is then given an *embedded agent*, called *result writer*, which formats, interprets and displays the result to the user on his portable appliance.

This scenario exemplifies the simplest use of Gypsy, but there are other issues that may arise and Gypsy addresses. For example, what happens if the user wants to recall his agent before the deadline is passed? He can launch a new agent that follows exactly the same path in order to catch up and find the original agent. It is probably more efficient, however, if this new agent starts at the latest known location of the original agent. Another issue involves more complicated tasks that consist of several simpler tasks. For example, what if the user wants to make hotel and theater reservations in addition to the flight reservation? Gypsy supports *supervisor agents* that consist of *worker agents*, each of which is responsible for a particular *task*. The supervisor agent uses a *constraint manager* which is responsible for ensuring that the results of the tasks are compatible, e.g., that the flight arrival date is the starting date of the hotel reservation and the hotel checkout date is the same as the flight departure date.

Figure 1 shows the main concepts of Gypsy as described in this section. Servers are grouped into regions. A region is an administrative unit which is administered using a remote administration tool. A log server in each region records log

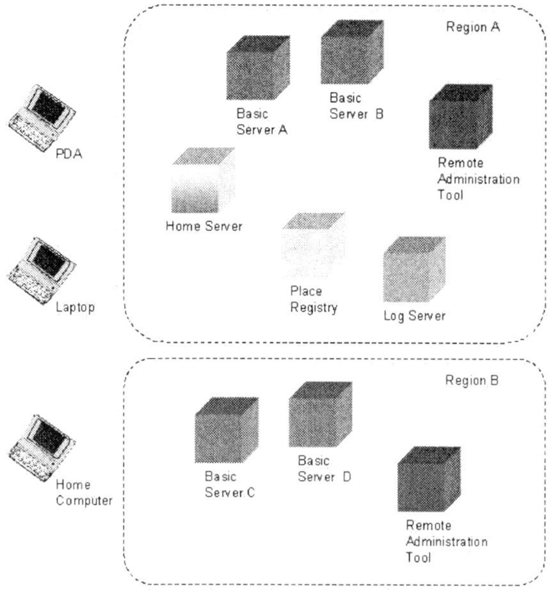

Figure 1. Gypsy Region Components

messages received from servers in the region.

In the following sections, we describe Gypsy's components and mechanisms in more detail.

3 Gypsy Concepts

Agents in the Gypsy environment travel between places. These places are located at servers where they provide special services to the visiting agents (Figure 2). A server is a process on a host and can run several different places. The server also provides underlying services like database systems for special places. Each server also has or knows a special place registry, which is accessible by the agents through the place interface. These place registries can be queried by mobile agents to find new interesting places to go to. The agent asks the current place to transfer it to the new place. The place hands over the agent to the server, which has at least one communication interface to transfer and receive mobile agents from the network. In the current implementation the agent itself does not know how it is transferred.

One of the main design goals of the Gypsy environment is the implementation of a flexible and dynamically extensible environment for experimenting with agent programming. Therefore, Gypsy has very simple servers, which can start and stop two different kinds of mobile agents: communicators and places. The benefit of these simple servers is to build manageable servers with nearly zero downtime which is important for running them in commercial industry not only on traditional hosts but also in embedded boxes such as telephone switches stored in remote locations. The

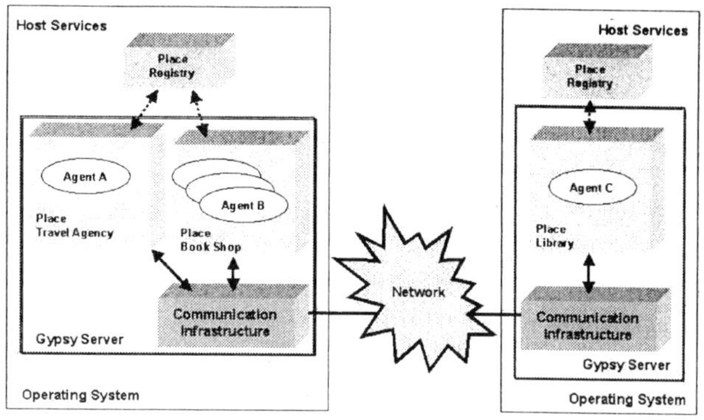

Figure 2. Gypsy Agent Systems

whole configuration and administration is done by a remote administration tool, which can launch new places and communicators to the server or upgrade and remove existing ones. A special classloader fetches the code when it is currently not installed on the server from given codebases.

3.1 Agents

A mobile agent is an object that visits agent-enabled servers in a computer network. A mobile agent in Gypsy is a Java *Runnable* object, therefore it can be executed as a dedicated thread at special places. The mobile agent consists of its code and its persistent state.

The Gypsy environment supports three different types of agents:

- one-hop agents
- multi-hop agents
- embedded agents

All the agents are implemented as *JavaBeans*. This permits a generic JavaBean-enabled user front-end where a user can compose and launch his agent simply by using drag & drop. It also permits the integration of new agents and components from third-party providers.

One-hop and multi-hop agents have a *GypsyAgentInfo* object containing attributes that describe the agent, its requirements and purpose to the server. These include a unique agent identifier, the version number, the manufacturer, the creation time, the owner name, the email address of the owner, the URI of the agent's codebase and, in the case of multi-hop agents, the URI of the home server of the owner.

One-hop and multi-hop agents also have *MessageManagers* to handle asynchronous and one-way communication between each other.

3.1.1 One-Hop Agents

One-hop agents can hop just once from one server to another. When these special agents arrive at the destination server, they will be started and fulfill their task until they are upgraded, removed or reach their deadline. Because their travel is limited, they can send only a simple status report back to their owner. One-hop agents are mainly used by the remote administration tool to transfer new functionality or upgrade existing functionality on the server.

Gypsy supports two types of one-hop agents: communicators and places.

Communicators

Communicators are one-hop agents which can communicate with other communicators of the same type over a network. Each server has one or more communicators. Because of the component-based design it is possible to implement new communicators for upcoming and promising transfer technologies. These new communicators can be sent to dynamically upgrade running servers to new transfer technologies without affecting their running places and other agents.

There are three different types of communicators. An *AdminCommunicator* enables the system administrator to maintain a server from a remote place. An *AgentCommunicator* transfers agents over a network to a remote location. A *UserCommunicator* enables a user to query the status of a special agent and to retrieve waiting agents on a network.

Currently there are two different kinds of agent communicators, one which transfers and receives the agents using Java RMI and one which uses MIME email attachments to send and receive agents. Additional communicators using various other techniques such as Secure Socket Layers (SSL), and CORBA MASIF [18] can be implemented easily.

The current implementation is focused mainly on communicating over a network using the Java Remote Method Invocation (RMI). An *RMIAgentCommunicator* uses the Java Remote Method Invocation (RMI) to transfer the state of an agent to a remote communicator. The communicator contacts the remote communicator and transfers the agent by calling the remote *receive* method from the remote communicator.

The *EmailAgentCommunicator* sends serialized agents as MIME attachment to mails either directly or by encrypting the serialized data using the Pretty Good Privacy (PGP) [6] program. Each email communicator has a special email address where a local monitor thread accepts incoming mails. Such a mail can contain the serialized state of an agent or a request for the public PGP key of this communicator to transfer an agent securely over the network.

To provide easy system administration, a special *AdminCommunicator* is used to add, upgrade or remove places and communicators from the remote administration tool. Each Gypsy server (except the user front-end) starts by default an *RMISysadminCommunicator*, which waits for incoming one-hop agents. Only agents of type *Place* or *Communicator* are accepted. The incoming agent is checked, and if it does not exist on the server, it is started. If an instance of the incoming agent is already running on the server but has an older version number, notification is given to terminate and the new agent is started.

Places

Mobile agents can only be executed at places. The places provide the interface to the underlying operating system services for mobile agents (e.g., a flight database). The Gypsy server hands over the incoming agent to the place. The place assigns a handle to itself for the mobile agent so that the agent has access to the place's infrastructure. Then the place runs the agent in the agent's own thread of control. When the agent has finished its task, it requests the place to transfer it to a different place.

Each place has a passive *Blackboard* where agents register with their ID, their next location and their deadline. Using this mechanism, special notification agents called *Messengers* can interpret these blackboard entries and follow the paths of agents in order to meet and notify them. The blackboard clears its entries based on the given deadlines of the agents, which means that other agents cannot contact them in any way in the future.

To facilitate system administration, Gypsy provides special script places to support the execution of scripts written in Java or Python. The scripts are transferred by *Worker* agents as a special task. The script place first checks the instance of the incoming agent to ensure that its task is of the correct type (e.g., *BeanShellTask* or *JPythonTask*), assigns the worker a handle and runs the agent. The agent runs its task as an independent thread and the task executes its script through the place's *exec()* method. The *BeanShellPlace* provides an embedded BeanShell interpreter [1], which makes the execution of scripts written in pure Java possible. The *JPythonPlace* provides an embedded JPython interpreter [11], which handles scripts written in pure Python or written with mixed Python and Java statements.

Each server has by default one *LogPlace* which runs incoming *LogMessenger* agents generated at that server. First it assigns the agent a default output stream, and then depending on the place configuration, the location of a centralized log server for this region. It then executes the agent. If the agent obtains a location of a centralized log server, it adds this to its itinerary.

To make detached computing possible, where the user front-end is disconnected from the net, the returning agents wait on a *UserPlace* at a home server until the user retrieves them. Each user must have a user place on a special home server to enable returning agents. The incoming agents are stored and the user can be notified by email or SMS message that the agent has returned, if the agent allows. The user can query his place for the number of waiting agents, the status of a special agent and can request the place to forward the agents to the user front-end.

When the agent returns to the user front-end it will be transferred to a special *ReturnPlace*. This place assigns the agent a handle and a *ResultWriter* based on the user's configuration. This result writer is an embedded agent which can interpret, format, and store the result and the history log of an agent. The agent checks if it is at the user's return place and executes the result writer. By default an *HTML-ResultWriter* is used which formats the result and launches the user's favorite HTML browser for displaying it.

3.1.2 Multi-Hop Agents

Multi-hop agents are the default agent model in Gypsy. They have the ability to hop between different locations on the basis of a fixed preset travel list or search for new, interesting locations to visit.

Multi-hop agents implement the interface *MultiHopAgent* or derive from the base class *MultiHopGypsyAgent*, which defines the common functionality. Multi-hop agents have an *Itinerary* containing a list of locations to visit and a history log to keep track of the status and failures during the agent's travel. Each multi-hop agent also has a *Result* object for storing the results obtained during its travel. The result is organized in a hierarchical tree containing the agent's ID, the server URI, the place on the server and the obtained result itself. The result can be interpreted by a special embedded agent called *ResultWriter*.

Gypsy supports two types of multi-hop agents: task-specific agents and supervisor agents.

Task-specific Agents

Task-specific agents fulfill a special task, e.g., find and book a hotel, or return a status report. The task functionality can be implemented in two ways. First, it can be programmed directly into the agent, e.g., a special lightweight agent like a *LogMessenger*, which therefore can be used as a standalone agent; second, it can be derived from the abstract class *Task*, which is an embedded agent. These tasks can be added to a heavyweight *Supervisor* or *Worker* agent to gain mobility.

The *Itinerary* of each task-specific agent has by default a simple travel plan implemented as a fixed list of locations to visit. If a task-specific agent has no home URI, it will be terminated at the last place on its list.

A *Worker* is a generic task-specific agent which carries and runs one *Task* with given constraints when it roams. Workers are necessary to decouple complex functionalities of a user task (e.g., search for a flight, search for a hotel)

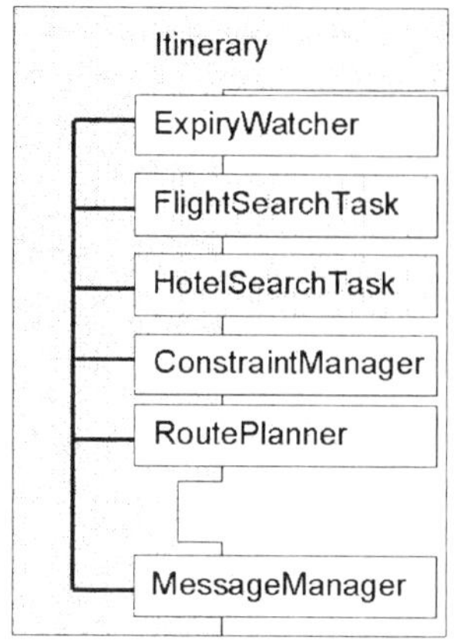

Figure 3. SupervisorAgent, Embedded Agents, and Tasks

from the mobility aspects. Each worker has a *Constraint-Manager* which monitors if the results of the task are fulfilled and sends the results back to its supervisor or owner. A worker with its task is the default mobile agent model in the Gypsy project.

For simple tasks it is useful to provide the possibility of lightweight agents without a constraint manager or a complex routing planner. An example of such an agent would be a *LogMessenger*, which carries and prints a log message. Lightweight agents have a predefined and statically programmed functionality and cannot be extended dynamically. These lightweight agents are mainly used for mobile messages and status reporters.

Supervisor Agents

Supervisor agents have a collection of embedded agents and tasks with their constraints, which are also implemented as JavaBeans. These agents and tasks can be plugged into a *Supervisor* dynamically by the user interface. This mechanism enables the user to choose lightweight or heavyweight implementations of special agents (e.g., travel plans by a simple list of hosts or by an intelligent routing mechanism) and the integration of special third-party vendor agents and tasks (Figure 5). Each supervisor also has a constraint manager which decides when the task has been fulfilled and can carry out transactions based on the given constraints (e.g., if you do not get the flight, do not book a hotel).

3.1.3 Embedded Agents

Embedded agents also fulfill specific tasks (e.g., a route planner) but they cannot travel of their own volition. Embedded agents are used as stationary agents on a server (e.g., a result writer) or are plugged into a mobile agent. An

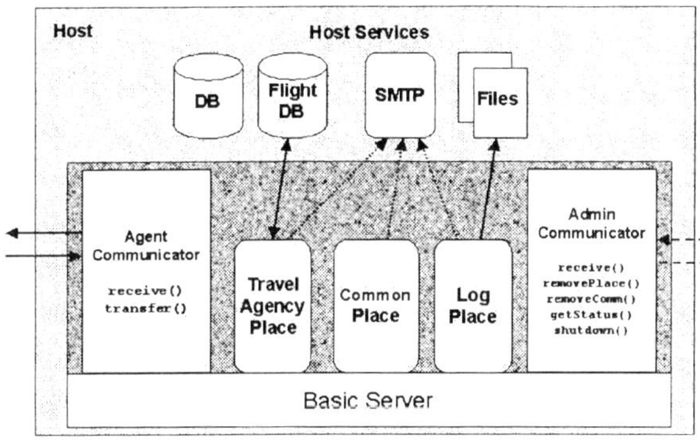

Figure 4. Basic Gypsy Server

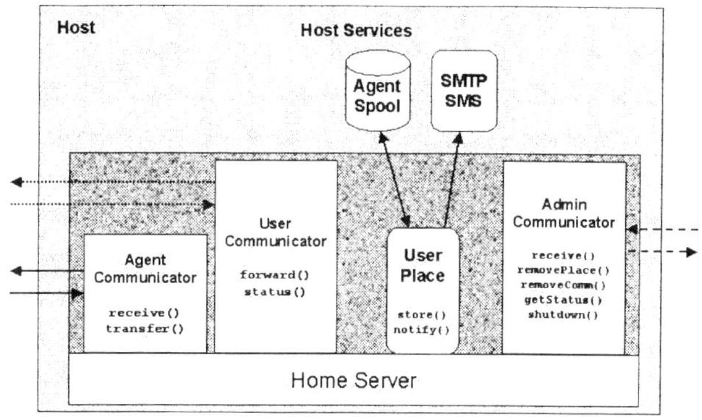

Figure 5. Gypsy Home Server

example of an embedded agent is a *RoutePlanner* which queries local place registries for new places to visit.

An example of a stationary embedded agent is the implementation of the *ResultWriter* interface. When an agent returns to the user front-end, the *ReturnPlace* which handles returning agents assigns a special result writer, e.g., an *HTMLResultWriter*. This receives the result of the returned agent, generates an HTML page and connects/starts an HTML browser for viewing and handling the results. Further implementations include *ODBCResultWriter*, which stores the result in a database, or other result writer capable of interpreting and evaluating the result object before presenting it to the user.

3.2 Servers

All servers are processes with their own Java virtual machine and can start and stop two different kinds of agents: places and communicators.

3.2.1 Basic Servers

An agent server offers one or more services to the mobile agent that enters it (Figure 4). Each server has an *AgentCommunicator* for transferring and receiving agents and handling the agent's messages to/from the owner or other agents. It has also an *AdminCommunicator*, where the system administrator can control and maintain this server through the remote administration tool. Each server has by default a *LogPlace* where the local log messengers move to print their entry and also one or more places for special tasks: a virtual shop, an interface to a special database, a waiting room, an agent meeting point, etc. The server knows the address of the local place registry and the local SMTP host, which are handed over to the places.

An incoming agent is checked by the network communicator for its special execution constraints e.g. resource requirements, expiration date, security issues, and so on before it is accepted. Then the agent is transferred to its desired place where the agent is actually executed.

3.2.2 Home Server

Gypsy provides home servers to support detached computing where the user front-end is disconnected from the network. A home server is a dedicated server at a host which is permanently connected to the network. A home server has a so-called user place for each local agent system user. Returning agents wait at this place to be retrieved by the user front-end (Figure 5).

In addition the home server has the communicators of the basic server, a *UserCommunicator* for communication with the user front-end. The user can query the status of a special agent from its place and request that all waiting agents be forwarded to his actual location.

3.2.3 Log Server

A log server is a centralized server in a region to which all *LogMessengers* can be forwarded. There all log messages of this region are stored in a database for further evaluation and system analysis. The log server has a *MySqlLogPlace* instead of the usual log place, which stores the messages in a file. This *MySqlLogPlace* receives the agent's message, inserts it into the database using JDBC and terminates the agent. The stored log entry contains the server URI, date and time, and the log message.

3.2.4 User Frontend Server

The user front-end also needs a server called *AgentManager* for transferring and receiving the user's agents. The user chooses the special tasks (e.g., *FlightSearchTask*, *HotelSearchTask*) to be fulfilled and fills out the corresponding forms, including special constraints and the name of the starting place. Then the tasks with their constraints are added to a supervisor and the agent is transferred by the local *AgentCommunicator*. If only one task is chosen, a worker will be used instead of a supervisor.

When an agent returns home, it is transferred to a *ReturnPlace* where it obtains the user's favorite result writer for interpreting, displaying and storing the agent's results.

3.2.5 Remote Administration Tool

The remote administration tool provides the centralized maintenance of all Gypsy servers inside a region. The region administrator can send new places or communicators to local servers to monitor and shutdown the servers and to remove agents.

3.2.6 Place Registry

Agents travel between places which can be identified by locations. A *Location* consists of the unique server name, the place name and a list of communicator URIs with which this place can be reached. The server is responsible for registering and unregistering its places and communicators at the place registry in the right format.

The place registry is a server which can be queried by agents to find places to visit. It stores a list of valid locations and corresponding properties. The *SimplePlaceRegistry* has its own proprietary format. In an advanced solution the entries are stored in Lightweight Directory Access Protocol (LDAP) server. The benefit of using LDAP is the ability to exploit available functionality, such as replication, and management tools.

3.3 Mobility

An agent in the Gypsy environment travels on its own volition between places according to its internal routing strategy. These places are called intermediate points on the agent's route. When an agent arrives at a place it gets a handle to its current place and at any time it can ask the place to transfer it to the next intermediate point on its route by calling *currentPlace.transfer(this)*. The place hands over the agent to the server, which gets the next intermediate point by calling the agent's *getNextPoint()* method. The server checks this point if the next place is on this server and transfers the agent to this place. If the next place is located on a different server, the server looks for compatible communicators of the next place and hands over the agent to the proper communicator by calling its *transfer()* method.

The agent terminates itself when no more intermediate points are left in its routing table and it has no home URI. Otherwise, it returns to its home server.

```
:
  [Read]
  *.html
  *.jpg
  [Write]
  /var/Gypsy/*.tmp
  [SystemClipboardAccess]
  yes
  [PropertiesAccess]
  no
  [Multicast]
  192.168.*.1     1234
  192.168.170.2
:
```

Figure 6. Example Configuration for the Security Manager

3.4 Security

The servers are protected against hostile agents through a special Java security manager and class loader. The server administrator can define runtime security policies such as file read/write access, hosts and ports to contact, etc. as shown in (Figure 6).

To protect the server from malicious code, the administrator can define a list of URIs from trusted codebases which are used by the secure classloader in the *AgentCommunicator*. The incoming agent will be revoked if the code cannot be retrieved from the given list. The agent communicator accepts only signed jar archives as valid codebases and stores them in its local cache.

The usage of the Supervisor-Worker pattern as described in [5] helps to minimize possible security attacks to roaming mobile agents. We have made the assumption that a company X runs secure servers in various regions. The supervisor agent with the list of the user's tasks and their constraints moves only between these secure servers. There, it splits up the tasks into subtasks, creates various workers, and assigns them their tasks and constraints. These workers can move to nearby untrusted hosts and perform their task. When their route is finished or the maximum status hops are reached, they send their result back to their supervisor. The supervisor merges the incoming results and checks the overall constraints. Based on this information it can create more new workers for unfulfilled results or move to the next host in its routing plan. Since the workers carry only a subtask, manipulation of the subtasks by malicious hosts does not affect the overall result as much as if one agent carries all the information.

4 Related Work

The work on Gypsy started in 1996, after a number of first-generation mobile agent systems had been built by different groups around the world. The current generation of such systems takes advantage of the knowledge and experience gained in these early systems. Gypsy, in particular, has been influenced by Aglets, D'Agents (Agent Tcl), Mole, and Voyager.

When we started, Aglets had the most advanced security solutions, both to protect the agent through proxy objects, and the idea of managing larger regions through a security context database. These ideas have influenced our security model.

The idea of the agent transfer protocol (ATP) [14] from Aglets [15], sending agents through email in D'Agents (Agent Tcl) [7], or socket connections as in Mole [21], led to our decision to decouple the transfer technology from the servers. The communicators in our design realize this idea.

Due the success of Java, many different language have been implemented in Java, e.g. Scheme and Python. Based on this we decided to support multiple languages through these language implementations, which mostly can interoperate with Java objects. Here we differ from ARA [20] which tries to support multiple programming languages on top of one proprietary virtual machine and system core.

Voyager [19] had the interesting idea of creating a virtual object, which is the contact point for the user to his agent and therefore responsible for keeping track of, and notifying, the roaming agent. This and the idea of supporting detached computing as in D'Agents (Agent Tcl) [13] led to the basic idea of our *UserPlace* at the home server. We go further and extend this user place to act as a user surrogate e.g. for e-commerce transactions, to track roaming agents, and to collect intermediate results.

Another novel feature of Gypsy is the simple, but powerful design of supervisor and worker agents [5], where (intelligent) stationary agents called tasks can be plugged in, transported over the net, and executed based on given constraints. This mechanism may be of use in the intelligent agent area. In this case Gypsy provides a stable, mobile agent environment, where applications can provide the tasks and easily gain mobility without having to deal with the low-level mobility aspects.

The dynamic subtask creation supported by supervisor-worker pattern contributes to the security model of Gypsy. In particular, it allows us to easily implement small tasks that are not worth tampering with.

5 Conclusion, status and future work

We have described the design of the Gypsy mobile agent system. A primary distinction of Gypsy is its component orientation both in the system environment and in agent construction. The basic component of the system is a mobile agent from which both the system components and user agents are built. Component orientation allows us to adopt a systematic design which is extensible, and in which ideas such as transport protocols or communication mechanisms from different systems can be imported in the form of plug-in components.

They Gypsy component model imposes a uniform architecture for all components. For example, as can be seen in Figures 3 and 4, agents and servers have nearly identical architectures based on a fixed minimal structure and specialized extension plug-ins.

Work on Gypsy started in 1996 and most components described in this paper have been implemented and are running. The *ConstraintManager* is currently just an interface and a dummy implementation. Our immediate future plans call for making JavaBean adapters to various existing constraint management solutions, so that the user can plug-in a favorite one. Currently, the user interface is not JavaBean-enabled, so that the programmer has to code new tasks into the program instead of the program dynamically reading given jar archives and building up the tasks as in the style of the Java BeanBox. Gschwind et al. [8] describes such a bean-oriented approach to mobile agent construction.

Like the constraint handling part, we will define interfaces for agent communication, and make adapters to existing solutions such as a reactive blackboard [2], tuple spaces [16], and the Knowledge Query and Manipulation Language (KQML) [4].

We will also focus on region based security solutions including hierarchical access control lists, where the system administrator can define local policies for his region or subregion. This policy will be stored in a context master database as proposed in [12].

We expect that the component-orientation of Gypsy supports these extensions in a straightforward way.

References

[1] BeanShell - A Java Scripting Environment. Open Object, Incorporated, 1999. `http://www.ooi.com/beanshell/home.html`.

[2] G. Cabri, L. Leonardi, and F. Zambonelli. The Impact of the Coordination Model in the Design of Mobile Agent Applications. *The Twenty-Second Annual International Computer Software and Applications Conference (COMPSAC '98)* (Vienna, Austria, August 19-21, 1998), August 1998.

[3] A. Carzaniga, G. P. Picco, and G. Vigna. Designing Distributed Appications with Mobile Code Paradigms. *19th International Conference on Software Engineering* (Boston, Massachusetts, May 17-23, 1997). ACM Press, May 1997.

[4] T. Finin, R. Fritzson, D. McKay, and R. McEntire. KQML - A Language and Protocol for Knowledge and Information Exchange. Technical report CS-94-02. University of Maryland, 1994.

[5] S. Fischmeister and W. Lugmayr. The Supervisor-Worker Pattern. *Pattern Languages of Programs (PLoP '99)* (Monticello, IL, August 15-18, 1999), August 1999.

[6] S. Garfinkel. *PGP: Pretty Good Privacy*. O'Reilly & Associates, December 1994.

[7] R. S. Gray, G. Cybenko, D. Kotz, and D. Rus. Agent Tcl. In *Mobile Agents: Explanations and Examples*. Manning Publishing, 1997.

[8] T. Gschwind, M. Feridun, and S. Pleisch. ADK—Building Mobile Agents for Network and Systems Management from Reusable Components. *First International Symposium on Agent Systems and Applications and Third International Symposium on Mobile Agents* (Palm Springs, California, October 2–5, 1999). Institute of Electrical and Electronics Engineers, October 1999.

[9] C. G. Harrison, D. M. Chess, and A. Kershenbaum. Mobile Agents: Are they a good idea? Technical report. IBM T.Journal Watson Research Center, 1995.

[10] M. Hauswirth and M. Jazayeri. A Component and Communication Model for Push Systems. *Proceedings of the ESEC/FSE 99 – Joint 7th European Software Engineering Conference (ESEC) and 7th ACM SIGSOFT International Symposium on the Foundations of Software Engineering (FSE-7)* (Toulouse, France, September 6–10, 1999), September 1999. `http://www.infosys.tuwien.ac.at/Staff/pooh/papers/PushIssues/`.

[11] JPython. Python Consortium, 1998. `http://www.python.org/jpython/`.

[12] G. Karjoth, D. B. Lange, and M. Oshima. A Security Model for Aglets. *IEEE Internet Computing*, **1**(4), July 1997. `http://computer.org/internet/ic1997/w4068abs.htm`.

[13] D. Kotz, R. Gray, S. Nog, D. Rus, S. Chawla, and G. Cybenko. Agent TCL: Targeting the Needs of Mobile Computers. *IEEE Internet Computing*, **1**(4), July 1997.

[14] D. B. Lange and Y. Aridor. Agent Transfer Protocol, March 1997. IBM Tokyo Research Laboratory Draft ATP/0.1.

[15] D. B. Lange and M. Oshima. *Programming and Deploying Java Mobile Agents with Aglets*. Addison Wesley, 1998.

[16] A. Lingnau and O. Drobink. An infrastructure for mobile agents: requirements and architecture. Johann Wolfgang Goethe University, Frankfurt am Main, Germany, 1995. Fachbereich Informatik (Telematik).

[17] C. Mascolo, G. P. Picco, and G. C. Roman. A Fine-Grained Model for Code Mobility. *7th European Software Engineering Conference* (Toulouse, France, September 1999). Published as O. Nierstrasz and M. Lemoine, editors, *Lecture Notes in Computer Science*, **1687**:39–56. Springer, 1999.

[18] D. Milojicic, M. Breugst, I. Busse, J. Campbell, S. Covaci, B. Friedman, K. Kosaka, D. Lange, K. Ono, M. Oshima, C. Tham, S. Virdhagriswaran, and J. White. MASIF - The OMG Mobile Agent System Interoperability Facility. *Mobile Agents - Second International Workshop, MA '98* (Stuttgart, Germany, September 1998). Published as Kurt Rothermel and Fritz Hohl, editors, *Lecture Notes in Computer Science*, **1477**. Springer, September 1998.

[19] Voyager Core Package: Technical Overview. ObjectSpace, Incorporated, March 1997. Technical White Paper.

[20] H. Peine and T. Stoplmann. The Architecture of the Ara Platform for Mobile Agents. *Mobile Agents - First International Workshop, MA '97* (Berlin, Germany, April 7-8, 1997). Published as Kurt Rothermel and Radu Popescu-Zeletin, editors, *Lecture Notes in Computer Science*, **1219**. Springer, 1997.

[21] M. Strasser, J. Baumann, and F. Hohl. Mole - A Java based Mobile Agent System. In M. Muehlhaeuser, editor, *Special Issues in Object Oriented Programming*. dpunkt Verlag, 1997.

[22] IKV++GmbH Informations und Kommunikationssysteme. *Grasshopper Development System, Release 1.1, Basics and Concepts*. IKV++ GmbH Informations- und Kommunikationssysteme, July 1998.

[23] J. White. Mobile Agents. General Magic, Incorporated, October 1995. Telescript Technical Whitepaper.

Towards Reference Architectures for Distributed Groupware Applications

Kurt Sandkuhl, Burkhard Messer
Fraunhofer Institute for Software Engineering and Systems Engineering ISST
Mollstr. 1, D-10178 Berlin, Germany
[Kurt.Sandkuhl | Burkhard.Messer]@isst.fhg.de

Abstract

Standard groupware products do not fulfill the specific requirements of various application areas, due to technical restrictions, lack of flexibility or non-availability of adapted interfaces. In view of this situation, development of groupware products for specialized application areas will continue to be necessary.

Our approach is to support this kind of software development projects by providing: a reference architecture for groupware applications as a guideline for software developers; reusable components and services; and design and architecture patterns. This paper presents a view concept for software architectures, a global reference architecture for groupware applications and an example from the application field of web-publishing.

1 Background

During the last decade, numerous groupware tools have been developed providing »standard« functionality for computer-supported cooperative work. Products like video conferencing tools, telecooperation platforms, group calendars or document management systems have become cooperative components of workplaces in distributed organizations. These tools provide adequate support for communication, collaboration and coordination of working groups within an office environment.

Where specialized groupware functionality is required, standard products are often not available or not suitable. Due to technical restrictions, lack of flexibility or non-availability of adapted interfaces, standard products do not fulfill the specific requirements of various application areas, for example:

- Telemedicine applications need »high resolution« video conferencing for angiographic and cardiologic purposes, see [3, 4].
- Systems management teams need decision support and collaboration functionality based on event correlation in order to efficiently solve problems in the area of trouble ticketing and configuration management.

In view of this situation, development of groupware products for specialized application areas will continue to be necessary. Our approach is to support this kind of software development projects by providing:

1. Reusable components and services enabling application-independent CSCW mechanisms
2. Design and architecture patterns for the creation of application-specific instances of components/services
3. A reference architecture for groupware applications as guideline and orientation for software developers.

This paper proposes a global reference architecture for groupware applications and an example from the application field of publishing. This work is based on experience in the areas of

- software reference architectures [17]
- distributed and service-based groupware systems [10, 11]

and is closely related to ongoing work in the area of distributed groupware operating systems [12].

2 Reference Architectures for Distributed CSCW Applications

An application architecture contains an abstract description of the application's structure and of the behavior and interrelations of its various components and interfaces. The application architecture is based on the application requirements, i.e. the requirements induced by the business processes.

If reference requirements are available for application domains, it is possible to create reference architectures.

1066-6192/99 $10.00 © 1999 IEEE

Reference requirements for groupware applications can be identified starting from typical functionality in the areas of communication, coordination and collaboration. These requirements are reflected in the CSCW components discussed in Section 2.3 below.

The advantage of reference architectures for software engineering lies in the reusability of entire architectures at design level. Where it is possible to isolate specific requirements within a reference architecture, the components needed to fulfil these requirements can be included in an application-specific version of the reference architecture. The design of a new application then involves combining those versions which fulfil the given requirements.

2.1 Views

A reference architecture as a software engineering product can be viewed from different perspectives according to the various requirements it has to fulfil. These views of the reference architecture support the development process of new applications. The view approach was introduced in CSCW some years ago, see [1] [13] and concentrates on the design aspects of groupware. Our proposal complements this design technique with software engineering approaches.

We propose four views of a reference architecture:

The **logical view** describes the structuring of a system: This view identifies components and services within an application domain, their inter-relationships and interfaces. Within a reference architecture for a specific application domain, the logical view is the most interesting part and will thus be discussed for CSCW in detail later. A framework as an example of a reference architecture can be described by defining an object model with the relevant classes and their relations. For groupware-oriented systems some other frameworks have been proposed, e.g. [7, 15, 18].

The **physical view** describes the distribution of the various software components on physical systems. This part of the reference architecture gives an abstract view of possible scenarios for the physical distribution of the various components. In addition to the choice of architecture, external conditions determined by the infrastructure also have a crucial effect on the efficiency of a system.

The **technology view** describes the technological properties of individual components of the proposed reference architecture and may recommend specific products. The relation between products/technologies and the proposed architecture is also considered here. The choice of architecture is often influenced by which products are available on the market or which are used in the application field.

So far we have not dealt with the use of architectures within the software development process itself. The development **process view** focuses, for example, on the question of how to turn an architecture into an application.

In addition to these examples, further views of a reference architecture are necessary depending on the system environment and its requirements, e.g. system management view or security view.

2.2 Architectures for Distributed Applications

In the area of distributed systems, several architectural approaches exist that are suitable for distributed applications. These approaches originate from different disciplines of computer science and telecommunication industries:

- distributed computing environments (DCE)
- distributed object systems (OMA, DCOM)
- intelligent telecommunication networks (TINA-C DPE)
- message queuing systems
- proprietary approaches, e.g. Oracle's Network Computing Architecture [14] or Sun Microsystems JAVA Computing [6].

These approaches are often referred to as »middleware«, which does not adequately describe the architectural elements of distributed applications. The 3-tier-architecture developed for structuring entire applications characterizes these features much better by emphasizing the architectural aspect.

The 3-tier-architecture is the starting point for our definition of a CSCW Reference Architecture in Chapter 3 (see [9] for another approach). It distinguishes three levels, dividing an application into data storage, business logic and frontend application:

- The top level contains the desktop applications, implementing the presentation of information and interaction with the user. These clients are implemented platform-independently. They use »business objects« to perform the user's transactions.
- The middle level implements most parts of the applications' functionality: the »business objects«. These objects implement services and can be distributed dynamically within the network during runtime. This level is often sub-divided into further levels for clear structuring of the increasingly complex processing logic, in which case the term multi-tier architecture is used.
- The bottom level contains data storage components. Possible systems within this level are distributed

database systems, information archives or data-warehouse services.

This model constitutes the basic construction plan for all further architecture concepts. The advantage of this approach lies in the possibility of isolating individual functions, which in turn enhances control of the system, both during the construction phase and for maintenance.

2.3 Reference Architectures: Logical View

Taking the 3-tier-architecture as the basic construction plan and views as a means of reducing the complexity of the development process, we concentrate here on the CSCW aspects. Our approach distinguishes between three levels:

- basic services for distributed applications
- components and services for CSCW
- domain-specific extensions of CSCW components.

Basic services

The »basic services« level includes various services relevant to distributed applications but not specifically tailored for CSCW:

- System management services for starting, stopping, configurating components and for fault and event management. In this context we propose a software component adding basic SNMP functionality to an application.
- Security services include authentication and authorization mechanisms for users and for components.
- Transaction services provide monitors and mechanisms for non-standard transactions.

CSCW services

Components for CSCW-support in distributed applications have been divided into three service classes with the following functionality:

(A) *Cooperation* in the sense of high level coordination: 1. Signalling (indicating classified events at different locations); 2. Negotiation (realization of a protocol set for use in different group situations); 3. Appointment (managing appointments made); 4. Planning (defining process plans with time schedules); 5. Workflow (enactment and controlling tasks according to the plans); 6. Scheduling (defining and using priorities in case of conflicts); 7. Workspaces (providing virtual views of shared objects within the group); 8. History (structured, timed database of all past events); 9. Access security (managing access rights to objects); 10. Membership (e.g. introducing new members, invitation); 11. Recovery (defines procedures to synchronize work after breakdowns or technological problems); 12. Information integration (Introduces and integrates new information into members' views).

(B) *Coordination* in the sense of scheduling access to shared resources: Reservation, allocation, de-allocation and optimization of resources; usage, mutual exclusion, and recovery after unresolved access conflicts; managing the involved transactions.

(C) *Communication* in the sense of providing communication media: Providing synchronous communication like video and audio conferences or asynchronous mechanisms like blackboards and chats. This service type includes data

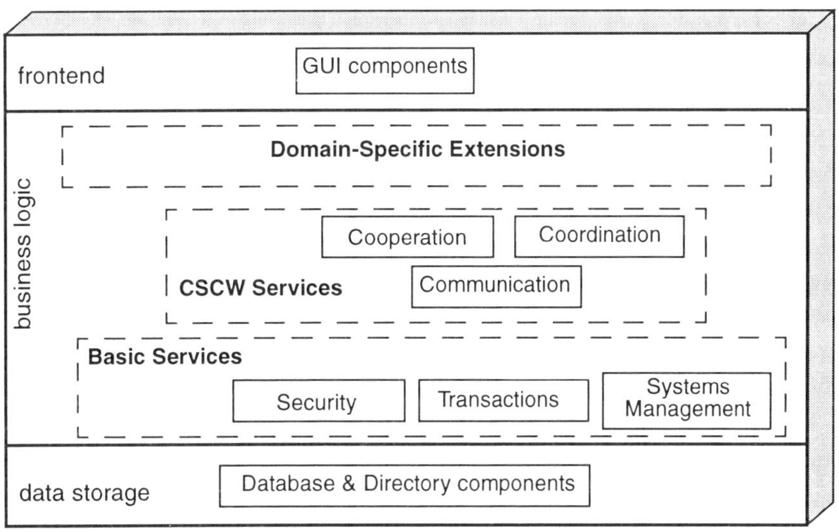

Fig. 1: Logical view of reference architecture

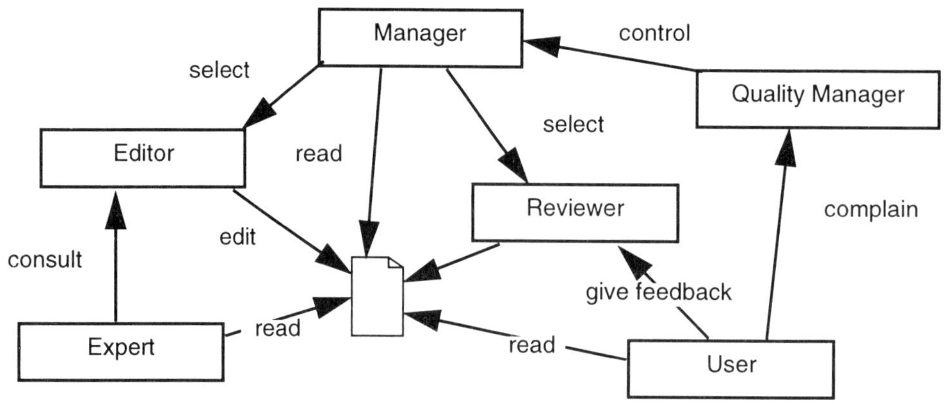

Fig. 2: Role diagram

conversion to overcome the heterogeneity of the involved platforms. Most of the components of this layer manage specialized communication channels.

Domain-specific extensions

The services provided by the basic services and CSCW services introduced above are not sufficient to support cooperative work in specific domains. In order to develop specialized CSCW-applications for telemedicine, electronic publishing or CAD, components encapsulating the relevant business logic have to be designed and implemented. These components are then added to the reference architecture as reusable elements. They use the CSCW-services introduced above or specialize them.

3 Example: Content Management

3.1 Application Domain

In this chapter, we demonstrate our reference architecture approach using the example of web publishing as a special case of content management. We assume that some documents with important content, e.g. maintenance descriptions and procedures for trains, should be published in a controlled way. In this application field, correctness of documents is very important, as several people perform maintenance activities without knowledge of the technical and scientific background. So the responsibility of the manager who allows the shipment of the document is high. Figure 2 above shows the role diagram of the group processes:

The goal of the group process is to update, correct and support the maintenance documents so that maintenance

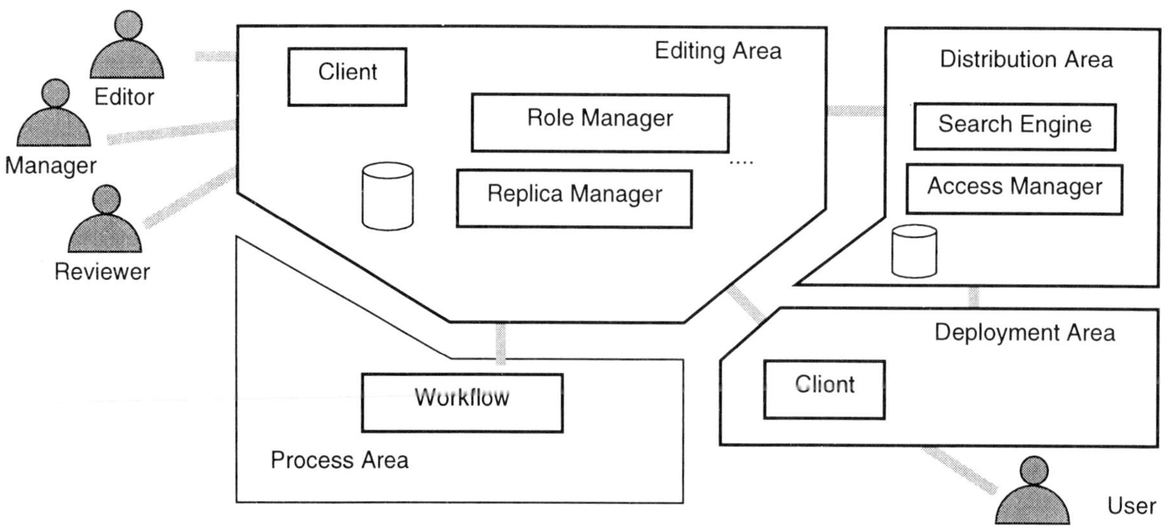

Fig. 3: Building blocks of group content management applications

can be performed in an efficient way. All copies of the documents must be under replica control; nobody except persons in the editor role has the right to modify the documents. If a new revision is published, all copies of the older versions must be replaced across the whole network, including disconnected mobile clients. Printed copies must also be removed, i.e. users who have printed out a copy must be requested to remove the outdated version. The replica system should therefore monitor the printing processes.

The next step is to use work process analysis to identify the building blocks of the supporting groupware application. Figure 3 shows four work areas and the corresponding building blocks.

This rough structure forms the basis for identification of domain-specific services within the logical view of the reference architecture. The HCI part with the complex presentation synchronization mechanism is not shown here, nor is the data tier with its transaction mechanisms.

The **Editing Area** contains all components to support the editing and reviewing process including replica management. This forms the base for editing tools. The **Process Area** contains components which support the working processes by providing quality management, e.g. checking fulfilment of predefined review procedures. Using components located in the **Distribution Area**, the replica manager ensures that documents are copied across the server network, e.g. FTP- or HTTP-servers. The main part is formed by tools like search engines and trader/ broker services. The **Deployment Area** contains components aimed at providing optimum user support. Users give feedback about the usability of the documents to the editors or to the responsible manager according the role model.

Process awareness is realized by the replica manager, which monitors document access data in the distribution area. Releasing a new version of a document triggers an update and propagation procedure based on replica descriptions. Accessing a document results in updating these replica descriptions. The replica database thus reflects the group situation from the document access point of view including access rights.

3.2 WebBook Prototype

In 1997 and 1998 the intranet of Deutsche Bahn AG[1] was planned, specified and implemented by Fraunhofer ISST. Part of this work was the implementation of standard intranet services, including the content management application »WebBook«. WebBook provides mechanisms for document management in intranets of distributed organisa-

1. German Railways

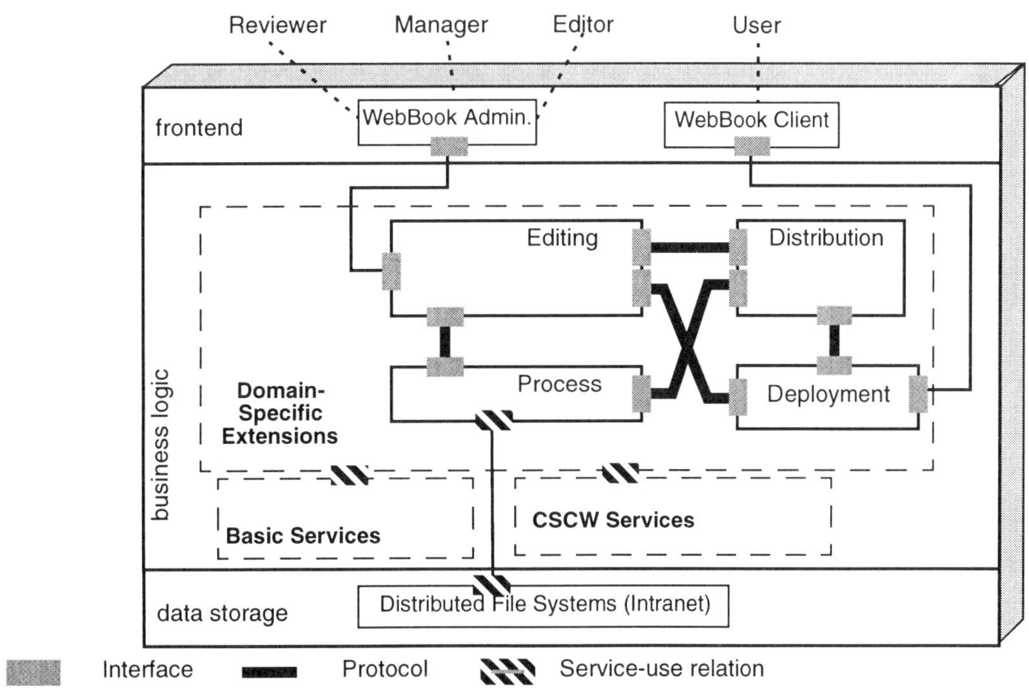

Fig. 4: Logical architecture of WebBook

tions. Using WebBook, editors of intranet documents can install their documents on various replication servers without having administrator permission. WebBook implements a combination of software distribution and joint editing functionality. In the context of content management, WebBook implements a subset of functionality described in 3.1.

Starting with the »building blocks« of content management (Figure 3), we conclude a reference architecture by abstraction, which is illustrated in Figure 4:

Introducing interfaces as defined protocol procedures, a reference architecture for a distributed publishing environment is established. With the necessary refinements, this architecture is common to the following application fields: installing/de-installing of software packages within intranets; writing short books/brochures where distribution is performed by printing houses and deployment by bookshops or e-commerce systems.

The next step is to provide hints or rules for refinement in order to construct the concrete architecture according to the application field requirements. This is shown in Figure 5 using the example of the editing area. The requirements are: a) full replica management, b) process enactment to control review processes, c) several common groupware tools like joint editing and video conferences.

This figure shows the following components:

- Client shell: Main interface to the client for login/logout/authentication etc.
- Application shell: Main component to control the whole editing/reviewing process. Starts tools within groupware environment, e.g. editor, video conferencing tool.
- Groupware Manager: Manages membership information, realizes invitation processes, assigns and changes member's roles, etc.
- Role Manager: Realizes roles (role types) by the capabilities/access rights to documents and to tools with role-dependent configuration.
- Replica Manager: Controls distributed copies including all version management and handling of partitioned networks (online, offline).
- Task ToDo: Workflow interface to the process area. Deals with workstep requests and receives results. For maximum freedom, the workflow only defines a rough outline of the process.
- Joint editing manager: Responsible for the management part of conference and shared tools (invitation, negotiation etc.) and the distribution of documents via the services of the distribution area, so all group members have the right access to the right documents.
- Joint editing tool/conferencing tool: These components realize the well known conference semantics.

In this architecture, every rectangle symbolizes a distributed functionality. Depending on the semantics, certain functionalities are implemented by several interconnected instances, e.g. shells, while others are realized by only one instance accessed by all members, normally the managers. The arcs symbolize a use relationship.

4 Conclusions and Outlook

Using a reference architecture as the basis for application development has significant advantages for commercial users. It provides a uniform framework within

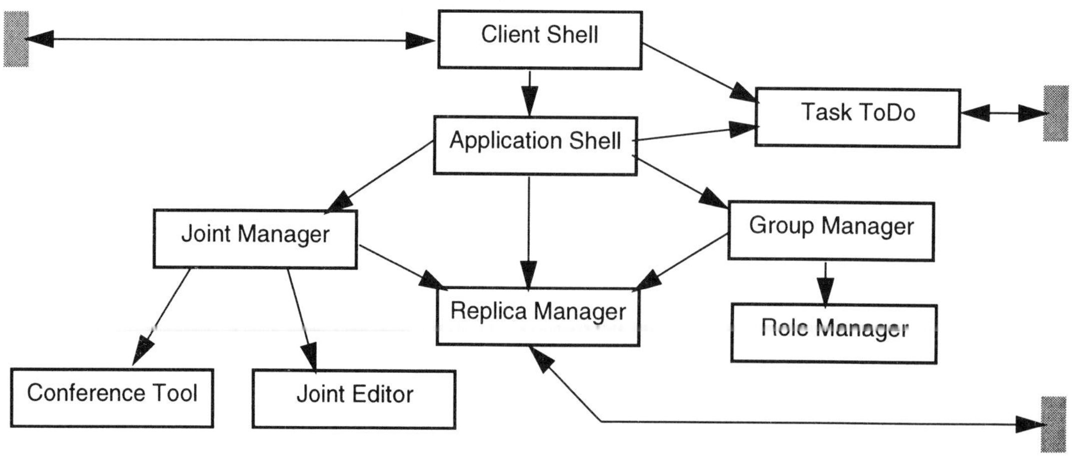

Fig. 5: Refinement of the editing area

which components are based on common technology and can be easily reused. The combination of components within a given solution takes place under »known« conditions. This leads to a reduction in the number of errors made in the development of new applications. A reference architecture brings together experience from past software development and makes it available to other developers.

Our approach has two advantages: A reference architecture based on the reference requirements of a broad application field stabilizes software development activities. This framework reduces the financial risk of software development. The second advantage is that the refinements within the framework have only a few differences. This allows a recursive approach. Within a given area, a second framework may be developed in order to increase the degree of reusability of complex components. The third level of framework is to structure the components themselves, which can be supported by using the technique of design patterns.

5 References

[1] Benfort Steve; Mariani, John; Navarro, Leandro; Prinz, Wolfgang; Rodden, Tom: MOCCA - An Environment for CSCW Applications.

[2] Bowers, J.M.; Benford, S.D. (Eds.): Studies in Computer Supported Cooperative Work. Elsevier Science Publisher, North-Holland, 1991

[3] Burkhard, H.-D.; Fellien, A.; Lindemann, G.; Messer, B.; Weckend, Th.: Case-Based and Agent-Oriented Techniques for Multimedia Medical Workplaces. Abstract of presentation on KI95, Bielefeld, September, 1995, printed in KI-95 Activities: Workshops, Posters, Demos, Extended Abstracts, Springer, 1995

[4] Burkhard, H.-D.; Klaus, R.; Lindemann-v.Trzebiatowskia, G.; Messer, B.; Weckend, Th.: Towards an Integrated Multimedia Medical Workplace via Agent-Oriented Approaches. Proceedings of CS&P ´95 Concurrency, Specification & Programming, Warschau, 1995

[5] Easterbrook, Steve: Coordination Breakdowns: Why Groupware is so difficult to design. School of Cognitive and Computing Science, University of Sussex, Falmer, Brighton

[6] Hopson, K.C.; Ingram, Stephen E.: Developing Professional Java Applets. Sams, 1996

[7] Kückes, A. (Ed.): The BERKOM Multimedia Collaboration Service (Release 1.9). Available from Berkom, Goslarer Str. 35, 10589 Berlin, Germany, see also http://www.deteberkom.de/, Feb. 1993

[8] Lenz, Richard; Kirsche, Thomas; Reinwald, Berthold: ASPECT - Specifying Consistency Requirements for replicated Data from an Applications Point of view.
In: Lenz, Richard; Wedekind, H.: Aspects of Advanced Data Management, Arbeitsberichte, Vol. 27, No. 5, University Erlangen-Nürnberg, December 1994

[9] Mansfield, Tim: User-tailorability in a locale-based collaboration System.
http://www.dstc.edu.au/worlds/Papers/Tailoring.html

[10] Messer, B.; Sandkuhl, K.: Towards adaptive Groupware: Dynamic Configuration Management of Groupware Applications. Second Int. Workshop on CSCW in Design, Bangkok, Thailand, Nov. 26-28, 1997

[11] Messer, B.; Sandkuhl, K.: Work Platforms: Basic Infrastructure for Groupware - A Conceptual Framework. 6th EUROMICRO Workshop on PARALLEL AND DISTRIBUTED PROCESSING, Jan. 1998 Madrid

[12] Messer, B.; Sandkuhl, K.: Concepts for Distributed Groupware Operating Systems. Proceedings HCI'99, Munich, August 1999

[13] Navaro, Leandro; Prinz, Wolfgang; Rodden, Tom: CSCW requires Open Systems. Spec. Issue of „Computer Communications", selected Papers of the Third IEEE Workshop „Future Trends of Distributed Computing Systems", Taipeh, Taiwan, 1992

[14] Network Computing Architecture (NCA). White Paper; Oracle Corp.; December 1996

[15] Popescu-Zeletin, Radu et al.: The Berkom Reference Modell. In: [16], pp. 421-471

[16] Ricke, H.; Kanzow, J. (Eds.): BERKOM Broadband Communication within the Optical Fibre Network. R.v. Dekker, Heidelberg, 1992

[17] Sandkuhl, K.; Faustmann, G.: Referenzarchitekturen für Intranet-Anwendungen. In: Vogt, F. (Ed.): Web Computing, Java, Corba & DCOM. Proceedings Online 99, Congress VI. Verlag Online GmbH, Velbert, 1999. (in German)

[18] Smith, H.T.; Hennessy, P.A.; Lunt, G.A.: An Object-oriented Framework for Modelling Organisational Communication. In [2], pp. 145-157

ENTER: The Personalisation and Contextualisation of 3-Dimensional Worlds

T. Guinan, G.M.P O'Hare, N. Doikov
Department of Computer Science, University College Dublin
e-mail: {Tom.Guinan, Gregory.OHare, NDoikov}@ucd.ie

Abstract

Within this paper we present the details of the ENTER (Environment which Totally Envelops the useR) system. The ENTER system seeks to provide a totally immersive 3-Dimensional environment which is highly configurable and personalised based on the perceived needs of an individual user. The use of agent-orientated modelling and design techniques has lead to a versatile and flexible system within which the constituent agents collaborate to realise the systems aims. The facility to dynamically reconfigure virtual worlds controlled by the agent entities lends to the technology being applicable for differing immersive environments. This system has in the first instance been cast in the arena of virtual shopping malls, but of course this represents but one potential application domain.

1. Introduction

This paper details research conducted within the ENTER (ENvironment which Totally Envelops the useR) project. The ENTER system seeks to provide a totally immersive 3-Dimensional environment which is highly configurable and personalisable based on the perceived needs of the individual user. Additionally like many other such systems the user is not merely immersed in a virtual world but also integrated into a virtual community with the associated evolution of inter-user relationships [1].

In the delivery of the ENTER system we have embraced an Agent-Oriented philosophy [2][3]. The system functionality is delivered via a community of software agents, which collaborate in opportunistic reconfiguration, and re-presentation of the 3-dimensional worldview.

Within the remainder of this paper we briefly examine the research baseline that has motivated this work. We subsequently introduce a high level overview of the ENTER architecture followed by a detailed consideration of each of the constituent agents. In section 5 we reflect on the issues associated with the dynamic reconfiguration within the context of a shared virtual community, section 6 offers some brief conclusions.

2. Related Research

The ENTER project draws upon three areas of research which it seeks to integrate in order to facilitate the pro-active delivery of information in 3-Dimensional (3D) space, those of Agent Oriented Programming (AOP) [2], Virtual Reality [4] and User Profiling. Agent Oriented Programming has been adopted in ENTER in an effort to ensure scalability and flexibility of system design, and draws upon much research already conducted in the area of multi-agent systems [2][5][6]. The use of virtual reality ensures the encapsulation of the agent-based architecture within a familiar and easy-to-use environment [7].

The chosen domain of ENTER is one of a Virtual Retail environment, there are numerous Internet sites that use a 3D metaphor for e-commerce [17][18] but there are none that offer personalization of a site based on users needs. Research into the usability of VR retail environments has proved very positive [19] with large retail chains adopting VR technology. VR technology research has to date been primarily focused on the creation of interactive training environments [7] and design modeling. The incorporation of VR techniques into the commercial domain lends to a very powerful and interactive marketing tool especially when coupled with artificial intelligence profiling techniques. Already user profiling and personalization of content proliferates throughout 2D web sites [8] and within ENTER we seek to use such techniques and to apply them to a 3-dimensional environment.

3. The ENTER Schematic Architecture

The ENTER system architecture as outlined in (Figure 1), adopts an agent oriented approach to its design and implementation. The system is broken down into different functional components known as Agents [9][10][16]. The ENTER community of interactive agents exhibit characteristics that conform to both strong and weak notions of Agenthood [11]. There are five agents described that interact with each other to facilitate the realisation of ENTER, these are a *Design & Build Agent* (D&B Agent), *Presentation Agent*, *Login Agent*, *Listener Agent* and *Analysis Agent*.

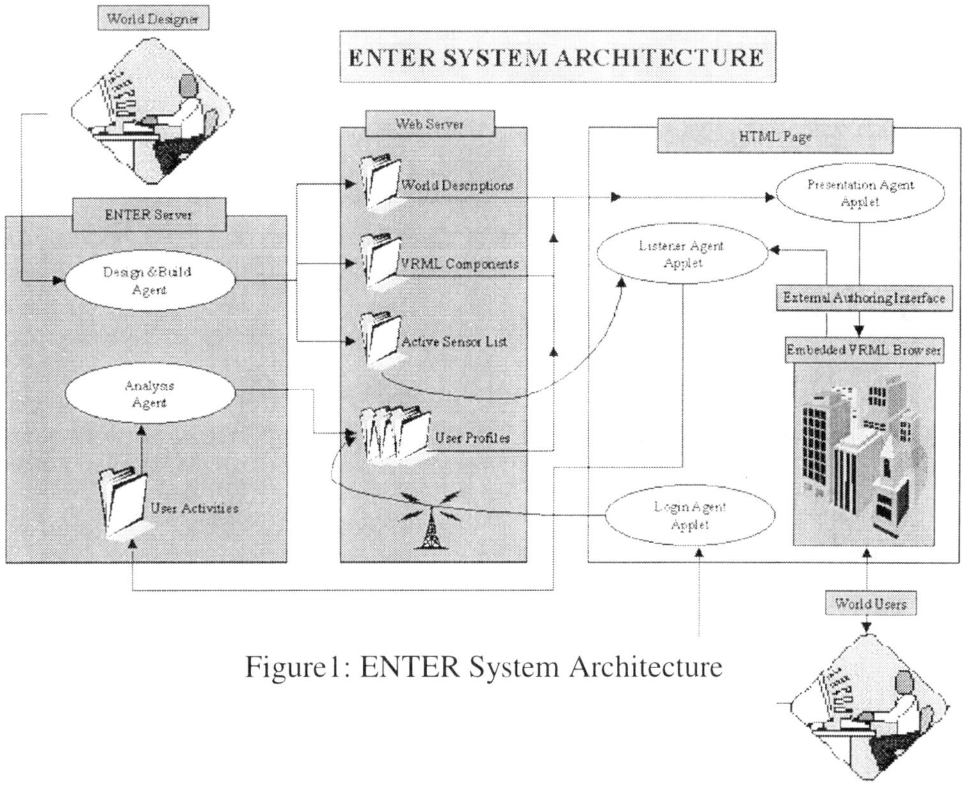

Figure1: ENTER System Architecture

Within ENTER worlds are initially created by a world designer through interaction with the *D&B Agent*. It is the *Presentation Agent* that is responsible for determining which particular view of a world is presented to a user and the actual displaying of this view. The presentation agent is able to interpret a unique user profile created and maintained by the *Analysis Agent* and the *Login Agent* respectively and manipulates the *world description files* where necessary. When the initial worldview is presented to a user, the *Listener Agent* monitors user activities and through the maintenance of user profiles the *Analysis Agent* indirectly informs the presentation agent of the user's interactions within the world. The *Analysis Agent* examines the user activities supplied by the *Listener Agent* which may lead to an update of the users profile, it then if deemed necessary prompts the *Presentation Agent* to dynamically reconfigure the world to suit a users perceived needs.

In order to describe the object's used by the world description files we utilise the Virtual Reality Modelling Language (VRML)[12]. VRML files can be viewed over the Internet in any standard web browser, there is also the ability to embed video, audio and objects called 'Sensors' within a VRML world. The sensors are used by the *Listener Agent* and allow us to monitor user activity and movements within a world. VRML allows the addition of script Nodes to add functionality to a scene, however in order for the agent community to control the VRML scene we make use of a set of JAVA classes known as the EAI [14] (External Authoring Interface). This set of classes can directly manipulate the CosmoPlayer [20] browser that displays the VRML scene thus allowing for VRML nodes to be dynamically added and removed from a scene and user actions to be monitored externally.

4. ENTER Agent Overview

4.1 Design & Build Agent.

The Design and Build Agent is charged with supporting the user in the rapid prototyping of the 3-dimensional

Worlds. At present the worlds supported in the construction process adhere to a physical metaphor, specifically buildings with associated exteriors and interiors. The user is guided through a series of steps which collectively specify the external view (figure 2), form and the nature of buildings and positions them using a grid with each cell in the grid having unique coordinates.

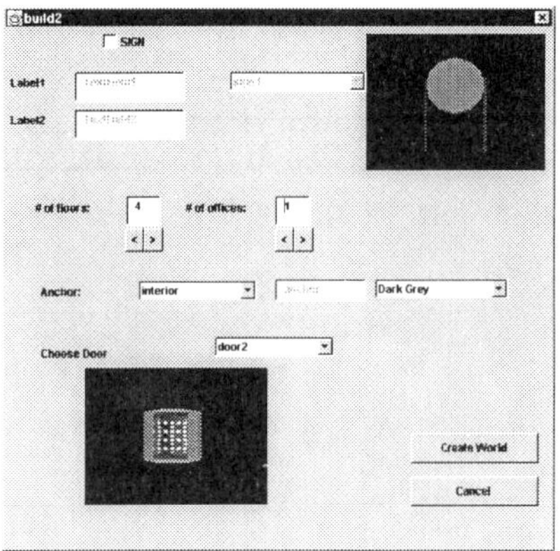

Figure 2: Exterior Interface

Each of the buildings is then populated with *contents* (Figure 3). The contents are selected from a *design palette, which* is contextualised given the nature and function of the building.

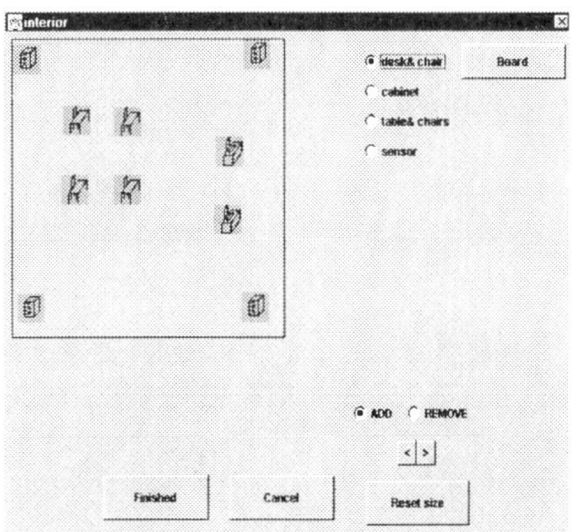

Figure 3: Interior Interface

For example a supermarket design pallet would typically contain shelves, products, trollys, cash registers and so forth while that of an office would typically contain desks, tables and chairs, filing cabinets and fax machines [15].The *D&B agent* draws upon a library of VRML components and produces world description files that describe the positioning of these components and their context within a world. The *D&B Agent* also facilitates the positioning of sensors that are used by the *Listener Agent* to accrue the raw data relating to user behavior. The VRML components, World Description files and the *active sensor list* are placed on a standard web server enabling access by the *Presentation Agent* over the Internet.

4.2 Presentation Agent.

The *Presentation Agent* is responsible for displaying a desired view of a given world. Central to the functionality of the *Presentation Agent* is its ability to understand the *World Description files*, which define the position and orientation of VRML components within the world, rather than reverting to a lower level VRML description of the scene. The presentation Agent is then able to manipulate the object types in the world description files using high level pre-defined *World Transform functions* including *inter alia:* Swap(ObjX , ObjY) , Move(Obj , Ref) , Rotate(Obj,Axis,Radians). Applying these functions to update the world description file can thus portray scene changes. The judicious choice of when and what transformations to apply is made by the presentation agent through interaction with the listener agent based on user events and the user profile, thus appropriate reconfiguration can be achieved. (Figure 4).

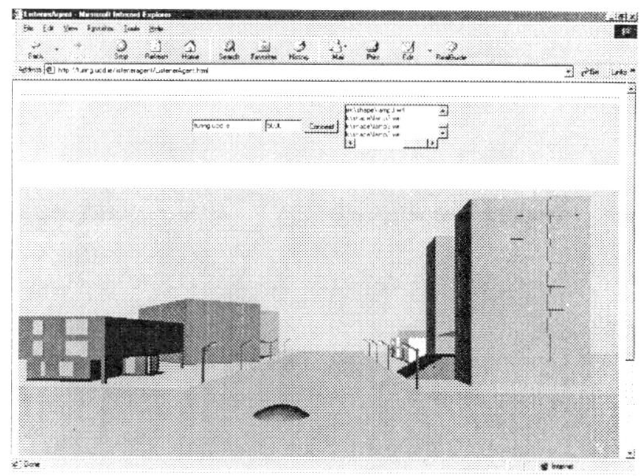

(i)Before Swap Activation

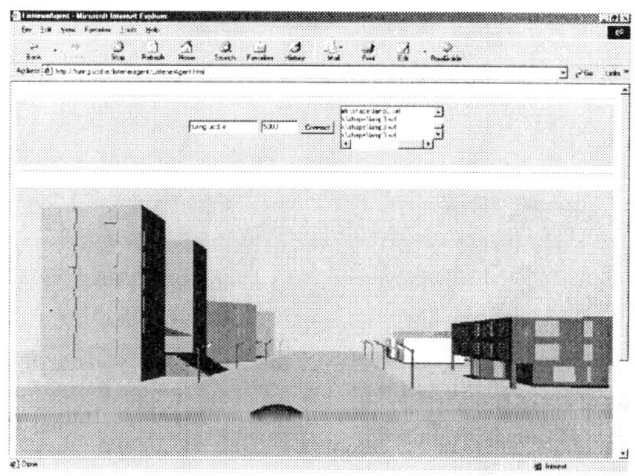

(ii)After Swap Activation

Figure 4: Dynamic Reconfiguration

There are 3 basic object types that are used to describe a world and which the presentation agent manipulates to provide alternate customised views. These are static objects, portal objects and composite objects.

Static objects:
Static objects constitute VRML components that have no functionality ascribed to them within the context of the scene description but may however have functionality within the scope of VRML for audio and video. For each static object the relative position of the object to a higher level VRML transformation is specified along with its orientation (whether it faces north, south, east or west). Each static object has an associated .wrl file that gives the 3-dimensional description of the object.

Portal Objects:
The portal object extends the static object type in that it has a destination World Description file associated with it. Portal objects are in essence standard VRML nodes with sensors attached. Standard VRML EventOuts [12] are registered by the *Presentation Agent* through the EAI and a new world description file is displayed.

Composite Objects:
These are a combination of both static and portal objects that are grouped together under a higher level VRML transformation in order that component objects can be manipulated within the world relative to one another. This enables buildings to be placed within a world, where the buildings themselves are static objects and the doors of the buildings are portal objects. Composite objects can themselves contain Composite objects which enables the creation of feature rich World Descriptions (Figure 5).

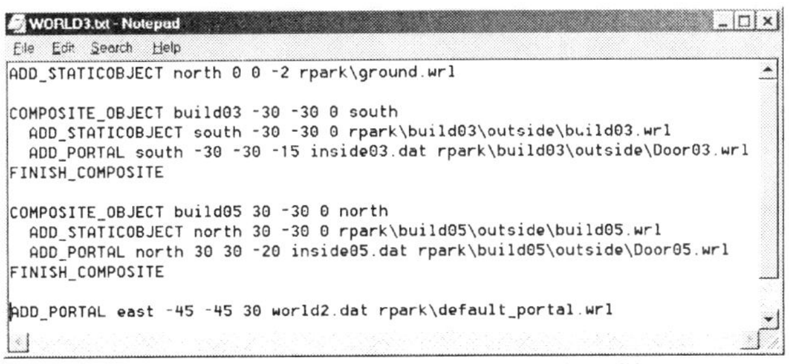

```
ADD_STATICOBJECT north 0 0 -2 rpark\ground.wrl

COMPOSITE_OBJECT build03 -30 -30 0 south
  ADD_STATICOBJECT south -30 -30 0 rpark\build03\outside\build03.wrl
  ADD_PORTAL south -30 -30 -15 inside03.dat rpark\build03\outside\Door03.wrl
FINISH_COMPOSITE

COMPOSITE_OBJECT build05 30 -30 0 north
  ADD_STATICOBJECT north 30 -30 0 rpark\build05\outside\build05.wrl
  ADD_PORTAL north 30 30 -20 inside05.dat rpark\build05\outside\Door05.wrl
FINISH_COMPOSITE

ADD_PORTAL east -45 -45 30 world2.dat rpark\default_portal.wrl
```

Figure 5: Sample World Description file.

4.3 Login Agent

The *Login Agent* is responsible for collecting initial information about users prior to their entry into the virtual world. This information is used either for creating a new user profile or accessing / updating an existing one. Within the ENTER system each world user is assigned a unique reference number which is used as a primary key to access their profile. The *Login Agent* intially accumulates all the personal details of a user e.g name, age, sex, nationality etc. (Figure 6) and this is used to instantsiate a generic user profile thus creating an initial user profile that can be updated if required.

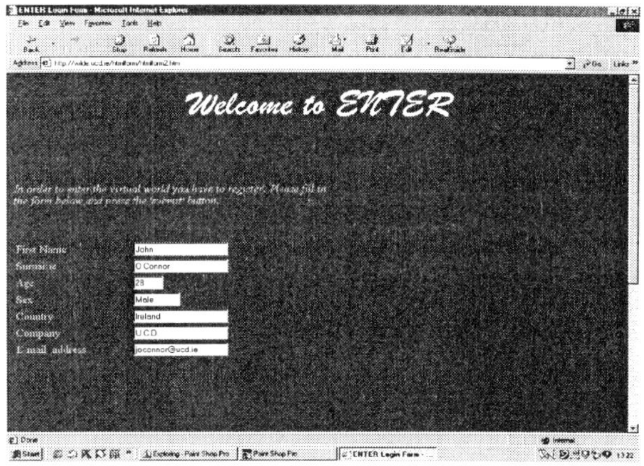

Figure 6. Personal Details

When an existing user logs on the *login agent* prompts the user to select their preference for that particular session (Figure 7) and these session preferences are reflected within the virtual world. The login agent collects the user login information through use of standard HTML forms and informs the analysis agent of any changes the user wants to make to their profile thus insuring that a user gets an optimised view relevent to their current interests.

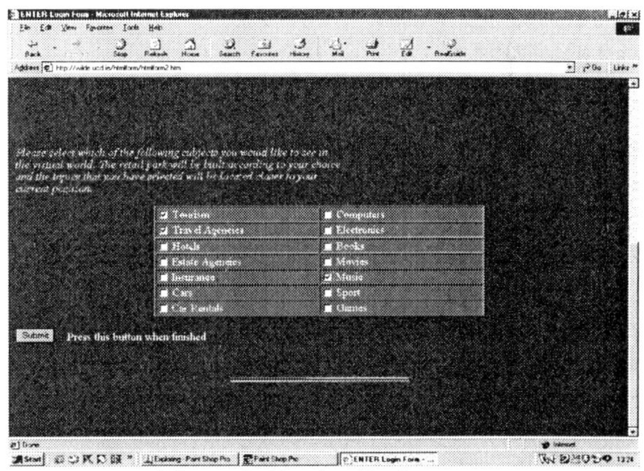

Figure 7. Session Preferences

4.4 Listener Agent

The *Listener Agent* collects information about a particular user's behavior within the virtual world by monitoring the activation of the sensors specified in the Active Sensor List. During the construction of the initial world view using the *Design and Build Agent* a facility is available to attach VRML sensor nodes to world components (doors, offices, buildings etc.) and an *active sensor list* is created. This list represents a simple text file that contains the unique names of all active tracking sensors used to monitor the user actions in the VRML world. This unique list is used by the *Listener Agent* to distinguish tracking sensors from sensors that are placed in the world that merely trigger simple actions.

To be able to receive events from the virtual world the *Listener Agent* is implemented as a JAVA applet embedded in the same page as the VRML browser for viewing the world. Both are connected and communicate through the EAI [14]. The unique sensor names are used as a reference to index a lookup table that stores a description of the sensor's location and context within the virtual world. In addition each sensor can provide the time of its activation which allows the *Listener Agent* to calculate how long a user spends in certain areas thus providing the *Analysis Agent* with a richer information set upon which to augment user profiles. The *Listener Agent* keeps a record of the user activities in a simple text file (Figure 8) referred to as the *user activity file* which the *Analysis Agent* parses and makes inferences on this in order to update the user profile.

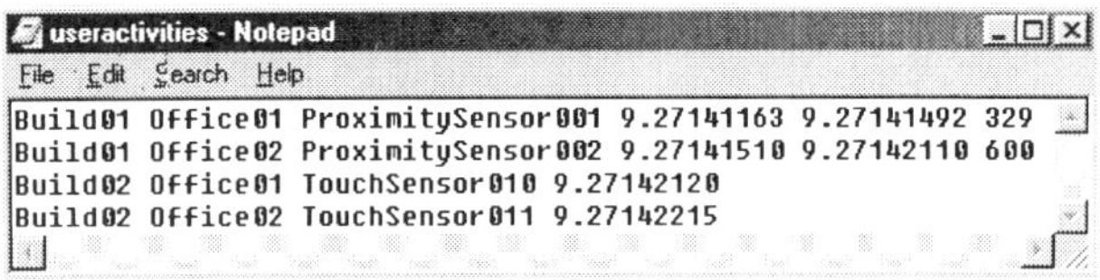


```
Build01 Office01 ProximitySensor001 9.27141163 9.27141492 329
Build01 Office02 ProximitySensor002 9.27141510 9.27142110 600
Build02 Office01 TouchSensor010 9.27142120
Build02 Office02 TouchSensor011 9.27142215
```

Figure 8: User Activity File

4.5 Analysis Agent

In order for the system to behave in a proactive and intelligent manner, meaningful assertions about an individual users preferred view of the virtual environment have to be made. The *Analysis Agent* is informed of user activities and movements from the *user activity file* supplied by the *Listener Agent.*This information is interpreted by the *analysis agent* and a user profile is constructed upon inferences made about the data. This user profile is utilised by the *presentation agent* to present a tailored view of the world according to the users tendencies.

User profiles are at present outputted using a weighting algorithm, where each subject is assigned a weight: a numeric value between 1 and 100 that represents user preferences, the higher the number the more the user is interested in that area. If a user spends a long time in a particular area e.g. HMV (Record Store) that areas weight can be incremented in the *user profile.*

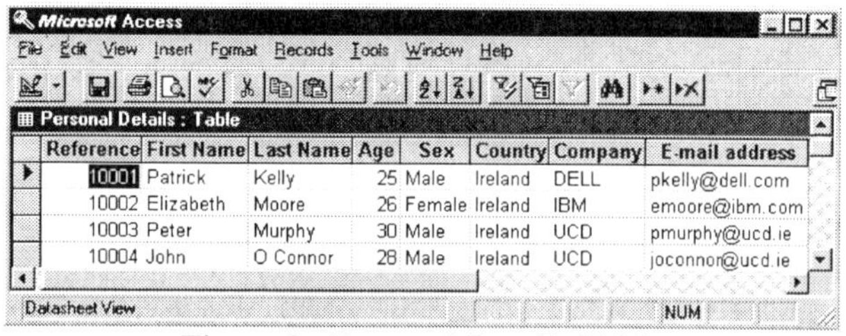

Reference	First Name	Last Name	Age	Sex	Country	Company	E-mail address
10001	Patrick	Kelly	25	Male	Ireland	DELL	pkelly@dell.com
10002	Elizabeth	Moore	26	Female	Ireland	IBM	emoore@ibm.com
10003	Peter	Murphy	30	Male	Ireland	UCD	pmurphy@ucd.ie
10004	John	O Connor	28	Male	Ireland	UCD	joconnor@ucd.ie

Figure 9: Personal Details Table

The resulting *user profile* produced by the *analysis agent* is at present stored in a simple database consisting of two tables that are indexed by the *presentation agent* using the user Reference Number as a Primary Key (Microsoft Access is the database of choice at present). The first table (Figure 9) stores the users personal details while the second table (Figure 10)stores the analyzed data. More than one table can be used when the system keeps a record of more than one browsing session. .

The adoption of an agent orientated design enables the easy incorporation of a higher level inference methodology such as Cased Based Reasoning [9] to construct the *user profile.* The format of the *user profiles* remains closely connected with the retail domain of ENTER, and as such can be easily adhered to by more advanced inference techniques.

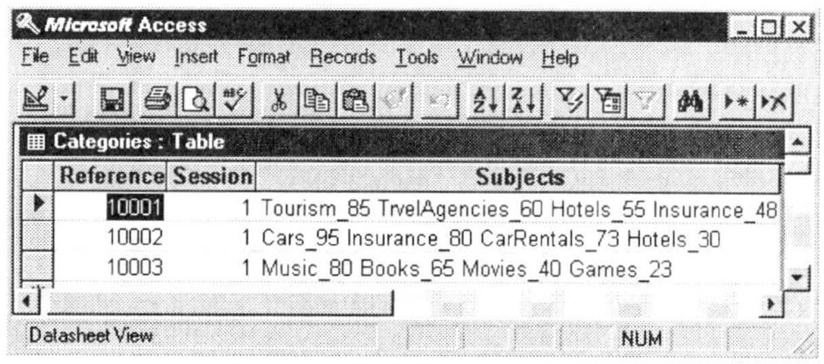

Reference	Session	Subjects
10001	1	Tourism_85 TrvelAgencies_60 Hotels_55 Insurance_48
10002	1	Cars_95 Insurance_80 CarRentals_73 Hotels_30
10003	1	Music_80 Books_65 Movies_40 Games_23

Figure 10: Weighted Data

5. Discussion

Within the ENTER system one of the key thrusts of the research was the ability to dynamically reconfigure the world within which the user is situated. In a shopping sense this is clearly not new. For many years now large supermarket chains have had a policy of frequent changes in product placement policies, with the specific aim of disorientating the user and thus causing them to be exposed to more products that they may ultimately be disposed to purchase.

Within the ENTER system we recognise, and take cognizance of, the fact that there exist differing classes of shopper. For example some shoppers, strekers are only interested in the efficient acquisition of a particular product. Others enjoy the social experience of the shopping activity and are less goal directed.

The dynamic world reconfiguration that we are able to achieve within ENTER would clearly only be activated in response to firstly certain events and secondly certain user classes.

Additional difficulties associated with user disorientation and the dynamic reconfiguration of regions of worlds within which other shoppers are currently situated are being addressed. Reconfiguration would generally only be a local operation effecting merely the immediate foreground of the particular shopper. Indeed it would more often than not be the situation that reconfiguration can only be achieved where co-occupation did not occur. However there is ultimately no reason why the same view needs necessarily to be presented to multiple users even if the co-occupy the same vicinity. Two users located in almost the same position could be presented with starkly differing worldviews. We need merely to ensure that the virtual community view remains consistent in that other shoppers that are within view are perceived by fellow shoppers.

6. Conclusion

This paper has presented the ENTER system an immersive multi-user 3-dimensional system. This system has in the first instance been cast in the arena of virtual shopping malls but of course this represents but one potential application domain.

System innovation manifests itself in three primary respects:

Firstly it offers user immersion in both a virtual world and that of a virtual community. On going research efforts have concluded that whilst user immersion in a virtual world is often beneficial, immersion and social inclusion in a virtual connected community is crucial. Social and professional relationships can emerge as recurrent encounters are made between avatars within the virtual world, recognition becomes more natural. In many environments shared experience maps, in the form of shared memories exist which can significantly empower group activity. Effective communication and collaboration with co-inhabitants is fundamental to effectiveness in goal accomplishment in all forms of reality.

Secondly it supports dynamic world reconfiguration so yielding personalised and contextualised user views. In the retail domain, information and service presentation based on perceived user needs are a key to market penetration. The classical world of retailing has long recognised the importance of product location. In the ENTER environment this can be achieved based upon an individual user profile where products and services most relevant to an individuals needs are assembled in the foreground while those of less relevance are pushed into the background.

Finally all of this is achieved through the judicious use of agent oriented techniques. A community of intelligent agents collectively monitor user interactions with the world and subsequently collates and analyses this, extracting features and updating user profiles based on this. Based upon these profiles tailored information presentation is delivered. At all times end user is blissfully unaware of the very existance of the agent community.

Current research focuses on potential view inconsistencies that may occur as users are presented with varying views of the same locality. We are currently investigating ways through which this may be addressed, such that certain common information layers can be presented consistently across all views of an environment, thus acting as referential anchors with personalised information merely overlaid on top, in essence a parallel reality.

This work has been supported through a Forbairt Applied Research Grant No. ARP/96/117.

References

[1] Jakobsson, Mikael,. *Understanding Social Interaction In Virtual Worlds,* TWLT 15, Proceedings of the Fifteenth Twente workshop on language technology, May 19-21, 1999 Enschede, The Netherlands.

[2] Shoham, Y., Agent-Orientated Programming, Artificial Intelligence, Vol. 60, 51-90, Elsevier Science Publishers, 1993.

[3] Nijholt Anton, *The Twente Virtual Theatre Environment:Agents and Interactions,* TWLT 15, Proceedings of the Fifteenth Twente workshop on language technology, May 19-21, 1999 Enschede, The Netherlands.

[4] Vacca, J.R., VRML: Bringing Virtual Reality to the Internet, Academic Press, 1996.

[5] O'Hare, G.M.P., Collier R., Conlon J., and Abbas S., Agent Factory: An Enviornment for constructing and Visualising Agent Communities, 9th Irish Conference

on Artificial Intelligence and Cognitive Science (AICS), 1998.

[6] R.W. Collier, G.M.P. O'Hare, B.R. Duffy, C.F.B. Rooney, R.P.S. O'Donoghue, Agent Factory: Building Social Robots Cognitive Science For The New Millenium, Dublin, 1999.

[7] O'Hare, G.M.P., Murphy A., Delahunty, T., Sewell K., *ECHOES*: A Collaborative Virtual Training Enviornment, TWLT 15 Interactions in Virtual Worlds (eds. Nijholt, A., Donke, O., Van Dijk, B.), Proceedings of 15th *TWENTE* Workshop on Language Technology, Enschede, The Netherlands, 1999.

[8] Smyth, B., Cotter, P., and O'Hare, G. M. P. (1998) Let's Get Personal: Personalised TV Listings on the Web. 9th Irish Conference on Artificial Intelligence and Cognitive Science. Dublin, Ireland.

[9] O'Hare, G.M.P. and Abbas, S., Commitment Manipulation within Agent Factory, *Proceedings of Decentralised Intelligent and Multi-Agent Systems, DIMAS '95*, 22-24 Nov. 1995, Cracow, Poland.

[10] O'Hare, G.M.P. and Jennings, N.R. (Editors.), *Foundations of Distributed Artificial Intelligence*, Sixth Generation Computer Series, Wiley Interscience Publishers, New York, 1996, 296 pages. ISBN 0-471-00675

[11] Wooldridge, M. and Jennings N.R., Agent Theories, Architectures and Languages: A Survey, in *ECAI Workshop on Agent Theories, Architectures and Languages*, Amsterdam, The Netherlands, August, *LNAI 890*, Springer Verlag Publishers ,1994.

[12] WEB 3d Consortium (The VRML Specification) , 1999 http://www.vrml.org/specifications

[14] External Authoring Interface Working Group, 1997

http://www.vrml.org/WorkingGroups/vrml-eai/ExternalInterface.html

[15] O'Hare G.M.P., Smyth B., Meehan T., Guinan T. and Cotter P., Enter: An Agent Based System for Pro-Active Information Delivery in Three Dimensional Spaces, *Ninth Artificial Intelligence/Cognitive Science Conference – AICS'98*, Department of Computer Science, U.C.D. Dublin, Aug. 1998

[16] Rao, A. S. and Georgett, M. P., Modelling Rational Agents within a BDI-Architecture, In J. Allen, R. Fikes and E. Sandwell (Eds.) Proc. of Third Inter'l Conf. On Principles of Knowledge Representation and Reasoning KR'92, Morgan Kaufmann Publishers, San Mateo, 1991.

[17] http://www.advances.com/vpark/

[18] http://www.vr-mall.com/

[19] http://www.vrweb.com/

[20] http://cosmosoftware.com

Session 5:
Computer Architectures

Tailoring a Self-Distributing Architecture to a Cluster Computer Environment *

Ronald Moore Bernd Klauer Klaus Waldschmidt

Technische Informatics, J. W. Goethe-University
P.O. Box 11 19 32, Frankfurt, Germany
{moore, klauer, waldsch}@ti.informatik.uni-frankfurt.de

Abstract

This paper analyzes the consequences of existing network structure for the design of a protocol for a radical COMA (Cache Only Memory Architecture).

Parallel Computing today faces two significant challenges: the difficulty of programming and the need to leverage existing "off-the-shelf" hardware. The difficulty of programming parallel computers can be split into two problems: distributing the data, *and* distributing the computation. *Parallelizing compilers address both problems, but have limited application outside the domain of loop-intensive "scientific" code. Conventional COMAs provide an adaptive, self-distributing solution to data distribution, but do not address computation distribution.*

Our proposal leverages parallelizing compilers, and then extends COMA to provide adaptive self-distribution of both data and computation.

The radical COMA protocols can be implemented in hardware, software, or a combination of both. When, however, the implementation is constrained to operate in a cluster computing environment (that is, to use only existing, already installed hardware), the protocols have to be reengineered to accommodate the deficiencies of the hardware. This paper identifies the critical qualities of various existing network structures, and discusses their repercussions for protocol design. A new protocol is presented in detail.

Keywords: Runtime Support Systems, Scheduling, Load balancing, Task and object migration, Cache Only Memory Architectures (COMAs), Cluster Computing.

*This work was supported in part with funds of the Deutsche Forschungsgemeinschaft under reference number WA 357/15-1.

1. Introduction

Parallel and Distributed Computing has always faced two significant problems: the difficulty of programming parallel computers and the cost of high performance hardware. For the classical "scientific computation" field, these problems are relatively small compared to the need for high performance. Further, the computation to be performed is typically regularly structured, and mapping data and computation onto the available hardware is relatively easy. However, if Parallel and Distributed Computing is to make significant inroads outside its traditional "scientific" application area, the hardware and software costs will have to be reduced:

On the one hand, *cluster computing* (e.g. [12]) leverages the huge installed base of network hardware to reduce hardware costs.

On the other hand, various approaches are making progress at decreasing the cost of producing parallel software. The problem here can, at a very high level of abstraction, be expressed quite simply: Programming parallel computers is hard, because data and computation have to be *distributed* amongst the available hardware. The distribution problem, in turn, consists of first deciding on the *granularity* of the entities to distribute, and second on positioning those entities in time and space.

Automatic parallelizing compilers can identify and distribute significant amounts of implicit parallelism in conventional "sequential" code (e.g. [16]). Nonetheless, these compilers are still largely restricted to regular control structures, typically loops, and simple data structures, typically arrays.

Help for programs with irregular structures is not entirely missing. The existence of a common address space, either in form of a SMP (Symmetric Multiprocessor) architecture or some form of a Distributed Shared Memory (DSM), reduces the complexity of *data* distribution significantly. COMAs (Cache Only Memory Architectures, see [3]) go even further by supplying an adaptive, *self-*

distributing common address space. COMAs do not however address the problem of *computation* distribution. Further, some computation distributions can be very detrimental to overall COMA performance [11].

To address these problems, we have proposed a radical COMA architecture, which we call SDAARC, for *Self Distributing Associative ARChitecture* [5, 6, 7]. This architecture leverages automatic parallelizing compiler techniques to identify parallelism in conventional code. Relatively sequential code segments are converted into *threads*, in the sense used in multithreaded architectures such as TAM [2] or P-RISC [9]. These threads are then mapped onto the available hardware using extended COMA techniques (see section 2, below). Thus, the *entire* distribution problem is addressed: both *data and computation* are distributed automatically, transparently and adaptively.

We are now in the process of implementing the SDAARC proposal on a small cluster of Linux PCs. While doing so, we have reexamined the coherency protocol published in [6] and discovered serious problems. These problems are discussed in a general fashion in section 3, and their implications for the protocol design are discussed in section 4. A new SDAARC protocol is presented in section 5. Conclusions are presented in section 6.

2. The SDAARC Proposal

In this section, we review the SDAARC Proposal as published in [7, 6, 5]. We first review conventional Cache Only Memory Architectures in section 2.1 to establish the necessary terminology, and then distinguish what is new in SDAARC in section 2.2

2.1. Conventional COMA

The concept behind COMAs builds on and extends the following simple realization: In every multiprocessor architecture where each processor has at least one private cache, the caches form a self-organizing, adaptive system, where data is transparently and dynamically mapped onto the processors.

COMAs extend this idea by augmenting each local memory with a *directory* and a *cache coherency protocol controller*. Thus augmented, each local memory is functionally equivalent to a cache, albeit a very large and rather slow cache. Compare figure 1. Since it leads to confusion to call these augmented memories "caches", they are instead referred to as *Attraction Memories* (AMs) in the literature [3]. A minimal COMA thus has a structure such as that illustrated in figure 1b. The augmentation can be done in hardware (e.g.[3]), in software, or in a mixture of software and hardware (e.g. [10]).

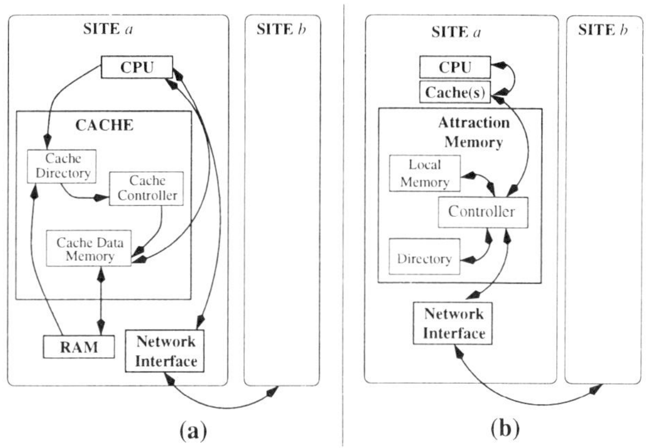

Figure 1. Two Parallel Memory Architectures: (a) A Cache Coherent Non Uniform Memory Architecture (CC-NUM), with exploded cache (cf. [4], fig. 1.6); (b) A minimal Cache Only Memory Architecture (COMA)

COMA relies on the programmer and/or the compiler to distribute computation amongst the processors. Whether a COMA will be able to distribute the data efficiently depends to a large degree on just how the programmer and/or the compiler distributed the computation. See [11] for a detailed discussion of COMA performance with various kinds of applications.

2.2. SDAARC: Radical COMA

The SDAARC Proposal [5, 6, 7] consists of two components: a low-latency network for parallel systems with migratory objects, and a run-time system for implementing a COMA which automatically and transparently distributes both data *and computation* at run-time. We consider the network proposal below (section 3). In this section we consider the run-time system.

The basic idea behind the SDAARC run-time system is fairly simple. If we can partition a program into a set of *grains*, and if each grain is associated with a data object, then we can use a COMA to distribute these grains. If we then execute each grain at the site where it is resident, we have effectively used COMA to distribute computation *by means of* distributing data. This approach is thus a hybrid between static and dynamic scheduling. Static scheduling is used to extract sequential grains, and dynamic scheduling is used to distribute these grains in space and time. We utilize compiler techniques from multiprocessor architectures [2, 9, 15] and thus refer to the grains as *microthreads* (a term established in [9]). The set of all microthreads represents a coarse-grain dataflow graph. See [5] for more details on how we extract threads.

Each microthread has a *frame* (actually a *framelet*, see [1]): a data structure which stores all the information necessary to execute the microthread. This includes all of the the microthread's arguments, and the addresses to which microthread's results should be sent.

Executing one microthread creates results which can be sent to other microthreads. If the recipients are *remote*, two courses of action are available: either we can simply send the data to the recipient framelet, leaving the recipient framelet where it is, or we can bring the recipient framelet to the argument. The first alternative (argument travels to framelet) is functionally equivalent to *active messages* [15]. The second alternative (framelet travels to argument) is more in the spirit of conventional COMAs. SDAARC employs *both*, leaving the decision up to the protocol controller. The controller thus *shops* for framelets for its site to store and (potentially) execute. For this reason, we call the controllers *brokers*, to distinguish them from the simpler controllers in conventional COMAs.

The distribution is thus driven by two sets of forces: sharing arguments leads to *attractive* forces, which bring related framelets together; congestion leads to *dissipative* forces, which evict framelets to balance the load. The entire system is thus constantly in flux, attempting to balance the contradictory goals of minimizing communication while maximizing parallelism.

So far, we have only considered framelets, and the only communication has been to exchange scalar arguments. A system with only framelets *could* be built, (see [8, 13] for one such system), but it would be extremely difficult to implement important classes of data structures. To allow arrays and other *random-access container* structures, we also need a *data partition*, which allows conventional COMA reads and writes to arbitrary addresses. Interestingly however, reads are now inherently non-blocking ("split-phase"), and the results of a read can be sent directly to a recipient framelet, and not (necessarily) to the processor which initiated the read.

SDAARC can, like other COMAs, be realized with or without special purpose hardware. The implications of various degrees of hardware support in the subject of the remainder of this paper.

3. Networks for COMAs

In order to better understand the constraints placed on protocol design by existing installed networks, we first review some of the networks suggested in the literature for COMAs with those widely available (section 3.1). With this background, we discuss the problems which various networks can cause for the correct operation of a COMA (section 3.2).

3.1. Example Networks

A set of network topologies which come into consideration for COMAs is presented in table 1.

Bus-based Networks:

A simple common bus, such as those used in SMPs, consists of one physical link shared by all of the processors and one bus arbiter. Hierarchical bus systems are possible. No special routing is available for COMAs. Collisions are possible at each stage of the network. All messages are broadcast on the non-hierarchical system. Hierarchical buses offer limited support for multicasting.

The DDM Bus: One of the first COMAs in the literature, the Data Diffusion Machine [3], used common buses, where each bus was augmented with a *directory*. Hierarchical systems can be built by adding buses and directories. All messages were sent first to the directory node and then from the directory to the recipients(s). The directories perform dynamic routing based on the current data distribution. Broadcasting is supported, but must also go over the directory. Hierarchical buses offer limited support for multicasting.

The SDAARC Network, as proposed in [7], used a two dimensional grid of buses. There are twice as many buses as processors. Each horizontal bus (compare illustration in table 1) carries output from exactly one processor, and each vertical bus carries input to exactly one processor. Every message must transverse first a horizontal and then a vertical bus. Collisions happen only on the vertical lines, and only when more than one processor sends to one recipient. The switches between the horizontal and vertical buses have small associative memories similar to the directories in the DDM. Hierarchical systems can be built by building grids of grids. Both broadcasting and multicasting are supported.

Fast Ethernet: (IEEE Standard 802.3, see e.g. [14]) is perhaps the most commonly used network technology for Cluster Computing today [12]. It presents an attractive tradeoff between cost and performance. Better still, it is already installed, or soon to be installed, in many locations, and is thus effectively "free".

In a flat (non-hierarchical) Ethernet system, each processor has dedicated links to and from a shared hub or switch (a.k.a. a "switched hub"). Collisions can occur at the hub. Hierarchies are possible, and are usually built through processors with two network connections

Network Type	Flat Topology	Hierarchical Topology
Common Bus	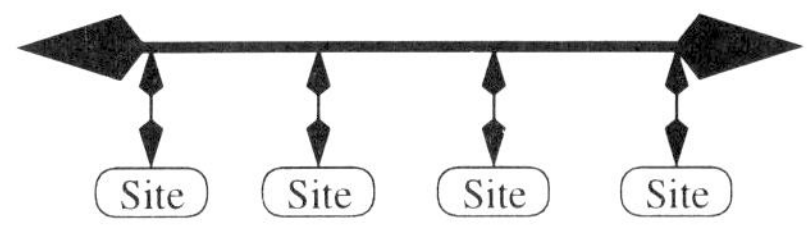	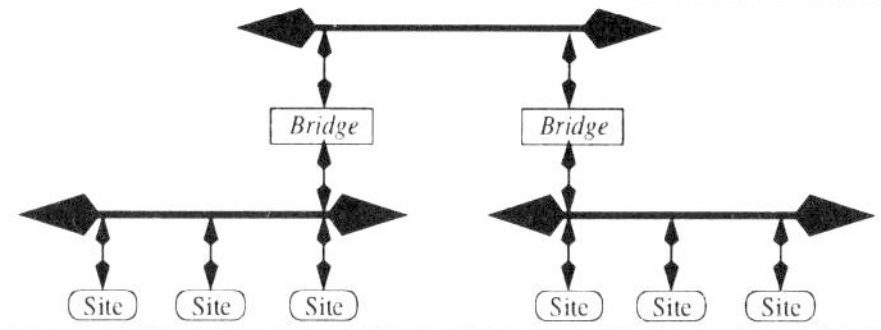
DDM Network	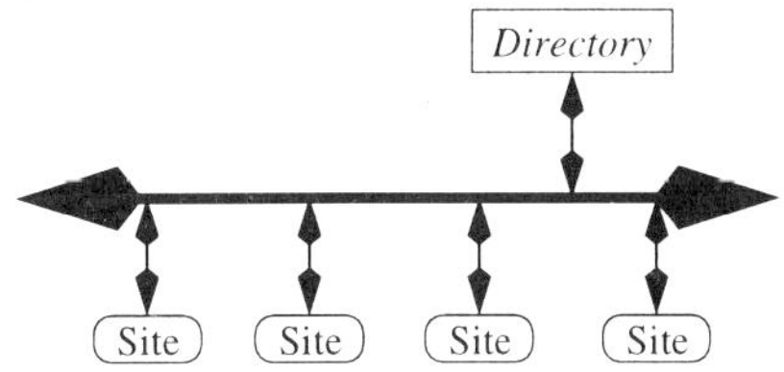	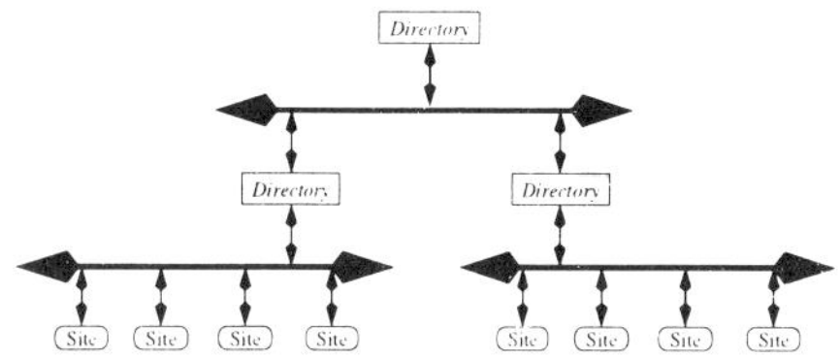
SDAARC Network	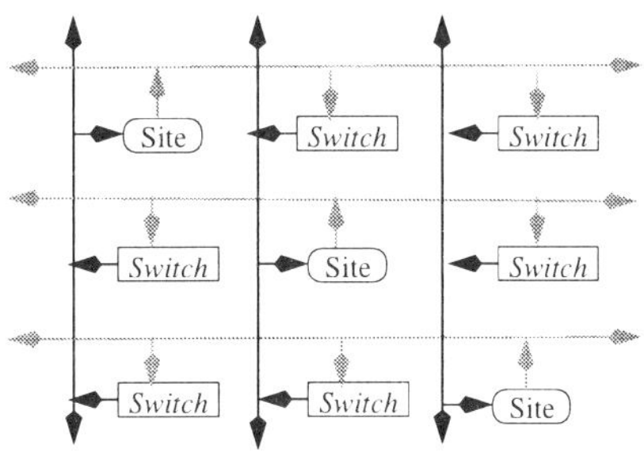	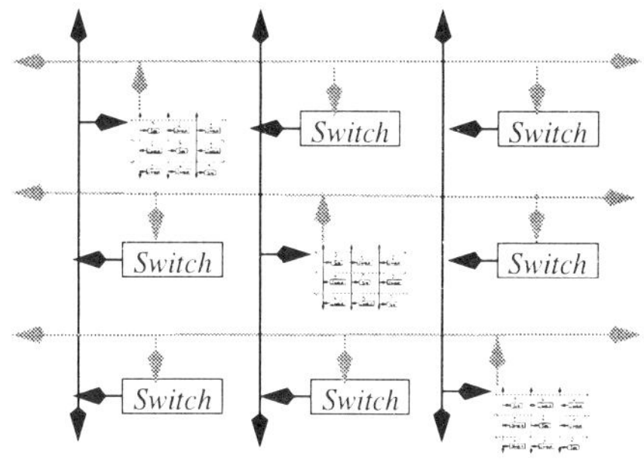
Ethernet	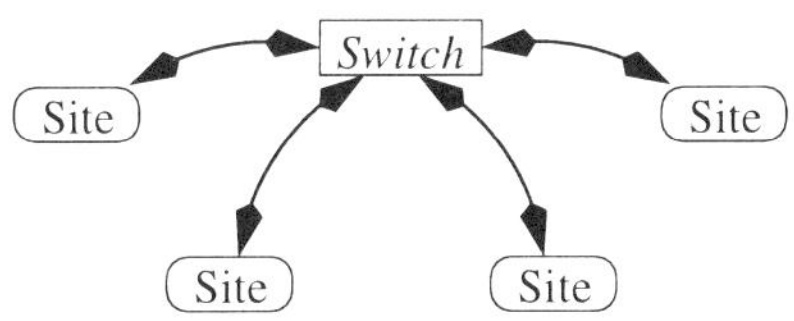	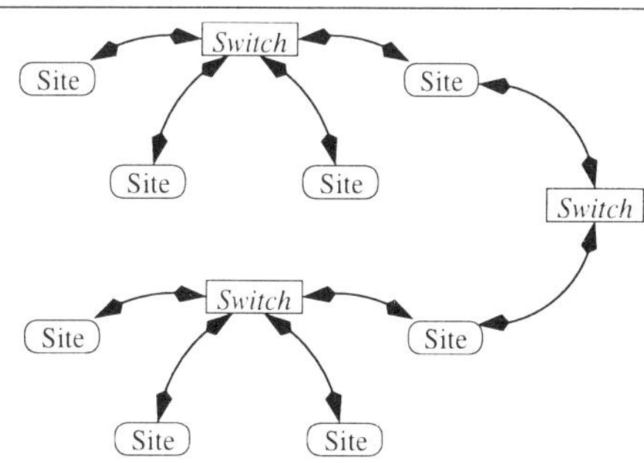

Table 1. Major Network types

(called *gateways*). No special hardware is available for accelerating COMAs. Support for broadcasting or multicasting is limited or nonexistent.

Other networks are of course possible and available. We focus on these networks since they represent two basic technologies found in non-COMAs (common buses and Ethernet), and two networks (DDM and SDAARC) explicitly tailored for COMAs. The important qualities in the two COMA-specific networks are:

1. *Associative switching;*
2. *Support for broadcasting;*
3. *Support for multicasting;*

We will examine why these features are important, and what can be done if they are missing, in the next section.

3.2. Problems Networks Make For COMAs

COMAs in general (and SDAARC in particular) present two novel problems for networks. Both problems arise since messages are (usually) addressed to migratory objects and not to physical sites:

1. Since an object can be *anywhere*, a message addressed to this object either needs to be sent *everywhere* where the object *could* be (each site then checks to see if the object is currently resident locally), or the message needs to be sent to some form of *associative switch* (such as those in the SDAARC or DDM networks)

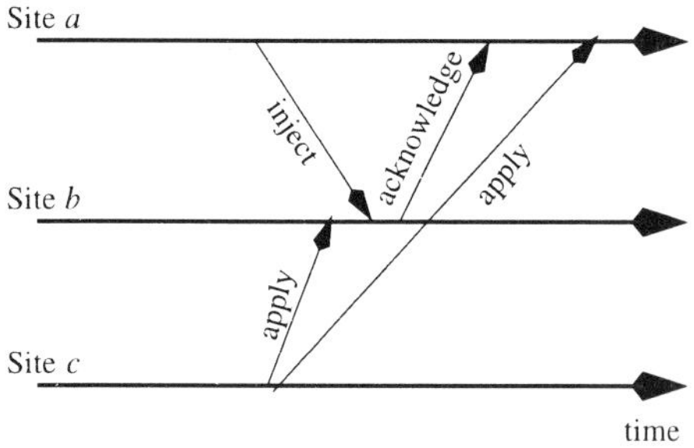

Figure 2. A message sent from Site c misses its recipient at both Site a and Site b.

which knows where to forward the message. All of these approaches use some form of broadcasting or multicasting. If neither broadcasting nor multicasting is particularly efficient, then care must be taken to reduce the network traffic as much as possible.

2. Even if we assume that a message can be successfully routed to all the sites where a recipient object is resident, we still need to take special care *during migration*. In its simplest form, the problem is that for some amount of time, the recipient object is *nowhere*.

In the general case, where we can assume next to nothing about the timing of messages sent across the network (we do assume at least that two messages traveling along the same path arrive in the same order they were transmitted) no matter how sophisticated the protocol is, a message can still miss its recipient. This problem is illustrated with a message sequence diagram in figure 2. The scenario is as follows: at some time, an object migrates from Site a to Site b. The two sites (a and b) can exchange any number of acknowledgments — we assume only that there is some amount of time *before* the total transaction reaches Site b, during which b refuses messages sent to the object; and some amount of time *after* the transaction, during which a believes that the object is safely moved away, and also refuses messages sent to the object. As such, it is possible for a third Site c to send a message to the object, such that the message arrives *before* the transaction at Site b and *after* the transaction at Site a.

4. Protocol Alternatives

We saw above (section 3.2) that the main challenge for a COMA protocol and network is to deliver every message to every copy of an object — even when that object is in the midst of migration. Depending on the characteristics of the network, several alternatives exist:

- Special COMA problems do not arise if the network resembles a common bus. If each message is broadcast, and no two messages can be in the network at once, then it is not possible for a message from a third party to send a message which arrives at one site *before* the migration, and at another site *after* the migration. In this case, we can use fairly simple COMA protocols. This approach breaks down, however, for any more complicated network, including a hierarchical bus system.

- For a hierarchical system with associative switches, it is sufficient if the associative switches note that an object is *leaving* during migration. There are then two possibilities: messages sent to an object in the *leaving* state can be returned to the sender, who then repeats the request (this is done in the DDM Protocol), or the message can be forwarded to the object's new home (this was done in the SDAARC Protocol in [6]). This requires, however, that a well-defined time exists when the *leaving* copy can be flushed out of the AM. Such a time can be derived for the bus-based networks, but does not exist for packet-switched networks such as Fast Ethernet (see section 3.1 above).

- Finally, given a network where we can assume virtually *nothing* about the timing of messages, the protocol must go to the greatest lengths to ensure that no object disappears from the system, even intermittently during migration. Such a protocol for conventional COMAs was introduced in [11] and is called COMA-F. COMA-F changes the concept of a *directory* in the following manner. Each site now has an extra data structure, called a *directory*, which stores information about a subset of the global address space. Given an address, any site can find the directory for that address, and the directory does not migrate. The directory stores the number and locations of all copies of each object in its subset of the address space. All messages are sent first to the directory, and then the site with the directory forwards the messages to the copies. If more than one copy of an object exist, one of those copies is *marked* (is in a state called *Master-Shared* in COMA-F). Unmarked copies can be dropped from the system at any time, but marked copies are returned to the site with the directory.

COMA-F is the only protocol known to the authors which can cope with a totally general network, and serves as the basis for our new protocol in the next section.

5. A SDAARC Protocol for an Existing Network

In the last section, we examined how various networks make various extensions to a simple COMA protocol necessary. At the end, we arrived at the COMA-F protocol [11], which makes the smallest set of assumptions about the network.

Like other conventional COMA protocols, COMA-F only provides a DSM. That is, it only provides support for read and write operations (and for operations occurring as a result of the protocol itself, such as object migration). We present a protocol in this section based on the more radical COMA envisioned in the SDAARC project and outlined above in section 2.2. We present definitions in section 5.1, and then present the major transactions in section 5.2.

5.1. Definitions

Using the terminology from section 2.1 above, We assume a system of Sites, where each site consists of a processor and an *Attraction Memory* (AM). For this protocol, we stipulate that an AM consists of the following data structures:

Local Tables: Two set-associative tables that associate global addresses onto a pair consisting of *state* and a local address. One table is used for framelets, and one for container objects.

Routing Table: (the "directory" in COMA-F) maps a set of global addresses onto lists of site numbers (or equivalently onto a site vector). The Routing Table must be full associative, since there is no way to evict an item from the Routing Table.

Every object is in the Routing Table at only one site. The mapping of addresses to sites is static: any processor can at any time compute *the* site where a given object is in the Routing Table. This is called the *home* site for this object.

Am object can be in one of 8 states: *Invalid, Routed, Exclusive-Owned, Exclusive-Borrowed, Original-Owned, Original-Borrowed, Clone-Owned* and *Clone-Borrowed*. An object is *Invalid* at a given site if it is neither in the Local Table or the Routing Table. An object is *Routed* if it is in the Routing Table but not in the Local Table. An object is *Owned* if it is in both the Routing and the Local Table, and *Borrowed* if it is in the Local Table but not the Routing Table. Further, the object is *exclusive* if it is only in the Local Table of this site, and otherwise either the *Original* or a *Clone*. Only one copy of an object can be in the *Original* state at any time, and at all times there must be at least one copy in either the *Original* or the *Exclusive* state. (the *Original* state is thus equivalent to the *Master-Shared* state in COMA-F, see above).

The broker receives *messages* either from the local processor or from the network. Messages can be of the following types:

Inject The AM is directed to store an object. Inject messages contain the state which the new object should have (thus there are *inject exclusive* messages and *inject original*, and so on).

Application Data is being sent to a migratory object. *Applications* come in three basic flavors:

- **Apply-Arguments** : One or more arguments are sent to a framelet;
- **Apply-Read** : A container object is directed to send data to one framelet, and a synchronization to another framelet (both of which are done with *Apply-Arguments* messages);
- **Apply-Write** A container object receives data, and is directed to send a synchronization to another framelet;

Delete The AM is directed to delete an object;

Evict: Used to notify the *home site* of object migration.

All Messages include information identifying the site which initiated the message, and also identifying the state in which the object is expected to be found.

5.2. Transactions

The rest of the protocol consists of a table cross-referencing states and messages. The transactions for object creation (*Inject*) and deletion (*Delete*) are relatively straight-forward and are not considered here in detail. We focus instead on *application* and *migration*. Examples of these transactions are illustrated in Table 2.

Table 2 illustrates four possible transactions.

In case (a), a CPU sends an *apply* message, and finds the recipient object in the Local Table and the Routing Table. The application can be performed without notifying any other site.

Cases (b) and (c) are more general. Here, the CPU's message must be sent to the *home site* (if not already there), and then forwarded to the object's current site(s). Sites with clones either update their copies (if a *write-update* protocol is desired) or invalidate them (if a *write-invalidate* protocol is desired). The site with the *Original* or the *Exclusive* copy decides, based on the current load distribution, whether to send a copy of the object to the site which initiated the *apply* (compare section 2.2 above), and if so, whether to keep a

<table>
<tr><td colspan="2">Key:
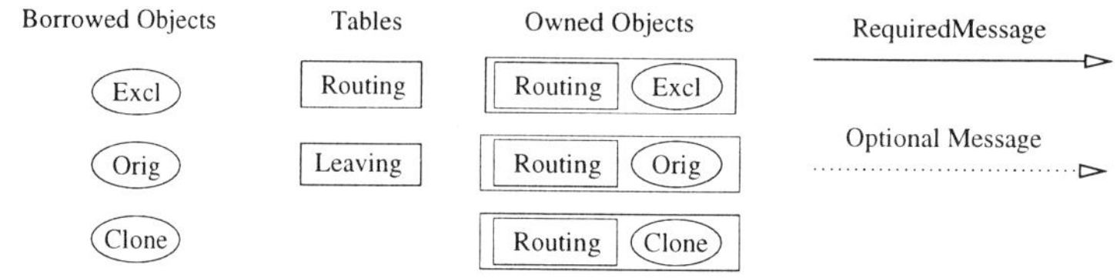
</td></tr>
<tr><td>(a) The Simplest Transaction: All data is local. No Network traffic is required.</td><td>
</td></tr>
<tr><td>(b) Object is in Exclusive-Borrowed state. CPU sends message first to home site (1). Home site forwards message to object (2). Object's site either simply accepts the message and performs the apply, or optionally sends the object to the initiating site (3a) with an inject message and updates the Routing Table (3b) with an evict message. The copy sent to the CPU can be in either Exclusive or Original (but not in Clone) state, and the existing copy goes either into Invalid or Clone (but cannot stay in original) state, respectively.</td><td>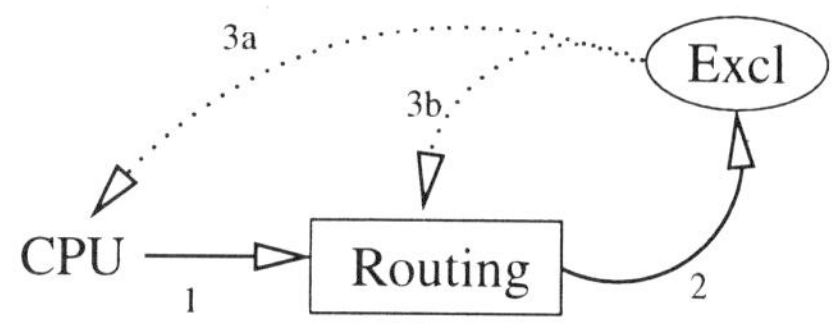
</td></tr>
<tr><td>(c) Object is in Original-Borrowed state. Exactly as above (b), except that the home site must also send updates to the copies in clone state (2b and 2c). These copies are either updated (write-update) or invalidated (write-invalidate). Updating never causes additional traffic from a clone however.</td><td>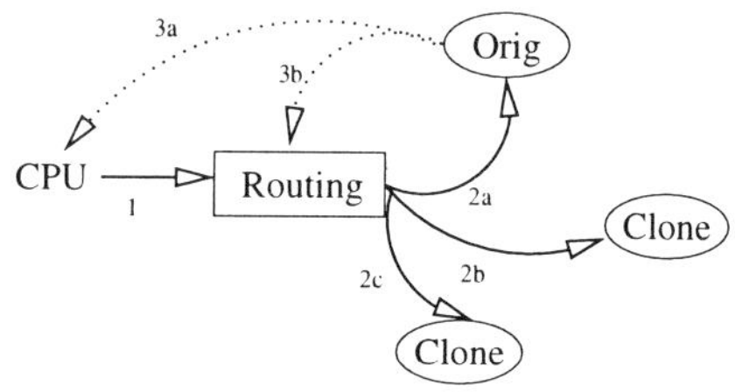
</td></tr>
<tr><td>(d) Two forms of Migration: An object in Exclusive or Original state is sent to another state, as in (b) or (c), above (1a and 1b). At some later time, the new copy is returned to the home site (2) with an evict message. The home site then elects a site and sends an inject message (3).</td><td>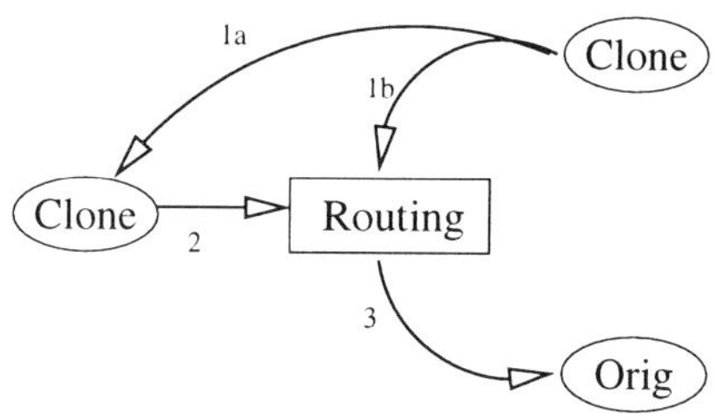
</td></tr>
</table>

Table 2. Examples of Atomic Transactions

copy for itself. Importantly, the site initiating the migration is allowed to send out an *exclusive* copy (and degrade its own copy to *invalid*), or to send out an *original* copy (and degrade its own copy to *clone*), but may not send out a *clone* and keep its own copy as *original*. This restriction is due to race conditions discussed below.

At any point, a site can decide to evict an object. This is illustrated in Table 2 (d). The *home site* must be notified, even if the object was in the *clone* state. When an *original* or *exclusive* copy is spontaneously evicted, it is sent back to the *home site*, which then either keeps it locally (in *exclusive-owned* or *original-owned* state), or sends it out again.

We need one final rule to cope with certain race conditions. See figure 3. We specify that any message sent from the *home site* is returned to sender if the message expected to find an object in either the *exclusive* or the *original* state, and does not do so (i.e., the object is in the *clone* or *invalid* state instead). These returned messages, upon arrival at the *home site*, are then redirected to the copy in the *exclusive* or *original* state.

Interestingly, this is sufficient to handle *all* transactions. More complicated exchanges are implicit in this specification. Thus, for example, a *read* to container structure is a chain-reaction of *apply* transactions. Migration can also cause chain reactions.

6. Conclusions and Future Work

In this paper, we have reviewed a proposal for a radical COMA which leverages parallelizing compiler tech-

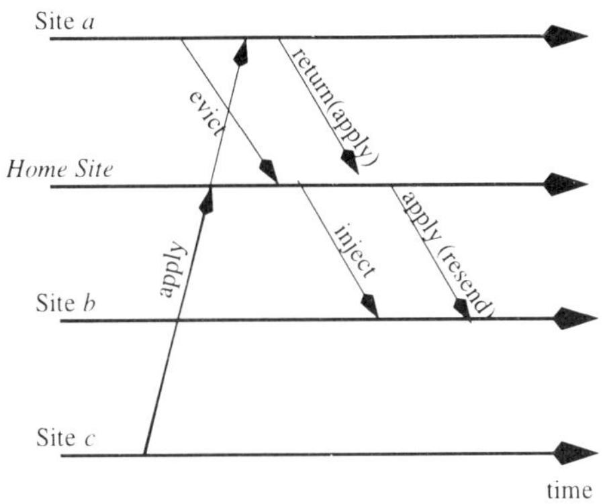

Figure 3. Race Conditions in the new SDAARC Protocol: An *Apply* is sent from site *c* to the *home site* and then on to site *a*. At about the same time, site *a evicts* the object, and the *home site* relocates the object at site *b*. The *apply* arrives too late at site *a*, is returned to the home site, and is then forwarded to site *b*. Compare figure 2 above.

niques and then extends COMA techniques to tackle the entire problem of distributing both data and also computation across a parallel and distributed computing system (whereas conventional COMA addresses only *data* distribution).

Since first publishing the SDAARC proposal in [7], we have made the following progress toward implementing it:

- A first prototype for the microthread extraction and code generation has been completed (preliminary thread extraction results have been published in [5]).
- Further, an distributed emulator has been written in Java and is being tested at the moment on a Beowulf cluster consisting of four Linux PCs and a dedicated Fast Ethernet network.

Initial experience with the emulator identified many of the problems discussed in this paper, and lead to the development of the protocol presented above.

References

[1] M. Annavaram and W. A. Najjar. Comparison of two storage models in data-driven multithreaded architectures. In *Eighth IEEE Symposium on Parallel and Distributed Processing (SPDP)*, pages 122–129, New Orleans, LA, Oct. 1996. IEEE, IEEE Computer Society Press.

[2] D. E. Culler, S. C. Goldstein, K. E. Schauser, and T. von Eicken. TAM — A compiler controlled Threaded Abstract Machine. In *Journal of Parallel and Distributed Computing, Special Issue on Dataflow*, June 1993.

[3] E. Hagersten, A. Landin, and S. Haridi. DDM — A Cache-Only Memory Architecture. *IEEE Computer*, 25(9):44–54, 1992.

[4] J. Handy. *The Cache Memory Book*. Academic Press, Inc., San Diego, CA, 1993.

[5] R. Moore, M. Klang, B. Klauer, and K. Waldschmidt. Combining static partitioning with dynamic distribution of threads. In F. J. Rammig, editor, *Distributed and Parallel Embedded Systems, IFIP WG 10.3 / WG 10.5 International Workshop on Distributed and Parallel Embedded Systems (DIPES'98), October 5-6, 1998, Schloß Eringerfeld, Germany*, International Federation for Information Processing, pages 85–96. Kluwer Academic Publishers, 1999.

[6] R. Moore, B. Klauer, and K. Waldschmidt. Automatic scheduling for Cache Only Memory Architectures. In *Third International Conference on Massively Parallel Computing Systems (MPCS '98)*, Colorado Springs, Colorado, Apr. 1998.

[7] R. Moore, B. Klauer, and K. Waldschmidt. A combined virtual shared memory and network which schedules. *International Journal of Parallel and Distributed Systems and Networks*, 1(2):51–56, 1998.

[8] R. Moore, S. Zickenheiner, B. Klauer, F. Henritzi, A. Bleck, and K. Waldschmidt. Neural compiler technology for a parallel architecture. In *International Conference on Parallel and Distributed Processing Techniques and Applications (PDPTA '96)*, Sunnyvale, CA, Aug. 1996.

[9] R. S. Nikhil. A multithreaded implementation of Id using P-RISC graphs. In *Proceedings of the Sixth Annual Workshop on Languages and Compilers for Parallel Computing*, pages 390–405, Portland, Oregon, Aug. 1993. Springer Verlag LNCS 768.

[10] A. Saulsbury, T. Wilkinson, J. Carter, and A. Landin. An argument for simple COMA. In *First IEEE Symposium on High Performance Computer Architecture*, pages 276–285, Rayleigh, North Carolina, Jan. 1995.

[11] P. Stenström, T. Joe, and A. Gupta. Comparative performance evaluation of cahe-coherent NUMA and COMA architectures. In *Proceedings of the 19th Anual International Symposium on Computer Architecture*, pages 80–91, Gold Coast, Australia, May 1992.

[12] T. Sterling, J. Salmon, D. Becker, and D. F. Savarese. *How to Build a Beowulf*. MIT Press, May 1999.

[13] J. Strohschneider, B. Klauer, S. Zickenheiner, F. Henritzi, and K. Waldschmidt. ADARC – Associative processors and processing. In A. Krikelis and C. C. Weems, editors, *Associative Processing and Processors*, pages 82–96. IEEE Computer Society Press, 1997.

[14] A. Tannenbaum. *Computer Networks*. Prentice Hall, 3rd edition, 1996.

[15] T. von Eicken, D. E. Culler, S. C. Goldstein, and K. E. Schauser. Active messages: a mechanism for integrated communication and computation. In *Proc. of the 19th International Symposium on Computer Architecture*, Gold Coast, Australia, May 1992. (Also available as Technical Report UCB/CSD 92/675, CS Div., University of California at Berkeley).

[16] M. Wolfe. *High Performance Compilers for Parallel Computing*. Addison-Wesley Publishing Company, 1996.

A Framework for Process Migration in Software DSM Environments *

Ivan Zoraja
Department of Electronics and Computer Science
University of Split
21000 Split, Croatia
E-mail: zoraja@fesb.hr

Arndt Bode
LRR-TUM, Institut für Informatik,
Technische Universität München, 80290 München, Germany
E-mail: bode@in.tum.de

Vaidy Sunderam
Department of Math and Computer Science
Emory University, Atlanta, GA 30322, USA
E-mail: vss@mathcs.emory.edu

Abstract

In this paper we prove that process migration can successfully be implemented for software DSM environments. We have developed a migration framework that is able to transparently migrate DSM processes, thereby preserving the consistency of running applications. The migration framework is integrated into the CORAL system, an online monitoring system that connects parallel tools to a running application. A special emphasis has been put on techniques and mechanisms for migration of shared resources and communication channels as well as internal monitoring data structures.

Currently, the migration framework migrates parallel processes based on the TreadMarks library. The Condor library has been utilized for the state transfer of a single process. In the computing environment consisting of eight nodes running TreadMarks applications, the migration framework brings 10 % overhead to Condor and grows almost linearly with added nodes. Although our first implementation supports TreadMarks applications, both the monitoring system and the migration framework are designed to be reusable and easily adaptable to other software DSM systems.

*Research supported by *German Science Foundation* SFB342, Subproject A1, *Department of Energy* grant DE-FG05-91ER25105, *National Science Foundation* grants ASC-9527186 and CCR-9523544 and *Army Research Office* grant DAAH04-96-1-0083.

1. Introduction

Load balancing presents an efficient technique to reduce the execution time of parallel applications and provide an even usage of computational resources. Generally, it incorporates load information management, distributed scheduling strategies and load migration mechanisms. Load information management deals with measurement, collection and evaluation of the load on computing nodes. Scheduling strategies make use of usually heuristic algorithms to take decisions which unit is to be migrated, what is the new target and when the migration should take place. Finally, migration mechanisms transfer load in forms of processes, threads or objects among computing resources and take care about the consistency of the running application.

The software DSM paradigm hides the distributed nature of the underlying hardware from the application programmer by providing an abstraction of shared memory in software. Thus, the programmer is not directly confronted with communication patterns which unless regular may impose a significant burden on him to manage the data movement – as it is in the *message passing* programming model. Instead, he or she is only required to ensure synchronization when accessing shared data. It is the task of the DSM runtime system to transparently manage the coherence of shared data by employing the underlying virtual memory and messages passing capabilities. There are a number of research activities focused on this very attractive research area exploring its adequacy for both high performance computing and commercial and business applications, but most of them have been undergone as experimental prototypes.

For the evaluation of our migration scheme we chose TreadMarks [1], a commercial product that presents the state of the art in the realm of software DSM systems. We utilize Condor [11] to checkpoint and restore the state of a single process. The migration framework is a part of the CORAL project, which provides online monitoring support to parallel tools and integrates load balancing, consistent checkpointing and performance analysis and is aimed to extend OMIS [12] to the DSM paradigm. The rest of the paper provides a background material on software DSMs, and discusses the impact of their implementations on process migration. Further, we discuss the differences between single and parallel process migration, describe the key features of our implementation and evaluate its effectiveness in terms of functionality and performance. Finally, we close the paper with a comparison to related systems, a discussion on our findings and suggestions for future work.

2. Software DSM Systems

Software DSM systems [27, 14] enhance the shared memory paradigm over a pool of workstation clusters and thus have become an appealing platform for development of parallel and distributed applications. Underlying communication patterns are hidden by runtime systems (RTS), which detect shared accesses using virtual memory mechanisms, user annotations or special compilers, and translate them to the underlying messages passing, thereby trying to minimize the overall system access latencies.

According to the structure of the shared address space and the sharing granularity, the following breakdown of software DSM systems can be obtained:

- **Page-based Systems** – support an unstructured address space at granularity of a page. In addition, these systems usually rely on virtual memory mechanisms to detect shared accesses. Typical representatives are TreadMarks, Cashmere [6], and Brazos [18].
- **Fine-grained Systems** – implement a fine-grained sharing and instrument memory operations to detect shared accesses. To insert the instrumentation code these systems make use of special compilers. Shasta [15] and Sirocco [16] are typical representatives.
- **Object-based Systems** – rely completely on the underlying messaging and provide structured address space at granularity which varies with user-defined constructs. Some systems require user annotations to detect shared accesses, while the others encapsulate data and operations and make use of proxies to determine sharing patterns. Typical examples are Linda [5] and Orca [2].

2.1. TreadMarks

TreadMarks is a commercial page-based DSM system which runs processes on UNIX or NT nodes that are connected by a common network. It implements several innovative features, including *lazy release consistency* and *multiple writer* protocol. TreadMarks buffers writes and propagates only modifications made on shared pages. In contrast to the *release consistency* model, where the propagation of page modifications is performed at the next release operation, TreadMarks postpones the propagation of differences (*diffs*) until they are really needed.

When TreadMarks releases a lock, it sends a message to the new acquirer. Among other information, the message contains notifications (*write notices*) for the pages that have been changed since the most recent time when the new acquirer released a lock. This strategy can substantially reduce network traffic and improve system performance. However, the system must maintain transitive information and, in order to validate pages, use a *vector timestamp* protocol to determine which modifications are needed to be obtained from other nodes. The timestamp protocol ensures the partial order of synchronization operations.

UNIX Aspects. Because our first implementation runs on Solaris 2.6 we give a brief insight into UNIX aspects of TreadMarks. The first TreadMarks process utilizes the `mmap` system call to establish the mapping between shared pages and its virtual address space. Further, according to the names in the configuration file, it starts processes on the given machines using either `rsh` or `rexec`. Among other arguments, the command line contains the beginning virtual address and its UDP communication ports. Each new process maps then the shared pages to the same virtual address, and connects the first process to obtain the ports of other new processes. After the ports have been obtained, the processes establish communication with each other.

Each process manages an array of page states and uses the `mprotect` system call to change the access protections on pages. An access to a non-valid page generates the `SIGSEGV` signal. The `SIGSEGV` handler consults internal data structures and in order to obtain page modifications sends messages to other processes. On remote nodes, the incoming message triggers the `SIGIO` signal. The `SIGIO` handler make use of the `select` system call to find out which process has sent the request and then consults internal data structures to construct a reply message which is then sent to the requester. Locks are implemented by sending a message to a manager, which forwards it to the last requester, thereby maintaining a distributed FIFO queue of requesting processes. Barriers are implemented by a central manager which gathers arrival and dispatches departure massages.

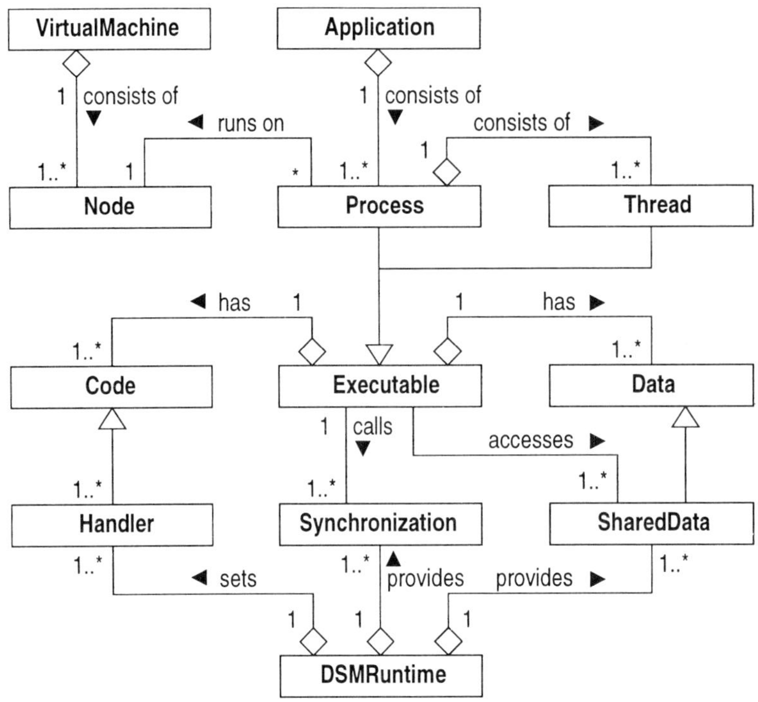

Figure 1. CORAL objects being monitored

3. The CORAL System

The CORAL [26] (**C**ooperative **O**nline Monito**r**ing **A**ctions **L**ayer) project is aimed at the design and implementation of online monitoring systems that support parallel applications based on the DSM programming paradigm. Figure 1 depicts the basic model of objects being monitored by CORAL. For the sake of simplicity only basic UML [4] relationships: dependency, association (aggregation) and generalization are used. Although the model is presented using UML – a well-established standard for modeling of object-oriented systems – the particular implementation can be realized in languages that are not object-oriented.

3.1. CORAL Objects

With respect to Figure 1, the class `VirtualMachine` represents the hardware platforms and system software on which applications run. It consists of several `Nodes` or clusters interconnected by a network. A node may contain several processors, private caches and local memory modules which are usually attached to a single bus. The `Application` class stands for a user application and consists of multiple processes that are represented via the `Process` class. The `Thread` class acts for both user-level and kernel-level threads. The `Object` class (not shown in the model) may be used to represent objects in sense of object-oriented languages. The basic building blocks for an application are the `Code` and `Data` classes. The first class contains operations in a programming or machine language while the second one describes data on which the operations are performed.

The `Executable` class encompasses the previous classes and may interact with other `Executables` through the DSM functionality that is represented via the `Synchronization`, `SharedData`, and `Handler` classes. The `Synchronization` class describes synchronization primitives that are implemented by DSM libraries and used by applications. The `SharedData` class describes data shared among multiple `Executables`. To this category belong lines, variables, pages, regions, tuples, and objects. For the sake of simplicity they are not depicted in the model. DSM mechanisms are represented via the `Handler` class.

3.2. CORAL Architecture

The CORAL monitoring system provides online monitoring support to parallel tools and integrates load balancing, consistent checkpointing, and performance analysis. It is itself a distributed application consisting of a control unit, called the CORAL Control Unit (CCU), local monitors, called CORAL Local Monitors (CLMs), and application wrappers (adapters), called Intruders.

The CCU gets requests from tools, performs needed checking to avoid possible deadlocks and starvations and distributes the requests to CLMs. Further, it gathers replies and sends them back to the tools. CLMs run on each node being monitored and, in addition to controlling the execution of the running application, gather load information from the current node and dispatch it to the CCU. CLMs make use of both shared memory segments and the `/proc` file system interface to control a running application and react on events generated in the application. Intruders are hooks into the target library, which monitor entering and returning from the library, perform actions given by CLMs, and send the requested information back.

The communication among monitoring components is accomplished through a fast and compact library, called Monitoring Communication Interface (MCI), which makes use of both TCP sockets and shared memory segments for local and remote communication, respectively. MCI is derived from the SCIPVM [25] library. In order to avoid disruption of local computing, potentially caused by monitoring components, and still preserve the effectiveness of the monitoring functionality, MCI implements interrupt-driven communication, buffering of early messages and multiplexing among multiple senders.

3.3. CORAL Startup

On startup, the CCU reads the DSM configuration file, starts CLMs on each specified node and, in order to perform load measurement, starts CLMs on some other nodes which are candidates for migration targets. CLMs establish communication with each other, create shared memory segments to talk to Intruders, and send shared memory identifiers back to the CCU, which writes them to the CORAL configuration file. The application to be monitored is linked against the DSM library, the Condor library and the Intruder library. While the intrusion library wraps DSM routines, it takes control at the application startup, reads the CORAL configuration file, and connects its local monitor. The monitoring system is started when all Intruders have been connected.

4. Process Migration

Process migration is a valuable mechanism for balancing of the load in a pool of computing nodes. Generally, process migration includes three phases:

Detaching Phase – encompasses actions to isolate the migree from its current computing environment, including the monitoring system and local and remote resources. All affected processes must be taken in a state in which the detaching of the migree does not cause any execution inconsistencies.

Transfer Phase – moves the migree to the target node. All information needed to restore the migree as well as internal data required by the monitoring system must be transfered.

Attaching Phase – reconstructs the process and its resources on the target node and updates other processes. Internal monitoring data structures should be updated and the application may continue execution.

Despite its indisputable advantages, process migration has not been widely used, especially because of its potential implementation complexity, heterogeneity of processor architecture, and lack of a common interface to the operating system. In the CORAL project, we employ Condor [11] as a legacy software for checkpointing and restoring the state of a single process, and implement a migration framework which performs the migration phases. The migration framework saves and reconstructs shared resources – in our case, shared data, communication channels, and internal monitoring structures that describe the objects being monitored.

4.1. Condor

Condor is a distributed batch processing system for UNIX environments. It provides a checkpointing library which allows a process to checkpoint itself by calling the `ckpt` routine, which writes the process state to a file or a socket. On a remote node, a new process reading the file or the socket is able to restore the state of the old one. From the operating system's perspective it is really a new process. The user code, in contrast, sees the restarting as the return from the `ckpt` call. Condor is able to manage text and data areas, shared libraries, mapped segments, signals, the processor state, and files. However, it does not deal with communication channels, `fork` and `exec` system calls, and mapped segments that are not visible through the `/proc` file system.

5. CORAL Migration Framework

In this paper we focus on the process migration framework and mechanisms needed to perform the migration phases defined in previous section. Figure 2 shows the scenario which takes place when a tool sends a request to the CCU to migrate process P_i from node N_i to N_j. The process to be migrated consists of four parts that are marked by letters I, A, D and C. They stand for Intruder, application code, the DSM library, and the Condor library, respectively. Full arrows denote messages exchanged using MCI, while the dotted ones describe other actions.

To perform the migration, the CCU sends a `MIGRATE` message to the appropriate local monitor (M_i) and a `PREPARE` message to all other monitors that are controlling

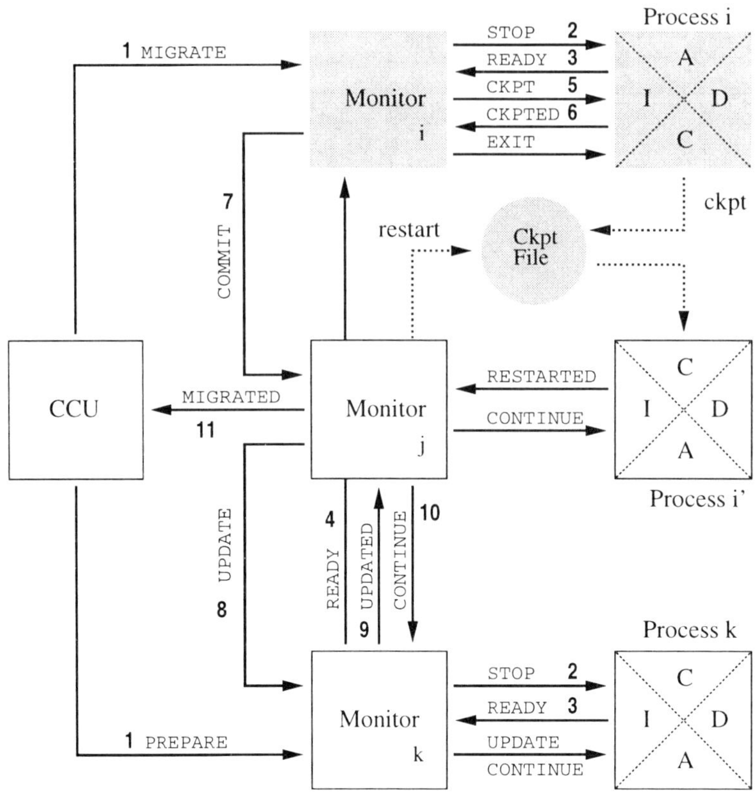

Figure 2. CORAL Migration Framework

DSM processes. Monitors send a STOP message to Intruders, which then try to find a point of execution that is safe for migration. In the current version we have adopted a simple strategy – the migration may be performed when all locks are released. messageThe idea behind this is deadlock avoidance. If a process holding a lock had been stopped, a potential acquirer would stay in an infinite loop requesting the lock which cannot be released and thus would not be able to reach the safe point. Since in real applications locks are acquired and released quite often, this constraint does not unnecessarily delay the migration. If the safe point has not been reached within a specified amount of time, an abort message is sent to the CCU, which aborts the migration by sending appropriate messages to CLMs. For the sake of simplicity these messages are not shown in Figure 2.

When the safe point has been reached, Intruders send a READY message to their monitors, which forward the message to the migrating node. At this point, M_i and its Intruder can save shared data and destroy communication channels and call Condor to perform the checkpointing. Condor writes the process state to a file and returns to Intruder, which sends a CKPTED message to its monitor and terminates P_i. M_i sends then a COMMIT to M_j, which makes use of the exec system call to start a new process, giving the name of the checkpointing file as a parameter. In the new process ($P_i^{'}$) Condor reads the checkpointing file, restores the process state and returns to Intruder, which connects M_j and restores its shared data and communication channels. M_j updates all other processes by sending an UPDATE message to all other monitors (M_k). After the resources have been restored on all nodes, acknowledgment messages are sent back to M_j, which allows the application to continue execution by sending a CONTINUE message to all the monitors. Finally, M_j sends a MIGRATED message to the CCU informing it that the migration has been successfully performed.

5.1. Shared Data

The migration of shared data strongly depends on the particular DSM implementation. Usually, in order to detect shared accesses, DSM libraries make use of virtual address management routines provided by the underling operating system. In CORAL, a local monitor makes use of the /proc process interface to obtain the process's address mapping and the shared memory interface to communicate with Intruders, which are linked into application processes.

In order to detach the migree from its current environment, CLM stops the process, reads its virtual address map, writes the map (an array of prmap_t structures) to the

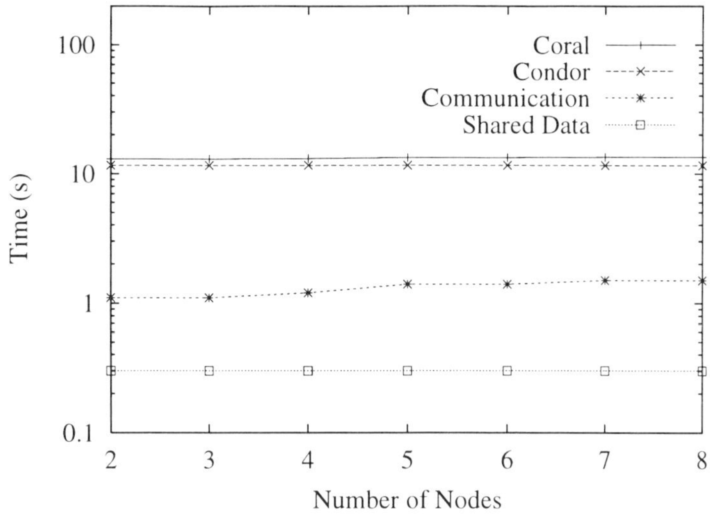

Figure 3. Average Migration Times

shared memory segment and allows the process to continue execution. When the intruder library gains control, it unmaps the shared pages from the process's virtual address space, saves the content and protection flags of each segment in a file, saves communication information, and yields control to Condor, which saves the state of the process. On the other node, after Condor has reconstructed the process state, the control is given to th intruder library. It then maps the shared data to the new process's virtual address space, updates page contents, sets the old protection flags, and finally connects its CLM.

5.2. Communication Channels

On workstation clusters, DSM libraries make use of TCP or UDP channels to communicate remote processes. In both cases on each side the communication channel can be identified by three resources: an Internet address, a port number, and a file descriptor. In the current version CORAL migrates connected UDP sockets, that are transparently utilized by the TreadMarks library and therefore are not visible through its API.

The scenario for destruction and construction of the communication routes is as follows: When Intruder gains control during the migration, it saves information about all communication channels to remote processes and destroys the channels. Since the migration is performed at safe points, a remote process can not asynchronously trigger a `SIGIO` handler that could use the resources. After resurrecting on a new node, the intruder library rebuilds the communication channels, connects its CLM and passes the new port numbers to it. The CLM distributes the new node name and the new ports numbers to all other monitors, which then update application processes. After all processes have been updated, the application is allowed to continue execution.

5.3. Monitoring Data

The design and implementation of the CORAL monitoring system is centered around the model of DSM objects being monitored shown in Figure 1. Each CLM, maintains data structures to keep information about the objects being monitored. Since the CORAL monitoring system allows multiple tools to observe and manipulate DSM objects at runtime, the monitoring data structures must also be transfered during the migration. This feature allows parallel tools to continue monitoring after migrations. For instance, process migration should be transparent for the performance analysis tool, while the performance data gathered by the monitoring system is preserved and transfered to the new monitor during the migration process. CORAL sends the monitoring information along with the `COMMIT` message.

6. System Evaluations

The primary objective of the migration evaluation has been to determine the times spent by the monitoring framework when doing specific tasks. The first category includes unmapping, transferring, and remapping of shared pages. The time needed to migrate communication channels, which includes destroying, rebuilding, and updating the communication channels, defines the second category. This category includes all other messages exchanged by CORAL itself and the time needed to reach the safe point for migration. Finally, the third category is the time consumed by Condor to perform the checkpointing and restarting of a single process.

The experiments were conducted on Solaris 2.6 machines interconnected by Fast Ethernet and running a Traveling Salesman application on one to eight nodes. Condor wrote the process state to a file using NFS. The average size the checkpoint file was 5 Mbtyes. The average size of shared data was 256 Kbytes.

Figure 3 shows the average times taken by Condor to migrate a single process and by CORAL to migrate shared data (mappings) and communication channels including monitoring data. Since we migrated only one process at a time the cost of Condor does not change with the number of nodes and amounts up to 90% of all CORAL cost. The number of pages accessed inside the common virtual address segment determines the amount of shared data, which must be migrated. This factor depends on the application access patterns. In our experiments we kept this factor constant by performing migration at the same point of execution. Finally, communication costs for destroying, establishing, and updating of communication channels grow almost linearly with added nodes.

7. Discussion

We have shown that process migration can be successfully performed in software DSM environments and presented an effective approach towards migration of shared data and communication channels including the internal monitoring data. In the realm of parallel and distributed systems, process migration have been implemented for the message passing [19, 24, 13] and hardware DSM (Origin 2000) systems. To balance the load in software DSM systems only page migration and replication [1, 6, 18], object migration and replication [2], thread migration [21, 10, 23], and loop scheduling [9, 17] have been utilized.

In contrast to page migration techniques where shared data (pages, diffs, regions, objects) are managed, thread migration moves code and data. By utilizing thread migrations false sharing can be reduced or even completely eliminated if all competing threads are co-located on the node where the shared page resides. However, if too many threads are located on the same node, the overhead of context switching and synchronization may degrade the system performance.

To perform loop scheduling some DSM systems combine compiler and runtime support to distribute the work of the parallel loops, trying to balance relative load of the processors and to minimize communication costs caused by data sharing. Source to source translations from a sequential program to a parallel DSM-based program is accomplished using special compilers. The sequential code is usually augmented with calls to the runtime library before parallel loops. Each time when the runtime systems gain control, they may change the number of loop bounds and therefore the amount of work that must be performed by individual tasks.

The primary disadvantage of the previous approaches is that the load balancing can only be performed inside the current computing environment. CORAL, in contrast, migrates processes and may include new nodes into the virtual machine and therefore avoid using nodes which have become overloaded after the application has been started.

The CORAL migration framework is similar to the CoCheck [20, 19] system, but CORAL is more complex. CoCheck deals only with communication routes that are directly available through the PVM [22, 3] or MPI [7, 8] libraries. CORAL, in contrast, must deal with shared data and communication routes which are not visible through the DSM API. Further, CoCheck uses the PVM Resource Manager and the PVM or MPI communication routines to perform interprocess communication, while CORAL implements a communication library which is not part of the system being monitored.

CORAL utilizes the Condor library as a legacy software for checkpointing and restoring the state of a single process via NFS. The current version of Condor spends about twelve seconds to checkpoint and restore a single process which makes use of virtual memory mechanisms. This is the biggest cost in the migration scheme. If virtual memory mechanisms are not employed, the measured time is about two seconds. In order to have TreadMarks and Condor working together we were forced to make some minor changes to the TreadMarks library. In particular we changed all `close` system calls to `syscall(SYS_close)`, since the `socket` system call is not wrapped by Condor and closing a socket results in a Condor runtime error.

8. Future Work and Conclusions

The design and implementation of the migration framework have proven to be very successful and beneficial. A number of issues concerning the migration of DSM processes as well as the integration of the monitoring framework into a monitoring system have been identified. While our results and findings so far are very promising and strongly motivate further investigations, we are going to continue our research along several dimensions.

One of the first enhancements to be undertaken is to investigate the integration of load balancing with performance analysis, checkpointing and debugging. We will further test our scheme for a larger cluster configuration, and explore interaction of migration mechanisms with scheduling strategies. A third modification involves using the socket option of the Condor library to transfer the state of a single process. It will lead to a more efficient and elegant solution, since the current transfer via NFS is very expensive and disruptive to the internal monitoring communications. Further, in order to get a better insight into migration potentials and benefits, we will repeat our experiments with real-world DSM applications. Finally, some long term work will be undertaken to compare process migration strategies with other load balancing techniques applied in DSM environments.

This paper has discussed issues and solutions for the migration of processes that support the DSM paradigm as a substrate upon which to construct process migration frameworks and integrate them into online monitoring systems. Most of our efforts in this regard have been to understand capabilities and limitations of process migration in DSM environments and to construct a migration framework in a manner such that any DSM system can easily be supported. In particular, although our first implementation is based on TreadMarks, the migration framework can be easily applied to other DSM systems.

References

[1] C. Amza, A. L. Cox, S. Dwarkadas, P. Keleher, H. Lu, R. Rajamony, W. Yu, and W. Zwaenepoel. TreadMarks: Shared Memory Computing on Networks of Workstations. *IEEE Computer*, 29(2):18–28, February 1996.

[2] H. E. Bal, F. Kaashoek, and A. S. Tanenbaum. Orca: A Language for Parallel Programming of Distributed Systems. *IEEE Transaction on Software Engineering*, 18(3):190–205, March 1992.

[3] A. Beguelin, J. Dongara, A. Geist, R. Manchek, W. Jiang, and V. S. Sunderam. *PVM: A User's Guide and Tutorial for Networked Parallel Computing*. MIT Press, 1994.

[4] G. Booch, J. Rumbaugh, and I. Jacobson. *The Unified Modeling Language User Guide*. Addison-Wesley, 1999.

[5] N. Carriero and D. Gelernter. Linda in Context. *Communication of ACM*, 32:42–51, April 1989.

[6] S. Dwarkadas, N. Hardavellas, L. Kontothanassis, R. Nikhil, and R. Stets. Cashmere-VLM: Remote Memory Paging for Software Distributed Shared Memory. In *Proceedings of IPPS '99*, April 1999.

[7] T. M. Forum. MPI: A Message-Passing Interface Standard, Version 1.1'. Technical report, University of Tennessee', Knoxville, TN, June 1995.

[8] T. M. Forum. MPI-2: Extensions to the Message-Passing Interface. Technical report, University of Tennessee, Knoxville, TN, July 1997.

[9] S. Ioannidis and S. Dwarkadas. Compiler and Run-Time Support for Adaptive Load Balancing in Software Distributed Shared Memory Systems. May 1998.

[10] A. Itzkovitz, A. Schuster, and L. Shalev. Thread Migration and its Applications in Distributed Shared Memory Systems . *The Journal of Systems and Software*, 42(1):71–87, July 1998.

[11] M. Litzkov, T. Tannenbaum, J. Basney, and M. Livny. Checkpoint and Migration of UNIX Processes in the Condor Distributed Processing System. Technical Report 1346, Computer Science Department, University of Wisconsin-Madison, April 1997.

[12] T. Ludwig, R. Wismüller, V. Sunderam, and A. Bode. OMIS – On-line Monitoring Interface Specification, Version 2.0. Technical Report 9, LRR - Techniche Universität München, 1997. Shaker Verlag.

[13] U. Maier, G. Stellner, and I. Zoraja. Resource Allocation, Scheduling and Load Balancing based on PVM Resource Manager. In *Parallel Computing: Fundamentals, Applications and New Directions (Proceedings of ParCo97)*, pages 711–718. Elsevier Publishers, 1997.

[14] J. Protić, M. Tomašević, and V. Milutinović. *Distributed Shared Memory: Concepts and Systems*. IEEE Computer Society, 1998.

[15] D. J. Scales and K. Gharachorloo. Shasta: A System for Supporting Fine-Grain Shared Memory Across Clusters. In *Proceedings of the Eight SIAM Conference on Parallel Processing for Scientific Computing*, March 1997.

[16] I. Schonias, B. Falsafi, M. D. Hill, J. R. Larus, and D. A. Wood. Sirocco: Cost-Effective Fine-Grain Distributed Shared Memory. In *International Conference on Parallel Architecture and Compilation Techniques*, October 1998.

[17] W. Shi, W. Hu, Z. Tang, and M. R. Eskicioglu. Dynamic Task Migration in Home-based Software DSM Systems. August 1999.

[18] E. Speight and J. K. .Bennett. Brazos: A Third Generation DSM System. In *Proceedings of the 1997 USENIX/WindowsNT Workshop*, August 1997.

[19] G. Stellner. CoCheck: Checkpointing and Process Migration for MPI. In *Proceedings of the International Parallel Processing Symposium*, pages 26–531. IEEE Computer Society Press, April 1996.

[20] G. Stellner and J. Pruyne. Resource Management and Checkpointing for PVM. In *Proceedings of EuroPVM'95*, volume 5, pages 131–136. Hermès, September 1995.

[21] Y. Sudo, S. Suzuki, and S. Shibayama. Distributed-Thread Scheduling Methods for Reducing Page-Threshing. In *Proceedings of the 6th IEEE International Symposium on High Performance Distributed Computing*, 1997.

[22] V. S. Sunderam. PVM: A Framework for Parallel Distributed Computing. *Concurrency: Practice and Experience*, 2(4):315–339, December 1990.

[23] K. Thitikamol and P. Keleher. Thread Migration and Communication Minimization in DSM Systems. *Proceedings of the IEEE*, March 1999.

[24] R. Wismueller, J. Trinitis, and T. Ludwig. OCM - A Monitoring System for Interoperable Tools. In *Proceedings of 2nd. SIGMETRICS Symphosium on Parallel and Distributed Tools SPDT98*, pages 1–9. ACM Press, August 1998.

[25] I. Zoraja, H. Hellwagner, and V. Sunderam. SCIPVM: Parallel Distributed Computing on SCI Workstation Clusters. *Concurrency: Practice and Experience*, 11(13):121–138, March 1999.

[26] I. Zoraja, G. Rackl, and T. Ludwig. Towards Monitoring in Parallel and Distributed Systems. In *Proceedings of SoftCOM '99*, pages 133–141, October 1999.

[27] I. Zoraja, G. Rackl, M. Schulz, A. Bode, and V. Sunderam. Modern Software DSM Systems: Models and Techniques. Technical report, SFB Report, LRR - Techniche Universität München, to appear.

PQE_HPF - A Library for Exploiting the Capabilities of a PQE-1 Heterogeneous Parallel Architecture

R. Baraglia, R. Ferrini, D. Laforenza, P. Palmerini, R. Perego
CNUCE-C.N.R. Institute
Via S. Maria 36 I-56126 Pisa (PI), ITALY
{baraglia,ferrini,laforenza,perego}@cnuce.cnr.it
palmerini@guest.cnuce.cnr.it

Abstract

Heterogeneous Computing is a special form of parallel and distributed computing where computations are performed using a single autonomous computer operating in both SIMD and MIMD modes, or using a number of connected autonomous computers. In Multimode System Heterogeneous Computing, tasks can be executed in both SIMD and MIMD simultaneously.

In this paper we present PQE_HPF, an HPF-based programming library which allows to exploit the MIMD and SIMD capabilities offered by PQE-1, a Multimode Parallel Architecture.

Two different implementations of a well-known application using HPF and PQE_HPF respectively were used to evaluate the overheads introduced over the machine's runtime system. Preliminary tests conducted by running the case study application on the first PQE-1 prototype show good results and encourage to dedicate more efforts to implement real production parallel codes on a similar architecture.

Keywords. *Heterogeneous Computing, Multimode Heterogeneous Systems, Task and Data Parallelism Integration, HPF.*

1. Introduction

Heterogeneous Computing (HC) is considered an important area of research since the mid 1980s. It is defined as a special form of parallel and distributed computing that performs computations using a single autonomous computer operating in both Single Instruction Multiple Data (SIMD) and Multiple Instruction Multiple Data (MIMD) modes, or using a number of connected autonomous computers [6].

According to [6], where a taxonomy of heterogeneous computing is presented, there are two types of HC: System Heterogeneous Computing (SHC) and Network Heterogeneous Computing (NHC). In SHC, an autonomous multiprocessor or multicomputer can execute one or more computational tasks in both SIMD and MIMD modes. An SHC can be build as a multimode and mixed-mode system. In multimode SHC, computations can be executed in both SIMD and MIMD simultaneously. In mixed-mode SHC, the execution mode is switched from MIMD mode to SIMD mode and vice versa.

A multimode SHC may be build as a hierarchical composition of basic architectural models (SMP/UMA, NUMA, SIMD, etc).

In this paper we present PQE_HPF, an HPF-based programming library implemented at CNUCE-CNR to exploit the MIMD and SIMD capabilities offered by PQE-1, a multimode SHC Parallel Architecture [17] [18].

This paper is organized as follows: in Section 2 the PQE-1 architecture is introduced; Section 3 presents some details of the PQE_HPF library; Section 4 introduces a well-known application chosen as a case study and shows some performance figures obtained by evaluating two implementations of the algorithm, obtained by using HPF and PQE_HPF, respectively.

Finally, in Section 5 some conclusions and future work are presented.

2. The PQE-1 Architecture

PQE-1 is a prototype machine developed within the framework of the Italian PQE2000 Project [5]. Several PQE-1 machines are currently operational in some Italian sites and, in particular, at the ENEA Research Center located in Casaccia (Rome).

One of the main aims of the PQE2000 Project is the realization of an architecture characterized by the hierarchical composition of several architectural styles. e.g. NUMA plus SMP at the outermost level, Processor in Memory

(PIM)/Active Memory at the innermost level [5].

PQE-1 represents a first step toward a complete PQE2000 architecture. As sketched in Figure 1 a PQE-1 machine is composed by MIMD and SIMD layers. PQE-1 connects a MIMD computer (Meiko CS-2) with more SIMD machines (Quadrics) [5]. Each SIMD component is connected to one of the MIMD nodes by a HiPPI channel. Quadrics machines can have different numbers of nodes, connected in a toroidal topology. Every SIMD node has its own local memory for real variables, which can be accessed by its nearest neighbors nodes, and a global memory for integer variables, shared among all the SIMD nodes.

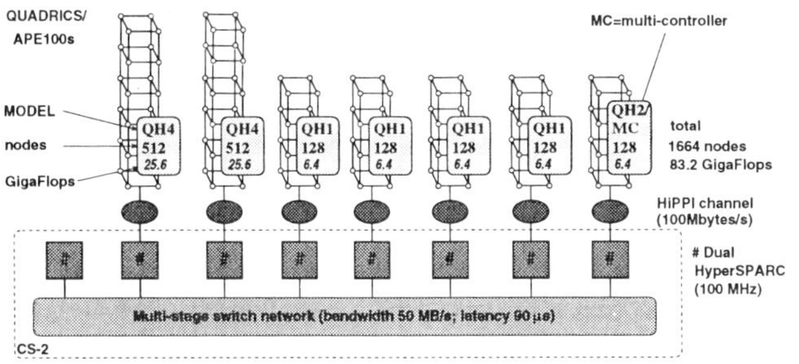

Figure 1. PQE-1 prototype

Many important parallel applications are composed of several cooperating sub-components, each of them adopting a particular form of parallelism (task, data, vector, dataflow, etc.). When the sub-components are coarse-grained and cooperate in asynchronous or loosely-synchronous way [10], this kind of applications can be more efficiently executed on a multimode SHC, like PQE-1. The advantage of exploiting both forms of parallelism is twofold. On the one hand the capability of integrating task and data parallelism in a single framework allows the number of addressable applications to be enlarged. On the other hand, the exploitation of parallelism at different levels may significantly increase the performances of algorithms which, by means of HPF alone, would exploit only a limited amount of data parallelism [15] [13] [3].

2.1. Programming the SIMD part of a PQE-1 architecture

To program the SIMD components a Fortran dialect, called TAO [14], is available. The most relevant peculiarity of this language is related to the data distribution strategy [14]. In fact, due to the SIMD machine's architecture, integer variables are always shared among all the SIMD nodes, while real variables can have different values from one node to another. This implies that real arrays stored in a single SIMD node can be thought of as part of global bigger arrays obtained by joining together all the arrays local to the single node. But it is also possible to think of the local arrays as copies of the same array, with different values. So, for example, if it is declared an array of N real elements, it is possible to think of a bigger array of $N \times$ `number_of_simd_processors` elements, distributed block-wise among the SIMD nodes, or of `number_of_simd_processors` copies of the same array.

To execute a program on a Quadrics machine, the following actions need to be performed [1], each one corresponding to the Quadrics Operating System command indicated in brackets:

- allocate the machine (`bootq`)
- load executable code into memory (`loadq`)
- start the execution (`runq`)

3. PQE_HPF

PQE_HPF was implemented to allow programmers to exploit the SIMD resources of PQE-1 from within their HPF programs, running on PQE-1's MIMD part. With PQE_HPF the HPF programmer is provided with all the mechanisms needed to allocate a Quadrics machine (the SIMD component in PQE-1), load a program, control its execution and perform basic read/write operations with SIMD node memories.

PQE_HPF is a library of HPF extrinsic procedures which handle communications among the MIMD nodes by means of MPI functions, and interact with the SIMD resource by means of calls to the Quadrics Run-Time System [12].

As was shown in Section 2.1, usage discipline for the SIMD resource is rather strict, therefore PQE_HPF functions cannot be called in any order. First it is necessary to allocate all the SIMD resources needed for our computation. Since in the PQE-1 architecture, Quadrics machines can have different number of nodes, PQE_HPF lets the programmer require resources specifying the number of SIMD nodes needed. For every successfully allocated machine a logic identifier is returned. Such identifier can be used by the programmer to addresses all other operations to that specific SIMD machine. After allocation, the Quadrics executable program has to be loaded into the SIMD node memories, so that TAO variables can be initialized and the program execution started on the SIMD resource. At this point the two parts of PQE-1 may run concurrently, executing different tasks. It is possible to know the program execution status on Quadrics nodes and, when it is finished, read back the results.

In Figure 2 is reported the *pseudo*-code of a general PQE_HPF program. Notice that the PQE_HPF support must be explicitly initialized (`PQE_Init()`) and released (`PQE_Close()`).

```
program pqehpf_model

include 'pqehpf.h'

[...]
call PQE_Init()                          ! Initialize PQE_HPF
ape = PQE_Processors(PQE_QH1)            ! Allocate 128 SIMD nodes
ret = PQE_Load(ape, 'tao_prog')          ! Load a program into SIMD memory
ret = PQE_Write(ape, a_hpf, a_tao)       ! Write to SIMD nodes memories
ret = PQE_Run(ape)                       ! Start execution on SIMD

while (PQE_Status(ape) == RUNNING) do
    [hpf computation]                    ! The two machines run together
end do

ret = PQE_Read(ape, a_hpf, a_tao)        ! Read from SIMD nodes memories
[...]
call PQE_Close()                         ! Release PQE_HPF

end program
```

Figure 2. Pseudo-code of a general PQE_HPF program.

3.1. Architectural issues of PQE_HPF

PQE_HPF functions can be divided into two categories: **Command Functions**, used to menage the SIMD resource, and **Communication Functions** which allow data to be exchanged between MIMD and SIMD processors. Command Functions are, for example, `PQE_Processors()` to allocate a SIMD resource, or `PQE_Load()` to load a Quadrics executable code into SIMD node memories. Communication Functions are `PQE_Write()` or `PQE_Read()` to excange data between MIMD and SIMD processors.

Command functions

To send a command to a Quadrics machine (such as `loadq` to load a program or `runq` to execute it), it is necessary to execute a system call to the Quadrics OS, from the MIMD node physically connected to the SIMD machine. We call such a node the `root` node for the specific SIMD resource. The operation of determining `root` is realized whenever a SIMD machine is allocated, by the function `PQE_Processors()`, which returns an integer, used to address all the PQE_HPF operations to a particular Quadrics machine.

Since only the `root` node can actually send commands to the specified machine, it is necessary to leave the *data-parallel* paradigm of HPF and let the MIMD nodes execute different actions. This is made possible in HPF by the use of extrinsic procedures [8] [2]. Every call to a Command Function is therefore a call to an extrinsic HPF procedure which is generally coded as follows:

```
extrinsic (hpf_local) PQE_command(ape)
if   (me == root(ape)) then
  result  = quadrics_system_call()
  broadcast(result)
else
  receive(result)
end if
return
end
```

Only the `root` node executes the actual Quadrics system call, and broadcasts the result to all the other nodes which, in turn, wait for the message. Note that this would not have been possible in an ordinary HPF subroutine, since the features of the language require single thread execution where instructions are executed at the same time by all the processors and scalar variables must have the same value across the whole partition of processors joining the computation. By means of this library of extrinsic functions, PQE_HPF provides a *natural* view, in the sense of HPF, of all the strictly *non-parallel* operations such as Quadrics system calls.

Communication functions

More complicated problems arise when data are written to - or read from - the SIMD node memories. The PQE_HPF functions used for these operations are `PQE_Write()` and `PQE_Read()`. These functions take four arguments and their general syntax is *PQE_Comm*`(ape, a_hpf, a_tao, PQE_MODE)`, where *PQE_Comm* can be either `PQE_Read` or `PQE_Write` . `ape` is the SIMD machine logic identifier, as returned by `PQE_Processors()`. `a_hpf` and `a_tao` are variables involved in the communication. Notice that `a_tao` is the SIMD nodes local variable, while `a_hpf` is an HPF variable which may be distributed among the MIMD nodes.

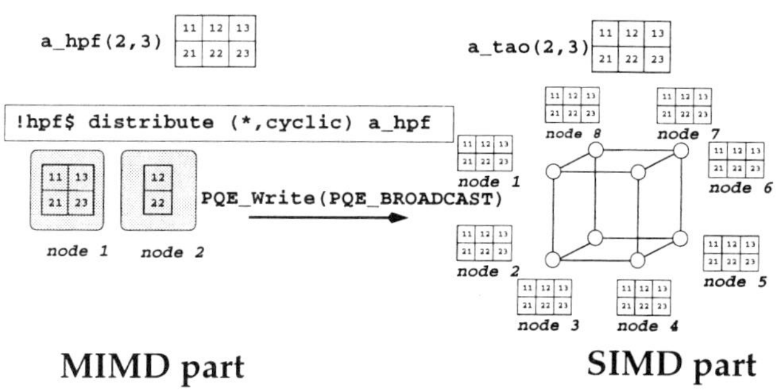

Figure 3. An example of data distribution for `PQE_MODE=PQE_BROADCAST`

The last argument, `PQE_MODE`, determines the kind of data distribution. When `PQE_MODE=PQE_BROADCAST` then the HPF variable `a_hpf` has to be replicated across all the SIMD nodes. This implies that `a_hpf` and `a_tao` must have the same number of elements, but possibly different shapes (see Figure 3). The other value allowed for

PQE_MODE is PQE_SLICEMD, which states that a_hpf should be distributed among the SIMD nodes. In this case the total number of elements in the HPF variable must be equal to the number of elements in a_tao, multiplied by the number of SIMD nodes (see Figure 4).

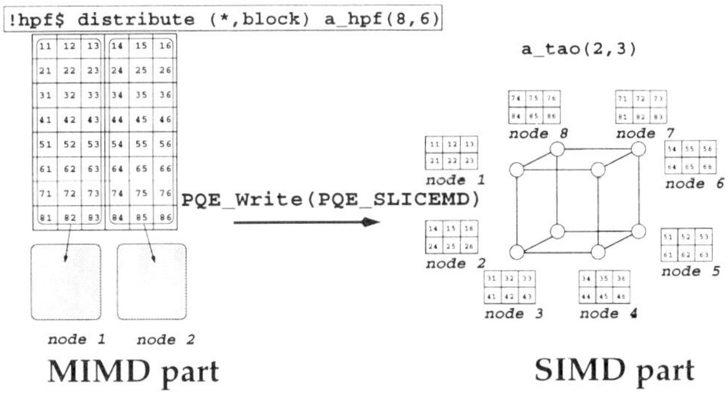

Figure 4. An example of data distribution for PQE_MODE=PQE_SLICEMD.

In both cases, to implement the Communication Function, it is necessary first to determine the correct mapping between the MIMD and the SIMD nodes, since data might be (and in general are) distributed differently, and then to perform an appropriate number of *basic-sends*. By *basic* we mean a call to the Quadrics system function that actually writes on the SIMD memories.

Of course there are different possibilities to handle data mapping and actual writing. The most relevant are scketched in the following. Suppose we have N elements stored in a_hpf on P MIMD processors, and we want to write these elements in the memory locations of the SIMD nodes corresponding to the variable a_tao in the TAO program. We adopt the following simplified linear model to describe communication times:

$$t^c = t_s + t_w \tag{1}$$

where t_s is the channel startup time and t_w is the time needed to send one word along the channel. We can have three possible solutions.

Case 1 Collect all the N elements in node root and perform only one basic-send of a message whose length is N. In the worst case we have $O(N)$ MIMD-MIMD communications and only one MIMD-SIMD communication. For this first solution, the total time spent in sending N words, distributed on the MIMD nodes, to the SIMD part, can be written as

$$T_1^c = N(t_s^{MM} + t_w^{MM}) + (t_s^{MS} + N t_w^{MS}) \tag{2}$$

where indexes ^{MM} and ^{MS} refer to MIMD-MIMD and MIMD-SIMD communications, respectively.

Case 2 Compute the intersections between the data present on every MIMD node and the slice of SIMD nodes where these data have to be written. In this way MIMD-MIMD communications are again $O(N)$, but the number of messages of one word sent to the SIMD nodes is also $O(N)$. The total communication time in this case is

$$T_2^c = N(t_s^{MM} + t_w^{MM}) + N(t_s^{MS} + t_w^{MS}) \tag{3}$$

Case 3 Redistribute block-wise the N data on the MIMD nodes. In this way every MIMD node has to write a contiguous block of data to a slice of SIMD nodes. This can be done in $O(P^2)$ operations for redistributions and $O(P)$ operations to send N/P-long messages. In this case

$$\begin{aligned} T_3^c &= P^2(t_s^{MM} + \frac{N}{P^2} t_w^{MM}) + \\ &+ P(t_s^{MS} + \frac{N}{P} t_w^{MS}) + P(t_s^{MM} + \frac{N}{P} t_w^{MM}) \end{aligned} \tag{4}$$

Actual values for t_s^{MS} and t_w^{MS} depend on the connection between the two architectures. For this theoretical analysis we consider the case of an HiPPI channel connecting the MIMD and the SIMD parts of PQE-1. For an 800 Mbps HiPPI channel we took $t_s^{MS} = 1000\mu s$ and $t_w^{MS} = 0.04\mu s$[1]. In Figure 5 we plot[2] equations (2-5) for $P = 1$ and $P = 4$. According to this model, the third solution has the minimum cost. For this reason we chose this strategy for implementing PQE_HPF communication fuctions.

On the available PQE-1 prototype, there is no HiPPI channel and the two components are connected via transputer links. In order to have an experimental measure of t_s^{MS} and t_w^{MS}, we plotted execution times for PQE_Write() for different message sizes. In Figure 6 experimental data are fitted with Eq. (5) and allowed to obtain $t_s^{MS} = 5000\mu s$ and $t_w^{MS} = 30\mu s$.

Finally, we studied the overheads introduced by data redistributions, measuring the cost of communications using PQE_HPF, as a function of the size of the message compared with the cost of communicating the same data using the Quadrics Run-Time support. Figure 7 highlights that the difference between the two curves is negligible for message sizes greater than 2 kbytes.

4. An application from physics: the Fermi-Pasta-Ulam β model

In the following sections we approach a problem from physics. The problem is to study the dynamical propreties

[1] Word length is 32 bit.

[2] Values for t_s^{MM} and t_w^{MM} were obtained from [9].

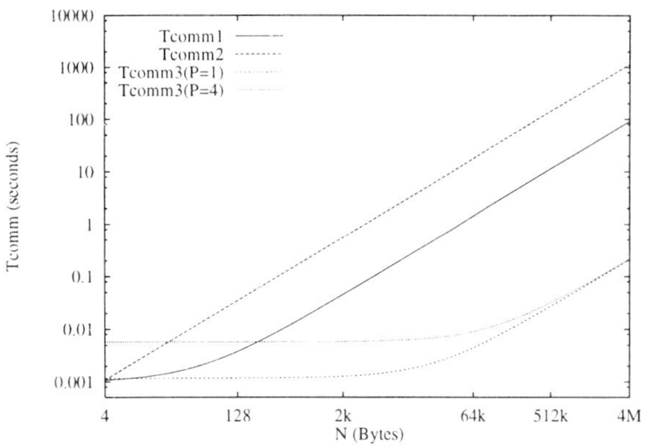

Figure 5. Expected communication times as a function of message size for the three cases of equations (2-5). The limit of 4 MBytes for the message size is imposed by the size of the SIMD node local memory. Values for the parameters are $t_s^{MM} = 87\mu s$, $t_w^{MM} = 0.08\mu s$, $t_s^{MS} = 1ms$, $t_w^{MS} = 0.04\mu s$.

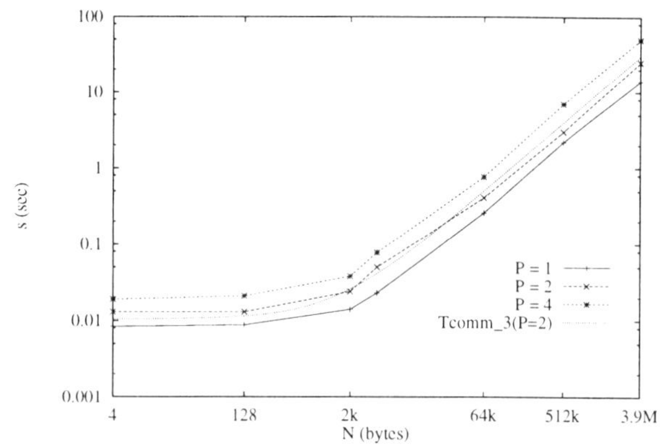

Figure 6. Communication times for PQE_Write as a function of message size. Data are stored in a one dimensional array distributed `CYCLIC` **on the MIMD part and replicated on the SIMD nodes. We also plotted the theoretical model with $t_s^{MM} = 87\mu s$, $t_w^{MM} = 0.08\mu s$, $t_s^{MS} = 5ms$, $t_w^{MS} = 30\mu s$, P=2.**

of a system with many degrees of freedom. It is a numerically intensive problem since it involves the solutions of a very high number of partial differential equations. The algorithm used for this problem, was implemented both in HPF and PQE_HPF, so to compare the results and have a measure of the possible advantages of HPF programming on PQE-1 platforms.

4.1. The Problem

The application we chose as a test-case is the study of the dynamical properties for a system with many degrees of freedom.

A characterization of these properties has important implications in the understanding of some macroscopic phenomena (such as phase transitions, for example) in terms of the microscopic properties of the system. Due to the complexity of such systems, numerical study remains one of the most effective tools of investigation. Here in particular we are interested in Hamiltonian systems and the way they reach their asymptotic, equilibrium state.

The system we chose is a Fermi-Pasta-Ulam (FPU) chain of N oscillators, coupled with anharmonic terms [7]. The model is described by the Hamiltonian

$$H(q,p) = \sum_{i=0}^{N-1} \left(\frac{p_i^2}{2} + \frac{(q_{i+1} - q_i)^2}{2} + \beta \frac{(q_{i+1} - q_i)^4}{4}\right) \quad (5)$$

with periodic boundary conditions $q_0 = q_{N-1}, p_0 = p_{N-1}$. For such systems the time τ needed to reach the asymptotic state where energy is equipartitioned among all the modes is

$$\tau = \tau_0 e^{(\frac{\epsilon_0}{\epsilon})^\delta} \quad (6)$$

where ϵ is the energy density and the constants ϵ_0 and δ are approximately 1. One problem of interest [16] is to establish the lower limit for ϵ within which equation (6) holds. This implies studying the system dynamics for low energies ($\epsilon < 0.001$).

To have a measure of energy equipartition we use the *spectral entropy* [11] given by

$$S(t) = -\sum_{k=0}^{N-1} w_k(t) \ln w_k(t) \quad (7)$$

where the probabilities w_k represent a measure of the energy in the k-th Fourier mode, i.e

$$w_k(t) = E_k(t) / \sum_l E_l \quad (8)$$

$$E_k(t) = \frac{1}{2}(P_k^2 + \omega_k^2 Q_k^2) \quad (9)$$

P and Q indicate the Fourier transforms of p and q, respectively. To determine whether we have equipartition or not, we use a normalized parameter

$$\eta(t) = \frac{S(t) - S_{\max}}{S(0) - S_{\max}} \quad (10)$$

which varies between 0 (no equipartition) and 1 (equipartition).

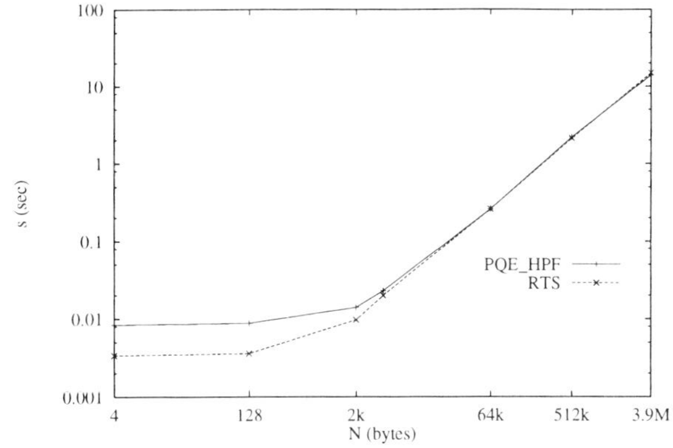

Figure 7. Latencies for writing to the SIMD nodes using PQE_HPF and the Quadrics Run-Time Support.

4.2. The Algorithm

Once the system has been initialized with only a small packet of modes excited, i.e. with an unequally distributed energy among the normal modes, we let the system evolve and measure the energy distribution until we can observe energy equipartition. As explained in the previous section, this is measured by the quantity η. The algorithm basically consists of a main temporal loop which gives the evolution of the system. During the evolution we want to measure η. This measurement is the most expensive computational part, since it involves two one-dimensional Fourier transforms (see Equation (9)).

For the evolution of the system we apply a simplectic algorithm of integration of the equations of motion. To work out η we need to perform basically two FFTs and a reduction operation.

The code has the following structure:

```
do NEXT (main loop)
  do NINT (internal loop)
    call evolve() ! system dynamics
  end do NINT
  call energy()    ! work out eta
end do NEXT
```

We decided not to measure η at every time step in order to speed up the simulation. The total number of iterations is hence given by $NINT \times NEXT$. Figure 8 plots $\eta(t)$ for different values of the energy density ϵ. As explained above, we are interested in the behavior of the system for low energies. This means $\epsilon < 0.001$. Figure 8 shows that for such energies, relaxation to equilibrium is extremely slow and a significant number of iterations in these cases is of the order 10^{10}.

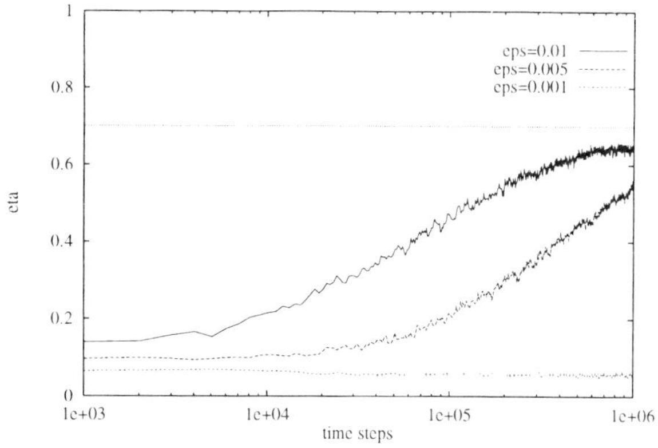

Figure 8. Results of simulations of an FPU chain with 2048 oscillators. The asymptotic state is reached for $\eta = 0.7$ due to fluctuations. Notice that in the curve corresponding to $\epsilon = 0.01$ it is not yet possible to see any energy exchange among modes in the observed time interval.

The number of oscillators N constitutes the size of the problem. In principle we would have to let $N \to \infty$. Scaling analyses (not reported here) showed that for our purposes $N = 2048$ can be considered as a good measure of such limit.

4.3. HPF version

Figure 9 highlights that the HPF version of the algorithm shows a rather good scaling up to 16 processors. The execution time of `energy` is two orders of magnitude higher than the execution time of `evolve`, due to the number of communications involved in a 1-dim Fourier transform. The prototype PQE-1 machine we have at our disposal has 4 MIMD nodes. Table 1 shows the execution times for the two subroutines, measured on the MIMD part of the PQE-1 architecture. The HPF codes were compiled using the Adaptor compilation system [4].

As can be seen, almost all the computational time is spent in the subroutine `energy`. With these values for the execution times, a significant simulation would last some years. Since we are not going to measure η at every time step, it would be useful to be able to perform a certain number of integrations while computing `energy`.

4.4. PQE_HPF version

To take advantage of the peculiarities of the architecture, the two components of PQE-1 have to work concurrently. So we deliver the execution of `energy` entirely to

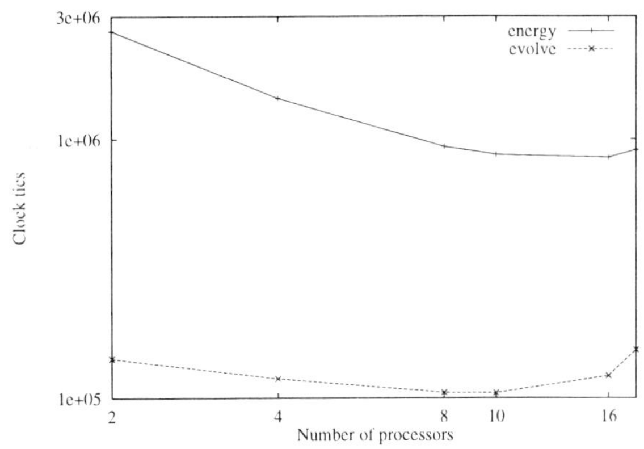

Figure 9. Execution times for the subroutines `evolve` and `energy` in clock ticks. In the x axis we have the number of processors. The simulation refers to a dataset of size 2048 and it was realized on a Cray-T3E.

Unit	MIMD nodes		
	1	2	4
`evolve`	0.041	0.042	0.041
`energy`	3.66	11.5	7.48
`main loop`	**3.70**	**11.6**	**7.52**

Table 1. Execution times (in seconds) of the two subroutines `energy` and `evolve` on the MIMD nodes of PQE-1 with $N = 2048$, $NEXT = 1$, $NINT = 1$. Values are averaged over 5 runs. Errors are never greater than 1%.

the SIMD part. We do not require it to run faster than on the MIMD one, here we want, above all, to exploit this form of task parallelism.

In order to overlap the two stages of the main loop (i.e. the internal loop and the call to `energy`), the algorithm must be changed as follows

```
do next (main loop)
  call energy_pqe_start()
  do nint (internal loop)
    call evolve
  end do nint
  call energy_pqe_stop()
end do next
```

The subroutine `energy_pqe_start()` is mainly concerned with writing data to the SIMD nodes and starting the program, while `energy_pqe_stop()` receives the result. Notice that to achieve more concurrency, we used two SIMD machines of 128 nodes, performing separately the two Fourier transform needed in Equation (9).

For the overlapping to be more effective, the workload between the MIMD and the SIMD part of PQE-1 has to be balanced. Balancing strictly depends on the TAO code, the latency of communications and other static and run-time issues. We manually tuned the program parameters so that the two machines spent the same amount of time for their computations. Experiments revealed that the SIMD implementation of `energy` takes about 10^3 steps of integrations in `evolve`, therefore we took $NINT = 10^3$.

In Table 2 are shown the execution times for the two subroutines, in the PQE_HPF and pure HPF versions. For this last case, `energy_stop` corresponds to `energy`.

Function	PQE_HPF		HPF	
	2	4	2	4
`energy_start`	0.13	0.23	-	-
`evolve`	37	46	43	43
`energy_stop`	0.90	0.45	12	8.5
`main loop`	**38**	**47**	**55**	**53**

Table 2. Execution times (in seconds) for the two subroutines `evolve` and `energy` using PQE_HPF and pure HPF. $N = 2048$, $NEXT = 1$, $NINT = 10^3$. In this case `evolve` is repeated $NINT = 10^3$ times.

We obtained a reduction of 30% with two MIMD nodes and 10% with four. What we have gained with the PQE_HPF implementation is the possibility of running the two parts of our algorithm concurrently.

Of course both codes, HPF and TAO, could be further optimized and fine-tuned. But, even in this first implementation the advantages of having the two components of a hybrid architecture working together are clear.

5. Conclusions

Many other different problems can be effectively ported onto the PQE-1 machine. At the moment of writing we are working on a reaction-diffusion problem of atmosphere modeling, and on some kernels for the spectral analysis of astronomical data.

The importance of the results shown in this work is above all the possibility of taking advantage of a hybrid machine, such as PQE-1. In fact, we found that the two parts of this architecture can work concurrently, achieving a form of task parallelism which, in our case, is controlled within the framework of a data-parallel language. In this sense PQE_HPF would appear to be a powerful tool for solving problems where different forms of parallelism are needed.

The PQE-1 architecture could thus be suited for a wider class of problems than the MIMD or SIMD parts alone are.

6. Acknowledgments

This work was founded in the framework of the PQE2000 project. We would like to thank Prof. Marco Vanneschi for his collaboration in the development of our project; Prof. Stefano Ruffo for his help in studying the application problem; the ENEA Computing Center of Casaccia (Rome, Italy) for providing us with the PQE-1 prototype and all the computational resources needed; thanks also to CINECA (Bologna, Italy) for allowing us to use a Cray-SGI T3E.

References

[1] Quadrics operating system. *Quadrics Supercomputer World*, 1995.

[2] M. Aiello, R. Baraglia, R. Ferrini, D. Laforenza, R. Perego, and M. C. Sechi. Integrazione di hpf con mpi e pvm per lo sfruttamento dell'eterogeneità in architetture mimd/simd. *CNUCE-CNR, TR PQE2000*, July 1997.

[3] H. E. Bal and M. Haines. Approaches for integrating task and data parallelism. *IEEE Concurrency*, (3), July 1998.

[4] T. Brandes. Adaptor programmer's guide. *GMD-SCAI Sankt Augustin, Germany*, 1997.

[5] P. S. Committee. Pqe2000 project: Architecture and software technology. *CNR-Alenia Spazio*, June 1996.

[6] M. Eshaghian. *Heterogeneous Computing*. Artech House, 1996.

[7] E. Fermi, J. Pasta, and S. Ulam. *Collected Papers of Enrico Fermi*. University of Chicago Press, Chicago, 1965.

[8] H. P. F. Forum. High performance fortran language specification version 1.0. 1993.

[9] I. Foster. *Designing and Building Parallel Programs*. Addison Wesley, 1995.

[10] G. Fox, R. Williams, and P. Messina. *Parallel Computing Works!* Morgan Kaufmann, 1994.

[11] R. Livi, M. Pettini, S. Ruffo, M. Sparpaglione, and A. Vulpiani. *Phys. Rev. A*, (31):1039, 1985.

[12] A. Monello. Rts user guide,. *Quadrics Supercomputer World*, 1998.

[13] S. Orlando and R. Perego. Colt-hpf a coordination layer for hpf tasks. *Concurrency, Practice & Experience (to appear)*, 1998.

[14] P. Paolucci, G. Todesco, R. D'Autilia, and S. Cabasino. The tao language.

[15] P.Dinda, T. Gross, D. O'Halloron, E. Segall, J. W. E. Stichnoth, J. Subholok, and B. Yang. The cmu task parallel program suite. *Technical Report CMU-CS-94-131, School of Computer Science, Carnegie Mellon University*, March 1994.

[16] S. Ruffo. The fput numerical experiment: time scales for the relaxation to thermodynamical equilibrium. *Symmetry and Perturbation Theory, Quaderni CNR*, page 188, 1998.

[17] M. Vanneschi. Variable grain architectures for mpp computation and structured parallel programming. *3rd International Working Conference on Massively Parallel Programming Models*, 1997.

[18] M. Vanneschi. Pqe2000: Hpc tools for industrial applications. *IEEE Concurrency*, (4):68, 1998.

A Case Study of Trace-driven Simulation for Analyzing Interconnection Networks: cc-NUMAs with ILP Processors*

V. Puente, J.M. Prellezo, C. Izu[†], J.A. Gregorio, R. Beivide

Abstract--

The evaluation of network performance under real application loads is carried out by detailed time-intensive and resource-intensive simulations. Moreover, the use of ILP processors in cc-NUMA architectures introduces non-deterministic memory accesses; the resulting parallel system must be modeled by a detailed execution-driven simulation, further increasing the evaluation cost.

This work introduces a simulation methodology, based on network traces, to estimate the impact that a given network has on the execution time of parallel applications. This methodology allows the study of the network design space with a level of accuracy close to that of execution-driven simulations but with much shorter simulation times. The network trace, extracted from an execution-driven simulation, is processed to substitute the temporal dependencies produced by the simulated network with an estimation of the message dependencies caused by both the application and the applied cache-coherent protocol. This methodology has been tested on two direct networks, with 16 and 64 nodes respectively, running the FFT and Radix applications of the SPLASH2 suite. The trace-driven simulation is 3 to 4 times faster than the execution-driven one with an average error of 4% in total execution time.

I. INTRODUCTION

Scalable distributed shared-memory (DSM) systems, represented by the cache coherent non-uniform memory access (cc-NUMA) systems, are emerging as the trend in building parallel systems since they provide much desired programmability. The network delay when accessing remote data is one of the basic overheads that limits parallel performance. Therefore, the design of interconnection networks that are optimized to handle DSM traffic is an important area of research.

The evaluation of interconnection network designs for a given parallel architecture is carried out via network simulation. In the first stages of design, networks are compared using synthetic loads, which provide a first approximation to real applications [2]. Notwithstanding, the analysis of the impact that the interconnection network has on system performance can hardly be forecast unless we use realistic application loads, similar to those the network is being designed to support.

The traffic in a cc-NUMA system, generated implicitly by the application's memory accesses, depends on the cache-coherent protocol used. Thus, precise loads can only be obtained by execution of the selected applications under a real or simulated system. The monitoring of a real system alters the network traffic, and it is constrained by the given network subsystem. In short, the extraction of realistic application loads can only be achieved using execution-driven simulations of the whole multiprocessor system with the high computational cost they entail.

This work tries to reduce the cost of evaluation of the interconnection network for a cc-NUMA system by introducing a new simulation methodology. Network traces are extracted from the execution driven simulation, processed to approximate the dependencies of cc-NUMA traffic, and then used by a trace-driven simulator to evaluate the network performance. This new methodology is compared with the original execution-driven simulation in terms of simulation cost and accuracy.

Our evaluation will show that the new proposal introduces an average error around 4%, and succeeds in reducing execution time by a factor of 2 to 4. We intend to use this trace-driven simulation as a partial substitute for execution-driven simulation, which should still be used in the latter stages of the design. The impact on the network design cycle will be quite large because of the cumulative speed-up in successive refinements of the router design.

The rest of the paper is organized as follows. Section 2 reviews the most relevant simulation methodologies for interconnection networks. Section 3 describes the trace-driven simulation with feedback. Section 4 describes the application of our methodology for performance evaluation and discusses the results and, finally, in Section 5 we draw some conclusions.

University of Cantabria, Spain, e-mail:{vpuente, prellezo, ja, mon}@atc.unican.es., [†]University of Adelaide, Australia, e-mail: cruz@cs.adelaide.edu.au

* This Work is supported in part by TI98-1162-C02-01.

1066-6192/99 $10.00 © 1999 IEEE

II. Application Loads for Analyzing Interconnection Networks.

Various simulation techniques can be used to model network loads in a cc-NUMA system, depending on the accuracy of the prediction desired and the complexity of the simulator itself. On one extreme of the scale, we can generate accurate network loads from a parallel application by simulating the complete parallel system, including each processor, the memory hierarchy and the network subsystem. By simulating the application, instruction by instruction, we can generate the exact memory references, and capture the requests passed from the memory simulator to its network interface. This method provides very accurate results, but the simulator itself is very costly in terms of both development and computation.

On the other extreme, we can make simulation more affordable by using an abstract model that reflects some statistical properties of current loads such as the random traffic model or other widely used permutation patterns. However, this approach does not capture the details of a specific application, and therefore, it cannot accurately predict its performance.

Trace-driven simulation is a third approach with a level of complexity in between the above two. The trace is a time ordered sequence of events (message generation events in our case) that happened during the execution of the application. If the trace is carefully extracted and processed, it can be powerful enough to represent all the necessary characteristics of the application load. We must use a detailed simulator to obtain an accurate trace, with the associated cost, but we can reuse the trace as many times as needed during the network design cycle.

Trace-driven simulation has been widely used in studies of memory hierarchies of uniprocessor systems. This strategy is limited by the characteristics of the simulated system. For example, memory traces assume that the sequence of addresses accessed is deterministic; this is correct for simple processors but is not applicable to ILP processors with out-of-order execution and non-blocking loads, which can cause large errors [6].

Like simple processors, message-passing architectures are easier to model using traces because of the deterministic and explicit ordering in which the messages are generated by the application. There is a large body on research of interconnection networks from this point of view [2]. However, network traffic in a cc-NUMA system is not deterministic because the characteristics of the network, contention for instance, will influence on the number of messages generated by the cache-coherent protocol. In addition, the processing nodes are ILP processors. Hence, the lack of trace-driven simulations for this environment.

For this reason, our first approach to model application workloads was based on an existing execution-driven simulator of a cc-NUMA machine with ILP processors called RSIM[3]. As our research is focused on network design, we substituted its simple network module NETSIM by our own network simulator SICOSYS [9], which takes into account the key parameters from the router's low-level implementation. The resulting system, RSIM-S reflects quite accurately the impact that a particular network design will have on the application's execution time [10]. The only drawback is the simulation time, e.g. simulating the execution of Radix on a 64-node machine takes approximately 11 hours on a R10000 processor at 200 MHz for the selected problem size. The volume of simulations required to refine and thoroughly test a new network design renders this approach unworkable, even for systems with a low number of nodes.

Recent studies have attempted to reduce the computational cost of execution-driven simulators in the context of analysis of memory hierarchies, using direct execution [5] which replaces full processor emulation with a functional and timing model. Another proposal modeled the benefits of ILP by increasing the clock rate of a simple processor by a factor equal to the ILP processor's peak instruction issue rate. However, such an approximation is a source of large errors as shown in [6].

Nevertheless, the complexity of the memory subsystem cannot be reduced in a similar way so we explore another avenue to speed up network simulation based on the use of traces. Trace extraction in a cc-NUMA system with ILP processors is not a straightforward process due to the non-deterministic characteristics of memory access and the influence of the network performance on the cache coherence protocol. Next section will describe our approach to trace extraction and post-processing.

III. Trace-Driven Simulation with Network Feedback (TDS-NF).

We proposed a new methodology for modeling the impact of network design on application loads. An application's network trace is obtained from the execution-driven simulator RSIM-S, which then feeds our network simulator SYCOSYS. We called this simulation strategy Trace-driven simulation with network feedback (TDS-NF). If the trace information is correct, the resulting trace-driven simulation will model the network effect on the application's execution time with an accuracy close to that of RSIM-S but with a much lower computational cost.

The network trace should reflect the key parameters of a network load: number of messages and their distribution both in time and destinations. Most traffic in a cc-NUMA system follows a reactive pattern: a remote memory request triggers the transmission of the requested data, and the processing of the received remote data may trigger other remote accesses. Similarly, cache coherence control packets are triggered by the movement of remote data. The application's trace should reflect this property by recording the time when a message is generated as relative to the message that triggered its generation as shown in Figure 1.

For example, Figure 1.(a) represents the communication of the processes P_1 and P_0, as observed during trace extraction. Process P_0 sends a message m_1 to process P_1 at time t_1, and, after some computations, process P_1 sends message m_2 at time t_2 as the reply to message m_1.

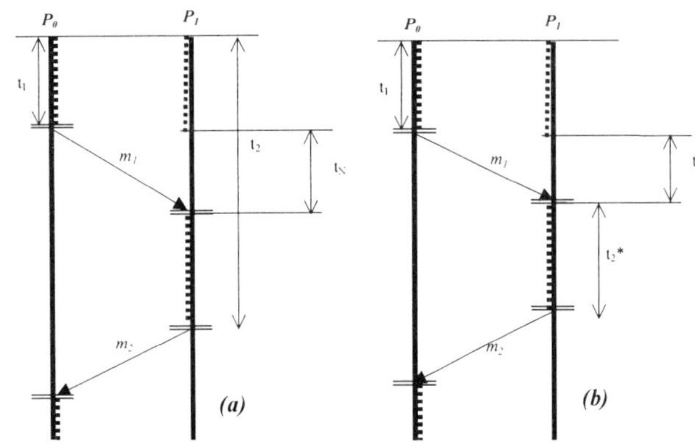

Fig. 1.- Scheme of (a) absolute temporization and (b) relative temporization.

The former trace, showing absolute times, does not encapsulate the impact of the network on the trace extraction. After the arrival of message m_1, which experimented a network latency of t_N units, process P_1 carries out some computations and generates message m_2.

Figure 1.(b) shows this dependency between network performance and the time generation for m_2, by making the time t_{2*} relative to the arrival of the message m_1. Thus t_{2*} only reflects the computation time, while t_2 includes also the communication cost.

In short, the generation time for each message depends on the current network status. Thus, we must provide a bi-directional flow of information between the network simulator and the module that interprets the trace to generate the remote memory references. This feedback mechanism distinguishes our approach from conventional trace-driven simulation of networks in which the message generator feeds messages to the simulator solely based on the trace information.

The goal of trace post-processing is to identify the time dependencies (t_Ni) ntroduced by the network employed when the trace was obtained. Thus, any change in network design will change the relative time at which messages are generated and delivered, and the trace-driven simulation will reflect its impact on the application's execution time.

Obviously, this temporization is oriented to reflect the changes in the communication subsystem. Severe changes in the processor architecture or in the memory hierarchy could invalidate previous traces as representative of the application loads for that new system.

A. Applying this methodology to cc-NUMA architectures.

1) Extraction of message dependencies.

Finding the correlation amongst messages described in the previous section is not an easy task in cc-NUMA architectures. It is not the application code that implicitly generates messages but the memory hierarchy subsystem. Furthermore, ILP processors that use non-blocking loads add complexity because message dependencies are then indirect.

To be able to deal with this problem we have ignored any changes in message ordering that are not causal. A first approximation consists of considering the last received message at that processing node as the cause of any outgoing messages. Figure 2 illustrates this approach. In this example, the reception of message m_{th} at node P_3 triggers this node to send three messages, two for node P_2 and one for node P_1. Let's assume that m_{th} was a request for a cache line located at P_3. Our approximation is correct in considering this reception as the trigger for m_1, the message that contains the data requested. The time t_2 models the time to access P_3's directory and locate the requested data. However, the remaining messages may or may not be related to the reception of m_{th}. They may be request messages or replies to previous requests.

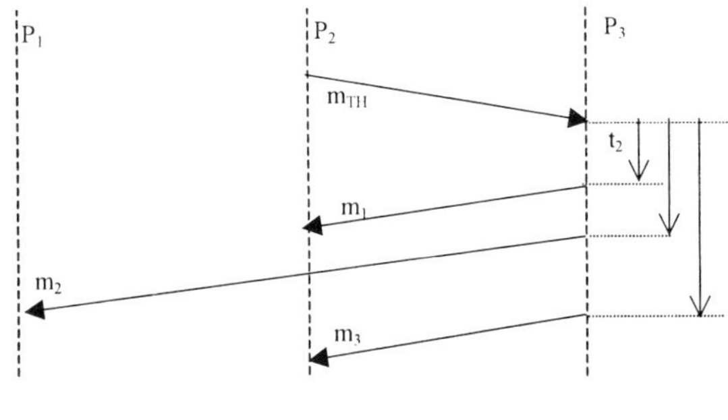

Fig. 2.- Initial approximation.

Due to the reactive nature of the DSM traffic, in which each request will trigger a reply, it is easy to identify such message pairs. A request message arriving at node *d* from node *s* will trigger, at least, one message reply from node *d* to node *s*.

Besides, we have to consider what is the trigger for the control packets that implement the cache-coherent protocol. This requires an in-depth analysis of the chosen protocol, which in our case is the invalidation-based MESI directory cache-coherent protocol.

Type of message received	*Type of messages triggered.*	
READ_SH	REPLY_SH	DATA
	REPLY_EXCL	DATA
	COPYBACK	COHERENCY
READ_OWN	REPLY_EXCL	DATA
	RELPY_EXCLDY	DATA
	COPYBACK_INVL	COHERENCY
	INVL	COHERENCY
UPGRADE	RELPY_EXCLDY	DATA
	REPLY_EXCL	DATA
	REPLY_UPGRADE	COHERENCY
	INVL	COHERENCY
ANY REPLY	READ_SH / READ_OWN / UPGRADE	

Table 1.- Trigger relationships between message types.

Considering all these criteria, we have constructed a table (see Table 1) that describes the correlation between the type of messages received and the set of messages it may trigger (only appear message types seen in the network).

As well as finding the trigger message based on this type of relationships, it is also necessary to compare both the source-destination pair and the memory addresses of the trigger and triggered packet.

This approach identifies the trigger for sending a data packet, but we still have to find a trigger for the original request. We have taken a rough approximation that consists of assuming that request messages are triggered by the last data packet received at that node.

2) Trace format

The trace extraction records one entry for each packet sent, containing the basic packet information and its generation time. The message label records the memory address that the packet is referring to.

During trace post-processing, the dependencies with other messages are identified as described in the previous section and three additional fields created: the *trigger label*, the *trigger delay* and the *trigger count*, as shown in Figure 3.

The trigger label indicates the message that must be received prior to this message generation. The trigger delay specifies the time elapsed between the reception of the trigger label message and that generation (t_2, as shown in Figure 2.(b)). The trigger count indicates the number of messages that will be triggered upon reception of this message at its destination. Both the message label and the trigger count will travel with the packet, carrying this causal information to the destination node. When the message reaches that node, we must search the messages whose trigged labels match the received message label. All messages found are trigged after their corresponding trigger delays.

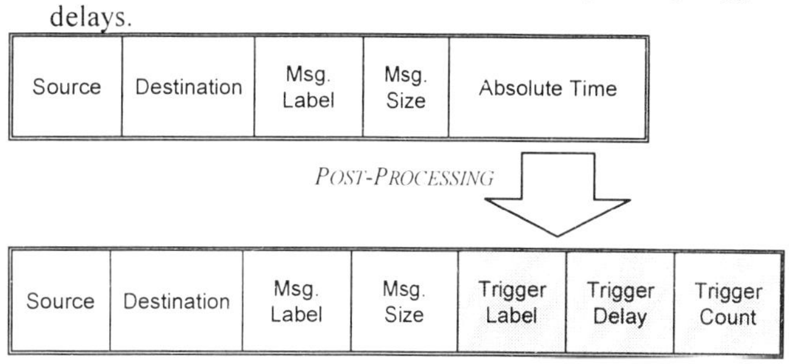

Fig. 3.- Trace entry format.

IV. VALIDATION OF TDS-NF METHODOLOGY.

A. Trace extraction.

As the previous section has described, we had to take some rough approximations in order to reduce the complexity of the cc-NUMA system with ILP processors. This fact may suggest that the level of accuracy of the network evaluation will drop when using trace files. Thus, we need to estimate the validity of these approximations by comparing the results of the trace-driven simulation with those of the accurate but time-intensive execution-driven simulation.

Figure 4 shows the process carried out to validate our methodology. As we mentioned before, we already have the simulator RSIM-S, which combines the cc-NUMA simulator RSIM with our own network module SICOSYS.

The trace is extracted from this simulator by capturing and post-processing all the references sent to the network interface as described in the previous Section.

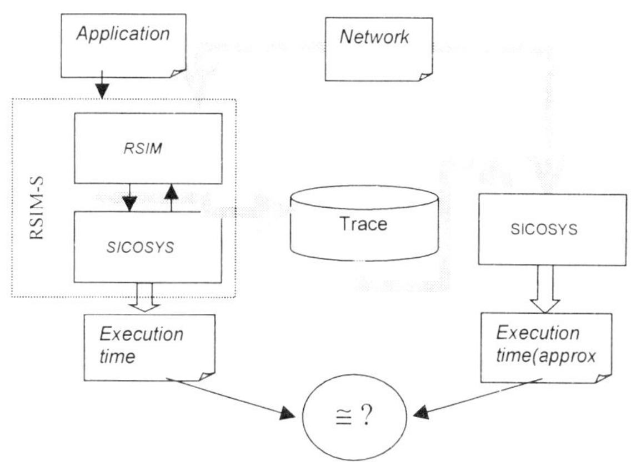

Fig. 4.- Trace extraction and validation of trace-driven results.

Once we have a trace that represents the load generated by one application, we can validate our new simulator in two phases. The first phase runs the trace-driven simulator using the same network configuration applied during trace extraction. As both simulators are emulating the same parallel system, the execution time should be similar, the more accurate the trace, the closer the results.

As we mentioned before, the advantage of having a trace which is independent of the given network configuration is that it will reflect the impact of changes to that network on the application's execution time. Therefore, the second phase runs the TDS-NF simulation with the same trace, after changing the network configuration. Again, we run the execution-driven simulation with the new network configuration and use its results as the baseline for accuracy, as shown in Figure 5.

All simulations run on a SGI Power Challenge LX, with MIPS R10000 processor at 200 MHz, 1 GB of RAM and 2 Mb of L2 cache. Both simulators were compiled and optimized by the C/C++ MIPSPro 7.2 compiler.

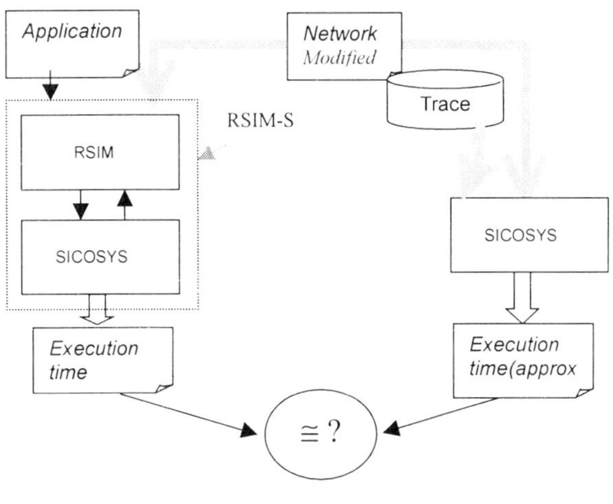

Fig. 5.- Validate the usage of the trace to analyze the impact of network changes.

B. Evaluation of TDS-NF for two applications: FFT y Radix.

We run the two-phase validation process for two applications - FFT and Radix, both from the SPLASH-2 suite [12].

We chose these applications because they are communication-intensive, so they are very sensitive to the characteristics of the interconnection network. We considered two system sizes: 16 nodes and 64 nodes. The problem size was 64K complex double points for the FFT, and 512K integer keys with a maximum radius of 512K for Radix.

The network does not play a critical role in the initialization and completion phases of parallel applications, so these two stages are eliminated to speed up testing.

The system configuration for the memory and processor subsystem is the default one provided by RSIM [3]: 600 MHz nodes with 32-byte cache lines for both L1 and L2. The size of cache coherence commands is 8 bytes.

The network configuration for the first phase is a 2D mesh with adaptive routing. Requests and replies share the same physical medium. The network channels are 4 bytes wide and the network rate is 275 MHz. The router uses Virtual Cut-Through (VCT) flow control and has two virtual channels: a deterministic one and a fully adaptive one. Each virtual channel has a buffer attached with capacity for 4 data packets (160 bytes).

Deadlock due to overflow of the consumption channel capacity is prevented by providing a large buffer size at the network interface's consumption ports (with N request-packet capacity for a network of N nodes), and restricting the number of pending memory references in face of a possible overflow.

The number of messages traced from each application under these conditions is shown in Table 2.

Radix		FFT	
16 Nodes	64 Nodes	16 Nodes	64 Nodes
564.189	1.220.718	311.985	342.107

Table 2.- Number of messages generated by each application under the two system sizes.

In the second phase of validation, we have considered three changes to the network configuration as follows:

- Change topology, from a 2D mesh to a 2D torus. The adaptive torus implementation is based on [11].
- Reduce the channel width from 4 bytes down to 2 bytes.
- Double the network clock rate.

These three changes in network configuration will have a significant impact on the application's execution time. We selected such severe changes so that any error introduced by the tracing mechanism will be magnified under such different scenarios.

Table 3 shows the set of results obtained from the validation process: the speed-up achieved by the TDS-NF simulation and the error in the execution time estimation when compared to the RSIM-S baseline.

Note that the differences in execution time between the TDS-NF simulation and the baseline are always less than 10%, for any of the 16 cases considered. As you can see in table 4, the average error is just above 4%. This level of accurracy is quite satisfactory considering the approximations discussed in section 3.

The *severe* changes in network configuration have a great impact on application execution time and this is reflected in the simulation results. For example, halving the router bandwidth resulted in a significant increment of the execution time of FFT-64 (16) by 70% (30%) as estimated by the execution-driven simulation, or by 65% (31%) as estimated by the TDS-NF simulation.

Obviously, the other two changes increased network performance and resulted in shorter execution time for all the applications. The largest average error corresponds to the networks with a clock rate of twice the original one. This may be due to our conservative correlation between messages which may not correctly model non-blocking accesses, but attributes to them false triggers that may delay their generation unnecesarily in a faster network.

The speed-up achieved by using traces ranges from 200% to 400%. For example, the time to *run* Radix in a 64 node system (RADIX-64) is reduced from 11 hours to 3 hours. We should point out that SICOSYS, being a low-level network emulator, exhibits a higher computational cost than other functional network simulators. On the other hand, it provides the necessary accuracy to model a particular VSLI router design. In short, SICOSYS complexity limits the speed-up (%) achieved by eliminating RSIM's memory hierachy and processor modules.

Considering the number of simulations needed for a complete network design, the time reduction is very considerable and clearly outweighs the cost of trace extraction and processing.

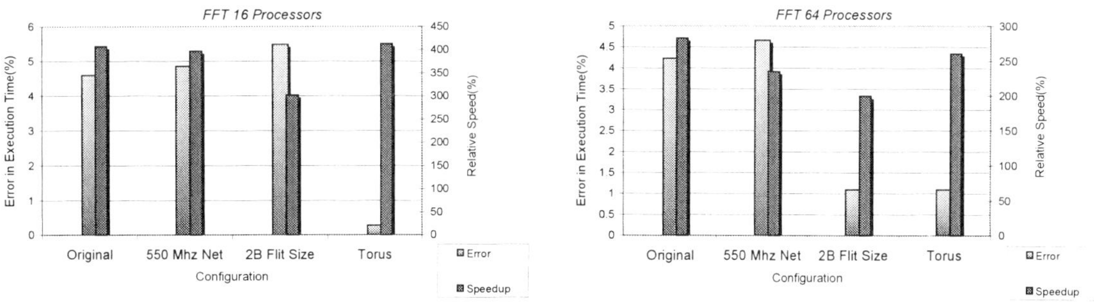

Fig. 6.- Relative error by the trace-driven simulation when compared to the execution-driven simulation for the FFT application.

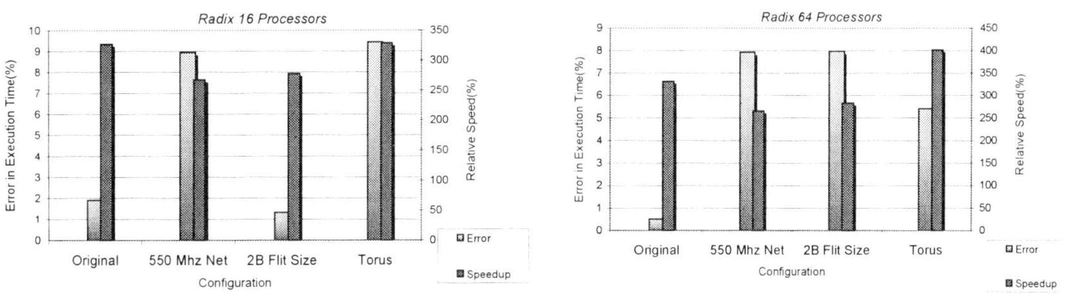

Fig. 7.- Relative error by the trace-driven simulation when compared to the execution-driven simulation for the Radix application.

Configuration	FFT16		FFT64		RADIX16		RADIX 64			
	Error (%)	SpeedUp (%)	Error (%)	SpeedUp (%)	Error (%)	SpeedUp (%)	Error (%)	SpeedUp (%)	Error (%)	SpeedUp (%)
Baseline	4.6	407	4.23	283	1.99	328	0.37	332	**2.8**	**338**
Net. Speedx2	-4.85	397	4.67	235	8.94	268	7.93	265	**6.59**	**291**
Flit Size/2	5.48	302	1.1	200	1.33	278	7.97	283	**3.97**	**265**
Torus Network	0.28	412	-1.1	261	9.45	330	5.76	402	**4.14**	**351**
Average	**3.80**	**379**	**2.75**	**245**	**5.45**	**301**	**5.55**	**396**	*4.37*	*311*

Table 3.- Speed-up and error obtained by the TDS-NF simulation when compared with the execution-driven simulation (average error calculated using absolute values).

	+20%Clock		-20%Clock	
	RSIM-S	TDS-NF	RSIM-S	TDS-NF
Radix 16 Processors	7.5%	8.69%	-5.63%	-1.5%
Radix 64 Processors	8.5%	6.45%	-10.1%	-15.5%
FFT 16 Processors	7.2%	8.7%	-4.6%	-10.0%
FFT 64 Processors	14.6%	11%	-15.3%	-13.3%

Table 4.- Change (%) in execution time estimated by simulation of a faster (slower) network.

We are interested in using traces to estimate the the impact of any network redesign on the execution time of parallel applications. Thus, we consider a more realistic variation of ±20% network speed.

Table 4 shows the variations obtained by the execution-driven simulation and the trace-driven simulation after increasing (decreasing) the network clock rate.

V.-CONCLUSIONS AND FUTURE WORK.

This paper has introduced a new methodology to analyze the effect that the interconnection network has on the performance of a cc-NUMA system with ILP processors.

A network trace of a given application is extracted from a execution-driven simulation, and processed to convert absolute-time references into network-relative ones. The processed trace encapsulates the reactive properties of DSM traffic. The message generator interprets this trace and the network feedback information to timely generate the remote memory references. This feedback mechanism distinguishes our approach from conventional trace-driven simulation. The same trace can be repeatedly used to evaluate the impact of different network configurations on the initial application at a much lower computational cost.

This methodology has been tested over direct networks (2D mesh and 2D torus) with 16 and 64 nodes, using the FFT and RADIX applications from the SPLASH2 suite. This approach significantly reduces computational times, 2 to 4 times, with a minimal loss of accuracy. The average error compared with the execution-driven simulation baseline is only 4.4%.

Considering the approximations made during trace processing, and the possibilities for further refining this trace extraction, the TDS-NF methodology is very promising. It can also be extended to model message-passing traffic.

VI.- REFERENCES

[1] M. S. Lam and R. P. Wilson, "*Limits of Flow Control on Parallelism*", Proc. 19th Annual International Symposium on Computer Architecture, May 1992.

[2] S. Chodenekar et al. "*Towards a Communication Characterization Methodology for Parallel Applications*" Proc. 3rd High Performance Computer Architecture, Feb. 1997.

[3] V. S. Pai, P. Ranganathan, S. Adve "*Rsim: An execution-Driven Simulator for ILP-Based Shared-Memory Multiprocessors and Uniprocessors*", IEEE TCCA Newsletter, Oct. 1997.

[4] A.S. Vaidya, A. Sivasubramaniam, C.R. Das, "*Performance benefits of virtual channels and adaptive routing: An application-driven study*", in Proc. of International Conference on Supercomputing, July, 1997

[5] H. Davis, S.R. Goldschmidt, J. Hennessy, "*Multiprocessor Simulation and Tracing Using Tango*", Proc. *Intl. Conf. On Parallel Processing*, 1991.

[6] M. Durbhakula, V.S. Pai, S. Adve, "Improving the Acuracy vs. Speed Tradeoff for Simulating Shared-Memory Multiprocessor with ILP Processors", Proc. *5rd High Performance Computer Architecture*, Jan. 1999.

[7] C.Holt, J. P. Singh, J. Hennessy, "*Application and Architectural Bottlenecks in Large Scale Distributed Shared Memory Machines*", Proc. 23rd Intl. Symp. On Computer Architecture, May 1996.

[8] M. Rosemblum et al., "Using the SimOS Machine Simulator to Study Complex Computer Systems", *ACM Transactions on Modeling and Computer Simulation*, 1997.

[9] J.M. Prellezo, V. Puente, J.A. Gregorio, R. Beivide, "*SICOSYS: an interconnection network simulator for parallel computers*" Technical Report available at http://www.atc.unican.es/ REPORTS/TR-ATC2-UC98.pdf, June 1998.

[10] V. Puente, J.A. Gregorio, C. Izu, R. Beivide and F. Vallejo, "*Low-level Router Design and its Impact on Supercomputer Performance*", Proc. of International Conference on Supercomputing, June 1999.

[11] V. Puente, J.A. Gregorio, J. M. Prellezo, R. Beivide, J. Duato, C. Izu, "*Adaptive Bubble Router: a Design to Balance Latency and Throughput in Networks for Parallel Computers*", Proc. of International Conference on Parallel Processing, Sept. 1999..

[12] S. C. Woo, M. Ohara, E. Torrie, J.P. Singh, A. Gupta "*The SPLASH-2 Programs: Characterization and Methodological Considerations*". Proc. of the 22nd International Symposium on Computer Architecture, June 1995.

Short Presentations 2:
Models and Languages

Scalability Analysis of Parallel Systems with Multiple Components of Work

E. Tambouris[1] and P. Van Santen
Department of Electronic and Computer Engineering
Brunel University
Uxbridge, UB8 3PH Middlesex, UK
{Efthimios.Tambouris, Peter.Van.Santen}@brunel.ac.uk

Abstract

In this paper, the generic fixed-value efficiency (fve) method is proposed to study the scalability of parallel algorithms with multiple components of work. The generic fve method is based on the isoefficiency method. Unlike isoefficiency however this method may be applied to parallel algorithm-machine combinations (parallel systems) where the relationship between the total work and its components is not predetermined by the decomposition method or any other factor. The objective of the method is to derive the relationships between the total work and its components in order for the efficiency of the parallel system to be preserved. The use of the method is demonstrated by analysing the impact of the sparsity of the input data on the scalability of a static state-estimator for power systems.

1. Introduction

Scalability analysis allows predicting performance of large machine and problem instances based on the known performance of small ones. A large number of metrics has been proposed for analysing scalability including isoefficiency function [1] scaled speedup [2] and isospeed [10]. It is now well-established that no single metric is better than the others as different metrics are more suitable under different conditions [3] [5] [9] [13]. For a comprehensive view of scalability the use of a set of metrics instead of a single one has been also proposed [5] [13]. In certain cases however a rapid evaluation of scalability is required. For these cases, isoefficiency analysis has been proved to be a useful tool [1] [4] [14].

The main objective of the isoefficiency analysis is to determine whether a parallel system can preserve its efficiency by increasing the work as the number of processors is scaled. Parallel systems are termed scalable if they can preserve efficiency and unscalable otherwise. Isoefficiency analysis is suitable for parallel algorithms where the relationship between the total work and its components is predetermined. Examples are some parallel algorithms derived from perfectly balanced domain decompositions. In these cases the work assigned to each processor cannot change. The objective of isoefficiency analysis is to determine whether the parallel system under investigation is scalable or not. For a certain number of processors, the analyst cannot experiment with different assignments of work to processors in order to increase efficiency.

For a certain class of parallel systems however the relationship between the total work and its components may not be implied by the decomposition method or any other factor. Examples are some parallel algorithms derived from a functional decomposition of the serial algorithm, such as the decomposed state-estimator for power systems [8]. The use of the isoefficiency method is not practical here, as all possible assignments of work to processors have to be defined and in turn analysed.

In this paper, the generic fixed-value efficiency (fve) is proposed. The objective of this method is to determine the relation that should hold between the growth rates of the total work and its components for the parallel system under investigation to preserve efficiency as the number of processors is scaled.

This paper is organised as follows. In section 2 the isoefficiency method is reviewed. In section 3, the model of parallel systems with multiple components of work is outlined. In section 4, the generic fixed-value efficiency (fve) method is introduced. In section 5, the proposed method is applied to analyse the scalability of a state-estimator algorithm for power systems. Conclusions and final comments are given in section 6.

2. Isoefficiency method

The size W of a problem may be defined as the work performed by an optimal (or the best known) sequential algorithm to solve the given problem on a single

[1] Now at Archetypon S.A., Sygrou Ave, GR- 176 72, Hellas. E-mail: tambouris@archetypon.gr

1066-6192/99 $10.00 © 1999 IEEE

processor. The overhead function $T_o(W, p)$ represents the sum total of all the overhead incurred by all the p processors during the parallel execution of an algorithm. The efficiency of a parallel system is given by

$$E = S / p = 1 / (1 + T_o(W, p) / W t_c)$$

where t_c is a machine-dependent constant. For a class of parallel systems, called scalable parallel systems, the efficiency can be maintained at a desirable value (between 0 and 1) provided W is increased as p is scaled. In order to maintain a fixed efficiency, W should be proportional to $T_o(W, p)$ or the following relation must be satisfied [1]:

$$W = K T_o(W, p) \quad (1)$$

where $K = E / ((1-E)\, t_c)$ is a constant depending on the efficiency to be maintained. The isoefficiency function of a parallel system is determined by abstracting W as a function of p through algebraic manipulations is equation (1).

For parallel systems where the overall overhead function T_o has multiple terms it can be very difficult or even impossible to obtain the isoefficiency function as a closed function of p. However, as p and W increase, the efficiency does not decrease if none of the terms of T_o grow faster than W. Therefore, if T_o has multiple terms, W is balanced against each term of T_o and the respective isoefficiency function for each individual term is computed. If at least one term yields no isoefficiency function the analysis terminates and the system is considered as unscalable. If all terms yield an isoefficiency function then the component of T_o that requires W to grow at the highest rate w.r.t. p determines the overall asymptotic isoefficiency function of the parallel system.

3. Parallel systems with multiple components of work

For a fairly large number of parallel systems, the amount of work at the parallel algorithm consists of multiple components. Parallel systems in this category include those where work is not equally balanced between processors, those with a serial component and those following the master-slave paradigm. They also include parallel algorithms derived from a functional decomposition of the best known sequential algorithm for the same problem. In these cases, assuming that the total work at the parallel algorithm is equal to the problem size W (i.e. there are no extra computations in the parallel algorithm) it is:

$$W = \sum_{i=1}^{p} W_i \quad (2)$$

where the growth rate of W_i is no faster than the growth rate of W (the term *no faster* as well as other order analysis terms which are used in this paper are defined in Appendix A). In this paper, it is assumed that the growth rates of the work components W_i with respect to W are not predetermined.

Other relationships between the problem size and the work components are also possible depending on the parallel system under investigation. For example, in a parallel system with a serial W_1 and a perfectly parallel W_p component, it is $W = W_1 + W_p$.

4. Generic fixed-value efficiency method

The generic fixed-value efficiency (fve) method can be applied to parallel systems where the relationship between the total work and its components is not predetermined. As a result, the total work may be distributed to the available processors in may different ways. The objective of the generic fve method is to derive the relationships between the total work and its components for the parallel system under investigation to be scalable.

In parallel systems with multiple components, the total work is related with its components as shown in equation (2). The overhead function T_o, which is a function of p and W, becomes a function of p and the components W_1, W_2, ..., W_p, i.e. $T_o(p, W_1, W_2, ..., W_p)$. Thus the main relationship for the generic fve method, i.e. $W = K\, T_o$ becomes:

$$W = K T_o(p, W_1, W_2, ..., W_p) \quad (3)$$

For generic fve analysis, the following set of relationships is examined:

$$W = K T_o(p, W_1, W_2, ..., W_p) \quad (4a)$$

$$W = W_1 + W_2 + ... + W_p \quad (4b)$$

There is a significant difference in the analysis of these two relationships. Equation (4a) is utilised to derive the isoefficiency function, i.e. the growth rate of W that is *required* for the parallel system under investigation to preserve efficiency. On the other hand, equation (4b) shows the *actual* growth rate of W thus posses a constraint on the relative growth rate of the work components in the parallel algorithm.

Equation (4b) suggests that W grows at the same rate as the fastest between the components W_i ($1 \le i \le p$). As the fastest component is unknown all possible cases are in turn examined. This gives a total of p cases where in case i the component W_i is assumed to be the fastest.

For each case, equation (4a) is then examined to reveal the conditions for the parallel system to be scalable. These conditions however should not violate relationship (4b).

5. Scalability analysis of a power systems state-estimator

A Decomposed State Estimator (DSE) program for power systems was made available by the Brunel Institute of Power Systems [6] for evaluation purpose of the fve method. This program implements the DSE algorithm reported by J. F. Marsh et al. [8]. The algorithm itself has two important characteristics. Firstly, it is based on the master-slave paradigm; additionally the amount of work in the master and each slave are not determined by the algorithm but rather by the input data. Secondly, different variations of the algorithm can be implemented based on the expected sparsity of the input data.

In this section, the generic fve method is used to analytically predict the effect of input data sparsity on scalability. The predictions are also verified by timing measurements obtained from porting the DSE program to a Parsytec GCel 3/512.

For clarity the relevant material relating to the power systems state-estimator reported by J. F. Marsh and M. Azzam [7] and J. F. Marsh et al. [8] is summarised in sections 5.1 through 5.3. A detailed account can be found in the appropriate references [6][7][8]. The performance analysis conducted to construct all necessary models is given in section 5.4. The generic fixed-value efficiency method is presented in section 5.5 while the convergence between theoretical predictions and timing measurements is shown in section 5.6.

5.1 The conventional least-squares estimator

In a steady state analysis of power systems operation, the objective is to estimate the states x of the system given a set of measurements z and an algebraic model relating z to x. Network states are nodal voltage magnitudes and phases while measurements consist of a selection of nodal voltage magnitudes, real/reactive nodal power injections and line flows. The power system is represented by a graph that essentially contains all available information on the relationship between z and x. This graph consists of n nodes interconnected by lines.

The relationship between measurements and states is represented by a set of algebraic non-linear equations of the form:

$$z = h(\chi) + u$$

where χ is the actual states of the system, h is the measurement function and u the measurement uncertainty ($\chi \in \Re^n$; $z, u \in \Re^m$ and $m>n$).

Assuming that measurements are assigned weights then the problem of Weighted Least-Squares estimation of χ is equivalent to finding the local minimum of the performance index:

$$J = \|z - h(x)\|^2_{R^{-1}}$$

by choice of estimate x. If the non-linear function $h(x)$ is approximated by a linear form obtained from a truncated Taylor-series expansion, then the conventional least-squares estimator (CSE) for the system states is given by convergence of

$$H^T(j)\, R^{-1}\, H(j)\, \Delta x\,(j) = H^T(j)\, R^{-1}\, \Delta z\,(j) \qquad (5)$$

where $\Delta x\,(j) = x(j+1) - x(j)$, $\Delta z\,(j) = z - h(x(j))$ and $H = \partial h / \partial x$ is the Jacobian matrix of $h(x)$. H and $h(x)$ are evaluated at $x = x(j)$ and j is an iteration index. The procedure terminates when a pre-defined function of $\Delta x(j)$ (such as $max \parallel \Delta x(j) \parallel$) falls below a predetermined threshold A_o .

5.2 The decomposed state estimator

The problem of reducing run times and also improving the robustness of state estimation can be addressed by hierarchical methods, such as the decomposed state estimator (DSE) [8]. In the DSE, the overall graph of n nodes is decomposed into k non-overlapping areas (figure 1). Lines which inter-connect areas are known as 'ties'. Areas that are directly interconnected by ties are said to be 'adjacent'. Ties are terminated at nodes termed 'boundary nodes'. The total number of boundary nodes is represented by n_b while the boundary states are represented by the vector x_b . In each area, all nodes other than boundary nodes are termed 'internal nodes'. For area i , the number of internal nodes is represented by n_{ir} while the internal states are represented by the vector x_{ir} .

The CSE method presented in section 5.1 is equivalent to the DSE method shown in figure 4 (Appendix C). Details on the derivation of the DSE and the mathematical equivalence of the two methods are reported by J. F. Marsh and M. Azzam [8].

In the DSE, the problem of state estimation is solved in two levels: the upper level is assigned to a single processor while the lower level is assigned to $(p - 1)$ processors working in parallel. At the upper level, the states x_b of the boundary nodes are computed. At the lower level the states x_{ir} of the internal area i are computed for all i; furthermore matrices required for computing the new x_b during the next iteration are also calculated. Communication is required between the upper and lower level but not within the lower level. The DSE consists of the repetition of consecutive entries to lower and upper level, continued to a defined convergence.

An appropriate model for implementing the DSE is the master-slave model where the master is assigned all computations at upper level while each slave is assigned the computations at each area of the lower level.

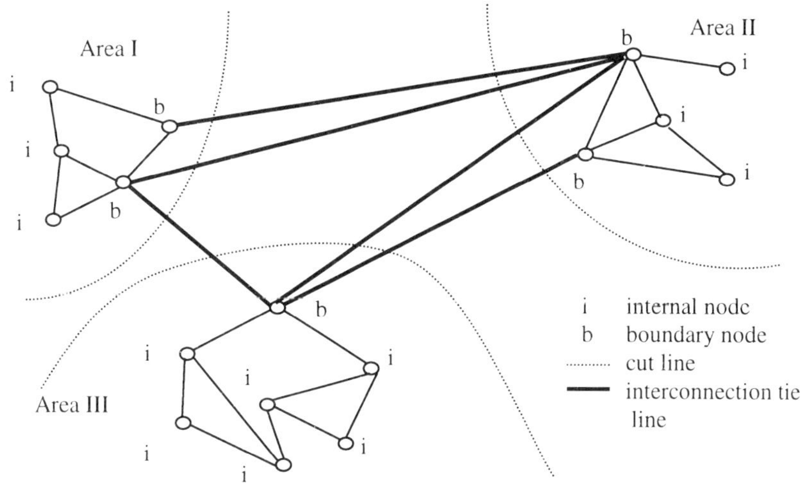

Fig. 1 Example of nodal definitions for network partitioned intro three areas

5.3 Sparsity of the input data

In most real-life power systems, each node is directly connected to a small number of other nodes hence the number of lines per node is small, usually around 3. Consequently, the Jacobian matrix H formed at the CSE is sparse and therefore programming techniques for sparse matrices can be used for the implementation of the CSE.

$$\begin{array}{c} z_1 \\ z_2 \\ z_3 \\ \vdots \\ z_k \end{array} \begin{bmatrix} H_{1r} & H_{11b} & 0 & H_{12b} & 0 & H_{13b} & \cdots & 0 & H_{1kb} \\ 0 & H_{21b} & H_{2r} & H_{22b} & 0 & H_{23b} & \cdots & 0 & H_{2kb} \\ 0 & H_{31b} & 0 & H_{32b} & H_{3r} & H_{33b} & \cdots & 0 & H_{3kb} \\ \vdots & \vdots & \vdots & \vdots & \vdots & \vdots & \ddots & \vdots & \vdots \\ 0 & H_{k1b} & 0 & H_{k2b} & 0 & H_{k3b} & \cdots & H_{kr} & H_{kkb} \end{bmatrix} \begin{array}{c} m_1 \\ m_2 \\ m_3 \\ \vdots \\ m_k \end{array}$$

dimension: n_{1r}, n_{1b}, n_{2r}, n_{2b}, n_{3r}, n_{3b}, …, n_{kr}, n_{kb}

Fig. 2 Block structure of the Jacobian matrix *H*

The Jacobian H has a block structure, shown in figure 2, which is fully exploited in the DSE [7]. As a result, computations at lower level are based on H_{ir}, the internal Jacobian matrix for area i, and H_{ib}, the boundary Jacobian matrix for area i, whereas computations at upper level are based on the boundary Jacobian matrix H_b which has the structure:

$$H_b = \begin{bmatrix} H_{11b} & \cdots & H_{1kb} \\ \vdots & \ddots & \vdots \\ H_{k1b} & \cdots & H_{kkb} \end{bmatrix}$$

It is expected that for 'clearly decomposable' graphs, i.e. those where $n_r >> n_b$, the Jacobian H_{ir} will be sparse thus programming techniques for sparse matrices could be employed at the DSE's lower level. Furthermore, the partitioning of the graph is unlikely to result in practice in any one subsystem being interconnected with more than four others [7]. As a result, when the number of areas is large (k>6) the Jacobian H_{ib} and consequently H_b are also expected to be block-sparse. Hence, programming techniques for sparse matrices could be also employed at the DSE's upper level.

In summary, sparsity programming techniques may be employed for implementing both the CSE and DSE depending on the structure of the global graph and the technique used to partition this graph into areas. Three cases have particular practical interest.

1. The global graph is large and is partitioned into a small number of large areas. Here, sparsity programming can be employed for the CSE and at the DSE's lower level but not at the DSE's upper level.
2. The global graph is very large and is partitioned into a large number of large areas. Here, sparsity programming techniques can be employed for the CSE and at both the DSE's upper and lower levels.
3. The global graph is dense and is partitioned into dense areas. Here, programming techniques for dense matrices are employed at both the CSE and DSE's upper and lower levels.

The employment of sparsity programming affects the performance of both the CSE and DSE. The storage required for a sparse matrix is usually proportional to the number of non-zero elements in the matrix. The execution time of computations, such as matrix multiplication or those required for solving a system of equations, depends on the number as well as the position of the non-zero elements in the participating matrices. For example, the result of a matrix multiplication between two sparse matrices may be a dense matrix as a result of the relative position of non-zero elements in the two matrices. In the general case, the execution time of computations, such as matrix multiplication or those required for solving a system of equations, is no slower (meaning linear or faster) to the number of non-zero elements in the participating matrices. It is therefore clear that the input data significantly affect the performance of sparsity programming methods.

5.4 Performance models

For simplicity, it is assumed that all areas have the same number of internal nodes n_r. Hence, it is:

$$n = n_b + (p-1)\, n_r \qquad (6)$$

The amount of work at the CSE is represented by W, the amount of work at the master by W_b and the amount of work at each slave by W_r. The total work W is a function of the number of nodes in the total graph n, the work W_b is a function of the number of boundary nodes n_b and the work at each slave W_r is a function of the number of internal nodes n_r and also a function of n_b. The exact relationship between work and input size depends on the sparsity of the input data. As all work involved various matrix operations it follows that work is in the best case $\Theta(n)$ for matrixes $n \times n$ that are sparse and $\Theta(n^3)$ for matrices that are dense [4].

The overheads in the DSE are due to load imbalance, communication and computation that is not performed by the CSE.

The overhead due to load imbalance consists of the overhead due to the slaves being idle while the master is performing computation, which is $(p\text{-}1)\ W_b$, and the overhead due to the master being idle while the slaves are performing computation, which is W_r. Hence:

$$T_o^{load\_im} = \Theta(p\ W_b) + \Theta(W_r)$$

The communication overhead is due to the two single-node broadcasts (steps 2* and 4* in figure 4) and the two global combine operations (steps 1* and 2a and 3* and 4). The performance of the global combine operation in steps 1* and 2a dominates all others. In this operations, matrix G is transferred thus the size of the message is $\Theta(n_b^2)$. If $\Theta(n_b)$ packets are formed where each has size $\Theta(n_b)$ then by using the recursive splitting algorithm [4] the communication overhead per processor is $\Theta(n_b^2) + \Theta(n_b \log p)$. Summing up over all processors, the total communication overhead is:

$$T_o^{comm} = \Theta(\ n_b^2\ p) + \Theta(n_b\ p \log p)$$

Extra computation in the DSE that is not performed in the CSE occurs in each slave. This is due to the inversion of matrix Ω (step 1 in figure 4) which is not required in the CSE and is $\Theta(W_r)$. Extra computation can also sometimes occur in the master. This is when programming techniques for sparse matrices are employed at the CSE but not at the upper level of the DSE (due to the fact that H_b may not be sparse enough). This contributes $\Theta(W_b)$ to the overhead function which however is slower than the $\Theta(p\ W_b)$ in $T_o^{load\_im}$ and thus is omitted. Hence, the overhead due to extra computation is:

$$T_o^{e\_work} = \Theta(p\ W_r)$$

Summing up all overheads and keeping dominant terms only, the total overhead is:

$$T_o = \Theta(p\ W_b) + \Theta(p\ W_r) + \Theta(\ n_b^2\ p) + \Theta(n_b\ p \log p) \qquad (7)$$

5.5 Generic fixed-value efficiency analysis

For generic fve analysis the expression $W = K\ T_o$ is examined. Since T_o contains multiple terms, W is balanced against each individual term (section 2). The following set of expressions is derived:

$$W = \Theta(p\ W_b) \qquad (8a)$$

$$W = \Theta(p\ W_r) \qquad (8b)$$

$$W = \Theta(\ n_b^2\ p) \qquad (8c)$$

$$W = \Theta(\ n_b\ p \log p) \qquad (8d)$$

In the DSE, the total work W, the work at the master W_b and the work at each slave W_r are not independent. Instead, they are related by equation (6) giving the relationship between n, n_b and n_r, i.e.

$$n = \Theta(n_b) + \Theta(p\ n_r) \qquad (8e)$$

Three cases are now examined based on the expected sparsity of the input data as suggested in section 5.3.

Theorem 1 presents the results from fve analysis when sparsity programming is employed at CSE and both the upper and lower level of the DSE. Since all matrices are sparse, the amount of work at the CSE is $W = \Theta(n)$, the amount of work at the DSE's upper level is $W_b = \Theta(n_b)$ and the amount of work at the DSE's lower level is $W_r = \Theta(n_r) + \Theta(n_b)$.

Theorem 1. The DSE is scalable when $n_r\ (p)$ is no slower than $n_b^2\ (p)$ for $n_b\ (p) = \Omega(\log p)$ and when $n_r\ (p)$ is no slower than $n_b \log p$ for $n_b\ (p) = o(\log p)$. The isoefficiency function is $\Theta(p\ n_r)$ which is $\Theta(p\ n_b^2)$ for $n_b(p) = \Omega(\log p)$ and $\Theta(n_b\ p \log p)$ for $n_b\ (p) = o(\log p)$.

Proof: The proof is given in Appendix B.

Theorem 2 presents the results from fve analysis when sparsity programming is employed in the CSE and DSE's lower level but not at the DSE's upper level (the proof is similar to the proof of theorem 1 and is omitted). The amount of work at the CSE is $W = \Theta(n)$. Matrix H_b is dense thus the amount of work at the DSE's upper level is $W_b = \Theta(n_b^3)$. Finally, matrix H_r is sparse thus the amount of work at the DSE's lower level is $W_r = \Theta(n_r) + \Theta(n_b)$.

Theorem 2. The DSE is scalable when $n_r(p)$ is no slower than $n_b^3(p)$ for $n_b(p) = \Omega(\log^{1/2} p)$ and when $n_r(p)$ is no slower than $n_b \log p$ for $n_b(p) = o(\log^{1/2} p)$. The isoefficiency function is $\Theta(p\ n_r)$ which is $\Theta(p\ n_b^3)$ for $n_b(p) = \Omega(\log^{1/2} p)$ and $\Theta(n_b\ p \log p)$ for $n_b(p) = o(\log^{1/2} p)$.

Theorem 3 presents the results from fve analysis when programming techniques for dense matrices are employed in both the CSE and DSE (the proof is similar to the proof of theorem 1 and is omitted). Since all matrices are dense, the amount of work at the CSE is $W = \Theta(n^3)$, the amount of work at the DSE's upper level is $W_b = \Theta(n_b^3)$ and the amount of work at the DSE's lower level is $W_r = \Theta(n_r^3) + \Theta(n_b^3)$.

Theorem 3. The DSE is scalable when $n_r(p)$ is no slower than $n_b(p) / p^{2/3}$ for $n_b(p) = \Omega(\log^{1/2} p)$ and when $n_r(p)$ is no slower than $(n_b \log p / p^2)^{1/3}$ for $n_b(p) = o(\log^{1/2} p)$. The isoefficiency function is $\Theta(p^3\ n_r^3(p))$ which is $\Theta(p\ n_b^3(p))$ for $n_b(p) = \Omega(\log^{1/2} p)$ and $\Theta(n_b\ p \log p)$ for $n_b(p) = o(\log^{1/2} p)$.

It can be reasonably assumed that the number of boundary nodes is linear to the number of areas (as each area contains on average the same number of boundary nodes). Since the number of areas is linear to p it follows that $n_b(p) = \Theta(p)$. In this case, for preserving efficiency, the number of internal nodes has to increase as $\Theta(p^2)$ (theorem 1), as $\Theta(p^4)$ (theorem 2) and as $\Theta(p^{1/3})$ (theorem 3) depending on the sparsity of the input data. These isoefficiency functions provide some interesting results on the scalability of the DSE and its relationship with the sparsity of the input data. It is first observed that none of the three cases examined is unscalable although the overheads incurred are large. It is also observed that the best scalability is achieved when all data are dense. In this case, the number of internal nodes has to increase at $\Theta(p^{1/3})$ to preserve the parallel system's efficiency. For example, it is assumed that a parallel system with $p = 4$ and $n_r = 20$ has a desirable efficiency. When p is scaled to 8 then this efficiency is preserved only if n_r is increased to 25. The scalability of the case where all data are sparse is not so good. For the same example, when p scales from 4 to 8 then n_r has to increase from 20 to 80 for the system's efficiency to be preserved. Finally, the scalability of the case where data are sparse at the CSE and DSE's lower level but not at the DSE's upper level is very poor. In the same example, n_r has to increase from 20 to 320 for the system's efficiency to be preserved.

5.6 An implementation of the DSE

An implementation of the CSE and DSE [6] was provided by the Brunel Institute of Power Systems for evaluation purposes. This program, initially written for a shared-memory parallel computer, was ported to the Parsytec GCel 3/512, a distributed-memory parallel computer with a mesh interconnection topology. More specifically, the parts of the program related to computations (initially written in FORTRAN) were ported with minor only changes. On the other hand, the parts to accomplish inter-processor communication were initially written using the PVM model, which has poor performance for the target architecture. To improve performance, the recursive-splitting algorithm was implemented using the more efficient message-passing model.

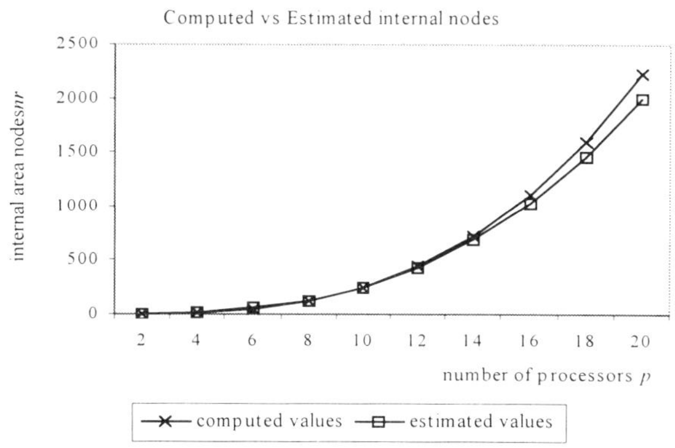

Fig. 3 Computed vs. estimated values of n_r

Timing measurements were obtained from solving the IEEE-30 node standard network and performance models were constructed for all sources of overhead. These models allowed computing an analytical expression for the number of internal nodes n_r that is required to preserve efficiency as p is scaled. This expression was thereafter projected to compute the values of n_r for large input sizes and number of processors. These computed values are presented in figure 3 together with values estimated from theorem 2. The convergence of these values illustrates the analytical power of the generic fixed-value efficiency method.

6. Conclusions

In this paper, the generic fixed-value efficiency (fve) method was proposed to evaluate the scalability of parallel systems with multiple components. The generic fve method is an extension of isoefficiency that is suitable for parallel systems where the growth rates of total work and its components are not predetermined. The method can be utilised to reveal the relation between the total work and its components for the parallel system to preserve efficiency. This method was demonstrated for a decomposed-state estimator for power systems on a distributed-memory parallel computer with a mesh interconnection topology. The results allowed the impact on scalability of the input data sparsity to be analytically estimates. These results were verified through timing measurements.

7. Acknowledgements

The authors would like to acknowledge the Brunel Institute for Power Systems (BIPS) for providing the source code of the CSE and DSE programs. Also Prof. Halatsis at the University of Athens for granting access to the Parsytec GCel 3/512 parallel computer. Finally, Dr. Marsh for his comments on the CSE and DSE algorithms.

8. References

[1] Gupta A. *Analysis and Design of Scalable Parallel Algorithms for Scientific Computing*. Ph.D. Thesis, Department of Computer Science, University of Minnesota, Minneapolis, MN. 1995

[2] Gustafson J. L. "The Consequences of Fixed Time Performance Measurement". *Proceedings of the 25th Annual Hawaii International Conference on System Sciences*, vol. 2, 1992, pp. 113-124.

[3] Kumar V., Gupta A. "Analyzing scalability of parallel algorithms on parallel architectures". *Journal of Parallel and Distributed Computing*, **22**, 1994, pp. 379-391.

[4] Kumar V., Grama A., Gupta A., Karypis G. *Introduction to Parallel Computing. Design and Analysis of Algorithms*, USA, Benjamin/Cummings, 1994.

[5] Martin I., Tirado F. "Relationships between efficiency and execution time of full multigrid methods on parallel computers". *IEEE Transactions on Parallel and Distributed Systems*, **8** (6), 1997, pp. 562-573.

[6] Marsh J. F., Zitouni S., Irving M. R. "Computational Aspects of Distributed State-Estimators for Power Systems". *12th IFAC World Congress*, 1993.

[7] Marsh J. F. "Structure of measurement Jacobian matrices for power systems". *IEE Proc., Pt. C.*, **6**, 1989, pp. 407-413.

[8] Marsh J. F, Azzam M. "MCHSE-a versalite framework for the design of 2-level power system state-estimators". *IEE Proc., Pt. C.*, **4**, 1988, pp. 291-298.

[9] Singh J.P., Hennessy J.L., Gupta A., "Scaling Parallel Programs for Multiprocessors: Methodology and Examples". *Computer*, July, 1993, pp. 42-50.

[10] Sun X-H., Rover D.T. "Scalability of Parallel Algorithm-Machine Combinations". *IEEE Transactions on Parallel and Distributed Systems*, **5** (6), 1994, pp. 599-613.

[11] Sun X-H. "The Relation of Scalability and Execution Time". *International Processing Symposium*, 1996. Also as NASA ICASE Report 95-62, Sep. 1995.

[12] Tambouris E., van Santen P., Marsh J. "Performance Evaluation of a Processor-Farm Model for Power Systems State-Estimators on a Distributed-Memory Computer". *Computing Systems in Engineering*, **5** (4-6), 1994, pp. 479-487.

[13] Tambouris E., van Santen P. "A Methodology for Performance and Scalability Analysis". *Lecture Notes in Computers Science*, vol. 1012, 1995, pp. 475-480.

[14] Tambouris E., Dimas E. "Scalability analysis of multiprocessor systems using stochastic models", *International Conference on Parallel and Distributed Processing Techniques and Applications*, vol. III, 1997, pp. 1448-1452.

Appendix A: Order Analysis Notation

Order analysis is used to classify functions by their growth rates. All functions analysed are from positive integers to positive reals. The order notation used in this paper is summarised in table 1.

Table 1 Order analysis notation

notation	description
$f = o(g)$	f is *slower* than g
$f = O(g)$	f is *no faster* than g
$f = \Theta(g)$	f is *about as fast* as g
$f = \Omega(g)$	f is *no slower* than g
$f = \omega(g)$	f is *faster* than g

The formal definitions of order notation follows:

- $o(g)$ is the set of f such that f/g approaches 0; i.e. $\lim_{n\to\infty}\{f(n)/g(n)\} = 0$.
- $O(g)$ is the set of f such that f/g is bounded above; that is, there exists C such that for all positive n, $f(n) < C\,g(n)$.
- $\Theta(g)$ is the set of f such that f/g is bounded above and bounded away from zero; that is, there exist C_1, C_2 such that for all n, $0 < C_1\,g(n) < f(n) < C_2\,g(n)$.
- $\Omega(g)$ is the set of f such that f/g is bounded away from 0; that is, there exists C such that for all n, $0 < C\,g(n) < f(n)$.
- $\omega(g)$ is the set of f such that f/g approaches infinity; i.e. $\lim_{n\to\infty}\{f(n)/g(n)\} = \infty$.

Appendix B: Proof of theorem 1

Since all matrices are sparse, the amount of work at the CSE is $W = \Theta(n)$, the amount of work at the DSE's upper level is $W_h = \Theta(n_h)$ and the amount of work at the DSE's lower level is $W_r = \Theta(n_r) + \Theta(n_b)$. Now equations (8) become:

$$W = \Theta(p\, n_b) \quad (9a)$$

$$W = \Theta(p\, n_r) + \Theta(p\, n_b) \quad (9b)$$

$$W = \Theta(n_b^2\, p) \quad (9c)$$

$$W = \Theta(n_b\, p \log p) \quad (9d)$$

$W = \Theta(n_b) + \Theta(p\, n_r)$ (9e)

Keeping dominant terms only these equations are reduced to the following set:

$W = \Theta(p\, n_r)$ (10a)

$W = \Theta(p\, n_b^2)$ (10b)

$W = \Theta(n_b\, p \log p)$ (10c)

$W = \Theta(n_b) + \Theta(p\, n_r)$ (10d)

The isoefficiency functions derived from equations (10a-c) are $f_1(p) = \Theta(p\, n_r)$, $f_2(p) = \Theta(p\, n_b^2)$ and $f_3(p) = \Theta(n_b\, p \log p)$ respectively. The growth rate of W, which is represented by $f_W(p)$, is conveyed from equation (10d), hence depends on the relative growth of n_b and $p\, n_r$. Therefore, two cases are examined.

(i) $p\, n_r$ is slower than n_b i.e. $n_r = o(n_b / p)$

In this case, the term n_b dominates the r.h.s. of equation (10d) and the growth rate of W is:

$f_W(p) = \Theta(n_b)$

We observe that one of the isoefficiency functions, namely $f_2(p) = \Theta(p\, n_b^2)$, is faster than $f_W(p)$ for all possible forms of $f_b(p)$. Therefore, the parallel system is fve unscalable.

(ii) $p\, n_r$ is no slower than n_b i.e. $n_r = \Omega(n_b / p)$

In this case, the term $p\, n_r$ dominates the r.h.s. of equation (10d) and the growth rate of W is:

$f_W(p) = \Theta(p\, n_r)$

The condition for the parallel system to be scalable is that $f_W(p)$ grows no slower than all isoefficiency functions. One of the isoefficiency functions, namely $f_1(p) = \Theta(p\, n_r)$, is always no slower than $f_W(p)$. Hence, the condition for the parallel system to be scalable is:

$f_W(p)$ is no slower than max $\{f_2(p), f_3(p)\} \Rightarrow$

$p\, n_r = \Omega(\max\{p\, n_b^2, n\, p \log p\}) \Rightarrow$

$n_r = \Omega(\max\{n_b^2, n_b \log p\})$

Now there are two different cases depending on which isoefficiency function is faster:

(a) n_b^2 is no slower than $n_b \log p$, i.e. $n_b = \Omega(\log p)$

Hence, $n_r = \Omega(n_b)$ and the isoefficiency function is $\Theta(p\, n_b)$

(a) n_b^2 is no slower than $n_b \log p$, i.e. $n_b = o(\log p)$

Hence, $n_r = \Omega(\log p)$ and the isoefficiency function is $\Theta(n_b\, p \log p)$. •

Appendix C: The Decomposed State Estimator

	Program DSE_upper_level /* executed in one processor (the master)	**Program DSE_lower_level** /* executed in $(p-1)$ parallel processors (the slaves) /* here shown for processor i
	Begin	Begin
0		Initialise $x_{ir}(0)$, $x_b(0)$. Read z_i. Set $j = 0$.
1		Compute: $h_i(x_{ir}(j), x_b(j))$; $H_{ir}(j)$; $H_{ib}(j)$; $\Delta z_i(j) = z_i - h_i$; $\Omega_{ir}(j) = H_{ir}^T R_i^{-1} H_{ir}$; $W_{ir}(j) = I - H_{ir}\Omega_i^{-1} H_{ir}^T R_i^{-1}$; $G_i = [W_{ir}\ H_{ib}]^T R_i^{-1} [W_{ir}\ H_{ib}]$; $g_i = [W_{ir}\ H_{ib}]^T R_i^{-1} \Delta z_i$.
1*	Receive $[G_i(j): g_i(j)]$ from lower level.	Send $[G_i(j): g_i(j)]$ to upper level
2a	$[G : g] = \Sigma\ [G_i : g_i]$ and $[G_i(j): g_i(j)]$.	
2b	Compute: $\Delta x_b(j)$ from $G(j)\,\Delta x_b(j) = g(j)$	
2*	Send $\Delta x_b(j)$ to lower level	Receive $\Delta x_b(j)$ from upper level
3		Compute: $\Delta r_{ib}(j) = \Delta z_i - H_{ib}(j)\,\Delta x_b(j)$ and $\Delta x_{ir}(j)$ from $\Omega_{ir}(j)\,\Delta x_{ir}(j) = H_i^T(j)\, R_i^{-1}\,\Delta r_{ib}(j)$. Set $j = j + 1$. Compute $x_{ir}(j)$; $x_b(j)$; If $\max \lVert\Delta x_{ir}(j)\rVert < A_0$ then slave_conv_flag:=TRUE
3*	Receive slave_conv_flag from lower level	Send slave_conv_flag to upper level
4	Compute: global convergence flag	
4*	Send global convergence flag to lower level	Receive global flag from upper level.
5	If global convergence not reached, then go to 1* else stop	If global convergence not reached, then go to 1 else $x_{ir}(j) = \mathbf{x}_{ir}$ and $x_b(j) = \mathbf{x}_b$
	End	End

Fig. 4 The decomposed state estimator (DSE)

Specification for Reactive Bulk-Synchronous Programming

Chen, Yifeng
Oxford University Computing Laboratory
Parks Road, Oxford OX1 6QD, UK
Yifeng.Chen@comlab.oxford.ac.uk

Abstract

This paper extends BSP to incorporate reactive (i.e. non-terminating) programming. We propose a semantic model for BSP which allows a process to have infinitely many supersteps. The semantics turns out to reveal the essential difference between BSP and sequential specifications. Based on the model, a specification language (called SSS) is proposed to support modularised programming and hide communication and synchronisation details in specification. The notion of public variable is proposed to substantially simplify reactive programming. The normal forms of BSP and SSS are identified and complete sets of laws for the two languages are given. Finally, a few refinement laws are used to provide a BSP treatment of the dining-philosopher problem which illustrates the power of BSP reactive programming. Much of the formalism presented in this paper can also be applied to non-reactive programming.

1 Introduction

1.1 BSP

The BSP model [15] provides an increasingly important paradigm bridging sequential and parallel programming, as shown by its recent popularity [13, 14, 6]. A BSP computer consists of several processors, each with its own local memory, connected by a network with an efficient barrier-synchronisation mechanism; and a BSP computation consists of a sequence of parallel supersteps, during each of which each processor executes local operations (steps). Communication between processors is completed only at the end of the superstep in which it was initiated. During a superstep, a variable can be accessed by more than one processor with *put* and *get* commands.

The following program is a sample BSP program containing *put* (sending value to a remote variable), *get* (copying a remote variable to a local one) and *sync* (synchronisation point) commands.

$$\left(\begin{array}{l} get\ x := y; \\ sync; \\ x := x+1 \end{array}\right) \Bigg\| \left(\begin{array}{l} y := 1; \\ sync \end{array}\right) \Bigg\| \left(\begin{array}{l} z := 2; \\ put\ x := z; \\ z := 10; \\ sync \end{array}\right)$$

The three *sync* commands set the synchronisation barrier at which communications are completed. At the beginning of the left-most process, x is set to be either 1 or 2 and then the local computation increases it by 1.

BSP has a simple cost model which makes the performance of a BSP program predictable. BSP also enjoys good portability and scalabilty.

Parallel programming is much more complicated than sequential programming. A popular approach to simplify parallel programming is to restrict communication interference and reduce non-determinism. For example, Object-Oriented programming protects the internal state of an object from being directly modified by outside processes; this can be viewed as some kind of spatial restriction on communications. In contrast, BSP imposes temporal restriction on communications, which protects the local state of a process before the next synchronisation command.

1.2 Reactive BSP

One of the criticisms of BSP is its lack of task parallelism. A BSP program was only allowed to produce a finite number of supersteps. Excluding reactive non-terminating processes does not free programmers from considering safety and liveness properties of a large parallel program. For example in some constrained optimisation problems, the constraints are safety properties, while the optimisation requirement is liveness property (or progress) which should be improved gradually until some precision requirement is achieved. Another example is computer simulation in which the final result is normally not interesting and termination is often artificially imposed and does not play an important role in the program. In practice, supercomputers are often used as distributed database servers or

1066-6192/99 $10.00 © 1999 IEEE

web-search engines. Reactive programming for networking, IO resource sharing or human-computer interfaces is inevitable in a large application. In general whenever we are not only interested in a computation's final result but also its intermediate states, non-reactive programming modeled by pre-post conditions becomes inadequate.

There are two ways to add task parallelism in BSP. One is to combine BSP with another language like CSP [8], but this would introduce unnecessary complexity. In this paper we extend BSP to allow non-terminating processes (called *Reactive BSP*, or RBSP). In RBSP, program behaviour with an infinite number of supersteps is no longer a bug. Such kinds of process can provide a useful service in a large application. RBSP is not as powerful as languages specialised for task parallelism. For example, to wait for a token from another process (easily done with synchronous communication in CSP), a process has to idle through a number of empty supersteps until its local state is modified by incoming communications and satisfies a guard condition (achieved by conditional empty loop $do\ b \rightarrow sync\ od$). However, in section 5, we will show a simple and straightforward RBSP solution to dining-philosopher problem. The advantage is that we may now include both data and task parallelism in one simple and unified programming paradigm.

1.3 Unifying Theories

In Unifying Theories [9], programs and specifications are predicates. The semantics of a sequential program is represented as a predicate $p(x, x', ok, ok')$ where ok records that the program starts properly and ok' records that the program has terminated properly. ok and ok' are not program variables, and so do not appear in any program text. For example, $ok \Rightarrow (x' = x + 1 \wedge y' = y \wedge ok')$ is the semantics of program $x := x + 1$ with alphabet $\{x, y, ok, x', y', ok'\}$. If the program $x := x + 1$ starts properly, it will terminate in a state x is increased by 1. A predicate A is a valid specification if it satisfies a few healthiness conditions. A healthiness condition is normally presented as an equation in the form of $A = L(A)$. For example, $A = (ok \Rightarrow A)$ is an healthiness condition.

[9] describes a principle called *parallel by merge* for parallel program semantics. The idea is that, once the shared variables are differentiated by labelling, the processes become disjoint, and they can be simulated in disjoint alphabets. The final effect of parallel execution is then defined by a merging operation, which shows how the final value of the shared variables is computed from the two results and the initial value of the shared variables.

This paper follows that approach and applies it to reactive BSP programming.

The first semantic model of BSP was given in [10]. It supported only terminating processes, did not encompass iteration nor recursion, and experienced difficulty in dealing with unbalanced supersteps in parallel composition. The model was improved in [12] where the latter problem was resolved by introduction of divergence at the end of the shorter process to match supersteps and some revision is made to parallel-by-merge. We now summerise the shortcomings still remaining.

2 Challenges

2.1 Non-termination

Use of either recursion or iteration raises the problem of non-termination. In past models of BSP [10, 9, 12] recursion has not been defined. The present paper clarifies and solves the recursion equation for BSP.

There are different kinds of non-termination, for example:

$$P \hat{=}\ do\ \ true \rightarrow skip\ \ od$$
$$Q \hat{=}\ ABT; sync;\ ABT; sync;\ do\ \ true \rightarrow skip\ \ od$$
$$R \hat{=}\ do\ \ true \rightarrow (ABT; sync)\ \ od$$

We suppose ABT to be the terminating specification that assigns variables with arbitrary values and executes arbitrary communication commands within a superstep. P diverges immediately. It is the worst specification (i.e. chaos) in the refinement ordering of BSP; its behaviour is totally chaotic. Q diverges after 2 legal supersteps. The rest of its behaviour is chaotic. R never diverges within finitely many supersteps. It is a reactive process with normal behaviour during each superstep.

BSP's non-termination problem is not just a semantic subtlety. It turns out to shape the form of BSP specification which is essentially different from sequential specification. In VDM [11], sequential specification has the form of (b, P). b is called *pre-condition* and P is called *post-condition*. It is defined as $(b \wedge ok) \Rightarrow (P \wedge ok')$ in [9]. However, in BSP, we do not have the law $P; chaos = chaos$ for feasible P (actually $P; chaos = P$ is true for any reactive process); there is no way to move chaos before a synchronisation point. Therefore, BSP specification has a more general form $(b_1, p_1, b_2, p_2, \ldots)$ (or $(b_1)_\perp; \langle p_1 \rangle; (b_2)_\perp; \langle p_2 \rangle; \ldots$) in which each b_i is an *intermediate condition* or a pre-condition for the rest of the specification and each $\langle p_i \rangle$ is a one-superstep specification (refer to section 4). (b, P) becomes a special case of BSP which certainly can not cover every application specifiable in practice.

2.2 Specification Challenge and Modularity

BSP is not a language directly suitable for specification. For example, we do not intuitively know what a $sync$ command does on the state of local variables unless communication commands before it are provided. Even with communication commands provided in a process (e.g. in $get\ x := y;\ sync$), it does not state anything certain about the process, as there can be communications from other processes modifying variable x before the beginning of the next superstep. There is no modularity of BSP's parallel composition. It is almost impossible to develop a BSP program from separate modules and compose them together with parallel composition.

A reasonable approach of specification is to state not only the commands in a process but also some constraints on the global communications in that superstep [12]. A typical constraint used in [12] is defined as $Empty(s) = putq_c = \lambda x.\{\} = getq$, which denotes no communication at all, i.e. *the bag of all communications is empty*. A specification allowing incoming communications is much more complicated. As concluded in [12], reasoning based on such kinds of specification has *tremendous complexity* and does not *scale up*.

This paper presents a specification language SSS, which makes BSP specification close to human intuition. SSS bridges the gap between high-level formal specification and BSP program code. One of the most important features of SSS is its modularity, which is justified by the fact that parallel composition can be defined as conjunction. A number of algebraic laws for SSS are presented. Safety and liveness properties can be properly expressed in SSS. Both soundness and completeness of the laws are provided. Details appear in section 4.

2.3 Other Challenges

One of the difficulties our semantics overcomes concerns the parallel composition of processes having different numbers of supersteps. Previous attempts broached that problem by producing divergence at the start of the processes or the end [12] of the shorter process's execution. In distributed computing it is essential to be able to combine reactive and terminating processes in parallel. We solve that problem by introducing empty supersteps and automatically appending those to the shorter process. The parallel composition no longer generates divergence.

A further challenge confronting BSP is its effectiveness in expressing distributed programs. With only asynchronous communication being completed at the beginning of the next superstep, how can the latest value of a variable be read immediately by another processor?

We introduce the notion of *public variables*. A public variable is a variable with copies on all processes. Modification to a public variable must be broadcast to all of its copies. Therefore, each public variable always has a unique value on all processes. Reading the local copy of a public variable is already accessing its latest value. This notion substantially simplifies reactive programming.

Our techniques are applied to the study of the well-known benchmark of the dining philosophers to demonstrate the advantage of BSP and SSS in reactive programming (section 5).

3 BSP language

BSP is usually embedded in a normal imperative language such as Fortran or C. The Guarded-Command language (*code*) abstracts such by containing only the basic imperative language operators. BSP commands can be embedded in code.

The following table lists the basic BSP commands we consider:

$chaos$	divergence (or $\perp$)
$skip$	no operation (or II)
$\mathbf{x} := \mathbf{e}$	local assignment
$P; Q$	sequential composition
$P \lhd b \rhd Q$	binary conditional
$P \sqcap Q$	non-deterministic choice
$var\ \mathbf{x}\ P$	variable block
$put\ \mathbf{x} := \mathbf{e}$	put $\mathbf{e}$ to variable $\mathbf{x}$
$get\ \mathbf{x} := \mathbf{y}$	get value of $\mathbf{y}$ into $\mathbf{x}$
$sync$	synchronisation
$\lvert P \rvert$	closure of process P
$P \parallel Q$	parallel composition
$do\ b \rightarrow P\ od$	iteration

Bold lowercase characters denote vectors of variables and italic lowercase single characters denote single variables. P and Q stand for BSP processes.

We follow the BSP World-Wide Standard Library [7] and employ the communication commands *put* and *get* (called bsp-put and bsp-get in [15]). The former copies its current local data into the local memory of its destination; it is buffered at each end and the data of communication are available only at the beginning of the next superstep. The latter achieves the reverse. The $sync$ command sets a synchronisation point, i.e. the end of a superstep. $|P|$ closes process P by excluding any communication with P's environment. Closure is always implied for a whole BSP program.

Semantic definitions can be found in [2].

BSP enjoys a number of algebraic laws in which A, A_1, A_2 and B are processes without synchronisation and $comm$, $comm_1$ and $comm_2$ are single communication commands:

$$\bot \sqcap P = P \sqcap \bot = \bot$$
$$\bot \| P = P \| \bot = \bot$$
$$\bot ; P = \bot ; A = A ; \bot = \bot$$
$$(P \lhd b \rhd Q); R = (P; R) \lhd b \rhd (Q; R)$$
$$(\mathbf{x} := \mathbf{e}_1;\ \mathbf{x} := \mathbf{e}_2) = \mathbf{x} := \mathbf{e}_2[\mathbf{e}_1/\mathbf{x}]$$
$$(\mathbf{x} := \mathbf{e};\ P \lhd b \rhd Q) = ((\mathbf{x} := \mathbf{e}; P) \lhd b[\mathbf{e}/\mathbf{x}] \rhd (\mathbf{x} := \mathbf{e}; Q))$$
$$comm;\ P \lhd b \rhd Q = (comm; P) \lhd b \rhd (comm; Q)$$
$$II \| P = P (\text{local variable list extended})$$
$$P \| Q = Q \| P$$
$$(P \sqcap Q) \| R = (P \| R) \sqcap (Q \| R)$$
$$(get\ \mathbf{gx} := \mathbf{gy}; \mathbf{x} := \mathbf{e}) = (\mathbf{x} := \mathbf{e}; get\ \mathbf{gx} := \mathbf{gy})$$
$$(\mathbf{x} := \mathbf{e};\ put\ \mathbf{px} := \mathbf{pe}) = (put\ \mathbf{px} := \mathbf{pe}[\mathbf{e}/\mathbf{x}];\ \mathbf{x} := \mathbf{e})$$
$$comm_1;\ comm_2 = comm_2;\ comm_1$$
$$(A; sync; P) \| B = (A \| B); sync; (P \| II)$$
$$(A; sync; P) \| (B; sync; Q) = (A \| B); sync; (P \| Q)$$
$$A_1 \| A_2 = A$$
$$(P \| Q) \| R = P \| (Q \| R)$$
$$do\ b \rightarrow P\ od = \textstyle\bigsqcap_{n \in \mathbb{N}} (((b)_\top;\ P)^\infty;\ (\neg b)_\top)$$

The laws in the table are semantically sound [2].

Finite BSP programs have the following normal form:

$$ST = put\ \mathbf{y} := \mathbf{e};\ \mathbf{x} := \mathbf{e};\ get\ \mathbf{x} := \mathbf{y}$$
$$PROC = II \mid (b)_\bot;\ ST;\ sync;\ PROC$$
$$NF = \textstyle\bigsqcap_{i \in I} (PROC_i;\ (b_i)_\bot;\ ST_i)$$

where $(b)_\bot \hat{=} II \lhd b \rhd \bot$. We suppose variable introduction and closure are applied on a whole program. The semantic equivalence between two BSP programs can be established by transforming them into the normal form with these laws (together with some laws for sequential computation) [2].

4 SSS Specification

This section presents the *Super-Step Specification language* (SSS for short). SSS bridges the gap between high level abstract specification and BSP implementation. Modularised programming can be achieved at this level.

Communication and synchronisation are invisible but implicit in SSS specifications. Thus programmers need not be bothered to decide which communication command to use when they are writing abstract specifications. It is an intermediate specification language, chosen for convenience, with no pretense at being as abstract as possible:

$$SSS = (b)_\bot \mid [p(\grave{x}, \acute{x})] \mid \langle p(\grave{x}, v, \acute{x}) \rangle \mid SSS; SSS \mid SSS \sqcap SSS \mid SSS \| SSS \mid do\ b \rightarrow SSS\ od$$

The semantics of SSS is based on the semantics of BSP.

The basic building block in this language is called *One-Superstep Specification* (or 1SS), $\langle p(\grave{x}, v, \acute{x}) \rangle$, in which $\grave{x}$ (the input, called *pre* x) denotes the initial state of local variables x, $\acute{x}$ (the output in the next superstep, called *post* x) denotes the final state of local variables, and v denotes the state of all global variables at the end of the current superstep. 1SS increases the superstep counter # by 1 like a *synchronisation* command, no communication is left uncompleted afterwards, and the predicate p specifies the relation among input, output and the global state at the end of current superstep. No communication is visible in 1SS.

$[p(\grave{x}, \acute{x})]$ denotes a terminating specification of local computation. Conditional chaos $(b)_\bot$ equals a *skip* if b is true in the current local state, but becomes *chaos* if b is false. Conditional miracle $(b)_\top$ is defined as $[b(\grave{x}) \wedge \grave{x} = \acute{x}]$. Therefore, $P \lhd b \rhd Q$ can be defined as $((b)_\top; P) \sqcap ((\neg b)_\top; Q)$.

A major advantage is that the parallel composition between two 1SSs becomes conjunction:

$$\langle p \rangle \| \langle q \rangle = \langle p \rangle \wedge \langle q \rangle.$$

Other laws are:

$$(a)_\bot; (b)_\bot = (a \wedge b)_\bot$$
$$[p(\grave{x}, \acute{x})];\ (b)_\bot = (\forall y . \neg p(x, y) \vee b(y))_\bot;\ [p(\grave{x}, \acute{x})]$$
$$((a)_\bot; P) \ \|\ ((b)_\bot; Q) = (a \wedge b)_\bot; P \| Q$$
$$([p]; P) \ \|\ ([q]; Q) = [p \wedge q]; P \| Q$$
$$(\langle p \rangle; P) \ \|\ (\langle q \rangle; Q) = \langle p \wedge q \rangle; P \| Q$$
$$\langle p \rangle = \langle p \wedge \grave{x} = x \rangle \quad \text{if } x \text{ is public}$$
$$[p]; [q] = [p; q]$$
$$[p]; \langle q \rangle = \langle p; q \rangle$$
$$\langle p \rangle; [q] = \langle p; q \rangle$$
$$\langle p \rangle \wedge \langle q \rangle = \langle p \rangle \| \langle q \rangle = \langle p \wedge q \rangle$$
$$\langle p \rangle \sqcap \langle q \rangle = \langle p \rangle \vee \langle q \rangle$$
$$\langle p \rangle \lhd b(x) \rhd \langle q \rangle = \langle p \lhd b(\grave{x}) \rhd q \rangle$$
$$[p] \| \langle q \rangle = \langle p[\alpha / \acute{\alpha}] \wedge q \rangle$$
$$II = (true)_\bot = (true)_\top = [\grave{x}, \acute{x}]$$
$$II \| \langle q \rangle = \langle q \wedge \grave{x} = x \rangle$$
$$[p] \| (\langle q \rangle; Q) = (\langle p \rangle \| \langle q \rangle);\ II \| Q$$
$$(P \sqcap Q) \| R = (P \| R) \sqcap (Q \| R)$$
$$do\ b \rightarrow P\ od = \textstyle\bigsqcap_{n \in \mathbb{N}} (((b)_\top;\ P)^\infty;\ (\neg b)_\top)$$

The laws in the table are semantically sound [2].

SSS has normal form:

$$PROC = II \mid (b)_\bot; \langle p \rangle; PROC$$
$$NF = \textstyle\bigsqcap_{i \in I} (PROC_i; (b_i)_\bot; [p_i])$$

which somehow reflects the general style of BSP specification. The semantic equivalence between two SSS specifications can be established by transforming them into the normal form with these laws (together with some laws for sequential computation) [2].

We shall use the following conventions to specify reactive processes.

$$\begin{array}{rl} P^0 \widehat{=} & II \\ P^n \widehat{=} & P; P^{n-1} \\ P^* \widehat{=} & \sqcap_{0 \le n < \infty} P^n \\ P^\bullet \widehat{=} & P; P^* = \sqcap_{1 \le n < \infty} P^n \\ P^\infty \widehat{=} & do\ true \rightarrow P\ od \\ P^\circ \widehat{=} & P^\infty \sqcap P^\bullet \end{array}$$

Thus a reactive specification S satisfying *safety property* p can be expressed as $S \Rightarrow \langle p \rangle^\infty$. S satisfying *liveness property* of p being repeated infinite times can be represented as $S \Rightarrow \text{Often}(p)$ where $\text{Often}(p) \widehat{=} (\langle true \rangle^*; \langle p \rangle)^\infty$. The following refinement laws ($\sqsubseteq \widehat{=} \Leftarrow$) will be used in section 5:

$$\begin{array}{rl} \langle p \rangle^\infty = & do\ true \rightarrow \langle p \rangle\ od \\ \langle p \rangle^* \sqcap \langle p \rangle^\infty \sqsubseteq & do\ b \rightarrow \langle p \rangle\ od \\ \langle p \rangle^\circ \sqsubseteq & (b)_\top;\ do\ b \rightarrow \langle p \rangle\ od \\ \langle p \rangle^* \sqsubseteq & var\ n :\in \mathbb{N} \\ & do\ n > 0 \rightarrow \langle p \wedge \acute{n} < \grave{n} \rangle\ od \\ \langle p \rangle^\bullet \sqsubseteq & var\ n :\in \mathbb{N} \\ & do\ n \ge 0 \rightarrow \langle p \wedge \acute{n} < \grave{n} \rangle\ od \\ (P; \langle p \rangle^*; Q)^\infty \sqsubseteq & (do\ true \rightarrow \\ & \quad P; \\ & \quad do\ b \rightarrow \langle p \rangle\ od; \\ & \quad Q \\ & od) \wedge \text{Often}(\neg b) \end{array}$$

5 Example: The Dining Philosophers

The problem of the dining philosophers is described in [4]. Five philosophers are seated in a circle. Each philosopher cycles through states *thinking*, *hungry* and *eating* denoted as t, h and e respectively. Neighbours can not eat at the same time. A hungry philosopher will eat eventually if thinking and eating are always done in finite time.

Let s_k ($k = 0, \ldots, 4$) be the public variable of philosopher k's state with type $\{t, h, e\}$. Neighbouring philosophers are able to access the latest state of philosopher k. The initial specification is:

$$\textbf{SPEC 1} \ \widehat{=} \ \Big\|_k \left(\begin{array}{l} \langle s_k = t \rangle^\bullet; \\ \langle s_k = h \rangle^\bullet; \\ \langle s_k = e \wedge s_{k^-} \neq e \wedge s_{k^+} \neq e \rangle^\bullet \end{array} \right)^\infty$$

In the definition, $k^- \widehat{=} k - 1\ mod\ 5$ and $k^+ \widehat{=} k + 1\ mod\ 5$. $\langle s_k = h \rangle^\bullet$ specifies the termination of the hungry procedure of each philosopher.

To refine this specification, we introduce 5 public variables $f_0, f_1, \ldots, f_4$ called *forks*. The 5 forks are located between neighbouring philosophers around the table. Each fork has two states: either l (belonging to the left philosopher) or r (right). A hungry philosopher k must have two forks to eat, i.e. $f_k = r$ and $f_{k^+} = l$.

$$\textbf{SPEC 2} \ \widehat{=} \ \Big\|_k \left(\begin{array}{l} \langle s_k = t \rangle^\bullet; \\ \langle s_k = h \rangle^\bullet; \\ \langle s_k = e \wedge f_k = r \wedge f_{k^+} = l \rangle^\bullet)^\infty \end{array} \right)^\infty$$

Theorem 1 $SPEC1 \sqsubseteq SPEC2$

The termination of thinking and eating is to be guaranteed by the user (if we consider the hungry phase to be the job of the operating system). Initially we suppose the termination of the hungry procedure to be unknown. A strategy is proposed and proved to ensure termination, i.e. *deadlock free* and *starvation free*.

$$\textbf{SPEC 3} \ \widehat{=} \ (acyclic)_\top; \Big\|_k \left(\begin{array}{l} \langle s_k = t \wedge stgy_k \rangle^\bullet; \\ \langle s_k = h \wedge stgy_k \rangle^\circ; \\ \langle s_k = e \wedge stgy_k \rangle^\bullet \end{array} \right)^\infty$$

where

$$\begin{array}{rl} stgy_k \widehat{=} & (s_k = t) \Rightarrow (f_k = l \Rightarrow \acute{f_k} = l) \wedge \\ & \qquad (f_{k^+} = r \Rightarrow \acute{f}_{k^+} = r) \\ \vee & (s_k = e) \Rightarrow (f_k = \acute{f_k} = r) \wedge \\ & \qquad (f_{k^+} = \acute{f}_{k^+} = l) \\ \vee & (s_k = h) \Rightarrow \\ & \left(\begin{array}{l} (f_k = r \Rightarrow \acute{f_k} = r) \\ \wedge (f_{k^+} = l \Rightarrow \acute{f}_{k^+} = l) \\ \wedge (s_{k^-} = t \Leftrightarrow (f_k = l \Rightarrow \acute{f_k} = r)) \\ \wedge (s_{k^+} = t \Leftrightarrow (f_{k^+} = r \Rightarrow \acute{f}_{k^+} = l)) \\ \wedge (f_k = r \wedge f_{k^+} = l) \Leftrightarrow \acute{s_k} = e) \end{array} \right) \\ acyclic \widehat{=} & \neg(f_0 = f_1 = \cdots = f_4). \end{array}$$

SPEC 3 requires proper initialisation. The directions of the forks form a priority graph. Condition *acyclic* is satisfied if there is no circle in the priority graph. In the case of improper initialisation, SPEC 3 becomes a miracle which still refines SPEC 2.

Informally the strategy is as follows: a thinking philosopher never obtains forks; a hungry philosopher never loses forks and he will obtain forks from adjacent thinking philosophers; only with both forks at hand does a philosopher begin eating. An eating philosopher holds the two forks tightly into the next superstep.

Lemma 1 *(acyclic safety)*
$SPEC3 \Rightarrow \langle acyclic \rangle^\infty$

Proof:
Let $stgy \widehat{=} stgy_0 \wedge stgy_1 \wedge \cdots stgy_4$.

$$\begin{array}{ll}
& \Big\|_k \left(\begin{array}{l} \langle s_k = t \wedge stgy_k \rangle^{\bullet}; \\ \langle s_k = h \wedge stgy_k \rangle^{\circ}; \\ \langle s_k = e \wedge stgy_k \rangle^{\bullet} \end{array} \right)^{\infty} \\
\Rightarrow & \|_k \langle s_k \in \{t,h,e\} \wedge stgy_k \rangle^{\infty} \\
= & \langle \mathbf{s} \in \{t,h,e\}^5 \wedge stgy \rangle^{\infty}
\end{array}$$

$$\begin{array}{ll}
& \langle stgy \wedge \mathbf{s} = (t,t,t,t,t) \rangle \\
\Rightarrow & \langle (\forall k.\, f_k = l \wedge s_k = t \Rightarrow \acute{f}_k = l) \\
& \wedge\ (f_k = l \wedge s_{k+} = t \Rightarrow \acute{f}_k = r) \\
& \wedge\ (\forall k.\, s_k = t) \rangle \\
\Rightarrow & \langle \acute{\mathbf{f}} = \mathbf{f} \rangle \\
\Rightarrow & \langle acyclic \Rightarrow ac\acute{y}clic \rangle
\end{array}$$

$$\begin{array}{ll}
& \langle stgy \wedge s_k = e \rangle \\
\Rightarrow & \langle \acute{f}_k = r \wedge \acute{f}_{k+} = l \rangle \\
\Rightarrow & \langle ac\acute{y}clic \rangle
\end{array}$$

$$\begin{array}{ll}
& \langle stgy \wedge \mathbf{s} = (h,h,h,h,h) \rangle \\
\Rightarrow & \langle (\forall k.\, s_k = h \wedge f_k = r \Rightarrow \acute{f}_k = r) \\
& \wedge\ (s_{k-} = h \wedge f_k = l \Rightarrow \acute{f}_k = l) \\
& \wedge\ (\forall k.\, s_k = h) \\
\Rightarrow & \langle \acute{\mathbf{f}} = \mathbf{f} \rangle \\
\Rightarrow & \langle acyclic \Rightarrow ac\acute{y}clic \rangle
\end{array}$$

$$\begin{array}{ll}
& SPEC3 \\
\Rightarrow & (acyclic)_{\top};\ \langle \mathbf{s} \in \{t,h,e\}^5 \wedge stgy \rangle^{\infty} \\
\Rightarrow & (acyclic)_{\top};\ \langle acyclic \Rightarrow ac\acute{y}clic \rangle^{\infty} \\
\Rightarrow & \langle acyclic \rangle^{\infty}
\end{array}$$

■

Lemma 2 *(deadlock free)*
$SPEC3 \Rightarrow \text{Often}(\exists k. s_k \neq h)$

Lemma 3 *(starvation free)*
For any k, $SPEC3 \Rightarrow \text{Often}(s_k \neq h)$

Theorem 2 $SPEC2 \sqsubseteq SPEC3$

We take a further step to introduce *do* loops in the specification.

$$\textbf{SPEC 4} \ \hat{=}\ \begin{array}{l} (acyclic)_{\top}; \\ (\mathbf{s} = (t,t,t,t,t))_{\top}; \\ \Big\|_k \left(\begin{array}{l} do \\ \quad true \rightarrow\ Thinking_k; \\ \qquad\qquad\quad Hungry_k; \\ \qquad\qquad\quad Eating_k \\ od \end{array} \right) \end{array}$$

$$\begin{array}{ll}
Thinking_k \hat{=} & var\ n :\in \mathbb{N} \\
& \quad do\ (n > 0) \rightarrow \\
& \qquad \langle \acute{n} = \grave{n} + 1 \wedge s_k = \acute{s}_k \\
& \qquad \wedge (f_k = l \Rightarrow \acute{f}_k = l) \\
& \qquad \wedge (f_{k+} = r \Rightarrow \acute{f}_{k+} = r) \rangle \\
& \quad od\ ; \\
& \langle \acute{s}_k = h \wedge (f_k = l \Rightarrow \acute{f}_k = l) \\
& \wedge (f_{k+} = r \Rightarrow \acute{f}_{k+} = r) \rangle
\end{array}$$

$$\begin{array}{ll}
Hungry_k \hat{=} & do\ (s_k = h) \rightarrow \\
& \quad if\ (lfree_k \wedge \neg rfree_k) \rightarrow \\
& \qquad \langle \acute{f}_k = r \wedge f_{k+} = \acute{f}_{k+} \wedge \acute{s}_k = h \rangle \\
& \quad [\!]\ (\neg lfree_k \wedge rfree_k) \rightarrow \\
& \qquad \langle \acute{f}_{k+} = l \wedge f_k = \acute{f}_k \wedge \acute{s}_k = h \rangle \\
& \quad [\!]\ (lfree_k \wedge rfree_k) \rightarrow \\
& \qquad \langle f_{k+} = \acute{f}_{k+} \wedge f_k = \acute{f}_k \wedge \acute{s}_k = h \rangle \\
& \quad [\!]\ (f_k = r \wedge f_{k+} = l) \rightarrow \\
& \qquad \langle f_k = \acute{f}_k \wedge f_{k+} = \acute{f}_{k+} \wedge \acute{s}_k = e \rangle \\
& \quad [\!]\ otherwise \rightarrow \\
& \qquad \langle f_k = \acute{f}_k \wedge f_{k+} = \acute{f}_{k+} \wedge \acute{s}_k = h \rangle \\
& \quad fi \\
& od
\end{array}$$

$$\begin{array}{ll}
Eating_k \hat{=} & var\ n :\in \mathbb{N} \\
& \quad do\ (n > 0) \rightarrow \\
& \qquad \langle \acute{n} = \grave{n} + 1 \wedge s_k = \acute{s}_k \\
& \qquad \wedge (f_k = \acute{f}_k = r) \wedge (f_{k+} = \acute{f}_{k+} = l) \rangle \\
& \quad od\ ; \\
& \langle \acute{s}_k = t \wedge (f_k = \acute{f}_k = r) \\
& \wedge (f_{k+} = \acute{f}_{k+} = l) \rangle
\end{array}$$

$$\begin{array}{ll}
lfree_k \hat{=} & s_{k-} = t \wedge f_k = l \\
rfree_k \hat{=} & s_{k+} = t \wedge f_{k+} = r
\end{array}$$

In SPEC 4, the thinking and eating procedures are simply simulated by empty terminating loops. Real users may have a more interesting implementation!

Theorem 3 $SPEC3 \sqsubseteq SPEC4$

From SPEC 4, we can derive a BSP program as follows:

$$\begin{array}{ll}
PROG \hat{=} & put\ \mathbf{s} := t,t,t,t,t; \\
& put\ \mathbf{f} := l,r,r,r,r; \\
& sync; \\
& Phil_0 \| Phil_1 \| \ldots \| Phil_4
\end{array}$$

$Phil_k \hat{=}$

$$
\begin{array}{l}
do\ true \rightarrow \\
\quad \left(\begin{array}{l}
var\ n :\in \mathbb{N} \\
\quad do\ (n > 0) \rightarrow n := n-1; sync\ od; \\
put\ s_k := h;\ sync; \\
do\ (s_k = h) \rightarrow \\
\quad if\ (lfree_k \wedge \neg rfree_k) \rightarrow \\
\qquad\qquad (put\ f_k := r;\ sync) \\
\quad\ [\,]\ (\neg lfree_k \wedge rfree_k) \rightarrow \\
\qquad\qquad (put\ f_{k^+} := l;\ sync) \\
\quad\ [\,]\ (lfree_k \wedge rfree_k) \rightarrow \\
\qquad\qquad (put\ f_k, f_{k^+} := r, l;\ sync) \\
\quad\ [\,]\ (f_k = r \wedge f_{k^+} = l) \rightarrow \\
\qquad\qquad (put\ s_k := e;\ sync) \\
\quad\ [\,]\ otherwise \rightarrow sync \\
\quad\ fi \\
od; \\
var\ n :\in \mathbb{N} \\
\quad do\ (n > 0) \rightarrow n : n-1; sync\ od; \\
put\ s_k := t;\ sync;
\end{array}\right) \\
od
\end{array}
$$

Theorem 4 $SPEC4 \sqsubseteq PROG$

6 Future Work and Acknowledgement

Our ultimate objective is to develop a comprehensive framework for specification and refinement calculus for reactive BSP programming. We are especially interested in performance, including load balancing, partition, and distribution.

This paper is part of the author's PhD thesis under the supervision of J.W. Sanders and He Jifeng. The author would also like to thank Quentin Miller, and David Lecomber for their encouragement, comments and discussions.

References

[1] K.M. Chandy and J. Misra. Parallel Program Desgin. Addison-Wesley, Reading, Massachusetts, 1998.

[2] Y. Chen, Reactive-BSP Semantics, Technical Report, Oxford University Computing Laboratory, 1999.

[3] O.J. Dahl, E.W. Dijkstra, C.A.R. Hoare, Structured Programming, Academic Press, 1972.

[4] E.W. Dijkstra, Two Starvation Free Solutions to General Exclusion Problem, EWD 625, Plataanstraat 5, 5671 Al Nuenen, The Netherlands 1978.

[5] E.W. Dijkstra, Guarded commands, non-determinacy and the formal derivation of programs, CACM, 18, 453-457, 1975.

[6] A. V. Gerbessiotis, C. J. Siniolakis and A. Tiskin, Parallel priority queue and list contraction: The BSP approach, In C. Lengauer, M. Griebl and S. Gorlatch, editors, Proceedings of Euro-Par'97, volume 1300 of Lecture Notes in Computer Science, pages 409–416. Springer-Verlag, 1997.

[7] M.W. Goudreau, J.M.D. Hill, K. Lang, M.F. McColl, S.B. Rao, D.C. Stefanescu, T. Suel, T. Tsantilas, A proposal for the BSP world-wide standard library (preliminary version), 1996. with program examples.

[8] C.A.R. Hoare, Communicating Sequential Processes, London, Prentice-Hall International, 1984.

[9] C.A.R. Hoare, J. He, Unifying Theories of Programming, Prentice Hall Europe 1998.

[10] J. He, Q. Miller, L. Chen, Algebraic Laws for BSP Programming, Euro-Par'96, LNCS 1124, 359-368 1996.

[11] C.C. Jones, Systematic Software Developement Using VDM. Prentice Hall, 1986.

[12] David Lecomber, Methods of BSP Programming, Oxford University Computing Laboratory DPhil thesis, 1998.

[13] W.F. McColl, Scalability, portability and predictability: The BSP approach to parallel programming, Future Generation Computer Systems 12(1996) 265-272.

[14] K. R. Sujikhan, J. M. D. Hill, Collection Types for Database Programming in the BSP Model, Tech Report, OXCL.

[15] L.G. Valiant, A bridging model for parallel computation, Comm. ACM, 33(8) (1990) 103-111.

First Steps in Metacomputing with Amica

Torsten Fink
Institute of Computer Science
Free University Berlin
Takustr.9, 14195 Berlin
tnfink@inf.fu-berlin.de

Stephan Kindermann
Department of Computer Science
University of Erlangen/Nuremberg
Martensstr.3, 91058 Erlangen
snkinder@informatik.uni-erlangen.de

Abstract

The metacomputing system Amica is a new approach to support the development of coarse grained applications for distributed, dynamic, heterogeneous systems (e.g. computers linked to the Internet). It aims at location-transparent and convenient design of distributed applications and at easy integration of legacy systems. Applications are described in the form of application graphs based on a predefined set of reusable components and connectors. This graph is dynamically interpreted using the Amica infrastructure.

Amica provides uniform access to computational resources using the well-known factory pattern. Additionally, a memory subsystem supports the location-transparent use of complex data objects which may be replicated to increase access speed. To transfer data, specific network resources can be used.

We report initial experiences using Amica for a computationally intensive real-world problem, the parallel simulation of cellular mobile systems. Measurements show that Amica, even in its premature stage, provides a convenient interface and sufficient efficiency to build distributed applications utilizing heterogeneous, dynamic resources.

1 Introduction

The dramatic improvement of networking technology in the last few years permits the collective usage of distributed computing and storage resources as a so-called metacomputer. The necessary communication and coordination between heterogeneous, distributed entities calls for a powerful infrastructure which supports the task of application development by providing transparent access to the resources.

The Amica[1] metacomputing system provides a set of coherent abstraction mechanisms to hide the heterogeneity of the computing hardware (ranging from high performance vector computers to special purpose systolic arrays), storage systems (database, file systems), and communication networks. Metacomputing applications are constructed on an abstract level as parallel application graphs (ApG) composed of well defined components and connectors. An ApG is then evaluated by an interpreter which interacts with the infrastructure.

Amica relies on the industry standards CORBA [12] and Java [8]. Based on wrapper/proxy techniques, existing libraries and software components (legacy systems) can easily be integrated and are accessible over CORBA-IDL interfaces.

This paper describes the parts of the metacomputing system Amica and their cooperation as well as an application to a real world problem: the simulation of cellular communication systems.

In section 2 the basic parts of the Amica system are introduced: the application part and the infrastructure. It is shown in detail how the infrastructure helps to abstract from the heterogeneous computing, storage, and communication resources. It is also shown how abstract metacomputing service requests are dynamically mapped onto the available resources.

In section 3 a complex real-world problem, the computation and storage intensive simulation of cellular communication networks, is formulated as an ApG based on a set of reusable components and connectors. Speedup and efficiency results using Amica to evaluate the graph on various numbers of WAN-connected workstations are given, showing the feasibility of our approach.

In section 4, Amica is compared to related work and its contributions are shown. In section 5, we conclude with a summary of our results and an overview about our current and future work.

[1] **A**bstract **M**etacomputing **I**nfrastructure for **C**oarse grained **A**pplications

1066-6192/99 $10.00 © 1999 IEEE

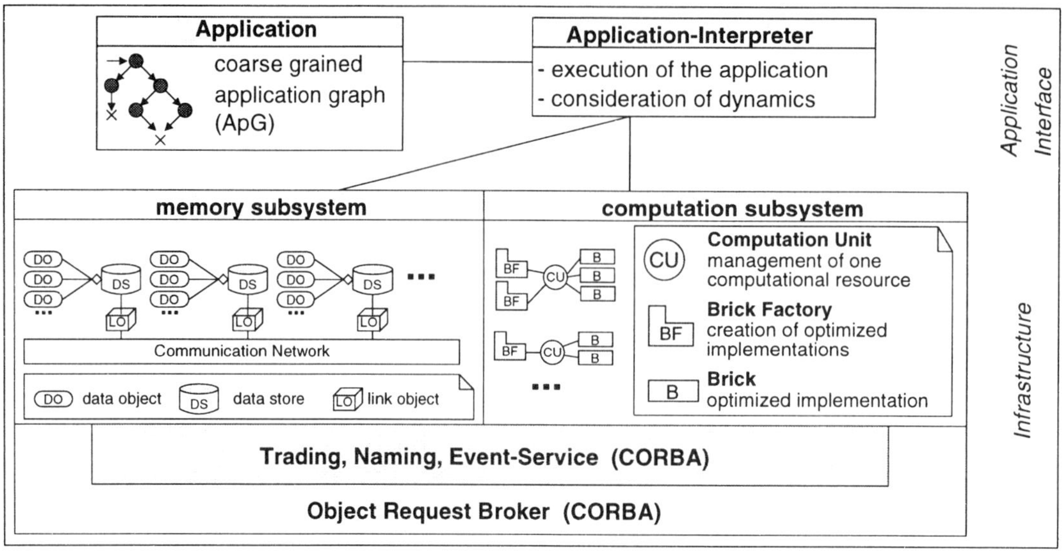

Figure 1. An Overview of Amica

2 Amica – An Abstract Infrastructure for Metacomputing

Figure 1 gives an overview of Amica. Two main independent parts can be separated: First the interface wherein metacomputing applications can be specified abstractly in so called application graphs (ApGs) and second a metacomputing infrastructure to serve the requests necessary to evaluate the ApGs.

An ApG is constructed using components representing abstract requests to the infrastructure for complex computational and storage services as well as user-provided functionality. Service requests and user components are linked together using a predefined set of connectors specifying the flow of control.

These abstract components and connectors are evaluated and translated to concrete infrastructure invocations by the application interpreter.

In a first step we implemented a small set of meta bricks resembling abstract computational service requests and connectors sufficient to specify and execute farm-type parallel metacomputing applications, see section 3.2 for a detailed example.

The main task of the infrastructure is to serve abstract computational and storage requests transparently despite of the heterogeneous, distributed basic computing, data storage and transmission capabilities of the metacomputer. To accomplish this, two mostly independent infrastructural subsystems have been implemented responsible for handling computation and data storage.

2.1 Computation in Amica

Abstract computational services (meta bricks) are provided by the computation subsystem of the infrastructure. These correspond to elementary services (called bricks) which are made available using the well known factory pattern: bricks are generated on demand by so called brick factories. Every brick factory is associated to exactly one basic computational resource (e.g. a workstation or a neurocomputer). The static and dynamic properties of this resource are represented by a computation unit. This computation unit also controls the execution of bricks using the associated resource.

As illustrated in figure 2, brick factories register themselves (along with the brick services they have to offer) to the broker component of the infrastructure. To resolve an abstract meta brick request the broker first looks for registered brick factories able to generate a suitable brick. The broker is implemented using the trading service from CORBA [17].

Then, according to a given cost function the best brick factory is selected. This cost function should estimate the running time of the brick based on the current load of the corresponding computation unit. In combination with the broker approach, dynamic load balancing is achieved.

But, in general it is not even possible to decide the termination of a function. Therefore sometimes other criteria must be used to characterize the performance of producible bricks. Some possible criteria are the maximum performance, current load, and/or the length of the queue of waiting bricks of the corresponding computation unit.

Having a reference to a brick factory, the dynamic map-

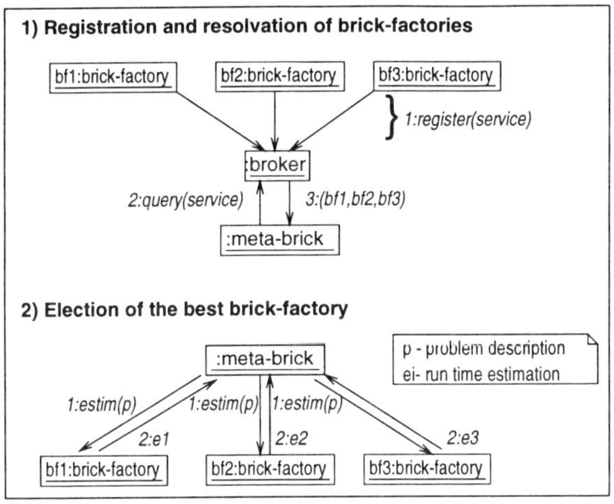

Figure 2. Brick factories: registration and selection

ping of an abstract service request (meta brick) to the concrete service on a specific hw/sw platform (brick) is illustrated in figure 3. The meta brick sends a request to the brick factory to generate a brick for a specific problem. The brick B1 is generated and registers itself at the corresponding computation unit. Because another brick B2 is currently running, B1 has to wait until B2 finish. Then, B1 does its computation, signals its termination to the computation unit and sends the results to the meta brick.

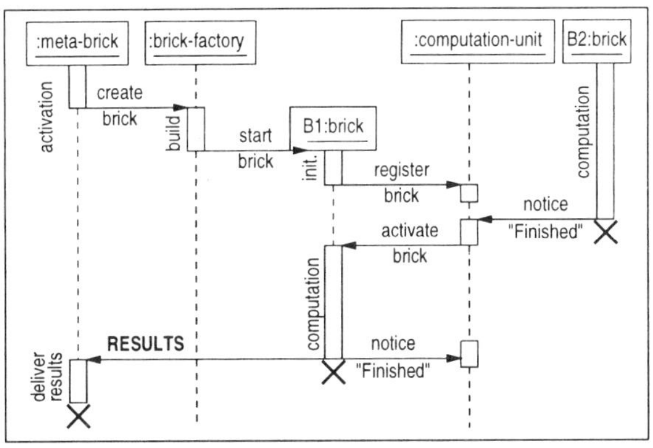

Figure 3. Exemplary call sequence of a meta brick (as UML sequence diagram)

A major advantage of this dynamic mapping from services to implementations is the possibility to implement abstract requests by highly optimized bricks. For example, the structure of the input data, which is not known at compile time, can be used to generate an efficient brick for a numerical algorithm on a massively parallel system.

2.2 Data Storage in Amica

Location transparent and easy access to the heterogeneous data storage resources of the metacomputer are provided by the memory subsystem of the infrastructure. Data is encapsulated in data objects which have unique identifiers. Data objects are placed in distributed data stores managing physical memory.

Data stores are linked together by link objects which represent the network capabilities of the metacomputer. Using the naming service to locate each other, the data stores build a transparent network. An application or a user only needs one arbitrary data store to access a data object. The data object is specified by its identifier, searched on all data stores, and its reference is returned.

Every data object has a unique identifier and offers methods to access and modify its content. Simple data types, as e.g. strings or numbers, as well as complex container data types, like bags (unordered multi sets of labeled elements of the same type), are currently supported. The methods of a data object are provided by CORBA interfaces. Therefore, every component which is implemented using a programming language supported by CORBA can use data objects.

To speed up the access time to a data object, it can be replicated. This is done transparently to the user. He receives the reference of the data object nearest to the data store where the data object was requested. Link objects are used to transfer data objects efficiently in the replication process.

Because data objects can be quite large and the CORBA communication protocol does not perform very well for large data packets, link objects support the use of special network protocols. Their design, which allows dynamic adding of new protocols, plus some measurements showing the gains in network performance are described in [6]. Additionally, the general design of link objects eases the integration of encryption of data objects before transferring them using unsecure networks (see [7]).

The consistency is maintained by a pessimistic protocol which uses the CORBA event service [16]. It permits an arbitrary number of concurrent read accesses, but before performing one write access all replicas are blocked. Pessimistic protocols do not perform very well and not all data types really need them. Therefore we encapsulated the consistency algorithm inside the data object. This way it can easily be replaced by other better performing protocols.

3 Application of Amica to Parallel Simulations

In the following section we use Amica to solve a parallel simulation application. First we introduce the problem arising in the context of mobile network optimization.

Thereafter the problem is translated to an application graph suitable for the application interpreter of Amica. The application is evaluated by Amica on WAN interconnected workstations.

3.1 Simulation of Resource Allocation in Cellular Systems

Efficient management and control of the scarce radio spectrum resource is of paramount importance to all mobile system operators. The radio spectrum is subdivided into channels (access ports between mobiles and their base station) and assigned to mobile users entering a system or moving within a system. In most systems nowadays a (quasi-) static channel assignment to cells is used requiring complex frequency (re-)planning. Future cellular systems need dynamic, self organizing channel assignment schemes to be able to cope with strongly varying traffic conditions as well as modifications in the infrastructure and the environment (e.g. the addition of new base stations and the erection of new buildings). A good overview of the great variety of different channel assignment strategies is given in [14]. Dynamic and self organizing features are motivated in [15]. Together with the wireless system research group at Lucent Technologies, Nuremberg we evaluate new channel assignment strategies in the project MONA (Mobile Network Analysis and Optimization). For this purpose we use a complex simulation tool called *Steam*.

A single simulation run needs tens of megabytes of data storage capacity and hours of processing time on modern workstations (Sun Ultra). To evaluate the effects and overall behaviour of a new channel allocation algorithm, we need hundreds of simulation runs. Therefore in a first step, we are interested in a coarse grain parallelization on a complete simulation run basis. The structure of the basic building block (the simulator program) of our parallel Amica application is quite simple: Two input files need to be read, one containing the simulation parameter settings and the other containing a huge floating-point array characterizing the radio propagation conditions (path loss) at each point of the cellular map. Relevant events within the simulation run are collected in a result event log file.

3.2 Distributed Simulation using Amica

As introduced in section 2 an application is given as an application graph (ApG) which is interpreted using the infrastructure of Amica. In a first step we implemented a small set of components and connectors, sufficient to specify a broad class of coarse grained metacomputing applications based on farm-type parallelism.

As illustrated in figure 4 we provide meta brick components which can be instantiated with an abstract service request to the computational subsystem of the Amica infrastructure. User bricks encapsulate and execute Java classes. This allows to adapt the internal application data to the format needed by the abstract services and vice versa. Additionally access to local resources, like printers or graphical user interfaces, can be integrated into the distributed application providing the option of real time visualization and interactive control.

We also developed some specialized user bricks to exchange data between local file systems and the memory subsystem of our infrastructure. In our visualization of ApG, strings inside of nodes denote identifiers of data objects used for in- and/or output.

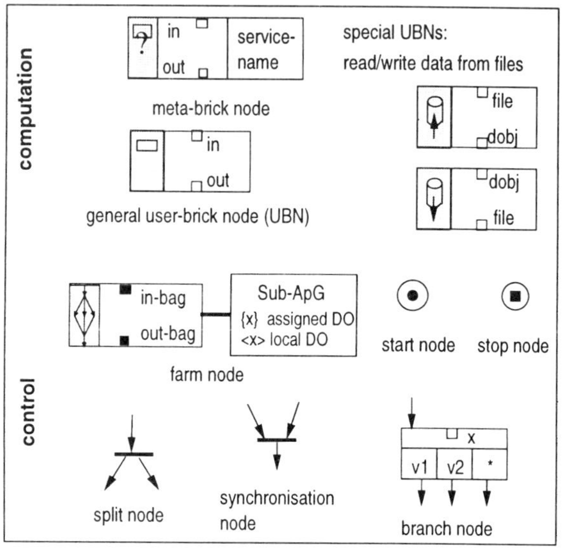

Figure 4. The different node types in application graphs

In our current implementation a small set of connectors is provided to wire the components with respect to control flow. We have connectors to start, stop, split, and synchronize the control flow. To be able to specify farm-type parallel control structures concisely, we also provide a farm connector. This connector instantiates an associated sub-ApG for each element of an input bag and collects the results in an output bag.

These components and connectors can now be instantiated easily to build up an ApG for our parallel simulation application which can be evaluated using Amica. Figure 5 shows the ApG of our example metacomputer application. First two user bricks are used to read files containing initialization data and a bag of parameter settings (`SignalF`, `ParaF`) into data objects of the Amica infrastructure (`Sdata`,`Pdata`).

After this the farm connector is activated and it starts

for each element in the bag `Pdata` of parameter settings one worker. The worker consists of one meta brick node looking for the simulation service called *Steam*. After all simulations finished, the individual result log data objects are merged together in a result log bag data object `Rlog` and written to a file. The name of this file is wrapped into `Rfile`.

The Steam service is essentially an execution of our simulation tool using the corresponding parameters. The tool was easily wrapped in bricks and brick factories and, thus, integrated in Amica. We implemented brick factories for Sun-Solaris and Linux platforms. To estimate the performance of a brick, we used, as a first approach, the length of the brick queue at the corresponding computation unit. A more precise cost function could be developed by analysing the run time behaviour of the simulator.

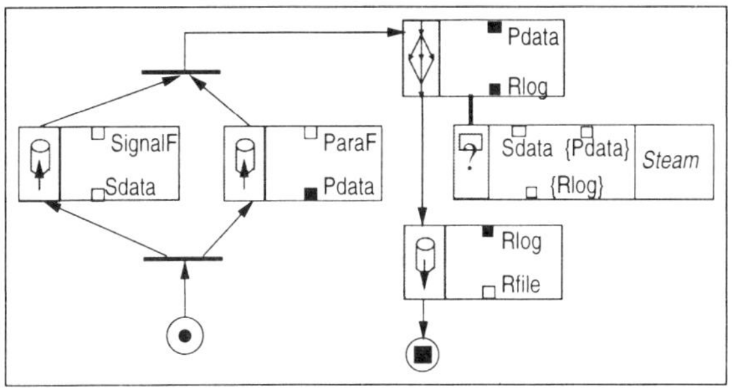

Figure 5. The ApG of the distributed simulation runs

3.3 Measurements

For the following measurements we used a varying number of workstations interconnected by a LAN (10 Mbit Ethernet) and a WAN (Internet, University of Erlangen - University of Jena). To achieve easily interpretable results, we concentrated on a homogeneous set of computing resources (SUN Sparc Ultra 1 workstations). As the individual simulations run in parallel without the need of synchronization and communication between the simulations, the maximum speedup S_o for n parallel simulations with the same need of computation time using p processors is $S_o = \frac{n}{\lceil n/p \rceil}$.

For the testing we used a bag of 10 parameter settings corresponding to 10 parallel simulation tasks. The simulations were done for a realistic, complex scenario with about 100 base stations, irregular cell deployment, and fluctuating traffic conditions based on hot spots. The generated path loss file which every simulation needs for initialization consists of approximately 18 MB. To get conservative results we have set the simulated time for a run to only 300 seconds (resulting in 20 minutes computation time). Realistic values here are 3000 seconds (corresponding to more than 3 hours simulation run time per task).

Figure 6 shows the results. On the left hand side the speedup, the maximum speedup S_o, and linear speedup is shown. Caused by the coarse granularity of our application, S_o is significantly smaller than linear speedup when p is no divider of 10. It is even constant for p in the range from 5 to 9. The speedup values are calculated in comparison to a dedicated workstation performing the simulations via batch processing without any communication overhead.

On the right hand side the absolute efficiency and the relative efficiency in relation to S_o is plotted. If p divides 10, the absolute and relative efficiency is equal, otherwise the absolute efficiency is smaller. The strong decrease of the absolute efficiency in the area where S_o is constant (5–9) is inherent in the problem. To avoid wasting computation power, Amica automatically maps idle workstations to other applications.

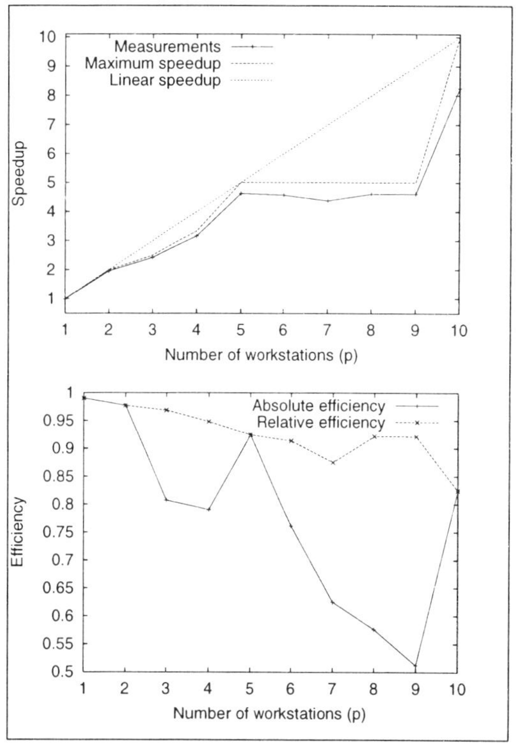

Figure 6. Speedup and efficiency for different numbers of workstations

Despite the big communication overhead caused by the input data which is transferred to every parallel simulation, we achieved a sufficient efficiency of more than 80% using 10 workstations. An increase of the simulated time frame to realistic values will directly improve the efficiency. Thus, complex simulation scenarios can be tested in hours instead of days. Because of the open architecture of Amica, every available computer can be integrated dynamically into the system and any number of applications automatically share all resources.

4 Related Work

There are many projects in the field of metacomputing using different approaches for different classes of applications. They can be ordered by the level of abstraction provided by their programming model.

One extreme is a heterogeneous programming model providing direct access to every resource of computation, communication, or data storage. The other extreme is a homogeneous model hiding distribution, fault behaviour, and heterogeneity. Amica uses an approach located between the extremes. In the following paragraphs we will compare three different aspects of Amica to related work.

The Application Interface
Amica uses a service-based approach to access the computational resources. The general control structure of the application is given as an arbitrary task graph and, additionally, Java code can be integrated.

UNICORE [1] provides abstract job objects which are represented as directed acyclic graphs. The nodes resemble tasks of specific classes (e.g. compile task, transfer task) and are thus more restricted than the general service nodes of Amica. Also the easy integration and local execution of Java code is not supported by UNICORE.

The system GIS [23] also uses process networks as programming model for service based metacomputing. Like UNICORE it is restricted to acyclic graphs. Different to Amica, GIS aims at the manipulation of geographical data and is specialized in the manipulation of streaming data.

The systems MoDis [5] and Juggle [19] provide a completely transparent and homogeneous programming model. In other systems the composition of an application into distributable parts is done explicitly, while the distribution itself is done transparently, e.g. in JavaParty [18] or Manta [22]. This approach eases the task of application development. But often the integration of legacy systems is difficult and, when applied to heterogeneous systems, the performance is not good.

Globus [9] offers direct access to the heterogeneous resources by uniform interfaces. Legion [11] provides a uniform object-oriented programming model with explicit distribution which wraps heterogeneous systems. These explicit approaches allow for maximum performance but impede the development of applications.

Computational Model
The computation subsystem of Amica provides a uniform, service-oriented access to computational resources based on servers and factories. Therefore it can use any back-end, like batch systems and libraries. Additionally the factory pattern allows to consider the properties of the input data to generate an optimal solution. For example the concrete dimensions of a matrix can be substituted into a general algorithm and fed into an optimizing compiler for a massively parallel computer.

There are some projects also based on servers, but they are more restricted in the type of services. ReGTime [4] only supports the execution of PVM applications, UNICORE and the Hypercomputer [20] are restricted to general batch systems. DISCWorld [13] offers general services like Amica but is not based on the factory pattern.

Some projects, e.g. RCS [2] or NetSolve [3], provide a library which is linked to an application and encapsulates a run-time system which uses distributed resources to compute a library function. A disadvantage of this approach is the difficulty of updating the library.

Data Storage and Communication
In Amica, communication is done by accessing variables which can be replicated to increase access efficiency. A particular feature of Amica is the direct use of network protocols to generate a distributed replica.

The data and communication model of Amica corresponds to the virtual shared memory model commonly used by distribution transparent programming models (e.g. Juggle, MoDis). Models with explicit composition often model the components as objects and communication as method invocation (JavaParty, Manta).

Explicit programming models offer support for typical communication patterns, like broadcasts and event channels (e.g. Nexus as part of Globus). Location-transparent and efficient data storage is provided by distributed file systems, like AFS [21].

5 Conclusion and Future Work

We have introduced the metacomputing system Amica and compared it to related approaches. The main contributions of Amica are the abstract, service based programming interface and the uniform wrapping of computational resources using the factory pattern.

Initial experiences using Amica for a real world application show the usability, flexibility, and performance of Amica when applied on coarse grained applications. Despite of a high communication overhead and an artificially reduced amount of computation we achieved a sufficient efficiency of 82% utilizing 10 workstations.

The embedding of the simulation program was straightforward. The application of general components like meta bricks, farms, and specialized data storage elements simplified the usage of the metacomputing environment. With little effort, a distributed and dynamic application was built which automatically utilized new computational resources at run time and shared the resources with other concurrent applications.

Our future work will be in several areas. The application graph (ApG) concept is currently extended into the following directions:

- First a more general and flexible specification of the architecture of metacomputing applications is necessary. We are currently adapting the architecture description language ACME [10] with its open semantic framework for our purposes.

- This extension will allow us to define different *views* of metacomputing applications, not only the control flow view supported in our current implementation.

- A concise formal semantics for all types of components and connectors that can be used to build up application graphs based on process algebra is currently developed. This has major advantages in an early phase of metacomputing application design: The ApG can be checked to provide a previously specified behaviour. Additionally we plan to use stochastic process algebras in the future to allow a performance prediction of metacomputing applications.

Currently the scalability of Amica is limited to a moderate number of resources. Therefore we will split the resources in different administrative areas. This also provides a basis for a security concept we are currently working on. Based on CORBA authentification we will build a prototypical environment to evaluate e-commerce scenarios in the context of metacomputing.

References

[1] J. Almond and D. Snelling. UNICORE: Secure and uniform access to distributed resources via the world wide web. Technical report, Forschungszentrum Jülich, Oct. 1998.

[2] P. Arbenz, W. Gander, and M. Oettli. The remote computation system. In H. Liddel, A. Colbrook, B. Hertzberger, and P. Sloot, editors, *High-Performance Computing and Networking*, number 1067 in LNCS, pages 662–667. Springer, Apr. 1996.

[3] H. Casanova and J. Dongarra. NetSolve: A network-enabled server for solving computational science problems. *The International Journal of Supercomputer Applications and High Performance Computing*, 11(3):212–223, 1997.

[4] B. Dreier, A. Huber, T. Ungerer, and M. Zahn. Trading computing power with ReGTime. *Journal of Systems Architecture*, 44:293–396, 1997.

[5] C. Eckert and M. Pizka. Improving resource management in distributed systems using language-level structuring concepts. *The Journal of Supercomputing*, 13:33–55, 1999.

[6] T. Fink, M. Gutzmann, T. Wolf, and W. Erhard. Entwicklung einer abstrakten Speicherkomponente für eine verteilte heterogene dynamische Infrastruktur in Java/CORBA. In C. Cap, editor, *JIT'98, Java-Informations-Tage*, pages 269–276. Springer, 1998.

[7] T. Fink, A. Krause, and W. Erhard. Einfluß von Sicherheitsanforderungen auf die Kommunikationsleistung im Metacomputing-System Amica. In C. Cap, W. Erhard, and W. Koch, editors, *Architektur von Rechnersystemen*, pages 45–54. GI, ITG, VDE Verlag, 1999.

[8] D. Flanagan. *Java in a Nutshell*. O'Reilly Inc., 2nd edition, Oct. 1997.

[9] I. Foster and C. Kesselman. Globus: A metacomputing infrastructure toolkit. *The International Journal of Supercomputer Applications and High Performance Computing*, 11(2):115–128, 1997.

[10] D. Garlan, R. Monroe, and D. Wile. Acme: An architecture description interchange language. Proceedings of CASCON '97, November 1997.

[11] A. Grimsaw and W. Wulf. Legion-a view from 50,000 feet. In *Proc. of the 5th IEEE Int. Symp. on High Performance Distributed Computing*, Aug. 1996.

[12] M. Henning and S. Vinoski. *Advanced CORBA Programming with C++*. Addison-Wesley, 1999.

[13] K.A.Hawick, H.A.James, C.J.Patten, and F.A.Vaughan. DISCWorld: A distributed high performance computing environment. In P. M. A. Sloot, M. Bubak, and L. O. Hertzberger, editors, *High Performance Computing and Networks Europe*, number 1401 in LNCS, Amsterdam, 1998.

[14] I. Katzela and M. Naghshineh. Channel Assignment Schemes for Cellular Mobile Telecommunication Systems. *IEEE Personal Communications*, pages 10–31, June 1996.

[15] R. Nettleton and G. Schloemer. Self Organizing Channel Assignment for Wireless Systems. *IEEE Communications Magazine*, pages 46–51, August 1997.

[16] OMG. Event management service, 1997. formal/97-12-11.

[17] OMG. Trading object service, 1997. Version 1.0, formal/97-12-23.

[18] M. Philippsen and M. Zenger. JavaParty–transparent remote objects in Java. *Concurrency: Practice and Experience*, 9(11):1125–1242, 1997.

[19] M. Schröder and F. J. Hauck. Juggle: Eine verteilte virtuelle machine für Java. In C. Cap, editor, *Java-Informationstage 1999*, pages 278–289. Springer, 1999.

[20] D. Tavangarian, P. Eschholz, M. Koch, C. Pitz, and S. Preuß. Hypercomputing: A concept for a network-based computer architecture. In *PDPTA'98*. CSREA Press.

[21] R. Többike. Distributed file systems: Focus on andrew file system/distributed file service (AFS/DFS). In *IEEE Symposion on Mass Storage Systems*, pages 23–26. IEEE Computer Society Press, June 1994.

[22] R. van Nieuwpoort, J. Maassen, H. E. Bal, T. Kielmann, and R. Veldema. Wide-area parallel computing in Java. In *ACM 1999 Java Grande Conference*, pages 8–14, San Francisco, CA, June 1999.

[23] D. Webb, A. Wendelborn, and K. Maciunas. Process Networks as a High-Level Notation for Metacomputing. In *Proc. of the Int. Parallel Programming Symposium (IPPS'99), workshop on Java for Distributed Computing, Puerto Rico*, Apr. 1999.

Parallel Programming with Data Driven Model

V. D. Tran, L. Hluchý, G. T. Nguyen
Institute of Informatics
Slovak Academy of Sciences
E-mail: viet.ui@savba.sk

Abstract

In this paper, we present a new powerful method for parallel program representation called Data Driven Graph (DDG). DDG takes all advantages of classical Directed Acyclic Graph (DAG) and adds much more: simple definition, flexibility and ability to represent loops and dynamically created tasks. With DDG, scheduling becomes an efficient tool for increasing performance of parallel systems. DDG is not only a parallel program model, it also initiates a new parallel programming style, allows programmer to write a parallel program with minimal difficulty. We also present our parallel program development tool with support for DDG and scheduling.

1. Introduction

Advances in hardware and software technologies have led to increased interest in the use of large-scale parallel and distributed systems for database, real-time, and other large applications. One of the biggest issues in such systems is the development of effective techniques for the distribution of tasks of a parallel program on multiple processors. The efficiency of execution of the parallel program critically depends on the strategies used to schedule and distribute the tasks among processing elements.

Task allocation can be performed either dynamically during the execution of the program or statically at compile time. Static task allocation and scheduling attempt to predict the program execution behavior at compilation time and to distribute program tasks among the processors accordingly. This approach can eliminate the additional overheads of the redistribution process during the execution. With the support of program models such as Directed Acyclic Graph (DAG), Iterative Task Graph (ITG), static scheduling can produce optimal or nearly optimal task schedule [1][2][5][8], because the scheduling process has enough time and information to consider. Unfortunately, static scheduling algorithms require exact data about execution times and communication delays of each task. In most cases, the data cannot be predicted because it depends on the actual loads of processors and interconnection networks. Furthermore, the behavior of many programs depends on their input data and cannot be determined at compile time.

On the other hand, dynamic task scheduling is based on the distribution of tasks among the processors during the execution, with the aim of minimizing communication overheads and balancing the load among processors. The approach is especially beneficial if the program behavior cannot be determined before the execution. However, the lack of program model for dynamic scheduling forces dynamic scheduler to make a "blind" decision, i. e. to assign tasks to processors only on the basis of load of processors, regardless of program structure [3][9]. That can lead to increasing communication, especially when tasks are fine-grained. Some dynamic scheduling algorithms are based on DAG, so they have the same restriction as DAG [10]. In the addition, the scheduling process also uses processor time and that increases the total execution time of the parallel program. The crisis of program models can threaten the existence of the dynamic scheduler: some approaches remove the separate scheduler and leave the task allocation for the program itself [6][7]. Finding a dynamic program model is the vital problem for scheduling and parallel programming in general.

2. Parallel program models

Most of static scheduling algorithms use a directed acyclic graph (DAG) to represent the precedence relationships and the data dependencies of tasks of a parallel program [1][5]. Each node of the graph represents a task and each edge represents the precedence relationship and communication between the tasks. DAG model is simple but it can represent only programs with static behavior and without loops. It cannot represent programs with loops or dynamically created tasks.

1066-6192/99 $10.00

In order to represent loops, the Iterative Task Graph (ITG) is proposed [2][14]. Each edge in ITG has a distance value d, which show the distance between tasks. If d is larger than 0, the parent task is connected with the child task in the next d-th iteration from the current iteration of the loop. Because d is constant, ITG can represent only a class of loops with constant distance called Uniform loops. Note that ITG represents only loops, not whole programs. For program with loops, we have to use a combination of DAG and ITG, but it is too difficult to manage, so it is very rarely used. Again, even the combination of DAG and ITG cannot represent all class of parallel programs with loops or with dynamical behavior.

For completeness we say some words about Task Interaction Graph (TIG) [11], which is widely used in mapping. TIG is similar to DAG, except that it does not consider the precedence relationship among tasks, so the edges in TIG are undirected. In scheduling, the precedence relationship is essential, so TIG is unsuitable for scheduling.

2.1. Data Driven Graph model

For a flexible model, which contains all advantages of the existing models and can represent also loops and dynamical behavior, we propose new approach to representation of parallel program called Data Driven Graph (DDG). The main ideas of DDG are following:

- Each task is defined by its input and output data. The set of input and output data creates a task interface, which hides all implementation details of the task. No relationship among tasks is explicitly defined. The tasks with the same output data are called producers of the data. Similarly the tasks with the same input data are called consumers of the data.
- A scheduler manages all tasks and data of the parallel program. It determines the relationship among tasks according to their interfaces, i.e. their input and output data. For backward compatibility with existing program models, the scheduler creates a graph by connecting producers and consumer of the same data.
- The behavior of the parallel program is defined by its data. A data on a processor is ready when it is produced by a task and is sent to the processor. When all input data of a task are ready, the scheduler will execute the task.

Fig. 1a shows the relationship among tasks in a classical parallel program with scheduler. Tasks interact directly with other tasks or via communication libraries (PVM, MPI). Each task must have information about the tasks it communicates with, so implementations of tasks are dependent and each modification of a task may affect all its neighbor tasks. Communication among tasks is asynchronous, so communication library must have some buffers, which require additional overhead. Scheduler has no control above communication, so optimization is very limited. It cannot move a task from a processor to another one or reuse data.

Fig. 1b shows the relationship among tasks in DDG model. Tasks are defined by their interface and all interactions among tasks are realized via scheduler. Scheduler has full control over communication. Implementations of tasks are independent and are hidden by tasks interface (TI). The relationship between task interface and task implementation is like the relationship between function calling and function implementation in HLL (High Level Language). The task interface of task A says "Task A reads data X and produces data Y" without

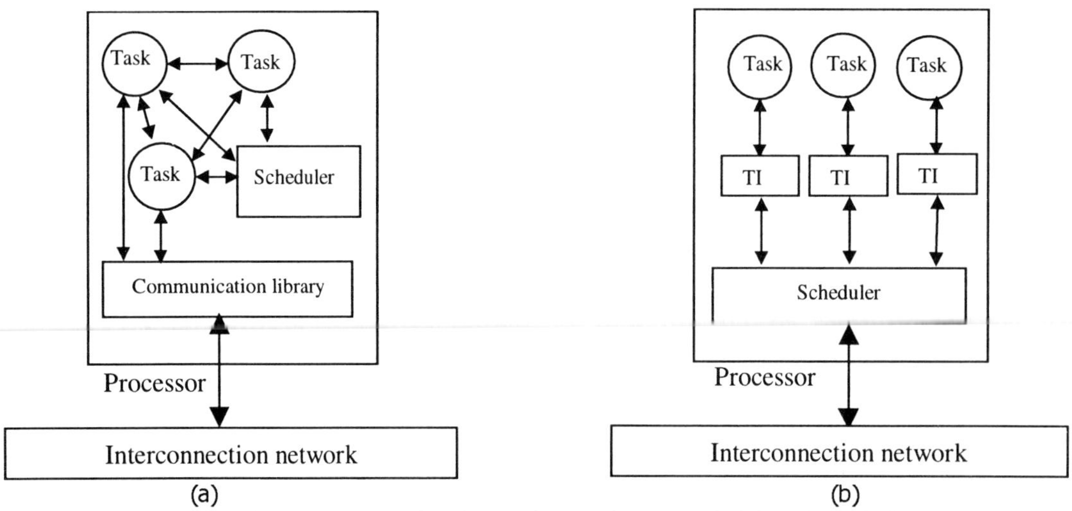

Fig. 1 The structures of tasks in classical approach (a) and DDG (b)

information how it is done, when the task implementation says "Tasks A reads a floating number and produces its square root" without information what real data it manipulates. That allows tasks to share their implementation, if they have the same functionality but manipulate with different data. The separation of task interface from task implementation is especially beneficial for tasks in loops and for dynamically created tasks, when tasks do the same work with different data and we do not know in advance, what real data they manipulate.

Moving the communication issue from tasks to scheduler is not a disadvantage for scheduler, on the contrary, this gives the scheduler more space for optimization. There are some optimizations, which can be done by the scheduler:

- Data packing: Tasks in scheduling are mostly fine-grained, so tasks exchange many small data and communication overhead may be very large. If a data is not needed immediately by other tasks on other processors, the scheduler does not send the data but waits and packs several small data to a large package then sends it at once to reduce communication overhead.
- Data reuse: There is at most one copy of each data on a processor. If several tasks on a processor require the same data, only one copy of the data is sent to the processor, what reduces the amount of communication in comparison with classical approach. The data may not be sent from the their producer but from the nearest processor, which contains its copy.
- Fault tolerance: The structure of DDG and values of data are the checkpoint of the parallel program. The scheduler can save them (e.g. each data has a copy on another processor) and restore the program in case of failure.
- Task migration: The scheduler has full control of tasks, data and communication, so it can move tasks in the waiting queue from a processor to another without the need of message redirection.

2.2. DDG versus DAG

Fig. 2 shows the similarities and differences between DAG and DDG. For the simplicity, each task is represented by one command line. At the first sight of the graphs (Fig. 2a), there is no difference except that DDG gives more information about communication. Because most of existing scheduling algorithms are based on DAG, the compatibility with DAG is very important for DDG. Despite that DDG uses a different method from DAG for definition, existing scheduling algorithms can

```
Example 1
task1: a=10
task2: b=a*2
task3: c=a+3
task4: d=b+c
```

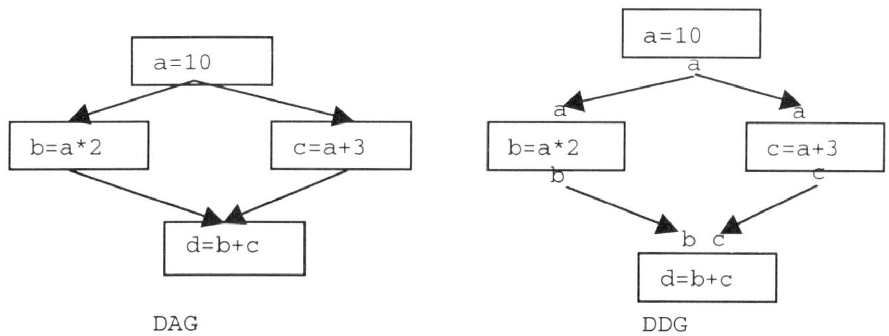

(a)

```
task1: from NONE                task1: input NONE
       to task2, task3                 output a
task2: from task1                      task2: input a
       to task4                        output b
    ...                                   ...
```

(b)

```
task1()                         task1(x)
    a = 10;                         x = 10
    send(task2, a)
    send(task3, a)
task2()                         task2(x,y)
    receive(task1, a)               y = x*2
    ...                             ...
main()                          main()
    create_task(task1)              create_task(task1, a)
    create_task(task2)              create_task(task2, a, b)
    ...                             ...
```

(c)

Fig. 2 Similarities and differences between DAG and DDG

be applied for DDG as for DAG.

The main difference is in the methods to define the graphs (Fig. 2b). Assume that a program has 1000 lines source code, each line represents a task and there is a command `c = a + b` at line 500. For DAG, the user has to search the first 499 lines to find, where `a` and `b` have to be received from and then search next 500 lines to find where `c` has to be sent to. For DDG, the user simply defines `input a, b, output c` and leaves all other work to the scheduler. Furthermore, the structure of DDG can be defined by the task interfaces in the source code. In Section 4, we will see that the scheduler does not need a separate DDG definition file, but uses the structures created by task interfaces.

The largest advantage of DDG is, however, the style of source codes (Fig. 2c). The source code of DDG is very similar to the source code of a normal sequential program. The task implementation does not contain any communication routines, which are typical of parallel programs. If the task creation `create_task(task1, a)` is replaced by function calling `task1(a)` , the source code of DDG is actually the source code of a sequential program. It means that transforming a sequential program to a parallel program in DDG is done with minimal difficulty. Programmers can write a parallel program in the style of the sequential program, which they are used to, then replace function calling by task creation. For DAG, the situation is different. Each task contains communication routines and has to know which tasks it communicates with and where the tasks are. That requires major modification in the source code when transforming a sequential to a parallel program. Programmers have to learn to use new communication libraries such as PVM, MPI or new parallel programming languages.

The absence of communication routines also makes parallel programs in DDG easier to modify, maintain and upgrade. The implementations of tasks are independent. Programmers can group several tasks into a large task, split a task into several small tasks or replace a task by another task with similar functionality without modification of other tasks. That allows programmers to work independently on a large shared parallel program. In DAG, each task is connected with several other tasks so each change in a task may require further modification in tasks connected with the task.

2.3. DDG and dynamic task creation

In classical approaches, a newly created task has to inform existing tasks about its existence and makes all necessary communication connection with existing tasks. That increases the communication overhead and requires a lot of work in the source code of the task. Furthermore, the scheduler has no information about communication between the new task and existing tasks, so it cannot produce a good schedule. In DDG, programming with dynamically created tasks is as easy as with static tasks. Tasks in DDG do not have an explicit relationship, thus adding a new task does not affect existing tasks. The new task can be created anywhere in the parallel program by adding the command like that `create_task(task2, a, b)`. The scheduler will add the new task to DDG, and schedule it. Existing tasks do not have to be notified about the newly created task.

2.4. DDG and loops

Loops are one of the largest problems in parallel programming, because they exist in every program and their parallelization is not completely solved. However loops can be simply presented in DDG and the scheduler will execute loops in parallel according to their data dependencies. Fig. 3 shows an example of a two-dimensional loop (Fig. 3a) and its DDG version (Fig. 3b). The dependencies of DDG tasks are shown in Fig.

Example 2

```
for i=1 to m
  for j=1 to n
    a[i,j]=(a[i-1,j]+a[i,j-1])/2
```

(a)

```
task1(x, y, z)
  z=(x+y)/2

main()
  for i=1 to m
    for j=1 to n
      create_task(task1,a[i-1,j],a[i,j-1],a[i,j])
```

(b)

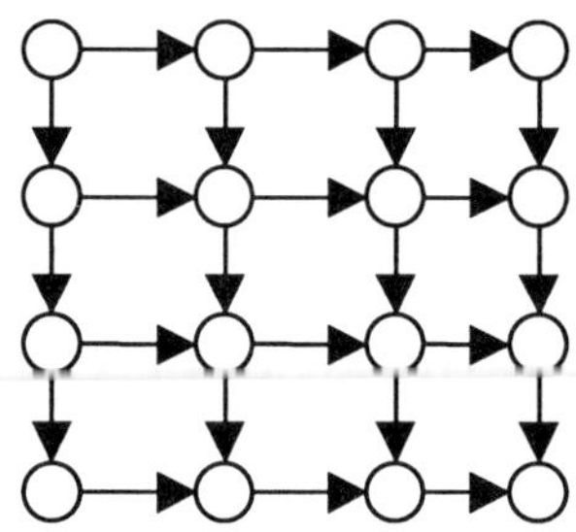

(c)

Fig. 3 DGG and loops

3c. With existing scheduling algorithms (linear task clustering [12], Dominant Sequence Clustering DSC [13]), the scheduler has no problem to assign tasks to multiprocessors and execute them in parallel.

In summary, the major advantages of DDG are:

- Program locality: Task implementations are independent, what makes program clear, flexible, easy to debug, modify and upgrade and allows programmers to work independently on a share program.
- Data reusable: If several tasks on a processor require the same data, only one copy of the data is sent to them. It can reduce communication between tasks.
- Dynamic behavior: Program with loops and dynamically created tasks can be represented as easily as static program without any additional problem.
- Backward compatibility: As the large amount of existing scheduling algorithms relying on DAG, the backward compatibility is a very important feature. The graph produced by DDG is compatible with DAG and we can use scheduling algorithms for DAG without modification.
- Clarity and simplicity of program design: For a large program, it is very difficult to design a DAG with thousands of nodes. It does not specify why a task is connected with other tasks and programmer loses his orientation in large DAG. DDG can be generated from code design and give more information about tasks.
- Modifiability: It is big problem to maintain a large DAG in order to keep synchronization with source code, when the program is changed. DDG is based on code design and each modification in code will be automatically reflected in DDG and vice versa.
- Smooth moving from sequential to parallel programs: The programming style of DDG is very similar the classic sequential programming style. Programmers do not have to learn new parallel programming libraries and languages such as PVM or MPI. Transformation from a sequential to a parallel program is done with minimal difficulty.

3. DDG Application Programming Interface

For demonstrating the advantages of DDG, we have implemented a set of routines in programming language C/C++ for programming in DDG. The aim of our implementation is to make a simple, robust and effective interface for DDG. All frequent errors, such as incompatibilities between task interfaces and implementations or attempts to modify input or to read output variables, have to be detected at compilation time. An example of programs in DDG API looks as follows:

```
void ddg_config(void)
{
  a = ddg_create_varriable(float);
  b = ddg_create_varriable(int);
  ...
ddg_create_task("task 1", task1,
             input(a), output(b));
  ...
}

void task1(import(float)x, export(int)y)
{
  y = x*10;
}
```

Each task is implemented as a function in C. As the program starts, it will call the `ddg_config()` routine, which contains definitions of variables and tasks. The `ddg_create_varriable(int)` creates an integer variable. The `ddg_create_task("task 1", task1, input(a), output(b))` creates a task with name "task 1", implementation in function `tasks1`, floating-point input variable `a` and integer output variable `b`. The name of task is useful for their identification in trace files, visualization graphs and resource files. The task implementation `task1(import(float) x, export (int) y)` shows that task1 has a floating-point input variable and an integer output variable. Macros input, output, import, export do not have only implementation functionality but also make the parallel program easier to read. All tasks created in `ddg_config()` are considered as "static" tasks, because they are created immediately when the program starts before scheduler running. The tasks created by other tasks are considered as "dynamic" tasks.

The classical `main()` function in C/C++ looks as follows:

```
void main()
{
  ddg_config();
  scheduler();
}
```

Note that the only work the user has do is to write `ddg_config()` and tasks functions and to link them with DDG API. Other functions, including `main()` and `scheduler()` are the part of DDG API. When parallel programs run, the scheduler will spawn on other processor, schedule and execute tasks in parallel. The presence of the scheduler in parallel programs also makes them more effective and easy to adapt to new hardware configurations. An optional trace file can be generated, which is used for visualization and other optimization.

Each program has also a separate resource file. The resource file contains the hardware configuration, optional task execution times and optional static task scheduling. The resource file makes programs in DDG API more flexible. If the task execution times are changed (e.g. when the size of input data is changed), the program does not have to be recompiled, but only the resource file has to be revised. Furthermore, the task execution times in the resource file can be generated from the trace file of the previous execution of the program. The user can give any execution times of tasks at the first time the program is running and uses the trace file to generate more accurate task execution times.

4. Scheduler

In Section 2, we assume that the scheduler will manage all communication. In this section, we will describe how the scheduler does it.

Scheduler in DDG consists of two parts: task management modules, which synchronize data, control communication among processors, supply proper data for tasks and execute tasks; and scheduling algorithms, which assign tasks to processors and determine priorities of tasks.

Scheduler has one task management module on each individual processor. The task management module maintains a structure of tasks and data on the processor such as in Fig. 4. When a task is created, the task management modules create a task structure (TS) which contains pointers to its input and output data and a pointer to the code of the task. When a task finishes, its output data is ready. The task management will check all consumers of the data. If a consumer is already assigned to another processor and the processor does not contain the data, the task management module will send a copy the data to the module on the processor. Each task management module has also a queue of task waiting for execution. If a consumer has all its input data ready, it will be assigned to the waiting queue. When a processor is idle, the task management module will choose the task with the highest priority from the waiting queue and execute it. The task management is a part of DDG API.

The scheduling algorithm can be performed statically once when the program starts or dynamically when a new task is dynamically created. Before the scheduling algorithm is performed, the task management modules generate a DAG from their data structure (Fig. 4) by connecting producers of a data to consumers and supply the DAG to scheduling algorithm. According to the result of the scheduling algorithm, the task management modules will assign priority to tasks and distribute them among processors.

The task management modules refer to the scheduling algorithm by an internal pointer so it is no problem to switch from a scheduling algorithm to another. There are several algorithms already implemented in DDG API (heuristic algorithms: HLF, LPF [15]; clustering algorithms: DSC [5], DCP [13]; iterative algorithms: simulated annealing[15], genetic algorithm [8]). The user can choose one of the built-in scheduling algorithms of DDG API or write his own algorithm and assign it to the scheduler.

5. Conclusion

This paper has presented the new program model DDG, which has many advantages over classical models DAG, ITG. The definition of DDG is simple, flexible,

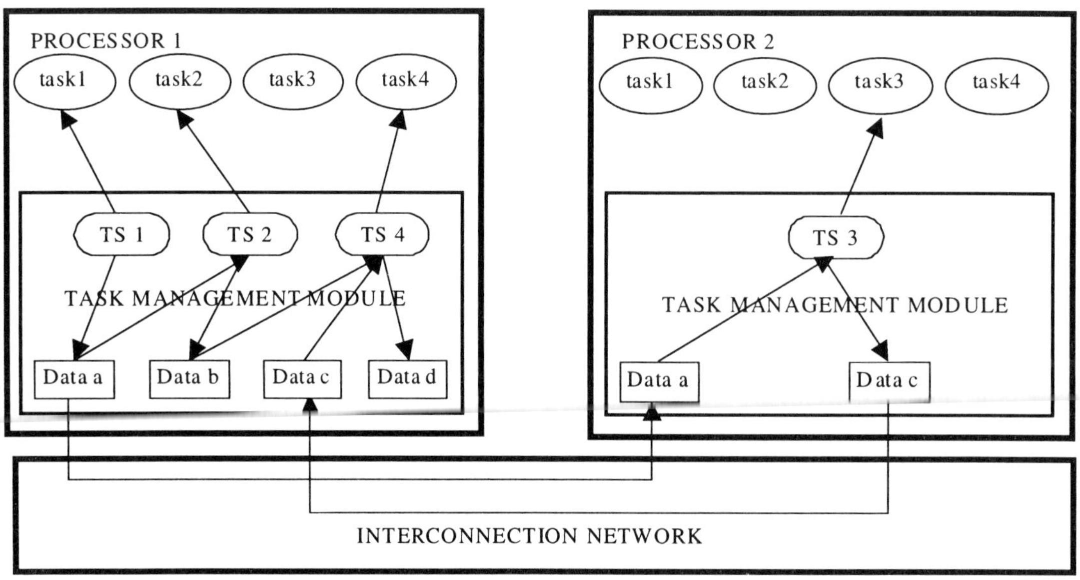

Fig. 4 Data structure in scheduler of Example 1

tasks in DDG are independent, easy to write and parallel programs in DDG are clear, easy to modify, maintain and upgrade. DDG model is also compatible with classical DAG model, so existing scheduling algorithms can be applied for DDG. DDG API initiates a new parallel programming style, allows programmer to write flexible, effective parallel program with minimal difficulty. DDG is not only a parallel program model, it also opens a new space for research and development in parallel programming. There is some work with DDG in future:

- Automatic parallelization: All modern compilers have already implemented data checking for each program block, i.e. which data is read or modified in the block. With minor modification, the compiler can produce codes in DDG format for each block. Linking the output codes with DDG API will allow program running in parallel without modification of the source code.
- System scheduler: In multiprogramming environment, the interference among different schedules can decrease system performance. In the addition, the effectiveness of each scheduling algorithm depends on hardware configurations. Both problems can be solved if each hardware system has its own optimized scheduler in DDG style. Parallel programs only add tasks to the system scheduler and the scheduler will executes tasks in the best order for the system.

Acknowledgements

We thank the Slovak Scientific Grant Agency which supported our work under Research Project No.2/4102/99.

References

[1] S. Darbha, D. P. Agrawal: Optimal Scheduling Algorithm for Distributed-Memory Machines, IEEE Trans. Parallel and Distributed Systems, vol. 9, no. 1, pp. 87-95, 1998.

[2] T. Yang, C. Fu: Heuristic Algorithms for Scheduling Iterative Task Computations on Distributed Memory Machines, IEEE Trans. Parallel and Distributed Systems, vol. 8, no. 6, pp. 608-622, 1997.

[3] W. Shu, M. Wu: Runtime Incremental Parallel Scheduling (RIPS) on Distributed Memory Computers, IEEE Trans. Parallel and Distributed Systems, vol. 7, no. 6, pp. 637-649, 1996.

[4] S. Ha, E. A. Lee: Compile-Time Scheduling of Dynamic Constructs in Dataflow Program Graph, IEEE Trans. Parallel and Distributed Systems, vol. 46, no. 7, pp. 768-778, 1997.

[5] Y. Kwok, I. Ahmad: Dynamic Critical-Path Scheduling: An Effective Technique for Allocating Task Graphs to Multiprocessors, IEEE Trans. Parallel and Distributed Systems, vol. 7, no. 5, pp. 506-521, 1996.

[6] C. D. Polychronopoulos, D. J. Kuck: Guided Self-Scheduling: A Practical Scheduling Scheme for Parallel Supercomputers, IEEE Trans. Computer, vol. C-36, no. 12, pp. 1425-1439, 1987.

[7] B. Hamidzadeh, D. J. Lilja: Self-Adjusting Scheduling: An On-Line Optimization Technique for Locality Management and Load Balancing, Proc. International Conference on Parallel Processing, Volume II: Software, pp. 39-46, 1994.

[8] D. V. Tran: Static Task Scheduling in Distributed Systems, Proc. International Scientific Conference Electronic Computers & Informatics, pp. 228-233, Slovakia 1998.

[9] M. Wu: On Runtime Parallel Scheduling for Processor Load Balancing, IEEE Trans. Parallel and Distributed Systems, vol. 8, no. 2, pp. 173-185, 1997.

[10] E. Maehle, F. Markus: Fault-Tolerant Dynamic Task Scheduling Based on Dataflow Graphs, Proc. IPPS'97, Workshop on Fault-Tolerant and Distributed Systems, Switzerland 1997.

[11] C. Lee, K. G. Shin: Optimal Task Assignment in Homogeneous Networks, IEEE Trans. Parallel and Distributed Systems, vol. 8, no. 2, pp. 119-129, 1997.

[12] A. Gerasoulis, T. Yang: On the Granularity and Clustering of Directed Acyclic Task Graphs, IEEE Trans. Parallel and Distributed Systems, vol. 4, no. 6, pp. 686-701, 1993.

[13] T. Yang, A. Gerasoulis: DSC: Scheduling Parallel Task on an Unbounded Number of Processors, IEEE Trans. Parallel and Distributed Systems, vol. 5, no. 9, pp. 951-967, 1994.

[14] L. Chao, E. H. Sha: Scheduling Data-Flow Graphs via Retiming and Unfolding, IEEE Trans. Parallel and Distributed Systems, vol. 8, no. 12, pp. 1259-1267, 1997.

[15] C. Coroyer, Z. Liu: Effectiveness of Heuristics and Simulated Annealing for the Scheduling of Concurrent Tasks – An Empirical Comparison, Proc. Parallel Architectures and Languages Europe PARLE'93, Lecture Notes in Computer Sciences no. 694, Springer-Verlag, pp. 452-463, Germany 1993.

A Knowledge-Based Approach to Scheduling Jobs in Metacomputer Environment

Jarek Nabrzyski, Juliusz Pukacki, Maciej Stroiński

{naber, pukacki, stroins}@man.poznan.pl
Poznań Supercomputing and Networking Center
ul. Noskowskiego 10, 61-704 Poznań, Poland

Abstract. The importance of metacomputing is without question. Only such a use of distributed resources, as in metacomputing, has the potential to maximize performance and cost effectiveness of a wide range of scientific and distributed applications. There are several projects that address the metacomputing area. Globus [Globus97], [Globus98], Legion [Legion], HPCM [HPCM98] are only a few examples. However, in most cases resource dynamics are not taken into account. In this paper we present a concept of the metacomputer management software based on the expert system techniques. The knowledge about some specific aspects of metacomputing, like system specific knowledge, communication networks parameters, architecture specialization, run-time scheduling techniques, optimal resource allocation etc. is kept and managed by different experts. They negotiate with each other to make up a common scheduling decision.

1. Motivation

Metacomputing is expected to bring a breakthrough in the increase of computing speed by such means as high level resource utilization, parallel computing and using high speed/low latency networks. Many ideas can be studied from previous experiences with current Cluster Management Software (CMS) packages like LSF, LoadLeveler, NQS and others. Of course, the existing knowledge will have to be extended to design and develop better and better metacomputer systems.
However, no one wants to reinvent the wheel. A good idea would be to build such an extensible system, which could be extended in a case when some new knowledge is learned. Some questions arise when we think of resource utilization within the metacomputer. Are there any good scheduling algorithms for metacomputing? Are the resources utilized on a high level? Do the scheduling algorithms take into account all the significant parameters? We will try to answer these questions in this paper. We will also present an extensible knowledge-based metacomputer management system based on the multi-expert approach.

The organization of the paper is the following. In section 2 we present the current methodology of job submission and processing on supercomputers based on some sample systems. Section 3 presents our concept of metacomputer management system

1066-6192/99 $10.00 © 1999 IEEE

(MMS) and finally section 4 contains some final remarks and description of our future work.

2. Methodology of typical CMS software

Currently several CMS packages have been developed by different vendors. The description of work of such CMS systems can be described in two main steps: processing the job description file and submission of the job.

- Step 1: Job Description File
- Step 2: Submit Job

Typically the CMS packages provide multiple queues, each being appropriate for different types of jobs. For example, a queue called "Parallel" could be used to service parallel jobs. This way the CMS administrator can setup special queues for CPU intensive jobs, jobs that need a rapid turnaround etc. The number of possible queue configurations depends on the profile of the typical job throughput on the system being managed.

The master scheduler is also responsible for ensuring that jobs complete successfully. It does this by monitoring jobs (using for example some monitoring agent) until they successfully finish. If a job fails, due to problems other than an application runtime error, it should reschedule the job to run it again. In most cases the CMS packages available on the market today use a very simple scheduling policy based on the FIFO model. The question is whether the model used for CMS systems is good enough for metacomputer management. We can distinguish between the following desirable features of MMS: (1) heterogeneous platforms support across OS and hardware platforms, (2) batch and interactive usage, (3) easy to use GUI, (4) scalability, (5) easy maintenance and support, (6) easy to manage, (7) reconfigure and administrate, (8) ease of submitting, (9) monitoring and controlling jobs, (10) support for all programming paradigms, (11) high level of security, (12) no single point of failure, (13) fault tolerant, (14) checkpointing, (15) process migration, (16) strong support for parallel applications, (17) quality of service.

In the next section we will describe the system which more or less fulfills all these requirements.

3. Global resource metascheduler

Having such complex environments as there are in a metacomputer, one would like to manage its policy for resource management and allocation. Establishing multicriteria based policy (CPU load, memory requirements, job priority, due dates etc.) for resource management and allocation is very far from being easy. The main task here is to organize an effective global scheduling of the systems involved in metacomputing to achieve the highest possible throughput, load balancing and reduced waiting times. Of course, all the above-mentioned features of CCS systems must also be provided by metacomputer management software.

Our approach to the metacomputer management is based on the above mentioned assumptions. Dynamic multicriteria scheduling is something which makes the system different from other existing ones.

The system is based on objects residing on different systems. Every object is composed of three layers. The first layer, called the visualization layer (VL), serves all the user interface functions. So, usually this layer will be present on graphical workstations. The layer allows a user to make use of different GUIs, based on Java (applets and applications), X/Motif, Web browsers etc. (see Fig. 1). The so-called Global Resource Manager is also located at this layer. It is responsible for receiving the submitted jobs from the user and make the first decisions about resource allocation. This process will be described in the next subsection.

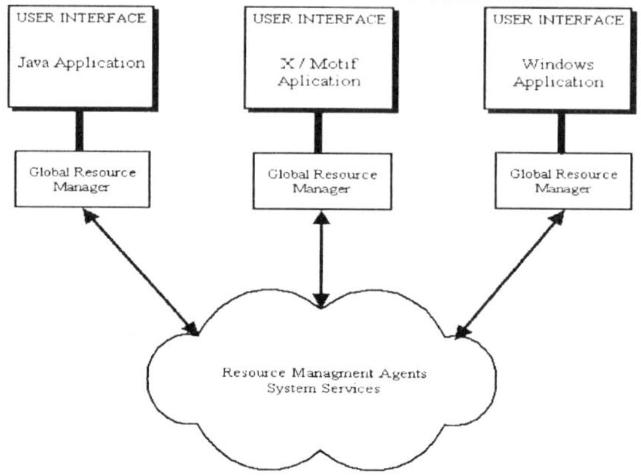

Fig. 1. The first layer of MMS

The second layer, called the management layer (ML), is composed of elements responsible for management and the allocation of resources. Finally the third layer, called system primitive services layer (PL), is responsible for performing low level services. Usually VL and ML use the PL layer for assistance operations. It is not necessary to install all the layers on every system. Computing-only hosts probably don't need any VL instances, but they will need the next two layers in order to be allocated for computing.

The central object of the presented architecture, the communication bus, provides a mechanism for communication between different layers on both a local and a remote basis. Between all the modules, communication channels are established allowing the user and administrator to control their jobs. Every action the user takes is responded with a reaction from the system.

From the resource management's point of view the second layer (ML), is the most important. It provides the scheduling mechanisms, resource and job control and monitoring, QoS etc. Figure Fig. 2 presents the basic architecture of the second layer and its co-operation with the Global Resource Manager (GRM).

Let's assume that a user submits a job to the system. The GRM placed in the VL reads the job description (given by a user) with its quality of service requirements and contacts all possible systems that can serve the job in a way required by the user. It

gathers information from the Information Agents (IA) placed on every system. IAs posses some information about the state of the systems they reside on.
It is possible that a job is dedicated for more than one architecture. A user can give a list of resource requirements concerning his job. It includes: default system architecture(s), number of processor, processor power, amount of memory, system-to-network interface, job due dates, job ready time, precedence relations for parallel jobs or several jobs co-operating with each other, communication QoS parameters etc. GRM and IAs then negotiate the parameters. For every user a priority is granted at the moment a user accesses the system. All these parameters have a direct influence on the first level scheduling algorithm. GRM is supported by an automated expert system possessing the knowledge from the past (historical knowledge) as well as general knowledge about the systems involved and scheduling policies for these systems. Metaknowledge about how to use facts and rules regarding the reasoning process is also stored in the knowledge base of the expert system. A user has the opportunity to express his preferences concerning different criteria.

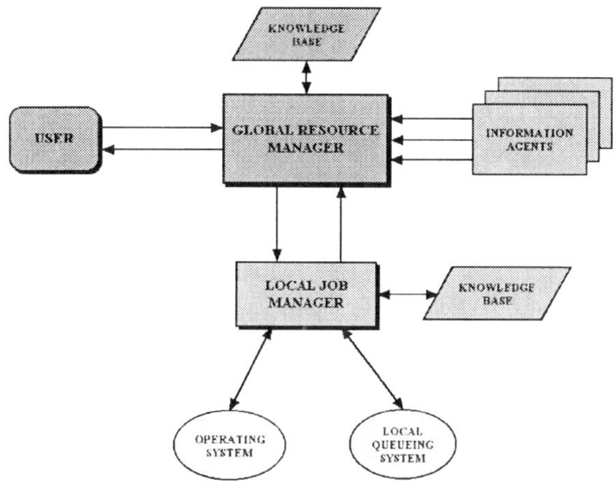

Fig. 2. Co-operation between Global Resource Manager and Local Job Manager

Depending on what is most important for the user, the system finds the best compromise resource allocation for the user's job. When the default architecture is chosen then the job is transferred to the default architecture's Local Job Manager (LJM). LJM is responsible for local resource allocation. It communicates either with operating system to start and control a job or with the local CMS software responsible. This solution was chosen to enable operations with other supercomputing centers, their load balancing policies, their autonomy etc. However LJB itself provides scheduling mechanisms for different architectures. It is also supported by the expert system. In both cases the knowledge bases are stored in separate files. They can be updated dynamically (automatically) or manually by the knowledge engineers. Thus, the scheduling policy can be changed without recompiling the whole system.

3.1. Scheduling

The scheduling problem in both cases (global and local) is transferred to the most general multiobjective multimode project scheduling problem [Slow94]. Simply stated the problem addressed is how to schedule precedence and resource-constrained jobs in order to find the best compromise solution, based on the user's and system administrator's preferences. In general these preferences are often contradictory. Resource constraints can concern: (i) the amount available at every moment, and (ii) the consumption over a given time period. If only constraint (i) is imposed we speak about renewable resources (processor, memory), if only (ii) is defined - about nonrenewable resources (processor time), and if both (i) and (ii) about doubly-constrained (network Bandwidth). The set of job execution performance measures is composed of time objectives (execution time, mean weighted flow time, mean weighted lateness) and cost objectives (e.g. weighted resource consumption, cost of the computation). The specific form of the scheduling problem examined here permits each job to be performed in several ways called operating modes, or simply modes. Each mode represents a different way of combining resources to accomplish a given job. thus, one job can be accomplished on one SGI Power Challenge with 12 processors or on several SGI Indigo2 workstations. The duration and resource requirements of each job mode are known a priori, and thus we can speak about resource-duration interactions. In this model a variety of multiple resource-duration interactions, such as using different technologies or types of resources to accomplish the same job can be expressed and evaluated.

3.2. Construction of compromise schedules - expert system approach

Heterogeneous environment of metacomputer makes it very difficult to make proper decisions concerning scheduling and mapping. Bad decision can cause the bottlenecks, some jobs might be not finished or even started. This is a common situation that occurs in the CMS systems or other metacomputer systems. Most of the approaches use very simple scheduling mechanism, usually oriented to some kind of applications, using only one criteria function, either cost or time based. The traditional algorithms were constructed for simple, homogeneous environments. They didn't take into account such aspects as: heterogeneity on hardware and software level, multicriteria aspects of scheduling and mapping, conflict resolution mechanisms etc.

In our system the scheduling problem is thought as an interactive search process involving the selection and sequencing of jobs (both waiting in queues and those already scheduled) and resources over time to achieve the total system objectives, subject to a set of constraints. These constraints are imposed on the whole metacomputer (given by metacomputer administrator in a form of rules) and on the every job (given by user in a form of job description file). The scheduling module of every Job Manager is organized as presented in the figure Fig.3.

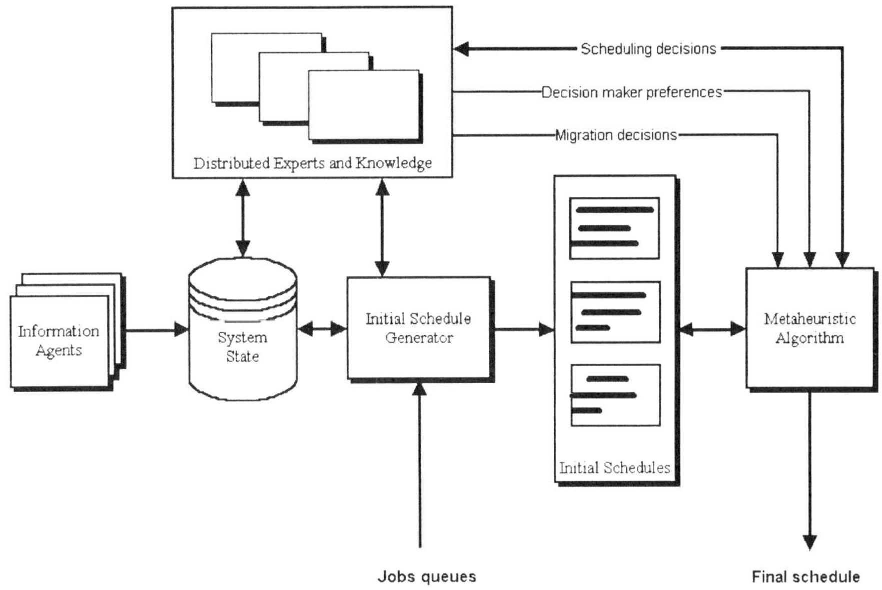

Fig. 3. Scheduling module of GRM and LJM

In general the scheduling module looks similar for both Global Resource and Local Job managers. The difference is hidden in the knowledge sources, as the particular problems to be solved are slightly different. Global Resource Manager needs the information about the load of different systems, as well as the information if there exist local CMS software or it is LJM, which controls the scheduling on particular system. The information agents give the information to GRM.

The scheduling is based on heuristic considerations since the optimal schedules for multicriteria problems are impossible to be found. These heuristic considerations are driven by metaheuristic algorithm (Tabu Search (TS)) which allows, together with expert system, to find a good schedule considering described preferences.

The expert system approach in the system is quite simple. We assumed that there doesn't exist any single expert that possesses the whole knowledge about a specific problem. That is why we have introduced several experts being responsible for different aspects of scheduling and resource management in such complex environments as metacomputer. This way the content of the knowledge base is easy to be managed. So we have experts responsible for networking aspects of metacomputing, job migration, resource allocation, memory management, I/O management, conflict resolution etc.

Every expert is represented in a form of a knowledge source (KS), which consists of its activation conditions, knowledge base and inference engine. All the experts communicate through the communication bus and negotiate the common decisions. They use some distributed object called blackboard, which they can access, write to, read from or delete information which is not valid any more. The blackboard is a specific distributed data structure, available to all experts, and it stores the active knowledge of the state of the scheduling process. The blackboard carries the problem observations (symptoms, i.e. objects with their values), local abstractions (data abstractions with their values), hypotheses and intermediate and final schedules. All problem features are known from the beginning and are incorporated into the system as knowledge bases and the initial contents of the blackboard. When a KS is activated it examines the current state of the blackboard and applies its (expert's) knowledge either to create a new hypothesis and write it on the blackboard, or to modify an existing one.

The system runs for every incoming job and reschedules the systems. The cost of job migration is taken into account and based on this the decision of whether it is worth migrating or not is made. Potentially, every incoming job can create some migration decisions. In general the migration cannot delay any of the scheduled jobs unless the higher priority jobs arrive.

The migration decisions are driven by the rules from the knowledge base. The expert knowledge says what kinds of job migrations are allowed on particular systems, how much the migration costs.

4. Final remarks

In the article we have described the metacomputer management system based on the artificial intelligence approach. The distributed expert system, which is the kernel of whole system, contains the specific knowledge about scheduling policies of global metacomputer and local subsystems. This knowledge is used by scheduling algorithms that co-operate with expert system to find compromise schedules for incoming jobs. The re-scheduling and job migration are supported taking into account the dynamics of the resources. Several modules of the system (GRM, LJM) were already tested in the environment and they gave promising results.

References

[Globus98] K. Czajkowski, I. Foster, C. Kesselman, N. Karonis, S. Martin, W. Smith, S. Tuecke. A Resource Management Architecture for Metacomputing Systems. Proc. IPPS/SPDP '98 Workshop on Job Scheduling Strategies for Parallel Processing,1998

[Globus97] I. Foster, C. Kesselman "Globus: A Metacomputing Infrastructure Toolkit", International Journal of Supercomputer Applications, 11(2):115-128, 1997.

[Legion] A.S. Grimshaw, A. Nguyen-Tuong, W.A. Wulf, "Campus-Wide Computing: Results Using Legion at the University of Virginia", UVa CS Technical Report CS-95-10, 1995.

[HPCM98] V. Sander, D. Erwin, V. Huber "High-Performance Computer Management in Java", proceedings of HPCN'98, Amsterdam, The Netherlands, April, 1998.

[CMS96] M.A. Baker, G.C. Fox and H.W. Yau, "Cluster Management Software", NHSE Review, Vol. 1, 1996, http://www.crpc.rice.edu/NHSEreview/CMS/

[Slow94] R. Słowiński, "Multiobjective Project Scheduling", in Advances of Project Scheduling, R. Słowiński, J. Węglarz (eds.), Kluwer Academic Publishers, 1994

[MMNS97] C. Mazurek, N. Meyer, J. Nabrzyski, M. Stroiński, High Performance Networking Infrastructure for Metacomputing, proceedings of PPAM'97 conference, Zakopane, September 1997.

[NSW96] J. Nabrzyski, M. Stroiński, J. Węglarz, Metacomputing at Pozna\'{n} Supercomputing and Networking Center, Proceedings of Parallel Programming Environments for High Performance Computing conference, Alpe d'Huez, 1996.

[BG96] T.B. Brecht and K. guha. Using parallel program characteristics in dynamic processor allocation policies. Performance Evaluation, 27(8): 519-539, October 1996.

[DAC96] A.C. Dusseau, R.H. Arpaci, and D.E. Culler. Effective distributed scheduling of parallel workloads. In Proceedings of the 1996 ACM SIGMETRICS conference on Measurement and Modeling of Computer Systems, pages 25-36, 1996.

[NVZ96] In Proceedings of IPPS'96 Workshop on Job Scheduling Strategies for Parallel Processing, pages 93-104, 1996.

[Par97] E.W. Parson, Using Resource Requirements in Multiprogrammed Multiprocessor Scheduling. Ph.D thesis, University of Toronto, Canada, 1997.

[Sev94] K.C. Sevcik. Application scheduling and processor allocation in multiprogrammed parallel processing systems. Performance Evaluation, 19:107-140

Consistency Requirements of Distributed Shared Memory for Lamport's Bakery Algorithm for Mutual Exclusion*

Jerzy Brzeziński Dariusz Wawrzyniak
Institute of Computing Science
Poznan University of Technology
Piotrowo 3a
60-965 Poznań, POLAND
brzezinski@put.poznan.pl *darek@cs.put.poznan.pl*

Abstract

As is well known Lamport's Bakery algorithm for mutual exclusion of n processes is correct if a physically shared memory is used as the communication facility between processes. An application of weaker consistency models (e.g. causal, processor, PRAM), available in replicated distributed shared memory (DSM) systems appealing due to possible performance improvement, may imply incorrectness of the algorithm. It raises consistency requirement problem, a problem of finding weaker consistency models of DSM that is sufficient for the algorithm correctness.

In this paper, consistency requirements of distributed shared memory for Lamport's Bakery algorithm for mutual exclusion of n processes are considered. It is proven that the algorithm is correct with a consistency model resulting from a combination of sequential consistency and one of the weakest consistency models, PRAM, without explicit synchronisation. The combination is achieved by specifying the consistency model with write operations on shared locations.

1 Introduction

Distributed shared memory (DSM) systems are usually based on replication ([9], [13]). A replica of DSM is made in a local cache of the node at which the access is required. This allows accessing the DSM simultaneously at different nodes, especially in case of read operations, which simply return a value of the accessed data from the local cache. On the other hand, replication raises the problem of replica consistency as write operations may change the values of the data in DSM.

The state of replicas is consistent if it obeys certain conditions, which are specified by a consistency model. The *consistency model* is a contract between the system and the application, which obligates the system to return an expected value to the application provided that the application accesses the memory following certain rules ([13]). To keep the consistent state of replicas according to the model, each replica of DSM must be updated after issuing a write operation. In other words, every write operation must be performed on each replica. Formally, the consistency models are defined by imposing some constraints on the order in which the write operations are performed. Potentially, the more restrictive the model is the more it guarantees, but the less efficient computation it allows, because additional synchronisation is required, which delays update of replicas. Strong (most restrictive) consistency models (atomic consistency, sequential consistency) ensure that the system behaves as if the memory were physically shared. Every algorithm that is correct with physically shared memory is also correct with these models. However, because of the restrictions the efficiency of computation may be significantly decreased. Weakening consistency, on the other hand, obligates the programmer to be careful when accessing the shared memory in their programs to keep to the rules of the contract in order to ensure application correctness.

This paper deals with consistency requirements of reliable DSM for Lamport's Bakery algorithm for mutual exclusion of n processes. It is shown that the Bakery algorithm is correct with a combination of sequential consistency and PRAM consistency. The combination is achieved by specifying the consistency model with write operations on shared locations. Detailed description of combining five basic consistency models: sequential consistency, causal consistency, PRAM consistency, processor consistency, and coherence is presented in [6].

* This work was supported in part by the State Committee for Scientific Research (KBN), Poland, under grant KBN 8 T11C 025 14.

1066-6192/99 $10.00 © 1999 IEEE

Consistency requirements of DSM for mutual exclusion algorithms have also been addressed in [2], [3] and [4]. In [2] Ahamad et al. have proven that processor consistency is strong enough for Peterson's algorithm, but too weak for Lamport's Bakery algorithm. Concluding the paper, they have stated that mutual exclusion algorithms require cooperation, which is provided either at a lower level (e.g. the level of DSM system) or explicitly at a higher level. Moreover, they have indicated that PRAM, causal and other consistency models that do not require cooperation in their implementation cannot provide mutual exclusion without cooperation at higher level. The problem is analysed in details by Attiya and Friedman in [4]. They distinguish fast consistency conditions (e.g. PRAM and causal) and prove that mutual exclusion algorithms based on fast conditions must be cooperative. They also state that classical solutions to the mutual exclusion problem (e.g. Peterson's algorithm, Lamport's Bakery algorithm) are non-cooperative, thus they are not correct with fast consistency conditions. Following the above reasoning, mixed consistency ([1]), is not suitable for classical mutual exclusion algorithms either, since it only offers PRAM consistency and causal consistency. In [3] they present an approach to supporting multiple consistency models, called hybrid consistency. Two kinds of read and write operations are distinguished in the model: weak and strong. Then they show that hybrid consistency is applicable to Peterson's algorithm for mutual exclusion of two processes. Every write operation in that application is strong, and every read operation is weak, i.e. write operations are observed in the same order by every process, and read operations return local values without synchronisation between processes. Our approach, in contrast, ensures correctness of the algorithm even though some write operations are PRAM consistent, i.e. have fast implementation. However, read operations in our approach are closer to strong reads in hybrid consistency.

The paper is structured as follows. In Section 2 an idea of DSM and formal definitions of basic consistency models applied to the Bakery algorithm are presented. Subsection 2.3 contains the definition of complex consistency, whose application to the Bakery algorithm along with correctness proofs is described in Section 3. Some concluding remarks are made in Section 4.

2 Basic definitions

Similarly to [12], DSM system is defined as a set of sequential processes $P_1, P_2, ..., P_n$, interacting via a set X of shared memory locations (read/write objects). Each process has its own replica of the whole set X, which is accessible for reading and writing. In other words, the shared locations are assumed to be fully replicated. A write operation of a value v into a location $x \in X$ issued by a process P_i defines a new value for this location and is denoted by $w_i(x)v$. Similarly, a read operation which obtains the value v is denoted by $r_i(x)v$. The set of all operations issued by P_i is denoted by H_i. Since the processes are sequential the set H_i is totally ordered by a *local order* relation, denoted by $\rightarrow_i$, according to the order of issuing the operations. The set H_i ordered by the relation $\rightarrow_i$ is called *local history*. H denotes the set of all operations in the system ($H = \bigcup_i H_i$). It is partially ordered by a *causal-order* relation, which is denoted by $\rightarrow$, and defined as follows:

$$\text{(i)} \quad \forall_{o1, o2 \in H} \left(\exists_{i=1..n} \; o1 \rightarrow_i o2 \Rightarrow o1 \rightarrow o2 \right) \tag{1}$$

$$\text{(ii)} \quad \forall_{x \in X} \; w(x)v \rightarrow r(x)v \tag{2}$$

$$\text{(iii)} \quad \forall_{o1,\, o2,\, o \in H} \left(o1 \rightarrow o \wedge o \rightarrow o2 \Rightarrow o1 \rightarrow o2 \right) \tag{3}$$

The set H ordered by the relation $\rightarrow$ is called *global history of execution*.

Because of full replication every read operation can be executed locally (the subsequent value can be obtained from the local replica). To keep the consistent state of the replicas the write operations have to be executed on each replica of the subsequent memory location. Thus, only write operations are important to other processes, because they change the state of replicas, while read operations report on the state to the issuing process. Hence, it is essential for each process to order all the write operations issued by the system (denoted by H_W) along with the local read operations. Because the processes are sequential, the operations are executed one after another, therefore they are totally ordered. A total order relation is called *serialisation*. The consistency models differ from one another in the orders in which operations issued by one of the processes are observed by other processes, i.e. the orders in which the operations are serialised by each process.

Formally, the consistency models are defined by imposing for each process P_i some constraints on the serialisation of the set $H_i \cup H_W$. The serialisation of $H_i \cup H_W$ is denoted by $\mapsto_i$. Independently of the consistency model the serialisation must satisfy the following condition, called *legality*[1]:

[1] For simplicity of formal definitions it is assumed that each write operation writes a value which is unique to a location.

$$\underset{\substack{w(x)v\in H_W\\ r(x)v\in H_i}}{\forall}\left(w(x)v \mapsto_i r(x)v \wedge \underset{o(x)u\in H_i\cup H_W}{\nexists} u\neq v \wedge w(x)v\mapsto_i o(x)u \mapsto_i r(x)v\right) \qquad (4)$$

A serialisation that satisfies the condition 4 is *legal.*

2.1 Sequential consistency

Sequential consistency guarantees that „the result of any execution (of a multiprocessor program) is the same as if the operations of all the processors were executed in some sequential order, and the operations of each individual processor appear in this sequence in the order specified by its program" ([8]). In the considered system model „operations of the processor" mean „operations of the process". Thus, the execution of operations on DSM is sequentially consistent if **for each P_i** there is a legal serialisation $\mapsto_i$ of the operations from $H_i \cup H_W$ satisfying the following two conditions:

(i) $$\underset{o1,o2\in H_i\cup H_W}{\forall} o1 \rightarrow o2 \Rightarrow o1 \mapsto_i o2 \qquad (5)$$

(ii) $$\underset{w1,w2\in H_W}{\forall}\left(\underset{i=1..n}{\forall} w1 \mapsto_i w2 \vee \underset{i=1..n}{\forall} w2 \mapsto_i w1 \right) \qquad (6)$$

The conditions state that the order of operations in the serialisations preserves causal order of operations and each process has to observe the same order of write operations. Figure 1 presents an execution, which is sequentially consistent because the processes can see the following sequence of operations: $w_2(x)1 \mapsto r_1(x)1 \mapsto w_2(x)2$.

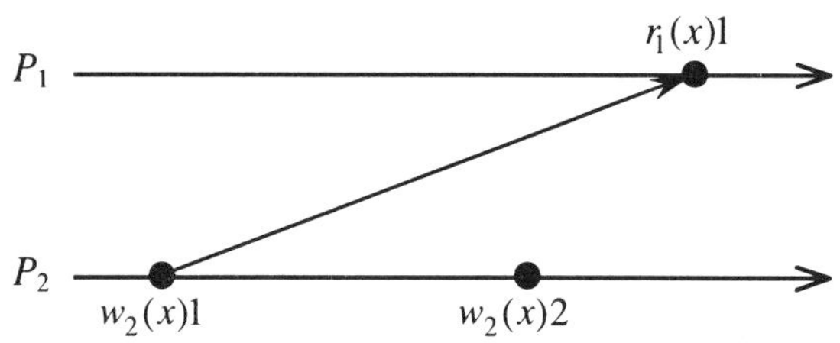

Figure 1. Sequentially consistent execution

2.2 PRAM consistency

PRAM consistency ([10]) guarantees that all processes observe write operations according to the local order of issuing, i.e. two operations are assured to appear in some order to other processes if they are issued in the order by the same process. Formally, the execution of operations on DSM is PRAM consistent if **for each P_i** there exists a legal serialisation $\mapsto_i$ of the operations from $H_i \cup H_W$ which satisfies the following condition:

$$\underset{o1,o2\in H_i\cup H_W}{\forall}\left(\underset{j}{\exists}\, o1 \rightarrow_j o2 \Rightarrow o1 \mapsto_i o2 \right) \qquad (7)$$

An example of PRAM consistent execution is presented in Figure 2. The process P_3 can see the following sequence of operations: $w_2(x)2 \mapsto r_3(x)2 \mapsto w_1(x)1 \mapsto r_3(x)1 \mapsto w_1(y)1$.

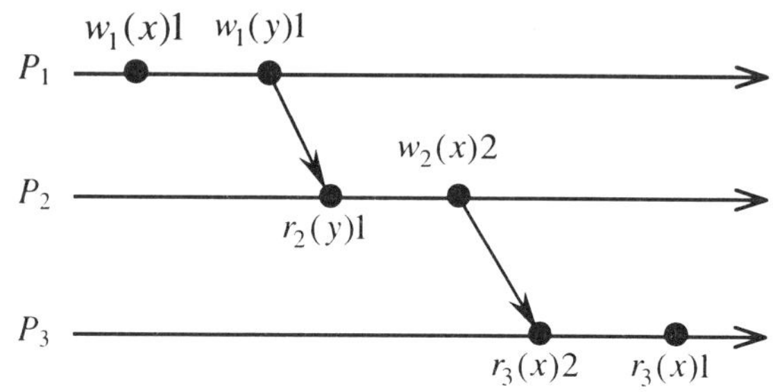

Figure 2. PRAM consistent execution

2.3 Complex consistency

Combining different consistency models raises two problems: how to specify the consistency criterion (object, write operations, read operations), and how to order operations belonging to different models. Consistency criterion can be specified along with the object declaration, which obligates the system to keep the criterion in respect to all operations on the object. This approach would be sufficient for the solution to the Bakery algorithm. However, to improve flexibility of the complex model the criterion can be specified with the operation, as in [1] and [2]. In case of read/write objects two kinds of operations are admissible, i.e. read and write.

According to the definitions above, the consistency model depends on the order of execution of write operations rather than on the semantics of read operations only. Especially, in the case of strong consistency models (e.g. sequential consistency) it is difficult to guarantee that a read operation will return a consistent value while neglecting the proper order of write operations, unless a multiversion replica of DSM is available in the local cache. Hence, the semantics of write operations has to be known before the value which is being written is read by another operation, and therefore in this approach the consistency criterion is specified with write operations.

Generally, our approach to supporting multiple consistency models, described in full in [6], allows combining sequential consistency, causal consistency, PRAM consistency, processor consistency and coherence.

It is an extension of the model presented in [5]. In that approach it is assumed that the serialisation of any two write operations must satisfy the conditions which are common to the definitions of the models specified with these operations.

Let CX(mod_1, mod_2, ..., mod_n) stand for the complex model resulting from the combination of mod_1, mod_2, ..., mod_n (mod_i denotes a basic model). To specify a model with a write operation let us also extend the denotation of write operation to $w_{mod,i}(x)v$, where *mod* determines the model. Moreover, let SEQ stand for sequential consistency, and PRAM stand for PRAM consistency. As it is easy to notice, the condition (7), defining PRAM consistency, is included in the definition of causal order, i.e. it is preserved in sequentially consistent executions. Thus, the condition is common to sequential consistency and PRAM consistency, thereby it is preserved in CX(SEQ, PRAM).

3 Lamport's Bakery Algorithm for Mutual Exclusion of *n* Processes

The idea of the Lamport's Bakery algorithm ([7], [11]) is based on assigning a number to a competing process in the first part of the trial section called doorway. The process indicates choosing the number by setting 1 to the corresponding entry of the *choosing* table. Then it determines the maximal value of the number assigned to other processes, i.e. the maximal value contained in the *num* table. It assigns to itself and writes to the corresponding entry of the *num* table the maximal value increased by one. After establishing its own number it writes 0 to the corresponding entry of the *choosing* table and starts checking the numbers chosen by other processes. The process waits on the critical section until its chosen value is less than another value greater than 0 in the *num* table (in case of equal values in the *num* table process identifiers are compared). The value of 0 in the *num* table states that the corresponding process is not involved in the competition.

The Bakery algorithm is proven to be correct, provided that write operations to the table *choosing* are sequentially consistent, and write operations to the table *num* are at least PRAM consistent (Figure 3).

```
shared
   choosing[1..n]: Boolean /* initially false */
   num[1..n]: integer /* initially 0 or 1 */
local
   test_i: Boolean
   k, mine_i, other_i, temp_i: integer
while true do
   w_SEQ(choosing[i])1                              } doorway     } trial section
   for k := 1 to n do
      /* mine_i := max(num[k] | k ≠ i) */
      if k ≠ i then
         r(num[k])temp_i
         mine_i := max(mine_i, temp_i)
   mine_i := mine_i + 1
   w_PRAM(num[i])mine_i
   w_SEQ(choosing[i])0
   for k := 1 to n do
      if k ≠ i then
         repeat
            r(choosing[k])test_i
         until test_i = 0
         repeat
            r(num[k])other_i
         until other_i = 0 or (mine_i, i) < (other_i, k)^2
   critical section
   w_PRAM(num[i])0          /* exit section */
   reminder section
```

Figure 3 Lamport's Bakery algorithm with CX(SEQ, PRAM) as executed by process P_i

Lemma 1

If two processes, say P_i and P_j, have left the doorway and have not left the critical section yet then when reading $r_i(num[j])other_i$ by P_i and $r_j(num[i])other_j$ by P_j either **($other_i = 0$ or ($mine_i$, i)<($other_i$, j)) and ($mine_j$, j)>($other_j$, i)**, or **($mine_i$, i)>($other_i$, j) and ($other_j = 0$ or ($mine_j$, j)<($other_i$, i))** holds[2].

Proof:

Sequentially consistent write operations have to be totally ordered, so the following interleavings of sequentially consistent writes are distinguished:

1) $w_{SEQ,j}(choosing[i])1 \mapsto w_{SEQ,j}(choosing[i])0 \mapsto w_{SEQ,i}(choosing[i])1 \mapsto w_{SEQ,i}(choosing[i])0$
2) $w_{SEQ,j}(choosing[i])1 \mapsto w_{SEQ,i}(choosing[i])1 \mapsto w_{SEQ,j}(choosing[i])0 \mapsto w_{SEQ,i}(choosing[i])0$
3) $w_{SEQ,j}(choosing[i])1 \mapsto w_{SEQ,i}(choosing[i])1 \mapsto w_{SEQ,i}(choosing[i])0 \mapsto w_{SEQ,j}(choosing[i])0$
4) $w_{SEQ,i}(choosing[i])1 \mapsto w_{SEQ,j}(choosing[i])1 \mapsto w_{SEQ,j}(choosing[i])0 \mapsto w_{SEQ,i}(choosing[i])0$

[2] $((mine_i, i) < (other_i, k)) \Leftrightarrow (mine_i < other_i$ or $(mine_i = other_i$ and $i < k))$

5) $w_{SEQ,i}(choosing[i])1 \mapsto w_{SEQ,j}(choosing[i])1 \mapsto w_{SEQ,i}(choosing[i])0 \mapsto w_{SEQ,j}(choosing[i])0$

6) $w_{SEQ,i}(choosing[i])1 \mapsto w_{SEQ,i}(choosing[i])0 \mapsto w_{SEQ,j}(choosing[i])1 \mapsto w_{SEQ,j}(choosing[i])0$

It is easy to notice that the case 1 is analogous to the case 6, the case 2 is analogous to the case 5, and the case 3 is analogous to the case 4. Hence, further analysis is restricted to the first three cases (Figure 4, Figure 5 and Figure 6), the order of write operations of different processes is indicated by the wide arrows).

In the case of the execution presented in Figure 4 sequential writes of P_j are perceived before sequential writes of P_i. Therefore, P_i reads from the table *num* the value written by P_j and writes a value, say v (the value is stored in $mine_i$), greater at least by one. Thus, before leaving the critical section by P_j $mine_i > other_i = num[j]$. From P_j's view point $other_j=0$ if the coherence protocol have not managed to update the Pj's replica, otherwise $other_j > mine_j$.

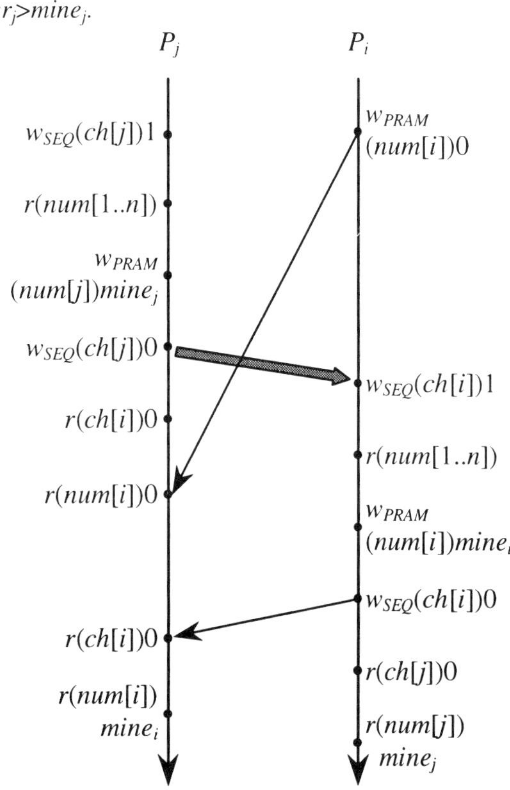

Figure 4 Mutual exclusion in case of $w_{SEQ,j}(ch[j])1 \mapsto w_{SEQ,j}(ch[j])0 \mapsto w_{SEQ,i}(ch[i])1 \mapsto w_{SEQ,i}(ch[i])0$

In the case of the execution presented in Figure 5, P_i reads from the table *num* and stores in $other_i$ the value $mine_j$ written by P_j. Because of $w_{SEQ,i}(ch[i])1 \mapsto w_{SEQ,j}(ch[j])0$ the operation $w_{SEQ,i}(ch[i])0$ must appear before $r_j(ch[i])0$, and thereby P_j reads from the table *num* and stores in $other_j$ the value of $mine_i$ written by P_i. Thus, $other_j = mine_i$ and $other_i = mine_j$, which means that $(mine_i,i)<(other_i,j) \Leftrightarrow (mine_j,j)>(other_j,i)$ or conversely $(mine_i,i)>(other_i,j) \Leftrightarrow (mine_j,j)<(other_j,i)$.

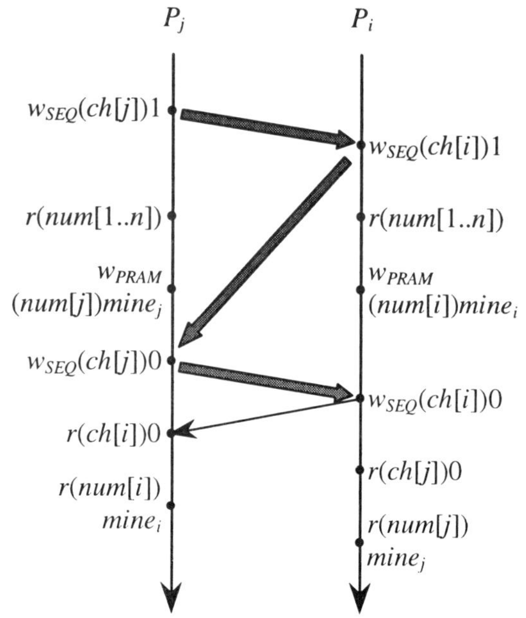

Figure 5 Mutual exclusion in case of $w_{SEQ,j}(ch[j])1 \mapsto w_{SEQ,i}(ch[i])1 \mapsto w_{SEQ,i}(ch[i])0 \mapsto w_{SEQ,i}(ch[j])0$

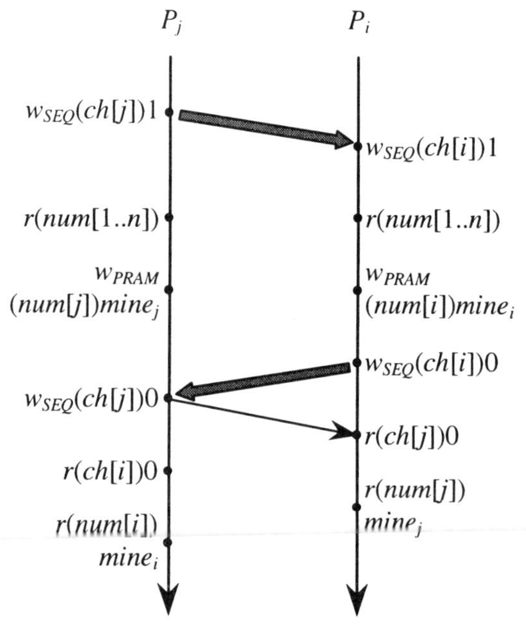

Figure 6 Mutual exclusion in case of $w_{SEQ,j}(ch[j])1 \mapsto w_{SEQ,i}(ch[i])1 \mapsto w_{SEQ,i}(ch[j])0 \mapsto w_{SEQ,j}(ch[i])0$

The execution presented in Figure 6 is similar to the one in Figure 5. Sequential writes of P_i appear between sequential writes of P_j. Therefore, P_j reads from the table *num* and stores in $other_j$ the value $mine_i$ written by P_i. Because of $w_{SEQ,j}(ch[j])1 \mapsto w_{SEQ,i}(ch[i])1 \mapsto w_{SEQ,i}(ch[i])0$ the operation $w_{SEQ,j}(ch[j])0$ must appear before $r_i(ch[j])0$, and thereby P_i reads from the table *num* and stores in $other_i$ the value of $mine_j$ written by P_j. Thus, $other_j = mine_i$ and $other_i = mine_j$, which means that $(mine_i,i)<(other_i,j) \Leftrightarrow (mine_j,j)>(other_j,i)$ or conversely $(mine_i,i)>(other_i,j) \Leftrightarrow (mine_j,j)<(other_j,i)$.

□

The lemma is obvious if the *num* table is physically shared. Note however, that each process has its own replica of the table *num*, which is updated by the coherence protocol in arbitrary finite time.

Theorem 1 Safety of the Bakery algorithm.

The Bakery algorithm with CX(SEQ, PRAM) satisfies mutual exclusion.

Proof:

Safety is proven by showing that only one of any two competing processes, say P_i and P_j, can enter the critical section. If P_i enters the critical section then $\underset{k=1..n}{\forall} \ \underset{other_i=num[k]}{\forall} \ other_i = 0 \vee (mine_i, i) < (other_i, k)$.

According to the Lemma 1, after reading $r_j(num[i])other_j$ by P_j the following condition must be satisfied $(mine_j, j)>(other_j, i)$, which prevents P_j from entering the critical section until P_i writes 0 to $num[i]$. As results from the algorithm (see Figure 3), P_i performs $w_i(num[i])0$ after leaving the critical section.

□

Theorem 2 Progress of the Bakery algorithm.

The Bakery algorithm with CX(SEQ, PRAM) guarantees progress.

Proof:

Progress for the exit section is obvious. Progress for the trial section is proven by contradiction. Let us assume that a number of processes want to enter the critical section, and all the processes are stopped in its trial sections while there is no process in the critical section. What can keep a process, say P_i, from entering the critical section are the repeat-until loops. The first one finishes after reading 0 from $choosing[j]$ (j=1..n, $j \neq i$). Since there is nothing to stop P_j from writing 0 to $choosing[j]$, the loop will be finished in a finite time. Let num_i denote the P_i's replica of the shared table *num*. The other loop finishes either after reading 0 from $num_i[j]$ or after reading a value, say $v1$, such that $(mine_i, i) < (v1, j)$. Assuming $(mine_i, i)>(v1, j)$ means that either P_j is in the critical section or is waiting on another process, say P_k, i.e. $(num_j[k], k)<(mine_j, j)$. From Lemma 1 $(mine_i, i)>(num_i[j], j) \Leftrightarrow (mine_j, j)<(num_j[i], i)$, which results in $(num_j[k], k)<(num_j[i], i)$. Since write operations to a particular entry of the *num* table are issued by one process, and the local order of the operations is preserved (they are PRAM consistent), every process eventually has the same value of each entry. Therefore, P_i does not block P_k from entering the critical section.

Extending the presented reasoning by induction to any number of processes results in the linear order of processes waiting on the critical section. Thus, one of them, say P_k, with the least value of the pair $(mine_k, k)$ enters the critical section. This guarantees progress.

□

Theorem 3 Lockout-freedom of the Bakery algorithm.

The Bakery algorithm with CX(SEQ, PRAM) is lockout-free.

Proof:

Let us assume that P_i waits for P_j to leave the critical section, i.e. it waits for $num[j]$=0 or $(num[j], j)>(num[i], i)$. After leaving the critical section P_j writes 0 to $num[j]$, which can be read by P_i. In case of $w_{SEQ,i}(ch[i])0 \mapsto w_{SEQ,j}(ch[j])1$ (Figure 7) even if P_i misses reading 0 from $num[j]$, because P_j managed to overwrite it in a next trial, the new value, say $v2$, written by P_j is greater than $mine_i$ ($mine_i$ is equal to $num[i]$). This results from the fact that P_j writes max(num[1..n])+1, thereby at least $num[i]$+1.

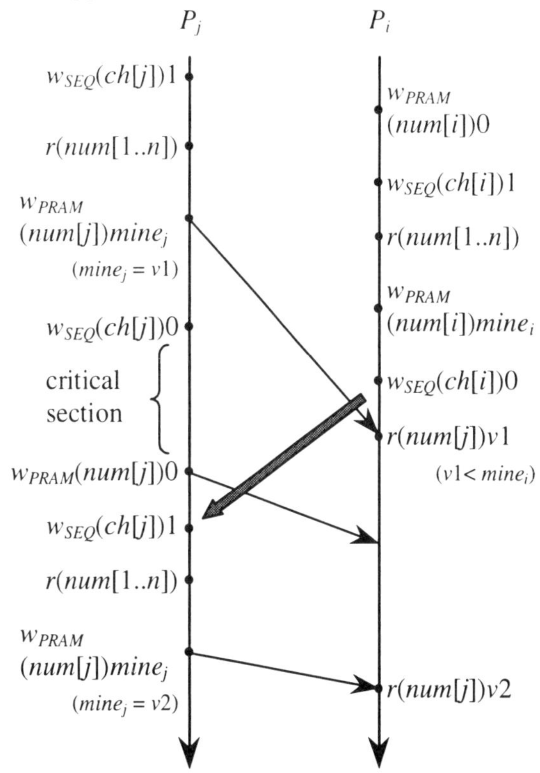

Figure 7 Lockout-freedom.

In the case of the reverse order (Figure 8) $r_i(num[j])$ would return $v2$. Depending on the order of $w_{PRAM,i}(num[i])$ and $r_j(num[1..n])$ $v2$ is either greater than $mine_i$ in case of $w_{PRAM,i}(num[i]) \mapsto_j r_j(num[1..n])$, or can be less than $mine_i$ if the operations occur in the reverse order (this is indicated by the dashed arrow in Figure 8). In the first case P_i enters the critical section before P_j, which suffices to prove the lockout-freedom. In the second case P_j can enter the critical section before P_i, however, since total order of sequentially consistent writes must be preserved $w_{SEQ,i}(ch[i])0 \mapsto_j w_{SEQ,j}(ch[j])0$, thereby also $w_{PRAM,i}(num[i])mine_i \mapsto_j w_{SEQ,j}(ch[j])0$. This means that in a next trial P_j will read the value of $mine_j$ from the table num, and P_i will enter the critical section before P_j. This way each process finally enters the critical section, which proves lockout-freedom.

□

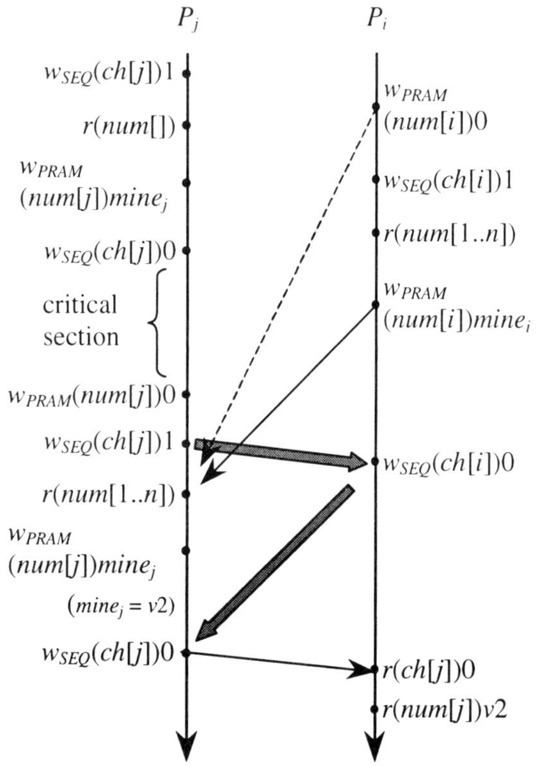

Figure 8 Lockout-freedom.

4 Conclusions

This paper has formally proven the correctness of Lamport's Bakery algorithm for mutual exclusion in a distributed shared memory system. It has been proven that a suitable combination of sequential consistency and PRAM consistency provides sufficient guarantees for the algorithms. Thus, it has been shown that the cooperation resulting in execution of write operations in the same order on each replica is not necessary for all memory operations, but only for some of them.

Further research will be aimed at analysing the weakest consistency requirements which ensure correctness of the algorithms. This may result in finding out requirements of new consistency models.

References

[1] Agrawal D., M. Choy, H.V. Leong, and A. Singh, "Mixed consistency: a model for parallel programming", *Proc. of the 13th ACM Symposium on Principles of Distributed Computing*, Los Angeles, 1994, pp. 101–110.

[2] Ahamad M., R. A. Bazzi, R. John, P. Kohli, and G. Neiger, "The power of processor consistency", Technical Report GIT-CC-92/34, Georgia Institute of Technology, Atlanta, December 1992.

[3] Attiya H., and R. Friedman, "A correctness condition for high-performance multiprocessors", Technical Report CS0767, Department of Computer Science, The Technion, Haifa, February 1994.

[4] Attiya H., and R. Friedman, "Limitations of fast consistency conditions for distributed shared memories", *Information Processing Letters*, 57, 1996, pp. 243–248.

[5] Brzeziński J., and D. Wawrzyniak, "Multi-criterion consistency model for distributed shared memory", *Proc. of the 6th IEEE Workshop on Future Trends if Distributed Computing Systems*, Tunisia, October 1997, pp. 202–207.

[6] Brzeziński J., and D. Wawrzyniak, "Supporting Multiple Consistency Models in Distributed Shared Memory System", *Proc. of DAPSYS98 Workshop on Distributed and Parallel Systems*, Budapest (Hungary), September 1998, pp. 83–90.

[7] Lamport L., "A new solution of Dijkstra's concurrent programming problem", *Communication of the ACM*, vol. 17, no. 8, August 1974, pp. 453–455.

[8] Lamport L., "How to make a multiprocessor computer that correctly executes multiprocess programs", *IEEE Transactions on Computers*, vol. C-28, no. 9, September 1979, pp. 690–691.

[9] Li K., and P. Hudak, "Memory coherence in shared virtual memory systems", *ACM Trans. on Computer Systems*, Vol. 7, No. 4, November 1989, pp. 321–359.

[10] Lipton R. J., and J. S. Sandberg, "PRAM: a scalable shared memory", Technical Report CS-TR-180-88, Princeton University, September 1988.

[11] Lynch N., *Distributed Algorithms*, Morgan Kaufmann Publisher Inc., San Francisco 1996.

[12] Raynal M., and A. Schiper, "A suite of formal definitions for consistency criteria in distributed shard memories", Technical Report PI n° 968, IRISA Rennes, November 1995.

[13] Tanenbaum A. S., *Distributed Operating Systems*, Prentice-Hall Inc., 1995.

Session 6:
Scheduling and Mapping

Session 6: Scheduling & Mapping

Session Chair: A.Antola

One of the most interesting and challenging aspects in parallel computation is the capability of formally representing the computation at a high level of abstraction in order to define optimal, high performance, scheduling and mapping algorithms partitioning and allocating the computation on the reference parallel machines. The papers presented in this session discuss this problem and present interesting computational models.

The first paper, "Modelling message-passing programs for static mapping" by C.Roig, A.Rippoll, M.A.Senar, F.Guirado and E.Luque, proposes a new model for mapping parallel programs: the Temporal Task Interaction Graph. With respect to current models, the proposed formalism explicitly captures the potential degree of parallel execution between adjacent tasks. Experimental results on its efficiency have been carried over by considering a number of different computational graphs and compared with the ones obtained by current literature models.

"Optimal scheduling for UET-UCT grids into fixed number of processors" by T.Andronikos, N.Koziris, G.Papakonstantinou and P.Tsanakas, is the second paper of the session and presents a possible solution to the problem of Unit Execution Time-Unit Communication Time (UET-UCT) scheduling for a task graph represented by a generalized n-dimensional grid, on bounded number of processors without allowing task duplication. The paper proves that the problem is low complexity tractable.

The third and last paper of the session "Groups in bulk synchronous parallel computing" by F.de Sande, presents an extension to the BSP model to allow the use of asynchronous BSP groups of processors. Processors groups are divided and synchronization is achieved through a generalization of the concept of barrier synchronization. The accuracy of the model and the optimality of the speedups are evaluated by considering three divide-and-conquer programs executed on a number of high performances supercomputers.

Modelling Message-Passing Programs for Static Mapping

C. Roig[1], A. Ripoll[2], M. A. Senar[2], F. Guirado[1] and E. Luque[2]

[1]Computer Science Department
e-mail:
{roig, fernando}@eup.udl.es
Universitat de Lleida
25001 Lleida - Spain

[2]Computer Science Department
e-mail:
{a.ripoll, m.a.senar, e.luque}@cc.uab.es
Universitat Autònoma de Barcelona
08193 – Bellaterra (Barcelona) - Spain

Abstract*

An efficient mapping of a parallel program in the processors is vital for achieving a high performance on a parallel computer. When the structure of the parallel program in terms of its task execution times, task dependencies, and amount communication data, is known a priori, mapping can be accomplished statically at compile time. Mapping algorithms start from a parallel application model and map automatically tasks to processors in order to minimise the execution time of the program. In this paper we discuss the current models used in mapping parallel programs: Task Precedence Graph (TPG), Task Interaction Graph (TIG) and we define a new model called Temporal Task Interaction Graph (TTIG). The contribution of the TTIG is that it enhances these two previous models with the ability to explicitly capture the potential degree of parallel execution between adjacent tasks allowing the development of efficient mapping algorithms. Experimentation had been performed in order to show the effectiveness of TTIG model for a set of graphs. The results are compared with the optimal assignment and the obtained using TIG model and they confirm that using the TTIG model, better assignments can be obtained.

1. Introduction

When a parallel program is executed on a distributed architecture, the assignment of tasks on processors is crucial to achieving good performance results.

Solving this assignment (mapping and scheduling problem) statically requires a modelling phase which analyses the code of the program and builds at compile time a model of the program, characterising the structure and the interactions of the tasks. The information obtained is represented by a weighted program graph including a node for each task of the program.

Two different models of the parallel programs are currently in use in the areas of mapping and scheduling: the *Task Precedence Graph (TPG)* [1], [2] and the *Task Interaction Graph (TIG)* [3], [4]. TPG is a directed graph where the nodes and directed edges represent the tasks and task precedence constraints respectively. On the other hand, TIG is an undirected graph where two tasks communicate if there is an edge between nodes. In this model, temporal dependencies in the execution of the tasks are not explicitly addressed: all the tasks are considered simultaneously executable and communications can take place at any time during the computation.

In both graphs, weights may be associated with the nodes and edges, representing computational and communication costs respectively. The choice of the program model depends on the abstraction level we are interested in, and on the structure of the computations.

The TPG model is well suited for computations where interactions take place only at the beginning and at the end of each task. On the other hand, programs in which communication among tasks can take place at any time are best modelled by a TIG.

Modelling the behaviour of the program by a weighted program graph with weights as *numbers* expressing the average amount of communication and computation required, has been the traditional modelling choice in the mapping and scheduling algorithms. The knowledge of these weights makes easier both, the formulation of the mapping problem and the development of algorithms for its solution. However, when the interactions between tasks take place not only at the beginning and at the end of each task, the knowledge of these weights is not significant and more information about the concurrent degree between tasks is needed in order to devise more efficient algorithms for the mapping purpose [5], [6].

* This work was supported by the CICYT under contract TIC 98-0433

1066-6192/99 $10.00 © 1999 IEEE

In this work we are concerned with the modelling of parallel applications which are designed by the programmer as a collection of communicating parallel tasks through explicit message-passing. The identity of all the tasks is known at compile-time. The paper addresses the design of a new model of parallel programs, which we call *Temporal Task Interaction Graph (TTIG)*. The TTIG combines the two predominant models used to represent parallel applications. This new model has the ability to explicitly capture the temporal behaviour of the tasks, making it useful as a unified abstraction in parallel programming environments for mapping and scheduling.

The remaining sections are organised as follows. In section 2 we discuss the role played by classical models in mapping parallel computations, and we show the necessity of defining a new model including information of program execution behaviour. Section 3 proposes the TTIG model and the methodology for building it. Section 4 presents some representative scenarios in which the new model TTIG plays an important part in the choice of good mapping, and we also illustrate the effectiveness of this model with a preliminary experimentation, finally in section 5 we comment on the main contributions.

2. Background and Motivation

In this section we briefly describe the problem arising in mapping parallel computations using traditional modelling and we underline the need for proposing new models in representing parallel programs, in order to devise new efficient mapping algorithms.

Parallel program design for distributed memory architectures can be divided into two steps. The first one is the decomposition of the problem into a set of interacting sequential sub-problems (or tasks) which can be executed in parallel. The second step is the assignment of these tasks to individual processors of the parallel architecture, also known as *mapping*, in such a way that the program execution time would be minimised. If the tasks of the parallel program have explicit precedence relationship we not only assign tasks to processors, but also have to define the order of execution of the tasks. In this case the mapping problem is referred to more specifically as the *scheduling* problem.

Consider the parallel program presented in fig. 1(a) where tasks T0, T1 and T2 communicate through the next explicit message-passing primitives:

- SEND(Tj,*msg*). A task executing this command transmits the message *msg* to task Tj.
- RCV(*msg*,Ti). A task executing this blocking primitive waits until it receives the message *msg* from task Ti.

Associated with each message there is a communication cost, c(*msg*), depending on the amount of data to be transferred.

In fig. 1(a) A,B,C,D,E,F,G,H represent the sets of instructions for each task, and t_N and c(msg_i) are the execution time and communication cost associated to each set of instructions *N* and message msg_i, respectively. Fig. 1(b) represents the corresponding Gantt chart for tasks T0, T1 and T2, assuming that each one is executed on a different processor. By the analysis of sets of instructions and communication primitives of fig. 1(a), it can be seen in the Gantt chart that task T0 starts executing the set of instructions A for 10 time units, then sends the message msg_1 to task T1 and continues executing the set of instructions B. Message msg_1 takes 10 time units to arrive at the receiving task, so task T1, after have been executing the set of instructions E, waits for 10 time units for the arrival of message msg_1 in order to be able to continue its execution and so on. From this Gantt chart we observe that tasks T0 and T1 are executed mostly in parallel, while task T2 begins its execution when T0 is almost finishing.

The temporal flow graph of fig. 1(c) represents the program execution behaviour corresponding to the previous Gantt chart. In this graph, dashed lines join sets of instructions inside each task that have to be executed sequentially, and continuous lines represent message transferences between neighbouring tasks and the communication costs associated. Using a traditional model, fig. 1(d) shows the TIG graph for the parallel program, where each node represents a task with its computation cost and edges joining communicating tasks, and have associated the corresponding communication cost. The weight of each task is the sum of all sets of instructions computation cost belonging to it (i.e. for task T0: $t_A+t_B+t_C+t_D=40$), and communication cost between two adjacent tasks is the sum of message cost involved in the transferences between them i.e. between tasks T0 and T1: c(msg_1)+c(msg_2)=10+10=20.

It can be observed that the temporal behaviour of the program shown in the Gantt chart. is not reflected by the TIG model and the same TIG could correspond to other completely different Gantt charts. It is obvious that when we are representing a parallel program with its corresponding TIG, we are losing some information about the execution program behaviour that would be very useful to know in the subsequent phase of mapping, because under the criteria of load balancing and minimum communication cost, no explicit effort can be made in using as many processors as possible of the architecture, at the same time.

A mapping policy would have to know some characteristics about temporal behaviour of tasks; i.e. for the parallel program of fig. 1(a), it would be useful to know that tasks T0 and T1 are able to execute concurrently an important part of its code and in consequence they can be assigned to different processors, but T0 and T2 are almost unable to be executed in parallel

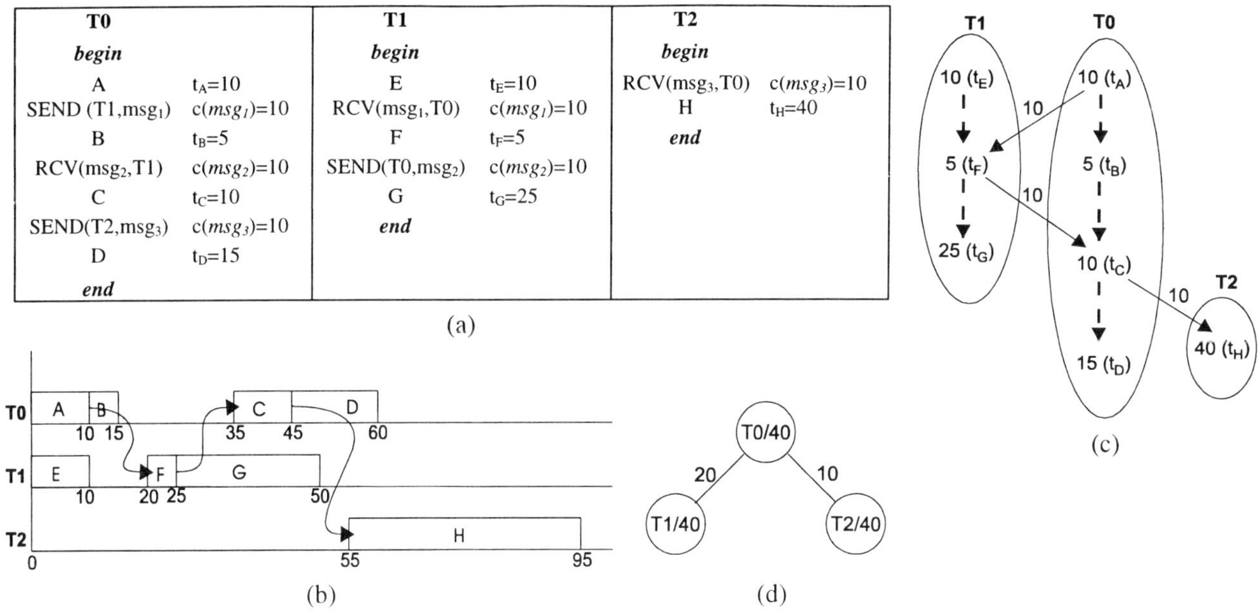

Figure 1. (a) Message-passing parallel program, (b) Gantt chart, (c) temporal flow graph and (d) temporal flow graph represented by TIG model.

so it may be a good decision to assign them to the same processor. Accordingly, a new model of parallel program should be proposed for the purpose of mapping, in order to capture the maximum *degree of parallelism* that two communicating tasks can achieve, considering their dependencies as a consequence of message-passing.

3. The Temporal Task Interaction Graph model

In this section we define a new model of parallel program representation called Temporal Task Interaction Graph (TTIG) and we describe the methodology for building it. No constraints are imposed on the structure of the program, but since it is a static approach, this model can be applied more effectively when program behaviour is loosely dependent on input values.

We define the TTIG for a parallel program as a directed graph G=(V,E) together with three maps, where:

- V={T0,T1,..,Tn} is the set of nodes, each node representing a task.
- E=(Ti,Tj) i,j∈{0,1,...,n} is the set of directed edges between tasks, representing their temporal relationship.
- w:V→**N** gives the execution time w(Ti) to each task.
- c:E→**N** associates a communication cost to edges, c(Ti,Tj) is the global amount of messages that have to be sent from Ti to Tj.
- For two connected tasks by a directed edge (Ti,Tj), p:E→[0,1] associates a normalised index p(Ti,Tj) representing the maximum degree of parallelism that Tj can achieve with Ti in its execution time, according to the existing dependencies and without considering any communication cost.

The TTIG model for a parallel program can be obtained with the following steps:

Step 1. Obtaining the Temporal Flow Graph of a parallel program.

The activity of a task in a message-passing parallel program can be seen as a sequence of periods of time during which the task is doing sequential computation of sets of instructions, and between them the task executes communication primitives. When a task executes a RCV primitive, it can enter into a wait state if the sending task hasn't already executed the corresponding SEND, or the message hasn't already arrived; so communication primitives indicate the existing precedences between tasks during execution. The first step for building the new parallel program model TTIG is to obtain the *Temporal Flow Graph (TFG),* indicating these periods of sequential computation inside each task and the communications established between them.

The TFG is a graph which reflects the execution and communication phases inside each task. Fig. 2 shows an example of TFG for a parallel program with six tasks {T0,..,T5}

Execution phases inside each TFG task are the periods of time during which the task is carrying out computation between the execution of communication primitives. We denote by $e\_p_r(Ti)$ the computation cost of execution phase *r* in task Ti, and E_P(Ti) the set of execution phases included in task Ti. In TFG of fig. 2 E_P(T1) has three execution phases with $e\_p_0(T1)=20$, $e\_p_1(T1)=15$ and $e\_p_2(T1)=35$.

Communication phases are intervals of time involved in the execution of communication primitives. We denote by $c\_p_r(Ti,Tj)$ the cost of communication phase *r* from Ti to Tj, and C_P(Ti,Tj) the set of communication phases established from Ti to Tj. In TFG of fig. 2 task T0 has four communication phases belonging to C_P(T0,T2) with $c\_p_0(T0,T2)=10$, $c\_p_1(T0,T2)=10$, $c\_p_2(T0,T2)=10$ and $c\_p_3(T0,T2)=10$.

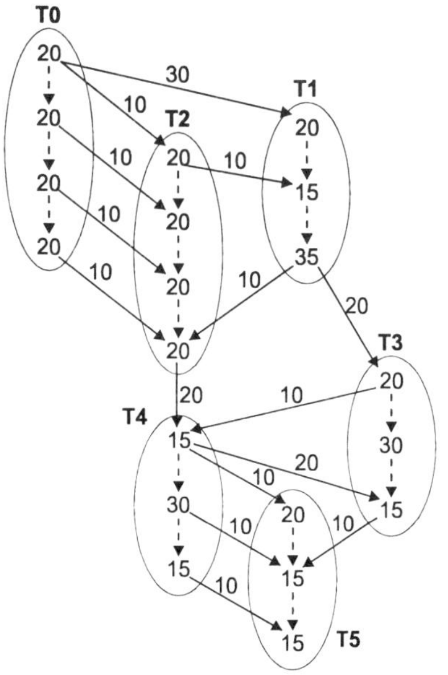

Figure 2. Example of Temporal Flow Graph.

The TFG of a parallel program can be obtained using current techniques for computation of the costs such as profiling, user estimates or compiler analysis of the program code [7], [8], [9].

Step 2. Calculation of task execution and communication costs between tasks.

Starting with the TFG obtained in step 1, the next stage is to calculate the global execution time of every task in the parallel program, and the global communication cost involved in the transferences between tasks due to the execution of communication primitives.

The execution time, w(Ti), of a task Ti can be calculated by:

$$w(Ti) = \sum_{r\in E\_P(Ti)} e\_p_r(Ti)$$

w(Ti) is the sum of the cost of all execution phases of E_P(Ti). For task T1 in the TFG of fig. 2: $w(T1)=e\_p_0(T1)+e\_p_1(T1)+e\_p_2(T1)=20+15+35=70$.

The communication cost c(Ti,Tj) from task Ti to Tj can be computed by:

$$c(Ti,Tj) = \sum_{r\in C\_P(Ti,Tj)} c\_p_r(Ti,Tj)$$

For two tasks Ti and Tj, c(Ti,Tj) is the sum of communication phases costs established from task Ti to Tj in the TFG graph. Communication cost between tasks T0 and T2 in the TFG of fig. 2 is:

$$c(T0,T2)=c\_p_0(T0,T2)+c\_p_1(T0,T2)+c\_p_2(T0,T2)+c\_p_3(T0,T2)=10+10+10+10=40.$$

Step 3. Degree of parallelism between tasks.

The next stage is to obtain the value of maximum potential degree of parallelism existing between adjacent tasks of the parallel program. For two communicating tasks Ti and Tj which transfer messages from Ti to Tj, the degree of parallelism, denoted by p(Ti,Tj), gives information about the percentage of Tj execution time that can be done in parallel with Ti, considering the existing dependencies due to message-passing between the two tasks.

The degree of parallelism between tasks is calculated considering only precedences due to communications, but without taking into account the associated communication cost. The incorporation of communication costs into the model will be considered in the mapping algorithm.

Given two communicating tasks Ti and Tj in a TFG graph, we simulate their execution starting at time t=0 considering their mutual precedences. We denote by e_i(Tj|Ti), the set of execution intervals of Tj, depending on Ti, i.e.:

$$e\_i(Tj \mid Ti) = \{[t_r^s, t_r^f]\}$$

where t_r^s, t_r^f are the starting and finishing times of the execution phase $r \in E\_P(Tj)$. Note that the intervals of e_i(Tj|Ti) are pairwise disjoint.

For tasks T0 and T1 of TFG in fig. 2, their execution simulation bearing in mind their mutual dependences and without considering any communication cost is that of fig. 3, so the execution intervals for these tasks will be the following:

e_i(T0|T1)={[0,20],[20,40],[40,60],[60,80]}
e_i(T1|T0)={[20,40],[40,55],[55,90]}

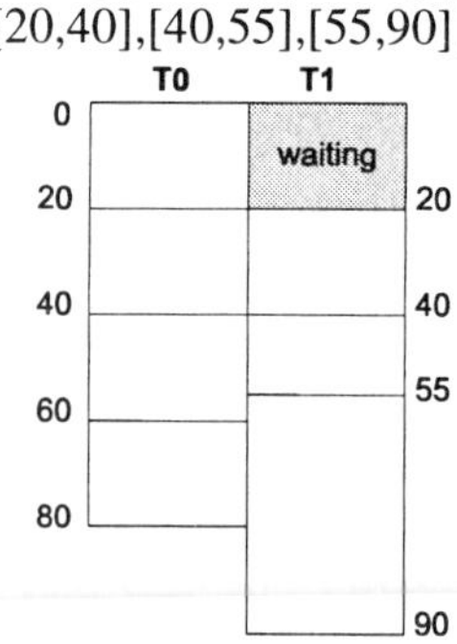

Figure 3. Execution simulation of tasks T0 and T1 of TFG of fig. 2, considering their precedences and without considering communication costs.

The Parallel Interval of Ti and Tj, denoted by PI(Ti,Tj), is the set of intervals of time while Ti and Tj can be executing concurrently.

$$PI(Ti,Tj)=\{[t_{i1},t_{i2}] \cap [t_{j1},t_{j2}] \mid [t_{i1},t_{i2}]\in e\_i(Ti|Tj), [t_{j1},t_{j2}]\in e\_i(Tj|Ti)\}$$

Note that $[t_{i1},t_{i2}] \cap [t_{j1},t_{j2}]$ either is empty or is in the interval $[\max(t_{i1},t_{j1}),\min(t_{i2},t_{j2})]$.

It can be observed that PI(Ti,Tj)=PI(Tj,Ti), because the Parallel Interval set contains common intervals of execution for both tasks. The Parallel Interval set for tasks T0 and T1 will be:

PI(T0,T1)={[20,40], [40,55], [55,60], [60,80], ∅}

The time of parallel execution of tasks Ti and Tj, denoted by TP(Ti,Tj), is the sum of the length of the intervals of PI(Ti,Tj). For tasks T0 and T1 of TFG of fig. 2:

TP(T0,T1)=(40-20)+(55-40)+(60-55)+(80-60)=60

The degree of parallelism p(Ti,Tj) for two tasks Ti and Tj in a TFG graph that communicate from Ti to Tj is calculated by:

$$p(Ti,Tj)=\frac{TP(Ti,Tj)}{w(Tj)}$$

i.e. p(Ti,Tj) gives the proportion of parallel execution that Tj can do with Ti. In the case of tasks T0 and T1 their parallel degree will be:

p(T0,T1)=TP(T0,T1)/w(T1)=60/70=0.85

Table 1 summarises the calculation of the following parameters, between the tasks (T0,T1) and (T0,T2) of the TFG of fig. 2: execution interval, parallel interval, time of parallel execution and degree of parallelism.

(Ti,Tj)	e_i(Ti|Tj)	e_i(Tj|Ti)	PI	TP	P(Ti,Tj)
(T0,T1)	[0,20] [20,40] [40,60] [60,80]	[20,40] [40,55] [55,90]	[20,40] [40,55] [55,60] [60,80] ∅	60	0,85
(T0,T2)	[0,20] [20,40] [40,60] [60,80]	[20,40] [40,60] [60,80] [80,100]	[20,40] [40,60] [60,80] ∅	60	0.75

Table 1. Execution interval sets, Parallel Interval, time of parallel execution and degree of parallelism for some tasks of the TFG in fig. 2.

Step 4. Obtaining Temporal Task Interaction Graph. With the parameters calculated in previous steps, the TTIG graph can be obtained. This is a directed graph where:

- Nodes represent tasks of parallel program with its associated execution time w(T).
- Edges indicate directed communications between tasks, and we associate two parameters to each one: communication cost, c(Ti,Tj), calculated in step 2 and the degree of parallelism, p(Ti,Tj), of successor task with its predecessor, calculated in step 3.

The representation of the TTIG model for TFG of fig. 2 is the graph of fig. 4.

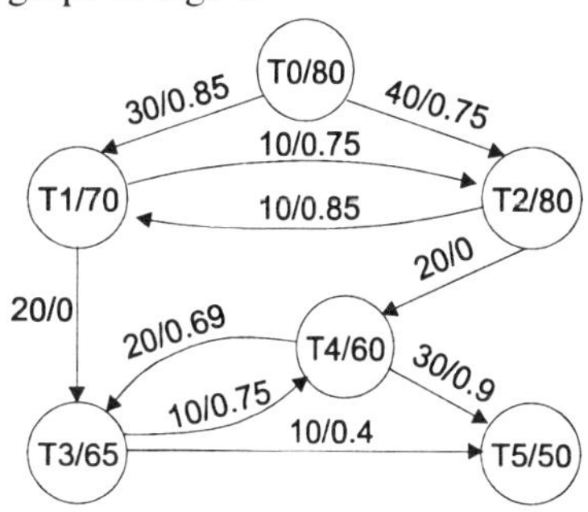

Figure 4. TTIG graph derived from TFG in fig.2.

The TTIG model integrates the two classical models TIG and TPG. In a TIG graph, adjacent tasks are considered simultaneously executable as it is the case of having a degree of parallelism of 1 between them in the TTIG, and on the other hand, in the TPG model there is a precedence relationship between adjacent tasks, and they have to be executed sequentially; this situation is indicated with a degree of parallelism of 0 in the TTIG. Moreover, with other values of degree of parallelism, any other situation can be stated in the TTIG graph, so this is a versatile model with no restriction about the temporal behaviour of the parallel program to be modelled.

4. Mapping a Temporal Task Interaction Graph

The objective in mapping a program graph to an architecture graph is the minimisation of the expected execution time of the parallel program on the target architecture. The quality of a given mapping will depend on the execution time of the parallel program. A mapping has better quality if the obtained assignment reduces the execution time of the application in comparison with its execution time with a different assignment. Thus, the mapping problem can be seen as an optimisation problem by defining a cost function that is directly related to the execution time and must be minimised.

In practice, the execution time of a program modelled using classical models like TIG is difficult to evaluate due to the appearance of run-time dependencies. Therefore, a set of cost functions have been proposed in the literature in order to simplify the real situation and facilitate use in a certain heuristic. One of the cost functions proposed for the TIG graph model is the *minimax* [3]. In the model of the minimax cost function, the cost incurred by each processor for a certain mapping f, known as *Processor*

Work Load (PWL), is the total cost due to the computation and communication of all the tasks mapped to it (PWL = computation cost + communication cost). Thus, the minimax cost function is defined as the maximum PWL for all of the processors. The objective of a mapping algorithm, resulting in the minimax criterion, would be to minimise the maximum Processor Work Load *(min(max cost(f))*.

In this section we show, using representative examples, that the classical model TIG and its associated cost function, finds poor efficient assignments due to the lack of information that the model provides. However, if the degree of parallelism between tasks included in TTIG model is used as a predominant parameter, better assignments are obtained. In the following examples we use the minimax cost function when the mapping is done using the TIG model, and the underlying system is a full-connected architecture with two processors {P0, P1}.

Example 1. Influence of degree of parallelism in the assignment.

Starting from a parallel program code, the TFG shown in fig. 5(a) and the TIG graph of fig. 5(b) are derived. Using the minimax cost function, the mapping of TIG graph in a two processor architecture will be tasks T0 and T1 to processor P0 and task T2 to P1. The assignment shown in fig. 5(c) obtains the best cost for the minimax function.

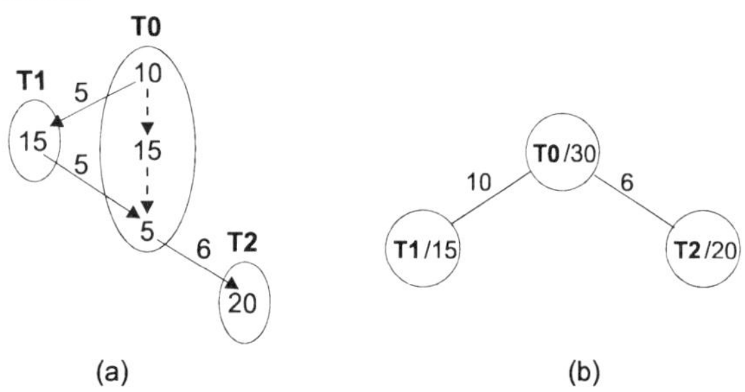

P0:T0,T1 P1:T2
PWL_0=comput(45)+comm.(6)=51 PWL_1=comput(20)+comm.(6)=26
cost(f)=51

(c)

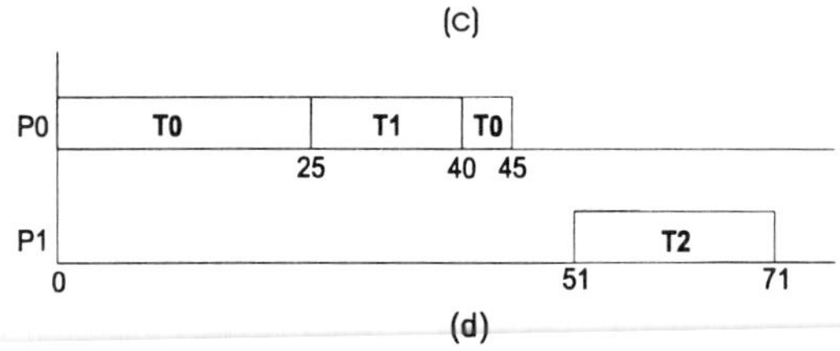

Figure 5. (a) TFG, (b) TIG model (c) TIG assignment and (d) execution simulation.

Fig. 5(d) shows the execution simulation of the program with the assignment of fig. 5(c). As can be observed this assignment brings about an important problem of efficiency at execution time, because it does not take advantage of potential system parallelism.

On the other hand, starting from the TFG graph of fig. 5(a), our approach will provide the TTIG graph of fig. 6(a). By the analysis of TTIG a mapping strategy will be able to decide, to assign tasks T0 and T2 to the same processor because the degree of parallelism is 0 and therefore task T2 is not able to start until T0 finished. With this assignment, fig. 6(b) shows the corresponding timing execution diagram.

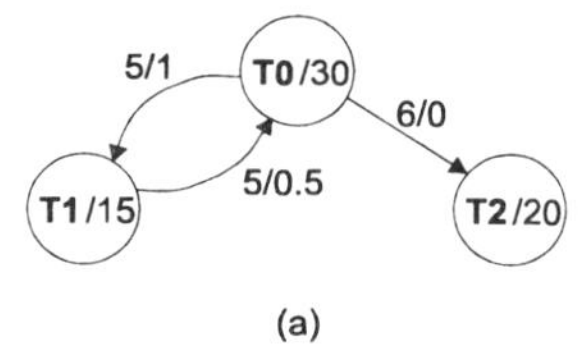

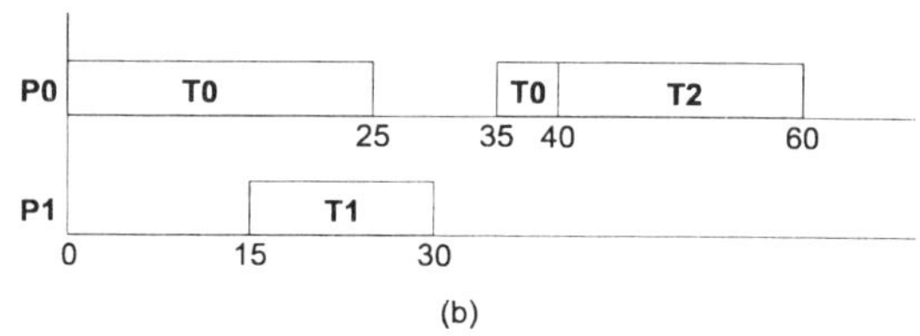

Figure 6. (a) TTIG model and (b) Execution simulation of TTIG assignment.

Example 2. Assignment sensitiveness to variations of the estimated costs.

It is worthwhile to underlining that estimated values for computation and communication costs associated to a graph can only give information about the behaviour of the program. Thus, if the behaviour of the program is not predictable, i.e. it shows great variation depending on the input values, the values of these weights have very poor significance, and dynamic solutions to the mapping are the most appropriate. However, assignments obtained for a TIG using a minimax cost function are strongly dependent on estimated values, and small variations can produce different assignments as we see below.

Suppose that we have a parallel program with the TFG of fig. 7(a), and the communication cost from task T0 to task T2 can be estimated with a little variation between 12 and 9, as it is shown in the edge of the graph. The corresponding TIG and TTIG models are represented in fig. 7(b) and fig. 7(c), respectively.

Considering that communication cost between tasks T0 and T2 is 12, the mapping of TIG will be P0:T0,T2 and P1:T1 with an associated cost(f)=70. The same task allocation would be derived for TTIG model because tasks T0 and T2 have to be assigned to the same processor given that its degree of parallelism is lower than that existing between T0 and T1.

On the other hand, if the communication cost from task T0 to T2 is estimated to be 9 instead of 12; the TIG assignment will be different: P0:T0,T1 and P1:T2 because this allocation provides a better value of the cost function cost(f)=69. The Gantt chart of this execution is shown in fig. 8.

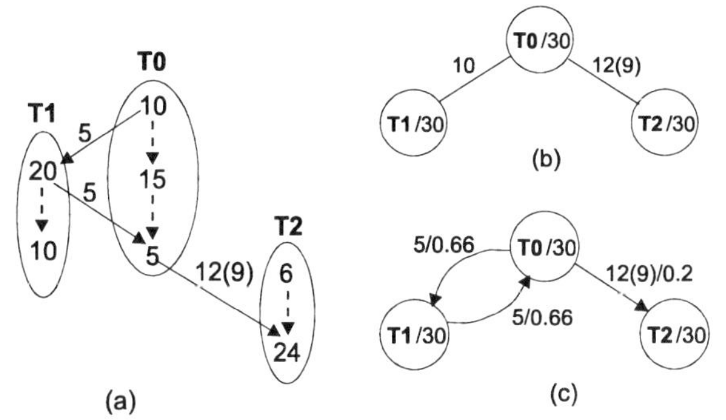

Figure 7. (a) TFG, (b) TIG model and (c) TTIG model of example 2.

However, this change in communication cost does not have any influence in task assignment when the TTIG model is considered, because the degree of parallelism between the tasks T0 and T2 is much lower, and therefore they will continue to be assigned to the same processor. fig. 9 shows the Gantt chart corresponding to this assignment.

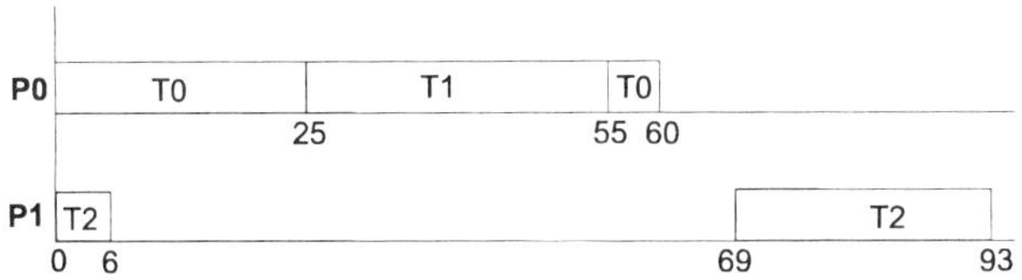

Figure 8. Gantt chart of TFG of fig. 7(a) under TIG assignment.

As can be seen, the TTIG model shows itself to be less sensitive than the TIG model to small changes in computation and communication cost values. This will therefore improve mapping quality and simplify the parameter evaluation tool.

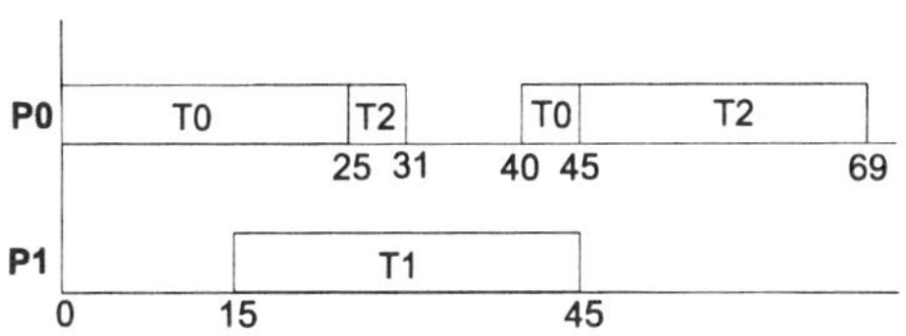

Figure 9. Gantt chart of TFG of fig. 7(a) under TTIG assignment.

Preliminary results

With the aim of testing the effectiveness of the newly defined model, we have done an initial experimentation on mapping parallel programs using the TTIG model. The performance obtained with the TTIG is discussed in comparison with that obtained using the classical model TIG, and also with the optimal assignment. The experimentation is done with a set of small synthetic graphs which exhibit either regular and irregular structures and assuming fully-connected architecture with different number of processors.

The mapping for each TIG graph was done using the heuristic CREMA, this is a mapping tool based on the minimax criterion, that provides excellents results compared with other mapping algorithms of TIG's existing in the literature [10]. We call **Ttig** to the global execution time obtained using TIG assignment.

The mapping approach of the TTIG graph was done taking into account the following criteria:

- Load balancing.
- Minimisation of communication cost
- Identification of more dependent tasks according to their degree of parallelism.

These criteria have been applied in the following way; first we determined the computational cost to be assigned to each processor, in order to achieve load balancing; after that, we analysed communication costs together with the degree of parallelism between tasks, in order to identify which are the more dependent tasks. Then, under the condition of load balancing and following the tasks of the TTIG in a qualitative order according to the edges direction, we have carried out the mapping, giving priority to the allocation of more dependent tasks to the same processor. We call **Tttig** the global execution time of the graph obtained under TTIG assignment.

In order to compare the efficiency of our results, an optimal allocation was computed using an exhaustive search of all possible combinations. Due to the NP-completeness of the search algorithm applied to obtain optimal allocations, we have restricted our experimentation to small graphs. We call **Top** the global execution time obtained using the optimal assignment of a graph.

Table 2 illustrates the performance obtained for the graphs evaluated using TIG assignment (Ttig), TTIG assignment (Tttig) and the optimal assignment. (Top). These times have been obtained using the parallel environment simulator [11].

The graphs used in this preliminary experimentation have 6 or 10 tasks, with a computation cost between 70 and 90 each. The ratio between the computation cost and communication cost is from 5 to 15, and the average degree of parallelism existing between the tasks of the graph is from 0.3 to 0.7.

In the analysis of the results obtained in table 2, we can observe that by the use of the TTIG model we can obtain significant improvements in the global execution time which can be up to 40% better compared with the time obtained using the TIG model (see gr2). We can also see that the graphs gr3, gr4 and gr5 have a lower difference for the values Ttig and Tttig, these correspond to graphs that exhibit a medium degree of parallelism between tasks less than 0.5, as long as the rest of the graphs have a medium degree of parallelism greater than 0.5. This means that when the medium degree of parallelism is decreasing in the graph, there is less option of executing the tasks simultaneously and indeed, the improvement in performance is not so significant.

Graph	n. tasks	n. proc.	Ttig	Tttig	Top
gr1	6	2	363	325	315
		3	342	305	293
		4	342	305	293
gr2	6	2	480	290	290
		3	340	270	270
		4	340	260	260
gr3	6	2	267	267	256
		3	256	256	248
		4	251	226	226
gr4	6	2	391	390	390
		3	405	325	325
		4	374	315	315
gr5	10	2	486	486	486
		3	511	447	447
		4	438	432	425
gr6	10	2	500	410	401
		3	370	345	345
		4	375	345	345
gr7	10	2	575	495	475
		3	505	400	385
		4	545	375	365
gr8	10	2	748	565	522
		3	463	463	441
		4	457	433	426

Table 2. Experimentation results.

Another aspect that is worth emphasising is that for each graph the value of Tttig time decreases as the number of processors increases, so using the TTIG model we obtain an execution time in accordance with the number of processors, as also happens with the optimal time.

In general, when the mapping is carried out using the TTIG model with the criteria previously indicated, the improvement in the performance is very significant, and in many cases the global execution time is near optimal or even equal to it. As the results are encouraging, we can conclude that the TTIG is a suitable model for representing message-passing applications, and new efficient mapping heuristics can be developed in future research, based on its characteristics.

5. Conclusions

This paper has investigated the problem arising in mapping parallel applications by using the traditional models Task Precedence Graph (TPG) and Task Interaction Graph (TIG). A new model, Temporal Task Interaction Graph (TTIG), has been proposed in order to represent parallel programs with message-passing.

The TTIG combines the two previous models currently in use in the areas of mapping and scheduling, and has the ability to explicitly capture the temporal behaviour of the tasks.

We have shown in this paper, that estimating the degree of parallelism between tasks at compile time is an important step towards the development of efficient mapping strategies. A mapping algorithm has to pay particular attention to the temporal behaviour of the program in order to make well-taken decisions: which tasks are able to execute concurrently on different processors in order to balance the workload processors, and which tasks should be allocated on the same processor to minimise the interprocessor communication cost.

The effectiveness of the new model has been established on a set of graphs and the results are very encouraging.

References

[1] Y-K. Kwok and I. Ahmad. Dynamic Critical-Path Scheduling: an Effective Technique for Allocating Task Graphs to Multiprocessors. *IEEE-Trans. on Parallel and Distributed Systems. Vol. 7, n. 5, pp. 506-521, May 1996.*

[2] H. Kasahara and S. Narita, Practical Multiprocessor Scheduling Algorithms for Efficient Parallel Processing. *IEEE Trans. Computers, vol. 33, no. 11, pp. 1023-1029, Nov. 1984*

[3] P. Sadayappan, R Ercal and J, Ramanujam. Cluster Partitioning Approaches to Mapping Parallel Programs onto Hypercube. *Parallel Computing 13 pp. 1-16, 1990.*

[4] Virginia Mary Lo. Heuristic algorithms for Task Assignment in Distributed Systems. *IEEE-Transactions on Computers. Vol. 37, n. 11, pp 1384-1397, Nov. 1988.*

[5] Chi-Chung Hui and Samuel T. Chanson. Allocating Task Interaction Graph to Processors in Heterogeneous Networks. *IEEE Transactions on Parallel and Distributed Systems. vol. 8, n. 9, pp 908-925, Sep. 1997.*

[6] M. A. Senar, A. Ripoll, A. Cortes, E. Luque. Clustering and Reassignment-base Mapping Strategy for Message-Passing Architectures. Int. Par. Proc. Symp&Sym. On Par. Dist. Proc. (IPPS/SPDP 98) 415-421. IEEE CS Press. USA, 1998

[7] T. Fahringer Compile-Time Estimation of Communication Costs for Data Parallel Programs. *J. Parallel and Distributed Computing, vol. 39, pp. 46-65, 1996.*

[8] M. Gupta and P. Banerjee Compile-Time Estimation of Communication Costs on Multicomputers. *Proc. Sixth Int'l Parallel Processing Symp,. Mar. 1992.*

[9] K. Kennedy, N. McIntosh and K.S. McKinley. Static Performance Estimation in a Parallelizing Compiler. *Technical Report TR 91-174, Dept. of Computer Science, Rice Univ., Dec. 1991.*

[10] M.A. Senar, A. Ripoll, A. Cortes, E. Luque, Performance Comparison of Strategies for Static Mapping of Parallel Programs. *High Performance Computing and Networking (HPCN97) Lecture Notes in Computer Science 225, 575-587. Springer. Germany, 1997*

[11] C. Roig. Scheduling Algorithms for Task Precedence Graphs with Variable Communication Delay and Execution Times (in spanish). *Master Thesis, Universidad Autónoma de Barcelona 1996.*

Optimal Scheduling for UET-UCT Grids Into Fixed Number of Processors

Theodore Andronikos, Nectarios Koziris,
George Papakonstantinou and Panayiotis Tsanakas
National Technical University of Athens
Dept. of Electrical and Computer Engineering
Computer Science Division
Zografou Campus, Zografou 15773, Greece
e-mail: {tedandr, nkoziris, papakon}@cslab.ece.ntua.gr

Abstract

The n-dimensional grid is one of the most representative patterns of data flow in parallel computation. Many scientific algorithms, which require nearest neighbor communication in a lattice space, are modeled by a task graph with the properties of a simple or enhanced grid. In this paper we consider an enhanced model of the n-dimensional grid by adding extra diagonal edges and allowing unequal boundaries for each dimension. First, we calculate the optimal makespan for the generalized UET-UCT (Unit Execution Time – Unit Communication Time) grid topology and, then, we establish the minimum number of processors required, to achieve the optimal makespan. We present the optimal time schedule, using unbounded and bounded number of processors, without allowing task duplication. This paper proves that UET-UCT scheduling of generalized n-dimensional grids into fixed number of processors is low complexity tractable.

1 Introduction

Task scheduling is one of the most important and difficult problems in parallel systems. Since the general scheduling problem is known to be NP-complete (see Ullman [15]), researchers have given attention to other methods such as heuristics, approximation algorithms etc. In their paper Papadimitriou and Yannakakis [13] proved the intractability of the general scheduling problem of a task graph with arbitrary communication and computation times and proposed a clever heuristic with guaranteed worst performance twice the optimum makespan. In addition to this, Gerasoulis and Yang have proposed in [10], [17] the Dominant Sequence Clustering, a low complexity heuristic for general task graph scheduling, which is based on the critical path of tasks. On the other hand, by restricting the general scheduling problem to instances with simple properties, we may come up with tractable solutions. For example, Jung et al. in [9] have presented a polynomial algorithm that finds the optimal makespan when the communication cost is constant and task duplication is allowed.

When both computation and communication times are restricted to have unit time length, it is known that scheduling general UET-UCT graphs with bounded number of processors is NP-complete, as Rayward-Smith proved in [14], or Picouleau in [13] by reduction from the unbounded UET-UCT instance. Even the case of unlimited processors, when no task duplication is allowed, is in general polynomially intractable [13]. On the other hand, using task duplication, Colin et Chretienne in [8] have presented a polynomial optimal schedule for arbitrary task graphs with UET and SCT (Small Communication Times, thus including UCT). Since the arbitrary task graph scheduling with UET-UCT and no duplication with unlimited processors is NP-complete, researchers have focused on special cases of DAGs. In [6] Chretienne presented an algorithm linear in the cardinality of the vertices of the graph, for optimal makespan on SCT in-trees and out-trees (thus covering UCT). In addition to this, there exist polynomial optimal solutions for Series-Parallel digraphs, bipartite graphs and trees with UCT as surveyed in [7].

This paper solves the problem of UET-UCT scheduling for task graphs having the form of a grid, on bounded number of processors, assuming no duplication. Grids and particularly generalized grids are typical task graphs, which model most of the signal processing algorithms and linear algebra methods such as matrix multiplication, LU decomposition etc. Although the general UET-UCT task graph scheduling problem into fixed number of processors is NP-complete, we restrict ourselves to grids which, as we prove, have low

1066-6192/99 $10.00 © 1999 IEEE

complexity tractable schedules. We extend the simple grid model of [4] by considering generalized n-dimensional grids. In [1], [2] we have proved that the problem of time and space scheduling for generalized grids is has a polynomial time closed formula solution, when unbounded number of processors are available. We have calculated the *optimal makespan* for UET-UCT grids and *optimal number of processors*, i.e., the minimum number of processors required to achieve the optimal makespan. In this paper we extend the scheduling strategy presented in [1],[2] by considering bounded number of processors. We present an optimal time and space scheduling policy for UET-UCT grids. Our schedule partitions the vertices of the grid into disjoint sets that lie on a family of parallel hyperplanes. Each hyperplane contains vertices, which are executed on different processors at the same time if unlimited processors are available. Since the number of available processors is less than the cardinality of vertices in most of the hyperplanes ("large hyperplanes"), we use a folding strategy for space scheduling. If m processors are available, we use shifts of m vertices for each execution step. Our method is based on the fact that for every "large" hyperplane, there are m vertices available for execution, which are ancestors of m already executed points of a previous hyperplane.

The paper is organized as follows: In Section 2 we give the notation and some definitions and in Section 3 we present the optimal UET-UCT makespan for n-dimensional generalized grids and the minimum number of processors adequate for the optimal makespan. In Section 4 we establish a tight lower bound for optimal makespan for UET-UCT grids when the number of processors is fixed and a polynomial scheduling strategy that realizes this lower bound, and, thus, is optimal. Finally, in Section 5 we present an illustrative example of a 2-D and a 3-D grid optimally scheduled on unbounded and fixed number of processors.

2 Preliminary Concepts

2.1. Notation

In the rest of the paper the following notation is used:

- N is the set of non negative integers (naturals).
- n is the dimension of the grid.
- G_U is the n-dimensional grid with terminal point $U=(u_1, \ldots, u_n)$.

2.2. Basic Concepts

The directed edges of a grid represent **precedence constraints** that have to be satisfied in order to correctly complete the tasks represented by the vertices. The formal definition of the schedule must reflect our intuition that a vertex **j** correctly begins its execution at instant k iff *all the vertices* $\mathbf{i} \in IN(\mathbf{j})$ *have completed their execution and communicated their results (if needed) to* **j** *by that moment.*

- The **initial segment** of N^n with **terminal point** $U=(u_1, \ldots, u_n) \in N^n$, denoted N_U, is the set $\{(k_1, \ldots, k_n) \in N^n \mid 0 \le k_i \le u_i, 1 \le i \le n\}$.
- In case n=1, the initial segment $\{k \in N \mid 0 \le k \le u\}$ is denoted N_u.
- Let $\mathbf{e}_i$ be $(\underbrace{0,\ldots,0}_{i-1},1,\underbrace{0,\ldots,0}_{n-i})$, $1 \le i \le n$. The (n-dimensional) grid vector set, denoted GVS, is the set $\{\mathbf{d}=(d_1, \ldots, d_n) \in N^n \mid \mathbf{d}=\lambda_1\mathbf{e}_1+ \ldots +\lambda_n\mathbf{e}_n, \text{ where } \lambda_i \in \{0, 1\} \wedge \sum_{i=1}^{n}\lambda_i>0\}$.

Definition 2.1. The generalized n-dimensional grid with terminal point **U**, denoted G_U, is the DAG with vertices the set N_U and directed edges the set $\{(\mathbf{i}, \mathbf{j}) \in N_U^2 \mid \mathbf{j}=\mathbf{i}+\mathbf{d}, \mathbf{d} \in GVS\}$. ■

Definition 2.2. We impose a **linear** ordering among the points of N_U, which we call **lexicographic ordering**. Let $\mathbf{i}=(m_1, \ldots, m_n)$ and $\mathbf{j}=(k_1, \ldots, k_n)$ be two points of N_U. We say that **i** is less than **j** and we write **i**<**j** iff $m_r<k_r$ for some r, $1 \le r \le n$, and, if r>1, $m_i=k_i$, $1 \le i \le r-1$. ■

In the rest of the paper we use the lexicographic ordering of the vertices, i.e., when we write **i**<**j**, we mean that **i** is lexicographically less than **j**.

Definition 2.3. For every vertex **j** of a grid G_U, we define the following sets:

(1) $IN(\mathbf{j}) = \{\mathbf{i} \in N_U \mid \mathbf{j}=\mathbf{i}+\mathbf{d}, \text{ where } \mathbf{d} \in GVS\}$, and

(2) $OUT(\mathbf{j}) = \{\mathbf{i} \in N_U \mid \mathbf{i}=\mathbf{j}+\mathbf{d}, \text{ where } \mathbf{d} \in GVS\}$. ■

Definition 2.4. A **schedule** for the grid G_U, denoted $S(G_U)$, is an ordered couple (TIME, PROC), where TIME and PROC are the **time** and **processor schedules**, respectively, defined as follows:

(1) TIME is a function from N_U onto N_k, for some $k \in N$, such that:

TIME(**j**)=t ⇔ the execution of task **j** begins at moment t, and

(2) PROC is a function from N_U onto N_m, for some $m \in N$, such that:

PROC(**j**)=r ⇔ task **j** is assigned to processor r, with the additional requirement

(3) $\forall \mathbf{i} \in IN(\mathbf{j})$ $\quad TIME(\mathbf{j})-TIME(\mathbf{i}) \ge \begin{cases} p, & \text{if } PROC(\mathbf{i}) = PROC(\mathbf{j}) \\ p+c, & \text{if } PROC(\mathbf{i}) \neq PROC(\mathbf{j}) \end{cases}$, where:

p is the processing time and *c* the communication delay. ■

Remark 2.1.

(1) In UET-UCT grids we assume *p*=1 and *c*=1.

(2) Condition (3) is necessary in order to ensure the **validity** of the schedule, i.e., that the precedence constraints are respected. ▲

Definition 2.5. Let TIME and PROC be functions from N_U onto N_k and N_m, respectively, for some k, m∈ N.

- The **makespan** of the time schedule TIME, denoted M_{TIME}, is k+*p*, where *p* is the processing time.
- The **processor-span** of the processor schedule PROC, denoted P_{PROC}, is m+1. ■

Clearly, the makespan gives the completion time of the last task and, hence, the time required for the completion of the whole grid, and the processor-span gives the number of processors required by the specific schedule.

Definition 2.6. We now give the following definitions:

- Assuming unbounded number of processors, a time schedule is optimal, denoted $TIME_{OPT}$, iff its makespan is minimal.
- In this case a processor schedule is optimal, denoted $PROC_{OPT}$, iff it realizes $TIME_{OPT}$ using the minimal processor-span.
- Assuming m processors, a time schedule is optimal, denoted $TIME_{m\text{-}OPT}$, iff its makespan is minimal among all time schedules that use m processors.
- Assuming m processors, a processor schedule is optimal, denoted $PROC_{m\text{-}OPT}$, iff it realizes $TIME_{m\text{-}OPT}$. ■

In [2] and [3] the following result was proved:

Fact 1. Let G_U be an n-dimensional generalized grid with terminal point **U** and let TIME be a time schedule for G_U. Then: M_{TIME} = TIME(U)+*p*, where *p* is the processing time. ❐

3 Properties of UET-UCT Grids

In order to achieve the execution of a grid in optimal time, we partition its vertices into parallel hyperplanes, taking into account the presence of communication delays. These hyperplanes contain the vertices that can be executed in parallel; if two points belong to the same hyperplane, they can be computed at the same moment and if they belong to successive hyperplanes they can be computed at successive moments.

Definition 3.1. Given the n-dimensional UET-UCT grid G_U, with **U**=(u_1, …, u_n), we give the following definitions:

- The **length** of G_U along the i-th dimension, 1≤i≤n, denoted L^i_U, is $2(u_1+ \ldots +u_{i-1}+u_{i+1}+ \ldots +u_n)+u_i$.
- $\Pi^i_k = \{(k_1, \ldots, k_n)\in N_U \mid 2(x_1+ \ldots +x_{i-1}+x_{i+1}+ \ldots +x_n)+x_i=k,\ k\in N\}$, 1≤i≤n.
- $\Pi^i_{\max} = max\{\,|\Pi^i_k| \mid 0\le k\le L^i_U\,\}$, 1≤i≤n. ■

Geometrically, Π^i_k consists of the common points of the grid G_U and the n-1 dimensional hyperplane $2(x_1+ \ldots +x_{i-1}+x_{i+1}+ \ldots +x_n)+x_i=k$.

Every vertex **j**=(k_1, …, k_n) of the grid has a **maximal** coordinate, i.e., a coordinate k_i for which $k_i\ge k_r$, 1≤r≤n. In [1] and [2] several important results for UET-UCT grids were shown. We state these results here, without proof:

Fact 2. Let G_U be an n-dimensional generalized grid with terminal point **U** and let **j**=(k_1, …, k_n) be a point of N_U with maximal coordinate k_i. The earliest computation time of **j** is $2\sum_{\substack{r=0\\ r\ne i}}^{n} k_r + k_i$.

This result demonstrates that in UET-UCT grids not all the n dimensions of the grid are equivalent. If our aim is to minimize the execution time of a vertex **j**, then we must pay special attention to the "maximal coordinate" of **j**, in the sense that the same processor must execute all points along this direction. This scheduling strategy has the effect of eliminating the communication overhead along this direction. Hence, in order to achieve the optimal parallel time of a UET-UCT grid, we have to give precedence to the maximal coordinate of the terminal point.

Fact 3. Let G_U be a UET-UCT grid with terminal point **U**=(u_1, …, u_n) and let $TIME_{OPT}$ be an optimal time schedule for G_U. Then, we have $M_{TIME_{OPT}} = 2(u_1+ \ldots +u_{i-1}+u_{i+1}+ \ldots +u_n)+u_i+1 = L^i_U +1$.

Fact 4. Let G_U be a UET-UCT grid with terminal point **U**=(u_1, …, u_n). Then, the following hold:

$$|\Pi^i_k| = \binom{n+\left\lfloor \frac{k}{2}\right\rfloor -1}{n-1} + \sum_{r=1}^{n}(-1)^r \sum \binom{n+\left\lfloor \frac{k}{2}\right\rfloor -(u'_1+1)-\ldots-(u'_r+1)-1}{n\text{-}1}$$

, $0\le k\le L^i_U$ and:

$$u'_i = \begin{cases} \left\lfloor \frac{u_i}{2} \right\rfloor, & \text{if k is even} \\ \left\lfloor \frac{u_i-1}{2} \right\rfloor, & \text{if k is odd} \end{cases}, \text{ and}$$

$u'_r = u_r$, 1≤r≠i≤n.

Fact 5. Let G_U be a UET-UCT grid with terminal point **U**=(u_1, …, u_n). Then, we have:

- $|\Pi^i_0| \le |\Pi^i_2| \le \ldots \le |\Pi^i_{2m_e}| \ge |\Pi^i_{2(m_e+1)}| \ge \ldots \ge \left|\Pi^i_{2\left\lfloor \frac{L^i_U}{2}\right\rfloor}\right|$,

  where $m_e = \left\lfloor \frac{L^i_U}{4} \right\rfloor$, and
- $|\Pi^i_1| \le |\Pi^i_3| \le \ldots \le |\Pi^i_{2m_o+1}| \ge |\Pi^i_{2(m_o+1)+1}| \ge \ldots \ge \left|\Pi^i_{2\left\lfloor \frac{L^i_U-1}{2}\right\rfloor+1}\right|$,

where $m_o = \left\lfloor \frac{\left\lfloor \frac{L^i_U - 1}{2} \right\rfloor}{2} \right\rfloor$.

Fact 6. Let G_U be a UET-UCT grid with terminal point $\mathbf{U}=(u_1, \ldots, u_n)$. Then, we have:

$$\Pi^i_{max} = \left| \Pi^i_{2\left\lfloor \frac{L^i_U}{4} \right\rfloor} \right|.$$

Fact 7. Let G_U be a UET-UCT grid with terminal point $\mathbf{U}=(u_1, \ldots, u_n)$, let u_i be a maximal coordinate of $\mathbf{U}$ and let $PROC_{OPT}$ be an optimal processor schedule for G_U. Then, we have:

$$P_{PROC_{OPT}} = \Pi^i_{max} = \left| \Pi^i_{2\left\lfloor \frac{L^i_U}{4} \right\rfloor} \right|.$$

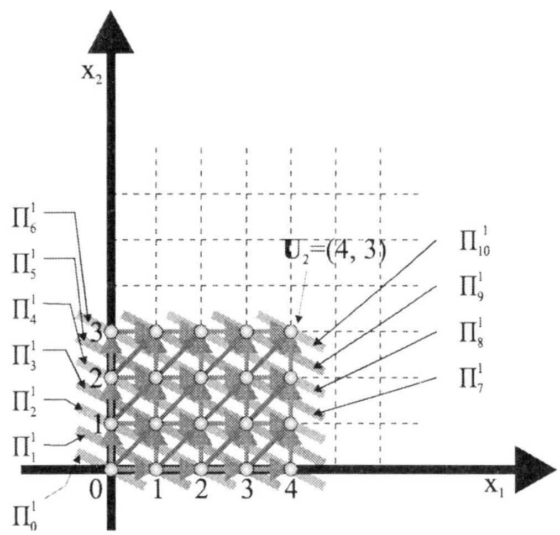

Figure 3.1. An optimal schedule for G_{U_2}.

Example 3.1. In this example we examine the issues involved in scheduling 2-dimensional grids using unbounded number of processors. Given an arbitrary **j** which is executed at time k, consider the set OUT(**j**). Under any optimal scheduling strategy, *at most one* **i**∈ OUT(**j**) will be executed at time k+1 and all others at later time instants. Obviously, the issue here is the selection of the **i** that will lead to the optimal makespan. As we have pointed out the maximal coordinate of the grid determines this selection.

Further, notice that in the UET-UCT case, due to the communication delays, there is no *unique* family of optimal hyperplanes for every grid. Instead, the family of optimal hyperplanes depends on the maximal coordinate of the terminal point. For G_{U_2} (see Figure 3.1) the optimal hyperplanes are $x_1+2x_2=k$, whereas for $G_{U_2'}$ (see Figure 3.2) the optimal hyperplanes are $2x_1+x_2=k$, $0 \le k \le 10$. ❒

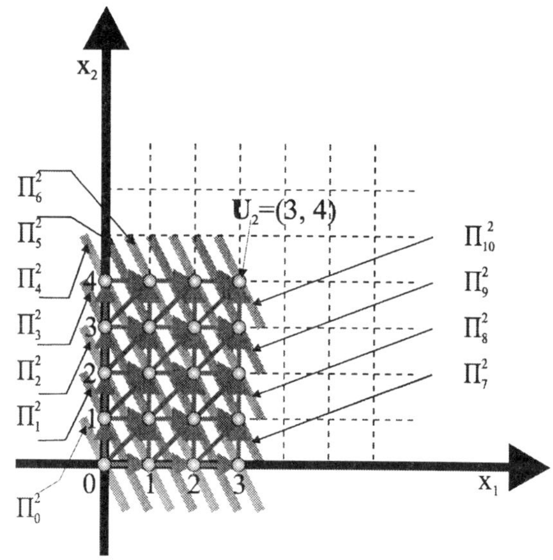

Figure 3.2. An optimal schedule for $G_{U_2'}$.

Example 3.2. The optimal schedule for the grid G_{U_3} is depicted in Figure 3.3 and Figure 3.4. We must stress the fact that in order to achieve the optimal time schedule for the terminal point, we are forced to execute a specific set of points *at a later time*. In the case of G_{U_3} these points are of the form $k_2\mathbf{e}_2+k_3\mathbf{e}_3$, where $0 \le k_2 \le 2$ and $0 \le k_3 \le 1$ (see Figure 3.3).

Table 1. The optimal time schedule for G_{U_3}.

	P_0	P_1	P_2	P_3	P_4	P_5
0	(0,0,0)					
1	(1,0,0)					
2	(2,0,0)	(0,0,1)	(0,1,0)			
3	(3,0,0)	(1,0,1)	(1,1,0)			
4		(2,0,1)	(2,1,0)	(0,1,1)	(0,2,0)	
5		(3,0,1)	(3,1,0)	(1,1,1)	(1,2,0)	
6				(2,1,1)	(2,2,0)	(0,2,1)
7				(3,1,1)	(3,2,0)	(1,2,1)
8						(2,2,1)
9						(3,2,1)

Notice that the vertices with the same y and z coordinate must be executed on the same processor, which means that the optimal time schedule must execute the vertices of Π^1_k at instant k, $0 \le k \le 9$ (see Figure 3.4). Consequently, we have $S_{TIME_{OPT}}(U_3)=9$. The optimal time schedule is given in Table 1. It is important to note that this schedule is not optimal in terms of processors. ❒

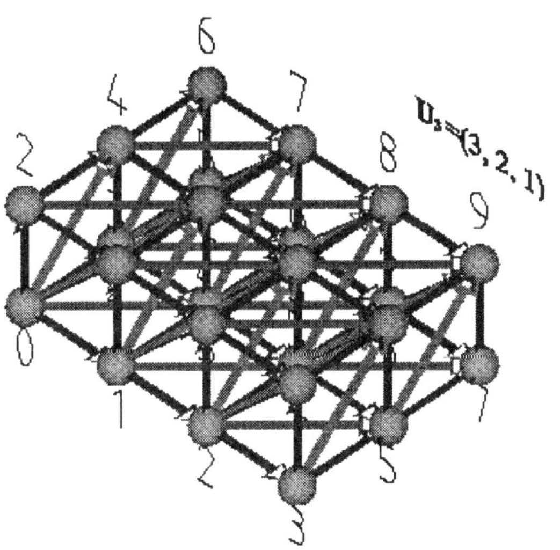

Figure 3.3. Execution Time for G_{U_3}.

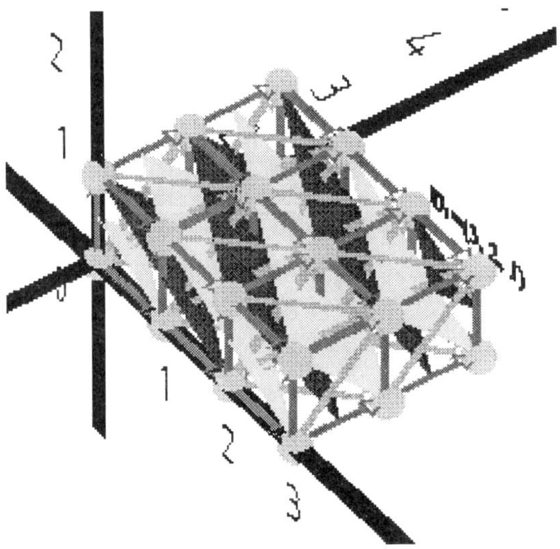

Figure 3.4. An optimal scheduling of G_{U_3}.

4 UET-UCT Grids & Fixed Number of Processors

4.1. Lower and Upper Bounds for the Optimal Makespan

In this section we establish lower and upper bounds for the optimal time schedule under the assumption that the number of processors is fixed. In the rest of this section we denote m the number of processors.

In the rest of the paper we assume that for the terminal point $\mathbf{U}=(u_1, \ldots, u_n)$ of the n-dimensional UET-UCT grid G_U we have $u_1 \geq u_2 \geq \ldots \geq u_n$. We can do that without any loss of generality because for every grid G_U, with terminal point $\mathbf{U}=(u_1, \ldots, u_n)$, there exists an isomorphic grid $G_{U'}$ in normal form with terminal point $\mathbf{U}'=(u_1', \ldots, u_n')$, where $(u_1', \ldots, u_n')$ is a permutation of $(u_1, \ldots, u_n)$. This assumption will greatly facilitate the statement of the subsequent results of this paper, regarding the UET-UCT case.

Lemma 4.1. Let G_U be a UET-UCT grid with terminal point $\mathbf{U}=(u_1, \ldots, u_n)$ such that $u_1 \geq u_2 \geq \ldots \geq u_n$. Let $\mathbf{i}_0 < \ldots < \mathbf{i}_p < \ldots < \mathbf{i}_{|\Pi^1_k|-1}$ and $\mathbf{j}_0 < \ldots < \mathbf{j}_q < \mathbf{j}_{q+1} < \ldots < \mathbf{j}_{|\Pi^1_{k+1}|-1}$ be the index points of Π^1_k and Π^1_{k+1}, respectively, $0 \leq k < L^1_U$, where $\mathbf{j}_q = \mathbf{i}_p + \mathbf{e}_1$ and $\mathbf{i}_p + \mathbf{e}_1 \notin N_U$. Then, the following hold:

(1) $q = |\Pi^1_{k+1}| - 1 \geq p$,

(2) $\left(\left(\bigcup_{r=(|\Pi^1_{k+1}|-1)-p}^{|\Pi^1_{k+1}|-1} IN(\mathbf{j}_r)\right) \bigcap \Pi_k\right) = \{\mathbf{i}_0, \ldots, \mathbf{i}_p\}$, and

(3) $\left(\left(\bigcup_{r=0}^{((|\Pi^1_{k+1}|-1)-p)-1} IN(\mathbf{j}_r)\right) \bigcap \Pi_k\right) = \varnothing$. ❐

The above Lemma says that any point $\mathbf{j}$ of Π^1_{k+1} either depends on the point $\mathbf{i}=\mathbf{j}-\mathbf{e}_1$ of Π^1_k or it does not depend on any point of Π^1_k at all. *Hence, the execution of* $\mathbf{j}$ *can begin at moment* t+1, *if the execution of* $\mathbf{i}=\mathbf{j}-\mathbf{e}_1$ *can begin at moment* t, *regardless of whether any point of* Π^1_k *other than* $\mathbf{i}$ *began its execution at* t (see Figure 4.1).

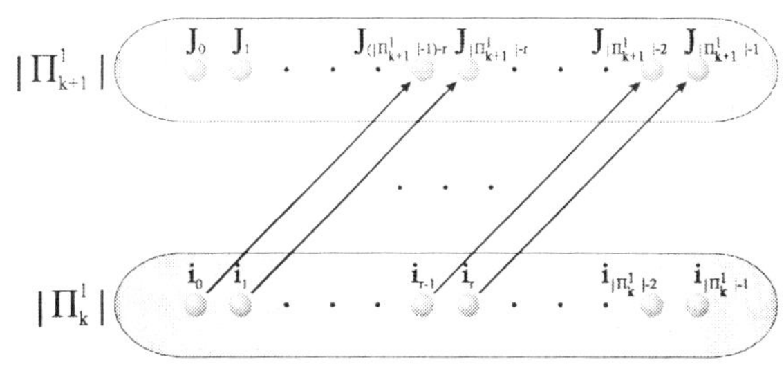

Figure 4.1. The Dependency Relation of Π^i_k and Π^i_{k+1}.

4.2. The Scheduling Strategy

What we have shown so far suggests the following optimal scheduling strategy:

Let $\mathbf{i}_0 < \ldots < \mathbf{i}_{p-1} < \ldots < \mathbf{i}_{|\Pi^1_k|-1}$ and $\mathbf{j}_0 < \ldots < \mathbf{j}_{|\Pi^1_{k+1}|-1}$ be the index points of Π^1_k and Π^1_{k+1}, respectively, $0 \leq k < L^1_U$, and let $\mathbf{j}_{|\Pi^1_{k+1}|-1} = \mathbf{i}_r + \mathbf{e}_1$. Suppose that at moment t the lexicographically first p points of Π^1_k $\mathbf{i}_0 < \ldots < \mathbf{i}_{p-1}$ are computed. We examine the following cases:

- p-1<r, where $\mathbf{j}_{|\Pi^1_{k+1}|-1} = \mathbf{j}^1_{OUT(\mathbf{i}_r)}$ and $\mathbf{j}^1_{OUT(\mathbf{i}_{r+1})}$ is undefined. Then **Lemma 4.1** asserts that at moment t+1 the first $(((|\Pi^1_{k+1}|-1)-r)+p) \geq p$ (obviously $r \leq |\Pi^1_{k+1}|$) points $\mathbf{j}_0 < \ldots < \mathbf{j}_{((|\Pi^1_{k+1}|-1)-r)+p-1}$ of Π^1_{k+1} are available for execution.
- p-1≥r, where $\mathbf{j}_{|\Pi^1_{k+1}|-1} = \mathbf{j}^1_{OUT(\mathbf{i}_r)}$ and $\mathbf{j}^1_{OUT(\mathbf{i}_{r+1})}$ is undefined. Then **Lemma 4.1** asserts that at moment t+1 all the points of Π^1_{k+1} are available for execution.

The conclusion is that either **at least** p points are available for execution, or **all** the points of Π^1_{k+1} are available for execution at moment t+1.

Utilizing the aforementioned optimal scheduling strategy, we derive the optimal makespan for any UET-UCT grid, as stated in the following Theorem:

Theorem 4.1. Let G_U be a UET-UCT grid with terminal point $\mathbf{U}=(u_1, \ldots, u_n)$ such that $u_1 \geq u_2 \geq \ldots \geq u_n$, let m be the number of processors and let $TIME_{m\text{-}OPT}$ be an optimal time schedule for G_U. Then the following hold:

- $TIME_{m-OPT}(\mathbf{U}) = r - 1 + \left\lfloor \frac{\sum_{k=r}^{L^1_U - r} |\Pi^1_k|}{m} \right\rfloor + r = 2r + \left\lfloor \frac{\sum_{k=r}^{L^1_U - r} |\Pi^1_k|}{m} \right\rfloor - 1,$
- $M_{TIME_{m-OPT}} = r - 1 + \left\lfloor \frac{\sum_{k=r}^{L^1_U - r} |\Pi^1_k|}{m} \right\rfloor + r + 1 = 2r + \left\lfloor \frac{\sum_{k=r}^{L^1_U - r} |\Pi^1_k|}{m} \right\rfloor,$

where r is the least natural such that $|\Pi^1_r| > m$. ❐

5 Case Study

Consider the grids G_{U_2} and G_{U_3}, of **Examples 3.1** and **3.2**, with terminal points $\mathbf{U}_2=(4, 3)$ and $\mathbf{U}_3=(3, 2, 1)$, respectively. The maximal coordinate of both terminal points is the first. The grids G_{U_2} and G_{U_3} are partitioned into the hyperplanes Π^i_k, whose cardinality is depicted in Table 2 and Table 3, respectively. Incidentally, one can also see that their optimal makespan is 10 and 9, respectively, when unbounded number of processors is available.

Table 2. The cardinality of Π^1_k for G_{U_2}.

Hyperplane	Cardinality
0	1
1	1
2	2
3	2
4	3
5	2
6	3
7	2
8	2
9	1
10	1

Table 3. The cardinality of Π^1_k for G_{U_3}.

Hyperplane	Cardinality
0	1
1	1
2	3
3	3
4	4
5	4
6	3
7	3
8	1
9	1

If we have only 2 processors available, then the following Table 4 and Table 5 depict the optimal time schedule for the grids G_{U_2} and G_{U_3}, respectively, based on the analysis of Section 4.

Table 4. The optimal UET-UCT schedule for G_{U_2}.

	P_0	P_1
0	(0, 0)	
1	(1, 0)	
2	(2, 0)	(0, 1)
3	(3, 0)	(1, 1)
4	(4, 0)	(2, 1)
5	(0, 2)	(3, 1)
6	(1, 2)	(4, 1)
7	(2, 2)	(0, 3)
8	(3, 2)	(1, 3)
9	(4, 2)	(2, 3)
10		(3, 3)
11		(4, 3)

6 Conclusion

In this paper we have proved that UET-UCT scheduling of task graphs having the form of n-dimensional generalized grids is not only low complexity tractable but it also has a general solution expressed with a closed formula for both time and processors. We have presented an optimal strategy for both time and processor scheduling of these grids with unit communication delays, having bounded number of processors. The proposed scheduling strategy for these UET-UCT graphs is proved to achieve the optimal makespan.

Table 5. The optimal UET-UCT schedule for G_{U_3}.

	P_0	P_1
0	(0, 0, 0)	
1	(1, 0, 0)	
2	(2, 0, 0)	(0, 1, 0)
3	(0, 0, 1)	(1, 1, 0)
4	(1, 0, 1)	(3, 0, 0)
5	(2, 0, 1)	(2, 1, 0)
6	(0, 1, 1)	(0, 2, 0)
7	(3, 0, 1)	(3, 1, 0)
8	(1, 1, 1)	(1, 2, 0)
9	(2, 1, 1)	(2, 2, 0)
10	(0. 2, 1)	(3, 2, 0)
11	(1, 2, 1)	(3, 1, 1)
12	(2, 2, 1)	
13	(3, 2, 1)	

References

1. Andronikos, T., Koziris, N., Papakonstantinou, G. and Tsanakas, P. Optimal Scheduling for UET-UCT Generalized n-Dimensional Grid Task Graphs, *Proceedings of the 11th IEEE International Parallel Processing Symposium (IPPS97)*, pp. 146-151, Geneva, Switzerland, 1997.
2. Andronikos, T., Koziris, N., Papakonstantinou, G. and Tsanakas, P. Optimal Scheduling for UET/UET-UCT Generalized n-Dimensional Grid Task Graphs, accepted, *to appear in Journal of Parallel and Distributed Computing, 1999.*
3. Andronikos, T., Koziris, N., Papakonstantinou, G. and Tsanakas, P. UET/UET-UCT Scheduling for Grids, *Technical Report CS-CSLAB-TR-7-96, Computing Systems Laboratory, Jul. 1996.*
4. Bampis, E., Delorme, C., and Konig, J.C. Optimal Schedules for d-D Grid Graphs with Communication Delays. *Symposium on Theoretical Aspects of Computer Science (STACS96)*. Grenoble France 1996.
5. Berman, G., and Fryer, K.D. *Introduction to Combinatorics*. Academic Press, New York, 1972.
6. Chretienne, P. A Polynomial algorithm to Optimally Schedule Tasks over a Virtual Distributed System under Tree-like Precedence Constraints. *Eur. J. Oper. Res.* 43, pp. 225-230, 1989.
7. Chretienne, P. and Picouleau C. (Ed.) Scheduling with Communication Delays: A Survey, *in* Scheduling Theory and its Applications *pp 65-90. John Wiley & Sons 1995.*
8. Colin, J. Y., and Chretienne, P. CPM Scheduling with Small Communication Delays and Task Duplication. *Oper. Res.* 39, pp. 680-684.
9. Jung, H., Kirousis, L., and Spirakis, P. Lower Bounds and Efficient Algorithms for multiprocessor Scheduling of DAGS with communication Delays. *Proceedings of 1st SPAA 1989, pp. 254-264,* and *Information and Computation 105, pp 94-104, 1993.*
10. Gerasoulis, A., and Yang, T. On the Granularity and Clustering of Directed Acyclic Task Graphs. *IEEE Trans. Parallel Distrib. Syst.* 4, 6, pp. 686-701, 1993.
11. Koziris, N., Andronikos, T., Economakos, G., Papakonstantinou, G., and Tsanakas, P. Automatic Hardware Synthesis of Nested Loops using UET Grids and VHDL, *Proceedings of the International Conference on High Performance Computing and Networking (HPCN97), Lecture Notes in Computer Science, Springer-Verlag,* pp. 888-897, Vienna, Austria 1997.
12. Papadimitriou, C., and Yannakakis, M. Toward an Architecture-Independent Analysis of Parallel Algorithms. *SIAM J. Comput.* 19, pp. 322-328, 1990. *Ext. Abstract in STOC 1988.*
13. Picouleau, C. Etude de Problems d' Optimization dans les Systemes Distribues. These, Universite Pierre et Marie Curie, 1992.
14. Rayward-Smith, V.J. UET Scheduling with Unit Interprocessor Communication Delays and Unlimited Number of Processors. *Discrete Applied Mathematics.* 18, pp. 55-71, 1987.
15. Ullman, J. NP-Complete Scheduling problems. *Journal of Computer and Syst. Sciences.* 10, pp. 384-393, 1975.
16. Varvarigou, T., Roychowdhury, V., and Kailath, T. Scheduling in and out Forests in the Presence of Communication Delays. *Proceedings of 7th International Parallel Processing Symposium, pp. 222-229, 1993.*
17. Yang, T. and Gerasoulis, A. DSC: Scheduling Parallel Tasks on an Unbounded Number of Processors. *IEEE Trans. Parallel Distrib. Syst.* 5, 9, pp. 951-967, 1994.

Groups in Bulk Synchronous Parallel Computing

Gonzalez J.A. [1], Leon C.[1], Piccoli F.[2], Printista M.[2], Roda J.L.[1], Rodriguez C.[1] and Sande F.[1]

[1] Departamento de E.I.O.C.
Universidad de La Laguna
Facultad de Matemáticas. Tenerife
casiano@ull.es
SPAIN

[2] Universidad N. de San Luis
Ejercito de los Andes 950
San Luis
mprinti@unsl.edu.ar
ARGENTINA

Abstract

An extension to the Bulk Synchronous Parallel Model (BSP) to allow the use of asynchronous BSP groups of processors is presented. In this model, called Nested BSP, processor groups can be divided and processors in a group synchronize through group dependent Collective operations generalizing the concept of barrier synchronization. A classification of Problems and Algorithms attending to their parallel Input-Output distribution is provided. For one of these problem classes, the called Common-Common class, we present a general strategy to derive efficient parallel algorithms. Algorithms belonging to this class allow the arbitrary division of the processor subsets, easing the opportunities of the underlying BSP software to divide the network in independent sub networks, minimizing the impact of the traffic in the rest of the network in the predicted cost. The expressiveness of the model is exemplified through three divide and conquer programs. The computational results for these programs in six high performance supercomputers show both the accuracy of the model and the optimality of the speedups for the class of problems considered.

1. Introduction

The Bulk Synchronous Parallel (BSP) model is a generalization of the widely researched PRAM model that was initially proposed by Valiant [9]. The initial formulation of BSP considered the possibility of machine decomposition. Careful attention was paid to this feature, and the BSP library standard document [4] mention this, but in the absence of any clear solution it was decided to exclude it from the standard. In this paper we present a proposal for Nested Bulk Synchronous Parallel Model (NBSP). In the NBSP model, processor sets can be divided using what we call Division Functions. Furthermore of computation and remote memory accesses, processors can perform group Collective operations implying all the processors in the set. Like in BSP, the computation takes place in steps bounded by the execution of group collective operations.

The remainder of the paper is organized as follows: section 2 introduces the NBSP model, stating its characteristics. The properties that the family of Division and Collective Functions have to hold are defined in that section. The laws that govern the time-cost of program execution under the model are also introduced.

The third section provides a classification of Problems and Algorithms attending to their parallel Input-Output distribution. For one of these problem classes, the called Common-Common class, we present a general strategy to derive parallel algorithms from a very compact formulation. These algorithms allow the arbitrary mapping of the processors in the division phase, easing the opportunities of the underlying BSP software to divide current high performance networks in independent sub networks minimizing the impact of the traffic in the rest of the network.

The power of these strategies is exemplified in that section. The comparisons show that there are opportunities for improvement in current implementations of Division Functions like those provided by MPI. Through the use of Division Functions, a skeleton for *common common divide and conquer* algorithms is derived. Experimental results for Cray T3E, Cray T3D, SGI Origin 2000, IBM SP2, Digital Alpha Server 8400 and a Hitachi SR2201 for the Fast Fourier Transform, the Quicksort and the Quickhull are shown and discussed in section 4. The actual and predicted times for a parallel FFT presented in this section show

1066-6192/99 $10.00

that there is no loss of accuracy relative to flat-BSP. Section 5 contains the conclusions.

2. The Nested BSP Computing Model

Let us consider a parallel computer made of a set $P=\{p_0, p_1, ..., p_{N-1}\}$ of memory-processor units connected through some kind of interconnection network. At any time, the processors are organized in a *hierarchy of processor sets*. At the beginning of the computation all the processors P of the machine belong the *root* set of processors. All the processors in a set execute the same *task*. Each processor in a *processor set* has associated two private variables, which we will refer as *NAME* and *NUMPROCS*. While each processor in the *set* has a different *NAME* value, all of them share a common value for the private variable *NUMPROCS*. This last value indicates the cardinality of its processor set.

The Nested Bulk Synchronous Parallel Model (NBSP) is determined by the tuple (N, Div, Col, g, L). N is the number of processors. *Div* and *Col* are respectively the set of division and collective functions. As in BSP, the communication power of a parallel machine is characterized by the bandwidth g and latency L parameters. Our experience shows that, besides the loss of simplicity, the advantages of introducing a family of latency and bandwidth values (one per machine size) are relatively modest. At any time, the processors are constrained to execute one of these three alternatives:

1. Any kind of sequential computation: assignments, loops, function calls, etc.
2. Operations $D \in Div$
3. Operations $C \in Col$

Let be $Q \subseteq P$ a set of processors executing a *task* T. Such an executing set Q will be referred to as a *leaf set*. The Division Functions have to be executed by *all* the processors in a leaf set Q. When the processors in Q execute a division function $D \in Div$ with arguments the tasks $T_i(in_i, out_i)$:

$$D(T_0(in_0, out_0), in_0, out_0, T_1(in_1, out_1), in_1, out_1, ..., T_r(in_{r-1}, out_{r-1}), in_{r-1}, out_{r-1})$$

the following sequence of events has to occur:

1. The *leaf set* Q is partitioned in r disjoint subsets $Q_0, ..., Q_{r-1}$:

$$Q = \cup_{0 \le i \le r-1} Q_i \, ; \, Q_i \cap Q_j = \emptyset \text{ if } i \ne j \ \forall 0 \le i, j \le r-1$$

On each processor $q \in Q_i$ the variable *NUMPROCS* is updated to $|Q_i|$ and variable *NAME* will hold consecutive and different values for the processors in Q_i. The processors in subset Q_i are assigned to the parallel task $T_i(in_i, out_i)$. In_i and Out_i are respectively the input and output data of task T_i.

2. Assign the input data in_i corresponding to the parallel task T_i to the processors in Q_i. After this step, the processor set Q becomes an inner node in the processor hierarchy and the new subsets Q_i will be leaf sets.
3. Execute the parallel tasks $T_i(in_i, out_i)$. Processors in Q_i perform the task T_i whose input data are in_i and whose results are out_i. From this point on, the term *task* will refer to each of the parallel processes T_i appearing as parameters in a division function D.
4. At the end of the execution of all the tasks T_i the subsets Q_i will join again to form the set Q and the output data out_i generated by the parallel tasks T_i is distributed among the processors.

The third component in the tuple defining the Nested BSP Computing Model is the group of collective functions *Col*. A collective operation $C \in Col$ performed by a leaf set of processors $Q=\{p_0, p_1, ... p_{k-1}\} \subseteq P$ is an operation $C(in_0, out_0, ..., in_{k-1}, out_{k-1})$ on a set of input data that has to be executed by all the processors p_i in Q. The computation in the NBSP occurs in steps that we will refer to as supersteps following the BSP terminology [4]. The cost $\Phi(T(in,out), N)$ of a NBSP program T executed by a set with N processors is obtained as the sum of the costs Φ_s of its supersteps. We consider two kind of supersteps. The first kind, called *normal* superstep has two stages:

1. Local computation and asynchronous messages or remote memory accesses.
2. Execution of a collective communication function C from *Col*.

As in BSP, the asynchronous communications and remote memory accesses performed during the first stage are made effective only at the end of the superstep. The second communication stage can be simply a processor subset barrier.

The cost Φ_s of a *normal* superstep s is given by:

$$\Phi_s = W + T_C = max\,\{W_i \,/\, i = 0,...,k-1\} + (g * h + L)$$

The first term (W) represents the computational cost, and T_C is the term associated with communications. $k = |Q|$ is the cardinal of the processor subset Q executing this superstep and W_i is the time invested in computation by processor i in this superstep. The number h is the h-relation of the superstep: the maximum number of messages communicated by any processor in Q, including those associated with the call to the collective function.

The second kind of superstep defined in the model is the *division* superstep. This *superstep* occurs when a division function $D \in Div$ is executed. The time or cost Φ_s is given by:

$$\Phi_s = g * h_{D,in} + L + g * h_{D,out} + L + max\,\{W_{D,i} \,/\, i=0,...,k-1\} + max\{\Phi(Task_0(in_0,out_0), P_0),..., \Phi(Task_{r-1}(in_{r-1},out_{r-1}), P_{r-1})\}$$

where $h_{D,in}$ is the h-relation produced by the input data distribution and $h_{D,out}$ corresponds to the resulting data interchange associated with D. The value $W_{D,i}$ is the computing time spent by processor i in the division and reunification. The value P_i is the number of processors assigned by D to $Task_i(in_i, out_i)$ that is, $P_i = |Q_i|$. The last term is the maximum of the times $\Phi(Task_i(in_i, out_i), P_i)$ recursively computed following the NBSP model for the r subsets.

The values of g and L can be obtained using the methodology explained in [8].

3. Strategies for the Implementation of Division Functions

Although the need of Division Functions appears in a wide class of algorithms, there is no doubt Divide and Conquer algorithms constitute a motivation for the introduction and formalization of Division Functions. The Nested BSP Computing Model makes easier the implementation of *common-common* Divide and Conquer algorithms. We say a problem to be solved in parallel is a *common-common problem* if initially, the input data are replicated in all the processors and at the end, the solution to the problem is required to be also in all the processors. A *common-common* Divide and Conquer is a divide and conquer algorithm that solves a *common-common* problem. The divide and conquer approach presented in Figure 1 to find the solution of a problem x proceeds by dividing x in subproblems x_0 and x_1 (function *divide* in line 6) and applying recursively the same resolution scheme. This recursive procedure ends when the subproblems are small enough, in which case, another procedure (*conquer*) is used to solve the problem.

```
1 procedure pDC(x: Problem; r: Result);
2 begin
3   if trivial(x) then conquer(x, r)
4   else
5   begin
6     divide(x, x0, x1);
7     PARALLEL(pDC(x0,r0),x0,r0,pDC(x1,r1),x1,r1);
8     combine(r, r0, r1);
9   end;
10 end;
```

Figure 1. General frame for a parallel divide and conquer algorithm

The call to the Division Function PARALLEL∈*Div* in line 7 of the code produces the parallel activation of two tasks (*pDC*) to solve each of the two subproblems in which the original problem has been divided. The PARALLEL Division Function divides the actual set of leaf processors in two subsets. Each of the subsets solve in parallel a subproblem x_i, and at the end of the division process, all the processors in the original set achieve the solution r combining the partial solutions r_0 and r_1. This procedure is applied recursively until there is only one processor in the leaf set. In this case, two sequential calls to *pDC* are made. Functions *trivial()*, *conquer()*, *divide()* and *combine()* in Figure 1 must be free of side-effects.

The code in Figure 1 is an example of the wide class of problems where the implementation of Division Functions $D \in Div$ can be made efficiently using only information local to the set of processors executing the function. Figure 2 shows a comparison between the cost of a *La Laguna C* [2] Division Function (label PAR-i) and the cost of *MPI_Comm_split* (label MPI-i). The figure represents the time in seconds of successive repetitions of the division functions varying the number of processors. We can observe that the cost is several orders of magnitude greater for the MPI Division Function. In fact, the three curves corresponding to *La Laguna C* Division Functions appear overlapped with the horizontal axis.

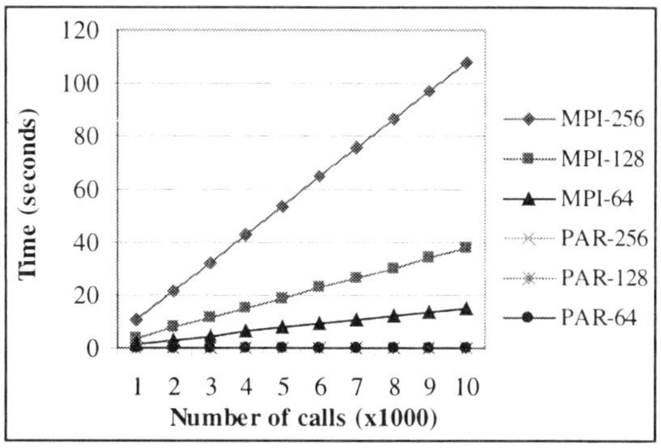

Figure 2. The cost of *MPI_Comm_split()* vs. *La Laguna C* Division Functions

3.1. A Division Function Scheme for *Common-Common* Divide and Conquer Algorithms

The underlying idea in our proposal for the implementation of Division Functions is the establishment of a relation among processors in the different sets produced by the division. Each processor q in a processor set Q_i produced by the division settles a partnership relation with one or more processors in the other subsets. This partnership relation determines the communication of the results produced by the parallel task T_i performed by processor set Q_i. The structure of divisions produced by the Division Functions and the partnership relation among processors give place to communication patterns among processors that are topologically similar to a hypercube. The number of divisions produced determines the dimension while the degree in each dimension is the number of parallel tasks (i.e. the number of subsets) created by the Division Function. Similarly with what occurs in a conventional k-ary hypercube a dimension divides the set in k subsets communicated through the dimension. Nevertheless, opposite subsets in a dimension may have not the same cardinality. We have named the resulting structures Dynamic Polytopes. The following paragraph, formally introduces this concept in order to settle the conditions that guarantee the correctness of the translation of the Division Functions.

3.2. Dynamic Polytopes

Let be $\Gamma = \{Q_0, .., Q_{m-1}\}$ a partition of a set Q. We will name complementary sets of Q_i to the sets Q_j with $j \neq i$. Let be $\boldsymbol{P}(A)$ the set of all subsets of set A.

For any $q \in Q_i$ we will name $G_j(q) \subseteq Q_j$ to the set of processors in Q_j to which processor q will send its results.

A *partnership relation* in Γ is any correspondence $G = (G_i)_{i \in \{0,...,m-1\}}$ where

$$G : Q \rightarrow \Pi_{i=0,...,m-1} \boldsymbol{P}(Q_i)$$
$$G_j : Q \rightarrow \boldsymbol{P}(Q_j)$$

In a conventional binary hypercube, the neighbor or partner of a node in a fixed dimension is unique, while in a partnership relation G a node may have more than one *partner* in one dimension. This is the reason why functions G_j take their values in $\boldsymbol{P}(Q_j)$ instead of Q_j.

We will say that the pair $(\Gamma, (G_i)_{i \in \{0,...,m-1\}})$ is a *neighborhood* if the following conditions are fulfilled:

Exhaustivity: for any $i, j \in \{0, ..., m-1\}$, any element in Q_j has a partner in Q_i:

$$\forall i, j \in \{0, ..., m-1\}: \cup_{q \in Q_i} G_j(q) = Q_j \qquad (1)$$

This condition guaranties that, in the algorithm to be presented in Figure 5, any processor q in Q_j receive the result of the execution of task T_i performed by the processors in Q_i.

Injectivity: $\forall i, j \in \{0, ..., m-1\}, i \neq j$

$$\forall q, q' \in Q_j, q \neq q' \text{ it holds } G_i(q) \cap G_i(q') = \varnothing \qquad (2)$$

This condition imposes that each processor q in a set Q_i receives the results of task T_j only from one of the processors in Q_j.

If $q \in G_j(q')$ we say that q is a partner of q' in the neighborhood defined by $(\Gamma, (G_i)_{i \in \{0,...,m-1\}})$.

A tree or hierarchy of neighborhoods H constitute a *Dynamic Polytope* iff it holds that:

1.- The root of the tree is the "trivial neighborhood" (Γ, G) where $\Gamma = \{Q\}$ and G is the identity function.

2.- If node T is labeled with the neighborhood $(\Gamma^d, (G^d_i)_{i \in \{0,...,r-1\}})$ such that $\Gamma^d = \{Q^d_0, .., Q^d_{r-1}\}$ is a partition of Q^d, then the children nodes of T are labeled with neighborhoods that partition the sets Q^d_i of Γ^d. Eventually, some of the sets Q^d_i of Γ^d may remain without division (in which case they are leaves in the tree).

We will name *dimension* of H to the depth of the neighborhood tree. The nodes at the same level d of the hierarchy H constitute what we will call a *dimension of the Dynamic Polytope*. A dimension is generically designated by the value of its level minus one, and therefore, the first trivial dimension (Γ, G) is dimension (-1).

Example: k-ary Hypercube

If k is a natural number, a k-ary d-dimensional hypercube is a graph with $p=k^d$ nodes. Dimension 0 defines a partition $\Gamma^0 = \{Q^0_0, ..., Q^0_{k-1}\}$ of the set $Q = \{0, 1, ... k^d-1\}$ in k subsets Q^0_s. Nodes whose least significant k-ary digit is s belong to Q^0_s. In general, each dimension (in the classical sense of the term) $i \in \{0..d-1\}$ determines a partition $\Gamma^i = \{Q^i_0, ..., Q^i_{k-1}\}$, where

$$Q^i_s = \{n \in Q \,/\, i\text{-th digit of } n \text{ is } s\} \text{ with } s \in \{0..k-1\}$$

Node q is connected in dimension $i \in \{0..d-1\}$ to nodes whose k-ary representation differs from q in the i-th k-ary digit. For any $n \in Q$ let be $n_{d-1} \ldots n_0$ the k-ary representation of n, then:

$$G^i : Q \rightarrow \Pi_{s=0,...,k-1} Q^i_s \qquad (3)$$
$$G^i_s : Q \rightarrow Q^i_s$$
$$G^i_s(n_{d-1} \ldots n_0) = n_{d-1} \ldots n_{i+1} s\, n_{i-1} \ldots n_0$$

Observe that in any dimension i of a k-ary hypercube the degree is $|\Gamma^i| = k$.

It is easy to see that the pairs $(\Gamma^i, (G^i_s)_{s \in \{0,...,k-1\}})$ obey the conditions that characterize the neighborhood concept in any dimension i.

Figure 3 shows a 2-dimensional ternary hypercube. This hierarchy of neighborhoods could be created by two nested calls to a Division Function. In this example, the first call has created three parallel tasks, and the second recursive call has divided again each subset in three new subsets. Each node in the tree represents a neighborhood, while processor subsets assigned to each task are represented by the shadowed nodes. The lines represent the partnership relations. Solid lines correspond to dimension zero while dotted lines correspond to dimension one. Observe that in this example, each node has two neighbors in each dimension. Each node has two solid and two dotted edges. Notice that the definition of Dynamic Polytope Dimension we have provided matches with the classical concept of dimension in a k-ary hypercube.

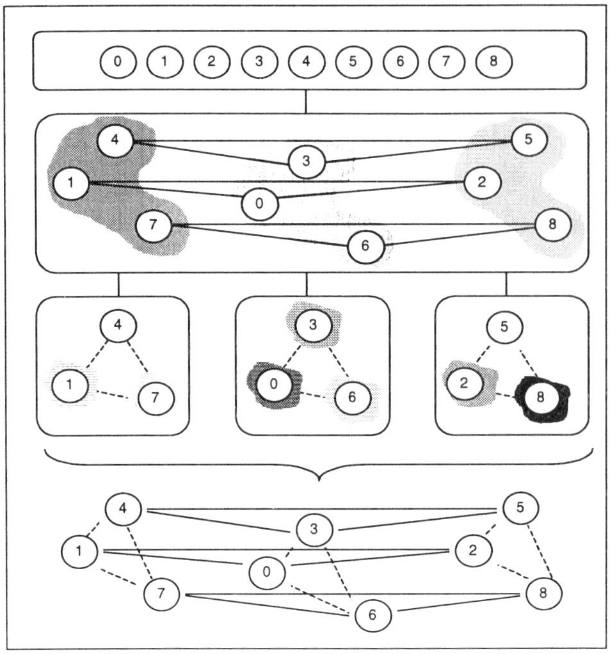

Figure 3. A Dimension Hierarchy for a 2-dimensional ternary hypercube

Example: A Dynamic Polytope

Figure 4 represents a hierarchy of neighborhoods, *(Γ^d, (G^d_j))* defined by the partitions Γ^d (different shadowed regions) and the partnership relations *(G^d_j)* (edges connecting processor nodes) for a 3-dimensional Dynamic Polytope.

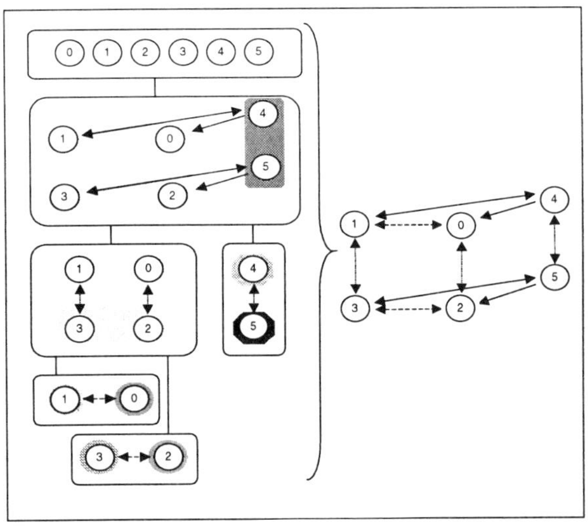

Figure 4. A Dimension Hierarchy for a 3-dimensional Dynamic Polytope

Solid lines correspond to the first dimension (first level in the hierarchy), fine dotted lines to the second dimension and coarse dotted lines to the third dimension. In the example of the figure, the nodes are always divided in two subsets, although not necessarily of the same size. This polytope would be produced by a binary Division Function if the amount of processors assigned to each task varies.

```
proc pDC(x: Problem; r: Result);
begin
if trivial(x) then
  conquer(x, r)
else
  begin
  divide(x, x0, x1);
  if (NUMPROCS > 1) then
    begin
    save(NUMPROCS,NAME, G^dim(NAME));
    dim++;
    compute(□^dim, G^dim);
    if NAME ∈ Q0 then
      begin
      pDC(x0, r0);
      send r0 to processors in G1^dim(NAME);
      receive r1 from j∈Q1 / G0^dim(j) = NAME;
      end;
    else /* in Q1 */
      begin
        pDC(x1, r1);
        send r1 to processors in  G0^dim(NAME)
        receive r0 from j∈Q0 / G1^dim(j) = NAME;
      end;
    dim--;
    restore(NUMPROCS, NAME, G^dim(NAME));
    end;
  else
    begin
    pDC(x0, r0);
    pDC(x1, r1);
    end;
  combine(r, r0, r1);
  end;
end;
```

Figure 5. Translation of the code in Figure 1; expansion of the PARALLEL call.

Precisely speaking, accepting $|Q^i_0| \geq |Q^i_1|$ and that $|Q^i_0|$ is multiple of $|Q^i_1|$, partnership functions G^i are given by the following expressions:

$$G^i_1(n) = (n - first(Q^i_0)) / |Q^i_1| + first(Q^i_1) \text{ for } n \in Q^i_0 \quad \textbf{(4)}$$

$$G^i_0(n) = \{j \text{ such that } (j - first(Q^i_0)) / |Q^i_1| + first(Q^i_1) = n\}$$

and analogously for the other case $|Q^i_1| \geq |Q^i_0|$.

As we can observe in Figure 3 for the case of a regular Hypercube, fixed a dimension, there is only one partner for each node in any complementary set. This is not true for the general case of a Dynamic Polytope. For example, for the first dimension, both nodes 4 and 5 have two partners (*partners(4)={0, 1}*; *partners(5)={2, 3}*) in the complementary set. The computational results of Figure 2 illustrate the advantages of using dynamic polytopes for collective computing.

3.3. Translation Scheme

Lets go back to the general frame of a common-common divide and conquer introduced in Figure 1. Figure 5 presents the expansion of the code corresponding to the PARALLEL Division Function. In general, each time a processor set is divided by the execution of a Division Function, a new dimension (Γ^{dim}, G^{dim}) is created. The creation of the neighborhood (in line 12) can be accomplished in time proportional to the number of tasks demanded (degree) using, for example, the policy described for a k-ary hypercube (equation 3). With such policy, the initial set of processors, Q is divided in two subsets $\Gamma^{dim} = \{Q_0, Q_1\}$ of equal size using constant time. Processors in Q_0 perform the task $pDC(x_0, r_0)$ and those in Q_1 execute $pDC(x_1, r_1)$. However, the optimal partition Γ minimizing load unbalance is the one satisfying:

$$|Q_0| / n_0 = |Q_1| / n_1$$

where n_i is the number of leaves in the tree of calls produced by the call to $pDC(x_i, r_i)$. We propose the use of Division Functions having as additional parameters weights, w_i, either provided by the user or by an heuristic function that estimate the quotient $|Q_i| / n_i$. Accurate heuristic estimations can be found for the cases considered in this paper: $w_i = 0.5$ for the *FFT*, w_i = length of the interval to sort for the quicksort and w_i = cardinal of the set of points for the quick hull algorithm.

Each of the processors q in Q_0 will hold in variable r_0 the result of $pDC(x_0, r_0)$. At the end of the execution of the parallel tasks, each processor $q \in Q_0$ sends the result r_0 to its partner processors in $G_1(q)$. Symmetrically, each processor $q' \in Q_1$ sends r_1 to its partners in $G_0(q')$.

Since the injectivity conditions of the dynamic polytope holds, only one message is received by each processor (lines 17 and 23 in the code of Figure 5). On the other side, the exhaustivity condition guarantees that at the end of the line 26 all processors in Q_i get a copy of the result r_{1-i}.

The cost of the code in lines 10-26 is dominated by the communication time:

$$D * max\{|r_0| * max_q(|G_1(q)|), |r_1| * max_q(|G_0(q)|\}$$

where $|r_i|$ represents the size of the results, $|G_i(q)|$ denotes the cardinal of $G_i(q)$ and D is a constant. The partnership relation G that maximizes the communication balance would be any that minimizes the number of partners each processor has. A solution is the policy exposed in equation 4 also used by the Division Functions of *La Laguna C*.

The time invested in a call to *pDC(x, r))* obeys the recursive expression:

$$\begin{aligned}\Phi(pDC(x,r), N) = W(divide(x, x_0, x_1)) + \\ W(\text{PARALLEL}) + \\ + max\{\Phi(pDC(x_0, r_0), N_0), \Phi(pDC(x_1, r_1), N_1)\} + \\ + g * max(|r_0| * max_q(|G_1(q)|), |r_1| * max_q(|G_0(q)|)) \\ + L\end{aligned}$$

where $N_i=|Q_i|$ and $N=|Q|$.

4. Computational Results

This section presents the computational results that we have obtained for the implementation under the *common-common* divide and conquer paradigm of some well-known algorithms: the Fast Fourier Transform (FFT) [1], the Quicksort sorting algorithm [6] and the Quickhull algorithm [7] for finding the 2D hull of a set of points. Since both the initial input data and the solution have to be stored in all the processors involved in the computation, the maximum speedup achievable is limited to be logarithmic in the size of the vector data. Since the data have to be stored in all the processors, the size of the data constitutes a lower bound for the time of any parallel algorithm. From this, it follows that

speedup ≤ Time sequential / Time spent moving Data input or output

considered in all the examples, the second expression takes order *log(Data Size)*.

In all the cases, the algorithms have been implemented using *La Laguna C* [2] and they have been executed in a wide range of parallel machines: Cray T3E and T3D, IBM SP2, Digital Alphaserver 8400, SGI Origin 2000 and Hitachi SR2201.

Figure 6 presents the speedup for the FFT algorithm using a 256K complex number vector as input data. The speed-up grows logarithmically when the number of processors increases. The Cray T3E is the architecture that presents a better performance.

Due to the regular nature of this algorithm, where the division stage separates the odd and even components of the input signal, the processor sets assigned to each subproblem have the same cardinality. If N is the number of processors that execute the algorithm, the communication pattern between complementary processor subsets has the configuration of a *log(N)*-dimensional hypercube.

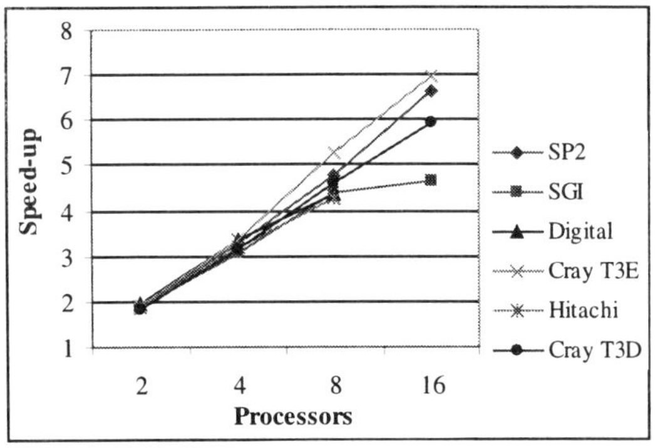

Figure 6. Speed-up for the FFT algorithm. Size of the vector: 256K

Figure 7 summarizes the results obtained for the Quicksort algorithm. In this case, the results correspond to the average of ten experiments changing the input data of the problem, that were generated according to a uniform random distribution. For the set of machines chosen for these experiments, the IBM SP2 is the one that presents better speed-up, while the poorer scalability corresponds to the Digital Alphaserver.

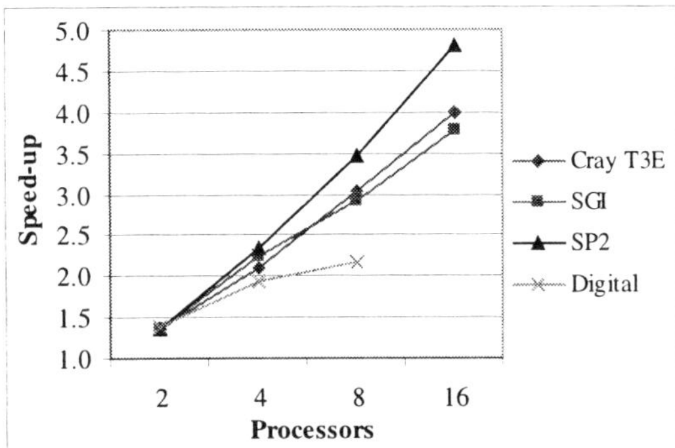

Figure 7. Speed-up for the Quicksort algorithm. Size of the vector: 7M

For this algorithm, the load balance between the processor subsets is achieved using *La Laguna C* Division Functions that assign processors to the parallel tasks proportionally to the size of the sub-vector to be ordered in each recursive call. The exact structure of the dynamic polytope produced by the Quicksort algorithm depends of the input data distribution.

The name of the Quickhull algorithm comes from its similarity with the Quicksort. In each division stage, the algorithm divides the input set of points in two subsets and goes ahead recursively until the set of points is small enough. The results are presented in Figure 8.

Figure 9 presents the actual and predicted times on a CRAY T3E for the considered FFT algorithm on 256KB vector. Singles value of g and L, independent of the number of processors, were used. As can be deduced from this experiment and the study of the capacity predictions using the flat-BSP model with the Oxford BSP library [5], the introduction of groups in BSP does not necessarily implies a loss of accuracy [3].

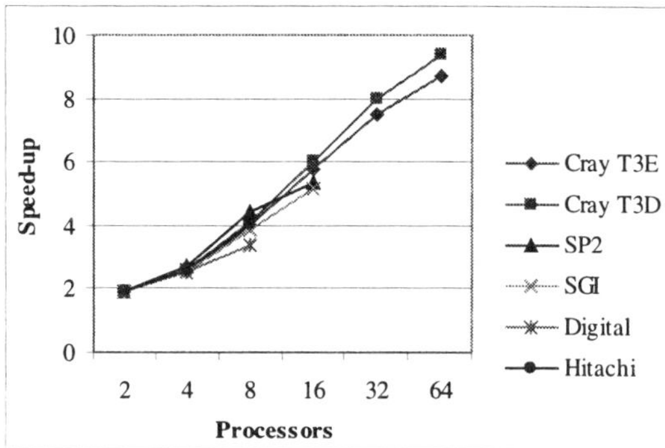

Figure 8. Speed-up for the Quickull algorithm. Number of points: 6M

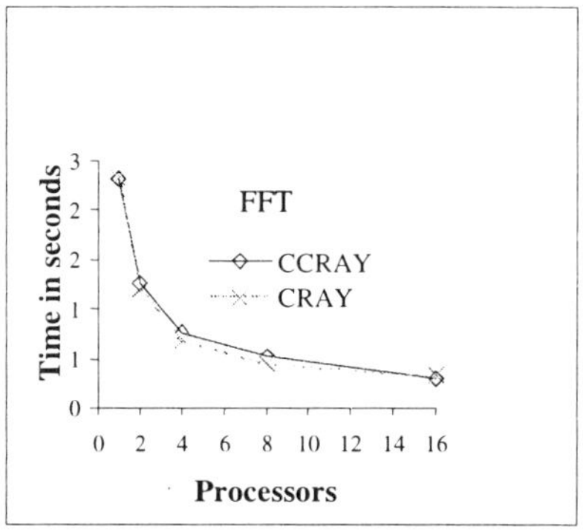

Figure 9. Real times versus Model prediction for the FFT. 256 KB

5. Conclusions

This paper presents the NBSP model whose main elements are Division Functions, Collective Operations and the Parameters that characterize the inter-processor communications. In this work we have focused our attention in the efficient implementation of Division Functions applied to a class of algorithms: *common-common* algorithms. The characteristic of this kind of algorithms is that both the initial input data and the solution have to be stored in all the processors involved in the computation. This fact limits the maximum speedup achievable. Since the data have to be stored in all the processors, the size of the data constitute a lower bound of the time of any parallel algorithm.

In our proposal for the implementation of Division Functions, we have managed two main aspects: how many processors to attach to each of the parallel tasks created by the function, and the design of the partnership relation among the processors. The cardinality of the subsets created influences the workload of the algorithm, while the partnership relations act on the efficiency of the communications. The formalization of these factors led us to the concept of Dynamic Polytope.

We have stated the conditions for the partnership relations to ensure the correctness of the implementation of any Division Function for a *common-common* problem. For the case divide and conquer algorithms, we have proposed partnership functions that guarantee not only the correct behavior of the algorithm but also its efficiency. An experimental example that the introduction of groups does not imply a loss of accuracy has been given.

Acknowledgements

We would like to thank to the following centers: CCCC (CESCA-CEPBA at (Barcelona), EPCC (Edinburgh), CIEMAT (Madrid). Also our acknowledgments to the following institutions: CYCIT (Spain), ULL (Canary Islands), UNSL (Argentina).

References

[1] Akl, S. G.: *The Design and Analysis of Parallel Algorithms.* Prentice-Hall (1989)

[2] de Sande, F.: *El Modelo de Computación Colectiva: Una Metodología Eficiente para la Ampliación del Modelo de Librería de Paso de Mensajes con Paralelismo de Datos Anidado.* PhD thesis. Universidad de La Laguna, (1998)

[3] Gonzalez J.A., Rodriguez C. , Roda J.L., Morales D.G.., Sande F., Almeida F., Leon C. *Performance and predictability of MPI and BSP programs on the CRAY T3E.*. Proceedings of the Euro PVM/MPI 99. Springer-Verlag. (1999.)

[4] Goudreau, Hill, Lang, McColl, Rao, Stefanescu, Suel, Tsantilas. *A proposal for the BSP Worldwide Standard Library. Oxford University Computing Laboratory.* (1996). http://www.bsp-worldwide.org/standard/stand2.htm

[5] Hill, J., McColl, B., Stefanescu, D., Goudreau, M., Lang, K., Rao, B., Suel, T., Tsantilas, Bisseling, R.: BSPLib: *The BSP Programming Library. Technical Report* PRG-TR-29-97, Oxford University Computing Laboratory (1997). www.bsp-worldwide.org

[6] Hoare, C. A. R.: *Algorithm 64: Quicksort.* Communications of the ACM Vol. 4, 321 (1961)

[7] Preparata, F. P., Shamos, M. I.: *Computational Geometry. An Introduction.* Springer-Verlag, New York (1985)

[8] Rodríguez C., Roda J.L., Morales D.G., Almeida F. *h-relation Models for Current Standard Parallel Platforms.* EuroPar'98. Springer Verlag. (1998)

[9] Valiant, L. G.: *A Bridging Model for Parallel Computation. Communications of the ACM*, Vol. 33(8), (1990) 103-111

Panel on Metacomputing

Panel on Metacomputing

Panelists: Vladimir Getov
Peter Kacsuk
Carl Kesselman
Konrad Kloeckner
Domenico Laforenza
Ferenc Vajda (moderator)

"Information technology will be one of the key factors driving progress in the 21st century - it is quite literally transforming the way we live, learn, work and play. Advances in the computing and communication technology will create a new infrastructure for business, scientific research and social interaction." [1]

"The grid is an emerging infrastructure that will fundamentally change the way we think about - and use - computing."[2]

As the first quotation emphasizes there are great and well established expectations on the future role of information technology. Our view on this process is ever changing and the topic of our panel is a good enough example of it. It is hard to find the proper meaning and scope of this term because very many partially overlapping areas are around. For example: Computational Grid (see our 2nd quotation), distributed supercomputing, high-throughput computing, collaborative computing, geographically distributed computing, network based computing, high performance cluster computing, etc.

Here we will use a very simple and not very specific term. A metacomputer consists of a numerous independent-computing resources, which are linked by interconnection networks. The term independent emphasizes the fact that the individual resources are not controlled by a single entity.

At the same time new application areas as virtual laboratory, teleimmersion, collaboratory, telemanufacturing, etc. have appeared.

Naturally, during the limited time available for a panel it is impossible to cover even a very small subset of the current and future issues of metacomputing. That is why we concentrate on very subjectively selected areas only, such as:

- Handling heterogeneity - is interoperability a possibility or an elusive dream?
- "Single computer image"
- How the different and used models and standards as multithreading, RPC, message passing (MPI, PVM), data parallelism (HPF), object oriented techniques (CORBA, Java RMI, DCOM), agents can be used in the new environment?
- The role of Java-based methods in distributed computing
- Toolkit vs. middleware
- Internet2, Qos, security, active networks, mobile agents
- Commodity metacomputing and DATORR (Desktop Access to Remote Resources)
- The effects (if any) of main line applications as network based electronic banking and commerce, multimedia, on- demand video and major computer companies' (as IBM, Sun, Oracle, Microsoft, HP) enterprise distributed architectures (NCF, Jini, etc.) on the development of metacomputing.
- Metacomputing in Europe (role, results and goals, EuroTools, European JavaGrande, W3C, main metacomputing projects)
- Is traditional HPCC and parallel computing are dead?
- Is it possible to set up a "brokerage" system for making idle resources of anonymous users of the Web accessible for distributed (meta)computing?

References:

[1] President's Information Technology Advisory Committee Interim Report to the President
National Coordination Office for Computing, Information and Communications, Arlington, Aug. 1998
[2} I. Foster and C. Kesselmann: The Grid: Blueprint for a New Computing Infrastructure
Morgan Kaufmann Publishers, 1999

1066-6192/99 $10.00 © 1999 IEEE

Keynote Address

Session 7:
Languages and Compilers

Languages and Compilers

Chairperson: Ferenc Vajda
MTA SzTAKI

Probably everybody is familiar with the old story of the three ways to do anything faster. I.e. work harder, work smarter or get help. The well-known meanings of these terms at the computers are: processor speed, methodology and parallel processing. In up-to-date computers parallelism appears at various levels both in hardware and software. Considering code granuality parallelism can be detected and implemented in instruction-level, data-level, control-level and task-level. It is naturally beyond the scope of this session to provide an overview of the different forms of parallelism. Let me give here only a few current categories: ILP (Instruction Level Parallelism), MPP (Massively Parallel Processing), SMP (Symmetric MultProcessor), SPMD (Single Program Multiple Data), distributed virtual memory, threads cluster, grid, etc.

Parallel programming models and tools play important role in efficient parallel systems developments and applications. They include languages and compilers. Not talking about old-new environments, based on languages as C++, Java or High Performance Fortran, parallel libraries as PVM or MPI, parallelizing compilers, etc. new ideas paradigms and methods appear day-by-day as optimizing, dynamic, Just-in-Time compilers, distributed object computing, mobile agents, etc.

The first paper of our session by G. Spezzano deals with CELLAR, an extension of the CARPET language to handle region based programming. The paper describes a new approach to extending the interaction among cells in a cellular programming environment.

The second paper of C. Leopold is titled "Generating Structured Program with a High Degree of Locality" Locality plays an important role in many computer-related topics e.g. virtual memory, cache memory, algorithm design, data structures, etc. The paper suggests a method and a tool called Instance-Based Locality Optimization . It defines and optimizes program instances and uses clustering to establish a locality-aware structured representation.

The paper of F. Bregier et al. Deals with irregular computation of distributed arrays in HPF2. The approach is based on the use of a directive characterizing and irregular prefix operation with support implemented in a library. The usefulness of the method was demonstrated in an interesting application.

The last paper of the session by P-J. Cagnard is on a parallel cellular programming model. It is a developed, more precise version of the BSP model for massively parallel fine-grained applications.

Parallel and distributed computing is moving from specialized to general purpose systems and I just hope that this session will provide a meaningful contribution in this process.

1066-6192/99 $10.00 © 1999 IEEE

CELLAR: A High Level Cellular Programming Language with Regions

Gianluigi Folino and Giandomenico Spezzano

ISI-CNR
c/o DEIS, Università della Calabria
87036 Rende (CS), Italy
{folino,spezzano}@si.deis.unical.it

Abstract

This paper describes CELLAR, a language for cellular programming which extends the cellular automata model through the concept of regions. Regions are spatio-temporal objects that define zones of the automaton (set of cells), containing interesting and meaningful data patterns or trends that can be defined as events. Each cell of the automaton can monitor regions for a given period and observe their evolution by global functions (max, min, sum etc.). Furthermore, each cell can have an associated attribute called its perception rating, that indicates how far that cell can 'see'. On the basis of this value and the cell's position in the cellular space, we can define the regions that are visible to the cell. Using these constructs, a cell can define significant events to extract data of interest in one or more regions and perform actions when an event is detected. In the paper, we show that regions simplify programming and allow the building of more complex models. After describing the main constructs of CELLAR, the paper illustrates the region-based programming model by describing the design of a parallel model of animal migration. Performance results of the model implemented on a Meiko CS-2 are also given.

1. Introduction

Cellular computing [1] is an emergent parallel programming paradigm based on the computational model cellular automata (CA) that is effective both for scientific and engineering computations and as a framework to enable fine-grained parallel computations.

A CA is composed of an array of interacting cells, either one-dimensional or multidimensional. Each cell can have a finite number of states. The states of all the cells are updated synchronously according to a local rule, called a *transition function*, according to which, the state of a cell at a given time depends only on its own state at the previous time step and the states of its "nearby" neighbors (however defined) at that previous step. Thus, the state of the entire automaton advances in discrete time steps. The global behavior of the system is determined by the evolution of the states of all the cells as a result of multiple interactions.

CA model has been applied to a wide range of practical applications such as freeway traffic flow, landslides, lava flow, particle dynamics, forest fire, and soil bioremediation. However, to support a larger number of real applications several extensions and modifications to the basic model have been proposed. A detailed description of these extensions is presented in [2]. The main changes concern: the possibility to have a more complex representation of the state of a cell instead of a few bits, temporal and spatial inhomogeneity both in the transition function and in the neighborhood, asynchrony so that each cell can in each step non-deterministically choose between changing its state according to the transition function or keeping its current state, complex time-dependent neighborhood (i.e. block rule), probabilistic and hierarchical transition functions. Moreover, many phenomena, especially those studied in biology, ecology and sociology, require information from other cells which do not belong to the cell's neighborhood.

Research activities on implementation of cellular automata models was mainly focused on algorithms and applications. For many years, the programming issues were not considered one of the major issues to be faced and solved. However, in recent years a number of cellular programming language such as CELLANG [3], CDL[4], CARP [5], and CEPROL [6] have been defined.

In our previous works [7,8,9] we defined and implemented a parallel cellular programming environment and a special language, named CARPET, to support both practical development of computational science applications and parallel algorithms in artificial intelligence. CARPET is a high-level language based on C with additional constructs to describe the rule of the state transition function of a single cell of a cellular automaton. The main features of CARPET are: the possibility to describe the state of a cell as a record of typed substates, the simple definition of complex neighborhoods (e.g., hexagonal, Margolus) that can be also time dependent and the specification of non-deterministic, time-dependent and non-uniform transition functions. In CARPET, the approach used in order to have a longer range of interaction among the cells consists in considering the cell's neighborhood within a larger radius. This method is very expensive because it significantly increases the overhead due to the communications.

This paper describes a new *region-based* approach for extending the interactions among the cells. Regions are spatio-temporal objects that define zones of the automaton (set of cells) containing interesting and meaningful data patterns or trends that can be defined as events. Each cell can monitor regions for a given period and observe their evolution by global functions (max, min, sum etc.). Moreover, each cell can define significant events that involve one or more regions and take actions when an event is detected. Occurrences of these events are automatically detected by runtime support system.

To exploit the concept of regions we defined and implemented an extension of the CARPET language, called CELLAR, with new constructs to handle region-based programming. The ZPL language also uses the concept of regions for expressing array computation [10].

The paper is organized as follows. Section 2 introduces the cellular programming model and presents the extension of the model with regions. Section 3 presents an overview of the CARPET language whereas section 4 illustrates the CELLAR language constructs for programming cellular algorithms using the concept of regions. Section 5 describes the programming environment and the parallel run-time system of CELLAR. Finally, section 6 illustrates the region-based programming model by describing the design of a parallel model of animal migration, and presents performance results.

2. Cellular programming model with regions

Cellular algorithms are performed by concurrent programs composed of numerous, fine-grained, iterative processes locally interacting according to usually simple rules (transition function). Local interaction between processes results in complex patterns of evolution of the state of the entire system. Termination of a cellular algorithm may be triggered by reaching a maximum number of generations or by finding an acceptable solution.

A problem can be described by a cellular algorithm defining the local transition function and the initial configuration of the state of each cell. Moreover, the global characteristics of the model, such as the border conditions or the size of the cellular array, must be defined. If the CA is homogeneous, the cellular algorithm is constituted by a collection of identical transition functions applied to all the cells of the automaton; otherwise, different transition functions must be defined for the non-uniform cells.

In traditional CA a cell can interact only with the cells defined within its neighborhood. CELLAR extends the range of interaction among the cells introducing the concept of region. Regions are spatio-temporal objects, statically defined, which allow a cell to know, by global functions (max, min, sum, avg, and, or, etc.), the behavior of a set of cells put within a defined area. At each iteration cells can update their own state not only with the state of the neighbor cells but also considering the global values obtained by global functions defined on substates of the cells of a region. A cell can also define events which involve variables, defined as substates of the cells of a region, and take actions when an event is detected. An event expression is composed of logical connectives (and, or, not) that combine the global functions applied to the event variables, where for each function it is checked if it is less-than, greater-than or equal to a constant value.

Each cell can have an associated attribute called *perception rating,* that indicates how far that cell can 'see'. On the basis of this value and the cell's position in the cellular space, we can define the regions that are visible to the cell. Figure 1 shows the region-based programming model used in CELLAR.

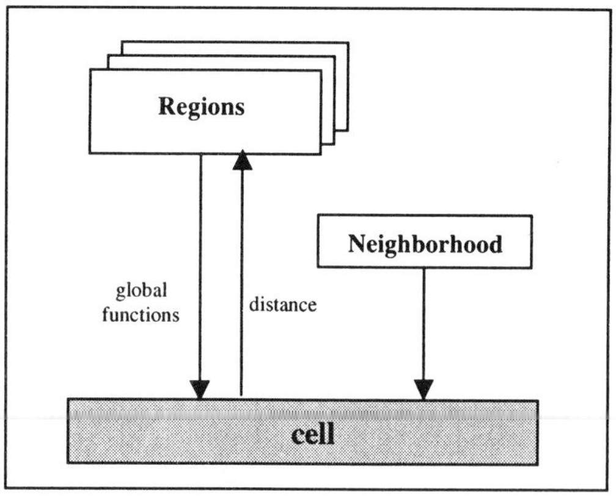

Figure 1. The CELLAR programming model with regions.

3. Overview of CARPET

The CARPET language allows to define the transition function of a cell of the automaton. It handles three kinds of objects: *state*, *neighborhood* and *parameters* that are defined inside the *cadef* declaration section.

State objects are passive entities composed of a set of typed substates. They are structured as a record in which the C basic types: *char*, *shorts*, *integers*, *floats*, *doubles* and mono-dimensional *arrays* of these types can be used to store the physical quantities of a model or the data structures of a parallel algorithm. The predefined variable *cell* refers to the current cell in the n-dimensional space under consideration. A substate can be referred appending to the reserved word *cell* the substate's name by the underscore symbol '_' (i.e, *cell_substate*). Cell substates are updated at each iteration only by the *update* function, in order to guarantee the semantics of cell updating in cellular automata. After an *update* statement, the value of the substate, in the current iteration, is unchanged. The new value takes effect at the beginning of the next iteration. The neighborhood of a cell is defined as the maximum number of cells that a cell can access in reading. For example, in a 2-dimensional automaton defining the radius equal to 1 the number of the neighbors can be up to 8. To define transition functions or neighborhood time dependent, the predefined variable *step* is used. Step is automatically updated by the system. Initially the value of step is 0 and it is incremented by 1 at each iteration. To allow a user to define spatially inhomogeneous CA, CARPET defines the GetX, GetY and GetZ operations that return the value of X,Y and Z coordinates of a cell in the automaton.

Parameter objects describe some global features of the system. CARPET allows to define global parameters and to initialize them to specific values. The value of a global parameter is the same in each cell of the automaton. Parameters can be modified by user interface (UI), described in section 4, during the automaton execution.

```
cadef
{
  dimension 2;   /* bidimensional lattice */
  radius 1;
  state (short value);
  neighbor cross[4]([0,-1]North,[-1,0]West,
                    [0,1]South,[1,0]East);
}
 int i; short N = 0;
{
  for (i=0; i<4; i++)
    N = cross_value[i] + N;
  if (N % 2 == 1)
    update(cell_value, 0);
}
```

Figure 2. The parity rule game.

The example in figure 2 shows how the CARPET constructs can be used to implement the parity rule program. In this example the cells can have '0' or '1' values only. Let us call N the number of '1' cells among the four nearest neighbors of a given cell. The transition rule is the following: given a cell, if N is odd, the new value of the cell will be 0; if N is even the cell's value does not change.

4. The CELLAR language

CELLAR is an extension of the CARPET language. It inherits all the CARPET constructs and extends the cellular programming introducing new constructs to handle the region-based model of programming.

In CELLAR, region objects are statically defined, inside the cadef section, by the **region** declaration and identified by the name of a vector with dimension equal to the number of regions defined in the automaton. Inside a region declaration, the areas of interest are enclosed in round brackets and separated by commas.

A *d*-dimensional region is defined by a sequence of indices which represent the geometric coordinates, the time period (starting time and ending time) in which the region is defined, and the interval of monitoring.

The following example defines three separated regions:

region zone[3] (*area1*(10,20,10,30, 0,0,10,300,5),
area2(50,60,10,20,0,0,10,300,5),
area3(10,20,40,50,1,1,10,300,5))

The region *area1* is a rectangular area defined by the x-y-z coordinates, and it is defined only during the time period from 10 to 300 with a monitoring interval equal to 5. The global behavior of the substates of the cells of a region can be observed by global functions that return a numerical value. CELLAR implements the functions *MaxRegion*, *MinRegion*, *SumRegion*, *AndRegion*, *OrRegion*, *AvgRegion*, which respectively allow to calculate the maximum, the minimum, the sum, the logical and, the logical or, and the average value of substates of the cells belonging to a region. Other functions can be added in the future. In the following example, the MaxRegion function is applied to the temperature substate

max = **MaxRegion** (area1_temperature, &success)

In the example given above the function MaxRegion assigns to *max* the maximum of the values that cells, belonging to the *area1* region, take for the temperature substate. The *success* variable takes a true value only if the function is performed during the time period specified. In the previous example, if the current iteration is 320, the value returned by the success variable is false and max equals to 0.

To know if a cell belongs to a spatial region we have defined the *InRegion* function. For example, the function:

val = **InRegion**(area1)

returns a true value if the cell belongs to the *area1* region; otherwise a false value is returned.

To check if a certain region can be monitored in the current iteration we have defined the *InTempRegion* function. In the following example

InTemp = **InTempRegion**(area1)

the *InTemp* variable is true if the current iteration is within the temporal window and the monitoring step is that defined for the *area1* region.

Regions that are visible to a cell are calculated by the *Distance* function. The *Distance* function returns the distance between the cell and the region considered. The Distance function is calculated by taking the integer part of the Euclidean distance between the coordinates of the cell and the coordinates of the cell that represents the center of a region. The center of a region is calculated by taking the average value of the three spatial coordinates. Distance function returns zero if the cell is within the region; otherwise it returns the distance value. The following example:

if (**Distance**(area1) < 20)

allows to check if the *area1* region is visible for the current cell. For example, the cell can define if the value returned from the Distance function is lower than 20 then the area1 region is visible where 20 represents its perception rating.

Significant events can be defined on one or more regions by defining expressions that contain the above defined functions. The basic event-action control structure of CELLAR is

if *<event-expr>* **then** < *action*>

An *event-expr* is an expression that combines the global functions defined on a region by basic numerical expressions as well as relational and logical operators. Actions consist of changing the value of some substates of the current cell or event definitions.

The example in figure 3 describes a simple simulation of the propagation of a forest fire and shows how the main constructs of the CELLAR language can be used. In this example each cell represents a portion of the land. Cells in the lattice can have values included between '0' and '2'. The ground is represented by '0' value, the tree is represented by '1' value and the fire is represented by '2' value. Fire spreads from a cell which is on fire to a von Neumann neighbour that has trees, but not on fire. The *area1* region represents the zone that must be controlled. A user-defined trigger on the *area1* region allows a user to monitor the presence of fire in the zone. The region is isolated when the fire is present. The fire is detected calculating the maximum of the *area1* region for the *land* substate because the fire is represented by '2' value. If the event is verified, then all the cells located at a distance from 30 to 20 from the region with the fire, change their value to *ground* in order to prevent the propagation of the fire. The *max* and *min* parameters can be changed to simulate different areas that isolate the region on fire.

```
#define ground 0
#define tree 1
#define fire 2
cadef
{
   dimension 2;
   radius 1;
   state (short land);
   neighbor cross[4]([0,-1]North,[-1,0]West,
                     [0,1]South,[1,0]East);
   parameter (min 20.0, max 30.0);
   region (area1(40,60,30,40,1,1,1,200,1));
}
int succ, dist;
{
 dist = Distance(area1);
  if((MaxRegion(area1_land,&succ)==fire) &&
       dist < max )&&(dist > min))
     update(cell_land, ground);
    else
     if((cell_land==tree)&&(North_land==fire) ||
        (East_land == fire) ||(West_land == fire)
          || (South_land == fire ))

        update(cell_land, fire);
          else
           if (cell_land== fire)
             update(cell_land, ground);
}
```

Figure 3. The forest fire simulation.

5. The parallel environment

The interactive parallel environment that allows the development and running of CELLAR programs on parallel architectures is called CARAVEL. The main goal of CARAVEL is to integrate computation, visualization and control into one environment to allow interactive steering of scientific applications [11]. CARAVEL consists of

- a graphical user interface (GUI) for editing, compiling, configuring, executing and steering the computation;

- a run-time support for the parallel execution of CELLAR programs;
- a load balancing strategy to evenly distribute the computation among processors of the parallel machine.

CARAVEL's GUI provides a *development window* for editing, compiling and configuring a cellular program and a *simulation window* for the running and the exploratory steering of the simulation.

To configure an application we use he *configure* menu of the development window defines the dimensions of the CA engine, the number of processes in which the CA is divided, the number of processors on which to allocate the processes and the numbers of folds which define the regions for the load balancing strategy described in the section 5.1.

When the simulation window is started the user can execute the simulation for a number of steps defined (by clicking the **go** button) or for an infinite number of steps (by clicking the **loop** button). During the execution of the simulation the results are visualised on multiple displays and the user can steer the computation stopping the execution of the application (by clicking the **pause** button), change parameters and/or the value of some substates and restart the execution. Figure 4 shows how the interface is used to change the value of a parameter. After entering the new parameter values, the user clicks on the **ok** button to send the steering command to the application which uses the parameter value for computations in the next time step.

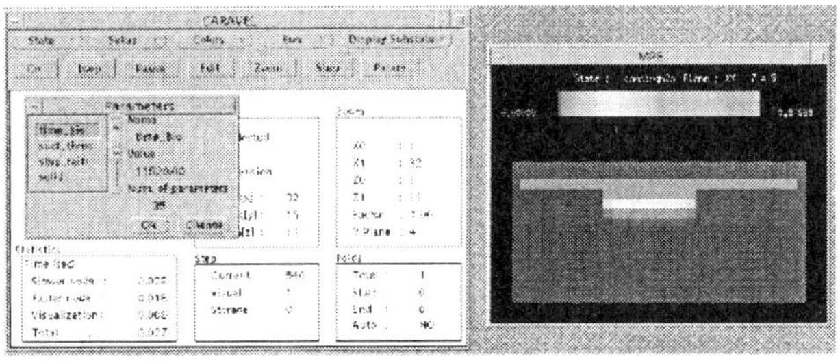

Figure 4. Simulation window of CARAVEL's GUI.

Moreover, the current version of CARAVEL allows

- to choose the colours that can be assigned to the cell substates to support the graphical visualization of their values;
- to change the visualization step to reduce the visualization time;
- to save at regular time the state of the CA in a file.

5.1. The parallel runtime system

The CELLAR run-time system maps CA programs on a parallel computer hiding the architecture issues to a user. Parallel computers are the best practical support for the effective implementation of high-performance CA [12]. The CELLAR run-time support is implemented as a SPMD (Single Program Multiple Data) program. The current implementation is based on the C language plus the standard MPI library and can be executed on different machines such as the Meiko CS-2, CRAY T3E and LINUX cluster of workstations. The concurrent program which implements the architecture of the system is composed by a set of *macrocell* processes, a *controller* process and a *GUI* process. Each macrocell process, which contains a strip of cells of the CA, runs on a single processing element of the parallel and executes the updating of the state of cells belonging to its partition. The synchronization of the automaton and the execution of the commands, provided by a user through the GUI interface, are carried out by the *controller* process. MPI primitives handle all the communications among the processes using MPI *communicators*. CARAVEL uses the capability of the MPE graphics library of MPI, that allows a set of processes to share an X display, in order to visualise the results of a simulation on line.

At each iteration, the region operations are performed in two steps. In the first step, the operations are performed on local data. Each processor performs that portion of the computation applicable to the index values of the data of a region stored in its memory. In the next step these data are combined using the MPI *AllReduce* function that applies the operations to local data and returns the final result to all processors. For example, in a SumRegion operation before the sum of the values stored on each processor is computed locally. Then these partial sums are combined and distributed to all processors. In this way, at the beginning of each iteration, the result is available for each cell of the automaton.

To improve the performance of applications that have a diffusive behavior such as CFD, the CELLAR run-time system implements the same load balancing strategy for mapping lattice partitions on the processing elements used in CARPET [13].

This load balancing strategy is a trade-off between the static and dynamic approach. In fact, the cells partitioning is static, whereas the amount of cells mapped on each partition is dynamic. In CARAVEL, the grid of cells is first divided into n vertical folds; each fold is then partitioned into N strips, where N is the number of processors of the multicomputer. The *i-th* strip of each fold is assigned to the generic processor P_i. To avoid useless computation the user may change, at run time, the set of folds on which the state transition function must be applied. Each macrocell process will compute only the strips of the specified folds. The set of active fold will be augmented or restricted just before some cells become active or passive. The choice of the active folds can be automatic including some tests.

6. Example: a parallel model of animal migration

We illustrate the CELLAR programming model by describing a parallel model of animal migration. The example is based on the NOYELP model developed by a group of modelers and biologists at the University of Tennessee [14]. NOYELP is a spatially-explicit individual-based model that simulates the search, movement and foraging activities of groups of animals across a landscape. The landscape is composed of a grid of cells where a cell represents a portion of the landscape. An initial quantity of available forage is assigned to each grid cell based on its habitat type and burn status at the beginning of each simulation. The algorithm used in NOYELP to simulate forage search and movement of the animals assumes that if an animal is located on a cell with available forage then the animal stops and grazes. Otherwise, the animal will search in concentric squares, up to a radius equal to the maximum moving distance, for another cell with available forage. NOYELP model does not consider some real features of the animals such as the possibility to use the sense of smell and the sight to determinate the availability of forage. In our model the animals can see in all directions up to a value equal to the perception rating and all the regions included within this radius can be monitored. We suppose that the forage is distributed only in some areas of the landscape defined as rectangular regions.

```
#define NumRegion 6
#define perception_rate 20
#define NumAnim 50

cadef
{
 dimension 2;
 radius 1;
 state(float forage, short animaldir[NumAnim]);
 neighbor Moore[8]([0,-1]North, [1,-1]NE,
         [1,0]East,[1,1]SE,[0,1]South,
         [-1,1]SW, [-1,0] West, [-1,-1]NW);

   parameter (thres_forage 0.1);

   region  sight[6](
     meadow1 (10,20,10,30 ,0,0,1,2000,5),
     meadow2 (10,20,10,30 ,0,0,1,2000,5),
     meadow3 (10,20,10,30 ,0,0,1,2000,5),
     meadow4 (10,20,10,30 ,0,0,1,2000,5),
     meadow5 (10,20,10,30 ,0,0,1,2000,5),
     meadow6 (10,20,10,30 ,0,0,1,2000,5));
}
```

Figure 5. The CELLAR declarations of animal migration model.

Figure 5 shows the CELLAR declarations for the model of animal migration. The cell state is composed of 2 substates which describe the quantity of forage and the moving direction of 50 animals. The cell's neighborhood contains 8 cells. Regions are six and represent the zones where is distributed the forage. They can be monitored each five iterations.

Figure 6 shows an outline of the transition function of the model. It is composed of two steps because CELLAR does not allow to modify the state of the neighbour cells. In the first step, for each cell where there are animals (cell_animaldir[k] != 0), we calculate the direction of movement of the animals. In the second step, the cell indicated as destination "transports" the animal from the neighbour site containing the animal toward itself.

If the cell contains animals and the value of the current iteration is included in the time period from 1 to 2000 and the monitor step is equals to 5 then the current cell calculates, by the *distance* function, its visible regions. For each visible region, by the *SumRegion* function, the available quantity of forage is calculated. If an animal is within a region and the amount of forage is greater than a threshold (*thres_forage*) then it stops and grazes, otherwise it moves at random within the region. However, if the quantity of forage available in the region is less than a threshold then the animal migrates to the nearest region that has an amount of forage above the threshold. An animal located outside a region moves in the direction in which the rate amount of forage/distance is maximized.

7. Performance

In this section we present the performance results of the CELLAR program that simulates the animal migration model. The model has been implemented on a Meiko CS-2 parallel machine. The CS-2 is a distributed memory MIMD parallel computer. It consists of *Sparc* based processing nodes running the *Solaris* operating system on each node, so it resembles a cluster of workstations connected by a fast network. Each node is composed of one or more Sparc processors, a communication co-processor, the Elan processor, that connects each node to a fat tree network built from Meiko 8x8 crosspoint switches. Our machine is a 12 processors CS-2 based on 200 Mhz *Hypersparc* processors with 256 Mbytes of memory on each processor and running Solaris 2.5.1. The model has been tested with different grid sizes and with six regions. Figure 7 shows a snapshot of migration animal model simulated by the CARAVEL environment. Table 1 shows the elapsed time of the execution of 100 steps, and the speedup measures of the parallel model implementation using different grid sizes on 1, 2, 4 and 8 processors. The performance showed for the 128x64 grid are better than the 64x128 grid. In fact, the automaton is subdivided along the x-axis and this implies that a smaller number of messages is exchanged between two consecutive partitions allocate on different nodes.

```
if (step %2 == 1)
{
 for (k=0; k < NumAnim; k++)
    {
     if (cell_animaldir[k] !=0 )
     {
      if((InTempRegion(meadow1)&&(InTempRegion(meadow2)&&
       (InTempRegion(meadow3)&&(InTempRegion(meadow4)&&
       (InTempRegion(meadow5)&& (InTempRegion(meadow6))
        {
         for (i=0; i < NumRegion; i++)
          {
           dist[i]= distance(sight[i]);
           if (dist[i] < perception_rate)
           {
             sum[i] = SumRegion(sight[i]_forage, &suc);
               see[i] = TRUE;
           }
           else
            see[i]=FALSE;
      }
     if ((InRegion(meadow1)|| InRegion(meadow2) ||InRegion(meadow3)||
          InRegion(meadow4) ||InRegion(meadow5)|| InRegion(meadow6))
      {
       if (cell_forage <= tresh_forage)
          dir = random_migration (dist,sum,see);
          else
            {
              grazes(cell_forage);
              dir = motionless;
            }
        }
       else
         dir = choose_direction (dist, sum, see);
       update(cell_animaldir[k], dir);
      }
     }
    }
       else /* movement rule of the animals */
       {
        for(k=0; k <NumAnimal ; k++)
         if (cell_animaldir[k] != motionless)
           {
           animtemp = 0;
             for (i=1; i<= 8; i++)
               if(moore[i]_animaldir[k] == i)
                    animtemp=i;
             update(cell_animaldir[k], animtemp);
           }
    }
```

Figure 6. The CELLAR transition function of animal migration model.

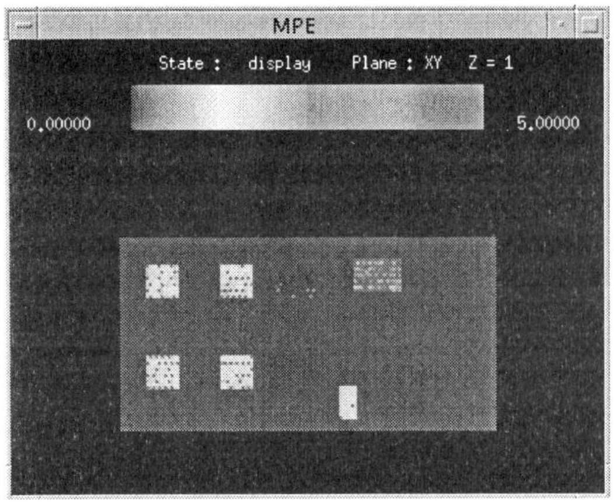

Figure 7. A snapshot of migration animal simulation.

PEs	64x64		64x128		128x64	
	Time (sec.)	Speedup	Time (sec.)	Speedup	Time (sec.)	Speedup
1	220.50	1	438.25	1	439.81	1
2	113.07	1.95	223.60	1.96	222.13	1.98
4	60.41	3.65	117.03	3.74	114.02	3.85
8	36.81	5.99	67.10	6.53	63.11	6.97

Table 1. Elapsed time and speedup for different grid sizes of the cellular automaton.

8. Conclusions

In this paper we have presented the constructs of the CELLAR language to extend the cellular programming with the concept of regions and demonstrated how this concept simplifies programming and allows the building of more complex models. The CELLAR programming environment offers to a user an interface that abstracts from underlying hardware and ensures portability and intellectual abstraction. The region-based programming model of CELLAR is used in the COLOMBO project within the ESPRIT framework. The main objective of this project is the application of parallel computing to the simulation of the bioremediation of contaminated soils using CA models.

Acknowledgements

This research has been partially funded by the CEC ESPRIT project n° 24907.

References

[1] M. Sipper, " The Emergence of Cellular Computing", IEEE Computer, vol.32, n. 7, July 1999.

[2] T. Worsch, Programming Environments for Cellular Automata, *Proc. Cellular Automata for Research and Industry (ACRI 96), Springer-Verlag*, London, pp. 3-12, 1997.

[3] J.D. Eckart, Cellang 2.0:Reference manual. ACM Sigplan Notices, vol. 27, n. 8, pp.107-112, 1992.

[4] C. Hochberger, R. Hoffmann, CDL – a Language for Cellular Processing. *In Proc. 2nd Intern. Conference on Massively Parallel Computing Systems*, 1996.

[5] G. Junger, *Cellular Automaton Tool user manual*, GMD,1994.

[6] F. Seutter, CEPROL – a Cellular Programming Language, *Parallel Computing*, vol. 2 , pp.327-333, 1985.

[7] G. Spezzano and D. Talia, A High-Level Cellular Programming Model for Massively Parallel Processing, in: *Proc. 2nd Int. Workshop on High-Level Programming Models and Supportive Environments (HIPS97)*, IEEE Computer Society, pp. 55-63, 1997.

[8] G. Spezzano, D. Talia and al. A Parallel Cellular Tool for Interactive Modeling and Simulation, *IEEE Computational Science & Engineering,* 3:3, pp. 33-43, 1996.

[9] Folino G., Pizzuti C., Spezzano G., Combining Cellular Genetic Algorithms and Local Search for Solving Satisfiability Problems, *Proc. of 10th IEEE International Conference Tools with Artificial Intelligence (ICTAI'98),* IEEE Computer Society, pp. 192-198 , 1998.

[10] Bradford L. Chamberlain, E Christopher Lewis, Calvin Lin, and Lawrence Snyder, Regions: An Abstraction for Expressing Array Computation, UW CSE Technical Report, UW-CSE-98-10-02, October, 1998.

[11] J.Vetter, K. Schwan, High Performance Computational Steering of Physical Simulations, *Proc. 11th International Parallel Processing Conference(IPPS'96),* IEEE Computer Society Press, pp.128-132, 1997.

[12] B.P Hansen, Parallel Cellular Automata: A Model for Computational Science, *Concurrency: Practice and Experience,* 5, pp. 425-448, 1993

[13] M. Cannataro, S. Di Gregorio, R. rongo, W. Spataro, G. Spezzano, and D. Talia, A Parallel Cellular Environment on Multicomputers for Computational Science, *Parallel Computing,* 21, pp. 803-824, 1995.

[14] E. Uziel and M.W. Berry, Parallel Model of Animal Migration in Northern Yellowstone Park, *Int. J. Supercomputer Applications and High Performance Computing,* vol. 9, n.4, pp.237-255,1996.

Generating Structured Program Instances with a High Degree of Locality

Claudia Leopold
Fakultät für Mathematik und Informatik
Friedrich-Schiller-Universität Jena
07740 Jena, Germany
claudia@informatik.uni-jena.de

Abstract

Memory hierarchy-consciousness is an important requirement for the design of high-performance programs. We describe a tool that supports the programmer in restructuring performance-critical code sections. The tool works with small program instances, which are obtained by fixing program parameters such as loop bounds, and rewriting the program as an operation sequence. The tool automatically reorders the operations for better locality, and respects data dependencies. It outputs the optimized program instance in a structured form. The user finally recognizes the locality-relevant structure and generalizes it to the program.

The paper focuses on recent advances in the development of our method. In particular, we introduce a hierarchical clustering scheme that highlights operation subsequences with much data reuse. The scheme is applied to the generation of structured optimized program instances in which the locality-relevant structure is easy to recognize. Experimental results are included.

1. Introduction

Due to the large and growing gap between processor speeds and memory speeds, the design of high-performance programs requires to be conscious of the memory hierarchy. In particular, one should avoid frequent access to the main memory, and instead try to reuse cached data as often as possible. Memory hierarchy-consciousness is a requirement for sequential and even more for parallel computation. Compiler optimizations can help, but the scope of most compiler optimizations is limited to nested loops and to a few transformations under consideration. Hence, memory hierarchy-conscious program restructuring is often a task for the programmer or algorithm designer, a task that can be time-consuming and difficult.

This paper suggests a tool that helps the programmer. The tool automatizes one of the human activities in algorithm/program design: developing solution ideas for a given problem by looking at small-input-size instances of the problem and thinking about efficient solutions for these instances. We believe the automatization of human activities to be crucial for closing the still large gap between the kind of optimizations that can be applied automatically and those that have to be applied manually. The work described here is a step in this direction.

Our work deals specifically with locality optimization in memory hierarchies. The distribution of data and computation in shared- and distributed memory parallel computers raises similar questions ([1] vs. [2]). We restrict ourselves to the simple case of sequential memory hierarchies here, but think that our approach can be generalized to the more involved case of interprocessor communication.

Locality is a gradual property of programs that reflects the level of concentration of the accesses to the same memory block, during program execution. A higher level of concentration corresponds to a higher degree of locality, and in tendency causes fewer cache misses, page faults etc.

The major component of our tool is an algorithm for the optimization of program instances (PIs). A PI is derived from a program, or typically from a performance-critical section of code, by fixing the input size and possibly more parameters. We fix those parameters that are required to unroll loops and resolve recursions in a way that the PI becomes a sequence of elementary or complex operations. This operation sequence is the starting point for the optimization algorithm, which reorders the operations and reassigns the data to memory blocks with the objective of maximizing locality. The rearrangement process is detailed later. Although the final arrangement found refers to a particular program instance, it gives hints for a restructuring of the program in general. It is the user's task to accomplish the generalization step from the instance to a program. Tool

1066-6192/99 $10.00

support for this step is provided in the form of a structured representation of the output operation sequence. We call our method Instance-Based Locality Optimization (IBLOpt).

This paper reflects the current state of the development of IBLOpt, with focus on recent advances. In particular, we introduce a hierarchical clustering scheme that highlights operation subsequences with much data reuse. We use the clustering scheme to establish a *locality-aware* structured representation.

The paper starts with an overview of related work in Sect. 2. Next, previously published work on IBLOpt [4, 5] is summarized in Sect. 3, to lay the groundwork for the rest of the paper. Sections 4 and 5 describe our recent advances, where Sect. 4 introduces the hierarchical clustering scheme, and Sect. 5 uses the scheme to improve the structured output. Section 6 gives experimental results for four example programs: a two-deep perfect loop nest, matrix transpose, matrix multiplication and mergesort. Section 7 finishes with conclusions.

2. Related work

There are two major areas of related work: compiler optimizations for locality, and memory hierarchy-conscious algorithm design.

Compiler optimizations for locality are an important research subject. A survey is, for instance, given in [6]. Most compiler optimizations use heuristics that reduce the number of cache misses via transformations such as loop permutation, loop distribution and loop tiling. The techniques for sequential memory hierarchies do in general resemble those suggested for symmetric multiprocessors and distributed-memory parallel computers (e.g. [2]). While earlier work has focused on code restructurings (e.g. [11]), more recent work also considers data reassignments, that is, storing arrays row-wise vs. column-wise, etc. (e.g. [1]). Most of the work is restricted to loop nests, where arrays are accessed via affine index expressions. It is a characteristic feature of the compiler optimization approach that program restructurings are based on a small set of transformations under consideration. If a program needs other techniques for improvement, the improvement will not be found. It is a prerequisite that compiler optimizations can be executed automatically and fast.

Memory hierarchy-conscious algorithm design has developed into an active research area during the last years. Its focus is on external memory algorithms (see [10] for a recent survey), and there is also some work on caches (e.g. [3]). The scope of this work is wider than the scope of our method, since locality optimization is combined with other tasks, particularly with the establishment of an algorithm's basic structure (choice of the operations to be carried out) and with the choreography of the data movement. The merit of our method is the provision of *automatic* support to the otherwise manual process of developing algorithmic ideas.

3. Instance–based locality optimization

3.1. Overview and tool

IBLOpt is an intermediate approach between algorithm design and compiler optimizations. It is neither restricted to a finite set of transformations nor to loop programs, and hence it has a broader applicability than current compiler optimizations. On the other hand, the scope of IBLOpt is narrower than the scope of algorithm design. IBLOpt has a higher time consumption than compiler optimizations, but can save human time during algorithm design.

The central concept of IBLOpt is that of a program instance (PI). A PI comprises a sequence of elementary or complex operations called statement instances (SIs). Each SI operates on a sequence of instantiated data (DIs). For data, instantiated means that the location is non-variable, e.g. $A[3]$ is a DI whereas A[i] is not. For simplicity, we assume all DIs to be the same size. Examples of SIs are "$A[5]$+=1" and "Merge sorted run at $A[1]\ldots A[4]$ with sorted run at $A[5]\ldots A[8]$". The SIs are taken as undivisible. We assume that there are no control dependencies between SIs, i.e., each SI is carried out exactly once, and branching is restricted to occurring within SIs. In addition to the SI sequence, a PI comprises an assignment of DIs to memory blocks. The assignment specifies which data are stored together in a memory block, it does neither specify the order within the block nor the identity of the block.

Our tool works in three phases: an instantiation, an optimization, and a generalization phase. In the instantiation phase, the user specifies the PI. Therefore, the user inputs the code section to be optimized, fixes the control flow-relevant parameters, and chooses the granularity of the SIs. Then, the system rewrites the PI as a sequence of SIs, by unrolling loops and resolving recursions. A data dependence graph [6] is derived automatically, too. In IBLOpt it is a directed acyclic graph, referred to as *dag*.

Next, in the optimization phase, the SIs are automatically reordered and the DIs are reassigned to memory blocks so that the PI is improved with respect to locality. The rearrangement is controlled by a local search algorithm that strictly obeys the data dependencies. To support the generalization phase, a second objective is regularity. Striving for regularity means that we favour operation sequences that can be written in a compact and intuitively appealing form using loops. The local search algorithm is detailed in Sect. 3.2. Its output is a locally optimal SI ordering for the PI, together with a structured representation thereof. In the structured representation, we allow for-loops with constant bounds.

Finally, in the generalization phase, the user inspects the SI ordering, to recognize the structural differences that make the suggested ordering superior to the initial ordering. After having found these differences, the user generalizes them to the program and writes down the improved program. The user can assess the quality of the new program by running the optimization algorithm on a different instance thereof.

Along with the PI, the user must also specify memory hierarchy parameters C, L. They denote the capacity and line size of a small hypothetical cache, which is assumed to be fully-associative and LRU. The parameters are used in the optimization process, and they are used to quantitatively assess the locality of our output PIs.

3.2. The optimization algorithm for program instances

The input of the optimization phase consists of a set S of SIs, a set D of DIs, a data dependence graph *dag*, and the memory hierarchy parameters C, L. The SIs are characterized by functions SD: $S \rightarrow D^*$, op: $S \rightarrow \mathbb{N}$ and V: $S \rightarrow \mathbb{Z}^*$. Here, *SD* assigns to s the sequence of DIs that are accessed by s. Further, $op(s)$ characterizes the operation carried out by s, and $V(s)$ is a sequence of numbers that appear explicitly in the notation for s. That is, *op* and V do together encode the textual string that denotes the operation in the PI. A more detailed explanation can be found in [4, 5]. The function *SD* is used for locality optimization, while *op* and V are needed for producing a structured output.

The output of the optimization phase comprises a schedule, which is an SI sequence where each $s \in S$ appears once, and a data assignment function *DB*, where $DB(d)$ is the number of the memory block to which $d \in D$ is assigned. The schedule is output in two forms: as an operation listing, and in a structured representation consisting of nested and consecutive `for`-loops with constant bounds. The optimization problem is constrained by the *dag*.

There are two objective functions: one for locality and one for regularity. The functions are combined in a way that is described later.

The locality function was introduced in [4], where two candidate functions were compared: OFL_{loc} and OFL_{cc}. The function OFL_{cc} measures the number of simulated cache misses, referring to the hypothetical parameters C, L. The function OFL_{loc} quantifies the intuitive notion of locality from Sect. 1. OFL_{loc} was established empirically and has quite a complex definition [4], omitted here. Briefly, OFL_{loc} is a sum where each summand assesses the access distance of a reuse tuple, which is a pair of successive accesses to the same memory block. The assessments follow the principle *the-closer-the-better*, which is in contrast to the *either-close-enough-or-not*–principle of OFL_{cc}. In [4], it was shown that OFL_{loc} outperforms OFL_{cc} with respect to the solution quality in local search, and that OFL_{loc} leads to more natural results. Hence, we use OFL_{loc}, and refer to OFL_{cc} chiefly for a clearer presentation of results. OFL_{loc} is to be maximized, while OFL_{cc} is to be minimized.

The objective function for regularity *OFR* was introduced in [5]. Regularity optimization aims at producing a schedule that can be written in a structured and intuitively simple form. Hence, the SIs should be arranged so that the sequence of values $op(s)$ and $V(s)$ exhibits regular patterns. *OFR* is a complex function omitted for brevity [5]. Briefly, it is based on the identification of loop structures in the schedule under consideration. To each recognized loop, some gain is assigned, and the gains are summed up. The summation takes only part of the loops into account, namely a maximal conflict-free subset. A subset of loops is called conflict-free if all the loops can be simultaneously realized in a single structured representation. The assignment of gains follows an empirically established formula; a greedy heuristic is used to select the maximal conflict-free subset of loops. The evaluation of *OFR* is more costly (in terms of computing time) than the evaluation of OFL_{loc}.

In the present implementation, regularity optimization is restricted to the SI sequencing aspect. Hence, we will usually assume *DB* to be fixed as standard row-wise storage order.

We have implemented a local search algorithm to approximately solve the optimization problem. The algorithm starts from a random schedule and repeatedly considers some neighbourhood of the current schedule. If a neighbour with a higher objective function value is encountered, the current schedule is replaced by that neighbour (at least the new neighbour is a candidate for replacement, see below). The neighbourhood comprises moves of consecutive SI groups as well as loop transformations (permutation, reversal, distribution, and a novel transformation called loop extension [5]). All intermediate schedules must respect the *dag*.

Locality and regularity are typically conflicting goals that must be traded off. [5] combines them in a two-step algorithm. In Step 1, locality has priority. Regularity comes in by choosing the next schedule from k locality-improving neighbours according to a weighted sum of OFL_{loc} and *OFR*. The weight is a parameter to be specified by the user. In Step 2, a neighbour must improve *OFR* and must not degrade OFL_{loc} too much (controlled by another parameter).

Step 2 of the algorithm is costly since *OFR* must be evaluated for many neighbours. This is one shortcoming of the algorithm. Another shortcoming is the algorithm's tendency to produce distracting structured representations. A structured representation is called *distracting* if it highlights another than the locality-relevant structure, and is hence misleading. An example is given in Sect. 4. This paper addresses the shortcomings.

3.3. Previous results and relevance for this paper

Reference [4] gives experimental results for about 15 example programs, mostly taken from the compiler research literature. The experiments referred to both the case that *DB* was fixed and to the case that *DB* had to be found. Regularity optimization was not covered. The results show that the local search algorithm compares well with compiler optimizations. The OFL_{cc} values achieved for example PIs were always the same or better than those of compiler optimized reference PIs. Due to the choice of the example programs, the improvements were often small. In two cases, the restructuring found for the PI was generalized into a restructuring of the program with a performance gain of about 20–30% over the compiler-optimized version. This performance gain was measured for realistic input sizes on a real machine.

Reference [5] gives some examples of PIs that were optimized for both locality and regularity. Due to the shortcomings mentioned above, the experiments were restricted to PIs with a very small input size. The examples show trade-offs between locality and regularity.

In particular the experimental results of [4] are still relevant for the modified algorithm suggested in the present paper. The suggested modification makes it easier for the user to recognize the differences between the original and the optimized PI in the generalization phase, the modification does *not* change the program that is found by the user. That is, if the user inputs the same PI to the different variants of the algorithm suggested in [4], [5] and the present paper, he or she will normally find the same optimized program. It is, however, much harder for the user to find the program on the basis of the [4] output than it is now. Since the locality optimization potential of the algorithm has already been assessed in [4], we do not repeat the experiments here, and instead concentrate on the quality of the output representation.

4. Hierarchical clustering

Figure 1 shows an output schedule that distracts the user from the locality-relevant structure. It refers to the example of 4 × 4 matrix transpose. For clearness, only half of the program is printed. Assuming row-wise storage order and a cache line size of two, the following pairs of data are stored in the same cache line: $A[0,0]$–$A[0,1]$, $A[1,0]$–$A[1,1]$, $B[0,0]$–$B[0,1]$, $B[1,0]$–$B[1,1]$, and so on.

In the example, locality is supported best by a program in which the matrix is divided into 2 × 2 sub-matrices that are transposed one after another. Although the operation

```
B[0,0] = A[0,0];
B[0,1] = A[1,0];
B[1,0] = A[0,1];
B[1,1] = A[1,1];
B[1,2] = A[2,1];
B[1,3] = A[3,1];
B[0,2] = A[2,0];
B[0,3] = A[3,0];
   ⋮
```

or, in structured representation:

```
FOR i:=0 TO 1 DO
  B[0,i] = A[i,0];
FOR i:=0 TO 3 DO
  B[1,i] = A[i,1];
FOR i:=0 TO 1 DO
  B[0,i+2] = A[i+2,0];
   ⋮
```

Figure 1. A distracting output for matrix transpose.

listing on the top exhibits this structure, the second for-loop in the structured representation distracts from it. To be of more help, a structured representation should put the first and the next four operations, respectively, into a separate loop nest. In other words, the locality-relevant structure of the example reads that the first four operations belong together, and the next four operations belong together. The operations belong together since their accesses concentrate on a small number of memory blocks, so that there is much data reuse.

In this section, a hierarchical clustering scheme is introduced that makes the locality-relevant structure explicit. Based on this scheme, distracting loops can be eliminated. Moreover, the clustering scheme on its own is a help in the generalization phase, and supplements the structured representation.

The clustering scheme is based on a locality-optimized schedule, and highlights groups of successive SIs with a high degree of data reuse. The groups, called clusters, are further agglomerated into larger clusters with a still relatively high degree of data reuse. The agglomeration proceeds hierarchically, producing a tree.

Our task resembles hierarchical clustering as studied in pattern recognition [7,9]. Since only *successive* SIs are agglomerated, we are particularly dealing with contiguity-constrained hierarchical clustering [8]. There are important differences: In pattern recognition, a set of objects is given where each object is characterized by some feature vector. The features belong to the individual object, i.e., they do not depend on other objects (not even for relational input data). In our case, data reuse is a property that only exists in the interplay of successive SIs. Additionally, our contiguity constraint is one-dimensional, whereas [8] handles two-dimensional constraints. Also, we agglomerate more than two objects/clusters per step if this is more natural. Hence, our clustering algorithm, although inspired by algorithms from pattern recognition, is quite different from these algorithms. Since our objective is stated vaguely (to find natural clusters that are helpful in the generalization phase), we assess our results empirically (in Sect. 6).

In the following, the clustering algorithm is outlined. Explanations are given below.

```
𝒞:= set of SIs;
for all c ∈ C do
    Determine the reuse factor f(c, succ(c))
repeat
    f* := ct · max_{c∈C} {f(c, succ(c))}
    while ∃c : f(c, succ(c)) ≥ f* do
        new := FormCluster(c, f*);
        (𝒞, {f(c, succ(c))}_{c∈𝒞})
        := UpdateClustersAndReuseFactors(new)
    end
until |𝒞| = 1
```

The reuse factor $f(c, c')$ characterizes the amount of data reuse between SI groups c and c'. Its definition considers all pairs of accesses to the same memory block with one access belonging to c and the other belonging to c'. The access in c must be the last access to that memory block in c, and the access in c' must be the first access to that memory block in c'. For each such pair, an access distance is determined as the sum of the number of accesses following the access in c, and the number of accesses preceding the access in c'. The access distance is assessed using the same *the-closer-the-better* function as in OFL_{loc} [4], and the assessments are summed up over all pairs. The resulting value is finally scaled with respect to the size of c and c'.

The scaling function is based on the intuition that the following combinations of c and c' should have the same reuse factor. (We describe each cluster by a list of memory block numbers. The list contains those memory blocks that are accessed within the cluster, in access order.)

- $c = (1),\ c' = (1)$,
- $c = (1, 2),\ c' = (2, 1)$,
- $c = (1, 2, 3),\ c' = (3, 2, 1)$,
- $c = (1, 1),\ c' = (1, 1)$, etc.

The combination $c = (1, 2, 3),\ c' = (3)$ should have a slightly lower reuse factor than the other combinations. The scaling function was empirically defined so that these intuitions are met.

The function *FormCluster*(c, f^*) forms a cluster *new* from two or more successive clusters around c (see below). *UpdateClustersAndReuseFactors* removes these clusters from $\mathcal{C}$ and replaces them by *new*. It also updates $f(\textit{new}, \textit{succ(new)})$ and $f(\textit{pred(new)}, \textit{new})$, where *pred* and *succ* denote the predecessor and successor clusters in the schedule.

The function *FormCluster* starts combining c with its successor. Then it repeatedly extends the current cluster by a neighboured cluster, as long as an appropriate neighbour exists. Let us w.l.o.g. consider a neighbour c_0 that precedes the cluster, and let us denote the current cluster by $\bar{c}$. c_0 is added to $\bar{c}$ iff either $f(c_0, \bar{c}) \geq f^*$, or if there is a direct sub-cluster $\bar{\bar{c}}$ of $\bar{c}$ with $f(c_0, \bar{\bar{c}}) \geq f^*$.

The algorithm outputs a tree consisting of the clusters found in intermediate steps (returned by *FormCluster*). The parameter $ct \in [0 \dots 1]$ (called cluster tolerance) is supplied by the user and controls the average cluster size. Clusters tend to be larger if *ct* is small.

5. The three–step optimization algorithm

The following three-step optimization algorithm avoids the shortcomings of the two-step algorithm from Sect. 3.2, and is used in the experiments of Sect. 6.

Step 1 of the algorithm corresponds to Step 1 of the algorithm from Sect. 3.2, that is, we reorder the schedule with locality as a primary and regularity as a secondary goal. In Step 2, the clustering is established as described in Sect. 4. The novel part is Step 3. It uses a modified function *OFR*' that assigns a gain to a loop only if the loop is non-distracting. A loop is non-distracting if for each cluster c and each loop iteration k, one of the following conditions holds: $c \subseteq k$, $k \subset c$, or $k \cap c = \varnothing$ (taking k and c as sets of SIs).

In addition, Step 3 restricts the neighbourhood of the local search algorithm to cluster-conform neighbours, i.e., to neighbours in which the SIs of each cluster are kept consecutive (the order may change). For the case that the neighbour is obtained by moving a group of consecutive SIs, it is easy to see that the neighbour is cluster-conform if and only if it can be produced by a reordering of the direct sub-clusters of some cluster. For the case of loop transformations, several clusters may have to be reordered in parallel. In any case, all cluster-conform neighbours can be generated in a systematic way. The number of cluster-conform neighbours tends to be much smaller than the original number of neighbours, at least if the cluster size is low. Since less neighbours need to be assessed in Step 3, the modification speeds up the algorithm. For the examples considered in this paper, the algorithm is speeded up to the extent that

Step 3 runs faster than Step 1.

As usual, Step 3 searches the neighbourhood in some deterministic, cyclic order. We replace the current schedule whenever a neighbour is found that fulfills the following three requirements:

- The neighbour improves *OFR'*.
- The OFL_{cc} value of the neighbour is at most $t3 \cdot OFL^1_{cc}$, where OFL^1_{cc} is the OFL_{cc} value of the schedule produced in Step 1, and *t3* is a user-supplied parameter (called tolerance for Step 3).
- Comparing the neighbour to the current schedule, the relation between the regularity gain and the OFL_{cc} loss (if any) is acceptable. The acceptance threshold is controlled by a user-supplied parameter *w3*. Expressed as a formula, we require

  $$OFR'_{new}/OFR'_{old} - 1 > w3 \cdot (OFL^{old}_{loc}/OFL^{new}_{loc} - 1)$$

  where *old* refers to the current schedule and *new* refers to the neighbour under consideration. *w3* is permitted to take any nonnegative real value.

Notwithstanding cluster-conformity, the neighbour may give rise to a different clustering if the new order permits the agglomeration of previously non-consecutive clusters. Larger clusters in tendency imply higher *OFR'* values. For a fair comparison between schedules, the clustering is *not* updated after a replacement of the current schedule. All we do is keeping the cluster coordinates up-to-date when the SIs have moved.

6. Experiments

This section gives experimental results for the following input PIs:

- 4×4 matrix transpose with $C = 8$ and $L = 2$ (Trapo),
- 4×4 matrix multiplication with $C = 12$ and $L = 2$ (Mult),
- Loop program in Fig. 2 with $N = 6$, $C = 4$ and $L = 2$ (Loop),
- Mergesort of $N = 32$ data with $C = 8$ and $L = 2$ (Morgo).

The mergesort input program is iterative, i.e., it makes $\lceil \log_2 N \rceil$ passes over the data where the i-th pass merges runs of length 2^{i-1} into runs of length 2^i (as in base mergesort from [3]). The program alternatingly writes to two arrays. Each SI is a merge of two runs, with some likely internal access order supposed.

```
FOR i:=0 TO N DO
   FOR j:=0 TO N DO
      f(A[i],A[j]);
```

Figure 2. Loop program taken from [11]

Figure 3 summarizes our results and shows the influence of the parameters *t3* and *ct*. Some exemplary outputs are depicted in Fig. 4–7. Each entry in Figure 3 stands for five runs with a different random initialization. The entries give OFL_{cc}/NoOfLines for the best of the five runs, and a symbol that characterizes the general impression from all the five runs. For clearness, identical entries are written only once. In the cases marked by '+', the five outcomes were, in our intuitive judgement, about as good as the example outputs given in Fig. 4–7. In the cases marked by '(+)', the structuring was improvable but the clustering was helpful. The symbol '–' marks cases where the clustering/structuring was of little help in the generalization phase.

For brevity, the influence of the parameter *w3* is not illustrated in Fig. 3. We found that the influence of *w3* is minor, provided that *w3* is set to a small value such as 0.0 or 1.0. If *w3* is set to a large value such as 100.0, then Step 3 let the operation sequence unchanged. All experiments were carried out with *w3*= 1.0. Appropriate values were also used for the parameters introduced in [4, 5].

The figures show that the clustering scheme does successfully highlight the locality-relevant structure and avoids distracting loops, provided that *ct* is set to an appropriate value. The trade-off between locality and regularity can be controlled by the parameter *t3*. For *t3*= 1.0, outputs with a very high degree of locality were produced. Slightly larger values of *t3* led to simpler solutions that may perform better in practice. The given *Mult* output with $OFL_{cc} = 40$ and the *Trapo* output correspond to compiler optimized programs. The *Loop* and *Merge* outputs generalize to programs that improve on compiler-optimized programs by about 20-30%, as shown in [4].

7 Conclusions

This paper has reported on recent progress in the development of the IBLOpt method. First, we have introduced a hierarchical clustering scheme that highlights the locality-relevant structure in an SI sequence. Second, we have applied the clustering scheme to produce a more meaningful structured representation of the final schedule, in which distracting loops are avoided. The new results are helpful in the generalization phase of our tool. The user finds the same optimized programs as with the [4, 5] version of IBLOpt, but the amount of human work needed for the generalization is reduced.

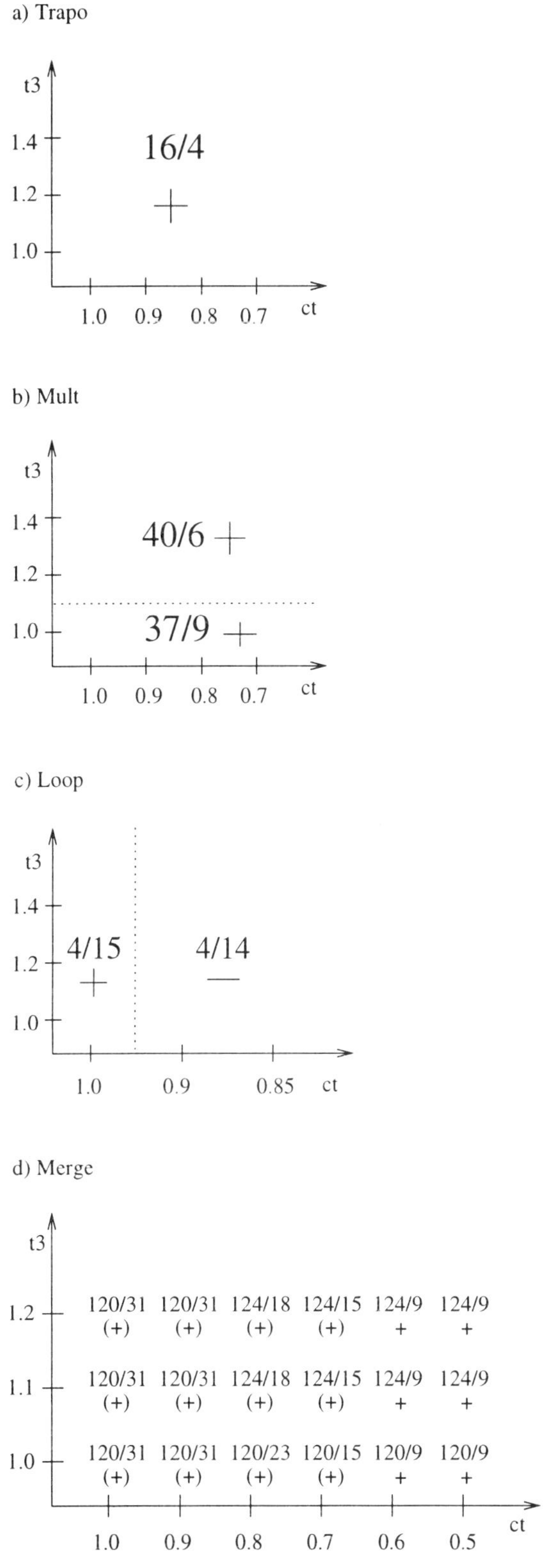

Figure 3. Results for various parameter settings.

```
f(A[0],A[4]); f(A[0],A[5]);
f(A[1],A[4]); f(A[1],A[5]);
f(A[4],A[0]); f(A[4],A[1]);
f(A[5],A[0]); f(A[5],A[1]);
f(A[0],A[2]); f(A[0],A[3]);
f(A[1],A[2]); f(A[1],A[3]);
f(A[2],A[0]); f(A[2],A[1]);
f(A[3],A[0]); f(A[3],A[1]);
f(A[0],A[0]); f(A[0],A[1]);
f(A[1],A[0]); f(A[1],A[1]);
f(A[2],A[2]); f(A[2],A[3]);
f(A[3],A[2]); f(A[3],A[3]);
f(A[4],A[4]); f(A[4],A[5]);
f(A[5],A[4]); f(A[5],A[5]);
f(A[4],A[2]); f(A[4],A[3]);
f(A[5],A[2]); f(A[5],A[3]);
f(A[2],A[4]); f(A[2],A[5]);
f(A[3],A[4]); f(A[3],A[5]);
```

```
FOR i2:=0 TO 1 DO
  FOR i1:=0 TO 1 DO
    FOR i0:=0 TO 1 DO
      f(A[i1],A[4+i0-2*i2]);
  FOR i1:=0 TO 1 DO
    FOR i0:=0 TO 1 DO
      f(A[4+i1-2*i2],A[i0]);
FOR i2:=0 TO 2 DO
  FOR i1:=0 TO 1 DO
    FOR i0:=0 TO 1 DO
      f(A[i1+2*i2],A[i0+2*i2]);
FOR i2:=0 TO 1 DO
  FOR i1:=0 TO 1 DO
    FOR i0:=0 TO 1 DO
      f(A[4+i1-2*i2],A[2+i0+2*i2]);
```

$OFL_{cc} = 4$ NoOfLines = 15

Figure 4. Example output for Loop: operation listing with clustering, and structured representation.

```
FOR i2:=0 TO 1 DO
  FOR i1:=0 TO 3 DO
    FOR i0:=0 TO 1 DO
      A[i1,i0+2*i2]=B[i0+2*i2,i1]
```

Figure 5. Example output for Trapo (structured representation only).

```
FOR i3:=0 TO 1 DO
  FOR i2:=0 TO 3 DO
    FOR i1:=0 TO 1 DO
      FOR i0:=0 TO 1 DO
        C[i2,i0+2*i3]+=
        A[i2,i1+2*i3]
        *B[i1+2*i3,i0+2*i3]
  FOR i2:=0 TO 3 DO
    FOR i1:=0 TO 1 DO
      FOR i0:=0 TO 1 DO
        C[3-i2,i0+2*i3]+=
        A[3-i2,2+i1-2*i3]
        *B[2+i1-2*i3,i0+2*i3]
```

OFL_{cc}: 37

```
FOR i4:=0 TO 1 DO
  FOR i3:=0 TO 1 DO
    FOR i2:=0 TO 3 DO
      FOR i1:=0 TO 1 DO
        FOR i0:=0 TO 1 DO
          C[i2,i0+2*i3]+=
          A[i2,i1+2*i4]
          *B[i1+2*i4,i0+2*i3]
```

OFL_{cc}: 40

Figure 6. Example outputs for Mult.

```
FOR i3:=0 TO 1 DO
  FOR i2:=0 TO 1 DO
    FOR i1:=0 TO 1 DO
      FOR i0:=0 TO 1 DO
        Merge two runs of length 1,
        first run starts at
        2*i0+4*i1+8*i2+16*i3
      END;
      Merge two runs of length 2,
      first run starts at
      4*i1+8*i2+16*i3
    END;
    Merge two runs of length 4,
    first run starts at 8*i2+16*i3
  END;
  Merge two runs of length 8,
  first run starts at 16*i3..16*i3+7
END;
Merge two runs of length 16, namely
0..15 and 16..31
```

OFL_{cc}: 120

Figure 7. Example output for Merge.

References

[1] M. Kandemir, J. Ramanujam, and A. Choudhary. A compiler algorithm for optimizing locality in loop nests. In *Proc. 11th Int. Conf. on Supercomputing*, pages 269–276. ACM Press, July 1997.

[2] M. Kandemir, J. Ramanujam, and A. Choudhary. Compiler algorithms for optimizing locality and parallelism on shared and distributed memory machines. In *Proceedings of the 1997 International Conference on Parallel Architectures and Compilation Techniques*, pages 236–247. IEEE Computer Society Press, 1997.

[3] A. LaMarca and R. E. Ladner. The influence of caches on the performance of sorting. In *Proc. 8th ACM-SIAM Symp. on Discrete Algorithms*, pages 370–379, Jan. 1997.

[4] C. Leopold. Arranging statements and data of program instances for locality. *Future Generation Computer Systems*, Elsevier, 14:293–311, 1998.

[5] C. Leopold. Regularity considerations in instance-based locality optimization. In *Workshop Proceedings Int. Parallel Processing Symp. and Symp. on Parallel and Distributed Processing, LNCS 1586*, pages 230–238, 1999.

[6] S. S. Muchnick. *Advanced compiler design and implementation*. Morgan Kaufmann Publishers, 1997.

[7] F. D. Murtagh. *Multidimensional Clustering Algorithms*. Physica-Verlag, Vienna, 1985.

[8] F. D. Murtagh. Contiguity-constrained hierarchical clustering. *DIMACS Series in Discrete Mathematics and Theoretical Computer Science*, 19:143–152, 1995.

[9] C. F. Olson. Parallel algorithms for hierarchical clustering. *Parallel Computing*, 21(8):1313–1325, Aug. 1995.

[10] J. S. Vitter. External memory algorithms and data structures. In J. Abello and J. S. Vitter, editors, *External Memory Algorithms and Visualization*. DIMACS Series on Discrete Mathematics and Theoretical Computer Science, American Mathematical Society, 1999.

[11] M. E. Wolf and M. S. Lam. A data locality optimizing algorithm. *SIGPLAN Notices*, 26(6):30–44, June 1991.

Asynchronous Progressive Irregular Prefix Operation in HPF2

Frédéric Brégier, Marie-Christine Counilh, Jean Roman
LaBRI, ENSERB et Université Bordeaux I, 33405 Talence Cedex, France

Abstract

In this paper, we study one kind of irregular computation on distributed arrays, the irregular prefix operation, *that is currently not well taken into account by the standard data-parallel language HPF2. We show a parallel implementation that efficiently takes advantage of the independent computations arising in this irregular operation. Our approach is based on the use of a directive which characterizes an irregular prefix operation and on inspector/executor support, implemented in the* CoLuMBO *library, which optimizes the execution by using an asynchronous communication scheme and then communication/computation overlap. We validate our contribution with results achieved on IBM SP2 for basic experiments and for a sparse Cholesky factorization algorithm applied to real size problems.*

KEY WORDS: *HPF2, irregular application, prefix operation, run-time support, inspection/execution mechanism, loop-carried dependencies*

1. Introduction

High Performance Fortran (HPF2 [10]), the standard language for writing data parallel programs, is quite efficient for regular applications. Nevertheless, efficiency is still a great challenge when irregular applications are considered.

In this paper, we study one kind of irregular computation on distributed arrays that we call irregular prefix operations. This kind of computation occurs in important irregular algorithms such as sparse Cholesky factorization.
Our goal is to propose a parallel implementation of this irregular operation that efficiently takes advantage of the independent computations arising in it. This implementation is based first on the use of a directive which specifies that a loop performs an irregular prefix operation; second, on an inspector/executor support, implemented in the C*o*L*u*MBO library, which optimizes the execution phase by using an asynchronous communication scheme and then communication/computation overlap.

This paper is organized as follows. In section 2, we define an irregular prefix operation on a vector. We present different ways of writing it in HPF2 and show the limits of these versions. Then, we present our `PREFIX` clause and directive for irregular prefix operation and we describe our implementation based on the inspection/execution approach. Finally, we present some related works. Section 3 describes our experimental work on IBM SP2. We present first some basic experiments in order to study and analyze the contribution of our approach. Then, we present an experimental study for sparse Cholesky factorization applied on real size problems, which confirms its interest. Finally, section 4 concludes and gives some perspectives to our work.

2. Progressive Irregular Prefix Operation

2.1. Definition

A prefix operation on a vector is an operation where each element of the output vector is a function of the elements of the input vector that precede it. For instance, the prefix sum of the input vector C of size N is the output vector X where:

$$\forall i \in [1, N]\ X_i = \sum_{1 \leq k \leq i} C_k .$$

Prefix operations are very useful in data parallel programming and they have been included in the HPF library. So, efficient parallel implementations of these operations are possible.

An *irregular prefix operation* is such that each element of the output vector is a function of an arbitrary subset of the elements of the input vector that precede it. For example:

$$\forall i \in [1, N]\ X_i = \sum_{k \in B_i} C_k \text{ where } B_i \subseteq [1, i] .$$

We define a *progressive irregular prefix operation* on one vector as an irregular prefix operation, where the input and output vectors are the same. More precisely, each output element $X(i)$ depends on the *output* values of the elements $X(k)$, $k \in B_i$ and $k < i$, and on the input value $X(i)$. So these values are computed by step (in worst case, step by step), so the *progressive* attribute. Moreover, functions can be applied to each element during the prefix operation (g) and to each element of the result (f). For instance:

$$\forall i \in [1,N]\ X_i = f(\sum_{k \in B_i} g(X_k)) \text{ where } B_i \subseteq [1,i]\,.$$

Progressive irregular prefix operations on distributed vectors (more generally arrays) are useful in irregular applications, for example in sparse matrix applications such as sparse Cholesky factorization. Our goal is to propose a parallel implementation that efficiently takes advantage of independent computations (if $j \notin B_i$ and $i \notin B_j$, then X_i and X_j can be computed in parallel).

2.2. Progressive Irregular Prefix Operation in HPF2

In this section, we present different ways of writing an irregular prefix operation in HPF2 and we show the limits and disadvantages of each of these versions.

Program 1 shows two Fortran codes with two nested DO loops. In Program 1(a), the B_i ($i = 1, N$) sets are replaced by a 2-dimensional array `B` where `B(i,:)` contains the `NB(i)` elements of the $B_i - \{i\}$ set. Program 1(b) uses a symmetric approach by using the 2-dimensional array `Bs` such that: `K ∈ Bs(I,:)` ⇔ `I ∈ B(K,:)` (so, elements in `Bs(I,:)` belong to `]I,N]`). In these programs, the `I` and `J` loops are not `INDEPENDENT` loops because each element of `X` is computed from some of the elements of `X` that precede it. These loops are no more `INDEPENDENT` loops with reduction statement since a reduction variable cannot be used in a reduction statement (more precisely, the reference `X(K)` is forbidden in the statement `X(I) = X(I) + X(K)`; cf. [10, pp. 71-76]). So, without any information about the properties of the loops, a HPF compiler will generate an inefficient serial SPMD code based on the *owner computes rule*.

```
DO I = 1, N                          (a)
   DO J = 1, NB(I)
      X(I) = X(I) + g(X(B(I,J)))
   END DO
   X(I) = f(X(I))
END DO

DO I = 1, N                          (b)
   X(I) = f(X(I))
   DO J = 1, NBs(I)
      X(Bs(I,J)) = X(Bs(I,J)) + g(X(I))
   END DO
END DO
```

Program 1. Prefix sum (a) and prefix sum in symmetric form (b)

In Program 2, we use a temporary variable (`TMP`) so that the inner loop `J` is an `INDEPENDENT` loop with reduction. This loop can be simply and efficiently implemented: each processor uses a private accumulator variable associated with the reduction variable and performs a subset of the `J` loop iterations. When it encounters a reduction statement, it updates its own accumulator variable. After the loop, the final value of the reduction variable is computed by combining the private accumulator variables using the reduction operator. In an MPI based implementation, the `MPI_Reduce` function could be used for this *combining operator*. But due to the indirect access (`X(B(I,J))`), the compiler will consider that all the processors take part in the collective communication at each iteration `I` even though it is not always necessary. So processors are synchronized at every iteration.

```
   DO I = 1, N                          (a)
      TMP = 0.0
!HPF$ INDEPENDENT, REDUCTION(TMP)
      DO J = 1, NB(I)
         TMP = TMP + g(X(B(I,J)))
      END DO
      X(I) = X(I) + TMP
      X(I) = f(X(I))
   END DO

   DO I = 1, N                          (b)
      TMP = 0.0
      TMP2 = 0.0
      DO J = 1, NB(I)
         if (X(B(I,J)) is local) then
            TMP2 = TMP2 + g(X(B(I,J)))
         end if
      END DO
      REDUCTION(TMP2, SUM)
      TMP = TMP + TMP2
      if (X(I) is local) then
         X(I) = X(I) + TMP
         X(I) = f(X(I))
      end if
   END DO
```

Program 2. Prefix sum with reduction (a) and its SPMD code (b)

Finally, the array prefix functions (`XXX_PREFIX`) and scatter functions (`XXX_SCATTER`) of the HPF library are not well suited to express irregular prefix operations and successive calls to these functions with appropriate mask vectors should be required. For example, the mask array that can be used in a prefix function to specify the elements of the vector that contribute to the result is not enough: here, each element of the result requires a specific mask (that represents the subset B_i).

None of the versions presented here can lead to a parallel implementation that allows parallel computations on some elements of the result. In the following section, we introduce a directive and a clause that may help a compiler to do so.

2.3. The PREFIX Clause and Directive

The PREFIX(*prefix-variable*) directive can precede a DO loop. It asserts the compiler that iterations in the following DO loop compute *prefix-variable* as the result of an (*irregular*) prefix operation.

The PREFIX(*prefix-variable*) clause is used with an INDEPENDENT directive and it asserts that the named variable is update in the INDEPENDENT loop by a series of operations that are associative and commutative. This clause is always relative to a declared surrounding PREFIX DO loop. The syntax of *prefix-variable* and *prefix-statement* is the same as *reduction-variable* and *reduction-statement* defined in HPF2. The difference between the REDUCTION and PREFIX clauses is that a reference to a PREFIX variable can occur in the operand part of a PREFIX statement. But, in this case, the PREFIX clause of the INDEPENDENT loop asserts the compiler that only final values (and not intermediate values) of the PREFIX variable are used within this loop. We consider Program 1 Version b. In this program, we know that X(I) gets its final value at iteration I (in the statement X(I) = f(X(I))), and that X(I) is never read before iteration I nor modified after this iteration. So we can use the PREFIX clause and directive to obtain Program 3.

```
!HPF$ PREFIX(X)
  DO I = 1, N
     X(I) = f(X(I))
!HPF$ INDEPENDENT, PREFIX(X)
     DO J = 1, NBs(I)
        X(Bs(I,J)) = X(Bs(I,J)) + g(X(I))
     END DO
  END DO
```

Program 3. HPF2/PREFIX code for an irregular prefix operation

In the following section, we show how a compiler can use the directive and clause introduced here.

2.4. Code Generation for a Prefix Do Loop

To implement INDEPENDENT loop with prefix statement, we use the same mechanism as for reductions (cf. section 2.3) by using a private accumulator variable that has the same shape than the PREFIX variable. For Program 3, on each processor, the private accumulator (cf. Program 4) is an array (TMP(1:N)). Unlike a reduction implementation, the combining operation is performed for only one element at a time of the prefix array variable. More precisely, the combining operation which computes the final value of X(I) from the local variables TMP(I) (Reduction (TMP(I), SUM)) must be performed within the external PREFIX loop; moreover, it must be executed after the last write access to each private variable TMP(I) and before the first read access to X(I).

In some simple cases, the compiler can determine the position of the combining operation. In Program 3, it may be performed at the beginning of iteration I since X(I) is read for the first time at the beginning of this iteration and TMP(I) is written only before iteration I (according to the PREFIX clause). But, in Program 4, this combining operation is still performed in a synchronous way. So, we propose to introduce asynchronism in communication in order to overlap communication by computation, and more precisely, to separate the send calls and the receive calls associated with the combining operation for X(I) so that:

1. the send call is performed independently and as soon as possible on each processor (i.e. when the corresponding private variable TMP(I) has its own final value),
2. the receive calls are performed as late as possible by the processor that owns X(I) (i.e. before its first read operation of X(I) outside a prefix statement).

```
TMP(1:N) = 0.0
DO I = 1, N
   REDUCTION(TMP(I), SUM)
   if (X(I) is local) then
      X(I) = X(I) + TMP(I)
      X(I) = f(X(I))
      DO J = 1, NBs(I)
         TMP(Bs(I,J)) = TMP(Bs(I,J)) + g(X(I))
      END DO
   end if
END DO
```

Program 4. SPMD pseudo-code for Program 3

To enable such an execution, an inspection step is required to determine when local computations on TMP(I) are over so that it can be sent, and which processor subset effectively contributes to the final value of X(I) (the owner of X(I) must receive only from these processors).

The inspection step (cf. Program 5(a)) consists in three parts. The first one only registers an array as a *prefix variable* (Insp_Prefix_Data). The second part is a local one: each processor scans its local accesses to the *prefix variable*. The calls to Insp_Prefix_Statement(X(Bs(I,J))) count the read/write accesses to X(Bs(I,J)) within the *prefix statement*; the Insp_Prefix_Access(X(I)) call determines which processor needs the final value of X(I). Finally, the third part (Insp_Prefix_Done) is in two steps: first, all processors gather their local information by using global communications; then each processor locally keeps only the relevant information.

The execution step (cf. Program 5(b)) uses two routines: Prefix_Statement and Prefix_Access. Each call

```
Insp_Prefix_Data(X(1:N))                        (a)
DO I = 1, N
  if (X(I) is local) then
    Insp_Prefix_Access(X(I))
    DO J = 1, NBs(I)
      Insp_Prefix_Statement(X(Bs(I,J)))
    END DO
  end if
END DO
Insp_Prefix_Done()

DO I = 1, N                                     (b)
  if (X(I) is local) then
    Prefix_Access(X(I))
          !receive: combining operation
    X(I) = f(X(I))
    DO J = 1, NBs(I)
      TMP(Bs(I,J)) = TMP(Bs(I,J)) + g(X(I))
      Prefix_Statement(X(Bs(I,J)))
          !send when ready
    END DO
  end if
END DO
```

Program 5. Inspector(a) / Executor(b) SPMD pseudo-code of Program 3

to `Prefix_Statement(TMP(Bs(I,J)))` decreases the counter resulting from the `Insp_Prefix_Statement(X(Bs(I,J)))` calls in the inspector step. When this counter reaches zero, the processor sends the value of its private accumulator variable `TMP(Bs(I,J))`. The `Prefix_Access(X(I))` call performs the receive operations and combines the received values to yield the final value of `X(I)`. Only one combining operation can appear for each prefix variable element (according to the `PREFIX` clause). So only the first `Prefix_Access` call for each element is required. Since all following accesses are on the same *prefix variable* element `X(I)` (excepting the access to the *prefix variable* for the *prefix statement*), the compiler can optimize the executor code by removing the subsequent `Prefix_Access` calls (which could have take place before the *prefix statement*). Anyway, all subsequent calls will be ignored by the run-time support.

So, the inspection/execution steps of Program 5 enable an "asynchronous execution of the prefix operation" where communication can be overlapped by computation. Note that Program 1(a) could also be written by using the `PREFIX` clause and directive. But, in this program, the last write access to the accumulator variable `TMP(I)` takes place just before the first read access to `X(I)`. So, in the corresponding SPMD code, the send and receive operations would take place side by side after the `ENDDO` of the `J` loop and before the statement `X(I) = f(X(I))`. Consequently, this version presents no overlap capabilities and looks like Program 2.

Note that if the global loop is declared as `PREFIX` but the `INDEPENDENT, PREFIX(X)` directive on the internal loop is omitted, the same inspection/execution scheme can be applied with a slight difference: the basic communication scheme is a broadcast (not a reduction) since the compiler will apply the *owner computes rule* on the internal loop (for Program 3 without the internal directive, `X(I)` will be broadcast). For simplicity, we omit this case in this paper.

We have implemented this inspection/execution scheme in our Co*Lu*MBO library. We have incorporated three implementation optimizations that are not shown, for simplicity, in the SPMD codes. The first optimization limits the size of the private accumulator array to its relevant part saving memory space. The second optimization consists in the scan of sections instead of single elements of the prefix variable array so as to save memory space and time. The third optimization consists in the reception of pending communications before the corresponding `Prefix_Access` call in order to avoid the saturation of the MPI communication buffers.

2.5. Related Work

To our knowledge, progressive irregular prefix operations have not been studied in the context of HPF or HPF-like languages as FortranD [16], Vienna Fortran [14] or HPF+ [3].

Inspector/executor paradigm has been widely used but for solving iterative irregular problems in which communication and computation phases alternate; indeed, in those kinds of applications, the cost of optimizations performed at the inspector stage can be amortized over many computation iterations at the executor stage. Major works include PARTI [16] and CHAOS [11] libraries used in Vienna Fortran and Fortran90D [15] compilers, and PILAR library [12] used in PARADIGM compiler [2]. These libraries are based on a `gather/scatter` approach and use the same optimized communication scheme on every (or at least many) iteration. So they do not address such asynchronous prefix operation since each iteration of the `PREFIX` loop has its own communication scheme.

The PILAR [13] library uses sections as minimal inspected elements, as our Co*Lu*MBO library does. This is necessary in order to produce an efficient inspector in most cases, since the minimal element considering in Fortran programs is often, at least, a section of array and not a single element.

3. Experimental Validations

3.1. Basic Experiments

This section studies the interest of our approach with some experimental validations achieved from the three SPMD codes given at Program 2, Program 4 and Program 5. Note that for Program 5, all measures will include inspector times. In our experimentation, the value of N is 1200 and X is a 2-dimensional array (300×1200) and has a (*, CYCLIC) distribution. The costs of functions f and g vary from 300 Flops to 400 KFlop. We also use various coefficients c of irregularity characterized by the ratio (in percent) of the number of elements in each subset B_i with the corresponding maximal possible number: so $c = 100\%$ means i elements in Bi ($B_i = [1, i]$ and B(I,J) = J, 1≤J<I); in general, c means $i \times c$ elements in B_i. So the lower the coefficient, the lower the irregularity or the number of elements in B_i.

We first compare Program 2 and Program 5 with a fixed cost for functions f and g (cost = 10 KFlop). We measure the time ratio of Program 5 compared to Program 2 both executed with various combinations of processor number p and coefficient c. Figure 1 gives the results achieved for p = 4, 8, 16 and c from 100 to 1%. For a fixed number of processors and a fixed function (f and g) cost, we define the *prefix balance coefficient* as the coefficient of irregularity such that Program 2 and Program 5 have the same execution time (time ratio = 1.0) (for example, this prefix balance coefficient is 4.6% for 4 processors and function cost = 10KFlop).

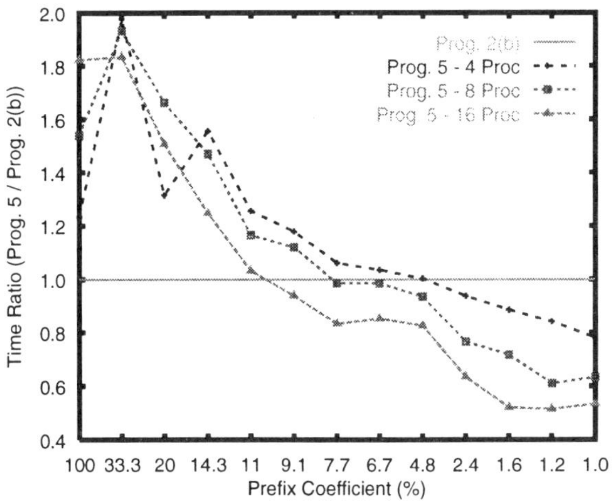

Figure 1. Time ratios vs. Prog. 2 with various coefficients of irregularity and processors ((f, g) fixed cost (10KFlop))

First of all, we can see that the lower the coefficient, the better the results of asynchronous prefix version (time ratio from 2.0 to 0.5). For Program 4, the time ratios compared to Program 2 (not shown) are always bad (from 6.0 with $c = 100\%$ to 2.0 with $c = 1\%$). This result shows the great interest of the asynchronous communication approach for the combining operation.

Figure 2(a) gives the prefix balance coefficient for various combinations of the processor number and function cost. For a fixed computation cost, one sees that increasing the number of processors increases the corresponding prefix balance coefficient. The reason is that the number of implied communications increases when more processors are involved, so there is more capability of overlapping communications by computations.

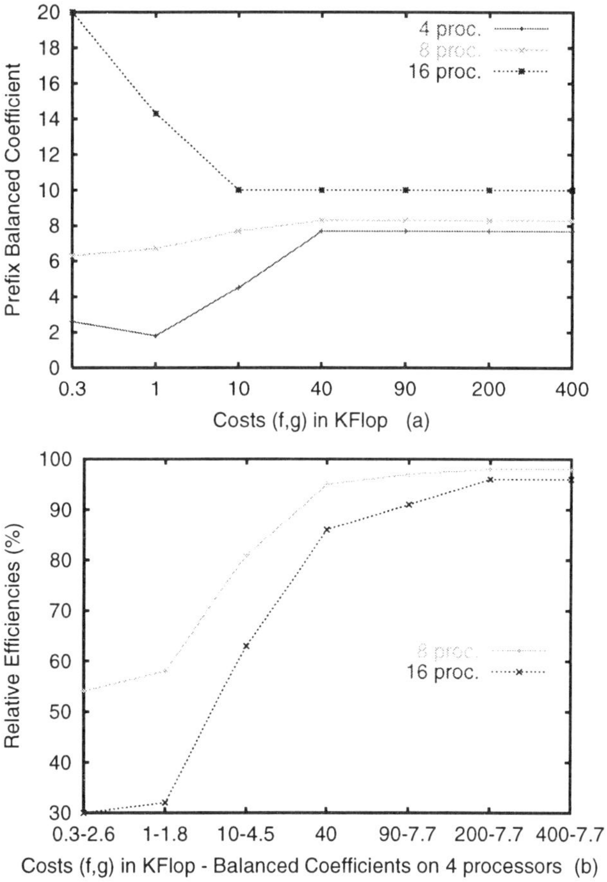

Figure 2. Prefix balance coefficients on various processors with various (f, g) costs (a) and Relative efficiencies compared to 4 processor times with fixed (f, g) costs (b)

If we fixed the number of processors, so increasing the elementary cost, the number of communications does not change but computations can better overlap communications since there are more expensive. To obtain again the prefix balance coefficient, we can therefore have more communications, so, with a fixed number of processors, the higher the elementary cost, the higher the prefix balance coefficient. We also observe that the prefix balance coefficient becomes stable (between 7 and 10%) after a certain elementary cost (40 KFlop). We suppose that this stability

is probably due to some overlap limitations or to some basic example specificities.
Another contradiction appears with the execution on 16 processors. It is in fact due to the lack of computation on so many processors, which introduces a scalability problem. Figure 2(b) presents the relative efficiencies of Program 5 with 8 and 16 processors compared to 4 processors with a coefficient of irregularity equals to the balanced prefix coefficient on 4 processors. With 0.3 and 1 KFlop and such low coefficients (2.6 and 1.8% respectively), there are low efficiencies (around 30%) on 16 processors. The computations have a very low cost, so only communications are taking into account in the relative efficiencies. Therefore, we measure in fact the relative efficiencies of asynchronous communications compared to synchronous ones. In order to obtain again the balanced prefix coefficient when there is a scalability problem, we must increase the amount of computations by increasing the coefficient, so the results on 16 processors.

Finally, we have measured the inspection cost with respect to a global execution. In our experiments, the inspection time represents between 1 to 8% of the global execution time. These good performances show the interest of the implementation optimizations performed in the inspector (cf. 2.4).

Shortly, these basic experiments show first that the lower the coefficient of irregularity, the better the performance of asynchronous prefix version, and second that efficiency is achieved even with only one executor step (unlike a standard inspector/executor approach which requires many executor steps to repay the inspector cost).

3.2. Cholesky Example

We describe here the experimental results we have obtained for an important computation arising in many scientific and engineering applications: the sparse Cholesky block factorization [8, 7, 1]. In this application, each column block is updated by some column blocks to its left on the sparse matrix; the subset $B_i \subseteq [1, i]$ of column blocks depends here on the sparsity structure of the matrix. More precisely, the structure of the application is closed to the extended HPF program presented in Program 3.

We then compare the three following versions of the Cholesky application:

- the `FIR` version (Program 6) is closed to the SPMD code in Program 4 using a reduction operation;
- the `FIP` version (Program 7) is closed to Program 5 using a specific inspection phase and an asynchronous communication scheme;
- the MPI version refers to a hand-made high-optimized MPI version presented in [9].

The `FIR` and `FIP` versions use other optimizations not presented in this paper for handling irregular applications in HPF2. In both versions, the sparse matrix data structure is represented by using the *tree notation*, introduced in [4], based on the derived data type of Fortran 90. This notation avoids indirect data accesses coming from the standard irregular programming style, so that both compile-time and run-times techniques can be more easily performed. Both versions use the *processor subset* optimization in order to restrict the scope of communications associated with each iteration only to the required processor subset [4]. Finally, they also use a *task scheduling* optimization (`SCHEDULE` directive) where each iteration of the outer loop is associated with a task. Due to the irregularity property of the prefix operation, some tasks are independent from other tasks and can be executed in parallel (or in any order). The goal of our task scheduler is to order the task execution so as to minimize the global execution time while respecting the dependence constraints [6].

```
!HPF$ SCHEDULE (J = 1:K-1, bj = 1:NB(J), &
     ANY(A(J)%BCOL(bj)%BLOC) in A(K)%BCOL(1)%BLOC)

 DO K = 1, NB_BLOC_COL
!HPF$ ON HOME (A(J), J = 1:K-1, &
   ANY(A(J)%BCOL(:)%BLOC) in A(K)%BCOL(1)%BLOC) &
                                            , BEGIN
   TMP%BLOC%VAL = 0.0
!HPF$ INDEPENDENT, REDUCTION(TMP%BLOC%VAL)
   DO J = 1, K-1
      Update A(K)%BCOL with A(J)%BCOL      ! (BLAS)
   END DO
   A(K)%BCOL(:)%BLOC%VAL += TMP%BLOC%VAL
   LLt A(K)%BCOL(:)%BLOC%VAL      ! (LAPACK + BLAS)
!HPF$ END ON
 END DO
```

Program 6. FIR HPF Pseudo Code

```
!HPF$ PREFIX (A(:)%BCOL(:)%BLOC(:,:)%VAL)

!HPF$ SCHEDULE (J = 1:K-1, bj = 1:NB(J), &
     ANY(A(J)%BCOL(bj)%BLOC) in A(K)%BCOL(1)%BLOC)

 DO K = 1, NB_BLOC_COL
!HPF$ ON HOME (A(K)), BEGIN
   LLt A(K)%BCOL(:)%BLOC%VAL      ! (LAPACK + BLAS)
!HPF$ INDEPENDENT, PREFIX(A%BCOL%BLOC%VAL)
   DO J = K+1, NB_BLOC_COL
      Update A(J)%BCOL with A(K)%BCOL      ! (BLAS)
   END DO
!HPF$ END ON
 END DO
```

Program 7. FIP HPF Pseudo Code

Two libraries have been developed to support these optimizations. The T*ri*D*en*T library [4] supports distributed trees. The C*o*L*u*MBO library supports all the inspector/executor techniques that we have designed especially for irregular processor subsets, irregular loop index inspection [4], task scheduling [6] and irregular prefix operations.
We currently use these libraries by writing HPF2 codes with

explicit calls to T*ri*D*en*T and C*o*L*u*MBO primitives. Then, we use the HPF compilation platform ADAPTOR [5] to obtain the final SPMD codes.

Matrix	C.B.	Col.	NNZ	NOp	Av. Coeff.
BCSSTK32	4286	44609	5.5 M	1.3 GFlop	0.368%
GRID 511	8216	261121	12 M	2.5 GFlop	0.121%
OILPAN	8024	73752	9.5 M	3.35 GFlop	0.129%
CUBE 31	1050	29791	8 M	5.5 GFlop	3.599%
CUBE 39	1129	59319	22 M	22 GFlop	4.518%

Figure 3. Properties of different sparse matrices

Experiments have been performed on IBM SP2 with 16 processors on various sparse matrices whose characteristics are described in Figure 3 (the number of Column-Blocks (C.B.), of Columns (Col.), of non zero elements (NNZ) and of operations (NOp)). The last column gives the average coefficient of irregularity. The average coefficient means that each column-block `I` has (on average since each column-block has its own subset B_i) `I` $\times c$ left-column-blocks which contribute to its irregular prefix operation. Matrices are distributed according to the *subtree-to-subcube* mapping [7] using an `INDIRECT` format; this mapping leads to an efficient reduction of communication while keeping a good load balance between processors.

Figure 4(a) gives the execution times obtained in seconds (for `FIR` and `FIP` versions, for global (inspection+execution) time and for execution time). The `FIP` versions are clearly better than the `FIR` ones (the gain varies from 3 to 62% for global time and from 0 to 35% for execution time). This great improvement comes from the asynchronous communication scheme, which allows communication/computation overlap. As noted in our basic experiments (cf. section 3.1), we can see that the lower the coefficient of irregularity, the higher the gain of the `FIP` version with regard to the `FIR` version. We can also note that the inspector time is proportional to the number of column-blocks (in accordance with the inspector SPMD code) and to the number of elements in B_i.

Finally, Figure 4(b) shows the time ratio of the `FIR` and `FIP` versions with regard to the MPI version. We can see that the ratio between the global time and the MPI time grows as the cost of the inspector time (from 1.2 for CUBE 31 to 3.5 for BCSSTK 32). However, when we consider only the execution time, the ratio is only about 1.11 to 1.18, except for the BCSSTK 32 (1.42, probably not enough work for a good scalability) for `FIP` and about 1.16 to 1.84 for `FIR`.

Ratio between regular HPF code and hand-made MPI code is generally about 1.50, and is worst in irregular application. So the results presented here show the great interest of our approach to obtain efficient irregular codes based on irregular prefix operations. This approach combines inspector/executor techniques for processor subset, task scheduling and asynchronous prefix operations.

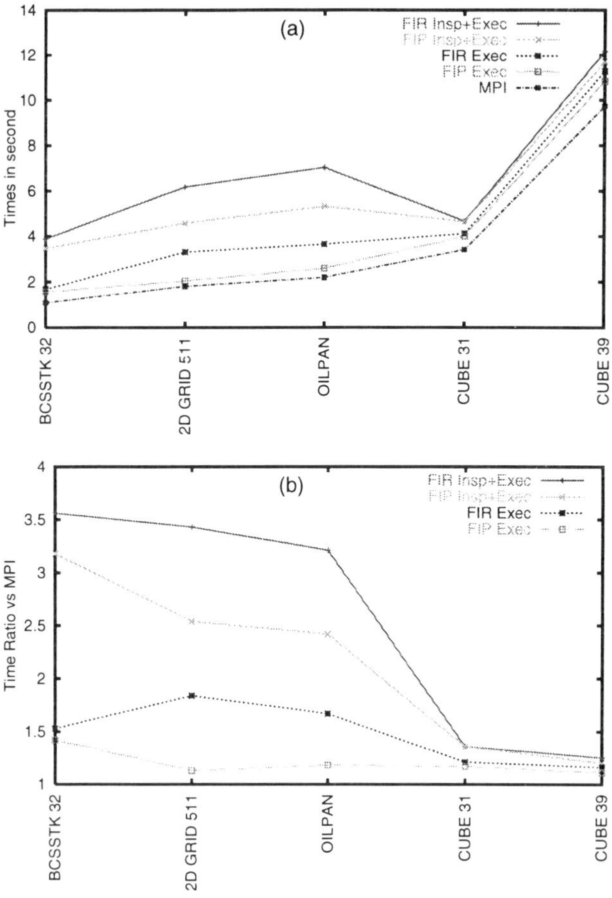

Figure 4. Times (a) and Time ratio (b) of Cholesky factorizations on different matrices on 16 processors

4. Conclusion

The new `PREFIX` clause and directive added to the HPF2 language with an appropriate inspector/executor mechanism enable an efficient implementation of *progressive irregular prefix operations*. The proposed execution optimizations are based on an asynchronous communication scheme and communication/computation overlap. The C*o*L*u*MBO library is our run-time support for this inspector/executor. The experimental results achieved on basic examples and on a sparse Cholesky factorization applied on real size problems show the great interest of our approach.

Our future work is to study some other kinds of irregular computations such as unbalanced computations, and to extend our approach to the new SMP architecture, which involves both message passing and shared memory programming styles. We have implemented a prototype source-to-source compiler, not shown in this paper, which is able to translate simple HPF2 codes with our new directives and clauses into HPF2 codes with the corresponding inspection/execution code. So, we also study the possibility to transfer our knowledge of its implementation into a real HPF compiler in order to allow the compilation of more complicated HPF2 source codes.

References

[1] C. Ashcraft, S. Eisenstat, J.-H. Liu, and A. Sherman. A Comparison of Three Column Based Distributed Sparse Factorization Schemes. In *Fifth SIAM Conference on Parallel Processing for Scientific Computing*, 1991.

[2] P. Banerjee, J. Chandy, M. Gupta, J. Holm, A. Lain, D. Palermo, S. Ramaswamy, and E. Su. The PARADIGM compiler for distributed-memory message passing multicomputers. In *The First International Workshop on Parallel Processing*, pages 322–330, Bangalore, India, Dec. 1994.

[3] S. Benkner. HPF+: High Performance Fortran for advanced scientific and engineering applications. *Future Generation Computer Systems*, 15(3):381–391, 1999. also in Tech. Report TR 99-1 from *Institute for Software Technology and Parallel Systems, University of Vienna*, with E. Laure and H. Zima.

[4] T. Brandes, F. Brégier, M.-C. Counilh, and J. Roman. Contribution to Better Handling of Irregular Problems in HPF2. In *Proceedings of EURO-PAR'98*, volume 1470 of *LNCS*, pages 639–649, Southampton, UK, Sept. 1998. Springer-Verlag. Also available as a LaBRI Research Report RR 120598, 1998.

[5] T. Brandes and F. Zimmermann. ADAPTOR — A transformation tool for HPF programs. In K. M. Decker and R. M. Rehmann, editors, *Programming environments for massively parallel distributed systems: working conference of the IFIP WG10.3, Ascona, Italy*, pages 91–96, Cambridge, MA, USA, Apr. 25–29 1994. Birkhauser Boston Inc.

[6] F. Brégier, M.-C. Counilh, and J. Roman. Scheduling loops with partial loop-carried dependencies. Submitted to Special Issue on "Parallel Computing for Irregular Applications", 2000.

[7] K. G. et al. *Parallel Algorithms for Matrix Computations*. SIAM, Philadelphia, 1990.

[8] A. George and J.-H. Liu. *Computer Solution of Large Sparse Positive Definite Systems*. Prentice-Hall, Englewood Cliffs, NJ, 1981.

[9] P. Henon, P. Ramet, and J. Roman. A Mapping and Scheduling Algorithm for Parallel Sparse Fan-In Numerical Factorization. In LNCS, editor, *Europar'99 Parallel Processing*, number 1685, pages 1059–1067, Toulouse, France, Aug. 1999.

[10] HPF Forum. *High Performance Fortran Language Specification*. Jan. 1997. Version 2.0.

[11] Y.-S. Hwang, B. Moon, S. Sharma, R. Ponnusamy, R. Das, and J. Saltz. Runtime and Language Support for Compiling Adaptive Irregular Programs on Distributed Memory Machines. *Software - Practice and Experience*, 25(6):597–621, 1995.

[12] A. Lain. *Compiler and Run-time Support for Irregular Computations*. PhD thesis, University of Illinois, 1996.

[13] A. Lain and P. Banerjee. Exploiting spatial regularity in irregular iterative applications. In *Proceedings of the 9th International Symposium on Parallel Processing (IPPS'95)*, pages 820–826, Los Alamitos, CA, USA, Apr. 1995. IEEE Computer Society Press.

[14] S. Mukherjee, S. Sharma, M. Hill, J. Larus, A. Rogers, and J. Saltz. Efficient Support for Irregular Applications on Distributed-Memory Machines. In *ACM SIGPLAN Symposium on Principles & Practice of Parallel Programming (PPoPP)*, pages 68–79, July 1995.

[15] R. Ponnusamy, Y. Hwang, R. Das, J. Saltz, A. Choudhary, and G. Fox. Supporting Irregular Distributions in Fortran 90D/HPF Compilers. *IEEE Parallel and Distributed Technology*, 1995. Technical Report CS-TR-3268 and UMIACS-TR-94-57.

[16] J. Wu, R. Das, J. Saltz, H. Berryman, and S. Hiranandani. Distributed Memory Compiler Design for Sparse Problems. *IEEE Transactions on Computers*, 44(6):737–754, 1995.

The Parallel Cellular Programming Model

Paul-Jean Cagnard
Swiss Federal Institute of Technology
Computer Science Theory Laboratory
IN Ecublens, CH-1015 Lausanne, Switzerland
cagnard@di.epfl.ch

Abstract

We present a synchronous parallel programming model designed for massively parallel fine grained applications such as cellular automata, finite element methods or partial differential equations. In this model we assume that the number of parallel processes in a program is much larger than the number of processors of the machine on which it is run. We present the computational model and the communication model. We introduce the virtual cellular machine, an abstract machine implementing this programming model which requires means to simulate efficiently the execution of many processes on a single processor, and to use the available communication bandwidth efficiently. Finally, we show an example program written in a prototype language designed for programming the virtual machine.

1. Introduction

Many parallel programming models have been proposed in the past years as alternatives to both message passing and data parallel programming. Among the most prolific class of alternate models there is the family of languages based on concurrent objects or actors. Concurrent object computation traces back to the actor model proposed by Hewitt [7], later improved by Clinger and by Agha [1].

In actor- or object-based models, parallelism of execution is expressed explicitly. These models allow to express the distribution of data explicitly and in a natural way. This opens interesting opportunities for automated data- and process-mapping.

Nearly all models based on concurrent objects or actors use asynchronous execution models, i.e., execution schemes where computation and message sending are not inherently automatically globally synchronised. As a consequence, communication has to be synchronized explicitly and each transaction between two objects must be implemented as a separate communication. Mail boxes or message queues have to be managed by the underlying system. This entails that communication is not easy to implement efficiently and concurrent object systems are often restricted to coarse grain parallelism for performance reasons. As a result, concurrent object programming, while finding a wider and wider acceptance for implementing distributed systems over wide area networks [5], is still seldom used to drive massively parallel high performance computers.

Bulk-synchronous computation was first introduced by Valiant [14, 15] with the Bulk Synchronous Parallel (BSP) model. Theoretical results [15] strongly suggest that it may be implemented efficiently on many parallel computer architectures.

In the following we will present a parallel programming model that can be seen as derived from the BSP model and other synchronous object-oriented models. We will present a virtual machine which runs processes according to this model. We will also present an example program written in a prototype language for our proposed model.

2. The parallel cellular programming model

A parallel cellular program is typically composed of a large number of fine grained processes, that is processes which execute only a small number of instructions. The computation model described below is inspired from the BSP model of computation [14]. It is more precise than the BSP model because it not only allows processes to communicate, but specifies what types of communications are allowed and how processes can communicate.

2.1. Computation model

A parallel cellular program is composed, as we have seen, of a given number of processes executing concurrently. Each process execution consists, using the BSP terminology, of a sequence of supersteps. A superstep is composed of two phases: a computation phase and a communication phase. Supersteps are separated by synchronization

1066-6192/99 $10.00

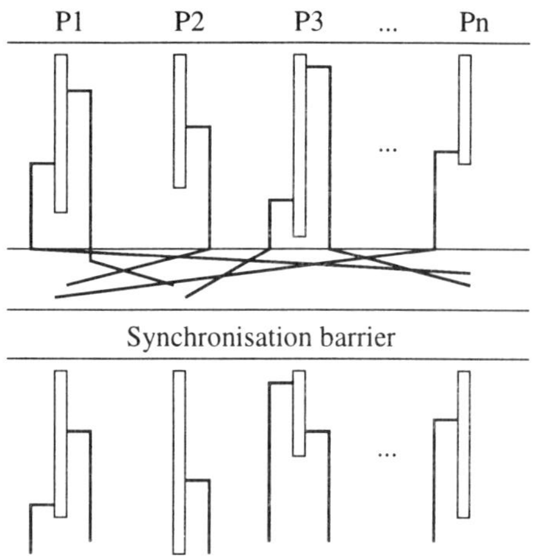

Figure 1. Program execution in the BSP model

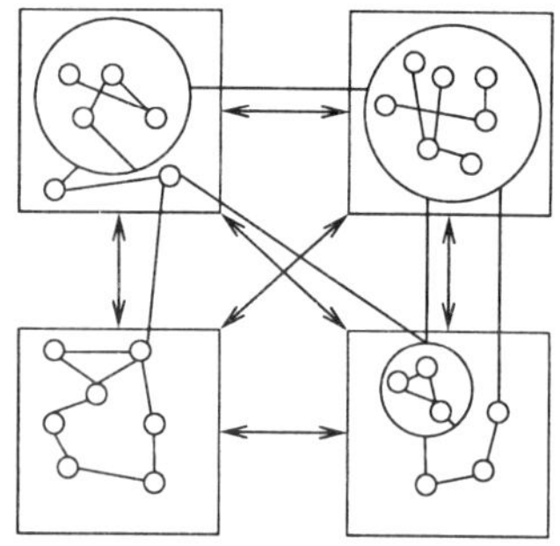

Figure 2. Program execution on four processors. Processors are represented by squares, processes by circles. Lines with arrows correspond to communication links provided by the underlying hardware or operating system, lines without arrows correspond to communication paths between processes

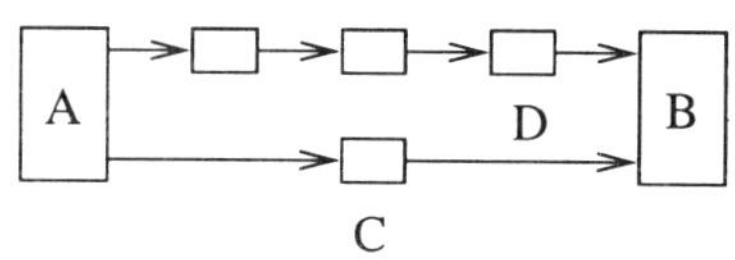

Figure 3. Reduced synchronisation frequency due to data dependencies

barriers. The execution of a program can be represented like in Fig. 1. During the computation phase of a superstep, a process executes computations which only manipulate data local to this process. These data can be local variables or data that has been received from another process. A process can send data to other processes in the course of a computation phase. The effective transmission of data between processes happens at the end of each superstep. This means that no data are exchanged during computation phases. This also implies that data sent from a given process P_1 to another process P_2 during superstep s, will only be available to the process P_2 at the beginning of the next superstep, that is superstep number $s + 1$. This type of delayed communication corresponds to the way cellular automata work. We will describe in more detail the communication model in the following section. We can observe that the parallel cellular model is an intrinsically distributed memory MIMD model.

Processes are not required to be executed in a flat structure where each process is at the same level as each other, and each process can "see" each other. Aggregates of processes can be constructed in order to build abstract processes whose behaviour is more complex than an elementary process but the rest of the program does not need to know how this behaviour is implemented. We can see an example of such a program in Fig. 2. This provides means for information hiding like in object oriented models. This also permits to use libraries of routines written following the same computation model, otherwise one would only be able to use either sequential external routines or parallel routines not following the superstep concept.

In a real world application, one may not want to synchronise all processes at the same frequency. In a program there is always a kind of global clock, this is the sequence of supersteps of highest frequency. A process may need to be synchronised or to communicate data every n supersteps only, not at each superstep for various reasons; it could present a complex behaviour that requires n supersteps to be computed, or it could have to wait n supersteps because of data dependencies like in Fig. 3 where process C has to send data only three times slower as the processes above itself in order to feed process B at the same pace as the chain of smaller processes.

Aggregates of processes and synchronism are the main characteristic features of the parallel cellular programming model. They enable developers to design programs in a modular and hierarchical way, starting from basic simple cells to more complex ones whose behaviour is represented by a network of interconnected cells which only act on their own local information. Thus reuse of already developed cells is encouraged, and the global architecture of a program can remain clear throughout development and provide a lot of information to the runtime environment in order to optimize execution speed.

Finally, is is to be noted that the number and kind of processes remain constant during execution of a program. This implies that processes can't be created nor destroyed at runtime.

2.2. Communication model

In a parallel program processes must be able to communicate in order to accomplish a useful task. They can communicate according to several models like message passing or direct remote memory access for example. In the parallel cellular model, processes exchange data in a way similar to that of the task channel model [3]. This means that they can only communicate through channels.

A channel can be viewed as a link connecting an output port of a process which produces data to an input port of a process that consumes data. Channels have the following properties:

- They are typed. A channel, like a local variable, is of a certain type, and only data of this type can be sent through this channel. The type of a channel can be any type allowed for a variable.
- They are directed. A channel can only carry data from an output port of a process to an input port of another process. If bidirectional communications are needed, two channels of opposite directions must be created between processes.
- They have a period which represents the minimal number of supersteps that must be executed before a new value can appear at the output of a given channel. This period corresponds to the inverse of the synchronisation frequency of the process that sends data through this channel.
- They are static. This has three consequences. First, the processes connected by a channel can't change during execution. Second, they must be declared before execution; channels can't be created at runtime. Third, channels can't be destroyed during execution.

A process can write as many different values into a given channel during a computation phase, but only the last written value will effectively be transmitted to the other end of the channel during the communication phase. Conversely, the output of a channel, which is the same as an input port of a process, always contains a valid value. This means that reading the content of a channel will never produce an error. This in turn implies that the same value will be available when reading a channel as long as no new value is sent through this channel. As data are effectively transmitted only between computation phases, the value a process gets when reading the contents of a channel doesn't change during a computation phase.

When processes are organized into aggregates, or groups, communications can only occur between processes or groups of the same grouping level or the level just above. We can distinguish two different cases involving communications with groups of processes. First, processes inside a group can communicate between them and with the group. Second, processes external to a group can communicate between them and with the group itself, not directly with any process inside the group. Thus a groups of process acts as a virtual process serving as an interface between the processes inside the group and processes outside of the group.

Three kinds of channels may connect processes:

- 1-1 channels, which connect a single process to another one;
- 1-n channels, which connect the output port of a single process to the input port of n other processes;
- n-1 channels, which connect the output ports of n different processes to the input port of a single process.

The first kind of channels implements one-to-one communications, the second kind is equivalent to multicasting because the same data is sent to the n receiving processes; this kind of channels is semantically identical to n 1-1 identical channels starting from the same processor. The third kind is a little more complex since n different values are sent to a single input port. We have thus defined two different semantics for these channels. One is equivalent to gathering, that is to say that the n differents values are combined into one using an operator associated with the channel. The other groups the n values into a set and the receiving process can extract individual values from this set, this is equivalent to a mailbox.

These different kind of channels, especially the n-1 channels, and their persistence are key characteristics of our communication model. Developers never have to worry whether a value is available in a channel or not because there is always one. Thus a program will never fail during communication operations. Persistent channels and synchronous communications provide a much simpler communication model to developers than traditional message passing, which can be considered as a low level communication model.

It is important to note that several different channels can exist between two processes. Since communications can only occur through predeclared channels, we can represent a program by a directed multigraph in which processes correspond to vertices and channels to edges. This level of abstraction enables a programmer to separate the description of the behaviour of the processes and the communication or interconnection topology. The use of graphical tools to design programs can thus be envisioned. Novis [4] is a tool that permits to design parallel programs graphically, but its goal was more oriented towards visual simulation than towards high performance.

Finally, we can observe that a process in the parallel cellular model can be viewed as an object in the sense of object-

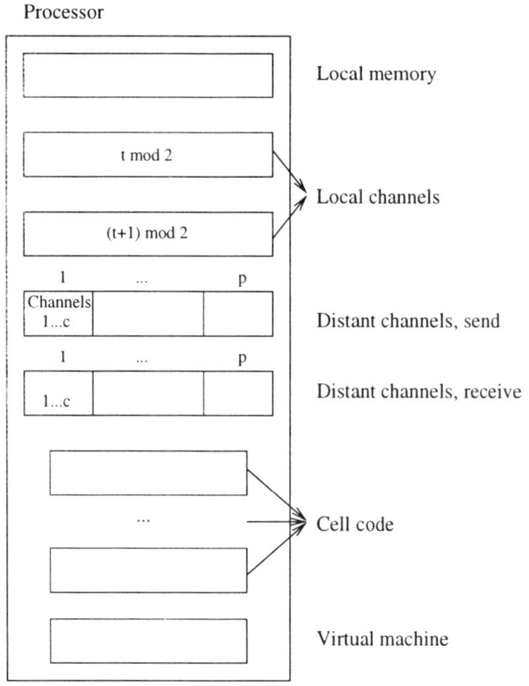

Figure 4. Architecture of the virtual cellular machine

oriented languages, with private data and code, and public data that are represented by channels.

3. The virtual cellular machine

The virtual cellular machine is the execution environment in which a parallel cellular program is run. Since we have assumed massively parallel fine grained programs, there will be much more processes than processors, so the virtual machine must find an efficient way to simulate execution of these processes on the available processors, and to use the available interprocessor communication bandwidth efficiently since fine grained programs tend to communicate a lot more than they compute. The general architecture of the virtual machine on one processor is represented in Fig. 4. The runtime provided by this virtual machine is fundamentally different from that of hardware cellular machines like, for example, the Connection Machine [9]. While the Connection Machine is a SIMD machine, permitting only the execution of identical programs on all processors, where all these processors act on a tiny part of a global data structure, our virtual cellular machine offers a kind of MIMD environment, where different processes can be executed on different processors, and where a single processor can run many processes in simulated concurrency. The most efficient way of simulating the concurrent execution of multiple processes on a single processor, especially since all processes must have finished their computation phases for the program to proceed, is looping through them. Thus on a processor one can find the instructions for all processes attributed to this processor. In addition there is some code for the management of the virtual machine, mainly to effectively send the data between supersteps. The virtual machine will thus execute in turn the code corresponding to every process that is to be run on a given processor, transmit data to other processors, and start again until the end of the program.

In order to use the interprocessor communication bandwidth efficiently, the data that are to be sent to another processor are grouped into contiguous locations in memory. Thus a single large message can be sent between two processors at the end of a superstep instead of many small ones. We can see in the figure that memory is divided into several specific zones. First there is a zone for local data which are manipulated by processes but never sent between processes. Then there are two zones used for data that corresponds to contents of channels connecting processes running on the same processor. In that case no interprocessor communication is needed and the data are only copied from one zone into the other at the end of a superstep. Of these two zones, one is the current data, available during computation phases, and the other is the future data, which will be available during the next computation phase. They play the roles of current and future data in alternance, in order to avoid copying whole zones of memory at each superstep. Then there is the zone of memory containing data to be transmitted to other processors. It is subdivided into smaller zones corresponding to a specific processor. In each of these smaller zones we have the data corresponding to individual channels. Finally there is the zone containing data received from other processors. We could have put the local communication memory zones into these last two, but for the sake of simplicity we have kept them as individual zones.

The virtual machine doesn't do any load balancing. It doesn't need to since processes can't be created or destroyed and the communication topology doesn't change at run time. This is the role of the compiler to place the processes on the processors, taking into account characteristics such as the computing load and the communication load of individual processes. The main idea is to let the programmer write a program according to the mathematical or physical model he uses. He doesn't need to artificially group smaller processes into coarser grained ones as he generally has to do and especially in ParCeL-1[16], this is the role of the compiler and the virtual machine, with the aid, if he so desires, of the programmer to force the placement of specific processes on certain processors.

4. An example program

We will present here a typical example of a massively parallel fine grained program: the simulation of moving particles on a discrete grid. We assume the reader is familiar with cellular automata. The simulation is elementary but sufficient to show the features of our computing model. Each particle has a position in the discrete grid and a speed that can be oriented in four directions: north, south, east ,and west. Each cell of the grid can contain only one particle at a given point in time, has four neighbours, from which particles can come and to which particles can go, handles the collisions between particles. Thus a cell can be empty or contain a particle with its own speed. Basic grid cells will be grouped into stripes in order to show aggregates of cells.

In this program, each cell corresponds to a process and each cell is connected to its neighbours by channels in both directions. As said before, the description of the processes can be entirely decoupled from the description of their interconnection topology. The behaviour of processes is described using an extension of the C language, and the topology is described in a graph file format called GML [10]. The language is under development and is called ParCeL-2. We could have extended any other language since we only need a few constructs to express parallelism and communication channels. Thus we benefit of all the basic work needed for the creation of a programming language.

Many languages exist already which can be used to program cellular automata or artificial neural networks, see [13, 2, 11] for example. But either they are too tied to their specific domain or their goal was expressiveness and dynamism rather than performance. In particular, cellular languages only allow to program regular grids of processes, not any desired topology; and neural network languages try to offer too much dynamism in the topology of processes, which leads to poor performance.

Here is the partial code of a typical basic cell from our simulation. Repetitive and unimportant parts have been removed. In particular, we assume that a function named `handle_collision` exists and computes the result of the collision of several particles at the place of a cell. The different `speed` variables encode the speed of particles moving away from the grid cell after a collision or of the particle present in the cell when no collision occurs. The `direction` variable stores the direction of movement of the particle in a cell.

```
celltype grid_cell
{
  IN  int N,S,E,O;
  OUT int N,S,E,O;
  int speed_N, speed_S, speed_E, speed_O;
  int speed;
  int direction;

  switch (handle_collision())
        {
        case 0 :
          write(N, speed_N);
          write(S, speed_S);
          write(E, speed_E);
          write(O, speed_O);
          break;
        case 1 :
          switch (direction)
            {
              case 0 :
                write(N, speed);
                break;
              ...
              case 3 :
                write(O, speed);
                break;
            }
        }
}
```

A stripe cell is composed of a rectangular part of the whole grid. In this case a stripe cell is only a structuring element, which means that it doesn't act on the data that pass through it; it hides the complexity of its behaviour. A compiler can optimize the execution speed of the whole program by flattening its structure. We assume that the whole grid is a torus. The various `inside` channels are the ones that come from and go to the basic grid cells hidden inside a stripe cell, while `outside` channels are the ones which enable communication with external cells.

```
celltype stripe
{
  int width = 1000;
  int height = 100;
  int i;

  IN  int inside_in_N[width],
          inside_in_S[width],
          inside_in_E[height],
          inside_in_O[height];
  IN  int outside_in_N[width],
          outside_in_S[width],
          outside_in_E[height],
          outside_in_O[height];
  OUT int inside_out_N[width],
          inside_out_S[width],
          inside_out_E[height],
          inside_out_O[height];
  OUT int outside_out_N[width],
          outside_out_S[width],
```

```
          outside_out_E[height],
          outside_out_O[height];

  for (i=0; i<width; i++)
    {
      write(outside_out_N[i],
        read(inside_in_N[i]));
      write(outside_out_S[i],
        read(inside_in_S[i]));
    }
  for (i=0; i<height; i++)
    {
      write(outside_out_E[i],
        read(inside_in_E[i]));
      write(outside_out_O[i],
        read(inside_in_O[i]));
    }
}
```

Here is the interconnexion topology. Again we have suppressed repetitive and unimportant parts. We can see the declaration of two nodes corresponding to two grid cells of the particle simulation, and the declaration of one channel from node number 1 to node number 2. We observe that channels are declared in the nodes as well as in the edges. This is due to the fact that input or output ports have to be present in the processes, or nodes, in order to be connected by channels, or edges. The hierarchical structure of the program appears in the `graph` declaration inside the first node. Connections between internal cells of type `grid_cell` can be seen in the declaration of the `edge` whose `id` is 1.1, while connections between cells of type `grid_cell` and cells of type `stripe` can be seen in the declaration of the `edge` whose `id` is 1.2.

```
graph [
  node [
    id 1
    type stripe
    inchannel inside_in_N int 1000
    ...
    inchannel inside_in_E int 100
    ...
    outchannel outside_in_N int 1000
    ...
    graph [
      node [
        id 1.1
        type grid_cell
        inchannel N int
        ...
        outchannel N int
        ...
      ]
      node [
        id 1.2
        ...
      ]
      edge [
        id 1.1
        source 1.1
        outchannel S
        target 1.2
        inchannel N
      ]
      ...
      edge [
        id 1.2
        source 1.1
        outchannel N
        target 1
        inchannel inside_in_S 0
      ]
      ...
    ]
  ]
  node [
    id 2
    ...
  ]
  ...
  edge [
    id 1
    source 1
    outchannel outside_out_N 0
    target 2
    inchannel outside_in_S 0
  ]
  edge [
    id 2
    ...
  ]
  ...
]
```

We ran a program with a grid of 1000×1000 cells on a network of 333 MHz Sun Ultra 10 workstations using MPI as a communication library. The speed-up we were able to achieve was nearly linear up to 16 processors, which is very satisfying considering that our virtual cellular machine is not much optimized yet.

5. Conclusion and future work

We have presented a programming model particularly well suited to the design of massively parallel fine grained applications. Cellular automata, partial differential equations and finite element methods are widely used for complex calculations or physical simulations, and we believe they can benefit from such a model with its associated language. Even programs using static neural networks may benefit from this programming model. Since programs are static in the sense that neither processes nor channels can be created, modified or destroyed at runtime, it is easy to represent a parallel program by a multigraph. Then we can use any graph algorithm like graph partitioning techniques to place processes on the available processors, unless the programmer decides he wants to place the processes himself.

We have implemented a first version of the virtual cellular machine that works for simple programs like the game of life or moving particles simulations. The first results are promising. We now have to study its behaviour with less regular programs, that is programs containing processes with varying computation and communication loads. This includes tests with real world applications like wave propagation[6] for example. Work is underway to use the virtual machine for linear algebra computations like matrix multiplication with systolic algorithms as described in [12].

It would be interesting to use the BSP library from Oxford university [8] instead of MPI as a communication layer.

Finally, work on a full compiler remains to be done. It should start from the descriptions of the processes and of their interconnections and build a graph representing the program. From there it can proceed to optimise placement of processes, and generate C code that can be compiled and linked with the virtual machine.

6. Acknowledgements

We would like to thank the Swiss National Science Foundation for supporting this work under grant 21-49519.96.

References

[1] G. Agha. *ACTORS, a model of concurrent computation in distributed systems.* MIT Press, 1986.

[2] J. D. Eckart. Cellang 2.0: Language Reference Manual. *ACM SIGPLAN Notices*, 27(8), Aug. 1992.

[3] I. Foster. *Designing and Building Parallel Programs, Concepts and Tools for Parallel Software Engineering.* Addison Wesley, 1994.

[4] E. P. Glinert and C. D. Norton. Novis: A visual laboratory for exploring the design of processor arrays. *Journal of Visual Languages and Computing*, 3(2):135–159, June 1992.

[5] R. Guerraoui. Les langages concurrents à objets. *Techniques et Sciences Informatiques*, 14(8):945–971, 1995.

[6] F. Guidec, P. Calégari, and P. Kuonen. Parallel irregular software for wave propagation simulation. *Future Generation Computer Systems (FGCS), N.H. Elsevier*, 13(4-5):279–289, Mar. 1998. ISSN 0167-739X.

[7] C. Hewitt, P. Bishop, and R. Steiger. A universal modular actor formalism for artificial intelligence. In *IJCAI-73*, 1973.

[8] J. M. D. Hill, B. McColl, D. C. Stefanescu, M. W. Goudreau, K. Lang, S. B. Rao, T. Suel, T. Tsantilas, and R. Bisseling. BSPlib: The BSP programming library. Technical Report May, Oxford University Computing Laboratory, 1997.

[9] W. D. Hillis. *The Connection Machine.* The MIT Press, 1985.

[10] M. Himsolt. *GML: Graph Modelling Language.* Universität Passau, 94030 Passau, Germany, Dec. 1996. Draft Version.

[11] H. Hopp and L. Prechelt. CuPit-2: A portable parallel programming language for artificial neural networks. In *1997 IMACS Conference on Applications of Computer Algebra*, 1997.

[12] W. F. McColl. Special purpose parallel computing. In A. M. Gibbons and P. Spirakis, editors, *Lectures on Parallel Computation. Proc. 1991 ALCOM Spring School on Parallel Computation*, pages 261–336. Cambridge University Press, 1993.

[13] G. Spezzano and D. Talia. CARPET: A programming language for parallel cellular processing. In *Proceedings 2nd Europ. School on PPE for HPC*, pages 71–74, Apr. 1996.

[14] L. G. Valiant. A bridging model for parallel computation. *Communications of the ACM*, 33(8):103, Aug. 1990.

[15] L. G. Valiant. Genaral purpose parallel architectures. In J. van Leeuwen, editor, *Handbook of Theoretical Computer Science*, chapter 18, pages 945–971. Elsevier Science, 1990.

[16] S. Vialle, T. Cornu, and Y. Lallement. ParCeL-1: a parallel programming language based on autonomous and synchronous actors. *ACM Sigplan Notice*, 31(8):43–51, Aug. 1996.

Short Presentations 3: Distributed Shared Memory Systems

Short Presentations 3: Distributed Shared Memory Systems

Session Chair: D. Laforenza

This session is dedicated to the Distributed Shared Memory Systems (DSMS) and it intends to contribute towards understanding some aspects of their design and implementation. A DSMS, otherwise known as Distributed Shared Virtual Memory, provides a view of logically shared memory over physically distributed memory. This approach avoids the programmer the concerns of explicit message passing when writing applications. The explicit message passing programming model imposes the programmer to be aware that there are different machines (nodes) in the compute platform, and data has to be explicitly sent across them.

Recently, the widespread availability of SMP (Symmetric Multi-Processors) nodes has led several vendors to consider their use as building blocks for DSMS. These systems exploit the SMP cache-coherence hardware to support fine-grain communication within a node, and use software to support communication across nodes at a coarser page-size granularity.

A key issue in designing an efficient DSMS is to reduce of the amount of communication required for coherent access. Most implementations use virtual-memory page protection and data replication or data migration policies to reduce the number of communications. Another important issue in designing a DSMS is the fault tolerance. In fact, the probability of failure of a DSMS increases with the number of nodes. Thus fault tolerance mechanisms must be implemented in order to allow processes to continue their execution in the event of failure.

The first paper *Self-Similarity in SPLASH-2 Workloads on Shared Memory Multiprocessors Systems* by J. Sahuquillo proposes the study of the self-similar properties of several SPLASH2 benchmarks. Each benchmark has been studied independently, and all exhibit a clearly self-similar behaviour. The results enable the construction of a self-similar memory reference generator that makes a wide variety of parallel workload traces in a flexible manner; as well as quickly

The second paper *Two Management Approaches of the Split Data Cache in Multiprocessor Systems* is by J. Sahuquillo. The paper proposes two new different approaches for increasing the L1 hit ratio in multiprocessor systems and a comparison with a conventional organization is given. Performance evaluation and hardware cost of these organizations are also calculated and compared with the cost incurred by the most common organization used.

The title of the third paper is *Evaluation of a Virtual Shared Memory Machine by the Compilation of Data Parallel Loops* by F. Baiardi et al. The authors introduce DVSA, Distributed Virtual Shared Areas, a virtual machine supporting the sharing of information on distributed memory architectures. DVSA supports the sharing of areas rather than of variables because this may result in better performances on architectures offering little or no hardware support for message exchange. The authors consider the implementation of data parallel loops and show that a set of static analyses based on the closed forms approach makes it possible to fully exploit the DVSA machine without incurring in too large overheads.

The fourth paper *Using Agent Wills to provide Fault-tolerance in Distributed Shared Memory Systems* by A. Rowstron describes the use of mobile objects to provide distributed programs coordinating through a distributed shared memory with tolerance to sudden agent failure, and in particular consider the increasingly popular Linda-like tuple space languages. The authors have integrated the use of agent wills into a Linda system without increasing the complexity of program writing.

The fifth paper is *The TIRAN: Approach to Reusing Software Implemented Fault Tolerance* by O. Botti et al. The TIRAN project develops a framework which provides fault tolerance capabilities to automation systems, with the goal of allowing portable, reusable and cost-effective solutions. Application developers are allowed to select, configure and integrate in their own environment a variety of software-based functions for error detection, confinement and recovery provided by the framework.

The last paper is *Combining Low-latency Communication Protocols with Multithreading for High Performance DSM Systems on Clusters* by L. Lefevre and O. Reymann. The authors show that by combining low latency communication protocols with multi-threading, high performance DSMS on top of clusters can implemented. In particular, they present the DOSMOS system, with experiments on various communication libraries (PVM,MPI) on various networks (Ethernet, Myrinet) and show high performance obtained.

1066-6192/99 $10.00 © 1999 IEEE

Self-Similarity in SPLASH-2 Workloads on Shared Memory Multiprocessors Systems[1]

J. Sahuquillo, T. Nachiondo, J.C. Cano, J.A. Gil, and A. Pont
Departamento de Informática de Sistemas y Computadores
Universidad Politécnica de Valencia
Cno. de Vera s/n 46071, Valencia (Spain)
{jsahuqui, tnachion, jucano, jagil, apont}@disca.upv.es

Abstract

The workload used for evaluating and obtaining performance results in shared memory multiprocessors are widely heterogeneous. Traces have been used over several decades and as computers systems grew in power, semantic benchmarks, like SPLASH2, became the most common workloads. Unfortunately, few benchmarks are available. Recently, self-similar studies have been performed in several computer domains. In this paper, we study the self-similar properties of several SPLASH2 benchmarks. Each benchmark has been studied independently, and all exhibit a clearly self-similar behaviour. The results enable the construction of a self-similar memory reference generator that makes a wide variety of parallel workload traces in a flexible manner; as well as quickly.

Keywords: self-similar behaviour, parallel workload, trace-driven simulator, execution-driven simulator.

1. Introduction

Multiprocessor shared memory systems (SMP) are recently growing in use and a large part of the computer industry is focussing on improving SMP performance. From the first pioneering studies, the workload used for obtaining and reporting SMP experimental results has been widely heterogeneous.

Traces were initially used as an economical workload for reducing the overall time spent on performing experiments. However, traces are obtained under a particular hardware organisation; and that means that traces are attached to a given organisation, and are liable to become useless if any parameter of the organisation changes (e.g. the cache size). Thiébaut et al [2] introduced techniques for producing synthetic address traces.

As computer hardware grows in power, semantic benchmarks like SPLASH-2 [1] have become the most common workload used in the open literature for SMP performance experiments. Execution driven simulators, such as Tango-Lite [3] or LIMES [4], have been developed to perform these experiments. These benchmarks are widely used by researchers, and their main drawback is the large amount of time needed to perform experiments.

In this paper we study the self-similar property of several SPLASH-2 benchmarks. For every benchmark we obtain the Hurst parameter using different statistical methods, like: R/S; variance-time; and periodogram analysis.

The remainder of this paper is organized as follows. Section 2 presents the motivations that led us to perform this work. Section 3 discusses work related with self-similarity behaviour. Section 4 gives a summary of the theory of self-similarity. Section 5 presents a summary of the characteristics of the benchmarks used. Section 6 contains the traces analysis and plots some of these results; and finally, section 7 concludes with the relation between SMP and self-similar workloads.

2. Motivation and Objectives

In this work we are not interested in studying typical parallel workload factors, like the structure of the parallel algorithm or how the data is distributed [1,5]. This paper focuses on studying the statistical properties of these workloads. Few parallel workloads are referenced in the open literature; we think that if a mathematical relation exited between these workloads, a method could be used to generate artificial workloads. The objective is not to replace to SPLASH-2 benchmark suite, but to produce alternative workloads for performing complementary, or

[1] This work has been partially supported by Research Grant GV98-14-47

collateral studies, where great detail is not needed. Note that many workloads could be generated – if they are artificially generated with a similar statistical behaviour.

From our viewpoint, every benchmark is a set of memory references (traces) generated by a multiprocessor. We used the LIMES simulator to obtain the memory references traces issued by the multiprocessor. To obtain the trace file the simulator is fed with both the multiprocessor architecture model and with the parallel SPLASH-2 workloads.

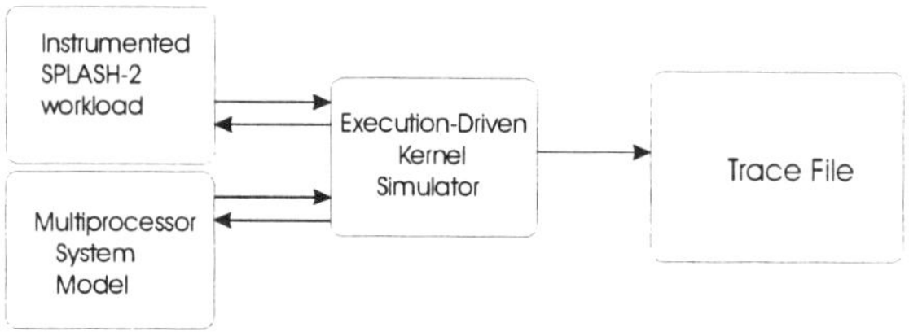

Figure 1. Block diagram of the trace-gathering process with an execution-driven simulator.

One trace file is gathered from each benchmark execution. Every file is carefully analysed to see if the self-similar property appears. Ideally, the property would appear in every benchmark. In these cases, it is possible to affirm that self-similar traces could be artificially generated in order to perform comparison studies. Thus, these artificial traces could be used to feed a trace-driven simulator for performing the studies. Figure 2 shows this process. The traces can dynamically feed the simulator (on-line) as they are generated; or after the total file trace is generated (off-line). The on-line method saves disk space and is preferable. In [6] a more detailed analysis of how the traces work is presented.

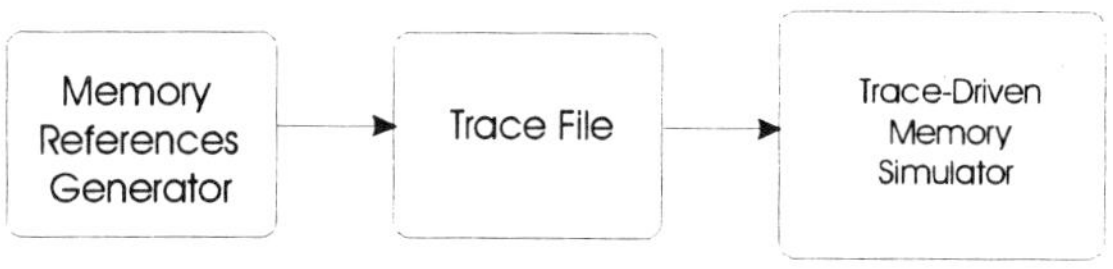

Figure 2. Block diagram of a study using a trace-driven memory simulator.

If traces are artificially obtained by a self-similar memory references generator, a wide set of memory references can be obtained in a flexible and rapid manner. The statistical properties of the traces would be the same as the SPLASH-2 workload exhibits. These traces could be used as a complementary workload to the SPLASH-2 in many studies. Obviously, there are studies where semantic workloads are needed.

3. Self-Similarity Related Work

From the first computer network self-similar studies to the present day, self-similarity has been widely applied in computer engineering fields; i.e. wide-area traffic [8], ATM networks [10], variable-bit-rate [9], and World Wide Web traffic [11].

Self-similarity could be attributed to the ON/OFF behaviour of traffic sources within their systems [12]. These ON/OFF periods have high variability or infinite variance, and this produces an aggregate workload (i.e. traffic). This workload is self-similar or long-range dependent: and shows how there is a relation between the parameters describing high variability (Noah Effect) and self-similarity (Joseph Effect) [12]. This originated the study of different aspects of the implications of long-range dependence for traffic modelling and network performance evaluation.

In [13] it was shown that the total file system traffic and individual classes of file system events (such as file opens, closes, writes, etc.) as seen by the server exhibit a self-similarity property. The self-similar nature of a file system traffic was used to show how to detect and predict idle period lengths. Further studies showed that total traffic on Ethernet LANs and WAN is self-similar. In [14,12,15] the self-similar nature of Ethernet traffic was studied. Leland et al. demonstrated that Ethernet traffic was self-similar in nature. Self-similarity is manifested in the absence of a natural burst length; traffic burst appears over a wide range of time scales. In this way, the self-similar process models network traffic much more closely than a Poisson process.

In [18] it is shown that increasing network bandwidth (one of the characteristics of highly self-similar traffic) can result in a smaller delay than when traffic is weakly self-similar. The study reveals that the degree of observed self-similarity is directly related to the heavy-tailedness of the file size distribution and therefore related to the transport layer mechanisms. In [16,17] it is shown that small buffer sizes, short time scales, and long-range dependence, have only a marginal influence.

Research about variable-bit-rate (VBR) video traffic has shown that the traffic exhibits long-range dependence, and this indicates self-similar nature. In [19] video sequence autocorrelation decays hyperbolically; this means that a long-range dependence exists and can be modelled using a self-similar process.

4. Self-Similar Stochastic Processes

In this section we define the self-similarity characteristic, discuss the mathematical definition of long-range dependence (Hurst effect [20]), and show some classes of stationary stochastic processes which can account for long-range dependence.

4.1. Definition of Self-Similarity

Intuitive description of self-similarity

The intuitive definition of self-similarity is that the process looks similar across all time-scales. As an example, Figure 3 shows six time series plots of the LU benchmark induced by the collected trace. Successive plots are refinements of the previous plots. The scopes of the refined plots were chosen by selecting some arbitrary intervals from a more detailed plot. There is significant burstiness.

The most outstanding characteristic of these plots is the fact that it is difficult to distinguish between them. They display a characteristic bursty behaviour that is independent of the time scale used. This burstiness provides strong evidence that the process is self-similar. This is because self-similar processes have heavy-tailed distributions where burstiness can be observed at all time scales.

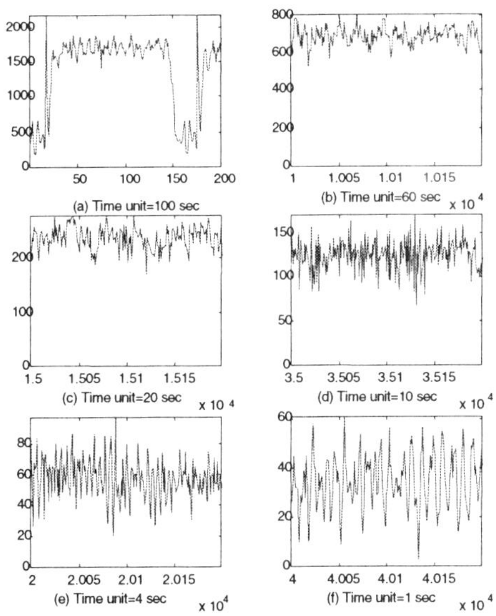

Figure 3. Visual demonstration of self-similarity

Mathematical description of self-similarity [A]

A covariance stationary stochastic process $X = (X_t: t \geq 0)$ is defined as a process with constant mean $\mu = E[X_t]$, finite variance $\sigma^2 = E[(X_t - \mu)^2]$, and an autocorrelation function $r(k) = E[(X_t - \mu)(X_{t+k} - \mu)]/E[(X_t - \mu)^2]$ $(k \geq 0)$ that depends only on k. In particular, we assume that X has an autocorrelation function like $r(k) \sim k^{-\beta} L_1(k)$, as $k \to \infty$, where $0 < \beta < 1$ an L_1 is slowly varying at infinity, $\lim_{t\to\infty} L_1(tx)/L_1(t) = 1$ for all $x > 0$.

For each $m > 0$, $X^{(m)} = (X^{(m)} : k > 0)$ denote a new time series obtained by averaging the original series X over non-overlapping blocks of size m – for each $m > 0$, $X^{(m)}$ is given by $X_k^{(m)} = 1/m\,(X_{km-m+1} + \ldots + X_{km})$, $k > 0$

Note that for each m, the aggregated time series $X^{(m)}$ defines a covariance stationary process; $r^{(m)}$ denote the corresponding autocorrelation function.

The process X is called self-similar with self-similarity parameter $H = 1 - \beta/2$ if the corresponding aggregated processes $X^{(m)}$ have the same correlation structure as X, i.e., $r^{(m)}(k) = r(k)$, for all $m > 0$ $(k > 0)$.

4.2. Estimating the Hurst Parameter

This subsection provides a brief description of the statistical methods for assessing self-similar: R/S analysis, variance-time analysis, and periodogram-based analysis.

R/S Analysis

For given observations (X_K: K = 1,2, ..., n) with partial sum $Y(n) = \sum_{i=1}^{n} X_i$ sample mean $\overline{X}(n)$ and sample variance $S^2(n) = (1/n)\sum_{i=1}^{n} X_i^2 - (1/n)^2 Y(n)^2$, the R/S statistic, or re-scaled adjusted range is given by:

$$\frac{R}{S}(n) = \frac{1}{S(n)}\left[\max_{0\leq t\leq n}\left(Y(t) - \frac{t}{n}Y(n)\right) - \min_{0\leq t\leq n}\left(Y(t) - \frac{t}{n}Y(n)\right)\right] \quad (1)$$

Hurst found that many naturally occurring time-series appear to be well represented by relation $E\left[R(n)/S(n)\right] \sim C_H n^H$, as $n \to \infty$, for fractional Gaussian noise or fractional ARIMA, with Hurst parameter H 'typically' about 0.73, and C_H a positive, finite constant not dependant on n.

To determine H using the R/S statistic, proceed as follows. For a given observation of length N, subdivide the series into K non-overlapping blocks, each of N/K size and computes the re-scaled adjusted range $R(k_i,n)/S(k_i,n)$ for each of the new 'starting points' $k_i = iN/K+1, i=1,2, \ldots$, which satisfy $k_i + n \leq N$. For values of n smaller than N/K, one gets K different estimates of R(n)/S(n). For values of n close to N, one gets fewer values; – as few as 1 when $n \geq N - N/K$. Next, one takes logarithmically spaced values of n, starting with $n \approx 10$. Plotting $\log(R(k_i,n)/S(k_i,n))$ versus $\log(n)$ results in the re-scaled adjusted range plot (pox diagram of R/S). The parameter H can be estimated by fitting a line to the points in the pox plot. Any short-range dependence in the series typically results in a transient zone at the low end of the plot – and so the answer is to set a cut-off point, and not use the low end of the plot for purposes of estimating H.

Usually, the very high end of the plot is not used either, because there are too few points to make reliable estimates.

The values of n that are situated between the lower and higher cut-off points are used to estimate H. For practical purposes, the most useful and attractive feature of R/S analysis is its relative robustness to changes in marginal distributions.

Variance-Time Analysis

From a statistical viewpoint for self-similar processes, the variances of the aggregated processes $X^{(m)}$ (m = 1,2 , ...) decrease linearly (for large m) in log-log plots against m with slopes arbitrarily flatter than −1.

To determine H using the variance statistic; we consider the aggregated series, obtained by dividing given series of length N by non-overlapping blocks of size m (we assume that both N and N/m are large), and averaging the series over each block. That is for m=1,2, ..., $X^{(m)}$ is given by:

$$X^{(m)}(k) = \frac{1}{m} \sum_{i=(k-1)m+1}^{km} X_i, k = 1,2,\ldots,\left[N/m\right] \quad (2)$$

We compute its sample variance,

$$\hat{Var}\; X^{(m)} = \frac{1}{N/m} \sum_{k=1}^{N/m} \left(X^{(m)}(k) - \overline{X}\right)^2 \quad (3)$$

The series $X^{(m)}$ scales like m^{H-1}; thus, if the series is Gaussian, or at least finite variance, the sample variance will be asymptotically proportional to m^{2H-2} for large N/m and m.

If (X_1, X_2, ...) are independent and identically distributed with finite mean and variance then the decrease in the variance (decaying variance) is around n^{-1}.
From (2) we obtain $Var(X^{(m)}) \sim a_1 m^{-1}$, as $m \to \infty$
If one observes:

$$Var(X^{(m)}) \sim a_1 m^{-\beta}, 0 < \beta < 1 \text{ as } m \to \infty \quad (4)$$

then the process has a slowly decaying variance. In (4) either the inter-event times cannot be independent or their variance is not finite.

One plots the sample variance of the aggregated series versus m on a log-log plot for successive values of m. The result should be a straight line with a slope of 2H-2. Actually, the slope is estimated by fitting a least-squares line to the points of the plot.

If the series has no longer-range dependence and finite variance, then H = 0.5 and the slope of the fitted line should be −1. Short-range effects can distort the estimation of H if the low end of the plot is used, and at the very high end of the plot there are too few blocks to get reliable estimates of the variance. Thus, in practice, these points are not used.

Periodogram-Based Analysis

The periodogram is defined as

$$I(v) = \frac{1}{2\pi N}\left|\sum_{j=1}^{N} X(j)e^{ijv}\right|^2, \text{i=1,2,..., q} \quad q = \frac{(N-1)}{2} \quad (5)$$

Where v is the frequency, N is the length of the series, and X is the time-series. In the finite variance case, I(v) is an estimator of the spectral density of X, and a series with long-range dependence will have a spectral density proportional to $|v|^{1-2H}$ for frequencies close to the origin. We thus expect a log-log plot of the periodogram versus the frequency to display a straight line with a slope of 1-2H.

5. Parallel Applications

The SPLASH-2 benchmark suite is a mixture of benchmarks carefully chosen to represent a great variety of scientific computations, as well as engineering and graphic computing. These benchmarks are widely used for comparison purposes in the most important references related to multiprocessor system performance studies. The suite consists of computational kernels and applications. The selected benchmarks in our work are three kernels (FFT, LU and Radix) and two applications (Barnes and FMM).

The FFT kernel (Fast Fourier Transform) is a representative kernel in applications that use spectral methods. The LU kernel is representative of many dense linear algebra computations. The integer RADIX sort kernel has a wide range of applications, like database management systems and aerospace applications. The Barnes application is an implementation of the Barnes-Hut n-body algorithm for solving a problem in galaxy evolution. The FMM application also simulates a system of bodies over a number of timesteps.

5.1 Benchmark Characteristics

Table 1 shows the problem size, the total read requests and write requests (expressed together as Memory References), the percentage of read requests (loads %) over writes , and write requests (stores %) over reads for each benchmark used. Finally, it shows the size of the file trace.

Bench-mark	Problem Size	Memory References	Loads (%)	Stores (%)	File Trace Size (Mbytes)
FFT	16 K points	3514603	59.4	40.6	67.2
Radix	2 K integers	1087218	82.0	18.0	11.9
LU	64x64 matrix 16x16 blocks	608232	68.5	31.5	13.0
FMM	64 particles	855444	79.7	20.3	11.9
Barnes	64 particles	932016	69.5	30.5	9.1

Table 1. Benchmark characteristics and file trace size.

To obtain the traces we examine a typical multiprocessor system with four processors, each having a 32-Kbyte two-way cache. We assume that each hit in the first level cache takes one cycle. The data buses are assumed to be 32-bit wide (one word). All the data transferred by the bus takes one cycle, except the first transferred word. If the main memory serves a request, it will take 16 cycles for the first word and an extra cycle for each additional word in the line. The Berkeley protocol [7] has been used for coherence maintenance.

6. Statistical Self-Similarity Analysis

In this section we study the self-similar nature of every chosen benchmark in a more rigorous way by using the statistical methods.

The first collected traces must be filtered to remove unneeded or redundant data. The resultant trace (filtered trace) contains the arrival patterns, the type of operation (load and/or store) studied, and the processor issuing the request. From these traces we can undertake the studies.

To study the self-similar behaviour from the different requests issued in the studied traces, we have made a top-down process.

Firstly, we made a global study of every considered benchmark, independently of the request sort and the issuing processor. Estimates of H were generated through R/S, variance-time, and periodogram-based analysis.

These statistical methods were used to determine whether the data behaviour is self-similar, or not. In the affirmative, the self-similar parameter H is given by the asymptotic slope (obtained by a simple least squares fit) which can take any value between ½ and 1. Table 2 shows the H parameter considering the global traces (RW).

		Hurst parameter estimates		
Benchmark	Request	R/S	Periodogram	Variance-Time
BARNES	RW	0.73	0.83	0.96
LU	RW	0.89	0.74	0.98
RADIX	RW	0.87	0.82	0.97
FFT	RW	0.99	0.63	0.80
FMM	RW	1.00	0.65	0.95

Table 2. Estimates of H from the global (reads and writes from any processor) traces.

The obtained results for every method clearly show a self-similar behaviour. All estimated Hurst parameters are between ½ and 1, confirming the presence of self-similarity.

Secondly, the initial collected traces were filtered again – but this time the objective was to obtain, independently of the issuing processor, the relative traces for the request sort, reads (R) and writes (W). In Table 3 we can see the results from this more detailed study.

		Hurst parameter estimates		
Benchmark	Request	R/S	Periodogram	Variance-Time
BARNES	R	0.74	0.76	0.96
	W	0.69	0.71	0.97
LU	R	0.89	0.68	0.98
	W	0.88	0.73	0.98
RADIX	R	0.87	0.79	0.96
	W	0.86	0.77	0.99
FFT	R	0.99	0.56	0.81
	W	0.95	0.55	0.87
FMM	R	0.95	0.58	0.94
	W	0.91	0.88	0.67

Table 3. Estimates of H for the benchmarks for read and write traces.

The above results confirm that SPLASH-2 benchmarks have a self-similar nature. We can suppose that traces relative to the request sort issued by the processors will also be self-similar in nature. For this reason, we performed the self-similar study from the split global trace (RW) in more specific traces: read and/or writes for every processor (P0,P1,P2,P3); in each benchmark. The differences between the results for each analysis method are related to the parameters that can be modified on the mathematical functions of each one of them. The R/S is the stricter formally. Anyway, they give near values, always inside of a same range ([½,1])

Table 4 shows the results corresponding to the LU kernel. The remains of the benchmarks used show a similar behaviour. This table shows the estimates of H for every statistic method and trace studied. The results obtained for each method clearly show a self-similar behaviour.

			Hurst parameter estimates		
Benchmark	Request	Processor	R/S	Periodogram	Variance-Time
LU	RW	P0	0.65	0.69	0.99
		P1	0.93	0.68	0.99
		P2	0.98	0.75	0.98
		P3	0.95	0.62	0.98
	R	P0	0.65	0.63	0.99
		P1	0.93	0.62	0.99
		P2	0.98	0.69	0.98
		P3	0.95	0.56	0.98
	W	P0	0.63	0.67	0.99
		P1	0.92	0.67	0.99
		P2	0.99	0.75	0.98
		P3	0.96	0.61	0.98

Table 4. Estimates of H corresponding for the LU kernel.

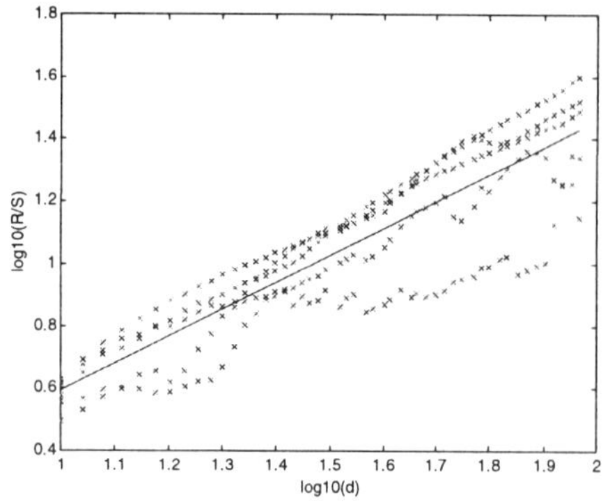

(a)

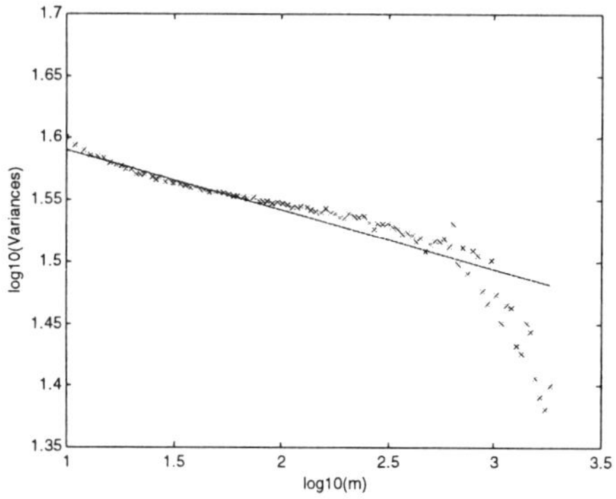

(b)

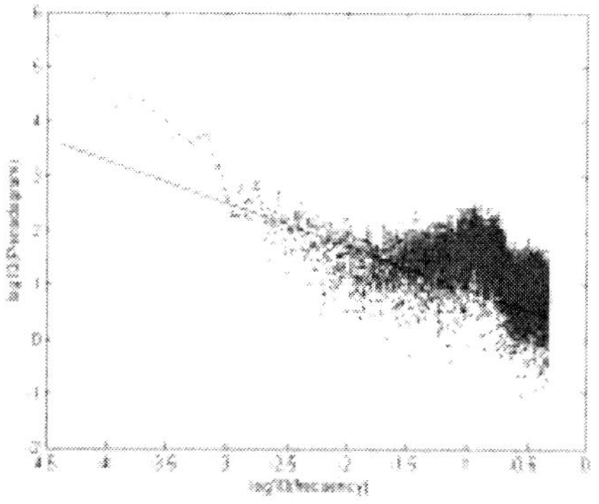

(c)

Figure 4.(a) R/S plot, (b) variance time plot, (c) Periodogram plot, for global radix trace. The asymptotic Hurst parameters are determined using the 'brushed' points. The dotted reference line corresponds to the slope, and is estimated by fitting a least-squares line to the points of the plot.

Graphically, Figure 4 shows this self-similar behaviour, where a R/S, variance time and periodogram plot are displayed for the radix global trace.

To round off this section on self-similarity analysis we show the aggregate R/S method. This has been also carried out for a more complete study. R/S analysis is able to identify the 'true test' short-range dependencies by a graphical method. If the R/S method for different time series $X^{(t)}$ is plotted by aggregating the original series over non-overlapping blocks of size t, and there are no short-range dependencies; then, the Hurst parameters calculated remain close to the original value (t=1). LU, Radix, Fmm and Barnes applications exhibit this property. As an example, Figure 5 shows the results obtained for a FMM kernel. This method could be inadequate for small data sets. However, for medium data sets, this method can be used to get an initial idea about dependencies in the data set. This small, and medium data set depends on the variability of the load, on our study, they are about $20 \cdot 10^3$ or less for small data set, and greater than $50 \cdot 10^3$ for medium data set.

a)

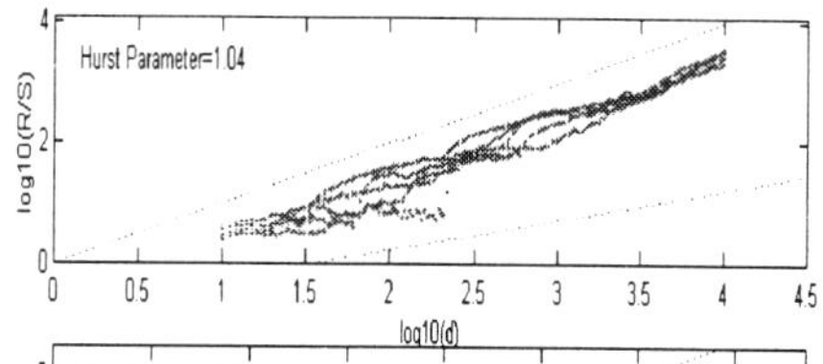

b)

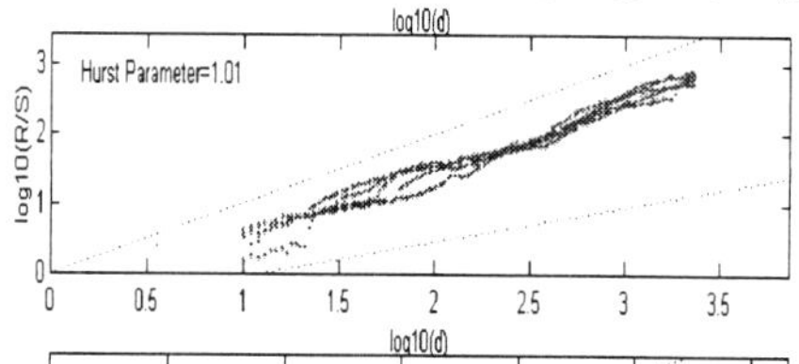

c)

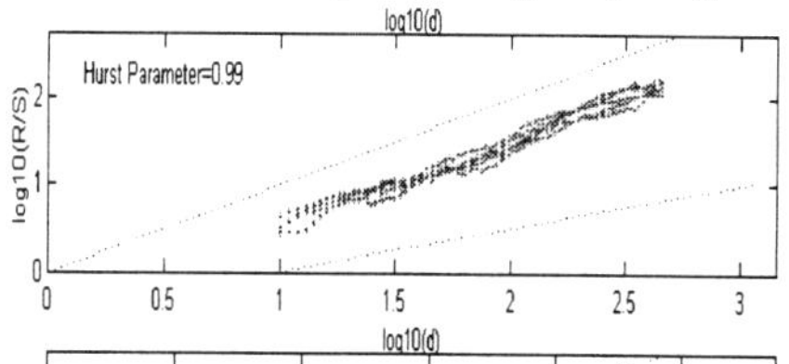

d)

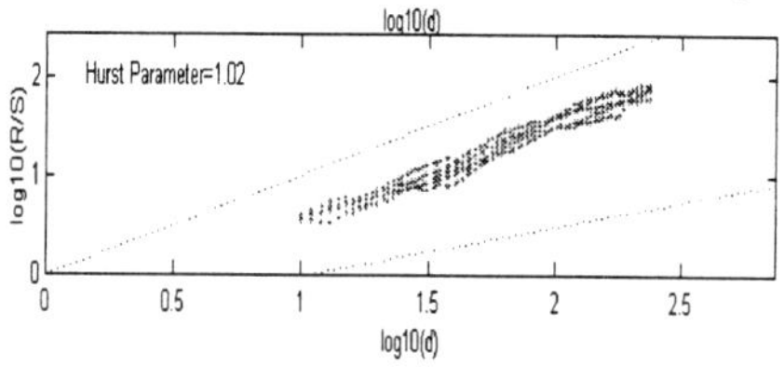

Figure 5. R/S plot with different aggregation levels (1, 10, 50 and 100), for FMM kernel. The levels are shown in increasing aggregation sizes from a) to d).

Once we have demonstrated that SPLASH-2 benchmarks have a self-similar behaviour in all the cases analyzed, we studied the hypothetically existent relation between cache size and the H parameter. For this study, we changed both the cache size and the problem size for every benchmark. The results obtained show that the self-similar property appears in the same manner, although no mathematical relation has found between the two variables.

In summary, we have demonstrated that SPLASH-2 benchmarks have a self-similar behavior in all the cases analyzed, and the influences of cache size and problem size on the H parameters are highlighted.

7. Conclusions

In this paper a detailed study of the self-similarity property in several SPLASH-2 workloads has been made in an SMP environment. We have examined this statistical property for an initial trace containing the entire memory requests issued by the processors. The results showed that this trace exhibited a self-similar behavior. Thus, for each selected benchmark we decided to perform a top-down analysis – reaching detailed analysis per processor and per request type. The results obtained were very encouraging for all the cases studied.

This statistical behaviour has been carried out with typical statistical methods as used in the open literature; the R/S, the variance and the periodogram methods. In addition, we have used the aggregate of the R/S – a more complete analysis. In all the methods used, the Hurst parameter remains inside the allowed interval. Also, the study shows that for traces around $50 \cdot 10^3$, the results are enough independents of the architecture parameters.

We have also looked into the possible mathematical relation between the cache size and the Hurst parameter; and arrived to a negative conclusion. Moreover, the H parameter values change with the problem size for a specific benchmark.

The most important conclusion of this paper is that a self-similar generator of memory references can be made and used to artificially generate request memory traces. These traces would have analogous mathematical characteristics to the SPLASH-2 benchmark suite and could be used to feed a trace-driven simulator (much faster than the execution-driven simulator) in order to perform comparison and evaluation studies. The main disadvantage of using traces is the large amount of disk space they need for storage. However, if traces were generated dynamically (on-line), this inconvenience would not appear. On the other hand, if traces were used, we would have a more flexible method to generate a wide variety of traces, while the actual number of parallel benchmarks used in the references are very limited.

As for future work, we plan to analyse an ideal memory requests generator; develop it; and connect to a trace-driven simulator.

References

[1] S. C. Woo, M. Ohara, E. Torrie, J. P. Singh, and A. Gupta, "The SPLASH–2 Programs: Characterization and Methodological Considerations," Proceedings of the 22nd ISCA, June 1995.

[2] D. Thiébaut, J. L. Wolf, H. S. Stone, "Synthetic Traces for Trace-Driven Simulation of Cache Memories," IEEE Transactions on Computer, vol. 41,no. 4, April 1992.

[3] S. Goldschmidt, "Simulator of Multiprocessors: Accuracy and Performance," Ph.D. Thesis, Stanford University, June 1993.

[4] D. Magdic, "Limes: A Multiprocessor Simulation Environment," IEEE TCCA Newsletter, March 1997.

[5] J. Hennessy and D. Patterson, "Computer Architecture: a Quantitative Approach," 2nd edition, Morgan Kauffmann, 1996.

[6] R.A. Uhlig, "Trace-Driven Memory Simulation: A Survey", ACM Computing Surveys, vol. 29, n. 2, July 1997.

[7] R.G. Sheldon, "Implementing a Cache Consistency Protocol," Proceedings of the 12th ISCA, 1985.

[8] V.Parxon and S. Floyd, " Wide-Area Traffic: The Failure of Poisson Modeling," IEEE/ACM Transactions on Networking, 3 (3), pp. 226-244, 1995.

[9] J. Beran, R. Sherman, M. S. Taqqu and W. Willinger, "Long-range Dependence in Variable-bit-rate Video Traffic," IEEE Transactions on Communications Vol. 43, pp. 1566-79, 1995.

[10] N. D. Georganas, "Self-similar ("fractal") Traffic in ATM Networks," Proceedings of the 2nd International Workshop on Advanced Teleservices and High-Speed Communications Architectures (IWACA ´ 94), pp. 1-7, 1994.

[11] M. E. Crovella and A. Bestavros, "Explaining World Wide Web Traffic Self-Similarity," Tech. Rep. TR-95-015, Computer Science Departament, Boston University, 1995.

[12] W. Willinger, M. S. Taqqu, R. Sherman and D. V. Wilson, "Self-Similarity Through High-Varibility: Statistical Analysis of Ethernet LAN Traffic at the Source Level," IEEE/ACM transactions on Networking, Vol. 5, 71-86, 1997.

[13] S.D. Gribble, G.S. Manku, and E.A.Brewer, "Self-similar in File-Systems: Measurement and Applications", ACM SIGMETRICS Performance Evaluation Review, Vol. 26, pp. 141-150, June 1998.

[14] W.E Leland, M. S. Taqqu, W. Willinger, D.v. Wilson, "On the Self-Similar Nature of Ethernet Traffic," IEEE/ACM Transactions on Networking, Vol 2, 1994.

[15] W. E. Leland, M. S. Taqqu, W. Willinge, and D. V. Wilson, "On the Self-similar Nature of Ethernet Traffic,"

SIGCOMM Symposium on Communications Architectures Protocols, pp. 183-193, 1993.

[16] M.Grossglauser and J.-C Bolot, "On the Relevance of Long-range Dependence in Network Traffic," Proceedings of the ACM SIGCOMM 96, pp. 15-24, 1996.

[17] B.Ryu and A.Elwalid, "The Importance of Long-range Dependence of VBR video traffic in ATM Traffic Engineering: Myths and Realities," Proceedings of the ACM SIGCOMM ' 96, pp.3-14, 1996.

[18] K.Park, G.Kim, M. Crovella, "On the Effect of Traffic Self-similarity on Network Performance," Proceedings of the SPIE International Conference on Performance and Control of Network Systems, 1997.

[19] J. Beran, R.Sherman, M. S. Taqqu, W. Willinger, "Long-range Dependence in Variable-bit-rate Video Traffic," IEEE Transactions on Communications 43, pp 1566-1579, 1995.

[20] B.B. Mandelbrot, "The Fractal Geometry of Nature", Freeman, New York, 1983.

Two Management Approaches of the Split Data Cache in Multiprocessor Systems

J. Sahuquillo, A. Pont
Departamento de Informática de Sistemas y Computadores*
Universidad Politécnica de Valencia
Cno. de Vera s/n 46071, Valencia (Spain)
{jsahuqui, apont}@disca.upv.es

Abstract

As processor speed continues, the gap between the processor cycle and the memory subsystem cycle is expected to grow. One solution to this growing problem is to maximize the first level (L1) cache hit ratio, therefore the mean memory access time can decrease. Several studies have been made in order to manage more efficiently the L1 data cache, both in uniprocessor both in multiprocessor systems. These studies seek two main objectives, to increase the L1 hit ratio and to reduce the chip area occupied by these caches. In this work we present two new different approaches for increasing the L1 hit ratio in multiprocessor systems and we compare with a conventional organization. Performance evaluation and hardware cost of these organizations are also calculated and compared with the cost incurred by the most common organization used.

Keywords: memory architectures, data cache management, multiprocessor systems, data locality.

1. Introduction

One of the main objectives when high performance computers are designed is to minimize the average data access time. This performance indicator is a measure of the time employed satisfying one load operation from the processor. Reducing this time is a crucial aspect for improving global performance.

To implement two cache levels is the most common hardware solution for reducing the average data access time. However, though current computers implement two cache levels, the first level (L1) cache management is usually the same as it was two or three decades ago.

Recently, new strategies have been proposed in uniprocessor systems in order to increase the L1 cache hit ratio and to reduce the average data access time. Some of them focus in prefetching techniques [1, 2]. These schemes load data from the memory to the cache before the data is referenced. Another schemes propose to manage the cache in a locality sensitive manner. There are two big approaches: bypassing the cache and splitting the cache. The aim of both approaches is to exploit the data locality. The first techniques propose schemes for bypassing the main cache the data infrequently referenced [3, 4, 5]. These techniques pursue to reduce the data pollution in the cache. The second approaches propose to split L1 cache in two independent and multi-lateral caches, in a manner that is sensitive to data locality [6, 7, 8, 9].

Several studies have been done in order to manage the L1 cache in an efficient way, but only a few of them show results for shared memory multiprocessor systems [10,11]. In this paper we have studied the impact of the splitting the L1 data cache in multiprocessor systems. We have chosen two different solutions to this subject and evaluated their performance and cost under different assumptions. In this work, we also present a new version of the algorithm used for the transference of the blocks between the different caches, where the state of the block is considered.

In this paper the average data access time, the bus utilization and the hardware cost have been calculated for a conventional organization and for the two models considering the split data cache. The remainder of this work is organized as follows: section 2 discusses the related work; section 3 presents the new algorithm and some concepts about the architecture modeled; section 4 includes the performance simulation results; section 5 shows the hardware cost incurred by this architecture and section 6 concludes with the advantages.

2. Related work

In the first level of conventional cache organizations there is only one data cache, and every line uses the same organization. Recent studies propose to classify the data in two groups. For example, temporal and spatial data, or another similar form, and the data are allocated and managed independently into two different and independent caches. Several architectures [6, 7, 8] have been proposed

* This work has been partially supported by Research Grant GV98-14-47

where different and independent caches coexist in the first level cache (L1).When two caches exist at the same level, the processor sends the memory reference request to both caches at the same time. If the request is a load instruction and hits in one of the two L1 caches, the neighboring cache must end the fetch.

If the request results in a cache miss, the second level (L2) cache will satisfy the processor. Different hypotheses are adopted in the studies depending on the author: such as the block size in the first level data caches; default cache in a cache miss (spatial or temporal); disjointed caches; etc.

2.1 The Dual Data Cache

As it is widely known a large line size (two tens of bytes) improves the data spatial locality. On the other hand, there are some data that exhibit a good temporal locality. These data do not need a large line size. Usually both data types coexist in the same applications. Recent studies [6,7] propose to split the L1 data cache in two independent caches which are sensitive to data locality.

The dual data cache [6] presented by González et al. is the first study published about the convenience of managing the first level data cache in a manner sensitive to locality. Figure 1 shows the block diagram for this architecture. Both spatial and temporal caches share a common second level cache. This diagram is the most usual in the current studies. In this scheme the spatial and the temporal caches have the same size line and the default cache is the temporal one. The model includes a hardware table for managing data locality.

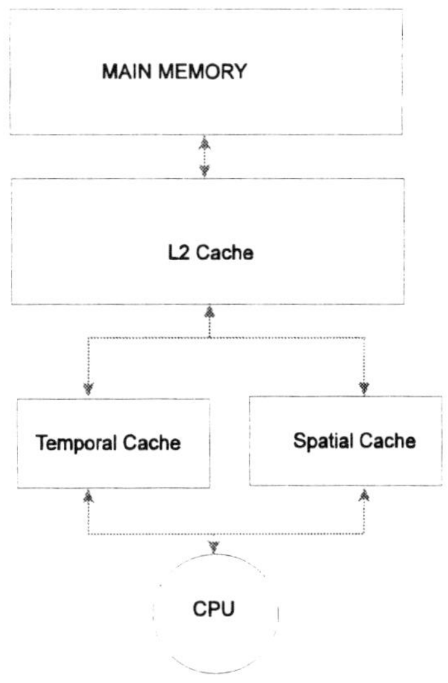

Figure 1. Dual Data Cache Organization

2.2 The STS Model

The STS cache [7] proposed by Milutinovic et al. split the L1 data cache into a temporal subcache (T1C) and a spatial subcache (SC). Only the T1C has a second level cache (T2C). The line size is four words for the spatial cache and only one word for the temporal caches. Every line in the spatial cache has two counters to decide if a line must be removed from the spatial cache and allocated in the temporal caches. SC cache is the default cache if a cache miss occurs. Figure 2 presents this architecture.

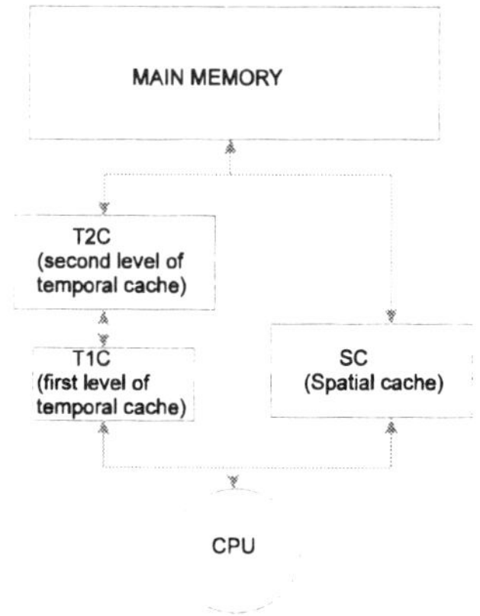

Figure 2. Organization of the Split Data Cache.

2.3 The NTS

Rivers and Davidson proposed the NTS cache [8]. The organization is similar to the dual data cache (figure 2), but the hardware algorithm and some additional hardware needed differ from the previous model. At run time the blocks are tagged as temporal and no temporal. When the block is allocated into one of the L1 caches, the block does not move to the another one. Only when the block is evicted and referenced again after, the cache controller decides by using the reuse information where the block must be allocated. The scheme incorporates a small table hardware structure for data reuse information management. Both L1 caches have the same line size and the default cache is the temporal cache.

3. System Organizations

This work focuses on shared memory multiprocessors using a split data cache in the first level. These systems need a protocol for data coherence maintenance and in this work some extensions of the Berkeley coherence protocol [12] have been used for this purpose. We have modeled two different approaches of the split data cache for multiprocessor systems and compared with a conventional organization of two level caches.

A detailed performance evaluation of the split data cache based on the ideas presented by Milutinovic for uniprocessors in [7] (SDC1) was presented in [10]. Figure 3 shows this organization. The model presents two caches in the first level cache: the temporal cache (T1C) and the spatial cache (SC). Only the temporal cache has a second level cache (T2C). Both the spatial part (first level) both the temporal part (second level) are connected to the bus. The size line of T2C and SC is 16 bytes (4 words) and the size line of T1C is one word. Also a 128 lines bus has been considered for transferring lines from SC to temporal caches.

In the organization proposed for SDC1 in multiprocessors [10] the blocks are initially looked as spatial, and then a run time algorithm decides if the block must be transferred to the temporal cache or not. Every line in the SC cache has two associate counters (X and Y). The Y counter is incremented when the line is referenced. The X counter is incremented if one word on the upper half of the line is referenced and decrement if the reference is for one word on the lower half. Each counter has a threshold associated. When the Y counter reaches its threshold, the value of the X counter is tested. If the X counter has reached its threshold the block is transferred from spatial cache to both temporal caches, if the SDC1 architecture is modeled or only to one temporal cache if we are considering the SDC2 configuration. Two 4 bit counters have been chosen for this work. Figure 4 shows the run-time hardware algorithm for this architecture.

In the SDC1 organization two bits state exits per block in the SC cache depending on the coherence protocol. The experiments show that in this organization better performance is obtained when the block is only transferred if it is in an ownership state.

```
Algorithm
Begin
If LOAD and state=MOD
     Read Xcount, Ycount values
     If (-X<Xcount<X)
          If (Hi) Increase(Xcount)
          Else Decrease(Xcount)
     If (Ycount<Y) Increase(Ycount)
     Else {          //Ycount=Y
          If ((Xcount=-X) or (Xcount=X))
               Make_transference to T1C and T2C
          Reset (Xcount, Ycount)
          }
               End
```

Figure 4. Run-time algorithm for moving the lines from SC to Temporal caches

In this paper we propose a new organization of the split data cache (SDC2) in order to achieve better performance reducing the bus utilization. Figure 5 shows this organization. This architecture is based on the original idea of González presented in [6] for uniprocessors.

Data are classified in temporal or spatial, but only in the first level caches. The L2 cache is common for the two first

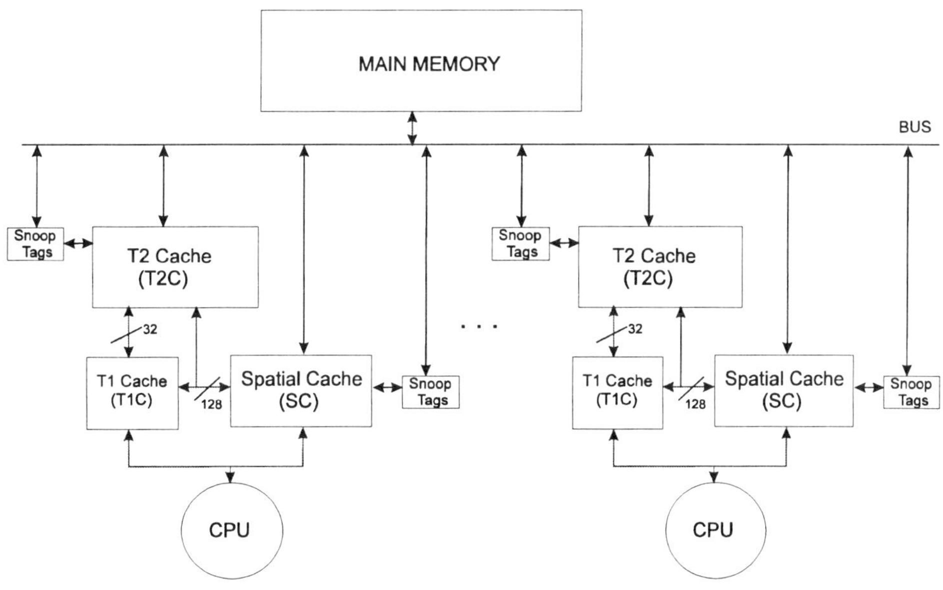

Figure 3. Organization of the Initial Split Data Cache **(SDC1)** in Multiprocessors Systems.

level caches. In order to make easy the block management we suppose that both first level caches have the same block size. This assumption means that there won't be a word duplicated in the two first level caches. For comparison purposes a 128 lines bus between the two levels cache memories has also been considered.

There are two great differences between the two discussed organizations, the first one is that the L2 cache is common for both first level caches, and the second one is that the SC cache isn't connected to the bus for coherence maintenance. The conventional organization can be understood as the SDC2 organization but considering a TC cache size of 0 bytes.

In the SDC2 organization the hardware determines when the block must be allocated in the temporal cache independently of its state, because only a valid bit per block exits in both first level caches.

obtained using the execution driven simulator LIMES [14] based on a parallel workload.

A conventional first level cache of size S is compared with a split data cache that assumes a spatial cache size of S/2 and a temporal cache size of S/8. In this study, 32 Kbytes has been chosen as the S value. The size of the second level (L2) cache of the conventional cache hierarchy is 128 KB and the size of T2C cache is 32 KB. T1C and TC caches have the same characteristics. All the caches modeled are two-way set-associative except T1C and TC caches which are four-way associative.

A 128-bit bus (four words) between SC and the temporal caches has been assumed for transferring the blocks. The temporal caches have four ports. All the first level caches that share a second level use a no-write allocate policy in the case of a write miss. The SC cache uses a write allocate policy.

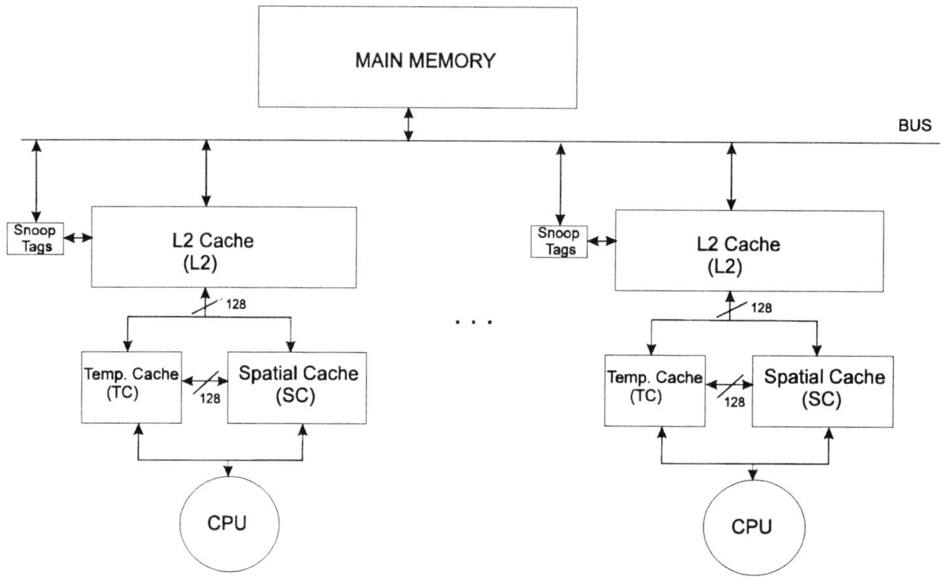

Figure 5. Organization of the Split Data Cache **(SDC2)** with a common L2 cache in a multiprocessor.

4. Performance analysis

Most of the performance results presented in the literature use the SPECfp95 benchmark because those studies have been done for uniprocessor systems. In the case of multiprocessors, it is very important to choose a parallel workload widely used in performance studies for comparison purposes. The SPLASH2 workload [13] is a set of parallel applications often used in the most important literature. Therefore, in our paper some applications of the SPLASH2 workload have been used, considering a problem size always exceeding 15 millions of read operations. Performance results have been

We assume that each hit in the first level caches takes one cycle and a hit in the second level cache of a conventional organization takes six cycles. Since T2C cache is four times less than L2 cache its access time has two cycles less. The data buses are supposed 32 bits wide (one word). All the transferred data by the bus take one cycle, except the first transferred word. The serving cache or main memory establishes the data transfer time of the first word. If the main memory serves a request it will take 16 cycles for the first word and an extra cycle by each additional word in the line. The non write allocate technique has been chosen as write miss policy when a miss occurs in the first level cache, because this policy offers better or slightly better performance than the write allocate [15].

In this work the following performance index have been chosen in order to know the system behavior: the mean data access time, the L1 cache hit ratio and the bus utilization. In this paper we only present the results for 2, 4 and 8 processors.

As previous work [10] we found that the SDC1 architecture usually offers better first level cache hit ratio than a conventional organization. Usually, the greater is the L1 cache hit ratio the lower is the mean data access time.

However, in the SDC1 model two caches with different access times are connected to the bus, and the miss penalty depends on the cache missing and the memory that serves the data. For example, the miss penalty is lower if a SC cache of a remote processor serves the miss than if the data is served by another T2C cache.

The L1 cache hit ratio and in consequence the mean data access time vary with the limit counter values. Moreover, the ideal limits of the counters are depending on the number of processors. These characteristics have been discussed in previous works [17].

As we said before in the present paper the organizations SDC1 and SDC2 have been modeled and evaluated, both use the same run-time algorithm without considering the block state. We are interested in comparing the mean data access time of these organizations with the values obtained for a conventional organization because this mean access time is one of the most relevant performance index.

In the SDC1 architecture the number of transferred lines from the SC cache to temporal caches are less than in SDC2 architecture because in SDC1 the lines are only transferred if they are in an ownership state.

All the results obtained are sensitive with the X-counter limit value [10]. If this value is reduced the number of lines moved from SC to the temporal part increases. As temporal part has two level caches the bus utilization is reduced. Therefore, the mean data access time is also reduced. On the other hand the number of transferred using the same X-counter limit value depends on the application.

As the aim of our experiments is to show that we can obtain similar or slightly better performance using the split data cache, we have not paid special attention to the ideal values of the counter limits.

Previous works [7, 10] have shown that for one and two processors both the SDC1 organization both the conventional organization performs very close. In this work we are interested in the impact of increasing the number of processors. Figure 5 shows the mean data access time for 2, 4 and 8 processors. Conventional and SDC2 organizations present very similar results independently of the number of processors. The differences in the results are usually less than 5 %. Sometimes the SDC2 organization performs better than conventional organization and sometimes vice-versa. However if we choose carefully the counters limit values we can achieve the SDC2 organization performs better than ever. But we are not interested in studying this aspect because the differences are minimal. The results obtained by SDC1 are similar to the other configurations but only for 2 and 4 processors. The performance decreases notably when 8 processors are considered in the SDC1 configuration.

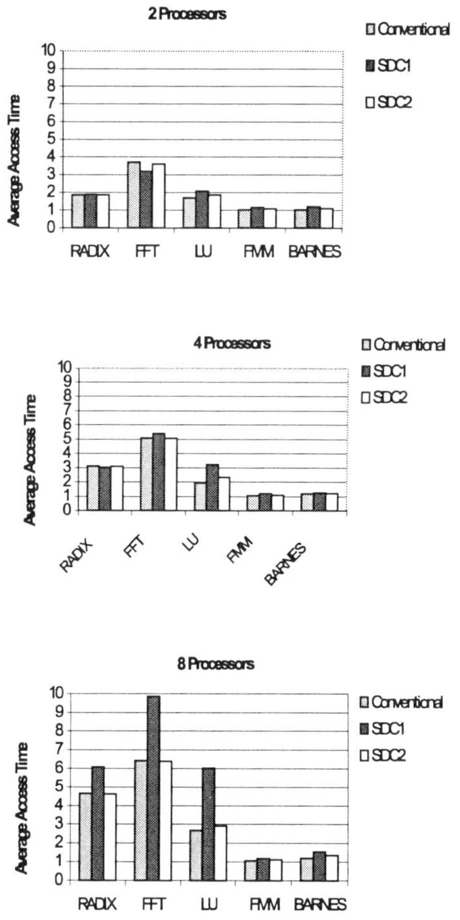

Figure 5. Comparative Average Data Access Time and for the Conventional Organization, SDC1 and SDC2 modeled.

Figure 6 shows that the bus utilization increases with the number of processors. As in previous results occur (Figure 5) SDC2 and the conventional organization present similar results. The bus utilization increases dramatically in the SDC1 organization that implies that this architecture is not suitable for more than four processors.

Resuming, the SDC2 configuration offers similar or slightly better performance than a conventional organization independently of the number of processors connected.

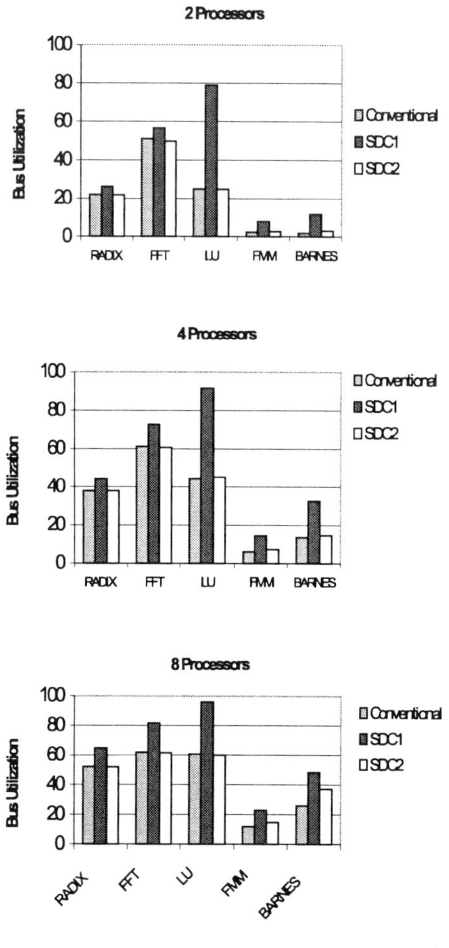

Figure 6. Comparative Bus Utilisation for the Conventional Organization, SDC1 and SDC2 modeled.

5. Hardware Cost

The additional hardware cost incurred by the split data cache in the first level cache is small compared to a conventional cache. For the 32 Kbytes a 2-way set-associative cache is used to generate the results presented in this paper, 18 bits of tags are used per entry (assuming 32-bit addresses). Because the line size is 16 bytes (4 words), the total cost of the tag array will be 18·2 K blocks, which result in 4.5 Kbytes. If a bit of valid per block is also considered the total cost is 36.75 Kbytes. In this account the cost of the logic control and the LRU bits have been ignored.

Table 1 shows the results of these accounts.

Data cost (bytes)	Tag Size (bits)	Tag Cost (bytes)	State-bit Total Cost (bytes)	Total Cost (bytes)
32 K	18	4.5 K	256	36.75 K

Table 1. Hardware Cost for a 32 Kbytes two-way set-associative cache.

For the 16 Kbytes a two-way set-associative SC cache is used, 19 bits of tags are used, what means 2432 bytes total array tag cost. The total array state bit cost for the SC cache is 2·1 K, which results in 256 bytes.

On the other hand, each line in SC cache has two counters of four bits respectively, that means a total of 1 Kbyte. For the 4 Kbytes four-way set-associative TC considered with a line size of 16 bytes, 22 bits of tags are used, that suppose a 704 bytes array tag cost. As there is a valid bit per line, it means a total of 32 bytes. Table 2 shows these results.

Data Cache	Data cost (bytes)	Tag Size (bits)	Tag Cost (bytes)	Valid-bit Cost (bytes)	Counter Cost (bytes)	Apprx. Total Cost (bytes)
TC	4 K	22	704	32		4.72 K
SC	16 K	19	2.375 K	0.125 K	1 K	19.5 K
						24.22 K

Table 2. Hardware cost for a Split Data Cache with a 16 Kbytes 2-way set-associate SC cache and a 4 Kbytes 4-way set-associate T1C cache and two 4 bits counters and a common L2 cache.

The approximate total cost incurred by the proposed model is 24.22 Kbytes that represents only around the 66 % over the cost needed by a conventional organization.

If only a second level cache exits in the temporal part, the spatial cache will have two block state bits that suppose a 0.25 Kbytes cost. On other hand as the spatial cache is connected to the bus, we have an additional snoop hardware cost.

Table 3 shows the results for a 4 bytes T1C line size. The total cost incurred by this architecture is 26.25 Kbytes that suppose around the 71.4 % over the cost needed by a conventional organization.

Data Cache	Data cost bytes	Tag Size bits	Tag Cost bytes	State-bits Cost bytes	Snoop Cost bytes	Count Cost bytes	Apprx Total Cost bytes
T1C	4 K	20	2.5 K	128	-		6.625 K
SC	16 K	19	2.375 K	0.25 K	2.625 K	1 K	19.625 K
							26.250 K

Table 3. Hardware cost for a Split Data Cache with a 16 Kbytes 2-way set-associate SC cache and a 4 Kbytes 4-way set-associate T1C cache and two 4 bits counters

6. Conclusions

The management and the performance evaluation of the split data cache for multiprocessors systems (SDC1) was introduced in [10]. This first study was done following the ideas presented by Milutinovic for uniprocessors in [7]. Some extensions in the cache coherence protocol were made in order to support that configuration in multiprocessors. The results showed that the SDC1 architecture improved the L1 cache hit ratio.

The experiments performed in this work show how this architecture performances worst than a conventional architecture if the number of processors increases, because the bus utilization increases notably. Therefore, under this assumption the mean data access time is also worse.

In this work a new configuration based on the idea presented by González in [6] has been also adapted to a multiprocessor system and carefully studied. This configuration (SDC2) uses a common L2 cache both for temporal data both for spatial data.

In the models done for SDC1 and SDC2 architectures we have used the same run-time hardware algorithm for the first level cache (if the block state is not taken in account). This run-time algorithm usually improves the L1 cache hit ratio respect to a conventional organization.

In this paper a detailed study about the performance and cost of the SDC1, SDC2 and the conventional configurations has been done. The mean data access time, the L1 cache hit ratio and the bus utilization for 2, 4 and 8 processors has been measured as performance index. In this study we have analyzed the impact of varying the number of processors in the system, and we have evaluated each performance index under these assumptions. Also the cost in bits of the first level caches has been calculated.

The results show that using the SDC1 split data cache we can achieve similar performance than in a conventional organization, but only under the assumption of a few number of processors (two or four). If more processors are considered the bus utilization increases notably, this implies that the mean data access time also will increase. In the SDC2 configuration proposed with a common L2 cache, the bus utilization is usually similar or slightly better than in a conventional organization independently of the number of processors connected to the bus. Therefore the SDC2 configuration seems to be more adequate for large-scale multiprocessors.

The most important conclusion of this work is that the chip area needed using the split data cache is very much smaller than a conventional cache. And in the case of the SDC2 organization the performance can be even improved independently of the number of processors. Therefore these models free up die area on the processor and this free area can be used for another processor optimization issues. On the other hand, the SDC2 organization also needs less die area than SDC1 because it does not need snoop tags for the SC data cache.

The approximately total cost incurred by the SDC2 represents only around the 66% over the cost needed by a conventional organization.

Actually we are working on the design of new architectures for study new run-time hardware algorithms.

References

[1] J.Tse and A.J. Smith, "CPU Cache Prefetching: Timing Evaluation of Hardware Implementations," *IEEE Transactions on Computers,* May 1998.

[2] N. Drach. "Hardware Implementation Issues on Data Prefetching," *ACM International Conference on Supercomputing*, June 1995.

[3] G. Tyson, M. Farrens, J. Matthews, and A.R. Pleszkun, "A Modified Approach to Data Cache Management," *Proceedings of Micro-28*, December 1995.

[4] T. Jhonson and W.W. Whu, "Run-time Adaptative Cache Hierarchy Management via Reference Analysis," *Proceedings of the ISCA-24*, June 1997.

[5] N. Jouppi, "Improving Direct-Mapped Cache Performance by the Addition of a Small Fully-Associative Cache and Prefetch Buffers," *Proceedings of the ISCA-17*, June 1990.

[6] A. González, Carlos Aliaga and M. Valero, "A Data Cache with Multiple Caching Strategies Tuned to Different Types of Locality," *ACM International Conference on Supercomputing,* Barcelona, Spain 1995, pp. 338-347.

[7] V. Milutinovic, B. Markovic, M. Tomasevic, and M. Tremblay, "The Split Temporal/Spatial Cache: Initial Performance Analysis", *Proceedings of the SCIzzL-5*, Santa Clara, California, USA, March 1996.

[8] J.A. Rivers and E.S. Davidson, "Reducing Conflicts in Direct-Mapped Caches with a Temporality-Based Design," *Proceedings of the 1966 ICPP*, August 1996.

[9] M. Prvulovic, D. Marinov and V. Milutinovic, "Performance Evaluation of Split Temporal/Spatial Caches: Paving the Way to New Solutions," Workshop Digest of ISCA/PAID-98, Barcelona, Spain, *June* 1998.

[10] J. Sahuquillo and A. Pont, "The Split Data Cache in Multiprocessors Systems: an Initial Hit Ratio Analysis," *Proceedings of the 7th Euromicro Workshop on Parallel and Distributed Processing,* Madeira, Portugal, February 1999.

[11] J. Sahuquillo and A. Pont. "The Filter Cache: A Run-Time Cache Management", *To appear in 25th Euromicro Conference.*

[12] R.G. Sheldon. "Implementing a Cache Consistency Protocol", *Proceedings of the 12th ISCA,* 1985, pp 276-283.

[13] S. C. Woo, M. Ohara, E. Torrie, J. P. Singh, and A. Gupta, "The SPLASH-2 Programs: Characterization and Methodological Considerations", *Proceedings of the 22nd ISCA*, June 1995.

[14] D. Magdic, "Limes: A Multiprocessor Simulation Environment", *IEEE TCCA Newsletter*, March 1997.

[15] J. Sahuquillo and A. Pont, "Impact of Reducing Miss Write Latencies in Multiprocessors with Two Level Cache", *Proceedings of the 24th Euromicro Conference,* Vasteras, Sweden, August 1998.

[16] J.A. Rivers, E.S. Tam, G.S. Tyson, E.S. Davidson and M. Farrens, "Utilizing Reuse Information in Data Cache Management," *Proceedings of the 12th ACM International Conference on Supercomputing*, July 1998.

Evaluation of a Virtual Shared Memory Machine by the Compilation of Data Parallel Loops*

Fabrizio Baiardi, Davide Guerri, Paolo Mori and Laura Ricci
Dipartimento di Informatica
Università di Pisa
{baiardi, guerri, mori, ricci}@di.unipi.it

Abstract

We introduce DVSA, distributed virtual shared areas, a virtual machine supporting the sharing of information on distributed memory architectures. The shared memory is structured as a set of areas where the size of each area may be chosen in an architecture dependent range. DVSA supports the sharing of areas rather than of variables because the exchange of chunks of data may result in better performances on distributed memory architectures offering little or no hardware support to information sharing. DVSA does not implement replication or prefetching strategies under the assumption that these strategies should be implemented by application specific virtual machines. The definition of these machines may often be driven by the compilation of the adopted programming languages.

To validate the assumption, at first we consider the implementation of data parallel loops and show that a set of static analyses based on the closed forms approach makes it possible to define compiler driven caching and prefetching strategies. These strategies fully exploit the operations offered by the DVSA machine and they noticeably reduce the time to access shared information. The optimizations strategies that can be exploited by the compiler includes the merging of accesses to avoid multiple access to the same area, the prefetching of areas and the reduction of the overhead due to barrier synchronization. Preliminary performance figures are discussed.

1 Introduction

Distributed virtual shared memory systems have been recently considered as a valid alternative to message passing ones, mainly to support applications requiring complex data structures and/or accessing data in irregular and data-dependent ways. A distributed virtual shared memory system emulates a shared memory at the software level on a distributed memory highly parallel architecture or on a workstation cluster. Current proposals differ in the way the shared space is structured, i.e. according to the types defined by the user or, at a lower level, as a set of segments. Furthermore, they often guarantee alternative consistency properties of the shared data [1, 8].

This paper introduces DVSA [2, 3], a virtual machine developed in the framework of the PQE2000 project [14]. DVSA supports a shared memory structured into a set of areas where the size of each area can be freely chosen in a predefined range depending on the underlying architecture. With respect to other shared memory abstract machines [9], DVSA is a lower level one because it is used as the target of the compilation of high level languages. A basic choice in the DVSA design has been to delegate to the compiler or to an higher level virtual machine, the detection and the management of data to be cached or replicated. Hence, even if the DVSA offers a rich set of operations on the areas, including both synchronous and asynchronous accesses and alternative strategies to preserve data consistency, it does not implement any data prefetching, caching or replication strategy. This does not imply that we neglect the importance of caching or prefetching strategies. Rather, we believe that effective strategies requires some information on the considered application and on the adopted programming language. Hence, these strategies can result in better performances if they are implemented on top of the basic functionalities to support information sharing.

To evaluate the effectiveness of this approach, we have considered the compilation of data parallel loops on the DVSA machine and shown how the strategies of interest may be defined during the compilation. Among the data parallel programming languages, HPF can be considered the most important one even if, recently, some interesting proposals for data parallel extensions of Java, based on the HFP model, have also been defined [4]. However, in the remainder of this paper we adopt HPF as the source language of the compiler.

*This work was partially supported by the Mosaico project.

1066-6192/99 $10.00 © 1999 IEEE

We show that most of static analyses defined for a data parallel language on a distributed memory architecture may be adopted for the DVSA as well. Obviously the returned information is exploited to define a different set of optimizations. In fact, now the main goal of the compiler is an optimal management of the data in the shared areas to minimize the overhead due to the accesses to the shared memory. As an example, multiple accesses to the same area should be avoided and asynchronous accesses to the shared memory should be exploited whenever possible.

Sect. 2 introduces the main classes of the DVSA operations. Alternative solutions for the implementations of data parallel loops are presented in sect. 3. Sect. 4 discusses some optimization strategies, while some preliminary performance results are presented in sect. 5. Related work and future developments are outlined in, respectively, sect. 6 and 7.

2 The DVSA Machine

As previously mentioned, the DVSA machine supports the sharing of information on a distributed memory architecture. The architectures of interest range from highly parallel systems, e.g. Meiko CS-2 or Cray T3-E, to workstation clusters. The main features of the DVSA machine are:

1. the data to be shared are partitioned into a set of user declared areas. The size of an area belongs to an architecture dependent range. An area is considered as an atomic entity that is read and updated through one operation;
2. caching and the prefetching strategies for the areas are delegated either to higher level virtual machines or to a compiler.

The choice of supporting the sharing of areas, i.e. of a set of data, rather than of elementary ones is related to our interest in portability of software layers developed on top of the DVSA machine. In several architectures, e.g. a workstation cluster, little hardware/firmware support for shared data is available. Furthermore, several architectures are characterized by a large cost to set up a communication. As a consequence, several data should be exchanged in each communication to reduce the overhead for each single data. On the other hand, a too large amount of shared data may easily become a bottleneck for the whole system, whenever several processes try to access data in the same area simultaneously. These considerations have led to the definition and design of a virtual machine where the user, in our case the developer of an higher level machine or of a compiler, can choose the size of a shared area in a range determined by the DVSA designer according to the physical architecture that is considered. Among the features of the physical architecture that determines the range where the size of an area can be chosen, we recall the topology of the interconnection structure among the processing nodes, the time to set up a communication, the communication bandwidth and the number of parallel communications that can be efficiently supported. Provided that DVSA(A), the machine developed on an architecture A, has been characterized through the range $[a, b]$ of the sizes of the areas it can efficiently support, any software layer developed on top of DVSA(A) may be ported without any loss of efficiency on DVSA(B), the DVSA machine implemented on an architecture B, provided that the range $[c, d]$ of DVSA(B) is such that $[a, b] \subset [c, d]$.

One of the problems to be considered when choosing the size of an area, within the architecture dependent range, is false sharing because as the size of an area decreases, the overhead due to this problem decreases too.

Another important assumption in the design of the DVSA is that caching and prefetching of areas should be either be implemented by higher level machines or driven by the code generated by a compiler. To validate this assumption, at least as for as concerns compiler generated code, we have considered the compilation of data parallel loops. While the static analyses and the optimization strategies are introduced in the following, the remainder of this section briefly introduces the main functions supported by the DVSA machine.

The most important classes of DVSA operations are:

- *Notification*
- *Access*
- *Synchronization*

Through operations in the *Notification class*, the processes declare the set of areas that will be shared and the size of each area. The processing node where an area is to be stored is chosen either by the programmer or by a default allocation procedure. In the current implementations, the allocator evenly distributes the areas among the local memories of the processing node. The operations in this class are also used to signal the termination of operations on an area. Each area is paired with an integer used to address it.

The *Synchronization class* includes operations to gain access, as a reader or as a writer, to an area. Only one process can gain access to an area as a writer, while several readers can share the same area simultaneously. This class also includes a function to implement a barrier synchronization among a user defined set of processes.

The *Access Class* includes operations to read or update an area; each operation may be synchronous or asynchronous and the access to the area may either be synchronized or unsynchronized. A *synchronous read/write* of an area waits till the operation is completed. Asynchronous read/write do not wait for the operation to be completed and they return an *handle*, i.e. an identifier, to test for their termination. As an example, a process may start an asynchronous read operation identified by a handle H, continue the execution of its program, and then wait for the completion of the operation identified by H only when its results are needed to continue the execution. Asynchronous operations enable an application to hide the latency of operations on the areas by overlapping them with some useful computation.

Each operation on an area may be *synchronized* vs. *unsynchronized*: *synchronized operations* preserve the consistency of the information in an area by scheduling the accesses through a *multiple readers-single writer* strategy. Some operations in this class merge an access to an area and a synchronization operation. As an example, one operation allows a process to gain exclusive access to an area as well as to read the area itself.

Unsynchronized operations directly access the shared area. Hence, they do not guarantee the consistency of the information. These operations have been introduced to avoid any synchronization overhead in all the cases where the semantics of the computation guarantees that no inconsistency can arise. An alternative strategy to guarantee a consistent access to an area introduces proper DVSA operations in the synchronization class after and before a sequence of unsynchronized operations.

Besides the mentioned ones, the DVSA also defines some *Utility operations* that return general information on the areas.

Two implementations of the DVSA machine are currently available: on the Meiko CS-2 and on a cluster of Linux workstations. Implementation on a Cray T3-E is currently under development.

In the following, we will describe in more detail the operations exploited by the compiler. Unsynchronized operations will be considered only.

3 Compilation of a data parallel loop

With reference to the forall loop, this section describes an allocation strategy of HPF data structures into the private memory of a process and into the shared areas. Then, two approaches to the compilation of a forall, a *static* and a *dynamic* one, are considered. For sake of simplicity, we consider the compilation of loops where the right hand side includes one reference to a data structure. The following section considers a right hand side with several references as well as the compilation of a sequence of forall statements.

3.1 Data Distribution

We consider the compilation of a data parallel loop:

$$\begin{aligned} &forall\ i = l : u : s \\ &\quad A[f(i)] = h(A[g(i)]) \end{aligned} \tag{1}$$

where f, g are linear functions and h is any function. As previously mentioned, we adopt an HPF like semantics for parallel loops and assume that the data is distributed through HPF like directives.

The first step of the compilation of loop (1) defines the distribution of data in the DVSA areas. Each HPF structure is distributed according to both an analysis of the accesses to its elements and to the program distribution directives. The data structures of an HPF program are partitioned into three classes:

- *replicated:* these structures can be replicated in the private memory of each process because they are not updated by the program;
- *private:* these structures are updated but not read: they are stored in the private memory of each process, according to the distribution directives;
- *shared:* these structures are both updated and read. Each one is stored in the DVSA areas according to the distribution directives.

Notice that if a data structure is both read and modified by the forall we consider the *whole structure* as shared, but this does not imply that each of its elements is shared. Sect. 4 introduces a more refined analysis to detect the shared elements of an array, i.e. those updated and read by distinct processes.

For each shared data structure, the compiler allocates a distinct area for each process of the program: each area includes the elements of data structure allocated to a process P according to the distribution directives. In the following, the *area corresponding to P* denotes the area including the shared data mapped to P by the distribution directives.

For the sake of conciseness, we will also assume that each area includes elements belonging to just one data structure and that all the elements of the same data structure associated to a process by the distribution directives can be stored in one area. The analysis shown in the following sections may be easily extended to overcome these constraints.

3.2 Code Generation: Run Time Resolution

To fully exploit the DVSA, the implementation of a forall should access each area once to read/write the data accessed in distinct iterations. In the following, we discuss the generation of code satisfying this requirement under the assumption that, as in most HPF compilers, the iterations of the parallel loop are distributed to the processes according to the *Owner Computes Rule*. Here and in the following by iteration we mean one instance of the body of the forall.

```
{*Phase1 : Area Detection*}
    Pid := my_index();
    for i := 1 to u step s do
        if Owner(f(i)) = Pid then
            begin
                It_set=It_set ∪ {i}
                R_set [area(g(i)]:=R_set [area(g(i)]∪ {g(i)}
                Pix_set:=Pix_set ∪area(g(i))
            end
{*Phase2 : Data Fetch*}
    ∀ Pix ∈ Pix_set do
        begin
            DVSA_read(Pix, LOC_Area);
            ∀ r ∈ R_set[Pix] do
                TEMP[r]:=LOC_Area(Disp(r))
            if Pix=my_area() then LOC_myarea:=LOC_Area
        end
    if my_area() ∉ Pix_set then DVSA_read(my_area,LOC_myarea)
    ⟨ synchronization barrier ⟩
{*Phase3 : Computation : each process modifies its area*}
    ∀ j ∈ It_set
        LOC_myarea(Disp(f(j))):= h(TEMP[g(j)])
    DVSA_Write (my_area(),LOC_myarea)
    ⟨ synchronization barrier ⟩
```

Figure 1. Code generated by the run-time resolution

Two strategies are possible for the compilation of a forall loop, according to the way the owner computes rule is applied [6]. The first one, *run time* resolution, evaluates at run time the owner computes rule. *Static* resolution, instead, evaluates the owner computes rule at compile time to determine the set of references of a forall. This section discusses *run time* resolution, while *static* resolution is described in the following one.

When adopting *run time* resolution, first of all each process applies the owner computes rule to discover which iterations it has to execute. Each process collects both the *indexes of these iterations* and those of *the array elements read* in these iterations. After this step, each process knows the areas to be read, and, for each area, the elements to be fetched. At this point, the areas are read and the proper elements are collected in a private data structure. When all the processes have terminated this step, each one performs the actual computation of the right hands side and then it updates its corresponding area.

The outline of the SPMD code generated by the compiler is shown in Fig. 1.

The function *my_index*, returns the identifier of the process executing the forall; the function *my_area* returns the index of the area corresponding to each process. The function *Owner(Ref)* returns the index of the process where the array reference *Ref* is mapped, while the functions *area(Ref), Disp(Ref)* return, respectively, the index of the area where the reference *Ref* is mapped and the displacement within that area: all the functions are defined in [5].

The object code includes three different phases, separated by synchronization barriers. In the first one, *Area Detection*, each process applies the owner computes rule and it builds three set of indexes: It_set, R_set[A] and Pix_set. It_set includes the indexes of iterations that modify the considered data structure, R_set[A] those of the elements referred by the iterations in It_set and that belong to the area A, while Pix_set includes the indexes of the areas A where R_set[A] is not empty.

In the second phase, *Data Fetch*, each area whose index belongs to *Pix_set* is copied into a local structure *LOC_Area* through the function *DVSA_read(x,y)* that reads the area indexed by *x* into the local variable *y*. The function implements a synchronous, unsynchronized access to the area. The indexes collected in the first phase allow each process to read each area once to gather all the data it needs. Read data are then copied in the local array TEMP: each element of A is stored in the corresponding position of TEMP, using its *global index*. The optimized version of the code compacts read data and uses *local indexes* to access them. In the third phase, *Computation*, each process performs the computations it has been assigned and modifies its corresponding area. To merge all these accesses into one DVSA operation, all the updates are first performed in a local structure y, that is then copied into the area through the function *DVSA_write(x,y)*. Also this function accesses the area in a synchronous, unsynchronized way.

The *synchronization barriers* among all the processes guarantee that all processes have fetched the data they need before any of them updates any area. This is a case where a protocol using an overall synchronization of the processes and unsynchronized accesses to the areas achieves a better performance than one using synchronized operations.

3.3 Code Generation: Static Resolution

To avoid the run time overhead proper of run time resolution, several static analyses may be applied. The most relevant ones [6] are those based on the computation of *closed forms*, on the definition of *automata* and on *linear integer programming* techniques.

The closed form approach [7] returns a description of each of the sets exploited by the run time resolution. In general, this description is parametric in the index of a process and in the number of the processes of the program. The only computation left at run time is the evaluation of the expression when the value of the parameters is known.

The closed forms approach can be applied only if the loop accesses an *Array Section* which may be described as a *slice*. A *slice* is triple *(f:l:s)* representing a sequence of elements, where *f* is the first element of the sequence, *l* is an

OWN[P]	=	indexes assigned to P by the HPF distribution directives
AREA[A]	=	OWN[P] where A is the area corresponding to P
		indexes of elements stored in Ar
WRITE[P]	=	OWN[P] ∩ f(l: u: s)
		indexes of the elements modified by P
LOCAL_IT[P]	=	f^{-1}(WRITE(P))
		iterations executed by P
READ[P]	=	g(LOCAL_IT(P))
		indexes of all the elements read by P
READ_AR[P,A]	=	READ[P] ∩ AREA[A]
		indexes of the elements read by P in the area A

Figure 2. Slices computed by the compiler

upper bound for the sequence, and *s* is the stride, i.e. the difference between two consecutive elements of the sequence. For instance, the slice *(1:30:2)* includes all the odd values in between 1 and 30. In [11], a slice calculus is defined based on intersection and linear transformation operators: the approach is simple, but it cannot be applied to loops accessing triangular or trapezoidal regions. In this case, integer linear programming techniques are required.

Let us consider the forall statement (1) again. The sets *It_set* and *R_set* of Fig. 1 can be statically computed through the slice calculus as follows. First the slice *OWN[P]*, describing the indexes of array *Ar* assigned to *P*, is determined according to the program distribution directives. The slice *AREA[A]* defines the index of the elements of *Ar* stored in an area *A* and is equal to *OWN[P]* if all the data assigned to a process are stored in a single area; otherwise it can be easily deduced by this slice. All other relevant slices are computed by the analysis through intersections and linear transformations as shown in Fig. 2. It is worth noticing that the slice *LOCAL_IT[P]* corresponds to the set *It_set*, while the slice *READ_AR[P,A]* corresponds to the set *R_set[A]* in Fig. 1. The computation of this information at compile time makes it possible to avoid the execution of the code labeled Phase1 in Fig. 1. In this way, both the iteration assigned to each process and the data to be fetched to execute these iterations are computed at compile time.

4 Optimizations

After describing how multiple accesses to elements in the same area may be merged into one DVSA operation, this section shows how area caching and prefetching may be driven through the output of proper static analyses.

4.1 Access Merging

The previous sections have considered a forall which refers just one element of one array in the right hand side. Let us now consider the more general case where the right hand side includes a set of references to the *same* array. Even now the fetches of different operands in the *same area* should be *merged* so that just one DVSA operation is invoked to access all the operands.

Example 4.1.1 *Let us consider the following forall statement:*

forall i = 1: 2:100
*B[i]=A[i]+A[2*i]-A[i+1]*

*The goal of this optimization is that each process reads through only one DVSA operation all the data it needs in the same area. These data are the elements corresponding to A[i], A[2*i] and A[i+1] in all the iterations assigned to P.*

◇

This optimization may be applied to both *run time* and *static* resolution. The latter requires the computation, for each process P and each area *A*, of the union of the slices *READ_Ar[P, A]* for all the references on the right hand side of the forall assignment. In the most general case, the union returns a set that includes, but may be different from, all the elements to be fetched because the slice calculus is not closed with respect to the union operator.

4.2 Area Prefetching

We consider now how the compiler can exploits a synchronous DVSA operations to overlap the fetching of an area with some useful computation. This is possible, for instance, if some arrays referred in the right hand side are replicated, while others are shared. Each process may execute iterations involving replicated data only while prefetching shared data. The remaining iterations are executed when shared data are available.

In the most general case, when any array is shared, a more refined static analysis can be defined to detect the shared elements of an array. We recall that, according to the analysis previously defined, an array is shared if it is referred by both sides of a forall assignment. Actually, only the elements updated by one process and read by some other ones are shared, while the remaining ones may be considered private. This requires a distribution of the data in the shared areas that stores an element of the array in an area only if is shared among several processes. In this way, each process performs *local computations*, i.e. computations involving local data only, while fetching an area. After shared data has been fetched, the process executes any remaining iterations. At the end, the process updates its corresponding area. This is shown in the following example.

Example 4.2.1 *Let us consider the following Jacobi code:*

> *Processors P(4)*
> *Integer A(100)*
> *Distribute A(BLOCK)*
> *Forall i=2,99*
> *A[i] := (A[i+1] + A[i-1])/2*

Even if A is referenced by both sides of the assignment, only the first and the last element of each block of A are shared. Furthermore, only the first and the last iterations assigned to each process refer shared data, while the remaining ones refer local data only. Hence, each process may prefetch data required by the first and last iterations while executing all the other iterations.

◇

The set of the indexes of the elements mapped into an area is now different from that of the indexes of the elements assigned to P. If Pnum denotes the number of processes, the shared elements corresponding to a process P are described by the slice:

$$\bigcup_{j=0}^{(Pnum)\wedge j\neq P} READ[j] \cap OWN[P]$$

The code generated by the compiler is shown in Fig. 3.

```
Pid := my_index()
∀ area A
    if READ_AR[Pid, A] ≠ 0
        Handles[A] := DVSA_Prefetch (A, new vtg)
< local computations execution >
∀ area A
    if READ_AR[Pid, A] ≠ 0
        DVSA_Wait (Handles[A])
< global computations execution >
```

Figure 3. Prefetch Optimization: code generated

The compiler exploits the function *DVSA_Prefetch* that reads an area in an asynchronous, unsynchronized way. The handles returned by *DVSA_Prefetch* are stored in the array Handles. After executing any local computation, this array is used to wait for the termination of the transfers. Each area is copied into a dynamically allocated local variable vtg.

4.3 Data Caching

In any solution proposed till now, each process updates at most one DVSA area, its corresponding one, while each area is updated by at most one process. This allows the process that updates an area to cache that area in a local variable. The process can update this variable and write it back into the area just before the last barrier of the forall. In this way, for instance, a process need not to read again an area A after an update of A.

4.4 Synchronization Optimization

Most of the optimization strategies to reduce the synchronization overhead of HPF programs may be applied to applications developed on top of the DVSA machine. In the following we focus on the minimization of the overhead due to barriers.

4.4.1 Barriers Elimination

In any previous implementation of a forall, synchronization barriers guarantee that any right hand side is evaluated before the updates on the left hand sides and that the execution of a forall starts only after the termination of any previous forall statement. These barriers may be avoided if either of the following holds:

1. the right and the left hand sides of the assignment are independent
2. two consecutive forall assignments are independent.

In the first case, the compiler checks that no array is referred in both sides of the forall assignment. In the second one, it checks that the array updated by a forall is not used by a successive assignment.

In the second case, to further reduce the synchronization overhead, rather than inserting a barrier after each forall assignment, the compiler splits the barrier execution. At the end of each forall, each process signals that it has terminated the execution of the forall. Furthermore, a process waits that the barrier has been reached by all other processes only when it executes a forall depending on the previous one. In this way, the execution of a process is suspended only if it is required by the program semantics.

4.4.2 Barriers Reduction

The barriers defined in the previous sections guarantee that *all* processes read data in the right hand side of a forall before *any* process modifies shared data.

However, the semantics of the forall only requires that a process updates an area A after all processes requiring data in A have read such data. This can be exploited provided that the compiler can determine the set of processes using each area: this information may be computed through the slice calculus.

In this way, the global barrier which synchronize all the processes of the program may be replaced by several barriers, each involving a subset of the processes only. The next example shows this optimization in the case of the Jacobi code:

Example 4.4.1 *Let us consider the Jacobi code again:*

```
Processors P(4)
Integer A(100)
Distribute A(BLOCK)
Forall i=2,99
    A[i] := (A[i+1] + A[i-1])/2
```

Each process P_i shares data only with processes P_{i+1} and P_{i-1}. Hence, P_i can modify its corresponding area only when both P_{i+1} and P_{i-1} have read these areas. A correct synchronization requires that Pi synchronize with P_{i-1} and P_{i+1} only, rather than with all the process.

◇

```
Processors P(4)
Integer A(N)
Distribute A(BLOCK)
Forall i= 2, N-1
    A[i] = 0.5*(A[i-1]+A[i+1])
```

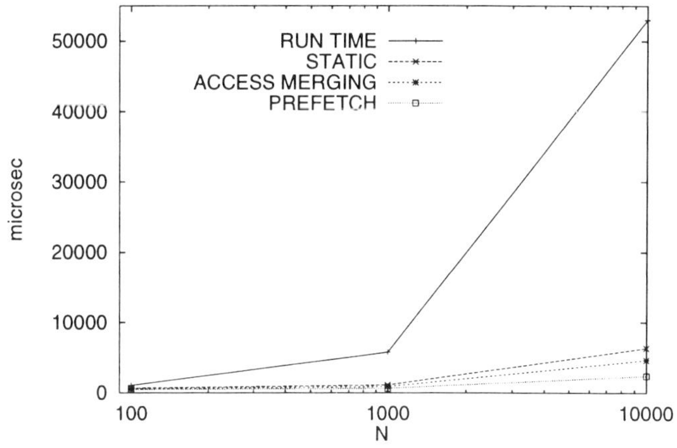

Figure 4. Execution times of alternative solutions.

5 Experimental Results

This section briefly evaluates the optimizations introduced in the previous sections. The execution times refer to the implementation of the DVSA on the Meiko CS-2.

Fig. 4 shows the execution times in μsec of several versions of the Jacobi code. Each version exploits one of the different optimization strategies previously discussed.

The execution times of the *run time* resolution and of the *static* one clearly show the effectiveness of the *static* one, especially as the size of the array increases. We also show the execution times achieved by applying the access merging and prefetch optimization strategies to the *static* resolution. We observe that, if the compiler exploits the DVSA operation to prefetch the data, then the execution time is reduced by 40% in the case of an array with 1000 elements and of more than 50% in the case of an array with 10000 elements. Fig. 5 also compares the performance of one global barrier against that of several barriers, each involving a subset of the processes. The latter solution decreases the execution time of the program by 40% with respect to the global synchronization barrier.

6 Related Work

According to our best knowledge, the only proposal of an HPF compiler for distributed shared memory architectures is that of [10], where a PGI-HPF compiler for distributed shared memory architectures is defined for the *Tempest* software distributed shared memory system. The *Tempest* system supports multiple cached copies of an area: the consistency of these copies is maintained by a consistency protocol. When considering this kind of systems, the most important problem in the definition of the compiler is the optimization of the system's coherence protocol through the information collected by the static analyses. For instance, a certain degree of controlled incoherence may be allowed provided that the compiler detects, through an analysis of data accesses, that the general coherence protocol may be bypassed. To apply this approach, when adopting the DVSA machine, each process has a private copy of an area in one of its local variables. The consistency of this copy is preserved by periodically reading/writing the corresponding DVSA area. As an example, a strategy similar to the one of *TreadMark* [1] may be adopted, where the consistency is guaranteed after each barrier. By applying this approach to a multigrid method, we have been able to achieve an increase of 20% in the speed up. However, in this case the number of iterations between two barriers has been chosen by the programmer. [13] extends some static analyses developed for data parallel languages compilers for message passing architectures to the case of the shared memory: the execution model of the considered loops is different from the HPF one. [12] proposes to share only selected

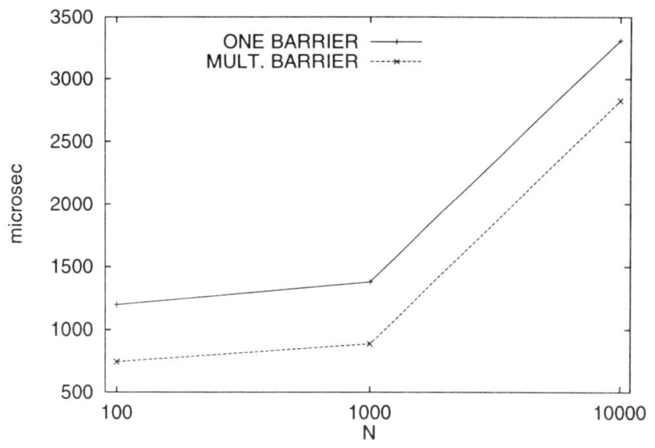

Figure 5. Execution times of alternative synchronization strategies.

arrays among the processes and to use the data distribution directives to balance the load distribution rather than to allocate the local parts of arrays.

7 Conclusions

This paper has presented some approaches to the compilation of data parallel loops and, in particular, it has shown that both proper distribution and static optimization strategies for the DVSA machine can be defined. This confirms that fairly simple machines, such as the DVSA one, can achieve good performances if paired with an optimizing compiler that drives the prefetching and the caching of data. Furthermore, multiple accesses to the same area may be merged into a single one. A critical feature to achieve good performances is the availability of unsynchronized operations. As shown by the forall compilation, in most cases these operation can be paired with proper synchronization constructs to minimize the synchronization overheads and reduce the overall execution time.

It is worth stressing that, because of the absence of both caching and prefetching strategies in the DVSA machine, no conflict can arise between the compiler strategies and those of the target machine. This simplifies the development of the compiler itself because the speed up due to an optimization strategy can be evaluated and alternative strategies can be compared in a more accurate way. Obviously, this does not imply that caching and prefetching strategies are not important. Our point is that, given the current state of the art, it is rather difficult to devise strategies where performance is independent of the considered application and of the programming tools that are used. Hence, caching and prefetching should be driven by the programming tools rather than frozen at the lowest machine level.

References

[1] C. Amza, A. L. Cox, S. Dwarkadas, P. Keleher, H. Lu, R. Rajamony, and W. Zwaenepoel. Treadmarks: Shared memory computing on networks of workstations. *Computer*, 29(2):18–28, feb 1996.

[2] F. Baiardi, C. Bernasconi, D. Guerri, L. Ricci, and L. Vaglini. Implementing concurrent paradigms through virtual shared areas. Technical Report 9, PQE2000 Project, apr 1999.

[3] F. Baiardi and D. Guerri. *Op_Memory Library User Manual.* PQE2000 Project, oct 1998.

[4] B.Carpenter, G. Zhang, G. Fox, X. Lin, and Y. Wen. HPJava: data parallel extensions to Java. *Concurrency: Practice and Experience*, 10(11-13), sep-oct 1998.

[5] C.Bernasconi. Compiling HPF on parallel architecture supporting virtual shared memory. Master's thesis, Department of Computer Science, University of Pisa, jul 1998.

[6] F.Coelho, C. Germain, and J. Pazat. State of art in compiling HPF. In *The parallel programming Model: Foundations, HPF Realization and Scientific Application*, number 1132 in Lecture Note in Computer Science. 1996.

[7] S. Gupta, S. Kaushik, S. Sharma, C. Huang, and P. Sadayappan. Compiling array expression for efficient execution on distributed-memory machines. *Journal of Parallel and Distribute Computing*, 32:155–172, 1996.

[8] L. Kontothanassis, G. Hunt, R. Stets, N. Hardavellas, M. Cierniak, S. Parthasarathy, W. Meira, S. Dwarkadas, and M. Scott. Vm-based shared memory on low-latency, remote-memory-access networks. In *Proc., 24th Annual Int'l. Symp. on Computer Architecture*, jun 1997.

[9] V. Milutinovic. Distributed shared memory systems. *Proceedings of the IEEE, Special Issue on Distributed Shared Memory*, 87(3):445–455, mar 1999.

[10] S.Chandra and J.R.Larus. Optimizing communication in HPF programs on fine-grain distributed shared memory. In *Proceedings of the Sixth ACM SIGPLAN Symposium on Principles and Practice of Parallel Programming, Las Vegas*, jun 1997.

[11] J. Stichnoth, D. O'Hallaron, and T. Gross. Generating communication for array statements: Design, implementation, and evaluation. *Journal of Parallel and Distibute Computing*, 21(1):150–159, apr 1994.

[12] T.Brandes. Compiling high performance fortran for shared memory and shared virtual memory systems. In *Proceedings of the 5th Euromicro Workshop on Parallel and Distributed Computing, London, UK*, pages 289–296, jan 1997.

[13] C. Tseng. Compiler optimizations for eliminating barrier synchronization. In *Proceedings of the Fifth ACM SIGPLAN Symposium on Principles and Practice of Parallel Programming, Santa Barbara, CA*, Jul 1995.

[14] M. Vanneschi. Heterogeneous HPC environment. In *Proceedings of Euro-Par98, Southampton, UK*, number 1470 in Lecture Notes in Computer Science, pages 21–34, sep 1998.

Using Agent Wills to Provide Fault-tolerance in Distributed Shared Memory Systems

Antony Rowstron
Microsoft Research Ltd.
St. George House, 1 Guildhall Street
Cambridge, CB2 3NH, United Kingdom.
antr@microsoft.com

Abstract

In this paper we describe how we use mobile objects to provide distributed programs coordinating through a persistent distributed shared memory (DSM) with tolerance to sudden agent failure, and use the increasingly popular Linda-like tuple space languages as an example for implementation of the concept.

In programs coordinating and communicating through a DSM a data structure is shared between multiple agents, and the agents update the shared structure directly. However, if an agent should suddenly fail it is often hard for the agents to make the data structures consistent with the new application state. For example consider if a data structure contains a list of active agents. In such a case, transactions can be used when adding and removing agent names from the list ensuring that that the data structure is consistent and does not become corrupted should an agent fail. However, if failure of the agent occurs after the name has been added, how does the application ensure the list is correct?

We argue that using mobile objects we can provide wills for the agents to effectively enable them to ensure the shared data structure is application consistent, even once they have failed. We show how we have integrated the use of agent wills into a Linda system and show that we have not increased the complexity of program writing. The integration is simple and general, does not alter the underlying semantics of the operations performed in the will and the use of mobility is transparent to the programmer.

1. Introduction

Using Distributed Shared Memory (DSM) as a communication and coordination mechanism for applications that are executing over the Internet is become increasingly popular. The concept of using DSM in such a framework has been explored in what could be called traditional DSM, in systems such as PerDiS[7], which quite literally provide a mechanism for moving and managing pages of shared memory between multiple machines. As well as the traditional DSM architectures there has been considerable interest in the last few years in the use of tuple space based coordination languages, with many new languages being proposed including WCL [13], PageSpace [5], TuSCon [11], MARS [2], Jada [4], TSpaces [19], KLAIM [10], Lime [12] and JavaSpaces [18]. These are all based around the original ideas contained in Linda [8, 3], where the processes which want to communicate and coordinate use a shared associative memory, or tuple space.

The domain we are interested in is systems that support asynchronous Computer Supported Collaborative Working (CSCW) applications, or in other words, systems where the DSM is persistent, and contains state that can be used after the agent that created the data has died. For the purposes of this paper we will assume that an agent is an entity (application, process, program or "agent") that is using a shared memory to communicate with other agents. The problem we aim to address is the one of sudden agent failure resulting in data structures in the memory being consistent (no dangling pointers etc.) but containing information that is incorrect, and in Section 2 we will demonstrate this problem in detail.

Traditional methods for providing fault tolerance, such as transactions, have been widely adopted in DSM systems, for example in PerDiS, TSpaces, JavaSpaces. However, with the current drive to use these infrastructures for highly distributed CSCW applications new demands are made by application programmers. These new demands include the need for more styles of fault tolerance. In the paper we describe our approach to providing a different layer of fault tolerance, which is used in conjunction with, not as a replacement for, traditional approaches.

The basic premise of the work is that if you can minimise

1066-6192/99 $10.00 © 1999 IEEE

the distance between a piece of code and the data it is acting upon then you can provide better fault tolerance. There is nothing new per se in this, and in client-server based applications manage this by having the shared state managed by a single server (or synchronised set of servers) which copes with failure of agents and maintains the shared state, which can only be access through the server interface. In DSM systems the agents share and manipulate the data directly, and there is often no server agent that has overall responsibility for the system. Indeed, the server could well be considered as the run-time system that supports the DSM, and it is a general infrastructure that supports a general-purpose access interface. In a client-server world the server can know what to do in the case of client failure, however, in the peer-to-peer world of DSM, the general system managing the shared memory has no notion of what should be done upon agent failure.

In this paper we introduce the notion of an "agent will" that simply is a piece of code that run-time managing the DSM can execute if it detects a failure with an agent.

In the next section presence notification is described which demonstrates the need for further fault-tolerance mechanisms, and in Section 3 the concept of agent wills is described in detail. Section 4 describes Linda, a comparison of this work with other work in the Linda field, and shows how agent wills are incorporated into a working Linda based system, showing the Java API used and briefly discussing the implementation. Finally, Section 6 describes future work and then we present our conclusions.

2. Presence notification

To demonstrate the general shortcoming with current DSM systems we consider the problem of "presence notification" [6] in a CSCW application. Presence notification is characterised as the need for an agent to know that another agent currently exists. For example, given a shared whiteboard application and the assumption that at some point in time there is more than one user sharing the same whiteboard it is quite conceivable that the application should maintain, on each user's screen, a list of people who are currently sharing that whiteboard. When someone starts the application their name is added to the list, when they close the application their name is removed. This list would be an example of presence notification.

If writing such an application using a client-server paradigm a server is written that manages the shared state, and the server can detect when it thinks an agent has failed and then remove the name from the list and propagate the change. The server knows what to do when the agent has been considered to fail, because the application programmer who created the server created the code to perform the necessary operations on the data structure. However, when using a DSM system the shared state would be stored by the underlying infrastructure providing the DSM, and the application writers create an agent that manipulates and monitors this shared state accordingly.

In a DSM system, although it is possible for the underlying infrastructure to detect that an agent has stopped responding, it is not easy for the agents to decide that another agent has failed. How this can be detected varies on the particular attributes of the DSM implementation. For example, in most tuple space based DSMs this is difficult/impossible to detect. This is compounded because multiple applications may share the same data structure, and then one application may not understand what to do to the data structure when another applications agent fails. This is especially true as there may be only one agent executing when the failure occurs, and therefore there are no other agents active. This is possible because many DSM systems provide persistence of data structures (all tuple space languages support persistence of tuple spaces) therefore; other agents will use the shared data structures in the future.

The problem is that the infrastructure supporting the DSM has no concept of what an application would like done when an agent fails (becomes disconnected, dies or whatever). In the shared whiteboard application example there is no real problem with the whiteboard. Whenever an update to the whiteboard is performed the program uses some fault tolerance mechanism (such as transactions) to update the whiteboard. If failure occurs in the middle of the transaction then the transaction aborts and the whiteboard is left in a consistent state. However, the presence notification data structure needs to be updated to reflect the agent has died. In other words, the shared data structure that contains the name of the user needs to have the name removed. But if the failure was unexpected how can the agent who died update the shared state[1]?

In order to overcome this problem we have examined the use of agent wills. The concept of agent wills is now described.

3. Agent wills

In order to overcome this we propose using mobile objects and to allow an agent to pass to the run-time supporting the DSM a piece of code that should be executed *should the system* think that the agent has failed. In this context, a mobile object is considered to be the code and internal state of the object, but not the execution point (in other words you can not pass a thread to the run-time system). The run-time stores the passed object, and this is called the "agent will". If the agent terminates normally then the will is discarded,

[1]The failure could have even occurred whilst the agent was trying to remove the name from the data structure.

but if the run-time decides that the agent has failed it executes a method within the object. It should be noted that the agent must decide when the agent has failed. The mechanism used to decide when failure has occurred will most likely be network dependent, and communication method specific. The object that is passed to the run-time system, implements an interface. The Linda embedding that is described in the next section is shown in Figure 1. The run-time system calls the method `will`.

If the will is executed it is able to update any shared data structures as though it was a normal agent. It can therefore, remove a name from a shared data structure, or even insert some state to indicate that the agent has disappeared rather than terminated normally. The application programmer creating the agent that dies is free to choose what operations are to be performed on the shared data structures.

The aim is that the application programmer should not perceive that the mobile code is being used, and the semantics of the operations performed in the will should be the same as though the operations are performed within the agent. Although the application programmer will hopefully not perceive this they are providing "small servers" that slot into the main server. The small server only provides one service which is called automatically on failure.

```
interface AgentWill{
  public void will(); }
```

Figure 1. The Java interface for a will object.

Having provided an overview of what an agent will is, let us now consider the addition of agent wills to a Linda system. Before describing the addition, we will provide a brief overview of Linda, and some background work on Linda systems.

4. Case study: Linda

Linda [8, 3] was the first tuple space based co-ordination language. In the nomenclature of Linda a tuple space is a mathematical bag (a multiset allowing for repetition of members), a tuple is an ordered list of typed elements (actuals), and a template is an order list of formals and actuals. Tuples are inserted and removed from a tuple space using an associative matching process. A template matches a tuple if they have the same number of fields, and all the actuals in the template match the actuals in the tuple and the formals in the template match the type of the corresponding actuals in the tuple. Basic Linda provides three primitives to enable access to a tuple space:

out(tuple) Insert a tuple into a tuple space.

in(template) If a tuple exists that matches the template then remove the tuple and return it to the entity performing the `in`. If no matching tuple is available then the primitive blocks until a matching tuple is available.

rd(template) If a tuple exists that matches the template then return a copy of the tuple to the entity that performed the `rd`. If there is no matching tuple then the primitive blocks until a matching tuple is available.

It should be noted that if multiple tuples in a tuple space match a template then the returned tuple is chosen non-deterministically. Although the original implementation only supported a single global tuple space, current tuple space based coordination languages support multiple tuple spaces in one form or another. In these implementations normally tuple space handles can be passed between agents in tuples. Also, the new generation, such as WCL, support a wide variety of access primitives, and support concepts like tuple streaming, event models, bulk movement of tuples and so forth. However, the exact primitives that a language supports and the styles of interaction with a tuple space are of no real consequence to the whether they can use the agent will concept. Any access primitives or coordination patterns that can be used by an agent can be used in the agent will.

Most of the new generation of coordination languages use a variety of mechanisms to provide fault-tolerance not found in the original Linda. Most languages that address fault-tolerance (such as TSpaces and JavaSpaces) use a transaction-based method of providing fault tolerance. The transaction model adopted provides fault tolerance for updating a data structure, where at the end of the transaction the data structure within the tuple space will be consistent. WCL uses the concept of mobility to provide the fault-tolerant properties which transactions address in traditional tuple space languages [14], and this work described in this paper is an extension of this work.

There are several other systems which look at the use of mobility within Linda systems, such as KLAIM [10], Lime [12], TuCSoN [11] and MARS [2]. Most of these systems attempt to expose the mobility of agents and to make it a feature that the application programmer explicitly uses. One of the main concepts of agent wills is that there is no concept of location. The application programmer has no notion of where or how an agent will is stored or executed.

There are two Linda based systems of particular interest at this point, both of which use reactive tuple spaces: TuCSoN and MARS. Reactive tuple spaces were first introduced in TuCSoN and they allowed sequences of non-blocking tuple space operations to be inserted into a tuple space. These sequences of operations are created using a logic language. The reactions are first class and persistent, so can be inserted and removed. These reactions were fired whenever a certain tuple operation in performed, such as tuple insertion, tuple removal or the use of a particular primitive. The operations which fire the reactions are all high level, not as low as agents failing, joining and so on. MARS extends the concept further incorporating mobility of agents. Agents can only access the tuple spacs which is physically present at the same location as the agent and therefore the agents migrate between one tuple space and the next in order to access them. Location is therefore explicit in MARS. The tuple spaces in MARS are reactive as well, and again the reactions are attached to tuple space access events as in TuCSoN. The reactions only refer to one tuple space, and in MARS are Java based.

There are many similarities but also many differences between the work described here and MARS and TuCSoN. It is guaranteed that an agent will is only ever executed once which is when an agent is thought to have died, whereas in MARS a reaction is persistent. MARS allows only administrator agents to add and remove (any) reactions, where as any agent can have a will but only they can manipulate their own will. The event that triggers a reaction is tuple space accessing whereas no tuple space access affects a will. A reaction in MARS could not be configured to fire when an agent dies and a reaction could not remove itself which is what would be required for the systems to provide an agent will. Different agents will probably not use the same agent will. Even, if "agent death" was added as an event it is unclear that each agent could configure its own agent will, because all reactions that reacted to "agent deaths" would fire. Also, an agent will can refer to multiple tuple spaces not just a single tuple space. There is no explicit notion of location with the will and so the programmer has no notion of where the will is being stored or managed. In the current Java implementation a will is associated with a tuple space, however, it can access any tuple space, and in future a new mechanism for managing agent wills may be added which is completely independent of the tuple spaces. Also, wills are presented as a general-purpose solution to the problem in DSM systems as a whole; Linda is used to demonstrate the concept. Indeed, it should be feasible to implement this on top of (as a service) many current Linda implementations (although this has not been attempted) without altering the underlying implementation at all.

5. Incorporating agent wills in Linda

5.1. Java API

In order to demonstrate the concept of agent wills we have implemented the system using our Java embedding of Linda. In order to demonstrate the concept of agent wills the Java language is a natural choice as it supports object serialisation and dynamic loading of class files which can be easily extended to support loading of the object code and current state across a network. The important point here is the use of a Virtual Machine, which allows heterogeneous machines to exchange executable code, and the ability to dynamically load code.

One of the aims of the system was to make the mechanisms providing the fault tolerance as transparent as possible. The application programmer should not need to worry about how the fault tolerance is provided. Indeed, it should be noted that in Linda the use of transactions alters the meaning of some of the primitives performed within the transaction. Mobile objects may also provide an alternative to the use of transactions in Linda based systems [14].

In order to show the API and how it is incorporated into the Java embedding of Linda consider the example code shown in Figures 2 and 3. They show an application that creates and uses an agent will and the object that acts as the agent will respectively. It should be noted there is no explicit mention of location anywhere in the two fragments of code.

In Figure 2 the class *TupleSpace* provides the interface to a single tuple space managed by the run-time, providing the methods `out,in`, and `rd` as would be expected, and also two extra methods `createWill` and `cancelWill`. A new object has to be created for each tuple space that is to be accessed, and the syntax of the constructor for the *TupleSpace* class has been simplified slightly for clarity. In the current implementation an agent can add a will to any tuple space, therefore it is potentially possible for a single agent to have multiple wills. This does not seem to be a problem and in many ways provides a more natural way of incorporating the concept into a Linda system. There is no reason why there could not be a single will attached to no particular tuple space.

A will is attached to a tuple space by calling the `createWill` method of the object that is acting as the gateway for accessing the tuple space. Once an object has been made a will any alterations to its internal state will not be reflected in the will that the system stores. If the internal state is updated then the object will have to be resubmitted as the will for this to be reflected in the will the system is storing. The `createWill` method requires an object that implements the AgentWill interface. The `AgentWill` interface is shown in Figure 1 and when the server wishes to execute a will it calls the method *will*. If there is already a will in place, currently, the will is cancelled and the new will is made the will. It may make sense though to raise an exception at this point and allow an agent to decide what they wish to do.

In Figure 2 line 9, the `cancelWill` method is called to remove the will. The `cancelWill` method means that an agent will can be put in place for short periods of time, or for the duration of a program. The lines 5-8 in Figure 2 insert a tuple into the tuple space with a name in it, then

```
public class TestWill {
  TupleSpace gts = new TupleSpace(''localhost",8989);

  public TestWill() {
    MyWill theWill = new MyWill(gts,"Antony");
    gts.createWill(TheWill);
    gts.out(new Tuple("Antony"));
      // do something
    t = gts.rd(new Template("Antony"));
    gts.cancelWill();
  }
```

Figure 2. Example - TestWill Class.

does something and before terminating removes the tuple containing the name. If run-time decides that the agent has died somewhere in between inserting the tuple and removing the name tuple then the will is executed. It should be noted that when the `createWill` method completes the will is *guaranteed* to be in place and usable. It should also be noted that although a will is notionally attached to a tuple space the will can access any tuple space that it has access to (the handles for the tuple spaces would have been passed in prior to the object being made a will), and can perform any of the Linda operations it wishes to.

For efficiency reasons we have also added a method called `executeWill` to the *TupleSpace* class. This causes the will to be executed, and blocks the current thread of execution until that has happened. This may seem a natural enough extension, but the implications are large, as a new style of programming becomes viable, which may or may not want to be encouraged (the movement of computation to the server may not want to be encouraged).

Figure 3 shows the will class. When it is instantiated the parameters it requires are passed in which are a tuple space handle and a string. All the `will` method does is to remove a tuple from the tuple space. The tuple it will remove is the name tuple, and thereby, even if the agent becomes disconnected before it can tidy the name state this agent will performs the task for it.

There is a restriction made on the object that is migrated; it cannot perform any I/O operations except through tuple spaces (in other words it can insert tuples that other agents read and then print or whatever but it can not perform I/O operations itself). In the current implementation if the will does perform I/O operations these are performed through the console of the server. We used to place a restriction that all instantiations of classes that are not in the standard JDK must be made *prior* to the object being passed as the parameter to a `createWill` method. This was because obviously the remote server cannot go back to request the class code when the agent is being executed. However, this restriction has been removed. Whenever an object is to be migrated, the class file is analysed and all potential class files are detected and packed with the object.

Another issue is that the agent may not have failed, just that the connection was transient. In this case, if the run-time has been over pessimistic about when an agent has lost connection and the agent attempts to perform more operations the current run-time implementation raises an exception in the agent. This means the agent can deal with it – which usually means they create another will and change back the state (in this example reinsert their name tuple). In the example of the presence notification, the other users will see the user disappear and then reappear. In the same example, another approach is to have the will remove the name tuple and insert another name tuple, but indicating in the tuple that the user has disappeared. The application then displays this information to the user, so a user knows when someone has purposely left the system, and when a fault has caused the user to leave the system. These are issues that the application programmer can decide upon.

5.2. Implementation

The current implementation uses a centralised server to provide support for the tuple spaces. A centralised server means all the tuple spaces are managed within a single process, but the agents can reside anywhere. Although many of the current WAN targeted tuple space based coordination languages use centralised servers some use distributed kernels, for example WCL [17]. In this section we provide an overview of how we implemented the current implementation. At the end of section we discuss how we intend to extend this for a decentralised kernel.

The main server is written in Java. When a will is passed to the server, the server creates an instance of the object passed as the will, which must provide an interface *AgentWill*. When the agent that sent it fails the will method of this object is called. When the object acting as the will is passed to the server, the server uses a new subclass of *ClassLoader* that attempts to find the class files locally (ei-

```
class MyWill implements AgentWill, Serializable {
  TupleSpace ts; String name;

  public MyWill(TupleSpace ts, String name) {
    this.ts = ts; this.name = name; }

  public void will() {
    ts.in(new Template(name));}
}
```

Figure 3. Example - The MyWill Class.

ther on disk or in a cache) and then remotely from the agent who provided the will. This is relatively simple and is the same method that is used in many Java based mobile object systems. The *ClassLoader* has been extended to determine which class files it may require in the future for a given (set of) class files. And retrieves these from the agent if required.

The wills are executed within a thread, with one thread being created for each will. This means that the wills can block whilst accessing a tuple space, without causing the kernel to stop, or the processing of other wills to stop. Indeed, in the current implementation a will could block forever.

As a slight aside, from an optimisation point of view, the *TupleSpace* objects detect whether it is running at the server or whether it is running remotely[2]. If it is running remotely then it opens up the necessary sockets to the server and if it is running under the same JVM as the server then it detects this, and is able to access the data structures used to store the tuples directly. This is important, because the migration and local execution of wills could increase the computational load on the server. This in turn would lead to worse performance of the server, and therefore of the system. However, by accessing the data structure directly many of the overheads of accessing a tuple space are removed [16]. This means that although running the will on the same JVM as the server increases the computational load, the server load is reduced so it appears roughly equivalent to performing the tuple space accesses remotely.

Figure 4 demonstrates the architecture of the Linda system used. The agent and the server process either run on the same or on different machines to the agent processes (normally a different machine). The server process maintains and manages all the tuple spaces, a cache of class files that the agent wills can use; and the agent wills. Although, the current implementation creates an active object as soon as the will arrives, another approach would be to only create the object when it was actually required. This means a will that is added and then removed incurs less of an overhead.

[2]Exploiting *transient* data types in Java.

5.3. Server fault tolerance

We have described how we provide fault tolerance for the application, but can this be implemented in a fault tolerance manner in the run-time system? Although not implemented in the current implementation, providing fault tolerance for the run-time system should be possible in a cheap and efficient manner. There is no need to check point the running code on the server, and this is good because this would require either modifications to the JVM being used or transformations of the class files. The first option is not acceptable and the second option would be time consuming if performed on the fly.

Instead, the server will checkpoint the tuple spaces as done in many Linda implementations [1] and the ClassLoader should create a local copy (on a persistent store) of all class files retrieved over the network and original state of the will should also be stored (on a persistent store). When the will is executed all tuples consumed and produced by the will should be stored and checkpointed as the tuple spaces are. If a total failure of the server should occur, the tuple spaces can be recreated; instances of all the wills can also be re-instantiated in their initial state. And the will method of the object called. When the will attempts to retrieve a tuple the stored tuples are re-returned and the produced tuples are discarded if they have already been produced. Once all the stored tuples have been used then normal operation can continue. This *must* be performed before any other operations on the tuple space are allowed in order to ensure that this is semantically correct. This also assumes that the will, given the same tuples in the same order, produces the same tuples in the same order.

We have discussed a centralised run-time system in this section. The implementation of this in a distributed kernel such as the one described in Rowstron [17] is quite feasible. There is an underlying assumption that if a particular server fails, then the sever will restart itself. We describe here the approach we are taking. Figure 5 shows the architecture. Each server is responsible for one or more entire tuple spaces.

In order to explain what happens lets us consider the

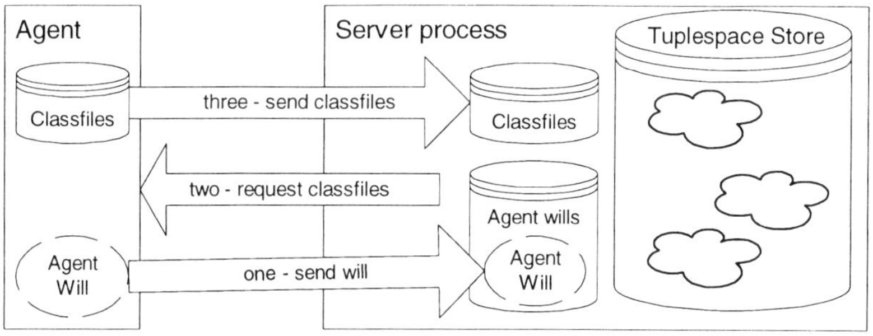

Figure 4. Architecture of the centralised system.

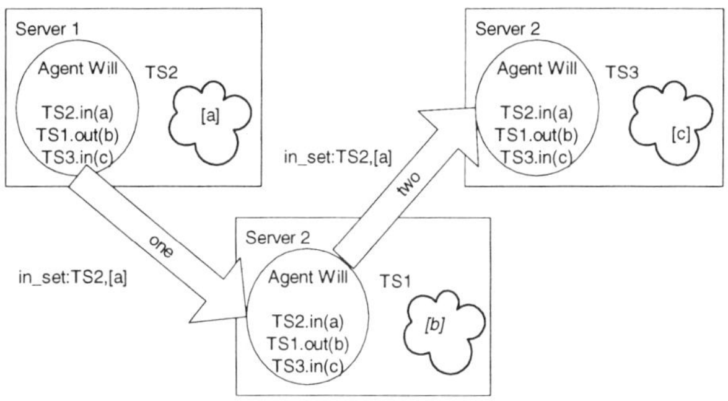

Figure 5. Architecture of the distributed system.

example in the figure. The agent will is attached to tuple space *TS2* initially. The agent will performs three operations: *TS2.in(a); TS1.out(b); TS3.in(c);*. The basic concept is that each time an agent will accesses a tuple space that does not reside on the local server, the agent will is moved to the correct server. So, in the example, the first statement of the agent will is executed, an *in*. The code is then moved to the location of *TS1*. The transfer of the state and classfiles is achieved in a reliable manner, using logs on a persistent store. However, the agent was in the middle of a method when the mobility became necessary. In order to migrate an executing code one would need to either augment the classfile or alter the JVM. However, because agent wills should be small we take an alternative approach. We create an *in_set* for the agent will and insert in the *in_set* a record of all the tuples consumed (and the order they were consumed) and a counter of the number of tuples produced by the will. When the agent will is moved, it is restarted, and the tuples in the *in_set* are returned as the results of the `in` and `rd` primitives, until the *in_set* is empty. The output tuples are discarded until the number of tuples produced matches the passed counter, which should incidently be when an operation that is local to the current server is performed. Any tuples consumed by the agent will are added to the *in_set* (in this case there are no tuples to be added as a tuple is inserted into the tuple space). When the next operation is performed, the agent will has to be migrated again, and this again transfers the state, code and the *in_set*. Again the agent will is executed, and the *in_set* is used to feed the agent will until all the entries in the *in_set* have been used once.

This approach provides a reliable, and fault tolerance approach to the problem, with low communication overhead. The same approach can be used to implement mobile coordination as described in Rowstron [15].

6. Future work

We are going implement the system using a distributed run-time system for Linda, using the method described in the last section. We also are currently considering two other issues: how much computation we allow a will to perform and how long, once it has been invoked, it should be allowed to run. We do not want agents to make their wills too computationally expensive. A will should, in general, perform a small number of accesses to the shared data structure then terminate. Wills that calculate pi to millions of decimal places are unacceptable, as they will degrade the performance of the servers managing the tuple spaces. Also, they can perform operations that block for example, awaiting a tuple. How long should a Will be allowed to exist? It is probable that the tuple garbage collection techniques described in Menezes et al. [9] can be extended to support garbage collection wills associated with tuple spaces as well.

7. Conclusions

We have identified and described a type of operation (person notification) that is common in CSCW applications that cannot easily be supported when using a DSM as the communication medium between agents. This is because the applications are written in a peer-to-peer style with the agents interacting directly with shared data structures.

We have proposed the use of mobile objects that we call agent wills that provide the ability for an agent to "tidy" the shared data structures, should the agent become disconnected from the underlying infrastructure. The will object has the ability to outlive the agent which created it.

We have shown that such as system has been implemented on top of a Linda implementation, and that it works. Also, it has been shown that this has been implemented in a fashion that makes then underlying method used to provide this transparent to the programmer. By making it transparent it does not increase the complexity of the program for the programmer.

We finally conclude that the use of agent wills in distributed shared memory systems is novel and provides a higher level of fault tolerance, and supports the use of a peer-to-peer style of distributed program.

Acknowledgements

I would like to thank all those who have discussed the ideas of agent wills, especially Stuart Wray. I would also like to thank my colleagues at Microsoft Research for their comments on the idea of mobile coordination and specific comments on this paper, including Marc Shapiro and Cedric Fournet.

References

[1] B. Anderson and D. Shasha. Persistent Linda: Linda + Transactions + Query Processing. In *Research Directions in High-Level Parallel Programming Languages*, LNCS 574, 1991.

[2] G. Cabri, L. Leonardi, and F. Zambonelli. MARS: A programmable coordination architecture for mobile agents. *To appear IEEE Internet Computing*, 0(0):0–0, 2000.

[3] N. Carriero and D. Gelernter. Linda in context. *Communications of the ACM*, 32(4):444–458, 1989.

[4] P. Ciancarini and D. Rossi. Coordinating Java agents over the WWW. *World Wide Web Journal*, 1(2):87–99, 1998.

[5] P. Ciancarini, R. Tolksdorf, F. Vitali, D. Rossi, and A. Knoche. Coordinating multiagent applications on the WWW: A reference architecture. *IEEE Transactions on Software Engineering*, 24(5):362–366, 1998.

[6] M. Day. Presence and instant messaging via HTTP/1.0: A coorindation perspective. In P. Ciancarini and A. Wolf, editors, *Coordination Languages and Models: Coordination99*, volume 1594 of *Lecture Notes in Computer Science*, pages 417–418. Springer-Verlag, 1999.

[7] P. Ferreira, M. Shapiro, X. Blondel, O. Fambon, J. Garcia, S. Kloosterman, N. Richer, M. Roberts, F. Sandakly, G. Coulouris, J. Dollimore, P. Guedes, D. Hagimont, and S. Krakowiak. Perdis: Design, implementation, and use of a PERsistent DIstributed Store. Technical report, QMW TR 752, CSTB ILC/98-1392, INRIA RR 3525, INESC RT/5/98, 1998.

[8] D. Gelernter. Generative communication in linda. *ACM Transactions on Programming Languages and Systems*, 7(1):80–112, 1985.

[9] R. Menezes and A. Wood. Garbage Collection in Open Distributed Tuple Space Systems. In *Proceedings of 15th Brazilian Computer Networks Symposi um - SBRC'97*, 1997.

[10] R. D. Nicola, G. Ferrari, and R. Pugliese. KLAIM: A kernel language for agents interaction and mobility. *IEEE Transactions on Software Engineering*, 24(5):315–330, 1998.

[11] A. Omicini and F. Zambonelli. Coordination for internet application development. *Autonomous Agents and Multiagent Systems*, 2(3):0–0, 1999. Special Issue on Coordination Mechanisms and Patterns for Web Agents.

[12] G. Picco, A. Murphy, and G.-C. Roman. Lime: Linda meets mobility. Technical Report Technical report WUCS-98-21, Washington University, Department of Computer Science, St. Louis, Missouri, 1998.

[13] A. Rowstron. WCL: A web co-ordination language. *World Wide Web Journal*, 1(3):167–179, 1998.

[14] A. Rowstron. Mobile co-ordination: Providing fault-tolerance in tuple space based co-ordination languages. In P. Ciancarini and A. Wolf, editors, *Coordination Languages and Models: Coordination99*, volume 1594 of *Lecture Notes in Computer Science*, pages 196–210. Springer-Verlag, 1999.

[15] A. Rowstron. Mobile co-ordination: Providing fault tolerance in tuple space based co-ordination languages. In *To appear Coordination'99*. Springer Verlag, 1999.

[16] A. Rowstron and A. Wood. BONITA: A set of tuple space primitives for distributed coordination. In *HICSS-30*, volume 1, pages 379–388. IEEE CS Press, 1997.

[17] A. Rowstron and S. Wray. A run-time system for the web co-ordination language. In *IEEE Workshop on Internet Programming Languages*, 1998. Chicago, USA.

[18] Sun Microsystems. Javaspace specification, revision 0.4. Final Specification., 1997.

[19] P. Wyckoff, S. McLaughry, T. Lehman, and D. Ford. TSpaces. *IBM Systems Journal*, 37(3):454–474, 1998.

The TIRAN Approach to Reusing Software Implemented Fault Tolerance

O. Botti
ENEL S.p.A., R&D, Via Volta 1, I-20093 Cologno Monzese (Milano), Italy
Tel: +39-02-7224-5553, Fax: +39-02-7224-5465, e-mail: botti@pea.enel.it

V. De Florio, G. Deconinck, R. Lauwereins
K.U.Leuven, Dept. Elektrotechniek (ESAT), Kard. Mercierlaan 94, B-3001 Heverlee, Belgium

F. Cassinari
TXT Ingegneria Informatica, Via Socrate 41, I-20128 Milano, Italy

S. Donatelli, A. Bobbio
Università di Torino, Dip. di Informatica, C.so Svizzera 185, I-10149 Torino, Italy

A. Klein, H. Kufner, E. Thurner
Siemens AG, Dept. ZT SE 2, Otto-Hahn-Ring 6, D-81730 München, Germany

E. Verhulst
Eonic Systems, Nieuwlandlaan 9, B-3200 Aarschot, Belgium

Abstract

Available solutions for fault tolerance in embedded automation are often based on strong customisation, have impacts on the whole life-cycle, and require highly specialised design teams, thus making dependable embedded systems costly and difficult to develop and maintain. The TIRAN project[1] *develops a framework which provides fault tolerance capabilities to automation systems, with the goal of allowing portable, reusable and cost-effective solutions. Application developers are allowed to select, configure and integrate in their own environment a variety of software-based functions for error detection, confinement and recovery provided by the framework.*

1 Industrial Motivations and Answers to the Market Needs

Market investigations with users and producers of automation systems have recognised the benefits offered by dependable systems, not only in the classical area of safety-critical tasks, but also in mission-critical ones, due to the high economic impact of failures. Moreover, dependable embedded systems were judged costly and difficult to develop and maintain, as they generally need strong customisation, impacting on the whole life-cycle, and requiring highly specialised design teams.

New proposals for fault tolerance (FT) should be based on pre-built and easily reusable solutions, customisable for different applications and portable on commercial and proprietary real-time operating systems (RTOS). The TIRAN project addresses these urgent needs raised from the market of real-time embedded automation systems.

Recent estimations (Embedded Software Association) show that the embedded software tools market is growing at about 30%/year and totals about 800 M US$ in 1998. Other investigations allows to estimate that at least 15% of all real-time applications are candidates for inclusion of fault tolerance.

TIRAN is a 24-month ESPRIT project, that has now reached the stage of full definition of the proposed solution, that will be developed on different platforms to allow an estimation of the reusability, and will be used on three different pilot applications to study its efficacy in making the applications more dependable. This paper describes the TIRAN solution and compares it with other approaches from the literature and/or from previous ESPRIT projects.

The TIRAN solution is built around a software framework which provides fault tolerance capabilities to automation systems. Application developers are allowed to select,

[1]ESPRIT Project 28620 TIRAN — "Tailorable fault tolerance frameworks for embedded applications".

1066-6192/99 $10.00

configure and integrate in their own environment a variety of software-based FT functions for fault masking, error detection, isolation and recovery, available in the framework. The framework includes techniques, tools and documentation to support the developers when combining the selected functions into their own fault tolerance strategies to obtain the required level of dependability.

The framework is basically a library of software elements which are parametric and support an easy configuration process. It is designed with the portability goal in mind: standard API are defined towards the application environment and towards the platform (e.g. RT-POSIX), most of the functions are intended to be platform and application independent and the cost to adapt the remaining ones is minimised. The adoption of FT functions from this framework significantly reduces the development costs of a new dependable system.

The Consortium will develop one single generic framework, providing its porting on different commercial RTOS (VxWorks, Windows CE) and micro kernels (Virtuoso, TEX), to be exploited in the pilot applications provided by the Consortium end-users and running on their corresponding target platforms.

The use of formal techniques to support requirement specification and predictive evaluation, together with the intensive testing on pilot applications, aims at guaranteeing the correctness of the framework, and to quantify the fulfilment of real-time, dependability and cost requirements, providing also valuable guidelines to the configuration process for the different users.

The paper introduces the target industrial environment (Sect. 2) and the user requirements driving the project activities (Sect. 3). The TIRAN approach is sketched in Sect. 4, and its positioning with respect to emerging FT trends is given in Sect. 5. Finally, the current status of the project is outlined in Sect. 6.

2 The Industrial Environment: Pilot Applications, Exploitation and Market Access

The TIRAN Consortium includes large European suppliers and end-users of mission critical systems in their application fields (energy and transport automation) that have an active role in the technology development and in the international standardisation process on the subject.

The Consortium involves the R&D Departments of ENEL (the main Italian electricity supplier, the 3rd largest world-wide) and of SIEMENS (the leading German company in the field of electrical engineering and electronics, one of the largest worldwide), EONIC Systems (B) (supplier of very high performance and application specific small RTOS for DSP processors and embedded ASIC cores), TXT Informatica (I) (provider of systems and services in many fields of real-time automation), the University of Leuven (B) and the University of Turin (I), particularly active on the R&D frontiers of fault tolerance and performance evaluation.

The project results, driven by industrial users' requirements and market demand, will be integrated with an existing off-the-shelf tool supplied by its producer (Virtuoso of Eonic Systems), will be ported onto commercial and proprietary RTOS (Windows CE, VxWorks, TEX), that will represent the basis for services offered by a system integrator (TXT), and are to be tested and adopted by two large end-user companies (ENEL, SIEMENS) within their application fields.

Pilot applications from Energy Distribution (ENEL, primary substation automation system) and Industrial Automation (SIEMENS, airfield light control system), bring a wide variety of requirements to the framework development and allow a deep validation of project results. Broad exploitation of results and market access are guaranteed in different sectors by the involved users, the technology providers and by third party association with market leaders. In addition, system providers (EONIC, TXT) bring in the project their typical customers' requirements from the fields of Space, Avionics, Automotive, Biomedical.

3 User Requirements

The first activity of the project has been the collection, classification of fault tolerance requirements of the partners, and their harmonization in terms of the features expected from the framework, their portability on different platforms, their performance and their configurability (see Table 1). Requirements have been split into functional and non-functional ones, where functional is here intended as "what is the functionality of the framework".

3.1 Functional Requirements

Requirements collected in this area have identified the FT features the TIRAN framework shall support.

The framework shall provide support for error detection. The types of errors taken in consideration include: communication errors (like corrupted messages, late or non-delivered messages, incorrect delivery order), processing errors, memory fault.

A detected error shall be contained to avoid affecting other parts of the system; isolation mechanisms that shall be supported by the framework include: output commitment, termination of faulty communication channels or processes or nodes, communication path reconfiguration, memory protection.

In addition, support for *fault masking* shall be provided by the framework: replication, voting and stable memory,

Functional	Error processing / Fault treatment	Error detection
		Fault containment / error isolation
		Fault masking
		Error recovery
	Monitoring	Target monitoring
		Fault injection
Non-Functional	Portability	Platform and RTOS independence
	Flexibility	Configurability and scalability
	Performance	Hard real-time
		Soft real-time

Table 1. Classification of user requirements.

applying both spatial and temporal redundancy.

An important feature to obtain a FT system is the possibility to restore/replace faulty components. The use of a "recovery language" will allow the user to define its own *recovery strategy*: following this strategy, the running system can check which kind of error has occurred in which part of the system, and start the most appropriate recovery actions, like terminate or restart a specific process or node, activate spare processes on different nodes, warn other processes about what happens, reintegrate a recovered node.

Since the typical use of such FT features is on embedded systems, it is important to provide mechanisms for *system monitoring*. Requirements for system monitoring include a communication mechanism with a host computer and the possibility to check the status of the embedded system, perform specific actions and simulate or inject faults for testing purposes.

3.2 Non-functional Requirements

The proposed FT framework is intended as a software solution, independent from hardware and operating system, scalable on a wide range of different target topologies, easily configurable, and open for interoperability with other commercial or user defined tools. From these goals, a set of additional requirements comes out.

Concerning *portability* of solutions: to allow a wide exploitability, the FT framework must be easy portable on different platforms, eliminating or reducing as much as possible the adaptation work. To obtain such a platform independence, different approaches have been adopted: adherence to appropriate standards (e.g. POSIX and its real-time extension); encapsulation of the operating system interface in a proper "adaptation layer" hiding the operating system peculiarities and providing to the upper level a stable and homogeneous interface. To concretely drive the implementation of the framework in a portable way, different pilot platforms have been selected on which a final evaluation and assessment will be performed. The selected platforms cover a wide range of embedded system including MOSAIC20 DSP platform with Virtuoso RTOS, Siemens SMP16 with Windows CE, PowerPC and embedded PC with VxWorks, Digital Alpha with TEX RTOS.

For what concerns *flexibility* requirements, the framework shall be easy adaptable to different user needs in terms of

- usage of the framework components in a stand-alone way or combined together;
- allocation of each component on different nodes;
- scalability from a single node to distributed/heterogeneous/differently connected nodes;
- parameterisation of the provided mechanisms in terms of data structures, size and number of replica.

The adoption of the proposed FT solution should not affect the *responsiveness* of the system, at least in absence of faults, i.e. the percentage of FT overhead must be negligible with respect to the application size and response time. Particular attention should be paid for those components that are positioned closed to the fault occurrence, i.e. masking, detection and isolation mechanisms, while a greater amount of overhead can be accepted for those mechanisms related to recovery actions, depending on the application specific real-time requirements.

4 The Framework Approach

TIRAN bases its fault tolerance strategy on the concept of "framework", which translates into the conjoint use of a layered system of fault tolerance mechanisms arranged into a library and of a sort of configuration tool by means of which the user expresses a number of recovery strategies. This is combined with a formal assessment of the performance of the framework approach centred around modelling and measurements associated with fault injection. These three elements are hereby described.

4.1 The FT Library

This part describes the generic fault tolerance entities for the TIRAN framework, i.e. in the library. This is to be accompanied by system-specific, kernel-specific and application-specific mechanisms. The system is made of three "layers": a *basic layer*, with entities related to error detection, fault containment, recovery, and fault masking mechanisms, a *control layer*, constituting a sort of "backbone" component for a coherent coordination of the entities in the basic layer, and a *monitoring and fault injection layer*, introduced for testing purposes and substantially given by a hypermedia distributed application.

The framework will be accompanied with a handbook providing:

- a characterisation of the library components in terms of FT coverage and performance overhead,
- strategies to be applied in assembling the mechanisms to meet dependability requirements,
- reports produced by validation and assessment carried out on the framework and its applications.

4.1.1 Basic Layer.

This part of the library will host basic mechanisms for error detection, fault containment, error recovery, and fault masking. The following list enumerates the mechanisms that will be considered for inclusion in the TIRAN framework, either implementing them or providing a suitable interface, public or for private use of the framework, to specific services supplied at driver, kernel, or hardware level (these latter are marked as "$\mathcal{I}$"):

- Error detection mechanisms
  - communication errors and mechanisms
    - corrupted messages: CRC, parity checking, checksums, retransmission, loopback testing ($\mathcal{I}$)
    - late or non-delivered messages: time-out ($\mathcal{I}$)
    - messages in disorder: checking packet numbers ($\mathcal{I}$)
  - processing errors and mechanisms
    - late or dead processes: watchdogs
    - corrupted processes: assertions, plausibility checks, range checks, history checks, authority checks ($\mathcal{I}$)
    - runtime errors (numerical exceptions): exception processing ($\mathcal{I}$)
    - memory violations, stack overflows: exception processing ($\mathcal{I}$)
  - memory faults:
    - transient errors (bit errors): error detecting codes, parity bits ($\mathcal{I}$)
  - mechanisms for diagnosis of latent errors
    - periodic tests: testing status of communication partners, memory scrubbing, monitoring of error history
  - Isolation mechanisms
    - output commitment: distributed synchronisation, voting, output delay
    - termination of a faulty process ($\mathcal{I}$)
    - disconnection of a faulty node ($\mathcal{I}$)
  - Recovery mechanisms
    - re-initialisation or establishment of new communication channels ($\mathcal{I}$)
    - re-initialisation or establishment of new process ($\mathcal{I}$)
    - re-initialisation of a node (reloading of kernel and/or application) ($\mathcal{I}$)
    - integration of a recovered node in the system ($\mathcal{I}$)
    - restoring the state in application: checkpoint and rollback, distributed atomic actions
  - Fault masking
    - data replication: distributed memory
    - voting
    - stable memory (conjoint use of temporal and spatial redundancy)
    - error correcting codes
  - Others
    - distributed synchronisation

These basic mechanisms rely on support from the kernel and the hardware, e.g., to allow memory protection or to have fault-tolerant communications.

4.1.2 The TIRAN Control Layer.

This layer is substantially given by a distributed tool which will play the role of backbone for the mechanisms in the basic layer, collecting all relevant information concerning the current structure and status of the user application and of the basic TIRAN tools. This application will also coordinate recovery and interpret user-defined recovery strategies. A prototypal implementation of this component, called DIR net (standing for "Detection, Isolation, Recovery net") has been developed within the ESPRIT project EFTOS[2] and

[2]ESPRIT Project 21012 EFTOS — "Embedded fault tolerant supercomputing".

discussed in [4]. This layer could also include a special component which, by means of, e.g., the count-and-threshold scheme, could be used to diagnose the nature of the witnessed faults, namely whether a given fault is temporary or permanent.

4.1.3 Monitoring and Fault Injection.

A special tool will serve as a monitor and software fault injector for debugging and testing purposes on embedded targets. The monitor will describe the structure of the system (user application plus TIRAN framework components) and will report in a hypertextual structure all the events taking place at the basic layer and at the control layer. This component will be also responsible for managing software fault injection services. These will include, e.g., task terminations, node reboots, illegal instructions generation (divide by zero, illegal memory access, etc.), actions resulting in value failures and violations of real-time constraints.

4.2 Configuration

While the overhead of including detection mechanisms in an application can be minimal, we experienced that a non-trivial, end-to-end strategy for recovering from faults, based on the pure library approach, does require large modifications to that application. For instance, the availability of a perfect-coverage trap handler, capable of intercepting any processor or communication exception, gives the developer but a powerful fault tolerance atom that must be nevertheless wisely integrated into a coherent, system-wide recovery strategy in order to actually enhance the resilience of the user application. This strategy usually results in the intrusion of a large percentage of non-functional code. This problem can be weakened, if not solved, by physically separating the specification of functional code, from that of the code for recovering from an erroneous condition. This is proposed via the use of a suitable "recovery language", by means of which the user can express strategies for recovery and reconfiguration. Special support towards design diversification (e.g., by means of recovery blocks) is under consideration. Further description of this approach and of its impact on transparency is given in Section 5.1.

4.3 Framework Validation and Evaluation

To prove the efficacy of the proposed framework it is important to assess the performance of the generic library and of its portings running on the different supported platforms. To reach these goals two techniques will be used in TIRAN: a probabilistic approach centred around modelling and measurements associated with fault injection.

A very nice study of available techniques for the validation and evaluation of dependability attributes has been done as part of the European project SQUALE (Security, Safety and Quality Evaluation for Dependable Systems) [2].

A probabilistic analysis has the advantages of allowing to treat the (intrinsic) probabilistic nature of faults, and of permitting the abstraction, in terms of probability, of a reality too complex to be treated and described in full details, but has the disadvantages of providing only probabilistic results (e.g. probability that a certain output will be produced before a given delay). Modelling allows to perform a quantitative analysis before the final system is actually built, and can therefore be used also as a development aid, to evaluate alternative solutions and to perform sensitivity analysis on different ranges of parameters. The models of the delivered version of the framework will be used to compute quantitative indices, providing the framework handbook with this characterisation.

Probabilistic modelling will be carried on using stochastic Petri nets [1]. Separate models for the library functions, the faults and the hardware characteristics will be developed and freely mixed to study different systems [6]. Simulations will be used when the type of stochastic delays considered, or the size of the resulting model does not allow an analytical solution.

Measurements of the system using software and physical fault injection on the pilot target environments will complement predictions providing a deep characterisation of the framework behaviour.

Petri net models of the library functions can also be used for validation, to prove 'classical' properties like absence of deadlocks and livelocks, as well as for proving properties expressed in temporal logic language [13].

5 Comparison with Other Works

This section positions TIRAN with respect to other emerging fault tolerance approaches and research projects. In order to compare different approaches we selected a number of attributes, i.e., positive aspects and qualities of each approach, and assessed each approach with respect to these attributes. Doing this we can position each approach and research project into a unique spectrum (see Fig. 1).

5.1 Relevant Attributes for Positioning

Five attributes have been selected, namely:

- Efficiency of the approach, measured by response times, what concerns error detection, isolation, and recovery,
- Transparency, or the separation of functional from dependability concerns, measured by lines of code (LOC) to be added or modified into an existing application in order to adopt the approach,

- Portability, measured by effort or LOC to be added or modified in order to allow the approach on a new platform,
- Cost of adoption for the target application developer, both at development and at maintenance times,
- Flexibility, i.e. the effectiveness of the approach with respect to different fault classes, different fault tolerance mechanisms, and to different end-user systems.

Four orthogonal approaches have been selected and will be assessed via the above attributes:

- System approach, i.e., the embedding of fault tolerance mechanisms into the hardware and/or the operating system.
- Library approach, or the embedding of fault tolerance tools into an application-level collection of functions.
- Conjoint use of metaobject protocols and of reflection, or modifying the semantics of an object-oriented language for a transparent adoption of fault tolerance methods.
- The Recovery Language Approach, viz., the conjoint use of a middleware backbone and a sort of secondary application layer for embedding and orchestrating recovery and configuration strategies and for managing design diversity.

Five ranking levels have been defined to measure the different approaches, ranging from low to high: low, low-to-medium, medium, medium-to-high, high.

The attributes and approaches constitute, in a sense, a *base* for discussing in more formal terms nowadays fault tolerance trends. TIRAN is finally assessed on the view of this base.

System Approach. Embedding fault tolerance in the hardware and/or in the operating system is typically characterised by:

- High efficiency, which makes it suitable if not mandatory for fulfilling hard real-time requirements,
- High transparency, as it does not involve the application level altogether,
- Good portability of the functional part of the user-application, bad portability of the features offered by the approach (ranking: medium),
- No development or maintenance costs (for the customer); typically higher costs for acquiring the target system with respect to general-purpose systems (ranking: low),
- Bad flexibility (a prefixed number and quality of dependability services are compulsorily offered to all customers; furthermore this approach does not include any fault tolerance support within the target application, so as argued in [12], it cannot reach full end-to-end fault tolerance). Moreover, this approach does not support means for tolerating design faults (ranking: low).

Project GUARDS [11] also makes use of this approach.

Library Approach. This approach consists in embedding a number of fault tolerance mechanisms and tools in the form of a library. The approach is characterised by:

- Medium efficiency (which makes it unsuitable for matching hard real-time requirements in its pure form),
- Medium transparency (the application programmer does not have to "re-invent each time the fault-tolerant wheel," though he/she is responsible for embedding the function calls of the library into the application, from detection-level tools through to complete recovery),
- High portability (in principle),
- Low-to-medium development and maintenance costs,
- Medium flexibility (as it lacks any system support).

Examples of this approach can be found in Project Isis [3]. Tools like, e.g., HATS [8], are purely based on the library approach.

Metaobject Protocols and Reflection. An elegant approach is given by metaobject protocols (MOP's) [9]. The idea is to open the implementation of an object-oriented language so that the developer can adopt and program different, custom semantics, adjusting the language to the needs of the user and to the requirements of the environment. The transparent addition and management of temporal and spatial redundancy is a typical example of this approach. The key concept behind MOP's is computational reflection, or the causal connection between a system and a meta-level description representing structural and computational aspects of that system. This causality translates into the possibility to adjust dynamically the structure and the operation of a system, e.g., to perform reconfiguration and error recovery. The basic object-oriented feature of inheritance can be used to enhance the reusability of the fault tolerance mechanisms developed with this approach. It is characterised by:

- Medium efficiency (someone questioned MOP's because of the inherent overhead of managing a different semantics; this overhead has been found to be negligible at least in some cases, see e.g., [10, 9]),
- High transparency (full separation of functional concerns from dependability concerns),
- Medium-to-high portability (requires custom languages, though often with strong resemblance with existing ones, like C++ or Lisp)
- Medium development and maintenance costs,
- Perhaps medium flexibility—no experimental or analytical evidence exists which allowed to evaluate the practicality and the generality of this approach. In other words, it is still an open question whether MOP's and reflection represent a practical solution towards the integration of *any* of the existing fault tolerance mechanisms into a given user application. Reflection and MOP's work at language level, giving means to modify the semantics of basic object-oriented language constructs like object creation and deletion, calling and termination of class methods, and the like. This means looking at the problem from a microscopic point of view. Some of the hitherto developed fault tolerance techniques fit perfectly with this approach—for instance, object redundancy can be easily managed with this approach. Some other techniques, specifically those who might be described as "the most coarse grained ones," like e.g., distributed recovery blocks, or those typical of digital systems (e.g. standby sparing), appear to be less suited for being efficiently implemented via MOP's and reflection. An architecture including this approach is Friends [7].

The Recovery Language Approach. This is the approach developed in the EFTOS framework [5]: a layered software system including a set of detection tools (Dtools), a control backbone coordinating detection, isolation and recovery (the DIR net), and a virtual machine executing recovery strategies, written by the user in a custom scripting language called Ariel. This language constitutes a sort of secondary application layer, devoted to the execution of system-wide recovery strategies, which comes into action whenever an error is detected by one of the basic fault tolerance elements of the EFTOS framework or of the underlying runtime systems. Only a minor number of changes need to be made to the original user application, as many of these fault tolerance methods can be transparently adopted—the bulk of the strategy to cope with errors is expressed in a separately defined, user-provided "recovery script". Such script is written in what we call a "recovery language", i.e., a custom language devoted to the management of the fault

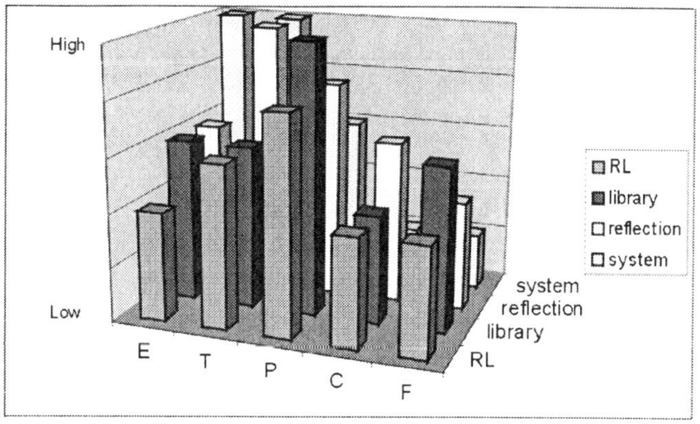

Figure 1. A ranking of the different orthogonal approaches according to the five attributes defined in §5.1.

tolerance strategies of the user and allowing to express scenarios of isolation, reconfiguration, and recovery, to be executed on meta-entities of the application with physical or logical counterparts (processing nodes vs. tasks or user-defined groups of tasks). Such strategy lets the user separately address the (non-functional) aspects of fault tolerance computing from those pertaining the (functional) behaviour that the user application should have in the absence of faults. Furthermore, the user is made able to tackle more easily and effectively any of these two fronts, e.g., to modify the fault tolerance strategy with only a few or no modifications at all in the functional part, or vice-versa, resulting in a better maintainability of the fault-tolerant application. Different developers, with specific knowledge, could act in each of these two application layers; e.g. a team with a FT skill could arrange the secondary application-level suitable for a wide class of applications. This approach is characterised by:

- Medium efficiency (as, in its pure form, it lacks hardware support for detection, isolation, and for managing redundancy),
- Medium-to-high transparency (full transparency is not reached, though there is a partial separation of design concerns, at least what recovery and reconfiguration are concerned),
- High portability (in principle),
- Medium development costs and low maintenance costs (low-to-medium),
- Medium flexibility (in its pure form).

TIRAN Positioning. TIRAN can be considered as a mixture of the library and of the recovery language approach for managing confinement-level, detection-level and isolation-level tasks, plus specific hooks to the underlying run-time system. The approach does not require object orientation and can be effectively used to add fault tolerance features to existing distributed or parallel applications. Thanks to specific system support for detection, isolation, and fault masking, one of the goals of TIRAN is also that of being able to fulfill real-time requirements. Furthermore, specific support towards managing design diversity could be included in a specific extension of the recovery language.

The approach allows the integration within the generic library of custom FT basic mechanisms (for masking, detection isolation, recovery) available at the system or software library level: this can have a positive impact on the flexibility and the efficiency without reducing portability. A goal of TIRAN is therefore to inherit or increase as much as possible the best performing attributes of the system and of the recovery language approach, and to reach a high degree of flexibility such that a large portion of the spectrum of fault classes can be effectively tackled.

6 Current Status and Outlook

Previous experiences within the EFTOS project [5] showed by running industrial prototypes the feasibility of the TIRAN framework approach and pointed out the major required improvements. TIRAN started with a revision of the industrial requirements to allow a wide usability of results and to promote the development of an industrial product. A suitable general architecture was identified to allow the satisfaction of a wide range of performance requirements, from soft to hard real-time. Relevant novelties concern the flexibility and portability issues, the adoption of market standards, the integration of the framework within commercially available solutions supplied by their producers, as well as the adoption of formal validation techniques. A first TIRAN "concept demonstrator" has been built and the development of the FT framework has started. The first prototype has been issued in October 1999. Portings on VxWorks and Windows CE are scheduled for March 2000, while the final release of the complete product and all its portings is planned for October 2000.

Acknowledgments. This project is partly sponsored by the ESPRIT-IV projects 28620 "TIRAN" and by COF/96/11. Geert Deconinck is a Postdoctoral Fellow of the Fund for Scientific Research - Flanders (Belgium) (FWO). Rudy Lauwereins is a Senior Research Associate of FWO.

The first Author wishes to thank Mr Piergiorgio Mirandola and Mr Roberto Meda for the fruitful discussions transferring years of experience on fault tolerance in the Energy field.

References

[1] M. Ajmone Marsan, G. Balbo, G. Conte, S. Donatelli, and G. Franceschinis. *Modelling with Generalized Stochastic Petri Nets*. J. Wiley, New York, N.Y., USA, 1994.

[2] Anonymous. SQUALE — Security, safety and QUALity Evaluation for dependable systems. Technical Report European commission project ACTS/AC097. Available at URL: `http://www.laas.research.ec.org/squale`.

[3] K. J. Birman. Replication and fault tolerance in the Isis system. *ACM Operating Systems Review*, 19(5):79–86, 1985.

[4] G. Deconinck, M. Truyens, V. De Florio, W. Rosseel, R. Lauwereins, and R. Belmans. A framework backbone for software fault tolerance in embedded parallel applications. In *Proc. of the 7th Euromicro Workshop on Parallel and Distributed Processing (PDP'99)*, pages 189–195, Funchal, Portugal, February 1999. IEEE Comp. Soc. Press.

[5] G. Deconinck, T. Varvarigou, O. Botti, V. De Florio, A. Kontizas, M. Truyens, W. Rosseel, R. Lauwereins, F. Cassinari, S. Graeber, and U. Knaak. (Reusable software solutions for more fault-tolerant) Industrial embedded HPC applications. *Supercomputer*, XIII(69):23–44, 1997.

[6] S. Donatelli and G. Franceschinis. *The PSR methodology: integrating hardware and software models*. LNCS, N. 1091. Springer Verlag, Osaka, Japan, June 1996.

[7] J.-C. Fabre and T. Pérennou. FRIENDS: A flexible architecture for implementing fault tolerant and secure applications. In *Proc. of the 2nd European Dependable Computing Conference (EDCC-2)*, Taormina, Italy, October 1996.

[8] Y. Huang and C. M. Kintala. Software fault tolerance in the application layer. In M. Lyu, editor, *Software Fault Tolerance*, chapter 10, pages 231–248. John Wiley & Sons, New York, 1995.

[9] G. Kiczales, J. des Rivières, and D. G. Bobrow. *The Art of the Metaobject Protocol*. The MIT Press, Cambridge, MA, 1991.

[10] H. Masuhara, S. Matsuoka, T. Watanabe, and A. Yonezawa. Object-oriented concurrent reflective languages can be implemented efficiently. In *Proc. of the Conference on Object-Oriented Programming Systems, Languages, and Applications (OOPSLA-92)*, pages 127–144, 1992.

[11] D. Powell. Preliminary definition of the GUARDS architecture. Technical Report 96277, LAAS-CNRS, January 1997.

[12] J. H. Saltzer, D. P. Reed, and D. D. Clark. End-to-end arguments in system design. *ACM Trans. on Computer Systems*, 2(4):277–288, 1984.

[13] K. Varpaaniemi, J. Halme, K. Hiekkanen, and T. Pyssysalo. Prod reference manual. Digital Systems Laboratory Report B 13, University of Technology, Helsinki August 1995. Available at URL: `http://saturn.tcs.hut.fi/pub/reports/B13.ps.Z`.

Combining low-latency communication protocols with multithreading for high performance DSM systems on clusters

Laurent Lefèvre and Olivier Reymann†
High Performance Networks and Multimedia Applications Support (RESAM)
Bat. ISTIL - Université Claude Bernard Lyon1 - France
†LIP, Ecole Normale Supérieure de Lyon - France
llefevre,oreymann@lhpca.univ-lyon1.fr

Abstract

With the development of clusters based on high performance networks, it is now possible to design efficient Distributed Shared Memory systems.

In this paper, we present the approach we choose to implement a high performance DSM system on top of a cluster by combining the use of low-latency communication protocols (MPI-BIP [12] on Myrinet networks) with multithreading approach (PM2 [11]).

We will present our approach called Distributed Objects Shared MemOry System (DOSMOS system), its design and experiments performed on various communication libraries (PVM,MPI) and on various networks (Ethernet, Myrinet).

1. Introduction

Since a decade, Distributed Shared Memory systems (DSM) show that a parallel programming environment based on shared memory can be useful on top of a distributed system. The purpose of Distributed Shared Memory systems (DSM) is to implement, above a distributed memory architecture, a programming model allowing a transparent manipulation of virtually shared data. Thus, in practice, a DSM system has to handle all the communications and to maintain the shared data coherence. By this way, with a Distributed Shared Memory model, programming a parallel application is much more easy than using message-passing approach because users do not have to manage communications between nodes. Distant data accesses are completely hidden to the application.

But demonstrating scalable results with DSM systems remains difficult because they need high performance architectures to provide good implementations. Management of coherence between data copies need low latency and high bandwidth.

With the development of cluster computing, Distributed Shared Memory systems will have a new role to play by providing easiness of programming a shared space combined with the performance of high speed networks.

In this paper, we present the approach we choose to implement a high performance DSM system on top of a cluster by combining the use of low-latency communication protocols (MPI-BIP [12] on Myrinet networks) with multithreading approach (PM2 [11]). In section 2 we describe the design of DOSMOS and in section 3 we analyze benefits for high performances with an implementation on a low latency communication protocol. Section 4 shows that adding multithreaded protocols can greatly improve raw performances of DSM systems.

2. Distributed Shared Memory System on high performance network

Distributed Shared Memory Systems (DSM) propose a interesting trade-off between the easy-programming of shared memory machines and the efficiency and scalability of distributed memory systems. Basically, a Distributed Shared Memory system is a mechanism that allows application processes to access shared data in a transparent way.

Since a decade, various software implementations have been proposed : Virtual Shared Memory systems (V.S.M.) merge into a single wide address space a set of memory pages distributed in the network (like Treadmarks[3]) and Object-based Distributed Shared Memory systems (D.S.M.) implement a software layer that automatically generates communications required to manipulate shared data (like LINDA[2]).

Other DSM have been proposed on top of clusters but most of them like Cashmere-2L[14], Brazos[13] or Avalanche Project[15] prefer to directly deal with hardware communicating layer regardless of portability. For more information on DSM systems, one can consult various bibli-

1066-6192/99 $10.00 © 1999 IEEE

ographies like [6].

2.1. DOSMOS system

The purpose of Distributed Shared Memory systems (DSM) is to implement, on top of a distributed memory architecture, a programming model allowing a transparent manipulation of virtually shared data. We have developed an original programming environment called DOSMOS system (**D**istributed **O**bjects **S**hared **M**em**O**ry **S**ystem)[4, 10]. DOSMOS is an object-based DSM system which allows processes to share in a transparent way a set of objects distributed and replicated over distant processors.

Basically, a DOSMOS application is composed of two types of processes: **Application processes (A.P.)** contain and execute application code; **Memory processes (M.P.)** manage the whole DSM system, i.e. they provide A.P. with the objects they request (see Fig. 1). The processes also maintain data coherence because for efficiency and scalability purpose, DOSMOS gives the opportunity to duplicate shared objects. It is clear that these replicas have to be kept coherent. DOSMOS implements a weak protocol: the release consistency (see Section 3.2.2). A barrier is also provided by DOSMOS to synchronize all processes on a given object.

Moreover Application processes can be grouped into groups and sub-groups in order to decrease cost of invalidation broadcasts and to optimize management of the data coherence. Groups managing and extra-group accesses are performed through dedicated **Link Processes (L.P.)**.

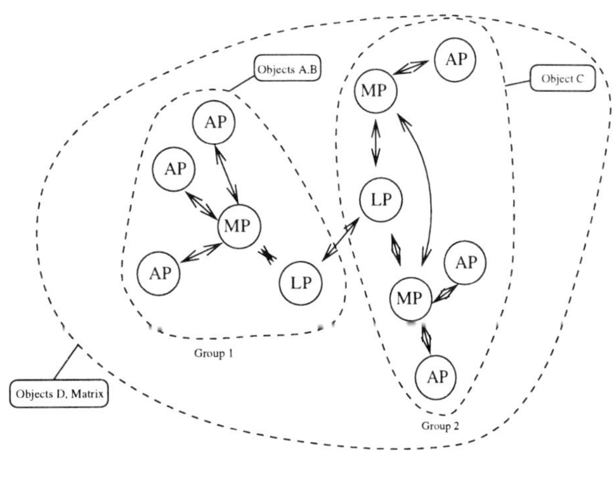

Figure 1. DOSMOS architecture

3. Adding high performance communications protocols

3.1. Why adding low latency protocols ?

By using a Distributed Shared Memory model, programming a parallel application is made easier but the added overheads usually penalizes applications to reach good performances.

Several communication protocols layers are now available for high performance networks. While VIA[5] proposes an unified portable API for high performance networks no free implementations of MPI are available. Low layer communication protocols like PM[9] or GM[1] implementing MPI are available on Myrinet networks. But none of these API provide performances compared to MPI-BIP.

MPI-BIP [12] is mono-process API layer based on zero copy protocols to efficiently send messages between nodes. It implements two strategies depending on message size. Small messages] are stored in a queue of fixed length on the receiving side. If the sender produces messages faster than the receiver consumes them, an overflow occurs and flow control is provided. MPI-BIP uses a credit based mechanism with piggybacking. Large messages are copied to main memory only when the receiver buffer is known (when the receive is posted). As long as no receive is posted, the bytes of a large messages fill the network buffers and the send can't complete. But, to ensure that the network is deadlock-free, Myrinet switches and boards use timeouts. A packet can be dropped if no data movements happen in the network buffers. Thus, a way to ensure that receives are already posted on the receiver when the send starts must be provided.

We experiment our DOSMOS DSM system with Myrinet[1] network (A 1Gb/s High performance network for clusters) on top of fragmented MPI-BIP[12] which provides a bandwidth of up to 66 MBytes per second for a latency of $8\mu s$.

3.2. Model of the MPI-BIP Dosmos version

3.2.1 Access to shared objects

To access to shared objects, Application Processes are provided with two basics operations :

- Object read : If an Application Process wants to read an object not present in its local memory (i.e. for which it does not own a copy) or invalidated, it sends a request to the Memory Process it depends on. If this MP manages a valid copy of this object on behalf of another AP, it transmits a copy of this copy to the AP "caller". On the contrary, if the MP does not own any valid copy of the requested object, it then forwards the request to another memory process of its group (the "owner" of the object, see section 3.2.2) (or of another group if needed) and waits for the object. When a copy of the object is returned to the MP, this latter transmits it to the AP caller. At last, objects tables (listing the available valid copies) are updated in order to improve further accesses to the same object.

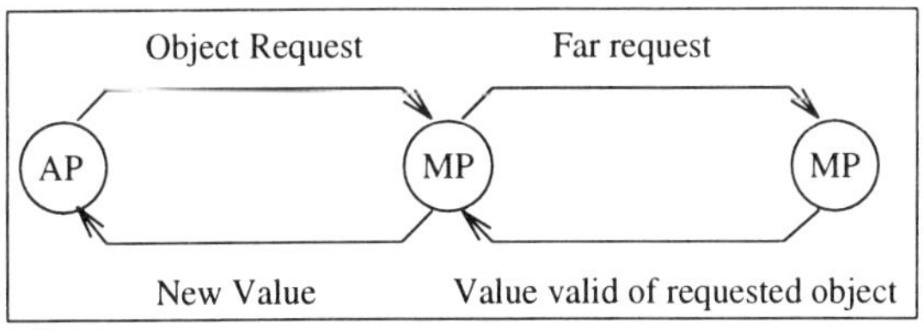

Figure 2. Object read

- Object write : DOSMOS implements a weak write protocol. Thus, when a processor modifies an object present in its local memory, it sends the new value to its dedicated memory process. This latter, depending on the invalidation protocol chosen, invalidates or sends the new value to the other processes. These invalidations are, of course, only transmitted to the processes that actually share the modified object.

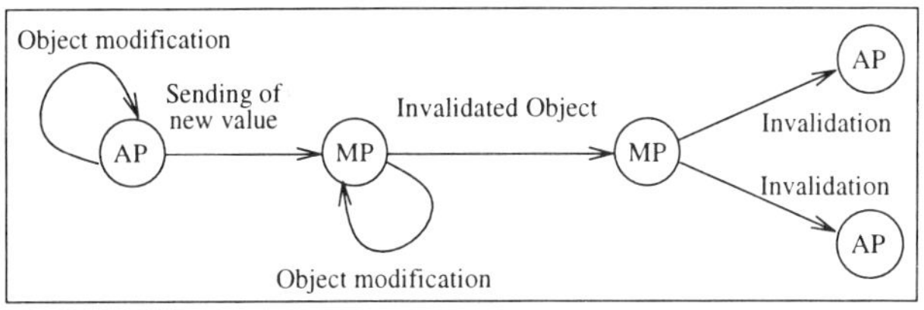

Figure 3. Object write

Invalidation protocols are used for maintaining the coherence of the distributed copies of a same object. They are a key point for any DSM system. Indeed a very important part of the efficiency of DSM systems depends on the efficiency of the invalidation protocols actually implemented.

We propose an adaptable strategy which integrates two invalidation protocols. When a large object (e.g., large arrays of data, matrices...) is modified, in order to avoid expensive communications, we only *invalidate* the copies of the object by sending a small invalidation message. But, on small objects like variables or short arrays of data, we directly update the copies by sending a *copy* of the object itself. So, by mixing these various strategies, the system tries to minimize the cost of the maintenance of the coherence of the copies.

3.2.2 Weak consistency implementation

The implementation of the maintenance of the shared data consistency is based on Release Consistency which provides two operators : *acquire* and *release*. With *acquire*, the user can set a Restricted Access Section (R.A.S.), where one process can access without any restriction to an object copy while the other processes can access to their local copies. But only one RAS can be active at a given time on an object. An RAS is terminated by using *release* operator which updates all object copies and unlocks the object.

Acquire an object

This operator is used when an application process wants to access to an object in an exclusive way, usually for a modification. Depending on the owner of the shared object (figures 4), the acquire request can pass through several processes before reaching the owner. An acquire can be performed only when the previous acquire on the requested object has been released.

After an acquire operation, the object is locked for calling process which is allowed to modify the object. Modifications done by the calling process are sequentially ordered. When waiting for the object release, the owner process is not held up. Thus, during this period of time, the owner process can continue to work, especially to reject write accesses from other processes.

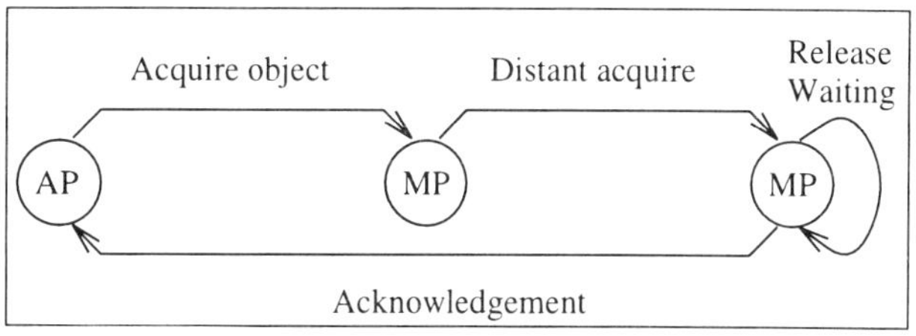

Figure 4. Acquire when the MP is not owner

Release an object

According to the release consistency model, releasing an object is the only way which ensures that an invalidation protocol will be triggered before the object is unlocked. Thus, after a process releases a previously acquired object any process can access the object. Copies of the released object are either invalidated or updated.

As it can be noted, these two operators have been implemented in the weakest way as possible in order to not to generate expensive communications and to ensure a good scalability to applications.

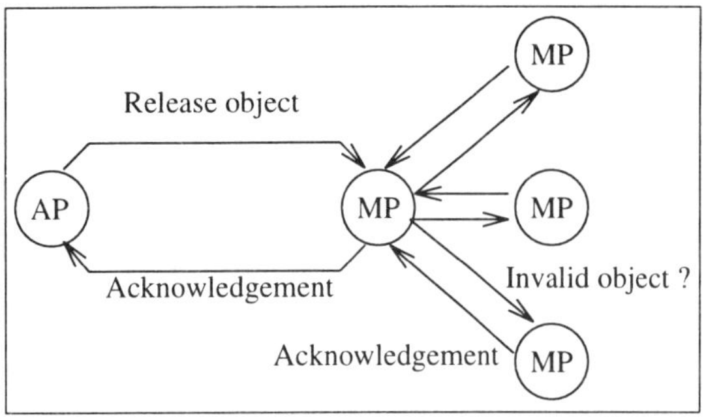

Figure 5. Release with modification

3.3. Performance measurements

This section presents a comparison of the raw performance obtained with DOSMOS depending on network used (Myrinet/Ethernet) and the communication library (PVM/MPI).

Our experiments have been made on top of a cluster of 12 Pentium Pro 200MHZ linked by an Ethernet Network or a Myrinet Network.

3.3.1 Shared Data Access time

Table 1 shows execution times of basic operations in DOSMOS when a process wants to access to remote data. We only tune read and acquire/release accesses because they are the most expensive operation due to a ping-pong communication on the network. On Ethernet networks, results in Table 1 are compared when A.P. and M.P. are mapped on the same processor (*Same*) or on different machines (*Diff*) (see Fig. 6). On Myrinet with MPI-BIP layer, A.P. and M.P. must be mapped on different processors (*Diff*).

On low performance networks (Ethernet), high latency is a limiting factor for DSM. MPI version shows bad results compared to PVM version due to the kind of polling method we use to manage AP requests. The benefit of weak consistency protocols (RAS) is not useful for Ethernet network applications based, while on Myrinet networks we see a good difference (41 μs instead of 68 μs). These are excellent results compared to raw latency ($8\mu s$) of MPI-BIP. As we perform a ping-pong communication, we only increase the latency with 25 μs (41 μs - 2*$8\mu s$), due to DOSMOS layer.

Table 2 shows the benefit of using a local copy directly present on Applications Processes (see Fig. 6). Compared to results of basic accesses without a local copy, we obtain better performance even of Ethernet networks. And the cost added to manage this local copy is around 2 to 5 μs when the process access to a remote object.

Management of distributed objects (consistency, invalidations, synchronization...) adds a latency to each distant access combined with latency of the network (Table 1). Distant operations concern A.P. which access a shared object managed by their M.P. while Long Distant operations involve one A.P. and two M.P. to access distant objects. Access to a distant object requires a ping-pong communication between two nodes (which takes around $16\mu s$ with MPI-BIP). An additional latency is added by DOSMOS to manage complex objects (like arrays) to provide splitting and transparent access to distributed arrays. As can be seen in Table 1 and 2 , the latency added by DOSMOS is kept reasonable and still compatible with the need of high performances by the applications.

3.3.2 Transfer rate

Using high performance networks is the only way to allow the transfer of big objects in DSM systems. We can see on figure 7, that using Ethernet network does not allow high data transfer possibility for a DSM like DOSMOS. Whatever, the message size, transfer rate remains under 1MByte per second.

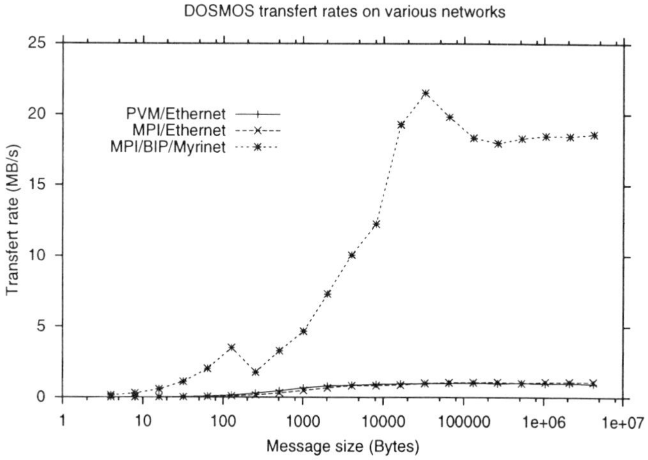

Figure 7. DOSMOS transfer rate depending of networks and communication library

By using MPI-BIP, transfer rates scale well depending on object size. The first scale around 128 Bytes message size is due to adaptative strategy of MPI-BIP to send small or large messages (see Section 3.1). We obtain the 22 MBytes/s best transfer rate for message of 64 KBytes. After this step, the latency remains around 17 MBytes due to cache management and DOSMOS layers.

These excellent results in terms of transfer rate make possible to use DSM systems for collaborative multimedia applications transferring large amount of data.

Access	Ethernet PVM Diff	Ethernet PVM Same	Ethernet MPI Diff	Ethernet MPI Same	Myrinet MPI/BIP Diff
Remote Read on MP	1200	750	2220	2150	68
Remote Read on MP within a RAS	1200	750	2220	2150	41
Long Remote Read on MP	2540	2050	3830	3810	130
Local Acquire	1170	730	1600	1600	60
Remote Acquire	3360	2670	3330	3860	130

Table 1. Comparison of execution times (in μs) of various operations depending of communication library and network : Without local copies on AP

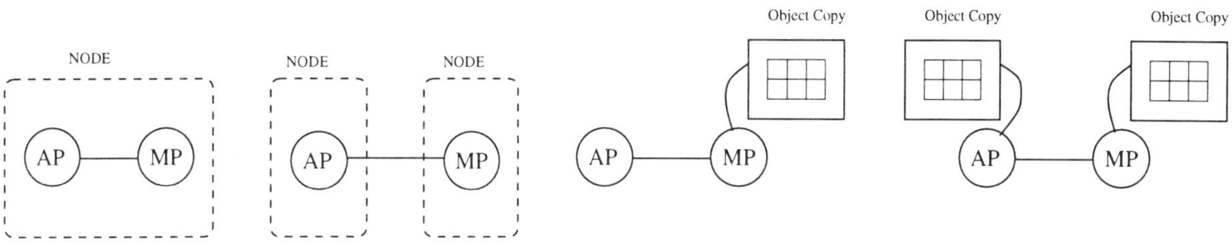

Figure 6. AP and MP on same or on different nodes and No copy vs Local copy on AP

4. Introduction of multithreading into DOSMOS

4.1. Why using multithreading ?

Before explaining why we chose to introduce multithreading techniques, we have to define their characteristics. Multithreading techniques allow to have several execution flows (lightweight processes or threads) in a heavy process (or simply process). A process can concurrently execute several hundred threads that share a common set of resources (process memory, file descriptors, signal routine tables,...). But each thread has his own program pointer and execution stack. Hence, due to the small size of the information that have to be stored, context switching of threads is very efficient. Another factor of that efficiency is that all data is stored in the process memory and there is no need to make a system call. Creating a new thread or switching to a thread can be done from 10 to 100 times faster than for a heavy process.

We developed a multithreaded version of DOSMOS in order to eliminate several limitations related with the use of heavy processes. The limitations addressed by introducing multithreading techniques into DOSMOS are the following ones :

1. The first limitation is that all processes on a same node have their own variable copies. This conducts to a waste of memory but also to an increase the cost of coherence maintenance due to the number of copies.
2. Communications between AP and MP on a same node call communication library routines. This is particularly expensive in comparison with sharing information via shared memory.
3. Heavy processes have high switching times.
4. The last limitation is due to the logical architecture imposed by DOSMOS. Actually, on some parallel architectures, only one process can be started on each processor (for instance, by using MPI/BIP). So Application Processes and their Memory Processes are always on separate processors. This leads to use the network for all communications and to waste processors.

By using the physical shared memory provided by the multithreaded techniques permits to resolve points 1 and 2. The outstanding efficiency of context switching improves point 3. Point 4 is simply addressed by putting the code of the DOSMOS processes into threads. This requires to redefine the implementation of all the protocols specified in DOSMOS.

4.2. Overview of the multithreaded execution support

We chose to use the PM2 (Parallel Multithreaded Machine) programming environment [11]. This one was developed by having in mind the same aims than DOSMOS (portability, efficiency, modularity, and extensibility). It

Access	Ethernet				Myrinet
	PVM		MPI		MPI/BIP
	Diff	Same	Diff	Same	Diff
Local Read on AP	20	20	280	280	21
Read within a RAS	0.7	0.7	1	1	0.7
Remote READ on MP	1300	830	2500	2470	70
Long Remote Read on MP	2550	2080	4250	4280	135
Local Acquire	1210	750	1660	1640	65
Remote Acquire	3320	2670	3410	4080	125

Table 2. Shared data access time (in μs) of various operations depending of communication library and network : With local copies on A.P.

also provides many features that are very interesting for implementing a Distributed Shared Memory system. Actually, PM2 allows to migrate threads from one node to another in order to balance the workload. The creation time of threads is reduced by using a cache of memory spaces that avoids doing a memory allocation. Thanks to the distributed management of threads, PM2 allows to create new lightweight processes on a remote processor. The idea is to use the notion of Lightweight Remote Procedure Call (LRPC). This approach permits to start the execution of a function (called a service) on any processor. Figure 8 shows the principle of LRPCs. Thread t1 starts a new thread (t2) on processor 2 which executes the requested service.

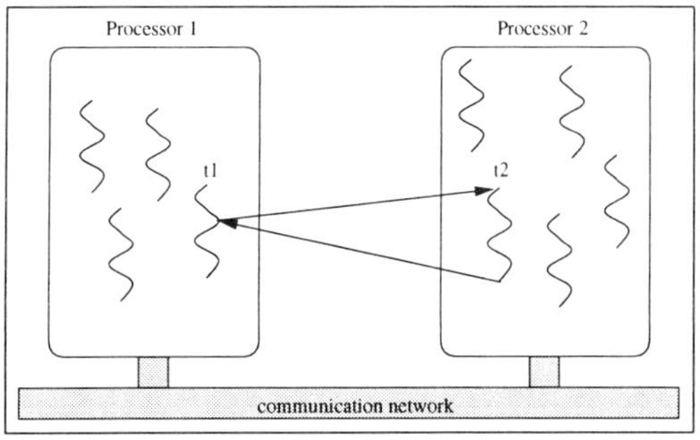

Figure 8. Principle of a Lightweight Remote Procedure Call

4.3. The model of the multithreaded version of DOSMOS

Using lightweight processes does not raise questions about the model proposed by our DSM system : we just have to consider Application Processes and Memory Processes as being lightweight processes. However, two major differences should be noticed :

- The approach based on heavy processes assumes that each process could have its own variable copy. Keeping such an assumption in a multithreaded environment is realistic in terms of efficiency. Hence, all tasks are becoming threads and all of them running in the same process share the same copy.
- In our model, the communications are explicitly made between two processes. For instance, an Application Process communicates directly with its Memory Process. Unfortunately, PM2 does not provide mechanisms that permit to directly communicate with a thread.

All these modifications require the definition of a new software architecture of a DOSMOS/PM2 application and also a complete redefinition of all the protocols specified to access shared data. The major changes between the implementation models is that in the heavy process based model all Memory Processes are created at the beginning and last until the end of the application when, in the multithreaded version, Memory Threads (MT) are created on demand to perform remote operations on shared variables. Figure 9 shows a software architecture composed by 11 Application Threads spread over 4 processors. One of the AT on processor 1 performs a read access on a remote copy. To do this, it starts a new Memory Thread (MT) that reads the value and returns it.

4.4. Performance measurements

This section presents a comparison of the raw performance (shared variable access time) obtained with the mono-threaded and the multithreaded version of DOSMOS.

4.4.1 Shared data access time

Table 3 shows the execution times for several operations on a shared variable. The introduction of multithreading tech-

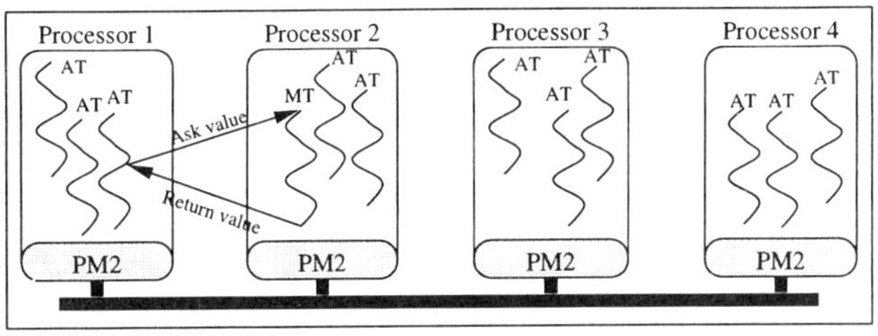

Figure 9. Software architecture of a DOSMOS/PM2 application in which an Application Thread performs a remote read

operation	Myrinet	
	MPI/BIP	PM2/MPI/BIP
local read	21	1
read within RAS	0.7	0.7
read using pointer	0.05	0.05
remote read	70	1
long remote read	135	150
local "acquire"	65	11
remote "acquire"	125	160

Table 3. Shared data access times (in μs) with or without multithreading

niques permits to severely reduce the access time in some cases. Thus, during a local read, the Application Thread can directly access the local memory without having to check if the copy is still valid. This divides the access time by more than 20. Read operations done within a RAS or by using a pointer spend the same time with MPI/BIP or with PM2/MPI/BIP because the work is the same in the two versions. The line representing the "remote read" results requires some explanations about this impressive reduction of access time. With the multithreaded version, remote reads are in fact local reads because there is only one variable copy for all threads on a processor and the AT can directly access the copy. It is the same for the local "acquire" operation. Concerning the accesses that really use the network (long remote read and remote "acquire"), a small overhead is introduced by PM2 due to the fact that only a PM2 system thread can access the network interface and thus an additional context switching is required.

4.4.2 Transfer rate

Figure 10 presents the transfer rates obtained for various variable sizes by using MPI/BIP and PM2/MPI/BIP. The first scale around 128 Bytes message size is due to adaptative strategy of MPI-BIP to send small or large messages (see Section 3.1). The results show that multithreaded version of DOSMOS increases transfer rate up to 28MBytes/s for 64KBytes messages. Actually, a read request generates twice more messages but the remote node has a shorter reaction time. Hence, for small messages (under 128 bytes), the mono-threaded MPI/BIP version is better and for large messages, transfer with multithreaded DOSMOS version is better than MPI-BIP version.

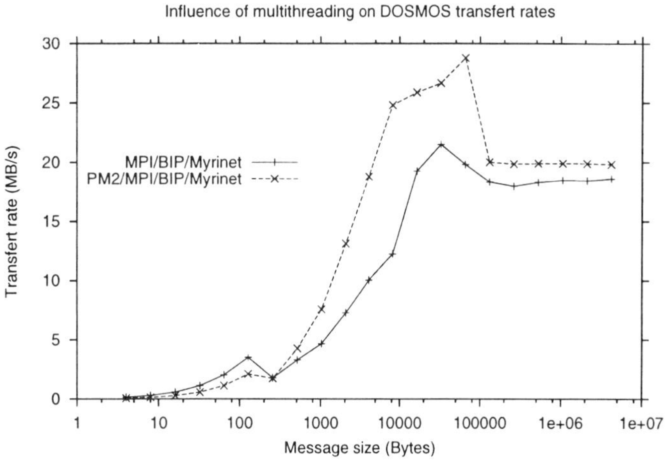

Figure 10. DOSMOS transfer rate with or without multithreading

We have compared our results with the remote access time of Cashmere-2L [14] that also uses a high performance network (Memory Channel [7]). This system shares 8KB memory pages and retrieves a copy from a remote memory in 824μs. In order to be able to compare, we measured the time spend for getting a copy of an 8KB variable with DOSMOS/PM2. It is done in 390μs, that is more than two times faster as with Cashmere-2L.

5. Conclusion and future work

With the development of cluster computing, DSM systems will have a new role to play by providing easiness of programming a shared space combined with the performance of high speed networks.

This paper presented the DOSMOS approach in response to the need of DSM for cluster computing and multi-clusters applications. DOSMOS tries to show that there is a huge future potential for DSM systems on top of clusters if they can benefit on high performance networks and multithreading environment. To be adapted to large aggregated networks and multi-clusters, we also propose hierarchical methods to efficiently share data between nodes.

DOSMOS is now available on top of PVM and MPI and can be used with Ethernet or Myrinet networks (MPI-BIP version). An SCI (Scalable Coherent Interface)[8] version of DOSMOS is currently under development for allowing experiments on multi heterogeneous clusters.

Using low latency protocols combined with High Performance networks greatly improves DOSMOS raw performances : time to access to a distant object remains small (68 μs) while transfer rate is not too reduced due to DSM layers (17 MByte/s). By adding, multithreading techniques, DOSMOS latency is improved for local accesses (1 μs) and for large messages we obtain a transfer rate up to 28 MBytes/s.

These result show that with high performance networks, low latency protocols and multithreaded environment, it is now possible to implement scalable and efficient DSM systems.

References

[1] Myrinet documentation : http://www.myri.com/scs/documentation.

[2] S. Ahuka, N. Carriero, and D. Glernter. LINDA and friends. *IEEE Computer*, 19(8):26–34, August 1986.

[3] Cristiana Amza, Alan L. Cox, Sandhya Dwarkadas, Pete Keleher, Honghui Lu, Ramakrishnan Rajamony, Weimin Yu, and Willy Zwaenepoel. TreadMarks: Shared Memory Computing on Networks of Workstations. *IEEE Computer*, pages 18–28, February 1996.

[4] Lionel Brunie and Laurent Lefèvre. New propositions to improve the efficiency and scalability of DSM systems. In IEEE, editor, *1996 IEEE Second International Conference on Algorithms & Architectures for Parallel Processing - ICA3PP '96*, pages 356–364, Singapore, June 1996.

[5] Dave Dunning and Greg Regnier. The Virtual Interface Architecture. In *Hot Interconnects V*, Stanford, USA, August 1997.

[6] M. Rasit Eskicioglu. A comprehensive bibliography of distributed shared memory. *ACM Operating Systems Reviews*, 30(1):71–96, jan 1996.

[7] R.B. Gillett. Memory Channel Network for PCI. *IEEE Micro*, 16(1):12–18, February 1996.

[8] D. Gustavson. The scalable coherent interface and related standard projects. *IEEE Micro*, 12(1), Feb 1992.

[9] Yutaka Ishikawa Hiroshi Tezuka, Atsushi Hori. PM:a high-performance communication library for multi-user paralllel environments. Technical Report TR-96015, RWC, 1996. http://www.rwcp.or.jp/lab/pdslab/papers.html.

[10] Laurent Lefèvre. Parallel programming on top of DSM Systems : An Experimental Study. In *Parallel Computing - Environments and Tools for Parallel Scientific Computing III*, volume 23 (1-2), pages 235–249. April 1997.

[11] R. Namyst and J.-F. Méhaut. PM2: Parallel multithreaded machine. a computing environment for distributed architectures. In *Parallel Computing (ParCo'95)*, pages 279–285. Elsevier Science Publishers, Sept 1995.

[12] Loïc Prylli, Bernard Tourancheau, and Roland Westrelin. Modeling of a high speed network to maximize throughput performance: the experience of BIP over myrinet. In *Parallel and Distributed Processing Techniques and Applications (PDPTA'98)*, Las Vegas, USA, 1998.

[13] E. Speight and J.K. Bennett. Brazos: A third generation DSM system. In *USENIX Windows/NT Workshop*, August 1997.

[14] R. Stets, S. Dwarkadas, N. Hardavellas, G. Hunt, L. Kontothanassis, P. Srinivasan, and M. Scott. CASHMERE-2L : Software Coherent Shared Memory on a Clustered Remote-Write Network. In *Proc. of the 16th ACM Symp. on Operating Systems Principles (SOSP'97)*, Saint Malo, France, October 1997.

[15] M. R. Wanson and L. B. Stoller. Shared memory as a basis for conservative distributed architectural simulation. Technical Report UUCS-97-005, Department of Computer Science, university of Utah, 1997. Avalanche Project.

Session 8:
Applications

Session 8: Applications

Session Chair: S. Smith

It is only when theory is put in to practise that the full nature of a problem can be realised. Whether a pioneering or a novel solution, the study of applications is most exciting and rewarding work. The discipline of parallel and distributed systems is a prime example, having a wealth of practical problems to reconcile and many different approaches to consider. This session considers three papers in three contrasting application areas.

The first paper is entitled *"Parallel simulated annealing for the set-partitioning problem"* by Z. J. Czech and considers a delivery problem which reduces to the NP-complete set-partitioning problem. Both sequential and parallel annealing algorithms to solve the problem are considered and the improvements to performance by applying parallelism demonstrated.

Wavelet packets are becoming a very popular technique within science and engineering. The second paper in this session is concerned with generalising existing wavelet packet algorithms, which are constrained to a number of processor elements equal to a power of 4. *"2-D Wavelet Packet Decomposition on Multicomputers"* by M. Feil, A. Uhl, considers several optimisations and generalisations, and compares their performance on an MIMD distributed memory architecture computer.

The final paper in the session is *"Towards Efficient BSP Implementations of BSR programs for some Computational Geometry Problems"* by C. Cerin and provides an interesting demonstration of how BSR (Broadcasting with Selective Reduction) can be used as a specification language and BSP (Bulk Synchronous Parallel model) primitives providing the means to implementation in software. Results are presented from implementations on a Silicon Graphics Origin2000 and a Bi-Pentium running Linux and encourage the development of automatic translation of BSR specifications in to efficient BSP implementations.

Parallel Simulated Annealing for the Set-partitioning Problem

Zbigniew J. Czech*
Institute of Computer Science, Silesia University of Technology
Gliwice, Poland
e-mail: zjc@polsl.gliwice.pl

Abstract

A delivery problem which reduces to the NP-complete set-partitioning problem is investigated. The sequential and parallel simulated annealing algorithms to solve the delivery problem are discussed. The objective is to improve the quality of solutions to the problem by applying parallelism.

Key words. *Delivery problem, set-partitioning problem, heuristic algorithms, parallel algorithms, parallel simulated annealing*

1. Introduction

A delivery problem (DP) which arose in a transportation company is investigated. It can be formulated as follows. There is a central depot of goods and n customers (nodes) located at the specified distances from the depot. The goods have to be delivered to each customer by using vehicles. The number of vehicles which can be used for delivery is unlimited, however in each trip which is effected during an eight-hour day a vehicle crew can visit at most k customers, where k is a small constant. Let $k = 3$. Then on a single trip the crew starts from the depot, visits one, two or three customers and returns to the depot. A set of routes which guarantees the delivery of goods to all customers is sought. Furthermore, the cost defined as the total length of the routes in the set should be minimized.

If a strong constraint is imposed on the magnitude of k (e.g. $k = 3$), then the DP reduces to the set-partitioning problem (SPP) which is NP-complete. Let $N = \{1, 2, \dots, n\}$ be a set of customers, and let $\mathcal{S} = \{S_1, S_2, \dots, S_q\}$, $q = \binom{n}{1} + \binom{n}{2} + \binom{n}{3}$, be a set of all subsets of N of size at most 3, i.e. $S_i \subseteq N$ and $|S_i| \leq 3$, $i \in M$, where $M = \{1, 2, \dots, q\}$. Every S_i represents a possible tour of a solution to the DP. Let c_i be a minimum cost (length) of the tour S_i. To obtain the solution to the DP we need to solve the SPP which consists in finding the collection $\{S_l\}$, $l \in M$, of minimum total cost such that every customer j, $j \in N$, is covered by the subsets in the collection exactly once. In other words, the intersection of any pair of subsets in $\{S_l\}$ is empty.

In this work we investigate the sequential and parallel versions of a simulated annealing algorithm to solve the DP. The objective is to improve the quality of solutions to the problem by applying parallelism.

Over the last years several approaches to parallelization of simulated annealing have been proposed. For overviews we refer to Aarts and Korst [1], Greening [10], Azencott [3], Boissin and Lutton [5], and Verhoeven and Aarts [17]. To our best knowledge no work was devoted to the the parallel simulated annealing algorithm for solving the delivery problem as defined in this paper.

In section 2 a solution space for the DP is discussed. Section 3 describes the sequential annealing algorithm. In section 4 the parallel annealing algorithms are presented. Section 5 concludes the paper.

2. Solution space

In order to find the solution to the DP we have to consider the sets of all possible routes for n customers. Given $k = 3$ it can be shown that the number of those sets is determined by the expression [6]:

$$n! \sum_{i=0}^{\lfloor n/3 \rfloor} \left(\frac{1}{6^i i!} \sum_{j=0}^{\lfloor (n-3i)/2 \rfloor} \frac{1}{(n-3i-2j)! 2^j j!} \right). \tag{1}$$

This means that for the number of customers from $n = 40$ to $n = 100$, which we consider, we have to "sieve" from $\sim 8 \cdot 10^{21}$ to $\sim 1.15 \cdot 10^{103}$ potential solutions, respectively. Surely, it is not possible in practice to search exhaustively through such enormous solution spaces.

*This research was supported in part by the State Committee for Scientific Research grant BK-245-RAu2-99.

In Figures 1 to 4 we show the suspected optimal solutions to the DP for $n = 100, 90, 80$ and 70 customers. These were obtained by multiple runs of the simulated annealing algorithms.

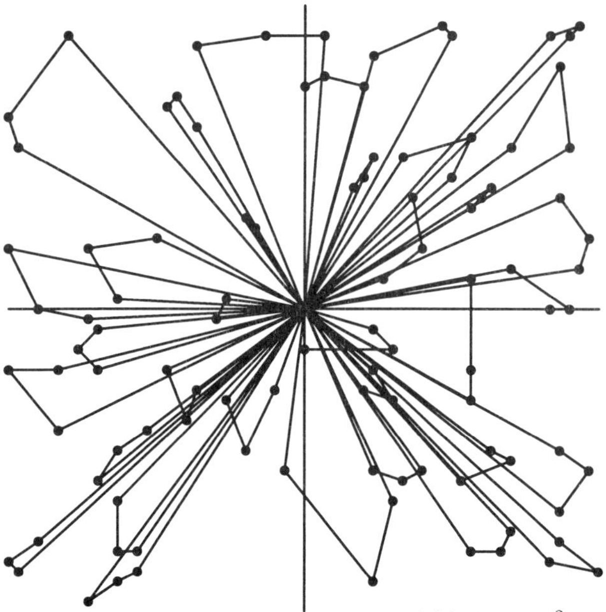

Figure 1. The suspected optimum solutions to the DP for $n = 100$ uniformly distributed customers in the 60×60 square with the depot in the center (the Euclidean distances between nodes are used).

3. Sequential annealing

The technique of simulated annealing which can be regarded as a variant of local search was first introduced by Metropolis *et al.* [13], and then used to optimization problems by Kirkpatrick *et al.* [11] and Cĕrny [7]. A comprehensive introduction to the subject can be found in [15]. The application of simulated annealing to solve the DP is as follows. Initially a solution to the problem is the set of routes of size 3 (last route may have less than 3 customers). The customers are grouped into the routes randomly. On every step a neighbor solution is determined by either moving a randomly chosen customer from one route to another (perhaps empty) or by exchanging the places of random customers between their routes. The neighbor solutions of lower costs obtained in this way are always accepted, whereas the solutions of higher costs are accepted with the probability

$$Pr = T_i/(T_i + \delta) \tag{2}$$

where T_i, $i = 0, 1, \ldots$ is the temperature of annealing which drops from a value $T_0 = cost(initial\_solution)/10^3$ according to the formula $T_{i+1} = T_i \cdot \alpha$, where $\alpha < 1$. Eq. (2) implies that large increases in solution cost, so called *uphill moves*, are more likely to be accepted when T_i is high. As T_i approaches zero most uphill moves are rejected.

The algorithm stops if equilibrium is encountered. We define that equilibrium is reached if the 20 stages of temperature reduction fail to improve the best solution. Contrary to the classical approach in which a solution to the problem is taken as the last solution obtained in the annealing process, we memorize the best solution found during the whole annealing process (cf. lines 14–17 of the *annealing_step* procedure).

Summing up, the annealing algorithm performs the local search by sampling the neighborhood randomly. It attempts to avoid becoming prematurely trapped in a local optimum by sometimes accepting an inferior solution. The level of this acceptance depends on the magnitude of the increase in solution cost and on the search time to date.

The cost of a single iteration of the **repeat** statement (lines 5–11) is proportionate to n^2, as the steps in line 7 and lines 9–10 are executed in constant time, and there is n^2 repetitions of the **for** loop (lines 6–8). It is difficult to establish analytically the number of stages, a, in the cooling schedule, i.e. the number of iterations of the **repeat** statement. In our experiments we found that for the number of customers $n = 40 \ldots 100$ and $\alpha = 0.95$, the number of stages did not exceed 200. Therefore the worst case time complexity of the sequential annealing algorithm is $\mathcal{T}(n) \leq 200n^2 = O(n^2)$.

The test results of 100 executions of the sequential annealing algorithm are shown in Table 1. These were obtained for the subsets of nodes of the test set of $n = 100$ uniformly distributed customers in the 60×60 square with the depot in the center. The columns of the table contain the cardinalities of the subsets (n), the suspected optimum solution value to the DP (Opt.), the best solution value found by the algorithm (Best), the average value of the solutions over 100 executions (Avg.), the standard deviation of the results (σ), the quality of the solution (expressed in per cent) measured by the ratio of the best (approximate) solution value obtained by an algorithm to the optimum (or suspected optimum) value (γ), and the number of times the optimum solution was obtained in 100 executions (H).

It can be seen from Table 1 that the probability of finding the optimum solution for larger n is low. For example, the minimum solution to the DP was found only once over 100 executions for the set of $n = 90$ customers, and it was not found at all for $n = 100$.

Sequential annealing algorithm

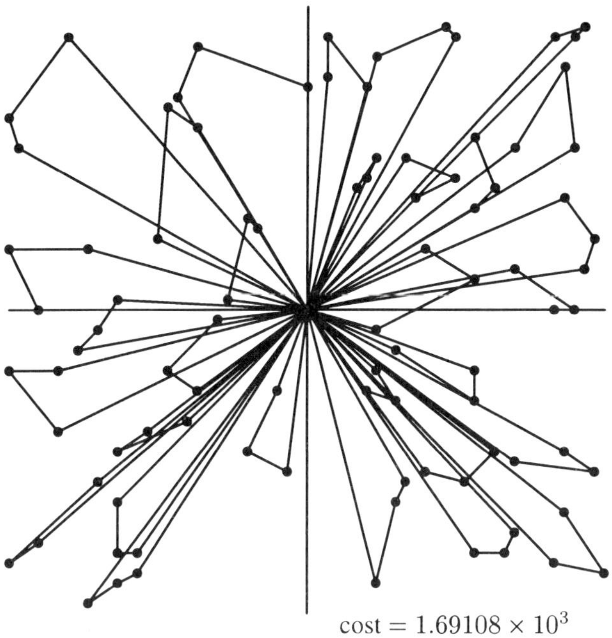

Figure 2. The suspected optimum solutions to the DP for $n = 90$ uniformly distributed customers in the 60×60 square with the depot in the center.

```
Create an initial, old_solution as the set of random
    routes of size 3;
best_solution := old_solution;
equilibrium_counter := 0; {set the equilibrium
    counter}
T := cost(best_solution)/1000; {initial temperature
    of annealing}
repeat;
  for iteration_counter := 1 to n^2 do
    annealing_step(old_solution, best_solution);
  end for;
  T := T · α; {temperature reduction}
  equilibrium_counter := equilibrium_counter + 1;
until equilibrium_counter > 20;
```

```
procedure annealing_step(old_solution,
    best_solution);
  Select randomly a customer;
  Select randomly a route (distinct from the
    customer's route selected in the previous line)
    from the set containing the routes of the
    old_solution and an empty route;
  if the route size is less than 3 then
    Create the new_solution by moving the
      customer into the chosen route;
  else
    Select randomly a customer in the route;
    Create the new_solution by exchanging the
      selected customers between their routes;
  end if;
  δ := cost(new_solution) − cost(old_solution);
  Generate random x uniformly in the range (0, 1);
  if (δ < 0) or (x < T/(T + δ)) then
    old_solution := new_solution;
    if cost(new_solution) <
        cost(best_solution) then
      best_solution := new_solution;
      equilibrium_counter := 0;
    end if;
  end if;
end annealing_step;
```

n	Opt.	Best	Avg.	σ	γ	H
40	819.0	819.0	823.9	11.17	100.00	49
50	982.2	982.2	987.9	11.11	100.00	28
60	1173.4	1173.4	1179.4	10.31	100.00	3
70	1364.7	1364.7	1376.8	13.14	100.00	6
80	1502.9	1502.9	1515.0	20.98	100.00	5
90	1691.1	1691.1	1701.3	6.20	100.00	1
100	1835.4	1836.8	1850.6	20.78	100.08	0

Table 1. Performance of the sequential annealing algorithm.

4. Parallel annealing

Let us assume that p identical processors are available and each of them is capable of generating its own sequential annealing sequence. The processors can be used either to speed up the sequential annealing algorithm or to achieve a higher quality of solutions to a problem. In this work we are interested in the latter goal.

There are several methods of parallelization of the sequential simulated annealing algorithm [3]. Among them are simultaneous independent searches and simultaneous periodically interacting searches. We shall discuss these approaches in the following subsections.

4.1. Simultaneous independent searches

The method of simultaneous independent searches consists in executing p independent annealing sequences and selecting the best solution among the solutions obtained by the processors.

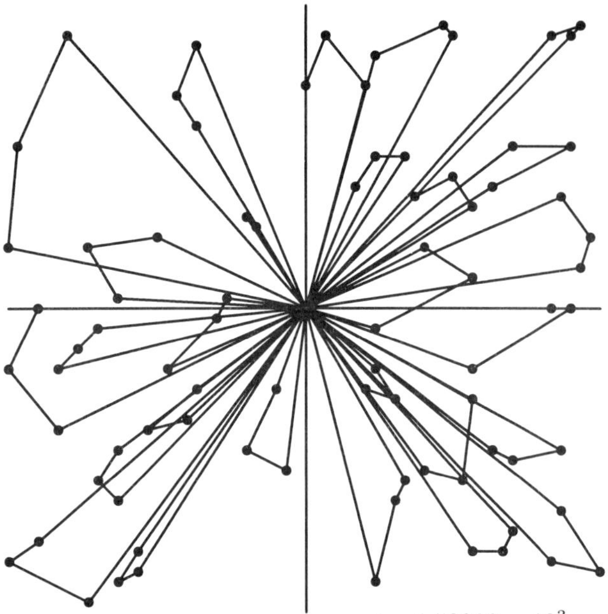

cost = 1.50293×10^3

Figure 3. The suspected optimum solutions to the DP for $n = 80$ uniformly distributed customers in the 60×60 square with the depot in the center.

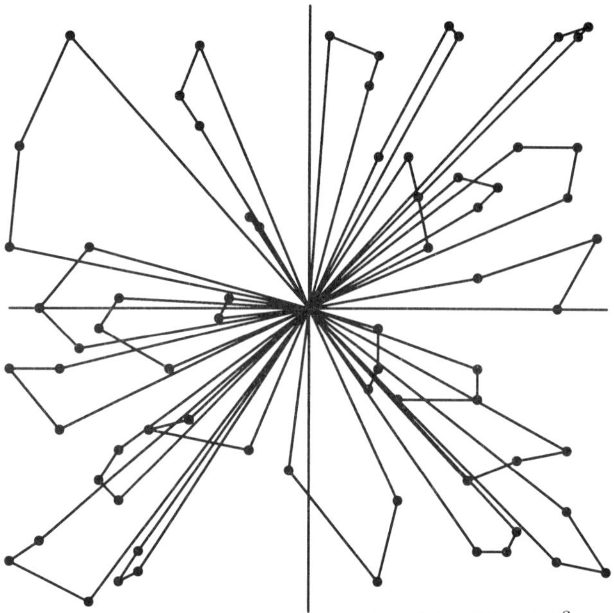

cost = 1.36471×10^3

Figure 4. The suspected optimum solutions to the DP for $n = 70$ uniformly distributed customers in the 60×60 square with the depot in the center.

Let E be the set of all solutions to the DP. A solution $X \in E$ is said to be a global minimum if

$$cost(X) = \inf_{j \in E}\{cost(j)\}.$$

Denote by $E_{\min}$ the set of all global minima. Let r be the total available time (expressed in annealing steps), and let $E_p = \{\bar{X}_r^{(1)}, \bar{X}_r^{(2)}, \ldots, \bar{X}_r^{(p)}\}$ be the set of p best solutions obtained by the processors after having performed r sequential annealing steps. The final solution to the problem is selected as the best solution in set E_p, what we denote

$$Y_r = \bar{X}_r^{(1)} \otimes \bar{X}_r^{(2)} \otimes \cdots \otimes \bar{X}_r^{(p)}.$$

Clearly we have

$$Pr(Y_r \notin E_{\min}) = \prod_{1 \le j \le p} Pr(\bar{X}_r^{(j)} \notin E_{\min}). \quad (3)$$

The Equation (3) indicates that the simultaneous independent searches improve a quality of the found solution since the probability that Y_r does not belong to the set of optimum solutions is less than a corresponding probability for an annealing sequence performed by a single processor. The open question, which we investigate in this work, is how much smaller this probability is.

A simultaneous independent searches algorithm written for a CREW PRAM model of computation is given below. The processors P_j, $j = 1, 2, \ldots, p$, carry out independent annealing searches using the same initial solution and cooling schedule as in the sequential algorithm (see section 3). At each temperature processor P_j executes n^2 annealing steps (lines 10–12) and then tests whether to update the *best_solution* with the *best_local_solution*$_j$ (lines 13–19). If such an update is made, the variable *equilibrium_counter* is set to 0. The searches stop when equilibrium is reached.

The worst case time complexity of the parallel algorithm is $\mathcal{T}_p(n) \le a(n^2 + p)$, since the cooling schedule gives at most a iterations of the **repeat** statement (lines 9–24) and the cost of every iteration is $n^2 + p$. That cost includes n^2 iterations of the **for** statement (lines 10–12) and p updates of the *best_solution* in the shared memory (lines 13–19). Note that the complexity of the parallel algorithm, $\mathcal{T}_p(n)$, is only slightly worse (by term p, $p << n^2$) as compared to the complexity of the sequential algorithm.

Simultaneous independent searches

---

1 **parfor** $P_j, j = 1, 2, \ldots, p$ **do**
2   **if** $j = 1$ **then**
3   Create an initial, *best_solution* as the set of

```
          random routes of size 3;
      equilibrium_counter := 0; {set the equilibrium
          counter}
      T := cost(best_solution)/1000; {initial
          temperature of annealing}
    end if;
    old_solution_j := best_solution;
    best_local_solution_j := best_solution;
    repeat;
      for iteration_counter_j := 1 to n^2 do
        annealing_step(old_solution_j,
            best_local_solution_j); {as in the sequential
            algorithm}
      end for;
      lock(best_solution); lock(equilibrium_counter);
      if cost(best_local_solution_j) <
            cost(best_solution) then
        best_solution := best_local_solution_j;
        equilibrium_counter := 0;
      end if;
      unlock(best_solution);
      unlock(equilibrium_counter);
      if j = 1 then
        T := T · α; {temperature reduction}
        equilibrium_counter :=
            equilibrium_counter + 1;
      end if;
    until equilibrium_counter > 20;
  end for;
```

The simultaneous independent searches algorithm was implemented in Ada95 and ran on a single-processor computer Sun Enterprise 450, 250 MHz. In the concurrent implementation, processor P_j performing an annealing sequence was represented by a separate Ada task. The tasks were executed via interleaving. The test results of 100 executions of the concurrent algorithm for $p = 2 \,..\, 5$ tasks are shown in Table 2. The same data sets as in the sequential experiments were used. The columns have the similar meaning as in Table 1.

It can be seen from Table 2 that the quality of solutions obtained increases with the number of tasks. When two or more tasks were executed the quality measure, γ, achieved 100 % for every n.

4.2. Simultaneous periodically interacting searches

As before, we assume that p identical processors are available and generate their own sequential annealing sequences. In this case, however, the processors interact with each other every s steps passing their best solutions found so far.

a) $p = 2$

n	Opt.	Best	Avg.	σ	γ	H
40	819.0	819.0	822.0	9.18	100.00	73
50	982.2	982.2	986.1	11.79	100.00	59
60	1173.4	1173.4	1176.7	7.58	100.00	8
70	1364.7	1364.7	1370.5	6.52	100.00	12
80	1502.9	1502.9	1508.7	6.38	100.00	7
90	1691.1	1691.1	1698.5	5.81	100.00	7
100	1835.4	1835.4	1842.7	4.16	100.00	1

b) $p = 3$

n	Opt.	Best	Avg.	σ	γ	H
40	819.0	819.0	819.4	1.41	100.00	85
50	982.2	982.2	983.5	5.66	100.00	79
60	1173.4	1173.4	1176.1	11.29	100.00	10
70	1364.7	1364.7	1370.2	11.95	100.00	15
80	1502.9	1502.9	1507.4	4.88	100.00	16
90	1691.1	1691.1	1696.6	4.54	100.00	11
100	1835.4	1835.4	1842.2	3.98	100.00	1

c) $p = 4$

n	Opt.	Best	Avg.	σ	γ	H
40	819.0	819.0	820.3	5.14	100.00	82
50	982.2	982.2	983.4	4.70	100.00	75
60	1173.4	1173.4	1175.6	8.97	100.00	14
70	1364.7	1364.7	1368.0	4.43	100.00	26
80	1502.9	1502.9	1505.8	3.04	100.00	21
90	1691.1	1691.1	1696.3	5.51	100.00	7
100	1835.4	1835.4	1841.2	4.02	100.00	1

d) $p = 5$

n	Opt.	Best	Avg.	σ	γ	H
40	819.0	819.0	819.7	3.49	100.00	91
50	982.2	982.2	983.0	2.99	100.00	82
60	1173.4	1173.4	1175.1	5.69	100.00	20
70	1364.7	1364.7	1367.5	4.18	100.00	22
80	1502.9	1502.9	1506.2	6.48	100.00	21
90	1691.1	1691.1	1696.3	4.18	100.00	13
100	1835.4	1835.4	1841.0	5.34	100.00	2

Table 2. Performance of the simultaneous independent searches for $p = 2 \,..\, 5$ tasks.

Suppose for a moment that the temperature T is fixed. Let $X_r^{(j)}(T)$, $j = 1, 2, \ldots, p$, $r = 1, 2, \ldots$ be the Markov chains for each of the processors, let $\mathcal{P}_T(X)$ be the realization of one step of the chain at temperature T and with starting point X, and let $\bar{X}_r^{(j)}$ be the best solutions found by processors $j = 1, 2, \ldots, p$ so far, i.e. between step 1 and r. We assume the following scheme of interaction:

$$\begin{aligned}
X_{r+1}^{(1)} &= \mathcal{P}_T(X_r^{(1)}),\\
X_{r+1}^{(j)} &= \mathcal{P}_T(X_r^{(j)}) \text{ for } j \neq 1, \text{ and if } r+1 \neq is,\\
X_{is}^{(j)} &= \mathcal{P}_T(X_{is-1}^{(j)}) \text{ if } cost(\mathcal{P}_T(X_{is-1}^{(j)})) \leq \\
& \quad cost(\bar{X}_{is}^{(j-1)}),\\
X_{is}^{(j)} &= \bar{X}_{is}^{(j-1)} \text{ otherwise.}
\end{aligned}$$

In this scheme the processors interact at steps is, $i = 1, 2, \ldots$ where each step consists in a single realization of the Markov chain. The chain for the first processor ($j = 1$) is completely independent. The chain for the second processor is updated at steps is to the better solution between the best solution found by the first processor, $\bar{X}_{is}^{(1)}$, and the realization of the last step of the second processor, $\mathcal{P}_T(X_{is-1}^{(2)})$. Similarly, the third processor chooses as the next point in its chain the better solution between $\bar{X}_{is}^{(2)}$ and $\mathcal{P}_T(X_{is-1}^{(3)})$. Clearly, the best solution found by the l-th processor is propagated for further exploration to processes m, $m > l$.

Now note that the temperature of annealing decreases according to the formula $T_{i+1} = T_i \cdot \alpha$ for $i = 0, 1, 2, \ldots$ There are two possibilities in establishing the points in which the temperature drops and the processors interact. Namely, we may assume that the processors interact frequently during each of the temperature plateaus, or that the temperature drops several times before an interaction takes place. In this paper the former approach is adopted.

The simultaneous periodically interacting searches algorithm written for a CREW PRAM model is shown below. The computations are similar to those in the simultaneous independent searches algorithm. However now the tasks interact every n steps in order to pass their best solutions.

The worst case time complexity of the algorithm is $\mathcal{T}_p(n) \leq a(n^2 + (p-1)n^2 + p)$. As compared to the previous algorithm the complexity is higher by a cost of communication. At each execution of the **repeat** statement there are n points of communication (cf. lines 12–21). The cost of a single communication is proportionate to $(p-1)n$, as $p-1$ messages of lenght $O(n)$ are sent and received.

Simultaneous periodically interacting searches

```
1   parfor P_j, j = 1, 2, ..., p do
2     if j = 1 then
3       Create an initial, best_solution as the set of
          random routes of size 3;
4       equilibrium_counter := 0; {set the equilibrium
          counter}
5       T := cost(best_solution)/1000; {initial
          temperature of annealing}
6     end if;
7     old_solution_j := best_solution;
8     best_local_solution_j := best_solution;
9     repeat;
10      for iteration_counter_j := 1 to n^2 do
11        annealing_step(old_solution_j,
            best_local_solution_j); {as in the sequential
            algorithm}
12        if number of annealing steps executed so far
            is a multiplicity of n then {interact}
13          if j = 1 then send best_local_solution_1 to
              processor P_2;
14          else {j > 1}
15            receive best_local_solution_{j-1} from
                processor P_{j-1};
16            if cost(best_local_solution_{j-1}) <
                cost(best_local_solution_j) then
17              best_local_solution_j :=
                  best_local_solution_{j-1};
18            end if;
19            if j < p then send best_local_solution_j
                to process P_{j+1}; end if;
20          end if;
21        end if;
22      end for;
23      lock(best_solution); lock(equilibrium_counter);
24      if cost(best_local_solution_j) <
          cost(best_solution) then
25        best_solution := best_local_solution_j;
26        equilibrium_counter := 0;
27      end if;
28      unlock(best_solution);
29      unlock(equilibrium_counter);
30      if j = 1 then
31        T := T · α; {temperature reduction}
32        equilibrium_counter :=
            equilibrium_counter + 1;
33      end if;
34    until equilibrium_counter > 20;
35  end for;
```

The simultaneous periodically interacting searches algorithm was implemented in Ada95 and ran for $p = 2..5$ tasks. The test results of 100 executions of the concurrent algorithm are shown in Table 3.

It can be seen that the simultaneous periodically interacting searches algorithm for $p \geq 4$ gives lower number of hits into the minimum for $n = 40 .. 80$ and higher number of hits for $n = 90 .. 100$ (Table 3) as compared to the corresponding values for the simultaneous independent searches algorithm (Table 2). Thus we conclude that the interaction of tasks improve the search in larger solution spaces.

In [3] C. Graffigne investigated a slightly different scheme of simultaneous periodically interacting searches. She conjectured that under some assumptions there is no need to add interaction between processors before last interaction. Her conjecture was supported by some experimental observations. The results from Table 3 show that this conjecture does not hold for our scheme of interaction.

5. Conclusions

As compared to the sequential algorithm the application of parallelism increases the quality of obtained solutions to the DP. For number of tasks $p \geq 3$ both the simultaneous independent searches and the simultaneous periodically interacting searches achieved the maximum quality measure $\gamma = 100\%$. This means that for 100 executions of the algorithms the optimum solutions to the DP was found at least once. The experimental results show that the simultaneous periodically interacting searches exhibit better performance in terms of finding the optimum solution for larger solution spaces comparing with the simultaneous independent searches.

References

[1] E. H. L. Aarts and J. H. M. Korst. *Simulated Annealing and Boltzmann Machines*. J. Wiley, Chichester, 1989.

[2] E. H. L. Aarts and P. J. M. van Laarhoven. *Simulated Annealing: Theory and Applications*. J. Wiley, New York, 1987.

[3] R. Azencott. Parallel simulated annealing: An overview of basic techniques. In R. Azencott, editor, *Simulated annealing. Parallelization Techniques*, pages 37–46. J. Wiley, New York, 1992.

[4] R. Azencott and C. Graffigne. Parallel annealing by periodically interacting multiple searches: Acceleration rates. In R. Azencott, editor, *Simulated Annealing. Parallelization Techniques*, pages 81–90. J. Wiley, New York, 1992.

[5] N. Boissin and J. L. Lutton. A parallel simulated annealing algorithm. *Parallel Computing*, 19:859–872, 1993.

[6] S. Cichoński. An application of simulated annealing to the set-partitioning problem. Technical report, Silesia University of Technology, 1998. (in print).

[7] V. Cĕrny. A thermodynamical approach to the travelling salesman problem: an efficient simulation algorithm. *J. of Optimization Theory and Applic.*, 45:41–55, 1985.

[8] F. Glover and M. Laguna. Tabu search. In C. R. Reeves, editor, *Modern Heuristic Techniques for Combinatorial Problems*, pages 70–150. McGraw-Hill, London, 1995.

a) $p = 2$

n	Opt.	Best	Avg.	σ	γ	H
40	819.0	819.0	821.6	7.35	100.00	67
50	982.2	982.2	986.5	11.33	100.00	57
60	1173.4	1173.4	1181.1	18.55	100.00	7
70	1364.7	1364.7	1374.1	20.44	100.00	14
80	1502.9	1502.9	1508.3	7.77	100.00	17
90	1691.1	1693.5	1708.3	8.77	100.15	0
100	1835.4	1839.1	1857.7	10.61	100.21	0

b) $p = 3$

n	Opt.	Best	Avg.	σ	γ	H
40	819.0	819.0	821.3	6.46	100.00	70
50	982.2	982.2	987.1	10.20	100.00	65
60	1173.4	1173.4	1178.4	15.53	100.00	13
70	1364.7	1364.7	1375.4	28.16	100.00	16
80	1502.9	1502.9	1508.8	9.46	100.00	22
90	1691.1	1691.1	1699.1	10.35	100.00	7
100	1835.4	1835.4	1845.9	16.34	100.00	1

c) $p = 4$

n	Opt.	Best	Avg.	σ	γ	H
40	819.0	819.0	822.6	9.17	100.00	62
50	982.2	982.2	986.8	12.89	100.00	64
60	1173.4	1173.4	1177.0	10.20	100.00	16
70	1364.7	1364.7	1370.6	10.59	100.00	22
80	1502.9	1502.9	1510.2	27.47	100.00	26
90	1691.1	1692.3	1697.6	7.90	100.00	10
100	1835.4	1835.4	1842.7	13.24	100.00	8

d) $p = 5$

n	Opt.	Best	Avg.	σ	γ	H
40	819.0	819.0	822.1	8.51	100.00	71
50	982.2	982.2	988.0	15.97	100.00	69
60	1173.4	1173.4	1176.8	9.68	100.00	17
70	1364.7	1364.7	1374.0	22.83	100.00	28
80	1502.9	1502.9	1509.0	13.14	100.00	20
90	1691.1	1691.1	1697.2	8.38	100.00	16
100	1835.4	1835.4	1843.4	13.29	100.00	7

Table 3. Performance of the simultaneous periodically interacting searches for $p = 2 .. 5$ tasks.

[9] C. Graffigne. Parallel annealing by periodically interacting multiple searches: An experimental study. In R. Azencott, editor, *Simulated Annealing. Parallelization Techniques*, pages 47–79. J. Wiley, New York, 1992.
[10] D. R. Greening. Parallel simulated annealing techniques. *Physica D*, 42:293–306, 1990.
[11] S. Kirkpatrick, C. D. Gellat, and M. P. Vecchi. Optimization by simulated annealing. *Science*, 220:671–680, 1983.
[12] R. Korf. Optimal path-finding algorithms. In L. Kanal and V. Kumar, editors, *Search in Artificial Intelligence*, pages 223–267. Springer-Verlag, 1988.
[13] N. Metropolis, A. W. Rosenbluth, M. N. Rosenbluth, A. H. Teller, and E. Teller. Equation of state calculation by fast computing machines. *Journ. of Chem. Phys.*, 21:1087–1091, 1953.
[14] J. Pearl. *Heuristics. Intelligent Search Strategies for Computer Problem Solving*. Addison-Wesley, Reading, Mass., 1984.
[15] C. R. Reeves, editor. *Modern Heuristic Techniques for Combinatorial Problems*. McGraw-Hill, London, 1995.
[16] M. M. Syslo, N. Deo, and J. S. Kowalik. *Discrete optimization algorithms with Pascal programs*. Prentice-Hall, 1983.
[17] M. G. A. Verhoeven and E. H. L. Aarts. Parallel local search techniques. *Journal of Heuristics*, 1:43–65, 1996.

2-D Wavelet Packet Decomposition on Multicomputers

Manfred Feil Andreas Uhl
RIST++ & Department of Scientific Computing
University of Salzburg, AUSTRIA
e-mail: {mfeil,uhl}@cosy.sbg.ac.at

Abstract

In this work we describe and analyze algorithms for 2-D wavelet packet decomposition for MIMD distributed memory architectures. The main goal is the generalization of former parallel WP algorithms which are constrained to a number of processor elements equal to a power of 4. We discuss several optimizations and generalizations of data parallel message passing algorithms and finally compare the results obtained on a Cray T3D.

1. Introduction

Wavelet packets [25] represent a generalization of the method of multiresolution decomposition and comprise the entire family of subband coded (tree) decompositions. Whereas in the wavelet case the decomposition is applied recursively to the coarse scale approximations (leading to the well known (pyramidal) wavelet decomposition tree), in the wavelet packet decomposition the recursive procedure is applied to all the coarse scale approximations and detail signals, which leads to a complete wavelet packet tree (i.e. binary tree and quadtree in the 1D and 2D case, respectively) and more flexibility in frequency resolution.

There are several possibilities how to determine the frequency subbands suited well for an application (the meaning of *suitable* depends on the type of application, e.g. signal/image compression [25], classification algorithms [18], etc.). The wavelet packet "best basis algorithm" [3] performs an adaptive optimization of the frequency resolution of a complete wavelet packet decomposition tree by selecting the most suitable frequency subbands for signal compression. The same algorithm employed with non-additive cost function is denoted "near-best basis algorithm" [21], if the subband structure is restricted to uniform time-frequency resolution the corresponding algorithm is denoted "best level selection" [25].

In the context of image compression a more advanced technique is to use a framework that includes both rate and distortion, where the best basis subtree which minimizes the global distortion for a given coding budget is searched [16]. Other methods use fixed bases of subbands for similar signals (e.g. fingerprints[11]) or search for good representations with genetic optimization methods [2, 1]. Recently, wavelet packet based compression methods have been developed [27, 12] which outperform the most advanced wavelet coders (e.g. SPIHT [17]) significantly for textured images in terms of rate-distortion performance. Therefore, wavelet packet decomposition currently attracts much attention and a thorough examination of parallelization possibilities is desirable.

Whereas a significant amount of work has been already done concerning parallel algorithms for the fast wavelet transform, only few papers have been devoted to parallel wavelet packet decomposition and its specific features and demands (e.g. subband based approaches for performing the best basis algorithm and the irregular decomposition into such a basis on parallel MIMD [8, 23, 24, 6] and SIMD [5] architectures, parallel wavelet packet decomposition in numerics [4] and corresponding applications [13, 14, 15, 10, 9]).

In this work we describe and analyze subband based algorithms for 2-D wavelet packet decomposition. It should be noted that the successive computation and availability of all frequency subbands of all decomposition levels is a must for all kinds of adaptive image processing applications. We base our implementations on algorithms described in [8, 6, 7] and focus on the generalization of these algorithms with regard to the number of used processor elements (PEs). Due to the subband structure inherent in 2-D WP decomposition (leading to 4^j frequency subbands at decomposition level j) former subband based algorithms are restricted to a number of PEs equal to a power of 4. We present first a more general version for processor fields of the size of a power of 2 and finally an algorithm for an arbitrary number of PEs. In the last section we analyze the results obtained on a Cray T3D in consideration of the used method of boundary treatment (zero padding vs. N-point symmetry).

2. The sequential WP algorithm

In this and the following sections we use a notation introduced in [8]. Suppose we have a two-dimensional signal $S = (n_{k,l})$ with size $0 \leq k < 2^{Xmax}$ and $0 \leq l < 2^{Ymax}$.

We begin our calculation with the initial subband ${}^0C^0_{k,l} = n_{k,l}$ and filter coefficients F and define every other subband recursively by the formula:

$$ {}^{4f_j+d}C^{j+1}_{k_{j+1},l_{j+1}} = \sum_{n_j,m_j} F(d, f_j)_{n_j-2k_{j+1},m_j-2l_{j+1}} * {}^{f_j}C^j_{n_j,m_j} $$

with the indices in the range:

$0 \leq j < jmax =$		$min(Xmax, Ymax)$
	...	last calculated level
$0 \leq f_j < 4^j$	...	index of subband in use
$0 \leq d < 4$	...	index of filter in use
$0 \leq n, m < filter\_length$	...	indices of filter coefficient
$0 \leq k_{j+1} < 2^{Xmax-(j+1)}$	...	coordinate of data-point in x-direction
$0 \leq l_{j+1} < 2^{Ymax-(j+1)}$	...	coordinate of data-point in y-direction

From a one-dimensional wavelet Ψ (defined by its filter g_n) and its smoothing function Φ (defined by its filter h_n) we obtain four two-dimensional filters by tensor products: $F(0)_{n,m} = h_n * h_m$, $F(1)_{n,m} = h_n * g_m$, $F(2)_{n,m} = g_n * h_m$, and $F(3)_{n,m} = g_n * g_m$. Simplifying, we may say that convolving the coefficients of a subband C^j at level j with 4 different filters $F(0) \ldots F(3)$ we obtain 4 subbands C^{j+1} at level $j+1$.

Fig.1 shows the data arrangement for levels $j = 0 \ldots 2$: at level j we get 4^j subbands, each with 2^{Xmax-j} by 2^{Ymax-j} coefficients.

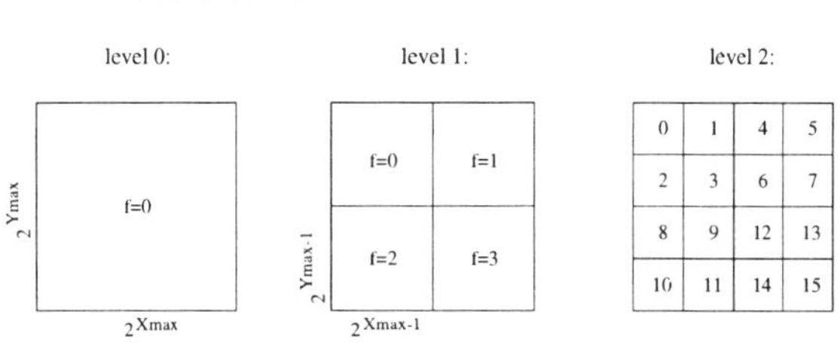

Figure 1. Data arrangement and labeling for a 2D wavelet packet decomposition

Further we have p PEs, on which we want to compute the two-dimensional wavelet packet decomposition of signal S in parallel.

3. WP Algorithms for MIMD architectures

In this section we discuss parallel algorithms for the two-dimensional periodic wavelet packet transform. The proposed algorithms assume that the size of PE memory is sufficient to keep the wavelet packet coefficients of all levels. For machines or applications which do not meet this condition a specific technique has been derived for parallel decomposition into any given basis [24].

The main difficulty of the development of a parallel WP implementation is the choice of an appropriate data distribution strategy that ensures a well balanced dispersion of the computational work. In the following subsections we show the most efficient strategies for architecture settings with:

- a number of PEs equal to a power of 4.
- a number of PEs equal to a power of 2.
- an arbitrary number of PEs.

For all of the following algorithms, two methods of handling the border data ($filter\_length$ coefficients of the neighbour PE are required to compute a single output coefficient at the border) can be used[26, 20]:

- *data swapping:* each PE computes only non-redundant data and exchanges these results with the appropriate neighbour PEs in order to get the necessary data for the next calculation step (i.e. the next decomposition level).
- *redundant data calculation:* in the initialisation step we do not only provide its share of the original signal to a PE but provide the entire data set to each PE which is required to compute also redundant data in order to avoid additional communication with neighbour PEs to obtain the border data.

In first experiments on the Cray T3D we found the redundant data calculation approach to be not competitive at all for this specific machine which is true also for different architectures[6], so we carried on our developments using the data swapping method. However, all the following algorithms are easily adapted to the second border treatment method if the architecture in question should require it.

3.1. WP algorithm for $p = 4^{jp}$

The most natural way to distribute the computational work of a WP transform can be found on an MIMD architecture with a number of PEs of a power of 4: we separate each level into 4^{jp} parts of equal size $2^{Xmax-jp}$ by $2^{Ymax-jp}$ and use the decomposition formula in two different ways depending upon whether level j is smaller or larger then jp. If $j < jp$, a subband at frequency f is not assigned to a single PE but is shared by PEs $p = 4^{jp-j} * f$ to $p = 4^{jp-j} * (f+1) - 1$. Therefore, in the initialisation step those 4^{jp-j} PEs will exchange their data in order to have the entire shared subband on each of them. Then, in the second step, they will calculate their own part of the subband they share at level $j+1$. If $j \geq jp$ each PE has 4^{j-jp} subbands and holds also the four children of each of them. Thus, no communication among PEs is needed and we will use the sequential algorithm on the subset of subbands each PE carries at level j. The overall communication amount is $O\left(\sum_{j=1}^{a-1} 2^{Xmax-a} * 2^{Ymax-a} * (4^{a-j}-1) * 4^{a-j} * 4^{j}\right)$.

In fig.2(a) we show the distribution of level 1 among 4 PEs. Now the entire output-subband resides on each PE; therefore, for the computation of the following levels no more communication is needed.

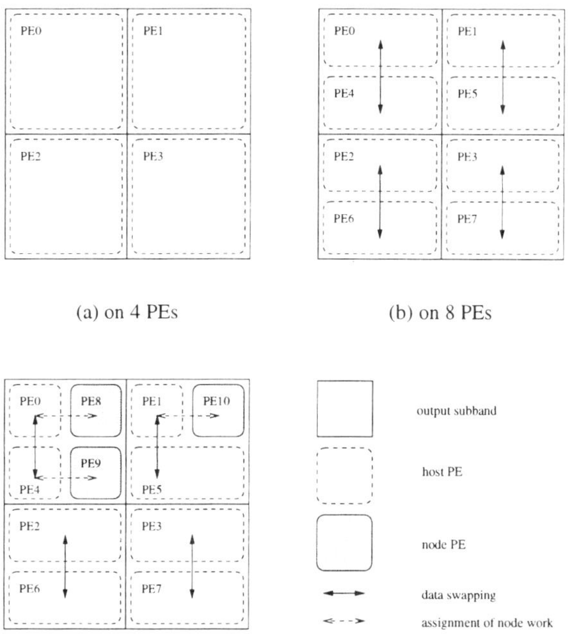

(a) on 4 PEs

(b) on 8 PEs

(c) on 11 PEs

Figure 2. Distribution of level 1

3.2. WP algorithm for $p = 2^{jp}$

The first generalization of the former algorithm deals with architectures where the number of PEs is a power of 2. For this case the algorithm does not need major changes, because without loss of generality we can assume that the computational work of two neighbouring PEs in a $p = 2^{jp} (jp = 2 * n, n \in \mathbf{N})$ setting is merged into one if $p = 2^{jp-1}$ PEs are used. For this number of processors we get a rectangular partitioning of data $(2^{Xmax-\lceil \frac{jp}{2} \rceil}$ by $2^{Ymax-\lfloor \frac{jp}{2} \rfloor})$ and an unequal number of communications in horizontal and vertical direction. The overall communication amount is

$$O\Big(\sum_{j=1}^{\lceil \frac{a}{2} \rceil - 1} 2^{Xmax-\lfloor \frac{a}{2} \rfloor} * 2^{Ymax-\lceil \frac{a}{2} \rceil} * (2^{a-2j}-1) * 2^{a-2j} * 2^{j}\Big)$$

Fig.2(b) shows the data distribution of level 1 among 8 PEs. For the computation of the next level, communication only between two vertical neighbours (arrows in the figure) is required.

3.3. WP algorithm for arbitrary p

The main contribution of this work is the development of a parallel WP algorithm which uses an arbitrary number of PEs.

To deal with the problem of how to integrate the PEs $2^{\lfloor \log p \rfloor} \leq i < p$ into the former setting of $2^{\lfloor \log p \rfloor}$ PEs i.e. to avoid the need of handling with fractions of subbands (which would introduce a huge amount of additional communication) we employ a variant of the well known "host-node" principle: PEs $0 < i \leq 2^{\lfloor \log p \rfloor}$, from now on denoted the "hosts", compute their part of the WP transform as described in the last subsection. Each other PE $(2^{\lfloor \log p \rfloor} \leq i < p)$, the "node", is assigned to a host and both share the computational work of one level: the node receives the input subband from its host, computes one half of the required subbands and sends the output back (see fig.2(c)).

The most important task is now to find a node assignment strategy which takes into account several points. These conditions are important to keep communication demand as small as possible:

- to avoid splitting of subbands or decomposition levels the nodes should change to a new host only at the beginning of a new level, and one node should be assigned to one host only and vice versa.
- the nodes should change their hosts as often as possible in order to distribute the computational work uniformly.
- the nodes should change their hosts as rare as possible in order to avoid exaggerating communication for sending the input data to the nodes resp. the output data back to the hosts.

After testing different strategies we found the following assignment scheme the most suitable one:

Let p be the number of processors. We divide now the processor pool in $h = 2^{\lfloor \log p \rfloor}$ hosts and $n = p - h$ nodes and compute for host h_i $(0 \leq i < h)$ the node assignment scheme for level j $(0 \leq j < jmax = min(Xmax, Ymax))$ by the following algorithm (n_k $(0 \leq k < n)$ is the node assigned to this host):

```
j=1; k=i
while (j<jmax) loop
  if (mod(k,m)<s) then
    assign node n_k to host h_i for THIS
      and the NEXT level
    j=j+2; k=k+1
  else
    no node for host for THIS level
    j=j+1; k=k+1
  end if
end loop
```

To show this concept clearer we demonstrate as an example a 9 level WP transform (full decomposition of a 512*512 pixel image) on 7 PEs (4 hosts, 3 nodes):

		levels								
		1	2	3	4	5	6	7	8	9
hosts	h_0	n_0	n_0	n_1	n_1	n_2	n_2	-	n_0	n_0
	h_1	n_1	n_1	n_2	n_2	-	n_0	n_0	n_1	n_1
	h_2	n_2	n_2	-	n_0	n_0	n_1	n_1	n_2	n_2
	h_3	-	n_0	n_0	n_1	n_1	n_2	n_2	-	n_0

Note that the duplicate assignment of one node to more hosts (e.g. n_0 in level 2) is no contradiction to the demand of non-partitioning of subbands or levels: h_0 finishes level 1 and 2 because of the help of n_0 in the same time as h_3 needs just for the first level. The node n_0 adopts partial work of h_0 in the first 2 levels, then switches to h_3 and continues with level 2. Therefore the amount of idle time is reduced to a minimum for each PE.

The communication amount is given by the formula for the former algorithm plus the transfers for each additional node PE:

$$O\Big(\sum_{j=1}^{\lceil \frac{\lfloor \log p \rfloor}{2} \rceil - 1} 2^{Xmax - \lfloor \frac{\lfloor \log p \rfloor}{2} \rfloor} * 2^{Ymax - \lceil \frac{\lfloor \log p \rfloor}{2} \rceil} * (2^{\lfloor \log p \rfloor - 2j} - 1) * 2^{\lfloor \log p \rfloor - 2j} * 2^j + 2^{Xmax - \lfloor \frac{\lfloor \log p \rfloor - 1}{2} \rfloor} * 2^{Ymax - \lceil \frac{\lfloor \log p \rfloor}{2} \rceil} * jmax * (p - 2^{\lfloor \log p \rfloor}) \Big)$$

4. Experimental Results

Our practical experiments were run on a 512-PE Cray T3D situated at the Edinburgh Parallel Computing Centre (EPCC). Each PE consists of a DECchip 21064 Alpha processor (150MHz) with 64Mb of memory, and the system has a peak performance of 76.8 GFlops. As message passing interface we used CRI/EPCC MPI[19], a native implementation of the MPI 1.1 Standard for the Cray T3D.

First we want to analyze if our scheduling algorithm behaves in reality as predicted by the theory. We decompose an image of 512 by 512 pixels into 9 levels and illustrate the required time for each level and PE in fig.3 (the figure shows just the 4 host PEs; hosts supported by nodes are shaded). We use the Daubechies W20 filter (20 filter coefficients) and run the algorithm on 7 PEs (4 hosts and 3 nodes). To investigate the effect of different boundary treatments we employed two classical methods, "zero padding" (the input signal is extended with zeros beyond the border) and "N-point symmetry" (the input signal is repeated with a period of N)[22]. This is important because the success of our scheduling algorithm is based on the assumption that the computation of each level needs roughly the same time in order not to induce a node to wait for its next host.

Fig.3(a) shows the scheduling results for the "zero padding" and confirms exactly this problematic behaviour: the compiler recognizes the large amount of multiplications with zero in higher levels and optimizes this calculations which leads to smaller time consumption and less efficiency for node supported hosts. The "N-point symmetry" method (fig.3(b)) assures the same computational demand for every level. Therefore, the synchronization between hosts and nodes works as expected (hosts with support of a node need roughly half the time as unsupported ones) and the algorithm shows better scalability although the absolute computation time is significantly higher as compared to the "zero padding" algorithm. It should be noted that the "zero padding" approach leads to severe border artifacts in image processing applications whereas the "N-point symmetry" assures constant quality across the entire image.

In fig.4 we show speedup results for the parallel algorithms executed on 1 to 128 PEs. As mentioned before, the redundant data calculation approach does not reach any considerable performance and was therefore neglected in further developments. The "zero padding" and the "N-point symmetry" show a nearly linear speedup in the first PEs but break out in irregularity later because of the difficulty to integrate each additional node in an equally efficient assignment pattern. Nevertheless, the "N-point symmetry" features the better scalability.

Note the jumps in speedup at power of 2 (denoted in the plot as $\times$ and $*$) which originate from the absence of node PEs and the corresponding reduced communication. At 128

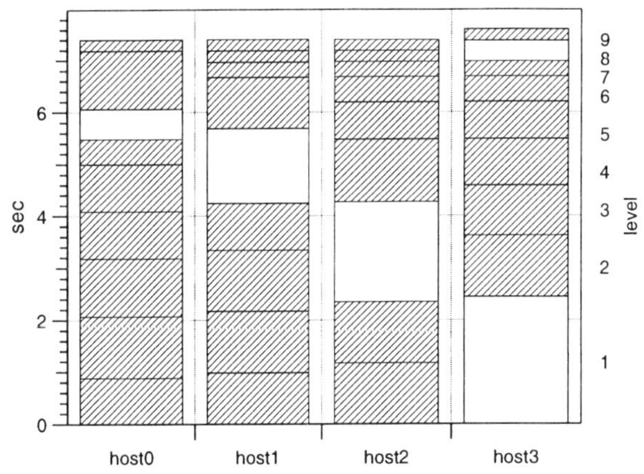

(a) using "zero padding"

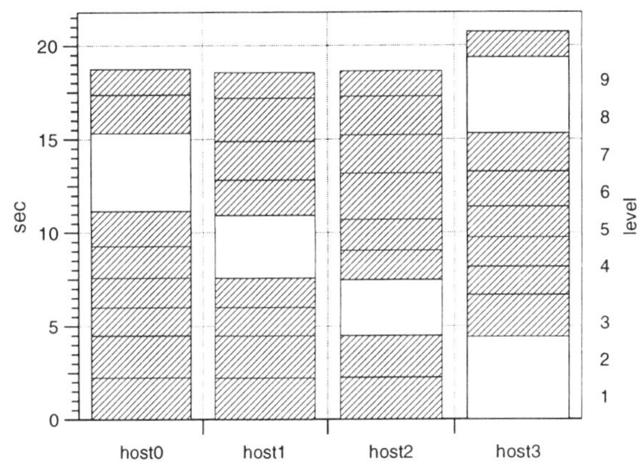

(b) using "N-point symmetry"

Figure 3. WP transform on Cray T3D (512*512 pixels, 9 levels)

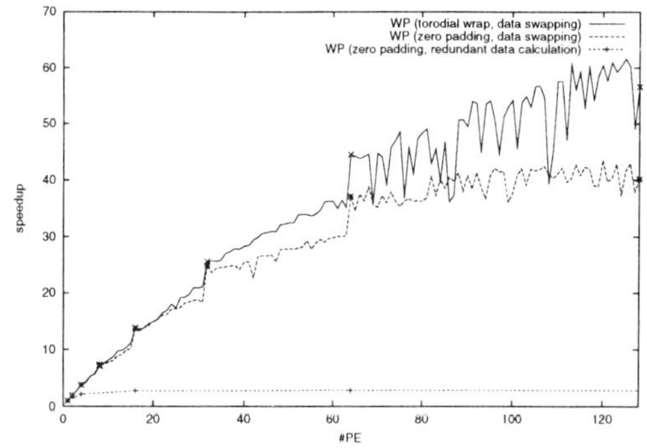

Figure 4. Speedup results on (512*512 pixels, 9 levels, W20 filter)

(=2^7) the expected jump is not exhibited in the plot because at deeper decomposition levels the advantage of exact subband-PE assignments is diminished by the higher communication demand. The obvious non-determinism in the plot for more than 64 PEs is a result of non-determinism in the operating system (e.g. different initialisation speed on different PEs).

5. Conclusion

In this study we presented a generalized parallel WP algorithm for MIMD architectures with an arbitrary number of processing elements. We showed that a satisfying performance can be obtained by employing the "host-node" principle. Further we pointed out the importance of the choice of the boundary treatment method.

Acknowledgements

The first author was partially supported by the Austrian Science Fund FWF, project no. P11045-ÖMA. Most of this work was accomplished in the course of a TRACS (Training and Research on Advanced Computing Systems) research visit at the Edinburgh Parallel Computing Centre (EPCC).

References

[1] A. Bruckmann, T. Schell, and A. Uhl. Evolving subband structures for wavelet packet based image compression using genetic algorithms with non-additive cost functions. In *Proceedings of the International Conference "Wavelets and Multiscale Methods" (IWC'98), Tangier, 1998.* INRIA, Rocquencourt, Apr. 1998. 4 pages.

[2] C. Chu. Genetic algorithm search of multiresolution tree with applications in data compression. In H. Szu, editor, *Wavelet Applications*, volume 2242 of *SPIE Proceedings*, pages 950–958, 1994.

[3] R. Coifman and M. Wickerhauser. Entropy based methods for best basis selection. *IEEE Transactions on Information Theory*, 38(2):719–746, 1992.

[4] S. Corsaro, L. D'Amore, and A. Murli. On the parallel implementation of the fast wavelet packet transform on MIMD distributed memory environments. In P. Zinterhof, M. Vajtersic, and A. Uhl, editors, *Parallel Computation. Proceedings of ACPC'99*, volume 1557 of *Lecture Notes on Computer Science*, pages 357–366. Springer-Verlag, 1999.

[5] M. Feil and A. Uhl. Wavelet packet decomposition and best basis selection on massively parallel SIMD arrays. In *Proceedings of the International Conference "Wavelets and Multiscale Methods" (IWC'98), Tangier, 1998.* INRIA, Rocquencourt, Apr. 1998. 4 pages.

[6] M. Feil and A. Uhl. Algorithms and programming paradigms for 2-D wavelet packet decomposition on multicomputers and multiprocessors. In P. Zinterhof, M. Vajtersic, and A. Uhl, editors, *Parallel Computation. Proceedings of ACPC'99*, volume 1557 of *Lecture Notes on Computer Science*, pages 367–376. Springer-Verlag, 1999.

[7] M. Feil and A. Uhl. Real-time image analysis using wavelets: the "à trous" algorithm on MIMD architectures. In D. Sinha, editor, *Real-Time Imaging IV*, volume 3645 of *SPIE Proceedings*, pages 56–65, 1999.

[8] E. Goirand, M. Wickerhauser, and M. Farge. A parallel two-dimensional wavelet packet transform and some applications in computing and compression analysis. In R. Motard and B. Joseph, editors, *Applications of Wavelet Transforms in Chemical Engineering*, pages 275–319. Kluwer Academic Publishers Group, 1995.

[9] C. Guerrini and D. Lazzaro. Parallel deconvolution and signal compression using adapted wavelet packet bases. In E. Hollander, G. Joubert, F. Peters, and D. Trystram, editors, *Parallel Computing: State of the Art and Perspectives*, volume 11, pages 617–624. 1996.

[10] C. Guerrini and M. Piraccini. Parallel wavelet-galerkin methods using adapted wavelet packet bases. In C. Chui and L. Schumaker, editors, *Approximation Theory VIII: Wavelets and Multilevel Approxiamtion*, pages 133–142. 1995.

[11] T. Hopper. Compression of gray-scale fingerprint images. In H. Szu, editor, *Wavelet Applications*, volume 2242 of *SPIE Proceedings*, pages 180–187, 1994.

[12] F. Meyer, A. Averbuch, J. Strömberg, and R. Coifman. Fast wavelet packet image compression. In *Proceedings Data Compression Conference (DCC'98)*, page 563. IEEE Computer Society Press, Mar. 1998.

[13] L. B. Montefusco. Parallel numerical algorithms with orthonormal wavelet packet bases. In C. Chui, L. Montefusco, and L. Puccio, editors, *Wavelets: Theory, Algorithms and Applications*, pages 459–494. Academic Press, San Diego, 1994.

[14] L. B. Montefusco. Semi-orthogonal wavelet packet bases for parallel least-squares approximation. *Journal of Computational and Applied Mathematics*, 73:191–208, 1996.

[15] L. B. Montefusco. Wavelet decomposition: a new tool for the construction of parallel algorithms. In E. Hollander, G. Joubert, and F. Peters, editors, *Parallel Computing: State-of-Art and Perspectives*, pages 383–390. Elsevier Science Publishers B.V., 1996.

[16] K. Ramchandran and M. Vetterli. Best wavelet packet bases in a rate-distortion sense. *IEEE Trans. on Image Process.*, 2(2):160–175, 1993.

[17] A. Said and W. Pearlman. A new, fast, and efficient image codec based on set partitioning in hierarchical trees. *IEEE Transactions on Circuits and Systems for Video Technology*, 6(3):243–249, 1996.

[18] N. Saito and R. Coifman. Local discriminant bases. In A. Laine and M. Unser, editors, *Wavelet Applications in Signal and Image Processing II*, volume 2303 of *SPIE Proceedings*, pages 2–14, 1994.

[19] T. M. S. G. Smith. *CRI/EPCC MPI for Cray T3D.* EPCC, May 1998. http://www.epcc.ed.ac.uk/t3dmpi/Product/index.html.

[20] S. Sullivan. Vector and parallel implementations of the wavelet transform. Technical report, Center for Supercomputing Research and Development, University of Illinois, Urbana, 1991.

[21] C. Taswell. Satisficing search algorithms for selecting near-best bases in adaptive tree-structured wavelet transforms. *IEEE Transactions on Signal Processing*, 44(10):2423–2438, 1996.

[22] C. Taswell and K. McGill. Wavelet transform algorithms for finite-duration discrete-time signals. *ACM Transactions on Mathematical Software*, 20(3):398–412, 1994.

[23] A. Uhl. Adapted wavelet analysis an moderate parallel distributed memory MIMD architectures. In A. Ferreira and J. Rolim, editors, *Parallel Algorithms for Irregulary Structured Problems*, volume 980 of *Lecture Notes in Computer Science*, pages 275–284. Springer, 1995.

[24] A. Uhl. Wavelet packet best basis selection on moderate parallel MIMD architectures. *Parallel Computing*, 22(1):149–158, 1996.

[25] M. Wickerhauser. *Adapted wavelet analysis from theory to software.* A.K. Peters, Wellesley, Mass., 1994.

[26] M.-L. Woo. Parallel discrete wavelet transform on the Paragon MIMD machine. In R. S. et al., editor, *Proceedings of the seventh SIAM conference on parallel processing for scientific computing*, pages 3–8, 1995.

[27] Z. Xiong, K. Ramchandran, and M. Orchard. Wavelet packet image coding using space-frequency quantization. *IEEE Transactions on Image Processing*, 7(6):892–898, June 1998.

Towards Efficient BSP Implementations of BSR Programs for some Computational Geometry Problems

Christophe Cérin
Université de Picardie Jules Verne
LaRIA, Bat Curi, 5 rue du moulin neuf
F-80000 Amiens - France
E-mail: cerin@laria.u-picardie.fr
Ph: (33)[0]322827875, Fax: (33)[0]322827502

Abstract

In this paper we present our investigations to implement some computational geometry problems (point in a polygon, intersection problem, convex hull) under the framework of BSR (Broadcasting with Selective Reduction) model of parallel computing, then under the framework of BSP (Bulk Synchronous Parallel model) programs. BSR is a (theoretical) model with the capabilities of PRAM models augmented with a broadcast mechanism. BSR offers concise notations that facilitates the specification part. BSP is suitable for concrete implementation because it also characterizes prediction in terms of a small set of machine parameters. So, instead of implementing in hardware the primitives of the BSR model we consider practical rules to translate BSR constructions into BSP ones. We also validate the discussion by translating BSR programs into BSP programs. We run them both on Silicon Graphics Origin2000 and on a Bi-Pentium 300MHz. The results encourage us to develop computational geometry problems starting from a BSR specification that is automatically translated into efficient BSP implementations. The results are pretty good and demonstrate that BSR can be used as a specification language which is implemented in software by BSP primitives.

Keywords: *foundations of parallel languages, broadcasting with selective reduction and bulk synchronous parallel models. Computational geometry parallel algorithms.*

1. Introduction and motivations

Many work has been done in the past to remedy the pitfalls (unitary communication cost versus long latency operations in used machines is the most frequently cited argument) of the PRAM (Parallel Random Access Memory) model of parallel computation. It is also required that a model should capture accurately the predicted performances of the machine for any algorithm to be executed on it. The PRAM model offered a rich framework for reasoning about the inherent parallelism of a problem and allowed to characterize problems for which poly-logarithmic (efficient) time solution can be obtained. It is also accepted that an efficient common global memory is not easy to build and not easy to scale for clusters of microprocessors. As a consequence a variety of alternative models have been proposed, each captures different aspects of "real" parallel machines. Among them, the promising BSP (Bulk Synchronous Parallel) model captures both communication latency and bandwidth through only two parameters. On the contrary, the BSR (Broadcast with Selective Reduction) model is derived from PRAM in the sense that it can be viewed as a PRAM equiped with a broadcast instruction. Under the same hypotheses about communication costs made for the PRAM, it offers a general framework in which many problems have constant time solutions and algorithms in the model are expressed with few symbols, in a concise way. Despite an attractive appearance, BSR has the default of not offering any implementation. In our work we propose to code BSR programs (corresponding to the problem to detect if a point is inside a polygon, the intersection of two polygons, the convex hull problem) into BSP pro-

1066-6192/99 $10.00 © 1999 IEEE

grams and we validate the approach by showing experimental results for these problems obtained on SGI Origin2000 and on a Bi-Pentium processor. Each implementation were developed with the BSP library from Oxford university and the Shared Memory `SysV` paradigm.
The organization of our work is as follows. In section 2 we introduce the BSR model and the BSP model through examples we code later in the paper. Section 3 introduce our transformation rules and our methodology. Section 4 is devoted to experimental results in order to validate our choices. Section 5 concludes the paper.

2. BSR and BSP models

2.1. BSR as a variant of a PRAM

Broadcasting with selective reduction (BSR) is a model of parallel computation introduced by Akl in [1]. It consists of n processors sharing m memory locations. The shared memory stores data and results and also serves as the communication medium for the processors. An interconnection unit (IU) allows the processors to gain access to the memory locations for the purpose of reading or writing. As in the PRAM (Parallel Random Access Machine) model, the BSR model is further specified by defining the mode of memory access (EREW: Exclusive read, exclusive write; CREW: concurrent read, exclusive write; CRCW: concurrent read, concurrent write). An additional type of memory access is permitted in BSR, namely a *broadcast* instruction by means of which all processors may gain access to all memory locations at the same time for the purpose of writing. Moreover, at each memory location, a subset of incoming broadcast data is *selected* and *reduced* to one value using a reduction operator (typically: min, max, prefix sum operations e.g. any arbitrary associative operator); this value is finally stored in the memory location.
The power an elegance of BSR were demonstrated by using it to obtain constant time solutions to a variety of problems including prefix sums, element uniqueness, sorting, maximal vectors, convex hull, measure of the union of a set of intervals, computing the Voronoi diagram, intersection of polygons, parenthesis matching, tree decoding and tree reconstruction from its traversals, the maximum sum subsegment ([2, 1, 3, 4, 5, 6, 7]). All of these algorithms have a constant execution time in the model! The number of processors is the only one parameter related to the input size and makes the originality of the model. Recently, Myoupo and Semé [8, 9] applied the BSR model for combinatoric problems on words and solved the maximum common subsequence of two sequences, the sequence alignment problem, the repetition of patterns. In [7], authors use the multi-criteria BSR variant for some computational geometry problems (which is not our point of view since we only use the elementary 1 criteria model); they provide a description of the circuitry implementing the multi-criteria paradigm but they do not provide any experimental results/implementations of their algorithms. Our work is the first paper to our knowledge about implementing parallel computational algorithms ([10, 11]) under the framework of BSR.
It is of particular interest to compare BSR with the PRAM. One important property of the PRAM is that in all of its variant, memory access is assumed to take constant time (this is part of the model). It is relevant that, in the literature, we do not take into consideration the mechanism necessary to provide such powerful capabilities. Consequently, all analysis of PRAM algorithms ignore both the size (e.g the gate number) of the interconnection unit linking processors to memory and the time required to gain access to an arbitrary memory location (both parameters are necessarily a function of the size of the memory). Results in [12] demonstrate that BSR requires no more resources asymptotically than the weakest variant of the PRAM (the EREW PRAM).

2.2. Notations for the BSR Model of Parallel Computation

A mathematical notation is used to describe the broadcast instruction. Let us define the following symbols:
n: the number of processors (numbered $1, \cdots, n$);
d_i: datum broadcast by p_i, $1 \leq i \leq n$;
σ: selection operation, taken from the following set $\{<, \leq, =, \geq, >, \neq\}$;
t_i: tab broadcast by p_i, $1 \leq i \leq n$ for criterion σ;
l_j: limit value broadcast by p_i, $1 \leq i \leq n$ for criterion σ;
$\mathfrak{R}$: binary associative reduction operation taken from the set $\{\sum, \prod, \wedge, \vee, \oplus, \cap, \cup\}$ denoting sum, product, and, or, xor, max and min respectively;
x_j: result of the broadcast instruction, $1 \leq j \leq n$;
The BSR broadcast instruction is denoted by:

$$x_j := \mathop{\mathfrak{R}}_{1 \leq i \leq n} d_i \mid t_i \sigma l_j, \text{ for } 1 \leq j \leq n$$

The semantics of the instruction is the following: memory locations x_j receive (in parallel for $1 \leq$

$j \leq n$) the single value obtained by the means of the binary associative operator $\mathfrak{R}$ applied to the set of all data "accepted"[1] by location x_j. We say that d_i is "accepted" by location x_j if $t_i \sigma l_j$ is satisfied. If no data is accepted then the value of x_j is not affected by $\mathfrak{R}$.

Examples: the all prefix sum problem is to compute $y_j = x_1 + x_2 + \cdots + x_j$ for $j = 1, 2, \cdots, n$. It can be done by the following broadcast operation: $y_j := \sum x_i \mid i \leq j$. A concurrent read operation (processor j wishes to read data x_j from processor p_j) can be done as follows: $y_i := \cap x_j \mid i = p_j$. Obviously the reduction operator has no matter in this special case. The effect of the next code is to store in y_j a count of the number of occurrences of the value of the jth input element among all inputs including itself: $y_j := \sum 1 \mid x_i = x_j$. The time of both algorithms is clearly in $\mathcal{O}(1)$ in the model.

2.2.1 Some computational geometry problems in BSR.

The three BSR programs we introduce now correspond to the straightforward implementations of basic "point/line properties". The advantage of BSR is that it allows to specify in a concise way properties of objects we deal with. Moreover, as we will see later in the paper it does not introduce severe penalties in the implementations.

Point in a polygon: To check if a point $P(x_p, y_y)$ which define a vertical line L_p is inside a polygon Q given by the array $Edge$ of his edges $e_i, 1 \leq i \leq n$, we simply write down the following BSR instruction:

$$R = \sum 1 | L_p \ intersects \ e_i \ above \ P$$

If R is odd then P is inside the polygon. The algorithm simply computes (in parallel) the intersection points between the vertical line L_p and the edges of Q (and return 1 if it is the case – then we add all the 1 values in the same broadcast instruction – then, if the sum is odd then the point is inside). The `intersects` operation corresponds to a straightforward trigonometric computation done in constant time and we does not exemplify it. Recall that the `intersects` operation in the current context is not part of the binary associative operators we deal in the model; it is simply a constant time testing (in order to select a point) operation. Two examples are given below to detect if $P(60, 26)$ is inside polygon of Figure 1 (left part) and to detect if $(59, 7)$ is inside polygon of Figure 1 (right part). In this case, 5 segments verify the criteria but not segment $(95, 6) - (1, 51)$: see Figure 1, left part again. On the right part of Figure 1 we see that P does not belong to the polygon.

[1] Sometimes, k criteria are used so select data; we say that we deal with a k-criteria BSR model.

Intersection of two polygons: Two polygons Q and R are said to *intersect* if an edge of Q crosses an edge of R. In the remainder of this paragraph, Q and R are given each by a array of size n of its edges. The BSR approach is based on a straightforward approach: for each edge of Q we determine whether it crosses one of the edges of R. According to the previous remark, a possibly BSR program is:

$s_i = \sum_{j=1}^{n} 1 | R_i \ intersects \ Q_j$
/* s_i = numb. of segment of Q that intersect R_i */
$T = \sum 1 | s_i > 0$
if $T > 0$ then printf("There is %d segments of R that intersect Q",T);

Once again, the `intersect` operation is done in constant time by the mean of a simple trigonometric computation.

Convex Hull: Given a set $S = \{p_1, p_2, \cdots, p_n\}$ of points in the plane, the *convex hull* of S, denoted $CH(S)$ is the smallest convex polygon that includes all the points of S. Many algorithms have been developed both for the sequential case [13, 14] and both the PRAM model of computation (see [15, 16, 17] for presentations of the main results). In [16], S. Akl provides some ideas of a BSR algorithm but the presentation is quite imprecise. We refine in deep the presentation here and we use only the "1-criteria" BSR. In [7], authors use the $k - criteria$ BSR to solve the problem.
Assume that the *extreme points* (the points with the maximal x coordinate, maximum y coordinate, minimum x coordinate and minimum y coordinate in S) have been determined as shown in Figure 2. We call these points $XMAX, YMAX, XMIN, YMIN$ respectively and we assume that no three points form a straight line. The fact that the extreme points are vertices of $CH(S)$ is obvious. Moreover we consider only points above line L defined by $XMIN$ and $XMAX$ (see Figure 2. To process with points below L it is sufficient to reverse the picture and to "apply" the algorithm that follows.

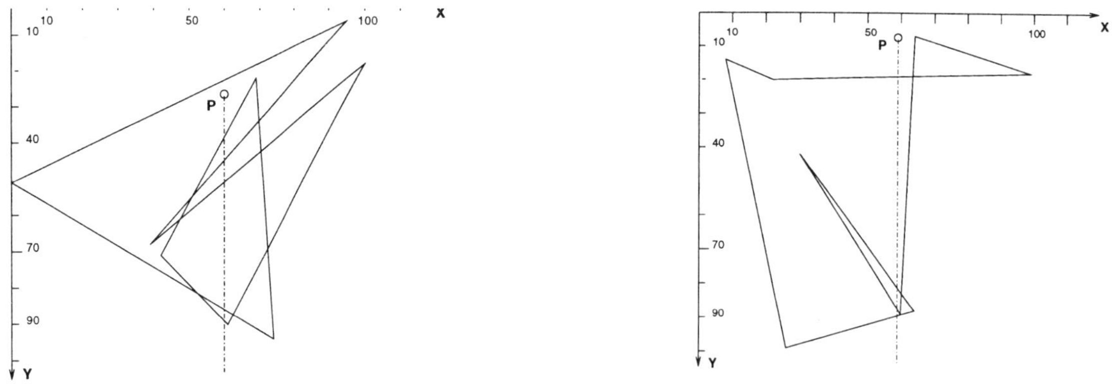

Figure 1. $P(60, 26)$ **is inside the left polygon.** $(59, 7)$ **is not! (right)**

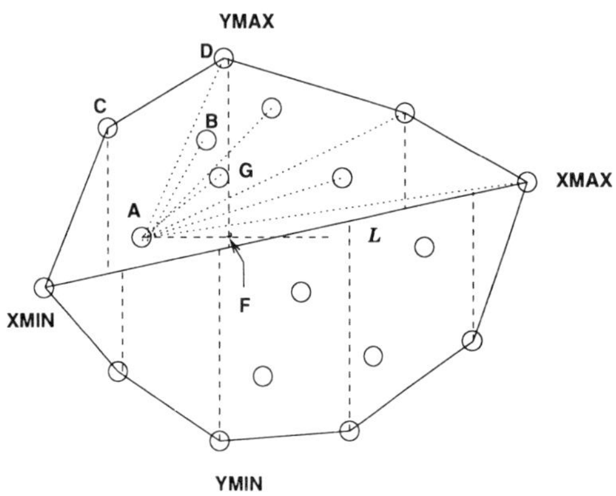

Figure 2. The convex hull of a set of points

Algorithm 1 *[BSR CONVEX HULL]*
Hypothesis: *no three points of S form a straight line*
Input: *set of n points stored in an array S*
Output: *the upper hull of S stored in array UH and the lower hull of S stored in array LH, both of size n*
Step 0: *Find points XMIN and XMAX. They define line L*
Step 1: *Divide S into $UH(S)$ (points above L) and $LH(S)$ (points below L)*
Step 2: *Sort the points by their x-coordinates.*
Step 3: *for each point q_i above L do*

- **(3.1)** *Among all points to the right of q_i, find the point q_j such that the line supporting the segment (q_i, q_j) forms the largest angle with the horizontal line that traverse q_i;.*
- **(3.2)** *Label all the points of S that fall below (q_i, q_j). (On Figure 2, take $q_i = A, q_j = D$ and consider also point F: the points B, G in the polygon defined by A, D, F should be labeled – note also that point A is itself labeled when we consider $q_i = C$);*

Step 4: *All unlabeled points form the upper hull;*
Step 5: *Consider $LH(S)$;Reverse the picture and redo steps 2,3,4 to find the lower hull.*

The different steps are implemented as follows: Step 0 is simply implemented by the following code:

$$XMIN = \bigcap S_i, XMAX = \bigcup S_i$$

Step 1 is implemented as follows:

$$UH_i = \vee S_i \mid S_i \text{ is above segment } XMIN, XMAX$$

$$LH_i = \vee S_i \mid S_i \text{ is below segment } XMIN, XMAX$$

with $\vee$ denoting the "set union" operation. Step 2 is going to be processing with the above BSR sorting algorithm. Step 3.1 is implemented as follows:

$$T1_i = \bigcup_{1 \le j \le n} \theta(UH_i, UH_j, XMIN, XMAX) \mid j > i$$

where θ is the predicate that return the angle between segment $(UH_i, UH_j$ and line $XMIN, XMAX$. In step 3.2 we label points that fall below (UH_i, UH_j):

$$T2_i = \sum_{1 \le j \le n} 1 \mid UH_q \in \text{polygon } (UH_i, T1_i, \text{XMIN,XMAX})$$

Step 4 is straightforward: it keeps unlabeled points from vector $T2$.

2.3. BSP: a concrete an efficient programming model

The *bulk synchronous parallel* model, introduced by Valiant [18] is a general-purpose model in which the properties of the parallel architectures are captured by four parameters: the number of processors p, the time to synchronize processors, l, the ability of a network to deliver messages under continuous traffic, g and the speed of the machine which can be ignored by expressing the other parameters in its units. The values of these parameters are obtained experimentally.

The BSP model can also be regarded as a generalization of the PRAM model and the ideal PRAM is obtained for $l = g = 1$ (unitary communication cost and no parallel slackness). For many interesting discussions about the validity of the model and the choice of parameters, see the following web list sites: `http://www.comlab.ox.ac.uk/oucl/groups/bsp` and `http://www.scs.carleton.ca/~palepu/BSP.html` for pertinent articles and discussions.

Note that we have experimented with a BSP impementation based on SHMEM for the Linux case and based on the efficient communication/synchronization primitives of the native machine for the Origin 2000. The reason is that the cost of synchronization, which by our best estimates can cause approximately a factor of 1,000 slowdown in the MPI (Message Passing Interface) implementation.

In BSP, programmers predict the run length of any computation in terms of the parameters defined above and they can rely on performance tools to automatically do the task. Thus, one advantage of BSP against some variants (CGM [19], LogP [20]) is that some librairies are available for a large platform number including cluster of PCs, and to effectively run BSP programs.

For the problem to decide if a point is inside a polygon, we quickly find that the time complexity of our algorithm is bounded by:

$$\lceil \log(n/p)+1 \rceil (10*n/p+g+l)+(n/p*g)+g+4l$$

We will compare this expected result with the practice later in the paper (see Figure 3). We notice for instance that our program has four synchronization primitives ($4l$ term) outside the main loop and iterate $\log(n/p)+1$ times.

3. Transformation rules

3.1. Methodology

In [3, 12] authors show how BSR can be optimally implemented "in hardware" according to a small set of combinational circuits. Recall that the main difference between BSR and PRAM is the availability of a *broadcast* instruction. It turns out that this instruction can be implemented in $\mathcal{O}(\mathcal{T}(n,m))$ time where $\mathcal{T}(n,m)$ is the time required for memory access in a PRAM having n processors and m memory locations. If $\mathcal{T}(n,m) = \mathcal{O}(1)$ as it is assumed in the PRAM, then algorithms on BSR run in constant time. Authors in [12] show how BSR can be implemented using an interconnection unit of size $\mathcal{O}(m \log m)$ for $n = \mathcal{O}(m)$. This is optimal in view of the $\Omega(m \log m)$ lower bound on the size of any interconnection unit connecting m processors to m memory locations [21].

In contrary, this paper deals with a software interface that implements in BSP terms BSR programs. In doing this, we view BSR as a specification language to express parallelism, and we consider BSP as a gateway between specification level and binary code.

In a first attempt, our methodology was to to translate one BSR instruction into a BSP function implementing the semantics of the BSR instructions. In doing this, a BSR program was translated into a "set" of sequential calls to BSP functions with an implicit synchronization point between each call. The BSR broadcast instruction was implemented by the following naive approach. Experimentally, we made the following decomposition assuming that we deal with $p < n$ processors and n, p are powers of 2: each processor received a chunk of the input data of size n/p, the processors reduced sequentially the problem by the means of some functions depending on the problem nature, then each processor passed the intermediate results to the next stage of a virtually binary tree of depth $\log p$ and p leaves. Thus the step number of iterations is bounded by $\log p$; internally, in each node the work is done sequentially (in linear or sometimes quadratic time complexity of n/p).

The methodology can exhibit some drawbacks. First of all, if the number of information we have to exchange between two processors at the end of the sequential reduction phase is not keep low (we mean below n/p), the cost of the associated communication becomes too important to obtain good performances. The right thing to do is to send few

short messages and preferably they should go directly to the final processor destination.
Precisely, our first methodology is convenient for the "point in a polygon problem" because in this case we only need to exchange between processors a constant number (1 at a time) of integers which represent the number of points that intersect the "sub-polygon" stored on the processor.
However, the previous methodology is not convenient for the implementation of the BSR program for sorting which is part of the convex hull implementation for the reasons we explained above: the rate of computation and communication is too important starting with the previous BSR sorting program. It turns out that we have implemented in BSP a new stable sorting based on the BSR specification.
The idea of the algorithm is also based on a technique referred as "sorting by regular sampling" [22]. All the discussion about theoretical arguments to explain why the "regular sampling" technique performs well in practice can be found in cited references above. The BSP implementation of sorting by regular sampling by Ronald Sujithan[2] is not *stable*. In contrary, our implementation is the first stable sorting implementation in BSP to our knowledge. A paper comparing different implementations and performance (from the point of view of time and cache utilization) of BSP sorting is going to be published and it can be obtained through the author.
So, a good methodology "verified" experimentally for many code we deal with is the following: initially, processor $i, 1 \leq i \leq p$ contains n/p data. Pick k pivots and broadcast them to the p processors in order to form $p * k$ partitions. Distribute data onto processor $j, 1 \leq j \leq p$) according to its partition number. Use an (optimal) sequential algorithm to solve the problem with your own partition(s).

4. Validating the transformation rules

Due to space requirement, we introduce now only one experimental result that enforce the validation of our approach. It is about the problem to decide if a point is inside a polygon; the other experiments reveal the same conclusions.
The codes were implemented on a Bi-Pentium 300Mhz, with a Linux multi-threaded kernel, and on the Silicon Graphics (SGI) Orign2000 available in Rouen (see `http://www.crihan.fr`), France. This machine is equiped with 64 processors (32 nodes with 2 processors), R10000 processors at 195Mz, $2 * 32ko$ primary cache, 4Mo of secondary cache, 1Go of RAM per node.

4.1. Point in a polygon

Figure 3 shows the results of our BSR-BSP implementation for the problem to decide if a point is inside a polygon on a Silicon Graphics Origin2000 configured as previously stated with estimated machine parameters values as follows: $p = 4, l = 1789, g = 20$. We observe good predictions. The small bias is possibly explained by the fact that the machine was shared with other jobs during our experiments (the workload was about 30%). Note that the x scale is a logarithmic scale! For instance on Figure 3, when we go from 64k points to 128k points (the point number is double), the extra computation time is only $0.065s$; that is to say 28% more important.
Both Figures 3 and 4 are obtained for codes that follow our first methodology approach (naive approach). On Figure 4, observed times include both the required time to broadcast initial data from processor 0 to others processors and the useful computation time along a "virtual binary tree". The curve on Figure 4 has two parts: for input sizes lower than 1Mb, the processor cache is not saturated because equation[3] $1M * 2 * 2 * 2 * sizeof(int)/16 < 4Mb$ holds; for input size greater than 1Mb previous equation does not hold i.e. the cache is saturated. However, in the range $[1M, 8M]$ we observe that doubling the input size increases the computation time by a factor of 35%-40%.
Figure 5 is about time performance of our algorithm developed according to our methodology we have refined in a previous section. We note that despite a workload of 70% comparing to 40% for the previous experiment and a processor number equals to 4 comparing to 16, the results are better by a factor of 5!

5. Conclusion

In this paper we presented our approach in order to translate BSR programs for three computational geometry problems into BSP programs. Comparing to the choice of re-developing a full parallel programming interface of BSR program according to a specific equipment, our approach reuses the

[2]see `http://www.comlab.ox.ac.uk/oucl/users/ronald.sujithan/`

[3]value $2 * 2 * 2 * sizeof(int)$ corresponds to the allocated memory size for one processor in our code

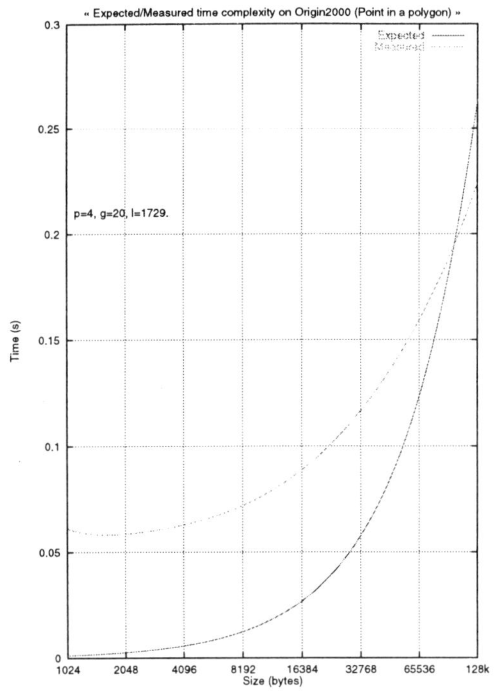

Figure 3. Expected and measured execution time for the problem to decide if a point is inside a polygon

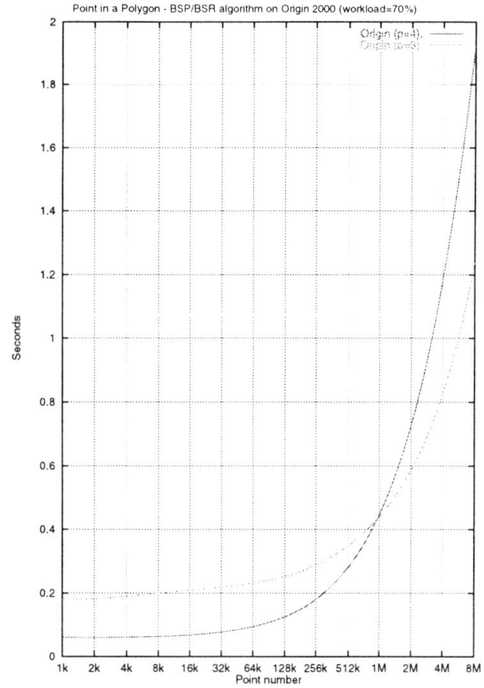

Figure 5. Execution time for the problem to decide if a point is inside a polygon (final approach)

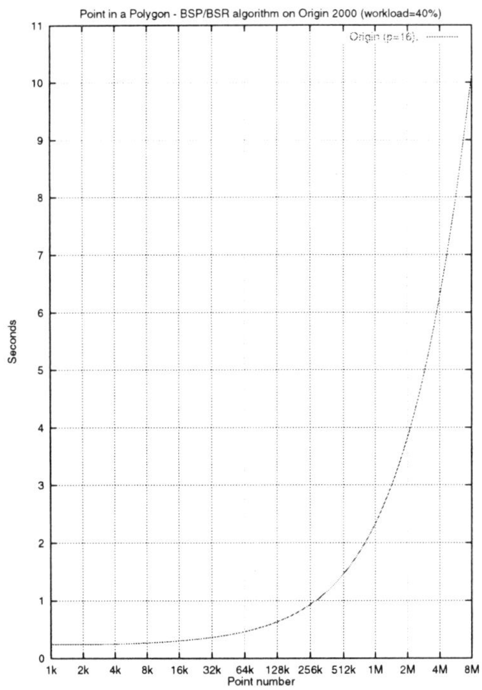

Figure 4. Execution time for the problem to decide if a point is inside a polygon (naive approach)

BSP framework which is known to provide efficient, easy to write programs and predictable results. Our work is the first attempt into a concrete coding of the very powerful, abstract and elegant parallel model namely BSR. We make the decision that BSR was used and will be used as a theoretical model, that is to say as a specification language and that BSP is a good candidate to implement the specification. The benchmarks demonstrate that our implementation choices do not provide important penalties in terms of execution time. Globally speaking our experiments are promising.

Another trial for further developments is related to an important problem in parallel software construction. It is named the *structure directed refinement* problem which is the ability to take into account the properties of the execution environment during the development of a parallel program. As it is accepted by the community, the broadcast and reduction operations can perform well or not depending of the exact processor number thus the necessity to tailor these primitives according to the equipment is inevitable. Before that, it is still necessary to augment the corpus of BSR/BSP computational geometry problems (25 BSR routines are currently available today) and to check if our methodology still performs well.

References

[1] Selim Akl and Grant R. Guenther, "Broadcasting with selective reduction", in *Information Processing*. Elsevier Science Publishers, 1989.

[2] Selim Akl, *The Design and Analysis of Parallel Algorithms*, Prentice Hall, 1989.

[3] Lorraine Fava-Lindon Selim Akl and Grant R. Guenther, "Broadcasting with selective reduction on an optimal pram circuit", *Technique et Science Informatiques*, 1991.

[4] Ivan Stojmenovic and S.G. Akl, "Multiple critera bsr: An implementation and applications to computational geometry problems", in *Proc. 27th Hawaii Int'l Conf. System Sciences*, Maui, Hawaii, Janvier 1994, vol. 2, pp. 159–168.

[5] Ivan Stojmenovic, "Constant time bsr solutions to parenthesis matching, tree decoding, and tree reconstruction from its traversals", *IEEE Transaction of Parallel and Distributed Systems*, vol. 7, no. 2, February 1996.

[6] Laurent Bergogne and Christophe Cérin, "Application of bsr model of computation for subsegment problems", in *Proceeding of 4th International Conference on High Performance Computing (HiPC'97)*, 1997, pp. 126–131.

[7] S.G. Akl and I. Stojmenovic, "Multiple criteria bsr: an implementation and applications to computational geometry problems", in *Proceedings of the Twenty-Seventh Annual Hawaii International Conference on System Sciences*, 1994.

[8] Jean-Frédéric Myoupo, *Parallélisme et répartition*, (coordinateur), Hermes, 1998.

[9] J.F. Myoupo and D. Semé, "Efficients parallel algorithms for the lis and lcs problems using the bsr model with a bounded number of selections", in *Intern. Symposium, of High Performance Computing, North Carolina*, 1998, oct.

[10] Atallah, "Parallel computational geometry", in *Parallel and Distributed Computing Handbook, McGraw-Hill, 1996*. 1996.

[11] M J Atallah and M.T. Goodrich, *Deterministic Parallel Computational Geometry*, In Synthesis of Parallel Algorithms, Morgan Kauffmann, 1991.

[12] Selim Akl and Lorraine Fava-Lindon, "An optimal implementation of broadcasting with selective reduction", *IEEE Transaction on Parallel and Distributed Systems*, 1993.

[13] R. L. Graham, "An efficient algorithm for determining the convex hull of a finite planar set", *Information Processing Letters*, vol. 1, no. 4, pp. 132–133, June 1972, See note [?].

[14] R. A. Jarvis, "On the identification of the convex hull of a finite set of points in the plane", *Information Processing Letters*, vol. 2, no. 1, pp. 18–21, Mar. 1973.

[15] Joseph Jájá, *Introduction to Parallel Algorithms*, Addison Wesley, 1992.

[16] Selim Akl, *Parallel Computation, Models and Methods*, Prentice Hall, 1997.

[17] Thomson F. Leighton, *Introduction to Parallel Algorithms and Architectures: Arrays, Trees, Hypercubes*, Morgan Kauffman Publishers, 1992.

[18] L.G. Valiant, "A bridging model for parallel computation", *Communiations of the ACM*, vol. 33, no. 8, august 1990.

[19] A. Fabri F. Dehne and A. Rau-Chaplin, "Scalable parallel computational geometry for coarse grained multicomputers", in *Proceeding ACM Symposium on Computational Geometry*, 1993, pp. 298–307.

[20] D. Culler R. Karp D. Patterson A. Sahay K.E. Schauser E. Santos R. Subramonian T. von Eicken, "Logp: Towards a realistic model of parallel computation", in *Proceeding 4th ACM SIGPLAN Symposium on Principles and Practices of Parallel Programming*, 1993, pp. 1–12.

[21] C. E. Shannon, "Memory requirements in a telephone exchange", *Bell Syst. Tech. J.*, 1950.

[22] Hanmao Shi and Jonathan Schaeffer, "Parallel sorting by regular sampling", *Journal of Parallel and Distributed Computing*, vol. 14, no. 4, pp. 361–372, 1992.

Short Presentations 4: Tools and Environments

Short Presentations 4: Tools & Environments
Session Chair: J. Bass

Welcome to this session of short presentations on tools and environments for the development of parallel and distributed software systems.

Approaches to the development of distributed software can be seen to lie on a continuum with two extremes. At one extreme is the use of some kind of distributed design methodology (i.e. a design method that does not impose a sequential solution) followed by elaboration of a distributed software implementation. At the other extreme are approaches that use sequential design methods (and possibly even legacy sequential implementations) from which distributed software can be extracted. This continuum can be seen to represent a tension between sequantial and distributed methods. Some researchers advocate producing distributed software from sequential language constructs (such as various flavours of high performance Fortran), where the distributed nature of the implementation is hidden from the programmer. However, this represents a very different paradigm from explicitly distributed design methods resulting in explicitly distributed implementations. The papers in this session describe novel and timely contributions to recent European research into distributed software development. These contributions are summarised below, not necessarily in the order they appear in the proceedings.

The paper by J. Cotronis ("Reusable Message Passing Components") considers an approach to the development of software using a run-time environment to communicate information from one processor to another. Message-passing environments such as PVM or MPI support the development of modules of sequential code that exchange data packets in the form of messages. Typically the architecture of such systems depends on a pre-determined communication topology. The approach proposed by J. Cotronis demonstrates the development of software modules that can be reused in different topological configurations.

The paper by C. di Napoli et al ("PVM Application-Level Tuning over ATM") also considers implements using message-passing run-time environments. Here the emphasis is on the underlying communication infrastructure, the efficiency of which has a dramatic effect on the performance of applications. In fact the authors show that careful selection PVM message-passing parameters (such as message fragment size) provide enhanced communication speeds when PVM executes over an ATM network.

In "A Performance Simulation Technique for Distributed Programs: Application to an SOR Iterative Solver", R. Aversa et al describes an approach to the performance prediction of message-passing systems. The approach uses static analysis of PVM code to reduce the time required to predict the performance of a PVM system. Thus, characterisation of the PVM system in terms of such parameters as CPU utilisation is available to the user.

The paper "Monitoriing and Debugging Message Passing Applications with MPVisualiser" by A P Claudio et al also assumes data exchange between software components using messages. In this paper, however, emphasis is on the analysis of an existing application. The visualisation tool comprises a trace/replay mechanism, a graphical user interface and a so-called visualisation engine.

The paper by N. Koziris et al ("An Efficient Algorithm for the Physical Mapping of Clustered Tasks Graphs onto Multiprocessor Architectures") presents a heuristic for mapping software in

1066-6192/99 $10.00 © 1999 IEEE

the form of task graphs onto hardware architectures. The "mapping problem" has been shown to be NP-Hard, precluding analytical solutions. Exhaustive search can be used to provide solutions for very small systems, or various forms of evolutionary computing (such as genetic algorithms or simulated annealing) have been advocated. In contrast, the heuristic proposed by N. Koziris et al first identifies a set of highly communicative tasks which are allocated to adjacent nodes in the multi-processor network. This set of highly communicative tasks forms what is described as a backbone, around which less communicative tasks in the system can be allocated to processors. The algorithm is presented which shows particularly favourable results where communications in the system a relatively balanced..

The work described in "Pipelining-based Tradeoffs for Hardware/Software Codesign of Multimedia Systems" by J. F. Perez Castellano et al is concerned with software development and hardware synthesis. In particular, the paper focusses on a tool for partitioning an abstract design into the hardware and software components. A novel approach using process-level pipelining is proposed.

A Performance Simulation Technique for Distributed Programs: Application to an SOR Iterative Solver *

R. Aversa[1], B. Di Martino[1], N. Mazzocca[1], U. Villano[2]
[1]Facoltà di Ingegneria - Dipartimento di Ingegneria dell' Informazione
Second University of Naples - Italy
[2]Facoltà di Ingegneria Informatica - Università del Sannio - Italy
{aversa,dimartin}@grid.unina.it, n.mazzocca@unina.it, villano@unisannio.it

Abstract

In this paper we present the application of an approach for the performance prediction of message passing programs, to a PVM code implementing an iterative solver based on the Successive OverRelaxation *method. The approach, based on the integration of static program analysis and simulation techniques, is aimed at significantly speeding up the time needed for simulating the execution of a message passing program.*

We show how the proposed technique can provide, in a reasonable elaboration time, the user for a characterization of iterative regular programs as the proposed one, in terms of idle-, cpu-, communication and synchronization time in Heterogeneous and Network Computing environments.

1 Introduction

Among the approaches to parallel software performance analysis and tuning, increasing interest are arousing techniques based on *Performance Prediction* [9], which, unlike dynamic evaluation techniques, do not require program execution on the target machine to deliver performance data. This can be particularly advantageous in the absence of the program or of the target computing environment. In the first case, performance prediction techniques make it possible to obtain an initial evaluation of partially implemented program designs (*prototype analysis*), for example if it is necessary to compare several possible algorithms and decompositions before writing any code. In the second case, it is possible to perform initial performance tuning even if the target architecture is not available at all (e.g., when it is still being implemented), or if its use is too expensive.

Performance prediction is usually based on static analysis or simulation techniques [9, 4]. The main disadvantage with static analysis techniques is the need for worst-case assumptions whenever programs characterized by irregular decompositions and data-dependent behaviour are being analyzed. These assumptions often turn out to be unrealistic. It should be noted that using of irregular decompositions is particularly usual in heterogeneous computing, since it is often the only way to get reasonable load balancing. As a consequence, even numerical algorithms which are notoriously data-independent and characterized by regular computing patterns, such as matrix-matrix multiply or fast Fourier Transform, may turn out to be hardly tractable by static analysis [15].

Previous research in this field has shown that a viable solution to some of the problems linked to the used of heterogeneous architectures is the development of parallel applications on a high-performance simulator, running on a workstation or on a scaled-down distributed environment rather than directly on the target computing system [2]. We have developed in the last few years PS, a simulator of PVM applications executed in heterogeneous environments [1]. PS is fed with traces collected by executing the program (or a prototype version of the program) on an execution host, a sequential or parallel computer that might be different from the final target environment. Traces are only used to derive the duration of the bursts corresponding to the execution of sequential code. The simulation of the network connecting the nodes in the target computer and suitable scaling of the duration of computation bursts make it possible to obtain performance indexes and diagrams corresponding to the program execution on several real or fictitious target systems. These systems may be different in the type and speed of computing nodes that compose them, in the interconnection networks used, in operating load conditions.

On the other hand, the simulation approach is time-

*This work has been partly supported by MURST, Italy (Project *MOSAICO* - "Design Methodologies and Tools of High Performance Systems for Distributed Applications") and by the Italian Regional Government (Regione Campania, L. 41/94, Project *Smart ISDN*).

1066-6192/99 $10.00 © 1999 IEEE

consuming, in terms of time needed both to produce the trace files, and to simulate a complete program execution on a target machine. In addition, the simulation complexity often grows non linearly with the data size of the program to be analyzed.

We have designed a technique [3], based on the integration of static program analysis and simulation techniques, which allows for significantly speeding up the time needed for simulating the execution of a message passing program, by reducing the computation complexity of the simulation. In particular, a static analysis of the developed code preceding the traced execution of the program reduces the time spent in producing the trace files, by avoiding the repeated execution of those loops, whose performance behaviour doesn't change with the iterations.

In this paper we present the application of this technique to a PVM code implementing an iterative solver based on the *Successive OverRelaxation* method. This is a parallel application showing a regular behaviour in terms of computational and communication structure, even though the interaction pattern is particularly complex.

This paper is structured as follows. In the following section we provide an overview of the technique we have designed, and an overview of the PS simulation environment. In section 3 we show how the described technique provides, in a reasonable elaboration time, for a performance characterization of iterative regular programs as the proposed one, in terms of idle-, cpu-, communication and synchronization time in Heterogeneous and Network Computing environments. Finally, we draw the conclusions and discuss the guidelines of our future research.

2 Overview of the hybrid approach

In this section we provide an overview of the approach we have devised, based on the integration of static program analysis and simulation techniques, which allows for significantly speeding up the time needed for simulating the execution of a message passing program. A more detailed explanation can be found in [3].

The simulation technique on which our approach is based, needs traces describing the program's behaviour, obtained by executing the program on a *execution host*, a sequential (or even parallel) computer different from the final target environment. The trace files record, for each spawned task, all the communication events and the actual sequence and duration of the CPU bursts - the intervals of time spent computing between two successive interactions with the PVM run-time support. The simulator converts these time intervals into the (predicted) duration of the corresponding CPU bursts in the target machine, while the simulation of the communication events and the interactions with the PVM daemon relies on a fairly complete and accurate model.

The static analysis of the code has been designed as a preprocessing phase for PS. Target of the Static analysis phase is to reduce the time needed for the trace generation by detecting those communication patterns and interleaved sequential code excerpts which are repeatedly executed, in order to execute them just once when producing the trace files. We have designed a technique for the automatic detection of interaction patterns in unstructured message passing parallel programs [8], on which the static analysis phase we are going to describe is based.

In order to better explain the approach we need to introduce the following definitions:

Definition 1 (Interaction Pattern Statements (IPS)) Interaction Pattern Statements (IPS) *is the set of statements that implements within one process any relevant communication interaction (*Interaction Pattern*)*[1] *with other processes. An IPS is made up of a set of* **Communication Statements** *(***CS***) and of control statements identifying the communication end-points (***Controlling EndPoint Statements**, *denoted with* **CEPS***). Thus* IPS = CEPS $\cup$ CS.

Definition 2 (Controlling Interaction Pattern Statements) Controlling Interaction Pattern Statements (CIPS) *is the set of statements belonging to one process that controls the execution of an interaction pattern* IPS.

In order to clarify the above definitions, these sets of statements are shown for the following example code:

if (mytid .eq. PROCS(1))
  do i = 2,nprocs
    `send(PROCS(i), somedata)`
else
  `receive(PROCS(1), somevariable)`

Here, the statements shown in bold font belong to the *CIPS* set; the statements in italics belong to the *CEPS* set, and the statements in courier belong to the *CS* set.

Definition 3 (Invariant interaction pattern) *is a set of point-to-point interactions that repeatedly occur during the program execution. This happens when the* CIPS *set includes iterative control statements.*

Definition 4 (Sequential Invariant Statements (SIS)) *or* Sequential Invariants *are the sets of statements, repeatedly executed and controlled by* CIPS *of an invariant interaction pattern, whose execution times are (roughly) invariant with respect to the iteration steps controlled by* CIPS.

[1]The concept of *interaction pattern* is purposely vague, since, as will be apparent later, there is no restriction on the communication schemes that one may wish to detect in a parallel program.

Definition 5 (Repeated Statements (RS)) *We finally define the set of Repeated Statements as* RS= IPS ∪ SIS.

The technique, we have designed, consists of three steps:

1. *Static analysis*: structural analysis (control and data dependencies) of the given parallel code (a single (SPMD) program or a set of programs, one per process) and identification of all the Invariant interaction patterns, and their corresponding set of statements IPS, CIPS, SIS and RS;

2. *Code restructuring and traced execution*: the goal of this step is to obtain a "thin code" version, where the *RS* statements are executed just once, so reducing the time spent by the traced execution. This phase consists in restructuring the sets of loop control statements of the *CIPS* by eliminating the loop headers of the loop constructs, maintaining the body and setting the loop induction variables to an arbitrary value (the legality of the computations of the produced code is not an issue in the simulation for performance). Such phase is not trivial, since, in some cases, the data produced in one of the suppressed iterations of a *RS* set could affect the control flow of following pieces of the code. On the other hand, the static analysis is able to detect the occurence of a such evenience, that can be corrected (with the help of the programmer) before generating the trace.

3. *Simulation*: The reduced traces can be post-processed by means of a further automatic or semi-automatic (user guided) action on the trace files in order to reproduce the repeated events suppressed by the code restructuring. This is obtained by fixing the number of iterations controlled by the *CIPS* sets. Such values might be, either statically determined or fixed by the programmer in order to obtain meaningful performance figures. This trace is then evaluated by the Simulator (PS), which takes into account the characteristics of the particular architecture chosen, models the static mapping processes/processors, the heterogeneity of the nodes, the interconnection topology and network load. In addiction PS can be used like an analysis tool since it allows the collection of aggregate and analytical indexes related to the heterogeneous system performance (e.g., efficiency, throughput, response time, individual processor utilization), or traces which can be processed off-line by a variety of tools for performance visualization and analysis (e.g., ParaGraph).

2.1 The Static Analysis Phase

Target of the Static analysis phase is to determine the Invariant interaction patterns and to identify, for each of them, the corresponding sets *IPS* and *CIPS*. In addition, the static analysis must determine if the sequential code which is repeatedly executed together with the interaction patterns has an execution time (roughly) invariant with respect to the iteration steps controlled by the *CIPS* (that is, a sequential invariant *SIS*). Finally, it must get ensured that the iterations shrinking applied to the candidate code excerpts *CIPS* would not affect the control flow execution of other pieces of code.

The analysis procedure is *static*; this introduces the restriction that the communication end-points must be determined at compile-time. Apart from communication end-points, the analysed code can be dependent on run-time data.

The analysis procedure starts with the generation of a structural representation of the code by means of a Program Dependence Graph (PDG) [10]. In particular, a PDG for each of the programs composing the parallel code is generated. There is instead only one PDG if the code is in SPMD form. This representation summarizes the control and data dependence information for the code to be analyzed.

2.1.1 Invariant Interaction Patterns detection

Definition 6 (Matching Communication Primitives) *Let $S(P, P_r)$ be a* send *statement belonging to process P and referring to process P_r. Analogously, be $R(Q, P_s)$ a* receive *statement belonging to process Q and referring to process Ps. The pair $\{S, R\}$ of send-receive point-to-point communication primitives is said to* match *if at some time during program execution they lead to a communication between P and Q.*

It can be easily proven that:

> A pair $\{S(P, P_r), R(Q, P_s)\}$ of send-receive communication primitives matches iff:
>
> - S and R are actually executed within their respective processes (i.e., if they are reached by the control flow of P and Q, respectively);
> - at the time of the execution of S and R, $P_r = Q$ and $P_s = P$.

The identification of an interaction pattern consists in the identification of a couple of matching communication primitives (point-to-point or collective), and of the statements which identify the end-points of the communication (i.e. the identity of sender and receiver process). We address to [8] for a detailed description of the interaction pattern detection technique. The output of this phase is given by the sets *IPS* and *CIPS* for each invariant interaction pattern detected.

2.1.2 Sequential Invariants determination

The transitive closure of the statements control dependent on the statements of *CIPS* is considered. This set, possibly without the statements of *IPS*, is the candidate *SIS*. The condition for it to be a sequential invariant is that the control flow paths determined by its execution remains invariant with respect to their iterated execution. This is achieved if the control expressions of branch and loop statements, and loop bounds of do-loop statements: (1) are not data dependence sinks of dependences driven by induction variables of the loop statements of *CIPS*; (2) are not data dependence sinks of loop-carried dependencies (or transitively dependent from), whose carriers are the loop statements of *CIPS*. Under these conditions, the statements executed during different iterations are always the same, thus taking roughly the same execution time.

2.1.3 Legality check for iteration shrinking

The iteration shrinking of a *CIPS* set does not affect the execution of another interaction pattern, controlled by *CIPS*', providing that: (1) no data dependence exists, with any of the statements controlled by *CIPS* as source, and (2) no data dependence exists, with any of the control statements of *CIPS*' or *SIS*' as sink.

In the case this condition is not fulfilled, the iteration shrinking could still be allowed by the user: the user is provided with visualization of the two code excerpts *CIPS* and *CIPS*' or *SIS*' affected by the dependence(s), and visualization of the corresponding data dependences between them, with related variables. The user then decides if the dependence(s) can be ignored, and the code excerpt *CIPS* restructured, or not.

2.2 Code restructuring and Simulation

Once identified the invariant interaction patterns and the related sets *CIPS*, a simplified version of the code is produced, where the communication patterns are executed just once. This is obtained by restructuring the sets of control statements *CIPS* by eliminating the loop headers of the loop constructs, maintaining the body and setting the loop induction variables to an arbitrary value (the legality of the computations of the produced code is not an issue in the simulation for performance).

The static analyzer and code restructuring steps produce a modified version of the distributed program in which is set to 1 the iterations number of all those loops whose body is independent (in a performance meaning) from the iteration count variable. However the real simulation phase must be preceded by a further automatic or semi-automatic (user guided) action on the trace files that fix the loop count number (*RS bounds*) of the executed invariant interaction patterns and sequential invariants. This number cannot, most of the times, be equal to one, because usually the repeated executions of the interaction patterns interfere with each other (with behaviour depending on the particular underlying interconnection network). As an example, the execution time (sequential computation time plus interaction time) can be affected by the execution of the interaction patterns in previous iterations. We must then determine values for the RS bounds which represent a "stable behaviour". Such values for the RS bounds can be:

- statically determined by the previous static analysis: in this case the RS bounds are fixed to the real values they get on a real execution and the simulated execution exactly reproduce the dynamic behaviour of the program;
- data dependent: such evenience needs the help of the programmer that can fix the RS bounds, according to his peculiar performance analysis requirements. For example, if the execution of a *RS* set was controlled by a convergence condition, the user could establish a bound value sufficiently high to obtain a stable behaviour and thus meaningful performance figures.

Some further details on the architecture and use of PS now follow. This tool makes it possible to simulate the execution of a distributed application, programmed in any language based on a message-passing paradigm on different heterogeneous computing environments (most typically, networks of workstations). The current implementation of PS is modelled on PVM and relies upon the existence of a daemon process but this limitation can be easily removed. The PS environment is both a performance *prediction* and *analysis* tool. It is a prediction tool, as the PS simulator makes it possible to obtain extrapolated performance data by estimating the behaviour that a parallel application would attain on different types of architectures from traces collected on a workstation or on a scaled-down distributed environment. It is also an analysis tool, since it allows the collection of aggregate and analytical indexes related to the heterogeneous system performance (e.g., efficiency, throughput, response time, individual processor utilization), or traces which can be processed off-line by a variety of tools for performance visualization and analysis (e.g., ParaGraph). In addition to this, it is also possible to evaluate the effect of such factors as time spent in blocks of code, processor speed, network latency and bandwidth on the overall application performance. PS is an integrated software package that allows to simulate a complete PVM application by combining predefined objects that reproduce the chosen heterogeneous computing platform: PVM hosts, inter-task communication subsystem (PVM daemons, TCP/IP protocol, network interfaces, physical interconnection medium), along with objects simulating the tasks making up the user program. In particular, the objects making up the simulation model of a parallel program should reproduce as faithfully as possible the sequence and timing of the interactions with the run-time support generated by the component tasks, when executed in the target computing environment. In order to do so, they are fed with traces describing the program behaviour on the *execution host*, a sequential or parallel computer which in general may be different from the final target environment. The traces enable PS to derive, for each spawned task, the actual sequence and the duration of the CPU bursts, i.e., of the intervals of time spent computing between two successive interactions with the PVM run-time support.

The use of PS is quite simple: once obtained the trace file of the application running on the *execution host*, the user needs only to choose the target distributed hardware architecture in terms of number and speed of the computing nodes and in terms of a given interconnection network. Several ready-to-use hardware configurations come with the simulator. Customizing the target hardware configuration for the simulation entails simply setting up two files, one containing information about the processing speed of every computing node for the given application, and the other containing the task-to-processor mapping. After that, the simulation can start: the duration of each CPU burst extracted from the trace files is computed to derive the duration on the final target, taking in account the effect of different machine speeds. All task interactions and network behaviour are, instead, simulated in great detail using the simulation kernel. The simulation model is able to consider packet collisions and the effect of external network load, which can be introduced by adding statistical interference with the messages transmitted by the computing nodes. The events and the timestamps representing the (simulated) execution of the program on the target environment are written into an output trace file. This file can be filtered and converted into the format required by Paragraph, a widespread program visualization tool. If the measured performance is not satisfactory, new hardware configurations or allocation strategies can be tried, however not entailing the collection of a new input trace file.

Figure 1 is a snapshot taken during one simulation session. The large window on the left is the graphical representation of the whole hardware/software system simulation model, consisting of four objects simulating the user tasks, four objects modelling the computing nodes of the network and its PVM run-time support, and a single object representing the Network layer. The lowest left window is an inside view of the object modelling a user task. The windows on the right side show some summaries of the simulated program execution.

3 The case study

In this section we present the application of the described technique to a code excerpt implementing the *Successive Over Relaxation* (SOR) method for iterative solution of systems of linear equations. The parallel implementation we are considering is described in [7]. It preserves the update ordering of the elements through a particular work distribution strategy. After updating its own elements, each processor computes partial sums for updating elements assigned to subsequent and preceding processors disposed in a pipeline fashion, using elements assigned to it only. As soon as these partial sums are computed, they are sent to the processors that will need them, so that these processors can start a new update step. This step now requires, for each element to be updated, only the computation of the partial sum of the elements assigned to that processor, and a final sum of the partial results received from the other stages of the pipeline.

A Fortran+PVM message passing code excerpt (in SPMD form) implementing the algorithm follows:

```
....
converged = .false.
do while (converged .eq.  .false.)
  do l = 1, nprocs
    firstj = (l-1)*NPERPROC+1
    lastj = l*NPERPROC
    if (l.ne.m) then
      do j = firstj,lastj
        tempa(j,m) = 0.0
        do i = (m-1)*NPERPROC+1, m*NPERPROC
          tempa(j,m) = tempa(j,m) + w(i,j)*x(i)
        enddo
      enddo
      call pvmfinitsend(PvmDefault,bufid)
      call pvmfpack(real4,
        tempa((l-1)*NPERPROC+1,m),NPERPROC,1,info)
      call pvmfsend(tids(l),any,info)
    endif
    if (l.eq.m) then
      do n = 1, nprocs
        if (n.ne.m) then
          call pvmfrecv(tids(n),any)
          call pvmfunpack(real4,
          tempa((l-1)*NPERPROC+1,n),NPERPROC,1,info)
        endif
      enddo
      do j = firstj,lastj
        tempa(j,m) = 0.0
        do i = (m-1)*NPERPROC+1, m*NPERPROC
          tempa(j,m) = tempa(j,m) + w(i,j)*x(i)
        enddo
        a = 0.0
        do n = 1,nprocs
          a = a + tempa(j,n)
        enddo
        x(j) = x(j) + a
      enddo
    endif
  enddo
enddo
```

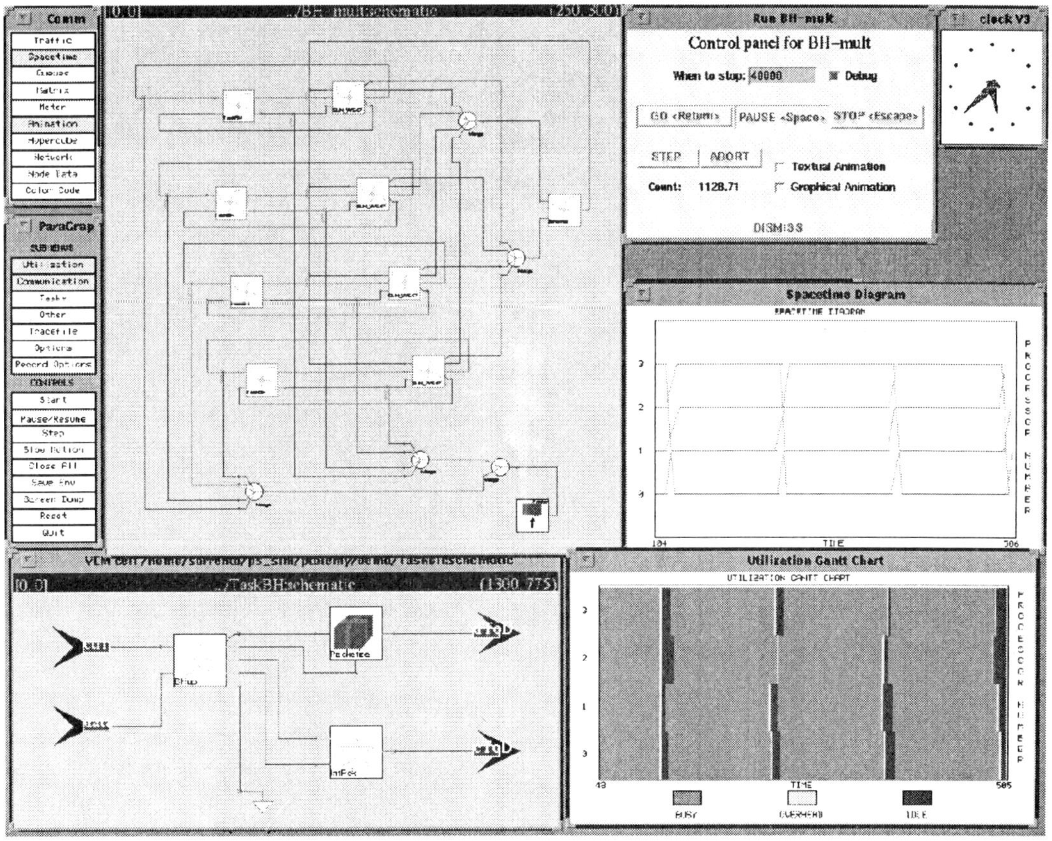

Figure 1. A screen dump of a PS simulation session.

```
....
```

Here `pvmf*` are calls to PVM routines for message packing/unpacking and point-to-point communication. `nprocs` is the number of processes, `m` the process identifier, `NPERPROC` the number of items owned by a process.

The detection of the invariant interaction pattern is performed as follows.

The Program Dependence Graph of the code is computed. The sets of statements *CEPS* for the two communication primitives `pvmfsend` and *pvmfrecv* are determined with a PDG traversing; they are highlighted in italics in the following:

```
....
  do l = 1, nprocs
     firstj = (l-1)*NPERPROC+1
     lastj = l*NPERPROC
     if (l.ne.m) then
       ....
       call pvmfinitsend(PvmDefault,bufid)
       call pvmfpack(real4,
          tempa((l-1)*NPERPROC+1,m),NPERPROC,1,info)
       call pvmfsend(tids(l),any,info)
     endif
     if (l.eq.m) then
       do n = 1, nprocs
         if (n.ne.m) then
           call pvmfrecv(tids(n),any)
           call pvmfunpack(real4,
           tempa((l-1)*NPERPROC+1,n),NPERPROC,1,info)
         endif
       enddo
       ....
     endif
  enddo
```

....

The interaction pattern detection technique performs the primitives' matching, and detects the two sets *CIPS* and *IPS*. The two sets are shown (the first in bold, the second in italics):

```
....
do while (converged .eq. .false.)
  do l = 1, nprocs
    firstj = (l-1)*NPERPROC+1
    lastj = l*NPERPROC
    if (l.ne.m) then
      ....
      call pvmfsend(tids(l),any,info)
    endif
    if (l.eq.m) then
      do n = 1, nprocs
        if (n.ne.m) then
          call pvmfrecv(tids(n),any)
          ....
        endif
      enddo
      ....
    endif
  enddo
enddo
....
```

From the *CIPS* set, the set *SIS* of candidate sequential invariants is determined. It is shown in italics:

```
....
do while (converged .eq. .false.)
  do l = 1, nprocs
    firstj = (l-1)*NPERPROC+1
    lastj = l*NPERPROC
    if (l.ne.m) then
      do j = firstj,lastj
        tempa(j,m) = 0.0
        do i = (m-1)*NPERPROC+1, m*NPERPROC
          tempa(j,m) = tempa(j,m) + w(i,j)*x(i)
        enddo
      enddo
      call pvmfinitsend(PvmDefault,bufid)
      call pvmfpack(real4,
        tempa((l-1)*NPERPROC+1,m),NPERPROC,1,info)
      call pvmfsend(tids(l),any,info)
    endif
    if (l.eq.m) then
      do n = 1, nprocs
        if (n.ne.m) then
          call pvmfrecv(tids(n),any)
          call pvmfunpack(real4,
          tempa((l-1)*NPERPROC+1,n),NPERPROC,1,info)
        endif
      enddo
      do j = firstj,lastj
        tempa(j,m) = 0.0
        do i = (m-1)*NPERPROC+1, m*NPERPROC
          tempa(j,m) = tempa(j,m) + w(i,j)*x(i)
        enddo
        a = 0.0
        do n = 1,nprocs
          a = a + tempa(j,n)
        enddo
        x(j) = x(j) + a
      enddo
    endif
  enddo
enddo
....
```

The *SIS* set fulfils the condition stated in sec. 2.1.2. It is worth noting that, even though the control flow paths determined by the inner do statements (e.g. the ones with `j` index) are not invariant with respect to the controlling do statement (with `l` index), the whole control flow path is instead invariant with respect to the controlling statement in *CIPS*.

The iterations determined by the statement in *CIPS* can thus be shrinked, in order to obtain a reduced trace, yet describing the communication behaviour of the application.

In order to fix an iteration count number (*RS bound*) sufficiently high to obtain meaningful performance figures for the simulation, without increasing it (and thus the simulation time) unnecessarily, we observed the speed-up value obtained by the simulation, at varying the iteration number. The simulation was performed for a set of two SUN Ultra 5 workstations (233 Mhz clock) connected with Ethernet bus; the simulated speed-up was obtained by considering the single node execution time of the parallel code as sequential time. We observed a substantial stabilization of the simulated speed-up for values of the iteration number bigger than 20. The simulated speed-ups were differing from the measured ones within a range of $5\% \simeq 10\%$ (real speed-up computed in the same way as for the simulated one, by considering the single node execution time of the parallel code as sequential time).

The simulation time was in the order of $\simeq 12sec$ (on a SUN Ultra 5) for the iteration number 20.

4 Conclusions and Future Directions

The native PS input preparation phase requires the complete and time-consuming execution of the PVM code on any available hardware configuration, possibly less powerful than the target one, or even on a single processor machine. Our approach, based on a static analysis of the code, allows to obtain in less time, when possible, equivalent (in a performance meaning) trace files feeding the simulator.

A prototype for the static analysis module has been built, with the use of the COCKTAIL Compiler Construction toolkit [12]. The syntax tree and PDG representations have been built with the use of the Ast and Puma [13] tools. Graph traversing routines, needed for the determination of controlling sets of statements and sequential invariants, have been implemented within the Puma environment.

The implementation of the invariant interaction patterns detection phase has been achieved utilizing the *Omega library* [16], a package for linear systems solving and set computation and manipulation.

We are currently implementing a graphical browser, using the DaVinci graph drawing toolkit [11].

We are currently investigating the viability to obtain automatically the values of the *RS bounds* which represent a "stable behaviour" for the simulated execution. Those values could be obtained either by means of analytical rules taking in account e.g. the pattern message sizes and network latency, or directly by automatically testing the simulated execution of just few iterations.

References

[1] R. Aversa, A. Mazzeo, N. Mazzocca, U. Villano. Heterogeneous System Performance Prediction and Analysis Using PS *IEEE Concurrency*, Vol.6, No.3, September 1998.

[2] R. Aversa, N. Mazzocca, U. Villano. Design of a Simulator of Heterogeneous Computing Environments. *Simulation Practice and Theory*, Vol. 4, May 1996, pp. 97-117.

[3] R. Aversa, B. Di Martino, N. Mazzocca, U. Villano, "Reducing Parallel Program Simulation Complexity by Static Analysis", Proc. of *1999 International Conference on Parallel and Distributed Processing Techniques and Applications (PDPTA'99)*, June 28 - July 1, 1999, Las Vegas, Nevada, USA, World Scientific Eng. Soc. (ISBN 1-892512-10-6).

[4] E. A. Brewer, W. E. Weihl. Developing Parallel Applications Using High-Performance Simulation. In Proc. 1993 ONR/ACM Workshop on Parallel and Distr. Debugging, 1993.

[5] A. Cimitile, A. De Lucia and M. Munro, "Qualifying Reusable Functions Using Symbolic Execution", Proc. of 2nd *Working Conference on Reverse Engineering*, IEEE CS Press, Toronto, Canada, Aug. 1995.

[6] F. Darema et al., "A single-program-multiple-data computational model for EPEX/FORTRAN", *Parallel Computing*, 7, pp. 11–24, 1988.

[7] B. Di Martino and G. Iannello, "Parallelization of Nonsimultaneous Iterative Methods for Systems of Linear Equations", *Lecture Notes in Computer Science* n. 854, Sett. 1994, Springer-Verlag eds.

[8] B. Di Martino, A. Mazzeo, N. Mazzocca, U. Villano, "Automatic Detection of Interaction Patterns for Parallel Program Analysis and Development", Proc. of 6th *IEEE Workshop on Program Comprehension*, Ischia (I), IEEE CS Press, 24-26 June 1998 (ISBN 0-8186-8560-3).

[9] T. Fahringer. Automatic Performance Prediction of Parallel Program s. Kluwer Academic, 1996.

[10] J. Ferrante, K.J. Ottenstein and J.D. Warren, "The Program Dependence Graph and its use in Optimization", *ACM Trans. Programming Languages and Systems*, 9(3), pp. 319-349, June 1987.

[11] M. Froehlich, M. Werner, "The Graph Visualization System daVinci - A User Interface for Applications", Technical Report n. 5/94, Department of Computer Science, Universitaet Bremen, September 1994.

[12] J. Grosh and H. Emmelmann, "A Tool Box for Compiler Construction", *Lecture Notes in Computer Science*, Springer - Verlag, n. 477, pp. 106-116, Oct. 1990.

[13] "Puma - A Generator for the Transformation of Attributed Trees", Compiler Generation Report n. 26, GMD Karlsruhe, July 1991.

[14] A. Geist et al.. PVM: Parallel Virtual Machine - A Users Guide and Tutorial for Networked Parallel Computing. MIT Press, Cambridge, 1994.

[15] A. Khokhar, V. K. Prasanna, M. E. Shaaban, C. Wang. Heterogeneous Computing: Challenges and Opportunities. IEEE Computer, 26(6):18-27, June 1993.

[16] W. Pugh, "A practical algorithm for Exact Array Dependence Analysis", *Communications of ACM*, 8(35), pp. 102-115, Aug. 1992.

[17] H. Zima and B. Chapman, *Supercompilers for Parallel and Vector Computers*, ACM Press, New York, NY, 1990.

Monitoring and Debugging Message Passing Applications with MPVisualizer

Ana Paula Cláudio[1], João Duarte Cunha[2], Maria Beatriz Carmo[1]
[1]Faculdade de Ciências da Universidade de Lisboa
Departamento de Informática, Campo Grande, Edifício C5, Piso 1, 1700 LISBOA, Portugal
{apc,bc}@di.fc.ul.pt
[2]Laboratório Nacional de Engenharia Civil
Av. do Brasil, 101, 1799 LISBOA CODEX, Portugal
jdc@lnec.pt

Abstract

MPVisualizer (Message Passing Visualizer) is a tool for the monitoring and debugging of message passing parallel applications with three components: the trace/replay mechanism, the graphical user interface and a central component, called visualization engine. The engine, which plays the main role during the replay phase, builds an object-oriented model of the application. Taking full advantage of inheritance and polymorphism the tool can be adapted to different message passing environments and different graphical environments, and easily re-programmed to detect specific predicates. The engine is also prepared to recognize race conditions.

1. Introduction

In parallel applications several processes cooperate with one another to achieve a common goal. To enable this cooperation the processes must communicate and one way of achieving this is the exchange of messages. Applications built using this type of communication are called message passing applications.

Having several processes running in parallel and communicating with one another gives rise to the so called race conditions which in turn may cause non-determinism. This is a serious trouble factor when debugging parallel applications, since bugs related to external events associated with inter-process communication may have different consequences in successive executions.

The tool described in this paper, MPVisualizer, Message Passing Visualizer, was mainly developed to aid in the detection of this kind of bugs.

Bugs concerning internal events, i.e. events involving one process only, can be detected using a sequential debugger. Compatibility with sequential debuggers is fully supported in MPVisualizer, as explained later.

The tool provides a graphical interface where the user can visualize the progression of the application's execution: processes, messages and communication events are displayed. Causal order [16] between communication events is preserved in the representation.

Furthermore, race conditions are automatically signaled and detection of specific predicates is possible.

The components of MPVisualizer are the trace/replay mechanism, the previously mentioned graphical interface and the central component, called visualization engine. The engine is the core of the tool and plays the main role during the replay phase: it builds an object oriented model of the application. Taking full advantage of inheritance and polymorphism, two important features have been built into the engine. First, it can be adapted to different message passing environments and different graphical environments. Second, it can be easily re-programmed to detect predicates related to communication events. Furthermore, MPVisualizer automatically detects race conditions.

2. MPVisualizer

This section describes the components of MPVisualizer, trace/replay mechanism, visualization engine and graphical interface, and explains the mechanisms used to detect predicates and race conditions. Section 2.1 describes the trace/replay mechanism. The visualization engine and the graphical interface, both closely related to the representation of the execution, are described in section 2.2.

2.1 The trace/replay mechanism

Due to race conditions, the internal work of a parallel application may be nondeterministic, that is, two successive executions of the same application with the same input may exhibit different behaviour. A trace/replay mechanism makes a particular execution of the parallel application repeatable, allowing cyclic debugging, a frequently used technique in sequential programs.

The trace/replay mechanism for applications based on the shared memory paradigm, described in [17], has been adapted for message passing applications and is one component of MPVisualizer. The basic idea of this mechanism is that, assuming the individual processes in the parallel application do not contain nondeterministic statements, if each process is supplied with the same input values, in the same order, during successive executions, it will exhibit the same behaviour each time. The mechanism includes two distinct phases: the trace phase and the replay phase. In the trace phase, minimal information is stored in order to minimize the probe effect, that is, intrusion. Although minimal, the stored information is sufficient to ensure that, during the replay phase, each process will consume the same messages, in the same order. For this reason, the observation of any individual process during replay, using a sequential debugger, will not change the behaviour of the whole application. This is why it is possible to integrate a sequential debugger with our tool.

The monitoring code is inserted in the standard libraries of the message passing software, which should not be modified by the common user. Application code is kept untouched but linking is different in the trace and replay phases. In the trace phase, the application under study must be linked with one modified library, the trace library; for the replay phase, it must be linked with a second modified library, the replay library. Therefore, during replay phase, the processes of the parallel application, hereafter called processes, will execute the routines of the replay library. These routines force the re-execution to respect the causal order of the communication events recorded during the original execution. They also force the processes to send blocks of data to a special process, named spy.

In MPVisualizer, observable events are not only communication events but also the beginning and ending of a process. During replay, each time an observable event occurs in a process, a data block (a structure with a field that identifies the sort of event) is sent to the corresponding process, that is, the spy process running in the same machine. This spy then sends the blocks to the so called main process[1], a kind of bridge between the parallel application and the object-oriented model of the application.

2.2. The visualization engine and the graphical interface

The visualization engine relies on a central object - instance of the GImanager class, explained below- to manage the object-oriented model of the application. The main process creates this object, and each time it receives a data block from a spy process, invokes the appropriate method of the object to notify the model of the occurrence of an event. Method selection depends on the type of the data block. For instance, if a given data block corresponds to a message sending the method "send_message" is invoked. This method creates a new message object, includes it in the model and takes care of all the necessary updates.

Any dependency on the message-passing software is therefore restricted to spy processes.

Figure 1 illustrates the classes in the model and their relationships. These classes belong to one of two groups. The first group, the kernel, includes the basic classes that do not depend on the graphical environment: manager, process, message, machine, spy, c_event (communication event) and its subclasses. They encapsulate the data and behaviour that are generic for any message-passing application. Comparing this version of the class diagram with the one described in previous stages of development [3] [4], a new group of classes has been included, namely c_event and its direct subclasses. The addition of these classes brings three sorts of benefits. First, considering that communication events, together with the beginning and the ending of processes, are the observable events, it is important that they correspond to objects in the model. Second, it became possible to distinguish between receive execution and message consumption. This is important for debugging purposes since a process can execute any sort of receive primitive and have no corresponding message to consume. Finally, using inheritance, the model becomes easily extendable to other types of communication primitives like, for instance, a blocking synchronous send [6] derived from the class send.

The second group, graphical classes, comprises the remaining classes, dealing with the graphical representation and derived from the ones in the first group. In order to achieve this, inherited methods are redefined, and new attributes and methods are added. The GImanager class has only one instance, the previously mentioned central object in the visualization engine.

Polymorphism plays an essential role in this group: GIentity contains a method named "draw", which is redefined in each of its subclasses.

The Display_controller class belongs to this group of classes and, as the name suggests, is in charge of managing the display where the graphical representation of the application is shown.

If the graphical environment changes, these classes have to be modified, maintaining the kernel classes unchanged.

All the objects created by the GImanager object during the construction of the model, are instances of graphical classes, that is, they all know how to draw themselves and how to react to user requests. More specifically, in what concerns processes and messages, GImanager creates instances of GIprocess and GImessage classes.

The distinction between GIprocess_intermediate and GIprocess as well as between GImessage_intermediate and GImessage is related to predicate detection and will be explained later.

The graphical interface, figure 2, comprises a main window where a time space diagram [16] represents the progression of the re-execution. There are specific symbols

[1] In the current implementation, communication between spies and the main process is socket based.

for processes, messages, and communication events. It must be strengthened that the symbols for communication events are displayed consistently with their causal order [16]. Horizontal and vertical scrollbars are used to access different parts of the time space diagram in the main window. Besides the main window, a popup window is opened every time the left mouse button is pressed when pointing at a symbol in the diagram. This window displays information about the object in the model that corresponds to the pointed symbol.

MPVisualizer supports observation during re-execution as well as post-mortem observation since the object-oriented model of the application remains accessible after the re-execution. In the present stage, post-mortem observation is available.

The trace/replay mechanism was implemented and tested on top of PVM [10]. The visualization engine and the graphical interface were implemented and tested using C++ and Motif.

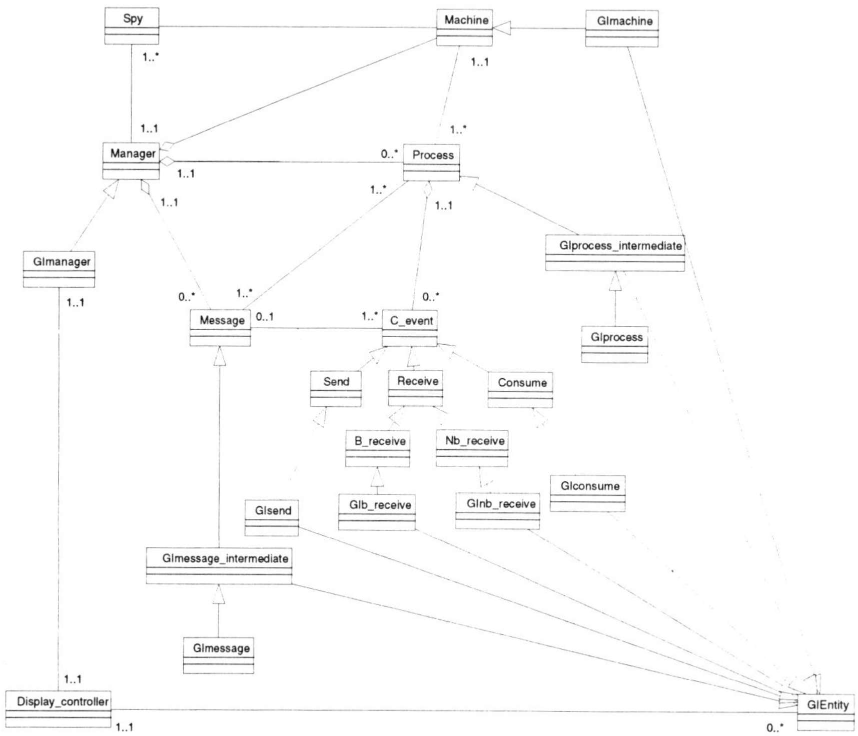

Fig.1 Class Diagram

2.3. Detection of race conditions

Race conditions are in the origin of potential non determinism in parallel applications. Therefore, when race conditions are detected, the user is notified and knows exactly which events are involved. This is a major feature in debugging.

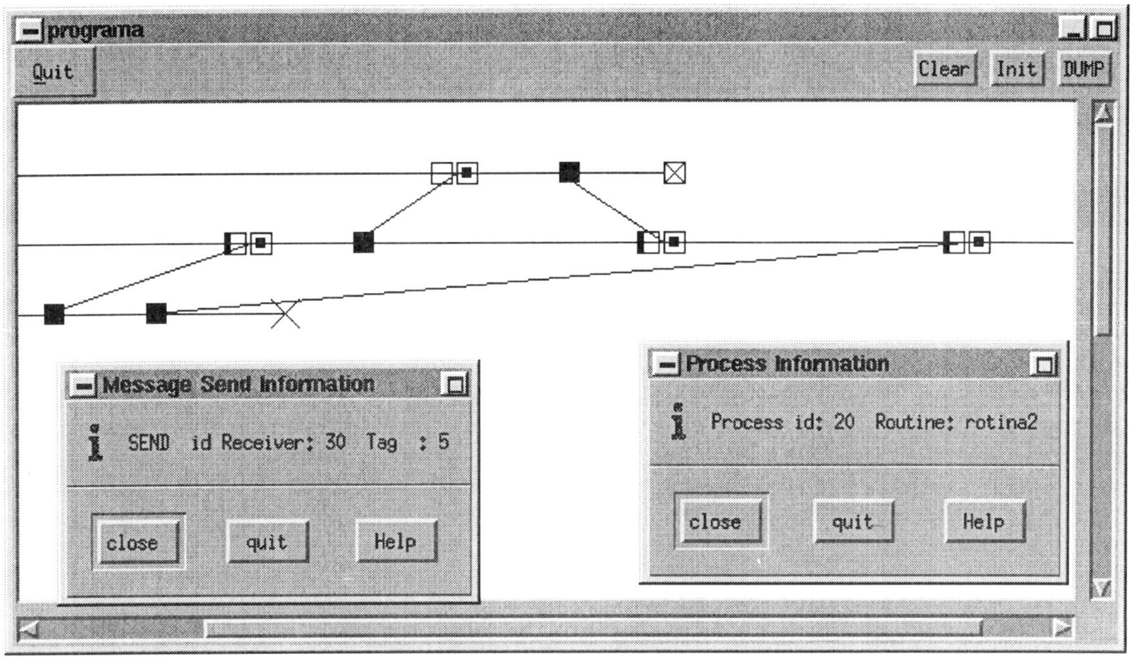

Fig. 2. The bottom windows give information about a process and a message sending. They are opened when the user clicks on top of a process symbol or a message blocking receive symbol, respectively. The graphic symbols used in the top window are:
—— process; ╲ message; ■ message sending; ⊡ message consumption;
□ non-blocking receive; ☒ blocking receive;
◧ non-blocking receive from any; ⊠ blocking receive from any

When two consecutive receive events that do not specify the sending process, called receive-from-any, occur in the same process, there is a potential race condition. However, as observed by Netzer and Miller [18], there are sequences of events that look like race conditions but are not real ones. Spurious race conditions can be eliminated as long as the causal order of the involved events is analyzed: if the first receive-from-any event "happens before" the send event that corresponds to the second receive-from-any, in the sense introduced by Lamport [16], then there is no real race condition.

In MPVisualizer, the code for race condition detection lies inside class Process; consistency of causal order between events is maintained with the help of vector timestamps [9].

Figure 3 shows a popup window which has been automatically opened when a race condition was detected.

2.4. Predicate detection

The kind of predicates that can be detected depends on the granularity of the observation performed by the tool. Therefore, in MPVisualizer, detectable predicates are those concerning communication events, beginning and ending of processes [3]. Classes involved in predicate detection are the ones closely related with these events, that is, GIprocess and GImessage. Predicate detection mode can be turned on or off whenever a re-execution is started. If the user wants detection mode on, he must re-program the class(es) involved in a specific predicate detection, GIprocess or GImessage or both. Consequently, the code of the tool has to be re-compiled. Otherwise (predicate detection mode off), GIprocess and GImessage are empty classes, just inheriting from their immediate ancestors, GIprocess_intermediate and GImessage_intermediate.

If we define a block as a sequence of instructions executed by a process between two consecutive observable events, a predicate concerning observable events remains true or false inside a block, and must be re-evaluated whenever an event occurs that may change its boolean value. For instance, if the predicate to be detected is "this process has consumed exactly one message with tag 2", methods concerning message consumption have to be redefined in class GIprocess: "m_consumed" and "m_consumed_any". Two attributes are added to the class, a counter for the consumed messages with tag 2 and a boolean for the logical value of the predicate. Basically, each redefined method invokes the method with the same name from its base class and updates the new attributes.

A button click on a block representation, causes the predicate popup window to open. This window contains a short predicate description and its corresponding boolean value inside that block (figure 3).

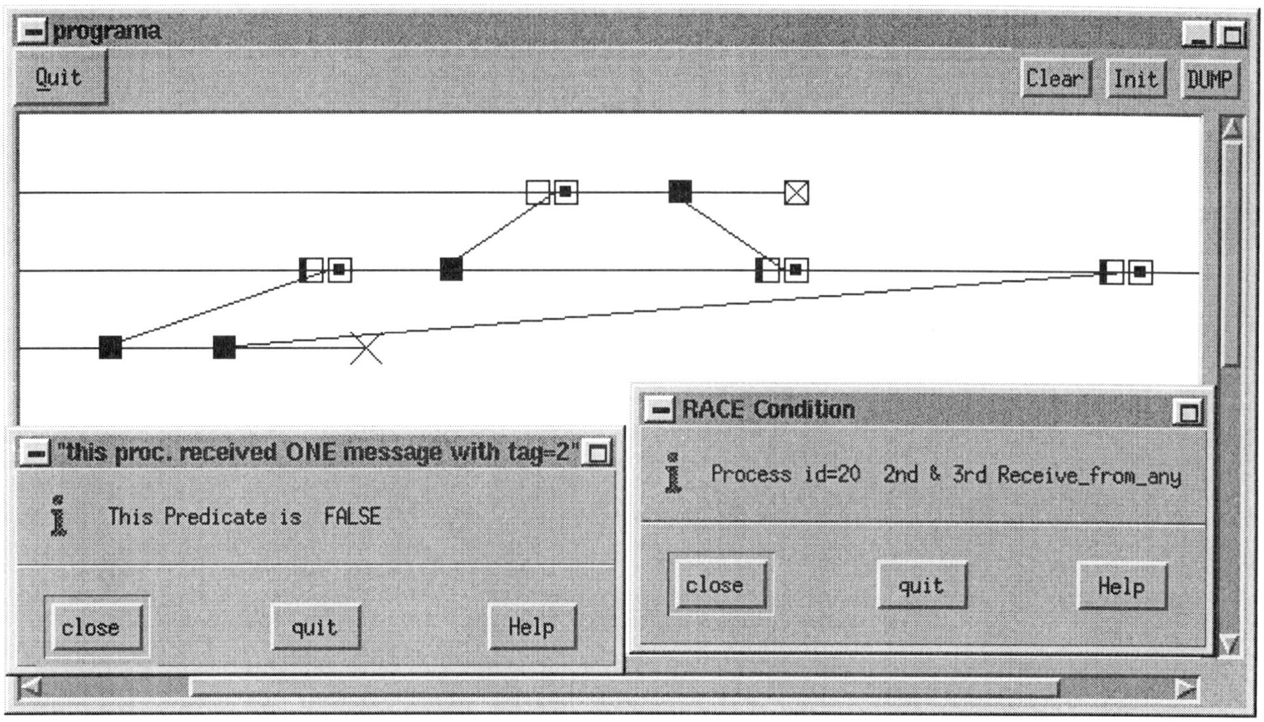

Fig.3. The RACE Condition window was automatically opened as soon as such a condition was detected; the other window concerns predicate detection (a synthetic description of the predicate is provided in the window's title) and is opened when the user clicks on top of a process block.

3. Distinctive features of MPVisualizer and similar tools

Using the terminology introduced by the *Parallel Tools Consortium*[2], program debuggers, together with execution trace visualizers and tools for performance tuning, form a group named *Execution Analyzers*. Two other groups of tools are *Source Code Analyzers*, used to analyze and convert serial programs to parallel code, and *Parallel Languages and Libraries*.

The usage of execution analysis tools is mandatory for programmers to obtain correct and tuned parallel programs and takes place after the usage of any tool from the other groups. Among those, debuggers have to be used before execution trace visualizers and tools for performance tuning.

The tool described in this paper, MPVisualizer, besides incorporating both a replay mechanism and a graphical representation to show the progression of the execution, includes a basic component, the visualization engine, which builds an object-oriented model of the message passing application. Taking full advantage of inheritance and polymorphism, the tool becomes adaptable to different message passing environments and/or to different graphical softwares and the object-oriented architecture makes the tool flexible enough to be extended with an important additional skill: predicate detection. Moreover, MPVisualizer automatically detects race conditions and allows observation during replay and in post-mortem mode.

In the following paragraphs a brief overview of other debugging tools is presented. These tools have been chosen because they support at least one of the following capabilities supported by MPVisualizer: incorporation of a trace/replay mechanism, fully featured graphical interface, predicate and race conditions detection.

p2d2 [13] is a *gdb* based portable debugger for parallel and distributed programs that has been tested on several hardware platforms for PVM and MPI programs. A large number of processes can be controlled simultaneously without requiring one window for each process. Control directives, such as "set breakpoint", can be directed to the set of all processes executing the same code. A 2-dimensional process grid gives a graphical overview of all the processes in the computation, each process corresponding to a single cell in the grid. The tool allows the user to program how information, including the process grid, should be displayed on the screen. For

[2] http://www.ptools.org

instance, the grid might be configured to represent running processes with green squares and stopped processes with red ones. Using the grid, the user can select individual processes or groups of processes for more detailed examination.

MAD [15] is intended for the debugging of parallel message passing programs and has been tested for MPI and nCUBE2. The tool generates an event graph representation providing a global view of the program's execution and traditional techniques such as breakpoints and program inspection can be used based on this graph. The graphical representation of an event is connected to its corresponding lines in the source code. The tool detects race conditions and allows record and replay. The user may change the order of the incoming messages and observe the consequences in the behaviour of the program, during an artificial program run.

DDBG [5] is a debugging tool integrated in the parallel software environment centered on the graphical programming language GRAPNEL [8]. It uses the *gdb* debugger to act as a process-level debugger and contains a central debugging user interface. This tool includes a trace/replay mechanism.

TotalView[3] is a debugger for single and multi-process programs in C, C++ and Fortran, supporting PVM and MPI. It includes a data visualization interface where data values are displayed using colour ranges.

pdbx[3] and pedb[3] are proprietary debuggers developed by IBM for programs running in its parallel environments and both provide support for MPI programs. pdbx is based on the sequential debugger *dbx*, but additional features for parallel programs are available. Process groups are permitted with breakpoints affecting all the processes in a given group. In pedb coloured animated executions and values of variables are displayed.

Xmdb[4] is a debugger for C, C++ and FORTRAN programs in PVM. A parallel program is debugged with respect to a single process and the user may control the messages that are delivered to this process. The tool supports any sequential debugger. A replay mechanism and a race detection mechanism are available.

XPVM[5] provides animated views to monitor the execution of PVM programs to assist in debugging and performance tuning. It also provides a trace/replay mechanism.

In the relatively large set of investigated tools, we have not found any that simultaneously covers all the capabilities of MPVisualizer.

[3] http://www.tc.cornell.edu/Parallel.Tools

[4] http://w4.lanl.gov:80/Internal/divisions/cic/cic8/para-dist-team/mdb

[5] http://netlib.uow.edu.au/pvm3/xpvm

4. Future Work

Planned future work is mainly focused on the level of observation of the tool and on the quality of the graphical interface.

MPVisualizer supports observation during re-execution as well as in post-mortem mode, as explained before. In order to make the observation during re-execution more powerful, we intend to introduce a breakpoint mechanism. The modified routines in the message passing library are those related to the observable events; these modifications will be extended to include a breakpoint mechanism, that is, a way to order a process to remain stopped in an observable event until explicitly told to continue. The process being stopped, may cause other processes to stop too. For instance, if a process is stopped when executing a send, the processes waiting for the corresponding message will be stopped when trying to consume it. This may produce a chain of stopped processes, in the limit, all the application processes.

Having in mind the granularity of the observation we can conceive a sort of global breakpoint: every process in the application will be stopped the next time it executes a communication routine. If a process does not stop, this means that it no longer depends on the other processes or interferes in their progression.

Undoubtedly, the observation of such phenomena helps the understanding of causal relations between a set of events in the application; therefore, the introduction of a breakpointing mechanism will be a major improvement in our tool.

Even though we consider the adopted graphical representation adequate, we are concerned with scalability aspects, since the volume of information can become overwhelming and the use of scrollbars may not be enough. Two complementary solutions may be adopted: to dynamically change the scale factor of the whole representation and allow the user to define zoom areas. This will allow the user to get a view of the whole and also a more detailed representation of a selected portion.

This type of solution is adopted, for example, in the Information Mural [14]. If we implement those facilities in our tool, they will be available both in re-execution and post-mortem observation mode. Otherwise, the Information Mural can be used in post-mortem mode, provided our tool produces, during re-execution, the necessary trace files.

The adoption of the tool proposed by Carmo et al. [2] is also possible in post mortem mode. This tool is a prototype for the visualization of both geometrical and non-geometrical data allowing, among other features, information filtering and zooming. Besides the zoom mechanism, we are mainly interested in using the filtering of information facility since this allows user attention to be focused on specific events or situations, for instance, race conditions.

PVM has gained wide acceptance [19] and Geist et al. even consider it a *de facto* standard [11]. This, however, does not invalidate our interest in testing MPVisualizer with other message passing systems, such as MPI [7], p4[1] and Parmacs [12].

References

1. Butler, R., Lusk, E.: User's Guide to the p4 programming system, Tech. Rep. ANL-92/17, Argonne National Laboratory, Mathematics and Computer Science Division, October 1992
2. Carmo, M.B., Cunha, J.D., Cláudio, A.P.: Visualization of Geometrical and Non-geometrical Data. In: Proceedings of the WSCG'99, Plzen, February 1999
3. Cláudio, A.P., Cunha, J. D., Carmo, M. B.: Debugging of Message Passing Parallel Applications: a General Tool. In Proceedings of VECPAR '98 - 3rd International Meeting on Vector Parallel Processing, Porto, June 1998
4. Cláudio, A.P., Cunha, J.D., Carmo, M.B.: MPVisualizer: a General Tool to Debug Message Passing Parallel Applications, in Proceedings of the HPCN'99, LNCS 1593, April 1999
5. Cunha, J., Lourenço, J., Antão, T.: An Experiment in Tool Integration: The DDBG Parallel and Distributed Debugger. In: Euromicro Journal of Systems Architecture, 2nd Special Issue on Tools and Environments for Parallel Processing, 1998. Elsevier Science Press
6. Cypher, R., Leu, E.: Message-Passing Semantics and Portable Parallel Programs. In: IBM Research Division - RJ 9654 (84094) January, 1994
7. Dongarra, J., Otto, S., Snir, M., Walker, D.:An Introduction to the MPI Standard. Tech. Rep. CS-95-274, University of Tenesse, 1995
8. Dózsa, G., Fadgyas, T., Kacsuk, P.: GRAPNEL: A Graphical Programming Language for Parallel Programs. In: Proceedings of uP'94: The EighthSymposium on Microcomputer and Microprocessor Applications, Budapest, Hungary, 1994
9. Fidge, C., Partial Orders for Parallel Debugging. In: Proceeedings of the ACM SIGPLAN/SIGOPS Workshop on Parallel and Distributed Debugging ACM SIGPLAN Notices, 24, 1 (Jan 1989), 183-194
10. Geist, A., Beguelin, A., Dongarra, J., Jiang, W., Manchek, R., Sunderam, V.: PVM: Parallel Virtual Machine. MIT Press, 1994
11. Geist, A.,Kohl, J., Papodopoulos, P.: PVM and MPI: a comparison of features. In: Calculateurs Paralleles, Volume 8(2), 1996
12. Hempel, R., Hoppe, H.-C., Supalov, A.: PARMACS-6.0 library interface specification. Tech. Rep., GMD, PostFach 1316, D-5205 Sankt Augustin 1, Germany, December, 1992
13. Hood, R.: The p2d2 Project: Building a Portable Distributed Debugger. In: Proceedings of SPDT'96: SIGMETRICS Symposium on Parallel and Distributed Tools, May 1996
14. Jerding, D., Stasko, J.: The Information Mural: A Technique for Displaying and Navigating Large Information Spaces. In: IEEE Transactions on Visualization and Computer Graphics, Vol. 4, NO. 3, July-Sptember 1998
15. Kranzlmüller, D., Hügl, R., Volkert, J., MAD - A Top Down Approach to Parallel Program Debugging, in Proceedings of the HPCN'99, LNCS 1593, April 1999
16. Lamport, L.: Time, Clocks, and the Ordering of Events in a Distributed System. In: Communications of the ACM, July 1978, Vol. 21, No. 7, 558-565
17. Leblanc, T., Mellor-Crummey, J.: Debugging Parallel Programs with Instant Replay. In: IEEE Transactions on Computers, Vol C-36, No. 4, April 1987
18. Netzer, R., Miller, B.: Optimal Tracing and Replay for Debugging Message-Passing Parallel Programs. In: Proc. of Supercomputing '92, pp. 502-511, Minnneapolis, November 1992
19. Skillicorn, D., Talia, D.: Models and Languages for Parallel Computation. In: ACM Computing Surveys, Vol. 30, No.2, June 1998

Pipelining-Based Tradeoffs for Hardware/Software Codesign of Multimedia Systems

Juan P. Castellano, David Sánchez, Onassis Cazorla, Álvaro Suárez
GAC (Architecture and Concurrency Group)
Dpto. de Ingeniería Telemática - Universidad de Las Palmas de G.C.
Campus Universitario de Tafira s/n - 35017- Las Palmas de G.C.
e-mail: {francis, alvaro}@cic.teleco.ulpgc.es

Abstract

In the last years, multimedia systems are present in an ever increasing number of applications. A software implementation often can not satisfy system timing constraints. This problem can be solved by adding specific hardware to the system. Lately, it has been developed some design methodologies for this type of hardware/ software systems. Our research group have developed a hardware/software codesign environment named GACSYS (GAC's Codesign System) for designing this type of systems. In this article, we present our Hw/Sw partitioning tool. Main contribution of our tool is the following: it supports process-level pipelining and takes into account system power consumption. Thus, system designer can explore the design space to make new latency, area and power trade-offs.

1. Introduction

In the last years, multimedia systems are present in an ever increasing number of applications. These systems process different types of information such as speech, images and data, and have a data-dominated processing. They have to execute many arithmetic operations. Moreover, they have also to satisfy some timing constraints.

In general, a software implementation of these systems does not satisfy system timing constraints. This problem can be solved by adding specific hardware to speed up system execution time so that some operations can be executed in parallel. Lately, it has been developed som design methodologies for this type of hardware/software systems. They are named as hardware/software codesign methodologies [1][2][3][4][5].

Our research group is developing a codesign environment named GACSYS (*GAC's Codesign System*) [6][7][8] (Figure 1) that is oriented to data-dominated applications. At present, we have mainly developed the following work: a) we have designed a new system specification language named VSS (*VHDL-based System Specification*). Our language supports high level statements to make easy system specification. VSS allows a designer to decrease system specification time. We have also developed a compiler to translate from VSS code to VHDL one. b) We have designed an intermediate representation to support VHDL specifications. It is based on the ASCIS (*Architectural Synthesis of Complex Integrated Systems*) data flow graph. We have also developed a compiler to generate the intermediate representation from VHDL code. c) We have developed a hardware/software partitioning tool that allows a better design space exploration.

In this paper, we present our hardware/software partitioning tool. Main contribution is the following:

- it supports process-level pipelining. Previous work on hardware/software partitioning does not support it. Process-level pipelining allows a designer to explore new design cost and latency tradeoffs.
- it makes use of design power consumption to explore design space. This parameter is important to design current systems and has not been used in previous work. Designer can use functional units with different supply voltage to explore area and power tradeoffs.

The structure of this paper is the following: in section 2, we present related work. In section 3, we describe our hardware/software partitioning tool. In section 4, we show some experimental results. Finally, we present some conclusions.

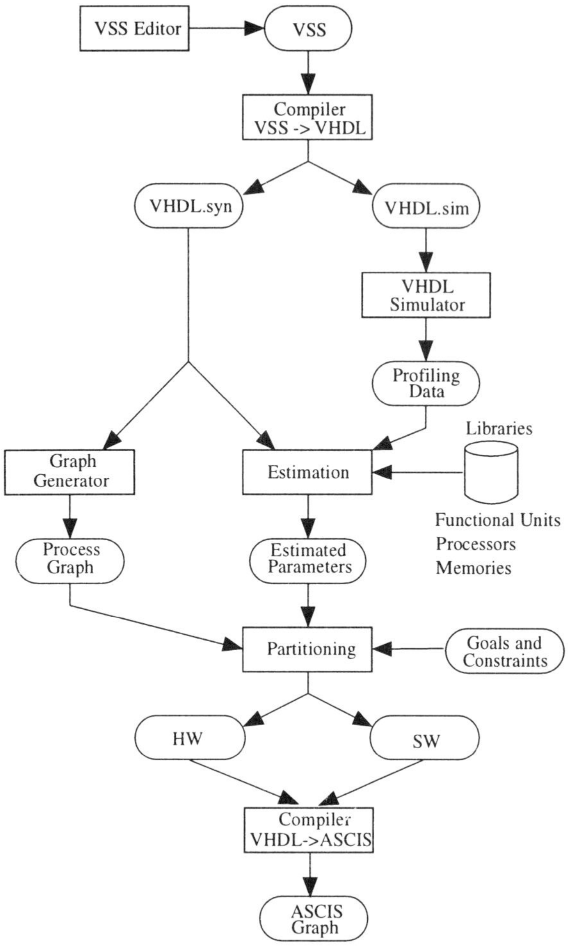

Figure 1. GACSYS codesign environment.

2. Related work

Previous work on hardware/software partitioning can be grouped into different classes by considering the following criteria: type of applications, representation model, target architecture, pipelining, granularity, partitioning strategy, optimization algorithm and cost function parameter .

Partitioning tools can be grouped into two classes depending on application type: a) control-dominated applications [1][9][10], and b) data-dominated ones [11][12][13].

We can also classify partitioning tools according to representation model: a) process DAG (*Directed Acyclic Graph*) [12][14][15], b) control and data flow graph (CDFG) [13], c) other types of graphs [1][16][17].

According to target architecture, we identify the following classes : a) tools based on monoprocessor architectures. Specific hardware modules can be used as coprocessors [1][9][16] or parallel processors [3][10][14][19]. b) Tools based on multiprocessor architectures [12][15][18].

Previous partitioning tools do not support process-level pipelining. We only have found one paper dealing with this topic [12]. Some papers mention it as future work [10].

Partitioning tools can be grouped into five classes according to grain size: a) process [10][12][14][15][18], b) subprogram [20], c) basic block [1][3][11][13], d) operation [21], and e) mixed grain [9][16][22].

We can also group previous work according to partitioning strategy: a) manual/interactive partitioning [20][21][22], and b) automatic partitioning. Later ones can be classified into the following classes: a) software-oriented (all processes are initially labeled as software) [1][11][12], b) hardware-oriented (vice versa) [3][23], and c) mixed tools (initial solution has hardware and software processes) [10][13][16][17][18].

Optimization algorithm can also be used to group partitioning tools. On one hand, there are tools that generate an optimal hardware/software partition by using algorithms such as ILP (*Integer Linear Programming*) [12][24], *branch & bound* [18], and dynamic programming [13][25]. However, these algorithms are not suitable for complex systems because they need an excessive computation time. On the other hand, there are tools based on heuristic techniques such as *clustering* [15][17][19][21], group migration [10][17], *simulated annealing* [1][11][12][16][17], and *ad-hoc* heuristics [14].

Finally, partitioning tools make use of different parameters to partition a specification. We can identify three groups: a) some tools only use system execution time [1][11][12][16][20], and b) other tools also consider design area [3][9][10][13][14] [15][17][18]. Majority of tools considers process communication time [1][3][9][10][11][12][13][14] [15][16][17][20]. However, some tools do not consider this parameter [18][25]. Anyway, previous tools do not consider system power consumption during partitioning process.

Main features of our tool are the following: *a) type of applications:* data-dominated, *b) representation model:* process DAG , *c) target architecture:* monoprocessor-based (specific hardware modules are used as parallel processors with local memory), *d) pipelining:* process-level, *e) granularity:* process-level, *f) strategy:* automatic partitioning, *g) optimization algorithm:* simulated annealing, *h) cost function parameters:* design execution time, area and power. Communication time is considered in the estimation phase (Figure 1).

3. Hardware/software partitioning

Our partitioning tool assigns a hardware or software implementation to each process of the input specification. Partitioning goal is to optimize design goals and satisfy design constraints. Partitioning input data are the following: a) input specification process graph (a node represents a process and an edge specifies process data flow), b) hardware and software parameter estimation such as system execution time, area and power, c) design goals and constraints (Figure 1).

Hardware and software parameter estimation is generated by using a tool that we have developed [26]. This tool gives us the following information (Figure 2):

process_1

Software estimations /* Pentium */

T (seg)	A (mm^2)	E (mj)
6.82e-7	2.96e+2	1.09e-2

Memory : RAM_3

Hardware estimations

Memory : RAM_1

3 /* Number of VHDL operators */

Functional Unit Configurations

N°	Code	T (seg)	A (mm^2)	E (mj)
* + >	* + + <			
1 1 1	3 1 5	1.5e-6	7.1e-1	1.9e-5
1 1 1	3 2 5	1.6e-6	7.4e-1	1.3e-5
1 2 1	3 1 1 5	1.9e-5	8.6e-1	1.9e-5
1 2 1	3 1 2 5	2.0e-5	8.6e-1	1.6e-5
1 2 1	3 2 1 5	2.0e-5	8.6e-1	1.6e-5
1 2 1	3 2 2 5	2.1e-5	8.6e-1	1.3e-5

Figure 2. Estimation phase output data.

- process name: next information corresponds to this process.
- software parameter estimation: estimated execution time (T), area (A) and energy (E).
- memories that have been used.
- number of different VHDL operators.
- functional unit configurations that can be used to implement the process in hardware. Configuration data is the following: a) number of functional units to implement VHDL operators, b) functional unit code, c) estimated design execution time (T), area (A) and energy (E).

Designer has to specify the following input parameters: a) maximum time to compute the process graph (T_E), b) number of pipeline phases, and c) design area or power upper bound. Given these parameters, design goals and constraints are the following:

- *Goals*: a) execution time of a pipeline phase must be as close as possible to maximum execution time. In this way, we avoid designs with unnecessary extra cost. This is a typical goal in digital signal processing system design. b) We must optimize design area or powe .
- *Constraints*: a) execution time of a pipeline phase can not be greater than maximum execution time. b) Design area or power upper bound must be satisfied.

Main contribution of our partitioning tool is the following:

- *it supports process-level pipelining* (Figure 3): previous work on partitioning does not consider this feature. We allow a designer to make a larger number of design cost (area or power) and latency tradeoffs.

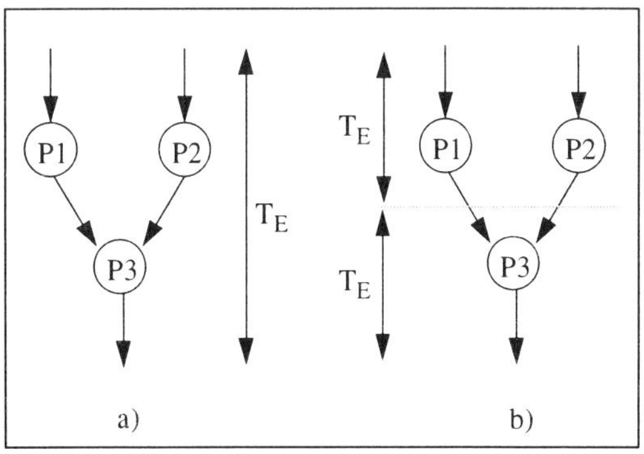

Figure 3. (a) Process graph without pipelining (b) process graph with 2-phase pipelining.

- *it considers design power consumption*: this parameter has not been considered in previous codesign environments. However, it is important to design current systems. We have supposed an implementation with CMOS technology. Thus, main power consumption is due to switching power [27][28][29]. We have also supposed power-down techniques (clock signal of some latches are disabled to avoid power consumption when a functional unit does not generate a useful result in a given cycle) [27][29][30].

3.1. Cost function

Cost function of our partitioning tool makes use of the following parameters: a) design area (A) and power consumption (P). b) Design execution time (T) that is not useful in each pipeline phase (Expression 1). This value is obtained by substracting maximum execution time (T_E) and pipeline phase execution time (T_F).

Given a pipeline schedule and a hardware or software process configuration, execution time of a pipeline phase depends on process schedule. We have named this scheduling process as virtual scheduling (Figure 4). Given a virtual schedule, Expression 2 shows how to evaluate execution time of a pipeline phase (T_{Fi}) (Pi represents one step of the virtual schedule).

In general, a virtual schedule step can have hardware and software processes. Thus, execution time of a virtual step is the maximum value among the following ones:

- slowest execution time among hardware processes ($max\{T_{Hw}\}$).

$$T = \sum_{i}^{Phases} (T_E - T_{Fi})$$

Expression 1. Execution time that is not used in pipeline phases.

$$T_{Fi} = \sum_{Pi} max\{max\{T_{Hw}\}, \sum T_{Sw}\}$$

Expression 2. Execution time of a pipeline phase.

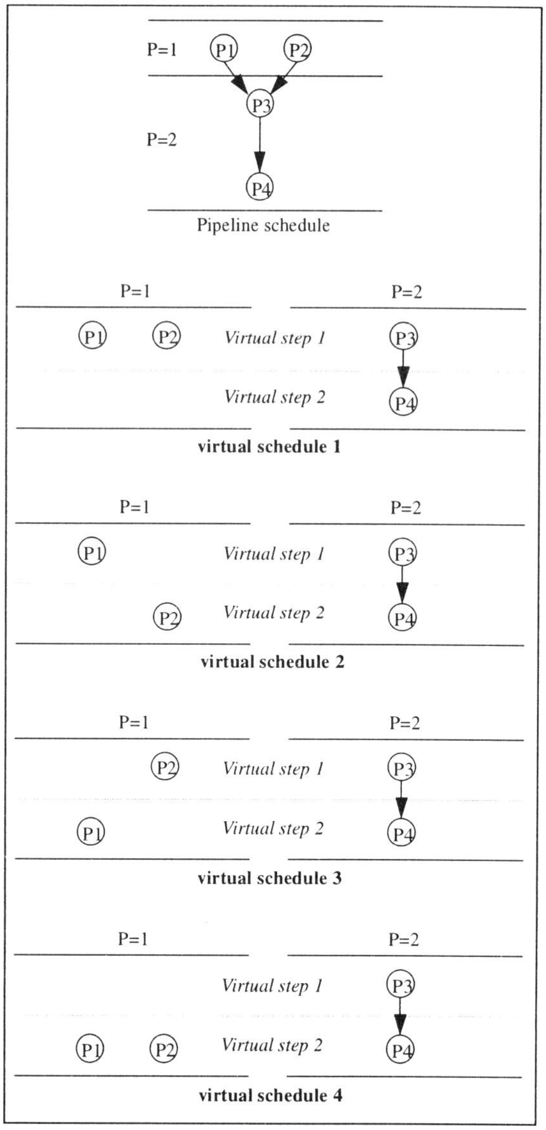

Figure 4. Example of different virtual schedules.

$$COST_P = \alpha \frac{P - P_{min}}{Range(P)} + (1-\alpha)\frac{T}{Range(T)}$$

$$COST_A = \alpha \frac{A - A_{min}}{Range(A)} + (1-\alpha)\frac{T}{Range(T)}$$

Expression 3. Cost function to optimize power ($COST_P$) or area ($COST_A$).

• software execution time. It is evaluated by adding each process execution time because we only have one processor (ΣT_{Sw}).

Expression 3 shows cost function that our partitioning algorithm uses. P_{min} and A_{min} represent minimum design power and area, respectively. Parameters are normalized by dividing them with corresponding value ranges. α weight allows a designer to give priority to design area or power.

3.2. Partitioning algorithm

Hardware/software partitioning is a NP-complete combinatorial optimization problem [31][32]. In general, we can not use methods that give us an optimal solution because they need an excessive computation time. Heuristic methods are an alternative to solve this problem. They allow us to make tradeoffs between computation time and solution quality. In short, they generate good solutions by using a reasonable computation time.

Our partitioning algorithm is based on simulated annealing [33][34]. We select this method following experimental results published in [17][19], where it is concluded that simulated annealing gives better results than other heuristic techniques do such as clustering or group migration.

Now, we describe main steps of our algorithm. First, algorithm generates an initial solution that has two components: a) initial pipeline schedule, b) hardware/software process configuration. Initial schedule is obtained by using an ASAP-based algorithm (*As Soon As Possible*) [35][36]. Initial configuration is randomly generated.

Once we have an initial (current) solution, annealing process is started. Algorithm selects a neighbour solution of the current one. It is randomly generated by selecting a process. Then, selected process is randomly changed from current pipeline phase to a new one. This change must consider process data dependences (Figures 5 and 6).

However, process phase change is not carried out each annealing process iteration. In this way, pipeline schedule remains stable various iterations. It allows remaining processes to adapt itself to process phase change. Finally, if neighbour solution cost is lower than current solution is, then first one is accepted as new current solution. On the other case, there is still a possibility to accept it that depends on both solution cost and annealing process temperature [33][34].

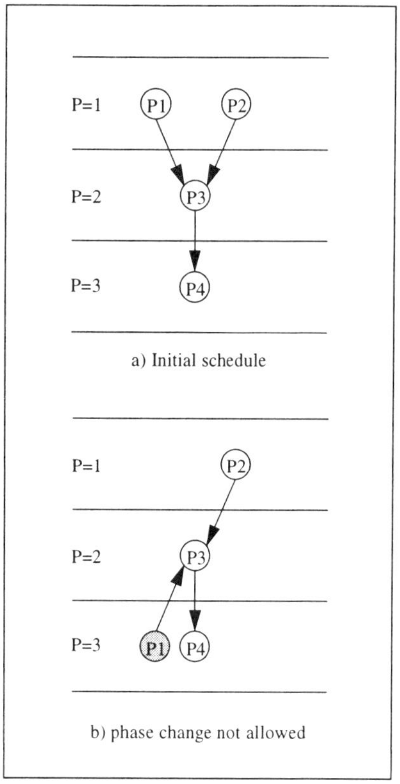

Figure 5. Example of process phase change.

We have also developed an exhaustive algorithm to get optimal solutions and evaluate our algorithm. However execution time was so high that it was not possible to get optimal solutions (even by using low complexity examples). In fact, some experiments were aborted after various weeks of computation. We have developed a semi-exhaustive algorithm to solve this problem. Algorithm is also based on simulated annealing but it is executed for all possible pipeline schedules.

4. Example

In this section, we present some experimental results. We have used a voice recognition system as example. This system generates a set of coefficients from a voice signal that is sampled at 8 KHz and packed in frames of 128 bytes. Thus, maximum graph execution time is 1.6E-2 seconds ($128 \cdot 800\ 0^{-1}$). System specification has eight processes (process graph is illustrated in Figure 7) and 2670 lines of VHDL code.

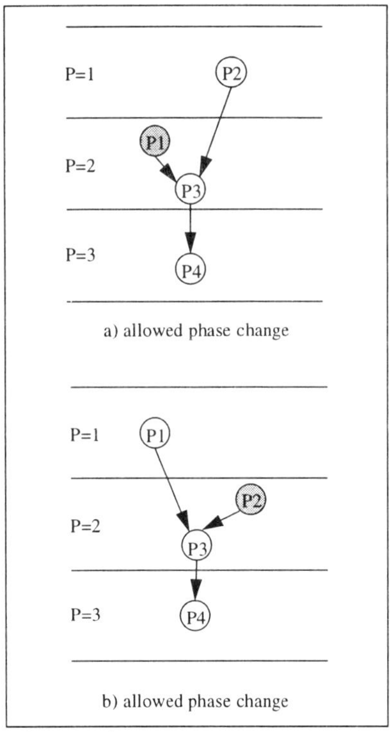

Figure 6. Example of right phase changes.

Now, we show some results to illustrate design space exploration. On the one hand, designer can make area and power tradeoffs. Figure 8 shows different design space solutions. System power consumption decreases as system area is increased. It is due to the following factors: a) if we increase design area, then functional units with lower supply voltage and higher area can be used, b) if design area is increased, then a larger number of processes can be implemented in hardware (Figure 9). It decreases processor power consumption.

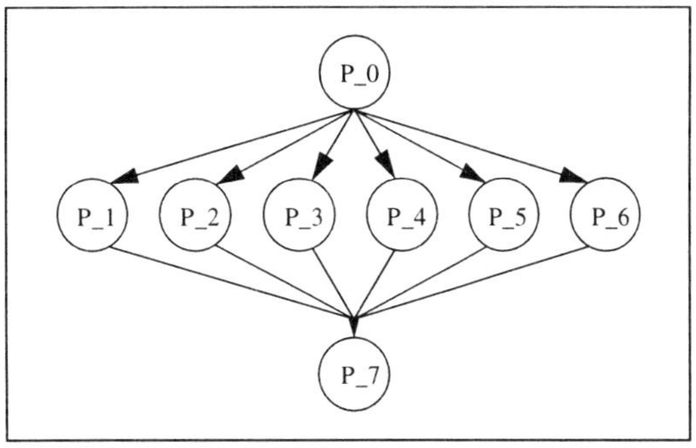

Figure 7. Process graph.

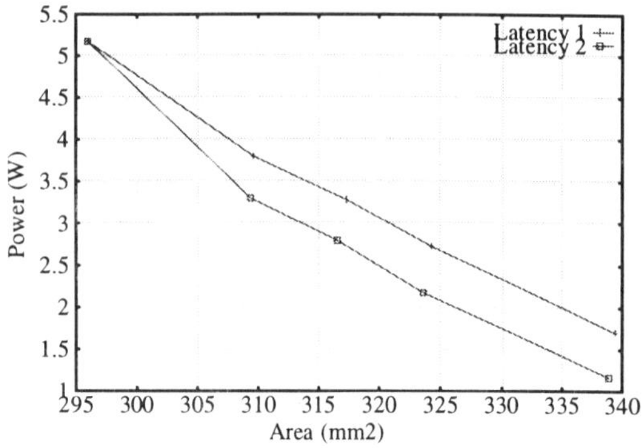

Figure 8. Process-level pipelining.

Moreover, designer can explore power and latency tradeoffs. Figure 8 shows design space solutions with different latency. It can be observed that designs with higher latency have a lower power consumption.

However, it is not always a good tradeoff to increase design latency. Figure 10 shows that designs with a 3-phase pipeline have equal power consumption than a 2-phase one has. In short, designer can select a hardware/ software partition among a set of solutions with different area, power and latency tradeoffs. For instance, designer could select a minimum power consumption partition if system under design is to be integrated in a portable equipment.

Finally, we have evaluated results quality by comparing our algorithm with semi-exhaustive one. Our results are close to those generated by semi-exhaustive algorithm (Figure 11). In particular, there is only a difference fro 5% to 10%.

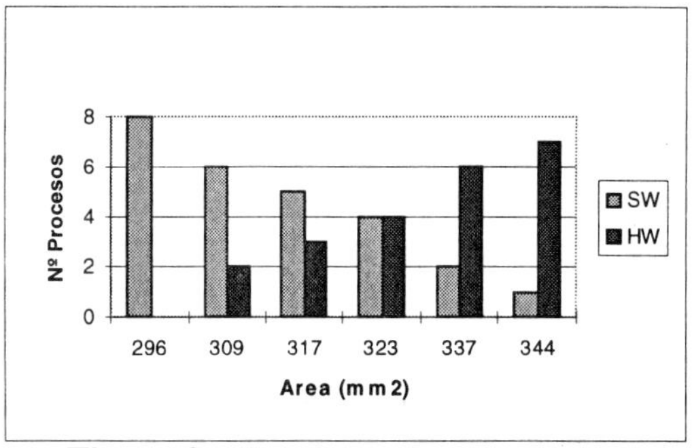

Figure 9. Hw / Sw process distribution.

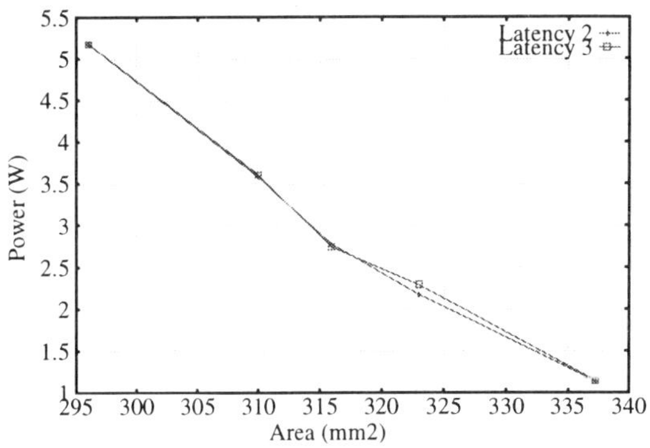

Figure 10. Process-level pipelining.

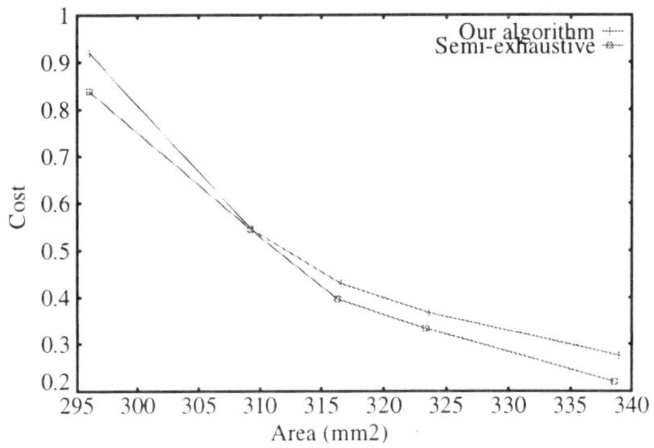

Figure 11. Results quality.

5. Conclusions

Our research group is developing a hardware/software codesign environment named GACSYS that is oriented to data-dominated applications. In this paper, we have presented GACSYS's hardware/software partitioning tool. Main contribution of our tool is the following: a) it supports process-level pipelining that is not supported in previous work on partitioning. This feature allows a designer to make new design cost (area or power) and latency tradeoffs. b) It makes use of design power consumption to explore design space. This parameter is not considered in previous work. This feature allows a designer to use functional units with different supply voltage. Thus, designer can explore new area and power tradeoffs.

We have recently got funds to develop a research project on hardware/software codesign of MAC and LLC protocols for wireless ATM LANs. However, our environment is not oriented to control-dominated applications. Thus, future work will be oriented to the extension of our system to support this type of applications. We will have to work on issues such as the following: a) our estimation tool is based on a message passing architecture. A shared memory architecture would be more suitable to design communication protocols. Moreover, this new model would have to account for memory access conflicts. b) Our estimation model does not consider process communication waiting time. It can not be obviated for communication protocols.

Acknowledgements

This work has been partially supported by Spanish Government by means of CICYT research project TIC98-1115-C02-02.

References

[1] R. Ernst, J. Henkel, T. Benner. *Hardware/Softwar Cosynthesis for Microcontrollers*. IEEE Design and Test of Computers, December 1993, pp. 64-75.

[2] D. Gajski, F. Vahid, S. Narayan. *A System-Design Methodology: Executable-Specification Refinement*. Proceedings of EDAC'94, 1994, pp. 458-463.

[3] R. K. Gupta. *Co-Synthesis of Hardware and Software for Digital Embedded Systems*. Kluwer Academic Publishers, 1995.

[4] T.B. Ismail, A.A. Jerraya. *Synthesis Steps and Design Models for Codesign*. IEEE Computer Magazine, February 1995, pp. 44-52.

[5] F. Balarin, M. Chiodo, P. Giusto, H. Hsieh, A. Jurecska, C. Passerone, A. Sangiovanni-Vincentelli, E. Sentovich, K. Suzuki, B. Tabbara. *Hardware-Software Codesign of Embedded Systems: The POLIS Approach*. Kluwer Academic Publishers, 1997.

[6] J. F. Pérez Castellano, Álvaro Suárez, J. C. Bordón. *Intermediate Representations of Concurrent VHDL-based Specifications*. Proceedings of 5th EUROMICRO Workshop on Parallel and Distributed Processing, January 22nd-24th, 1997, London, United Kingdom, pp. 66-71. ISBN 0-8186-7770-8.

[7] J. F. Pérez Castellano, O. Cazorla, J. C. Bordón, Álvaro Suárez. *A VHDL-based Hardware/Software Codesign Approach*. VHDL User's Forum in Europe, SIG-VHDL Spring'97 Working Conference, Toledo, Spain, April, 1997, pp. 159-170. ISBN 84-8102-158-X.

[8] Juan P. Castellano, David Sánchez, Onassis Cazorla, Juan Bordón, Álvaro Suárez. *GACSYS: a VHDL-based Hw/Sw Codesign Tool*. The Second International Workshop on Design and Diagnostics of Electronic Circuits and Systems (DDECS'98). Szczyrk, Poland, September (2nd - 4th), 1998, pp. 293-299. ISBN 83-908409-6-0.

[9] A. Balboni, W. Fornaciari, D. Sciuto. *Partitioning and Exploration Strategies in the TOSCA Co-Design Flow.* Proceedings of the International Workshop on Hardware/ Software Codesign, 1996, pp. 62-69.

[10] C. Carreras, J. C. López, M. L. López, C. Delgado-Kloos, N. Martínez, L. Sánchez. *A Co-Design Methodology Based on Formal Specification and High-level Estimation.* Proceedings of the International Workshop on Hardware/ Software Codesign, 1996, pp. 28-35.

[11] J. Becker, R. W. Hartenstein, R. Kress. *Two-level Partitioning of Image Processing Algorithms for the Parallel Map-oriented Machine.* Proceedings of the International Workshop on Hardware/Software Codesign, 1996, pp. 77-84.

[12] A. Bender *MILP Based Task Mapping for Heterogeneous Multiprocessor Systems.* Proceedings of the EURODAC, September 1996, pp. 190-197.

[13] P. V. Knudsen, J. Madsen. *PACE: A Dynamic Programming Algorithm for Hardware/Software Partitioning.* Proceedings of the International Workshop on Hardware/Software Codesign, March 1996, pp. 85-92.

[14] A. Kalavade, E. Lee. *A Global Criticality/Local Phase Driven Algorithm for the Constrained Hardware/Software Partitioning Problem.* Proceedings of the International Workshop on Hardware/Software Codesign, 1994, pp. 42-48.

[15] W. Wolf, J. Hou. *Process Partitioning for Distributed Embedded Systems.* Proceedings of the International Workshop on Hardware-Software Co-Design, March 1996, pp. 70-76.

[16] P. Eles, Z. Peng, A. Doboli. *VHDL System-Level Specification and Partitioning in a Hardware/Software Co-Synthesis Environment.* Proceedings of the International Workshop on Hardware-Software Codesign, 1994, pp. 49-55.

[17] F. Vahid, T. dm Le. *Towards a model for hardware and software functional partitioning.* Proceedings of the Fourth International Workshop on Hardware-Software Co-Design, March 1996, pp. 116-123.

[18] J. G. D'Ambrosio, X. Hu. *Configuration-Level Hardware/ Software Partitioning for Real-Time Embedded Systems.* Proceedings of the International Workshop on Hardware-Software Codesign, 1994, pp. 34-41.

[19] F. Vahid, D. Gajski. *Clustering for improved system-level functional partitioning.* Proceedings of the 8th International Symposium on System Synthesis, France, 1995, pp. 28-33.

[20] M. Theibinger, P. Stravers, H. Veit. *Castle: An Interactive Environment for HW/SW Co-Design.* Proceedings of the International Workshop on Hardware/Software Codesign, 1994, pp. 203-209.

[21] E. Lagnese, D. Thomas. *Architectural Partitioning for System Level Synthesis of Integrated Circuits.* IEEE Transactions on Computer-Aided Design, July 1991.

[22] T. B. Ismail, K. O'Brien, A. Jerraya. *Interactive System-level Partitioning with PARTIF.* EDAC'94, 1994, pp. 464-468.

[23] A. Kalavade, A. Lee. *A Hardware-Software Codesign Methodology for DSP Applications.* IEEE Design & Test of Computers, Vol. 10, Nº 3, 1993, pp.16-28.

[24] R. Niemann, P. Marwedel. *Hardware/Softwar Partitioning using Integer Programming.* Proceedings of the European Design and Test Conference, 1996, pp. 473-479.

[25] A. Jantsch, P. Ellervee, J. Öberg, A. Hermani, H.Tenhunen. *Hardware/Software partitioning and minimizing memory interface traffic.* Proceedings of the EURODAC, 1994.

[26] D. Sánchez, J. P. Castellano. *Herramienta de Particionado Hardware/Software para Codiseño de Sistemas.* Proyecto Fin de Carrera, ETSIT, ULPGC, Enero 1999.

[27] A. Chandrakasan, A. Sheng, R. W. Brodersen. *Lower-Power CMOS Design.* IEEE Journal of Solid-State Circuits, 1992, pp. 472-484.

[28] A. Raghunathan, N. K. Jha. *Behavioral Synthesis for Low Power.* Proceedings of the International Conference on Computer Design: VLSI in Computers and Processors, 1994, pp. 318-322.

[29] R. S. Martin, J. P. Knight. *Power-Profiler: Optimizing ASICs Power Consumption at the Behavioral Level.* Proceedings of the DAC, 1995, pp.42-47.

[30] E. Macii, M. Pedram, F. Somenzi. *High-Level Power Modeling, Estimation and Optimization.* In Proceedings of the 34th DAC, June 1997, pp. 504-511.

[31] M. R. Garey, D. S. Johnson. *Computers and Intractability: A Guide to the Theory of NP-Completeness.* W.H. Freeman and Company, 1979.

[32] D. S. Hochbaum. *Approximation Algorithms for NP-hard Problems.* PWS Publishing Company, 1997.

[33] S. Kirkpatrick, C. D. Gelatt, M. P. Vecchi. *Optimization by Simulated Annealing.* Science, Vol. 220, Nº 4598, pp. 671-680, May 1983.

[34] K. A. Dowsland. *Modern Heuristic Techniques for Combinatorial Problems.* Ed. by C. R. Reeves, McGraw-Hill, 1995, ISBN 0-07-709239-2.

[35] D. Gajski, N. Dutt, A. Wu, S. Lin. *High-Level Synthesis: Introduction to Chip and System Design.* Kluwer Academic Publishers, 1992.

[36] P. Michel, U. Lauther, P. Duzy. *The Synthesis Approach to Digital System Design.* Kluwer Academic Publishers, 1992.

PVM Application–Level Tuning over ATM

Claudia Di Napoli Maurizio Giordano Mario Mango Furnari
Francesco Vitobello
Istituto di Cibernetica CNR
Via Toiano, 6 - I-80072 Arco Felice, Naples, Italy
{C.Dinapoli, M.Giordano, M.MangoFurnari, F.Vitobello}@cib.na.cnr.it

Abstract

The use of software packages that allow for distributed application computing is becoming more and more attractive due to the advent of high speed computer networks as well as of high performance general purpose workstations. Nevertheless it is well known that the success of cluster–based parallel computing depends on the performance of communication among processors, which in turn depends on the physical network architecture, protocols, and interface software. In this paper we present the results of our investigation into an efficient use of PVM software package in real distributed application settings over ATM networks. In particular we will show that the tuning of PVM network parameters, done at application–level, improves communication performances on ATM networks without using a native ATM PVM implementation that directly adopts the ATM Adaptation Layer instead of TCP/IP.

1. Introduction

Distributed computing has always been very challenging since it involves many different research areas. In the last years it has become even more attractive due to the use of software packages allowing for distributed application computing based on networks of workstations. The possibility to use network of workstations as a single parallel virtual machine is stimulated by the advent of high speed computer networks as well as of high performance general purpose workstations at reasonable costs.

Among the software packages that have been developed in the last decade to implement distributed applications on top of cluster of workstation, *PVM* (*Parallel Virtual Machine*) [6] is one of the most used. Parallel applications can be written on top of PVM library and executed over a network of heterogeneous machines viewed as a single parallel machine, since PVM automatically handles all communication operations like message buffering, transmission and routing, data conversion, and task scheduling across the network.

Since communication between processors is one of the critical points in networked computer systems, high–speed switched networks, such as ATM, instead of traditional broadcast networks, such as Ethernet, are expected to significantly increase the communication performances for networks of workstations [3].

Asynchronous Transfer Mode (*ATM*) [2] is a network standard. It specifies a *cell–switched* network where data is fragmented in small data units, named *cells*, each containing 48 bytes of information and a 5 byte header that provides switching and control information. Moreover ATM is *connection–oriented*, which implies that *virtual channels* must be established between source and destination prior data transmission.

To achieve better performances on high–speed networks several sources of overhead must be discovered and reduced. Hardware overhead is mostly caused by host network interface board, signal propagation delay, host bus architecture and network switch. Software overhead occurs in the interactions among operating system, device drivers and higher layer protocols. These interactions are sources of significant overhead for the communication [8, 16, 18].

The PVM software package is based on the *BSD Socket* programming interface [12], the *Transmission Control Protocol* (*TCP*) and the *User Datagram Protocol* (*UDP*) as transport protocols.

Researches have been carried out in implementing PVM directly on top of ATM [11] and *Hippi* [9], avoiding the TCP/IP layers. The results obtained showed that, although this new implementation provides increased communication throughput, the maximum achieved throughput is still far below the full potential of high–speed networks.

In our experimentations with PVM applications, we showed that it is possible to improve PVM communication performances over ATM networks just by tuning the PVM *message fragment size* parameter at the PVM application

1066-6192/99 $10.00 © 1999 IEEE

```
/*
 * PVM "echo_server" program
 */

main ()
{
   /* initialize */
   ...
   /* activate "echo_client" program & get id */
   pvm_spawn("echo_client",...,&client_id);

   for (i = 1; i <= n; i++) {
      timer_start(...);

      /* pack message into send buffer */
      pvm_initsend(...);
      pvm_pkbyte(msg, m, 1);

      /* send message to client */
      pvm_send(client_id, MSGTAG);

      /* receive message from client */
      pvm_recv(client_id, MSGTAG);

      /* unpack message from receive buffer */
      pvm_upkbyte(msg, ,m, 1);

      timer_stop(...);
   }
   pvm_exit();
}
```

```
/*
 * PVM "echo_client" program
 */


main ()
{
   /* initialize */
   ...
   /* get "echo_server" program id */
   server_id = pvm_myparent();

   for (i = 1; i <= n; i++) {

      /* receive message from server */
      pvm_recv(server_id, MSGTAG);

      /* unpack message from receive buffer */
      pvm_upkbyte(msg, m, 1);

      /* pack message into send buffer */
      pvm_initsend(...);
      pvm_pkbyte(msg, m, 1);

      /* send message to server */
      pvm_send(server_id, MSGTAG);

   }
   pvm_exit();
}
```

Figure 1. The ping–pong program.

program interface (PVM API) [7]. The results obtained in measuring the time spent in communication for a ping–pong program, built *ad hoc* for the experimentations, were encouraging. In fact they showed that fixing opportunely the PVM fragment size, it is possible to improve up to 30 per cent the communication costs.

In order to validate these results, it was decided to verify if they can be obtained also in the case of real PVM distributed application settings. In particular we considered a PVM distributed application designed according to the *Cellular Automata* approach [15] simulating the melting and solidification of a silicon sample.

The rest of the paper is so organized: Section 2 reports the preliminary tests based on the ping–pong program, the hardware setup, the parameter used for tuning and the experimental results. Section 3 describes the Cellular Automata application used in carrying out our experimentations to validate the preliminary results. Section 4 sketches the PVM distributed implementation of the considered application. Section 5 gives the results regarding the improvements obtained in communication costs. Finally some conclusions and future works are reported in Section 6.

2. A preliminary test: the ping–pong program

The communication measurements carried out in [7] took into account only the effective network communication without considering the message (un)packing time, since in the test application the communication was affected mainly by the message transit over the network. In real distributed application settings the time spent for packing and unpacking messages becomes relevant and so it was necessary to carry out some preliminary tests in order to verify if the same results can be obtained also in this case.

The new preliminary measurements were based on a ping–pong test performed by two PVM programs, a *server* and a *client*, exchanging data messages on a peer–to–peer (TCP) connection. Figure 1 shows the code for server and client programs of the ping–pong test.

The server program starts running on the *server* host and it spawns the client program on another host of the parallel virtual machine, that is the *client* host. Each program gets the task identifier of the other process needed for exchanging data. On each ping–pong transmission, the server packs a message of a chosen size into the sending buffer and sends it to the client; the client, upon reception, unpacks the message from the receiving buffer, packs it again in the sending buffer and sends the same message back to the server; the server, upon reception unpacks the returned message; the ping–pong is iterated to get statistics from the measurements. The time is measured in such a way that the (un)packing time on both server and client programs is taken into account.

2.1. Hardware setup

The hardware used for our experiments is a cluster of SUN SPARCstations 20. Each machine, equipped with the Solaris 2.5 operating system, has a Fore Systems SBA-200E ATM adapter connected to a Fore Systems LE155 ATM switch.

SBA200E [4] is characterized by a raw bandwidth of 155 Mbit/sec; the physical layer format is *Synchronous Optical Network (SONET) Synchronous transfer mode 3c (STS-3c)*. It is a hierarchy of optical signals that are multiples of a

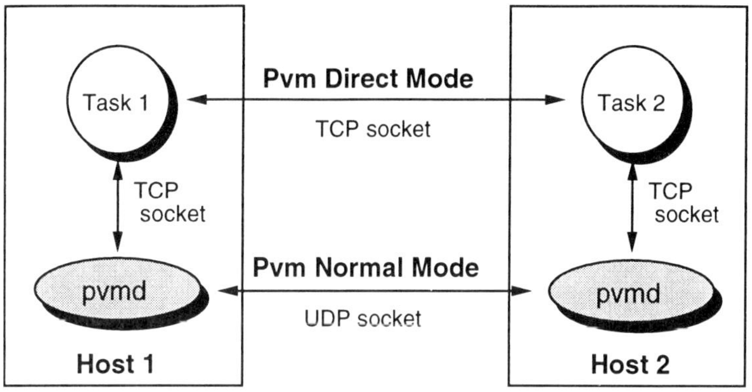

Figure 2. PVM communication modes.

basic signal rate of 51.84 Mbit/sec (*STS-1*) [14]. LE155 ATM workgroup switch [5] has a non-blocking switching capability of 2.5 Gbit/sec. The switch provides up to 16 ports connectivity, each running at speeds of 155 Mbit/sec.

The ATM switch is configured in such a way to use a bidirectional *Permanent Virtual Circuit* (*PVC*) with a bit rate of 155 Mbit/sec between the two workstations. When running test programs on ATM, the network was dedicated.

The communication stack used is a *Classical IP over ATM* (*CIOA*) [10]. IP datagrams are encapsulated using IEEE 802.2 LLC/SNAP and are segmented into ATM cells using ATM Adaptation Layer type 5 (AAL5).

2.2. PVM parameter tuning

PVM communication mode. PVM provides both a task–to–task *normal mode* and *direct mode* communication. PVM daemons communicate each other through UDP sockets. In normal mode tasks communicate through their associated PVM daemons, and the connection to them is via TCP sockets. In direct mode tasks communicate each other directly using a TCP socket. These two communication modes are shown in Figure 2.

PVM task–to–task direct mode communication provides better performances [17, 6] since it is based on peer–to–peer TCP connections. Nevertheless, the main drawback of direct mode communication is scalability: there is a small number of TCP connections that the operating system may support at the same time.

PVM message fragment size. PVM messages are assembled without assigning a maximum length ahead in time. Message packing functions allocate dynamically memory in steps using *data buffers* (message *fragments*) to store the data, and *fragment descriptors* to chain data buffers together. From now on we refer to the data buffer size as *message fragment size*.

2.3. Communication measurements

We measured the *round–trip time* (*RTT*) and the *throughput* between two SUN SPARCstations 20 interconnected by a 155 Mbit/sec ATM LAN.

The RTT is defined as the time a message takes to go from the source to the destination host and return back. We chose to measure the RTT in order to avoid synchronization between the two machines. Throughput (or *data rate*), is defined by the number of bytes sent divided by half of the RTT. If m is the number of bytes sent in a message, the throughput is calculated as follows:

$$throughput = \frac{(2 * m * 8)}{RTT} \; [Mbit/sec]. \qquad (1)$$

The ping–pong transmission is iterated 1000 times to collect samples of RTTs and compute the mean RTT value and throughput.

We run the test program varying both PVM message size and message fragment size: the message size ranges from 4 bytes up to 1 Mbyte, while the message fragment size ranges from 512 bytes (the minimum allowed) up to 1 Mbyte. We measured RTTs using the PVM direct mode communication. We used SUN OS *Solaris-specific timers*, timing routines with a resolution of 1 microsecond.

2.4. Preliminary test–bed results

We split the test–bed experiments in two sets. The first includes measurements of RTTs between the server and client programs running on the above described hardware setup. We consider in each RTT measurement also the message (un)packing time spent by both programs (see the code in Figure 1). In the second set of experiments we measured the same quantities where the RTT accounts only for data transmission. This is done by slightly modifying the ping–pong program in such a way that the client, upon reception,

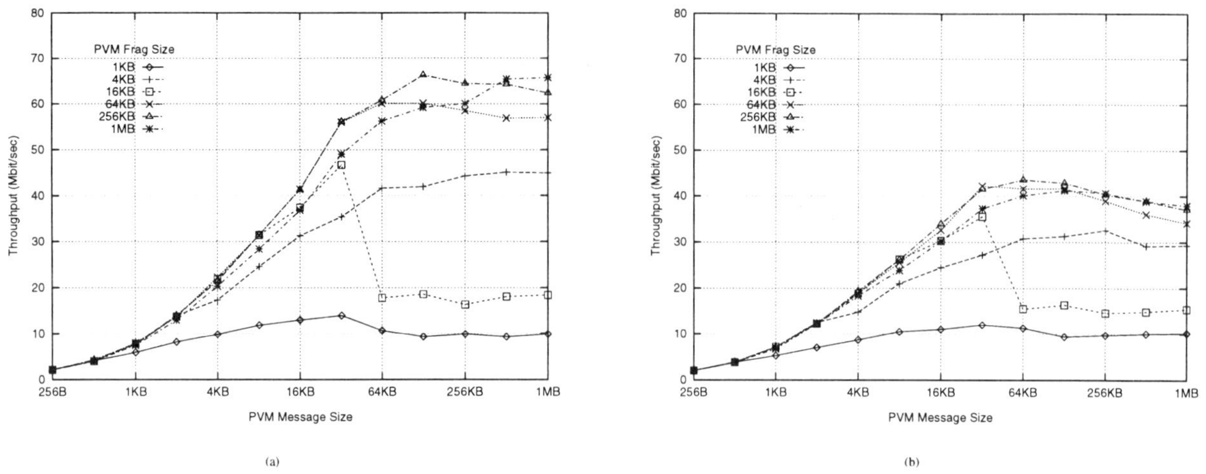

Figure 3. Throughputs varying message fragment size and message length, without (a) and with (b) packing (unpacking) time.

sends immediately a pre-packed message, while the timers in the server program embody only the send and receive operations.

The results of these two sets of measurements are shown in Figure 3, where we report throughputs for the two sets of experiments. In both cases we gain when varying the message fragment size. If we consider only the time spent for data transmission without (un)packing time, the maximum achievable throughput with the message default fragment size is around 45 Mbit/sec, while we go over 60 Mbit/sec for fragment size greater than 64 Kb with a gain of about 30 per cent. The maximum achieved throughput is 67 Mbit/sec for a message size of 128 Kb and a fragment size of 256 Kb.

This is due to the PVM dynamic allocation of messages: multiple fixed–size data buffers are chained together to hold unlimited sized messages. Choosing larger message fragment sizes the time required to assemble and manage large messages is significantly reduced. This caused better throughput values with respect to the case when message default fragmentation size was used (4 Kb).

If we consider also the time needed for (un)packing data (from) to communication buffers, the maximum achieved throughput with the default fragment size is 32 Mbit/sec, while the maximum gain reaches the 30 per cent for fragment sizes greater than 64 Kb.

This second set of preliminary tests shows that although we considered the time spent for message (un)packing, the gain in percentage did not vary significantly. Absolute throughput values are lower than the ones obtained in the previous case because the time is increased by the (un)packing time. Since this time increases with message size, this overhead is balanced using larger fragment sizes. In fact the fragment size affects also the (un)packing time.

In both sets of experiments we observed a sensible degradation of throughput when using a fragment size of 16 Kb. This is an anomalous behaviour which is likely not to be dependent on the parameters we are considering in these experiments. This is why it needs a different investigation that should take into account the OS implementation. In fact, in a related work [13], the communication tests used to benchmark a cluster of Linux-based workstations presented a similar behaviour that was proven to be due to the OS.

3. Cellular Automata application

In order to verify the results obtained for the ping–pong test in a real application setting, we considered a simulation application, since performances are a critical point in simulation activity.

The application simulates the interaction of bubbles and drops with a solidification front in a microgravity environment [1]. The experiment setup is based on a solid sample of silicon contained in a closed cell to be melt and then solidified under different thermal conditions (temperature gradients, heat exchange through the boundary walls).

The model adopted for the simulation of the considered physical system is two dimensional, and it is represented, according to a *Cellular Automata* (*CA*) approach [15], as a matrix of elements (CA cells) bounded by two lateral walls and two plates.

In particular the sample is represented by a cellular automaton consisting of three *properties* [1]: one represents the container, and the other two represent the cell state, i.e. the temperature and the phase defined as the percentage of

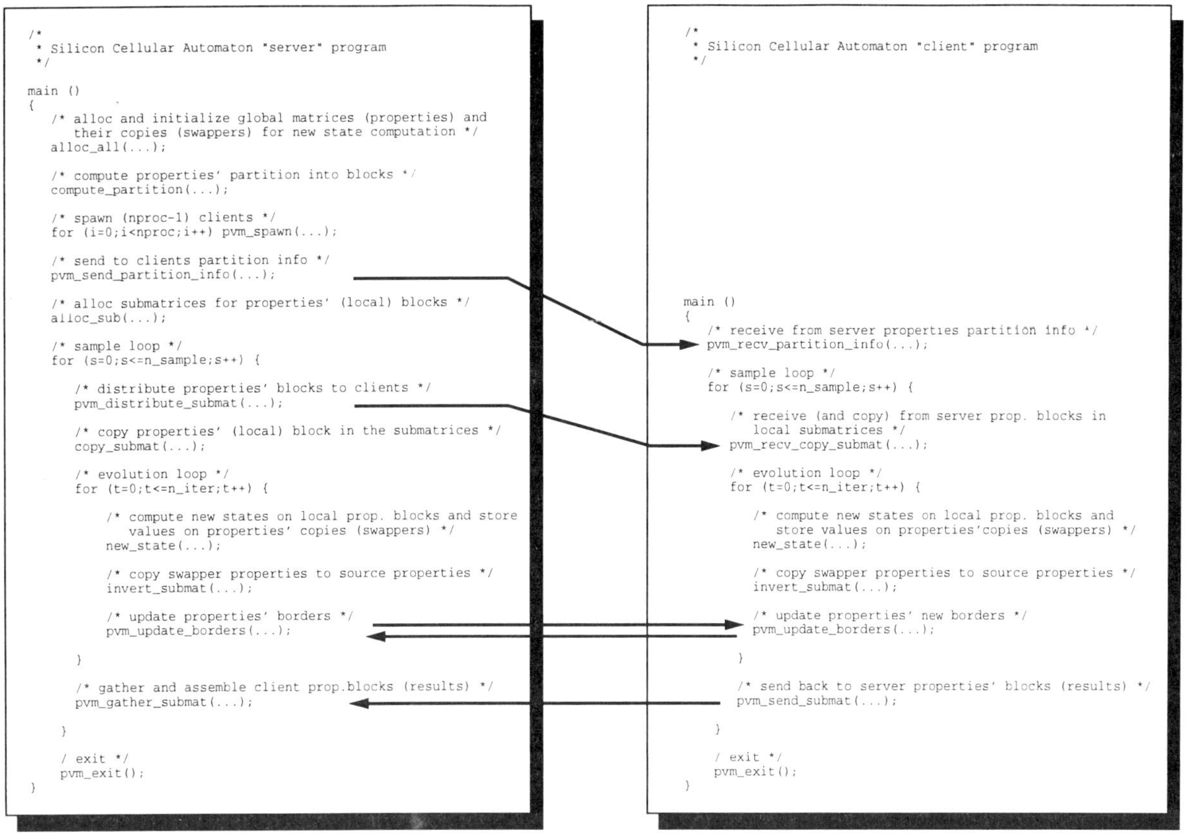

Figure 4. The Cellular Automata master and slave programs.

the solid phase content. The cellular automaton has a four–neighborhood topology, i.e. each cell value is affected only by the cell values individuated by the *North East West South* (*NEWS*) topology, while the border condition is *adiabatic*.

Each cell exchanges heat by diffusion with its neighbours; at each step the heat exchanged is computed to determine the new temperature. If the temperature evolution crosses the melting point, the phase transition is modeled as follows: part of the computed heat exchanged is available for the phase transition; then the corresponding phase variation can be evaluated. Once the transition is completed, the cell temperature can change again according to the Fourier law. This behaviour has been implemented in terms of the cellular automaton *transition function* iterated for a number of times fixed at each program execution.

4. Cellular Automata PVM implementation

The algorithm before described was re–implemented to allow for a distributed execution of the code according to a message–passing paradigm. The algorithm is suitable for a distributed implementation based on a *SPMD* (*Single Program Multiple Data*) paradigm since, according to the Cellular Automata model, the transition function (i.e. a single control flow) is applied, at each time step, at the same time on the three properties of the cellular automaton. According to the CA approach, the transition function represents local rules which depend only on the state of each automaton cell and a finite number of neighbour cells, so the model can be easily implemented according to the SPMD paradigm.

The distributed version of the code, see Figure 4, has been designed according to a *master/slave* programming model. The master program is responsible for allocating and initialising the automaton properties (i.e. the matrices representing the system temperature, phase, and container). Then it spawns the slave programs according to the configuration of the parallel virtual machine, calculates the matrix distribution according to the available processors, and distributes the individuated matrices' blocks among the slaves. Once completed these operations, the master starts acting as the other slaves whose execution consists of applying the transition function, iterated for the fixed number of times, on the local data of the corresponding matrices.

At each time step, the slaves communicate according to the automaton topology and border conditions in order to update the borders of each matrix portion to proceed in the

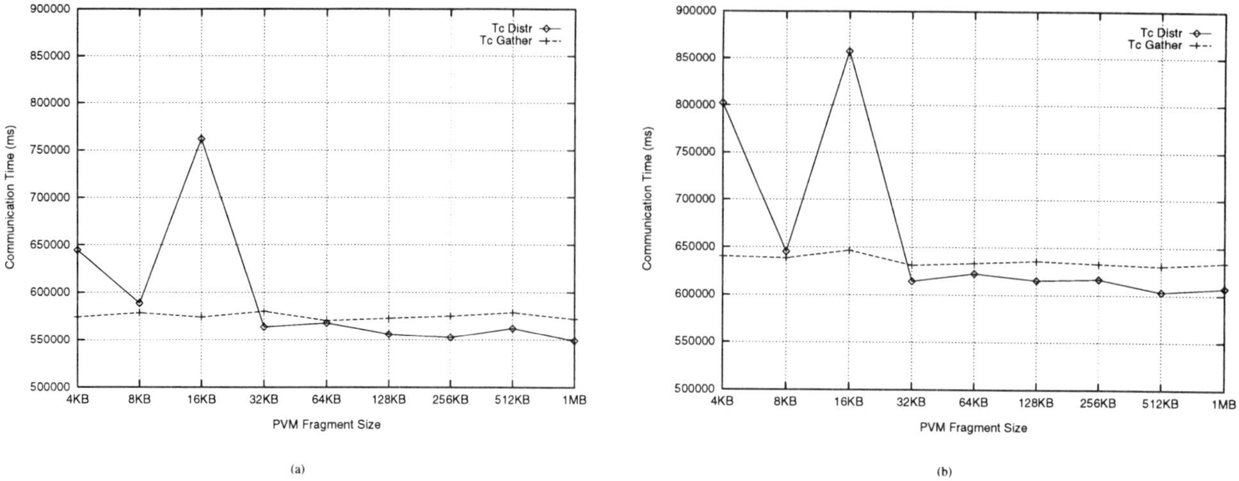

Figure 5. Silicon program running on 3 nodes (a) and 4 nodes (b) - Property distribution and gathering times vs PVM fragment size.

computation of the next automaton state. In fact the new cell state is computed using (i.e. reading values of) the immediate neighbour cells.

In the property distribution, the master sends the slaves matrices' blocks including the borders belonging to contiguous blocks. So, at each time step, border updating implies data exchange (i.e. communication) between "owners" of contiguous matrices' blocks. At the end of the transition function execution for the fixed number of time steps, the master gathers the matrices' blocks calculated by each slave to obtain the final automaton state.

Of course the matrix distribution and gathering are the most expensive operations from the communication cost point of view since they involve a greater amount of data exchange. Nevertheless, in the simulation activity it is important to have the possibility to check the state of the system evolution in order to adjust physical system parameters to tune the system behaviour.

This is why it was necessary to sample the automaton state after a fixed number of time steps (sampling step). In this case the distribution/gathering operations need to be repeated at each sampling step to guarantee the possibility to access the system dump. This adds even more communication costs and so the improvements of communication overhead becomes even more crucial in these applications.

5. Cellular Automata experimental results

We fixed the automata property size to 1024 x 1024 cells. The hardware in the silicon program experiments is the one used in the preliminary tests: we used the same workstation type, operating system and network connection. Only the number of nodes in the parallel virtual machine is different.

The silicon program experiments were divided in two sets: in the first, we run the master/slave program on a 3-node virtual machine, while in the second set a 4-node configuration was used. In both sets we varied the PVM message fragment size doubling it from 4 Kb to 1 Mb. Figures 5(a) and 5(b) report the obtained results.

First, we have to underline that in both experiments we detected the same anomalous behaviour found in the preliminary tests when using a fragment size of 16 Kb. As mentioned before, this result cannot be explained in the context of the application–level tuning parameter treated in this work, but should be correlated to the OS implementation.

In both figures we report two communication times measured in the silicon application execution: the first (*Tc distr*) is the time spent by the master to distribute automata properties' blocks to slave programs. the second time (*Tc gather*) is spent to receive them from slaves. In both communications we varied the PVM message fragment size from 4 Kb (default value) to 1 Mb.

When using 3 nodes, in the distribution and gathering steps the message size was 2.8 Mb, while with 4 nodes it was 2.1 Mb. For the other message transfers involving the automaton border update we used the default fragment size value: in fact, in this communication step the message size is 8 Kb, thus increasing the fragment size does not imply communication improvements.

As shown in Figure 5(a), with the default fragment size the total distribution time is about 650 sec and it decreases down to 550 sec for fragment size greater than 128 Kb; after this point the slope maintains this value until the maximum fragment size is reached. The gain in this range is about 18 per cent with respect to the time obtained with the message default fragment size.

In the same plot we report the gathering time which is not affected by the parameter tuning: slave programs send back to the master the properties' blocks in an asynchronous way, while the master sends them to the slaves in "one shot". Therefore, in the distribution phase the communication subsystem is busier than in the reception phase where messages are scattered when transmitted to the master. The fragment size tuning has a very low effect when the node processor is less overloading the communication subsystem.

Figure 5(b) reports the same measurements with 4 nodes. Communication times are higher than the previous case since the number of messages exchanged in the distribution and gathering phases increases, while the size is still large (2.1 Mb). Nevertheless, with a greater number of slaves the gain observed in the previous experiments increases up to 30 per cent when the fragment size is greater than 32 Kb with respect to the default size. The slope decreases sharply even varying the fragment size from the 4 Kb to 8 Kb. Again the gathering time is not effected by the parameter tuning.

This second set of measurements has shown gains comparable with those observed in the ping–pong tests. Moreover, the gain obtained with a larger parallel virtual machine lets us suppose that the improvements coming from tuning are more significant when the communication subsystem is busier, i.e. when large messages are sent across the network in short time ranges.

6. Conclusions

The goal of this paper is to evaluate the possibility to improve communication costs in distributed applications built using the classical TCP/IP PVM implementation over ATM networks. The obtained results confirmed our expectations on the necessity to exploit first the full potential of standard PVM software package at the application–level. In fact, as we showed in our experimentations, it is possible to gain in communication performances without using the PVM implementation native on ATM.

Of course, in real distributed application settings the communication time spent in (un)packing messages affects in a considerable way the total communication costs. Anyway some preliminary tests (still in progress) convinced us that this time can be drastically reduced using faster processors. In this case we expect a further improvement in communication costs.

Anyway this work stimulated us to proceed our investigations in order to verify the possibility to obtain the same improvements in communication just with the tuning of PVM parameters at the application–level, but using network infrastructures more affordable compared to ATM, as for example *FastEthernet*.

References

[1] L. Carotenuto, F. Mele, M. Mango Furnari, and R. Napolitano. Pecans: A parallel environment for cellular automata modeling. *Complex System Journal*, 10:23–41, 1996.

[2] M. de Prycker. *Asynchronous Transfer Mode solution for broadband ISDN*. Ellis Horwood series in Computer Communications and Networking, 1991.

[3] J. Dongarra and T. Dunigan. Message-passing performance of various computers. Technical Report CS-95-299, Oak Ridge National Laboratory, 1997.

[4] Fore Systems Inc. *ATM SBus Adapter User's Manual*, 1996.

[5] Fore Systems Inc. *ForeRunnerLE ATM Workgroup Switch Install. Manual*, 1997.

[6] A. Geist, A. Beguelin, J. Dongarra, W. Jiang, and R. Manchek. *PVM: Parallel Virtual Machine - A Users Guide and Tutorial for Network Parallel Computing*. MIT Press, 1994.

[7] M. Giordano, M. Mango Furnari, and F. Vitobello. Interaction between pvm parameters and communication performances on atm networks. In *Proceedings of The Fourth International ACPC Conference*, number 1557 in LNCS, pages 586–587, Salzburg, Austria, February 1999.

[8] Z. Haas. Protocol structure for high-speed communication over broadband isdn. *IEEE Networks*, 5(1):64–70, January 1991.

[9] J. Hsieh, D. Du, N. Troullier, and M. Lin. Enhanced pvm communications over a hippi local area network. In *Proceedings of The Second Intern. Workshop on High-Speed Network Computing*, Honolulu, Hawaii, April 1996.

[10] M. Laubach. Rfc 1577: Classical ip and arp over atm. 1994.

[11] M. Lin, J. Hsieh, D. Du, J. Thomas, and J. MacDonald. Distributed network computing over local atm networks. *IEEE Journal on Selected Areas in Communication, Special Issue of ATM LANs: Implementations and Experiences with a Emerging Technology*, 13(4):733–748, May 1995.

[12] M. K. McKusick, K. Bostic, M. Karel, and J. Quarterman. *The Design and Implementation of the 4.4BSD UNIX Operating System*. Addison Wesley, 1996.

[13] W. Salamon and A. Mink. Linux clusters. *Linux Journal*, pages 105–109, June 1999.

[14] A. Schmidt. *Multiprotocol over ATM*. Manning, 1997.

[15] T. Toffoli and N. Margolus. *Cellular Automata Machines: A New Environment for Modeling*. MIT Press, 1987.

[16] T. Von Eicken, T. Culler, S. Goldstein, and K. Schauser. Active message: a mechanism for integrated communication and computation. In *Proceedings of the 19th Annual Intern. Symposium on Computer Architecture*, pages 256–266, Gold Coast, Australia, May 1992.

[17] H. Zhou and A. Geist. Faster message passing in pvm. In *Proceedings of 9th Intern. Parallel Processing Symposium*, pages 67–73, Santa Barbara, California, April 1995.

[18] M. Zitterbart. High-speed transport components. *IEEE Network*, 5(1):54–63, January 1991.

Reusable Message Passing Components

J. Y. Cotronis

Department of Informatics, University of Athens, Panepistimiopolis, 15771 Athens, Greece
cotronis@di.uoa.gr

Abstract

Reusability of executables is an integral part in the design and implementation of message passing programs, as from the same executable component a number of interacting processes are spawned. In practice, reuse of executables within an application is usually achieved when processes execute within a specific regular topology and within a specific message passing environment (e.g. PVM, MPI). We propose the design and implementation of reusable message passing components, which are independent of the target message passing environment (MPE) and may be used in any topology, whether regular, partially regular or irregular. We define virtual process communication interfaces independent of any topology. Process topologies are established by associating compatible communication interfaces.

1. Introduction

In sequential programming reuse of components is considered as using already developed software artefacts in future applications. But in parallel programming reusability is an integral part of the design and implementation of a single parallel program. It is very common and many times desirable for processes to be spawned from the same executable. This is certainly true in message passing programming, where the SPMD model is the extreme case, in which all processes are spawned by the same executable component. The task a designer of a message passing program faces is to express in a single component the appropriate interactions of all the processes, which will be spawned from it, considering all their possible positions in the topology and additionally, for any size of the topology. Then the design has to be implemented using a message passing environment, such as PVM [6] or MPI [9] or Parix [10].

Process topologies in message passing applications are implicitly specified, but explicitly programmed within components. Topologies are formed by considering processes as nodes and communications channels between processes as arcs. Communication channels, i.e. the passing of messages from one process to another, in point-to-point communication are expressed by symmetric calls of send and receive operations in two processes. Each of the send or receive operations in one process has as parameter the identifier of the other process (e.g. tid in PVM and rank in MPI). Other parameters, which are common in both sides, include an integer value tagging the message and an implicit or explicit context. Process topologies are implicitly specified by such pairs of symmetric calls, but must be explicitly programmed by manipulating process identifiers in the calls. If the topology is regular, e.g. a grid or a ring, the designer develops functions, which take a process identifier and return the identifiers of its communicating processes. These functions are usually parameterised to return the identifiers processes in any size of the regular topology.

There are three problems with this approach. The first is that the implementation effort does not only depend on the application design, but also on the target Message Passing Environment (MPE), such as PVM and MPI. Each MPE requires different implementation techniques for programming the same design, because of the process management models they assume. Each MPE is suited for specific types of process topologies, those being closer to its process management model. For example, PVM favours tree and MPI ring or grid topologies. Topologies not well suited to an MPE may certainly be implemented, but require more complex programming. Additional effort is required for parameterizing topologies not well suited to a particular MPE [1, 2, 3, 4].

The second problem is that this approach is only suitable for regular topologies. There are many topologies, which are not globally regular but only partially or locally regular or even altogether irregular. In such cases, general functions returning the identifiers of the communicating processes cannot be derived and consequently ad hoc programming methods are used.

The third problem is that programming communication channels based on symmetric calls of send and receive operations which directly use specific process identifiers limit the reuse of components, as the processes spawned from them may operate only within specific topologies.

In this paper we present the design of reusable message passing components, which are independent of the target

1066-6192/99 $10.00 © 1999 IEEE

MPE and may be used in any topology, whether regular, partially regular or irregular. We define generic process communication interfaces independent of any topology, which processes use in the parameters of point-to-point and group operations. We establish process topologies by associating compatible communication interfaces.

This paper is structured as follows: In section 2 we present the requirements for generic point-to-point process interfaces and demonstrate their use in constructing regular, partially regular or irregular applications. In section 3 we design open process interfaces for point-to-point, as well as for group communication and barrier synchronisation. In section 4 we implement reusable components. In section 5 we outline the composition of reusable components in the Ensemble methodology [1, 2, 3, 4]. Finally, in section 6 we present our conclusions and plans for future work.

2. Process communication interfaces and process topologies

The physical analogy to the reusable components we try to construct is manufacturing of components, which are assembled or composed to make different products. Another analogy is Lego toy components, in which the same pieces are used to make different constructions. The reason for being able to reuse such components is the design of their interfaces, which permits components to be plugged together. Our objective is to be able to specify such interfaces for processes in a message passing environment. Let us examine the requirements for such process interfaces in point-to-point communication.

2.1 Process interface types for point-to-point communications

We may consider point-to-point communication interfaces as consisting of a number of abstract communication ports, through which messages may be sent and received. We may distinguish two main types of interfaces depending on the way these ports are related and managed.

Fixed number of ports. This is the simplest interface type and has the same number of ports in all processes. Typical example is the interface of processes in a ring topology, where all processes have two such interface types for connecting to the previous and next processes, each having exactly one port (figure 1).

Variable number of ports. An interface type may involve a variable number of ports, which are managed in a semantically similar way. We may distinguish two cases. The first has a variable, but bounded number of ports. The number of ports in this case may be any number within a fixed range from 0 or 1 up to any number N. The interface of a process spawned from a component having such an interface type has a number of ports within the specified range. Typical example is the interface of processes is in a grid topology, where all processes have four such interface types, for North, South, East and West each having either none or one port (figure 1) depending on its position on the grid.

The second case of a variable number of ports has an unbounded number of ports. The number of ports in this case may be any number from 0 or 1 up to any number. Interface processes spawned from a component having such interface types have any number of ports. Typical example is the interface of a master process, which may have any number of slave processes (figure 1).

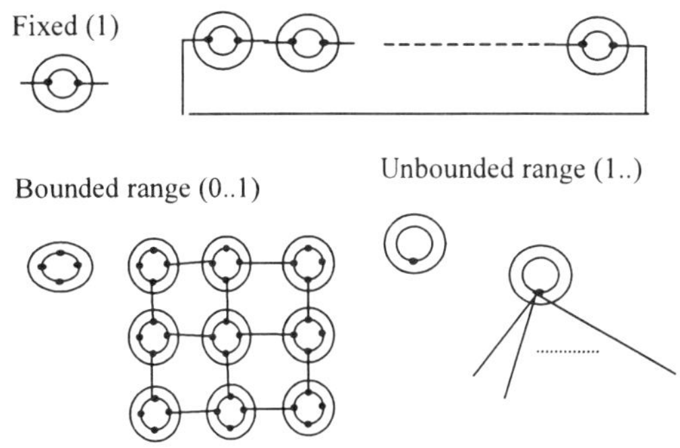

Fig. 1: The three process interface types exemplified in components used in regular topologies

2.2 Examples of partially regular or irregular topologies

The three process interface types have already been used in examples (fig. 1) of regular topologies. Let us now give some examples of processes having the same three interface types and construct locally or partially regular and irregular topologies.

Locally or partially regular topologies. There are topologies, which are not globally regular, but contain nevertheless regular topologies. We demonstrate such a topology by the application Get Maximum. The requirement is simple: Selector processes get an integer parameter and require the maximum of these integers.

We design the following solution, called Selector-Servers-in-Ring: Selectors are connected as client processes to some associated Server processes. Each Selector sends its integer parameter via its single port of interface type Out (type fixed to 1) to its associated Server and, eventually, receives the required maximum via its single port of interface type In (fixed to 1) from the same Server. Servers receive integer values via their Cin ports (unbounded type) from their client Selectors and find the local maximum. Servers are connected in a ring. They find the global maximum by sending via Pout port (fixed to 1) their current maximum to their next neighbour Server in the ring, receiving via Pin port (fixed to 1) a value from their previous Server neighbour, comparing and selecting the maximum of these two values. Servers repeat the send-receive-select cycle M-1 times, where M is the size of the ring. Finally, Servers send the global maximum via Cout ports (unbounded) to their client Selector processes. The topology or process communication graph (PCG) of the design is depicted in fig.2.

Note that Server processes have ports of two types of interfaces: Pin and Pout are fixed to 1 and are used to construct the ring of Servers, and Cin and Cout of the unbounded variable type, used to construct the client/server topologies with Selectors. The design is partially regular, as each Server is associated with its own Selectors by a regular server/client topology and Servers are associated in a regular ring topology.

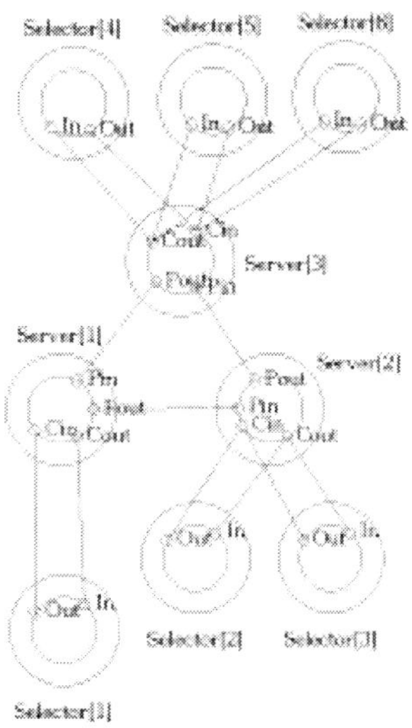

Fig. 2. The Selector and Server in a ring design

We may add to the design more Selectors to any Server by scaling the Server's interface accordingly and setting the appropriate channels. We may also add more Servers in the ring. Implementing reusable components for this type of topology involves the problems we noted in the introduction.

Irregular topologies. There are also topologies, which are completely irregular. For example, consider an implementation of a PDE solution by message passing, but partitioning data into irregular blocks (fig. 3), possibly for load balancing.

The process topology obtained by allocating these irregular blocks to processes is itself irregular (fig. 4). This type of topology is very difficult to implement. Certainly there are not general methodologies for constructing reusable executables in irregular of topologies.

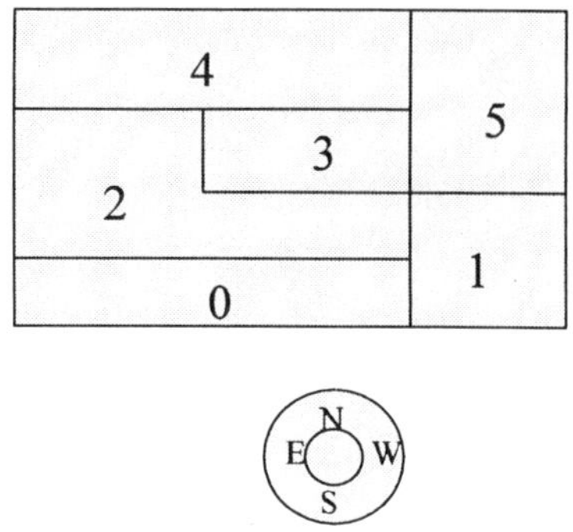

Fig. 3: Irregular partition and component

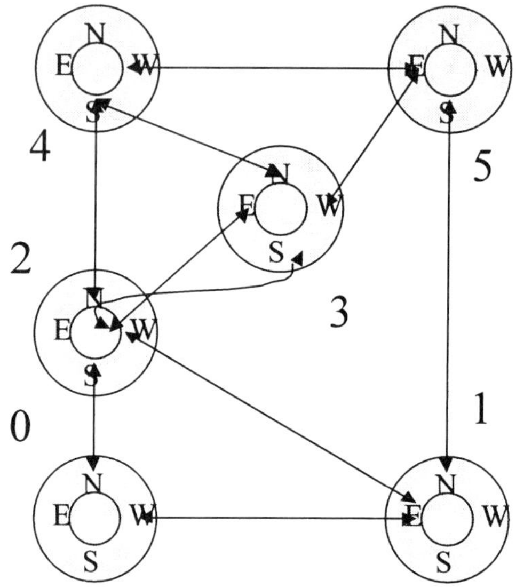

Fig. 4: Irregular topology with six processes

In this section we have demonstrated that, at least at the design level, we may construct process topologies with three generic interface types. In the sequel we will present the implementation of these interfaces and the construction of reusable components.

A topology is then composed in three simple steps: spawn processes, scale their interface if necessary and specify communication channels by setting port information.

3. Implementation of open process interfaces

In this section we implement open process interfaces (OPI) for point-to-point as well as for collective communications. The implementation will be on top of specific MPEs and in spite of their syntactic and semantic differences the OPIs may be applied to any MPE.

3.1 Point-to-point communications

The notion of a port is not explicit in message passing interfaces, but implicit because send and receive operations use process identifiers as parameters identifying the receiver and respectively the sender process. The notion of a communication channel is also conceptual and refers to the passing of a message from one process to another, as determined by the symmetric send/receive calls.

Single port and arrays of similar ports. We first make the notions of port and communication channel explicit. We consider a port as being a structure which holds information of the recipient or the sender process, used respectively by send and receive operations. In PVM3.3 for example, a port would be defined as a structure `struct port={int tid, msgtag;}`, which holds pairs of (tid, msgtag) the parameters denoting message destination in send and respectively, origin in receive operations. A channel between two ports p1 and p2 exists if : they belong to processes tid1 and tid2 respectively, they have a common msgtag, and the tid of p1 is tid2 and the tid of p2 is tid1 (i.e. p1.msgtag=p2.msgtag ^ p1.tid=tid2 ^ p2.tid=tid1). A port in PVM3.4 as well as in MPI would have an extra field for the context of the message (communicator in MPI) and a channel between two ports would additionally require that the ports have a common context.

Ports of the same type (such as the Cin and Cout ports of Server) form arrays, the number of which is a variable in general and has to be dynamically allocated. We define the structure

```
struct port_type
        {int portcount; port_struct *port;}
```

which is a header element with two fields, one for holding the actual number of ports (portcount) and a pointer to the actual array of ports of the process to which it belongs. Note that the above declaration is independent of any specific message passing interface. The differences are hidden in the declaration of a single port.

Structure of Ports and its use in point-to-point communication routines. Finally we define the complete interface as an array of port_types as

```
struct *port_type Interface;
```

Such port_types are associated with the interface types of components, e.g. Pin, Pout, Cin, Cout of Server and In, Out of Selector.

In the body of the components all send and receive operations in processes refer to ports, identified by the appropriate port type and the port index within the type. In PVM for example, tid and msgtag parameters of pvm_send and pvm_recv routines should refer to tid and msgtag of a port P of type T, i.e. Interface[T].port[P].tid and Interface[T].port[P].msgtag, respectively. Alternatively, we may hide pvm_send and pvm_recv calls within wrapper routines, i.e. `Wsend(T,P)`, `Wrecv(T,P)`, where T is an index to an element of Interface and P and index of a port within this element. With this convention sending to the i'th port of Cout may be written as `Wsend(Cout,i)`.

We have achieved developing message passing code without referring explicitly to processes, but to ports. Ports are virtual at compile time as they do not have any values. Also their actual number in each port type may be unspecified at compile time. This is what makes process interfaces open and scalable and the code that uses such interfaces reusable. In section 4 we explain how the number of ports and their values are set at run time.

3.2 Collective communications

We may apply the idea of defining point-to-point communication parameters in a virtual way to collective communications, namely barriers and groups. In the way we have given virtual names, namely port types, for specifying the parameters of point-to-point communication, we may also give virtual names to barriers and groups.

Single Barrier or Group and its use in collective communication. For a virtual barrier in PVM we only need the simple structure

```
struct barrier_type {char *group;}
```

and for a group the structure

```
struct group_type {char *group; int msgtag}
```

Each process spawned from the component will be able to participate in a barrier or group the actual name of which will be stored in `*group`. This way we distinguish between the fact that every process spawned from the same component should participate in a barrier or group, but each process may in principle participate in a different barrier or group. The name of the actual barrier or group and the msgtag must be provided dynamically at run time time. Consider the case of an SPMD application where the processes are spawned from the same component form a tree topology and we require that processes on each level of the tree use the same barrier. The component specifies that each process spawned from it participates in a barrier, but not any specific barrier and certainly not the same barrier. In principle, each process may participate in a different barrier.

3.3 General Interface Structure

The complete interface structure is declared as

```
struct *g_type Interface;
```

where `g_type` is a union structure of the three cases above

```
union g_type
  {  struct port_type;
     struct barrier_type;
     struct group_type;}
```

All barrier and group parameters of collective routine calls in the body of the components will refer to the corresponding element of the general interface structure. E.g. a PVM broadcast call will be

```
Info=pvm_bcast( Interface[T].group,
                Interface[T].msgtag)
```

and a barrier call will be

```
Info=pvm_barrier(Interface[T].group, count)
```

4. Implementation of Reusable Components

Reusable message passing components should only compute results and do not involve any process management or assume any topology in which they operate. If message passing routines in the code use the virtual interface ports, barriers and groups we constructed in the previous section they already have this property.

Of course we must pass information to the interface of each process upon its creation to establish the required process topology. We assume at this stage that the process topology is somehow specified externally. Many design tools such as Trapper [12], Grade [7,8], EDPEPPS [5], etc. provide features for specifying process topologies. We assume also that there is a "loader" program which interprets such topology designs and establishes the actual process topology in three steps: spawns processes in the topology, provides the actual number of ports of each port type of each process and finally provides values to ports, groups and barriers.

The aforementioned design tools do not make such clear distinction between the process as it looks from the outside (used to specify the process topology) and the code of the processes from inside. In other words they do not use reusable components. In section 5 we describe the Ensemble methodology, which makes this distinction clear, makes use of the reusable components and may be integrated in any of the design tools mentioned before.

4.1 Implementation of open interfaces

Looking components from inside, we need to implement two aspects to make them reusable: setting the number of ports of each interface type and set values for the fields of ports, barriers and groups.

Setting number of ports. As processes are spawned, the actual number of ports for each port type may be passed by the loader programme as command line parameters. The first procedure processes call is MakePorts, which reads these parameters and allocates space for the appropriate number of ports and sets the portcount field to the appropriate value for each port type in array Interface.

Setting Interface with communication parameters. Processes then get the values for the communication parameters for each port. Processes set actual values to their interface by executing a routine, called SetInterface. Each MPE requires its own implementation of the SetInterface routine. In MPI, as process identification (rank) is known at compile time, it is possible to pass it in their command line parameters. In PVM, where process identifiers tid are dynamically determined, it is not possible in general to pass to a process at the time of its spawning the tids of its neighbours, as these may have not been spawned yet. In PVM the "loader" program sends messages with the tids of the neighbouring processes as data. Symmetrically, the SetInterface receives these messages and updates the interface.

The Main Body of Reusable Components. Having constructed and set values to the interface the components may proceed with the application computations. A common Main for all program components, which may be seen below has been developed. The application computations for each component are coded in RealMain routine.

```
/* Common Main for all reusable components */
void main(argc,argv) int argc; char **argc;
{  MakePorts(Interface);
   SetInterface(Interface);
   RealMain(Interface,argc,argv);}
```

The programmer has only to write the RealMain routine.

4.2 Code parameterisation

Sometimes the number of messages sent or received depends on the size of the topology (local or global) a process belongs to. For example, for the servers of fig. 2 to operate correctly they must repeat the send-receive-select cycle M-1 times, where M is the size of the ring they belong to. These parameters are not application parameters, in the sense that they are not demanded by the requirements of the problem. They are introduced from the particular design of the solution, and for this reason are called design parameters. Since design parameters depend on the discrete topology size are always non-negative integers and may be passed as command line parameters to the spawned processes, together with any application parameters. The first action of `RealMain` routine is to read the design and application parameters.

4.3 Reusable components

We have now completed all the elements of the reusable components. The `RealMain` of the Selector and Server programs are outlined in fig. 5.

For convenience, we have abstracted PVM send and receive routines by using `send(T,P,What)` and respectively `receive(T,P,What)`, to indicate that message What is sent to, and respectively, received from port P of type T. The same wrapper routines may call MPI routines if the target MPE is MPI, thus hiding all differences and maintaining one source code of components for any MPE.

5. Composing message passing applications

We have used such reusable components in the Ensemble methodology and its tools for the design and implementation of message passing programs independent of any message passing environment. Ensemble specifies a common software architecture, which is depicted in figure 6, for all message passing programs on any MPE.

An application in Ensemble is an "ensemble" of reusable executable program components and of a script which specifies the application processes (to be spawned from the reusable program components), their topology (or Process Communication Graph-PCG) and the mapping of processes onto the virtual architecture. The programmer specifies the PCG and encodes the source programs (using abstract communication routines as in 4.3) independent of the target architecture and MPE. By compiling and linking with the appropriate libraries the reusable executables (within the specific architecture and MPE) are obtained. The programmer also specifies the resource allocation (mapping of processes to processors, data files, etc.)

Universal (within an MPE) tools, PCG-Builder, Annotator and the Loader program, interpret the script and compose the message passing application by spawning application processes and establishing their communication channels relieving the programmer of a complex task.

Ensemble has been applied [1,2,3,4] to compose applications in PVM, MPI and Parix, three very different MPEs; each requiring its own techniques for reusable components and its own loader program. Using the Ensemble methodology applications may be ported without much difficulty to other message passing environments and in certain cases automatically. Process Topologies or PCGs are either represented by the Ensemble script language or directly by GrEnT, a simple Graphical Ensemble Tool, demonstrating that it is possible to integrate the Ensemble methodology in existing graphical environments supporting the design, implementation and debugging of message passing programs.

The Ensemble script describing the topology of the design of Get maximum application is shown in fig. 7. The first section of the script headed by Components specifies the components to be used and their interface. The second section headed by Processes specifics the processes with the appropriate number of ports and values for their design parameters. The third section headed by Channels specifies port associations. The application parameters are specified under a separate section.

To demonstrate the reusability of the components we give another design to the same problem (fig. 8). We modify the topology into a tree. Server[1] and Server[2] have the same clients as in the previous design. Server[3] now has Selector[6] as its client but also Server[1] and Server[2], connected through their Pin and Pout ports. Server[3] has no connections to its Pin and Pout ports. Sever[1] and Server[2] receive values from their clients and find their local maximum; they send their local maxima to their Pout port, which is connected to a Cin port of Server[3]. Server[3] finds the global maximum, and as it is not connected in a ring, it does not perform any send-receive-select cycle over its Pin and Pout ports; it sends the global maximum to its clients. The two Server clients receive and select the global maximum and send it to their Selector clients.

Further information on Ensemble may be found on the Web site http://www.di.uoa.gr/~ensemble.

<table>
<tr>
<td>

```
        /* Selector Code */
#define In   0
#define Out  1



void RealMain(Interface,argc,argv)
   struct port_types *Interface;
   int argc; char **argv;
{  GetParams(N);
   send(Out,1,N);
   receive(In,1, Max);
}
```

</td>
<td>

```
                    /* Server Code */
#define Pin  0
#define Pout 1
#define Cin  2
#define Cout 3

void RealMain(Interface,argc,argv)
   struct port_types *Interface;
   int argc; char **argv;
{  GetParam(M);
   LMax=0;
   for (j=1;j<=Interface[Cin].PortCount;j++)
     {receive(Cin,j,V); if (V>LMax) Lmax=V; }
   Gmax=Lmax;
   for (i=1;i<=M-1;i++)
   { send(Pout,1,GMax);
     receive(Pin,1,V);
     if (V>GMax) Gmax=V}
   for (j=1;j<=Interface[Cin].PortCount;j++)
   Send(Cout,j,Gmax)}
```

</td>
</tr>
</table>

Fig. 5: The code of selector and server

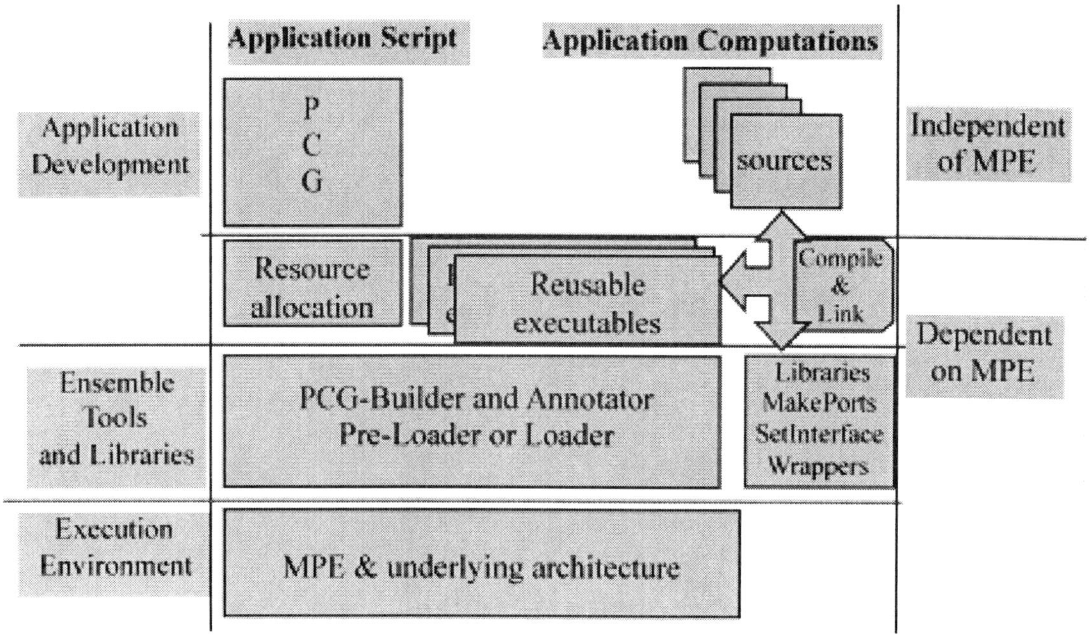

Fig. 6: The Ensemble software architecture

```
APPLICATION Get_Max_Selector_Servers_in_Ring;
  PCG
  Components
    Selector    range: In, Out [1..1]
    Server      range: Pin, Pout [0..1], Cin, Cout [0..]; DParams M;
  Processes
    Selector[1], Selector[2], Selector[3],
    Selector[4], Selector[5], Selector[6] #ports = In:1, Out:1;
    Server[1] #ports = Cout, Cin:1, Pout, Pin:1; DParams M=3;
    Server[2] #ports = Cout, Cin:2, Pout, Pin:1; DParams M=3;
    Server[3] #ports = Cout, Cin:3, Pout, Pin:1; DParams M=3;
  Channels
    Selector[1].Out[1] -> Server[1].Cin[1];    Server[1].Cout[1] -> Selector[1].In[1];
    Selector[2].Out[1] -> Server[2].Cin[1];    Server[2].Cout[1] -> Selector[2].In[1];
    Selector[3].Out[1] -> Server[2].Cin[2];    Server[2].Cout[2] -> Selector[3].In[1];
    Selector[4].Out[1] -> Server[3].Cin[1];    Server[3].Cout[1] -> Selector[4].In[1];
    Selector[5].Out[1] -> Server[3].Cin[2];    Server[3].Cout[2] -> Selector[5].In[1];
    Selector[6].Out[1] -> Server[3].Cin[3];    Server[3].Cout[3] -> Selector[6].In[1];

    Server[1].Pout[1] -> Server[2].Pin[1];
    Server[2].Pout[1] -> Server[3].Pin[1];
    Server[3].Pout[1] -> Server[1].Pin[1];
  ----------------------------------------------------------------
  APPLICATION PARAMETERS
    Selector[1]: "6"; Selector[2]:"999"; Selector[3]:"7";
    Selector[4]:"8"; Selector[5]:"9"; Selector[6]:"5";
```

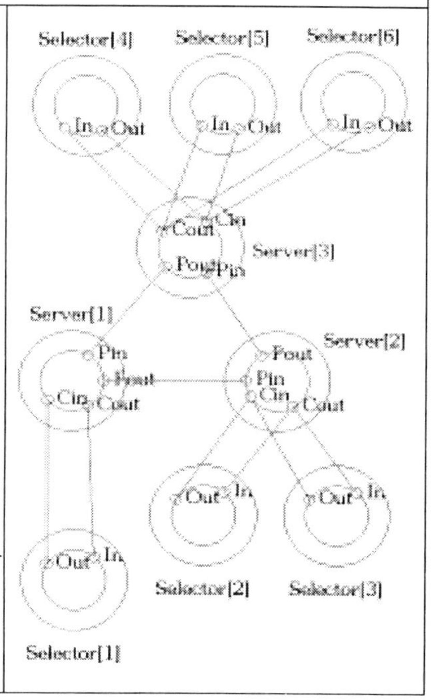

Fig. 7: The Ensemble script defining topology for the Selectors and Server in a Ring

APPLICATION Get_Max_Selector_Servers_in_Tree;

Components

```
Selector   range In[0..1], Out[0..1];
Server     range Pin,Pout[0..1], Cin, Cout[0..] DParams M;
```

Processes

```
Selector[1], Selector[2], Selector[3],
Selector[4], Selector[5], Selector[6] #ports In:1, Out:1;
Server[1] #ports Pin:1, Pout:1, Cin:2, Cout:2 DParams M=2;
Server[2] #ports Pin:1, Pout:1, Cin:3, Cout:3 DParams M=2;
Server[3] #ports Pin:0, Pout:0, Cin:3, Cout:3 DParams M=2;
```

Channels

```
Selector[1].Out -> Server[1].Cin;   Server[1].Cout -> Selector[1].In;
Selector[2].Out -> Server[1].Cin;   Server[1].Cout -> Selector[2].In;
Selector[3].Out -> Server[2].Cin;   Server[2].Cout -> Selector[3].In;
Selector[4].Out -> Server[2].Cin;   Server[2].Cout -> Selector[4].In;
Selector[5].Out -> Server[2].Cin;   Server[2].Cout -> Selector[5].In;
Selector[6].Out -> Server[3].Cin;   Server[3].Cout -> Selector[6].In;

Server[1].Pout -> Server[3].Cin;
Server[3].Cout -> Server[1].Pin
Server[2].Pout -> Server[3].Cin;
Server[3].Cout -> Server[2].Pin;
```

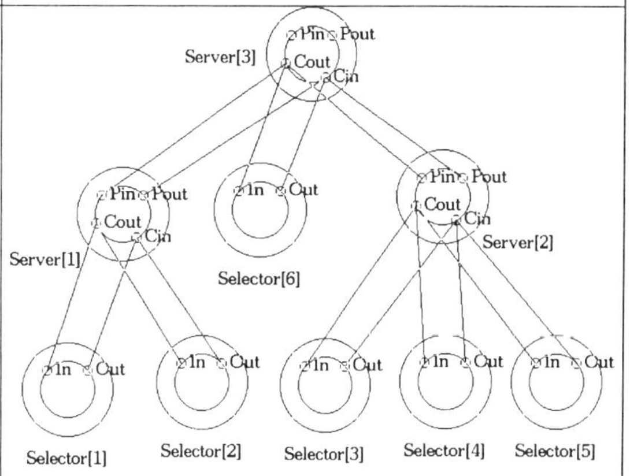

Fig. 8: The Ensemble script defining topology for Selectors and Server in a Tree

6. Conclusions

We have designed and implemented reusable message passing components, which do not rely on any specific topology. The reusable components have open and scalable interfaces, which may be used to compose and scale any topology, be it regular, irregular or locally regular.

We have demonstrated their reusability within the Ensemble methodology by implementing two designs of the Get Maximum problem, which reuse the Selector and Server components; it was sufficient to change only the topology of the application.

The reusable components and the Ensemble architecture may be integrated into any tools supporting the design, implementation and debugging of message passing applications.

7. References

[1] Cotronis, J.Y.: Efficient composition and automatic initialization of arbitrary structured PVM programs. IFIP Proceedings of the 1st Workshop on Software Engineering for Parallel and Distributed Systems, (held in association with ICSE 96), Berlin, March 1996.

[2] Cotronis, J.Y.:Efficient Program Composition on Parix by the Ensemble Methodology. In: Proc. 22nd Euromicro Conference 96, Computer Society Press, 1996.

[3] Cotronis, J.Y.: Message--Passing Program Development by Ensemble.In: Bubak, M., Dongarra, J. (eds.): Recent Advances in PVM and MPI. LNCS Vol. 1332, Springer--Verlag, Berlin Heidelberg New York (1997) 242—249

[4] Cotronis, J.Y.: Developing Message--Passing Applications on MPICH under Ensemble.In: Alexandrov, V., Dongarra, J. (eds.): Recent Advances in PVM and MPI. LNCS Vol. 1497, Springer--Verlag, Berlin Heidelberg New York (1998) 145—152

[5] Delaitre T., Zemerly MJ, Justo G R, Spies F and Winter S (1998): EDPEPPS: An Environment for Optimal Parallel Software Design,*Journal of Computers and Artificial Intelligence,* 17(5), pp. 405-416, 1998.

[6] Geist, A. , Beguelin, A. , Dongarra, J. , Jiang, W. , Manchek, R. , Sunderam, V.:PVM 3 User's guide and Reference Manual. ORNL/TM--12187, May 1994

[7] Kacsuk, P., Dózsa, G. and Fadgyas, T. (1996) Designing Parallel Programs by the Graphical Language GRAPNEL, *Microprocessing and Microprogramming,* 41, 625-643.

[8] Kacsuk, P., Dózsa, G., Fadgyas, T. and Lovas, R. (1998) The GRED Graphical Editor for the GRADE Parallel Program Development Environment, in *Proc. of HPCN98, International Conference on High-Performance Computing and Networking,* 728-737.

[9] Message Passing Interface Forum (1994) MPI: A Message Passing Interface Standard.

[10] Parsytec Computer Gmbh.:Report Parix 1.2 and 1.9 Software Documentation.1993

[11] Scheidler, C. and Schafers, L. (1993) Trapper: A graphical programming environment for industrial high-performance applications, *in Proc. of PARLE'93: Parallel Architectures and Languages Europe,* Munich, Germany.

An Efficient Algorithm for the Physical Mapping of Clustered Task Graphs onto Multiprocessor Architectures

Nectarios Koziris Michael Romesis
Panayiotis Tsanakas George Papakonstantinou

National Technical University of Athens
Dept. of Electrical and Computer Engineering
Computer Science Division
Computing Systems Laboratory
Zografou Campus, Zografou 15773, Greece
e-mail: {nkoziris, mromes}@cslab.ece.ntua.gr

Abstract

The most important issue in sequential program parallelisation is the efficient assignment of computations into different processing elements. In the past, too many approaches were devoted in efficient program parallelization considering various models for the parallel programs and the target architectures. The most widely used parallelism description model is the task graph model with precedence constraints. Nevertheless, as far as physical mapping of tasks onto parallel architectures is concerned, little research has given practical results. It is well known that the physical mapping problem is NP-hard in the strong sense, thus allowing only for heuristic approaches. Most researchers or tool programmers use exhaustive algorithms, or the classical method of simulated annealing. This paper presents an alternative approach onto the mapping problem. Given the graph of clustered tasks, and the graph of the target distributed architecture, our heuristic finds a mapping by first placing the highly communicative tasks on adjacent nodes of the processor network. Once these «backbone» tasks are mapped, there is no backtracking, thus achieving low complexity. Therefore, the remaining tasks are placed beginning from those close to the «backbone» tasks. The paper concludes with performance and comparison results which reveal the method's efficiency.

1. Introduction

In the last years the evolution in the fields of VLSI technology and computer networking has given raise to the utilization of distributed computing systems. Distributed computers are attractive to many demanding applications since they provide the user with modularity, scalability and low cost decentralized processing power. Nevertheless distributed computing has a sound drawback which discourages application developers to use it. The existence of many parallel processors is not fully exploited because of the interprocessor communication overhead. The degradation of optimal speedup when the number of processors increases is caused by the excessive sometimes amount of messages between non-neighboring cells.

Researchers have already focused on such low-performance problems and proposed various methodologies to the optimal parallelization of the given programs. Experience has shown that an effective solution to the general task graph scheduling problem onto a given architecture is a multistep approach which includes the task graph description of the problem, efficient scheduling of the tasks onto a virtual fully connected parallel machine, merging tasks into larger clusters and finally assigning clusters into the physical processor topology.

As far as the task graph scheduling with precedence constraints is concerned, the most widely used model is the directed acyclic graph with edges and nodes having various weights. Node weights represent computation time for the corresponding tasks, while edge weights are communication requirements between tasks. Each edge direction gives a set of precedence constraints which should be preserved. The general task graph scheduling problem with communication delays is NP-COMPLETE as presented in [9]. Sarkar [10], Gerasoulis and Yang [3] presented good heuristics for solving the task graph scheduling problem with arbitrary communication costs.

All previous researchers were supposing unbounded or bounded number of processors with CLIQUE topology.

This hypothetical topology is far away from the realistic case. Modern distributed memory parallel systems are organized in different topologies, including hypercube, mesh or ring architectures. There is a strong need for efficient placement of clustered tasks into the real processor network. The mapping of virtual into real topologies is called the physical mapping problem or the task allocation problem.

The task allocation problem can be optimally solved in special cases such as two-processor distributed systems, or linear array of any number of processors. If the target architecture contains two processors, then the task allocation problem is stated as a maximum flow minimum cut problem [11] which can be polynomially solved using, for example, the Ford-Fulkerson algorithm. There also exists a heuristic presented [7], which addresses the general m-processor problem using the 2-way min cut algorithm m times.

Most of the theoretical work on mappings considers structured graphs like grids, hypercubes, trees, etc [8]. An increasing number of applications demand methods dealing with irregular graphs. The general mapping problem is unfortunately NP-complete, thus allowing only for efficient heuristics.

Our paper deals with the intractable problem of cluster allocation onto parallel architectures, by proposing an alternative approach to the above mentioned methodologies. We model any target parallel architecture by a non-directed graph with unitary edge weights only. This representation retains the meaningful only details of the target. Next, the graph of tasks is depicted as a non-directed graph with various edge costs and node weights resulting from clustering heuristics as the one proposed by Gerasoulis in [3]. The task assignment procedure starts by tracing the clusters which are most likely to be placed in neighboring places, where the maximum number of links is available. This step ends by placing these backbone clusters into these places. For each of the backbone clusters, the algorithm creates sets of neighboring clusters which are candidate for placement into the adjacent cells of every preassigned backbone cluster. The algorithm ends when all clusters are assigned.

In the remainder of this paper the following are presented and further elaborated: Section II reviews the multistep approach of task graph scheduling with precedence constraints using a specific topology distributed architecture. Section III presents the proposed graph model for the parallel architecture and the utilized cost function for evaluating different physical mappings. In section IV we outline the steps of the proposed algorithm. Finally section V the proposed algorithm is compared to other approaches in terms of efficiency and the outperforming results are shown.

2. The Multistep Approach

The general scheduling problem of an arbitrary task graph with communication delays onto a fixed size and connection pattern distributed architecture is NP-COMPLETE. El-Rewini et H. Ali in [1], [2] proved this NP completeness by representing the problem of task allocation onto distributed system with a split graph. The task allocation is therefore equivalent to a weighted clique graph partitioning which is NP-COMPLETE, thus proving inherent intractability. In order to find efficient methods, researchers have followed a multistep approach, where each step addresses a limited instance of the general problem. The successive steps are outlined as follows: *task clustering*, *cluster merging* and *physical mapping*.

2.1. Task Clustering - Scheduling a task graph with communication delays onto a bounded/unbounded CLIQUE of processors.

First the task graph with computation/communication costs and precedence constraints is scheduled onto a fully connected network of processors. The classical CLIQUE architecture is therefore used as a target having limited or unlimited number of processors [4]. Researchers, in this first step, propose algorithms which minimize the maximum makespan, disregarding the actual processor's topology. Even when the makespan metric is to be minimized, the scheduling problem remains NP-COMPLETE in the majority of general cases. Papadimitriou et Yannakakis in [9] have proved that the classical scheduling problem of a task graph with arbitrary communication and computation times is NP-COMPLETE. They proposed a 2-optimal approximation algorithm. In addition to this, Sarkar in [10], Gerasoulis in [3] proposed faster heuristics with acceptable performance. All these algorithms perform the same initial step: Cluster the tasks into large nodes, so that the grain of the parallelism is increased and the use of distributed processors is minimizing the task graph makespan. The resulting topology, by applying this initial step is a graph of clusters. Inside every cluster there exist several tasks which are time scheduled in the same processor and have zero intracommunication overhead. As far as clusters intercommunication is concerned, this is the summation over all tasks intercommunication overhead for all clusters. This organises the set of tasks into clusters with the following property: Each cluster contains all tasks which are to be executed on the same processor. This step is called *task clustering*.

2.2. Cluster Merging into p physical clusters

In this step, the set of clustered tasks is mapped onto a clique of bounded number of processors. Since the set of clustered tasks is larger than the number of available processors, this step assigns two or more clusters to the same processor. Sarkar in [10] has proposed a scheduling heuristic with $O(|V|(|V|+|E|))$ complexity, where $|V|$ stands for the number of nodes and $|E|$ for the number of edges. A lower complexity heuristic which is used in PYRROS [12] is the work profiling method. It merges clusters which have approximately the same arithmetic load.

2.3. Physical Mapping of p physical clusters onto p network connected processors.

While so much effort has been done concerning the first steps, the final step of cluster allocation onto the physical processor topology has not given considerable attention. Few researchers such as Bokhari have presented some heuristics. Many scheduling tools which such as OREGAMI or PYRROS or PARALLAX use heuristics or approximation algorithms which are sometimes efficient. For example Gerasoulis et Yang in Pyrros [12] use Bokhari's heuristic which is based onto simulated annealing. This algorithm starts from an initial assignment, then performs a series of pairwise interchanges by reducing the cost function and stops after $O(p^3)$ steps.

In Oregami's [6] MAPPER, a tool for task allocation onto distributed architectures, a greedy heuristic is used, called the NN-Embed. It currently supports only mesh and hypercube processor networks thus limiting its potential use. Even in the case of those two architectures, it uses a rather simple method, by listing all edges in ascending order of their weights and assigning them to the processor's network edges.

2.4. The NN-Embed Algorithm

Given a task graph, it first constructs a list of all the edges in the graph, sorted by weight. The heuristic then traverses this list in linear time and for each edge, assign endpoints as follows:

- If both nodes have already been assigned, do nothing
- If only one node has been assigned, then assign the other node to the closest free processor
- If neither node has been assigned, randomly choose a free processor and assign one node to it and the other to its closest free neighbor.

The sorting step needs $O(|E|\log|E|)$ time, and the rest is $O(|E|)$. It is a fast heuristic, but it is limited to hypercube and mesh topologies.

Obviously, it has poor performance in many cases because it is based on single-edge adjacency, and it does not take into account any set of adjacent nodes. In Example 5, we apply both our method and the NN-Embed, and the outperforming results of the proposed heuristic are shown.

In PARALLAX [5], all task allocation heuristics assume fully connected networks of processors. Only the mapping heuristic considers arbitrary processor interconnection topology. It uses a modified list scheduling technique with priorities, by taking into account the communication delays. The node's priority in the list is its level.

In [8], Monien and Sudborough reviewed results on mapping specific task graphs into the most popular parallel architectures.

3. Graph Models

Our problem considers two graphs: The graph of virtual processors, or equivalently the graph of clustered tasks, defined as $G_c(V_c, E_c)$ and the graph of physical processors, defined as $G_p(V_p, E_p)$.

Definition 3.1: Consider two graphs and $G_w(V_w, E_w)$ where V is the set of nodes and E is the set of edges with $|V_w| = |V_p|$, we define the following function $F_m: V_w \rightarrow V_p$ as the physical mapping function :

$$\forall\, v_w, v_w' \in V_w \text{ with } (v_w, v_w') \in E_w,$$
$$\exists\, (F_m(v_w), F_m(v_w')) \in E_p$$

Let us define some topological parameters for the processor graph/network:

- *Hop* is the unit distance between any two directly connected processors in the network
- *Distance* between two processor nodes u and v is called the number of hops in the shortest path connecting u and v. *Distance* is represented by dist(u,v).

The following formula defines the cost function used to evaluate the different mappings:

Cost Function for a mapping F_m:

$$CF(F_m) = \sum_{(v_w, u_w) \in E_w} dist(F_m(v_w), F_m(u_w)) \times comm(v_w, u_w)$$

where:

- $dist(F_m(v_w), F_m(u_w))$ is the shortest path in the processor graph between the 2 processors-nodes where the tasks v_w and u_w are mapped.
- $comm(v_w, u_w)$ is the total communication cost between the tasks v_w, u_w

The following properties characterize the efficiency of a mapping from G_w to G_p:

Edge-dilation is the maximum distance in G_p an edge of G_w has to be routed. Formally:

Edge-congestion is the maximum number of edges from G_w routed via an arbitrary edge (or node) of G_p

In most theoretical works dealing with the physical mapping problem, minimizing edge dilation and edge congestion are the primary goals. Our objective is therefore to find the mapping F_m which minimizes CF_m, or formally:

Definition 3.2: A mapping F_m^{opt} with respect to Cost Function CF() is called optimal if:

$CF(F_m^{opt}) = \min \{ CF(F_m) \mid F_m \in MAP\}$,

where MAP is the set of all possible mappings

3.1. Example

Consider the G_c (V_c,E_c) with c_{ij} costs shown in figure 1, and the processor graph $G_p(V_p,E_p)$:

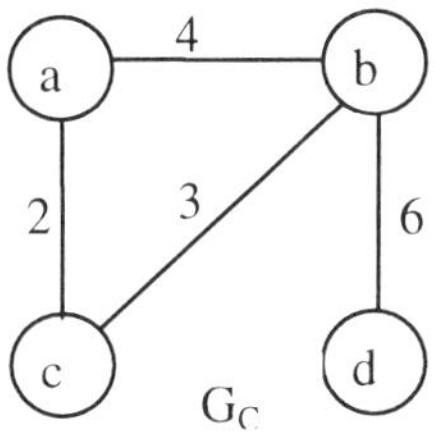

Figure 1. The Cluster Graph

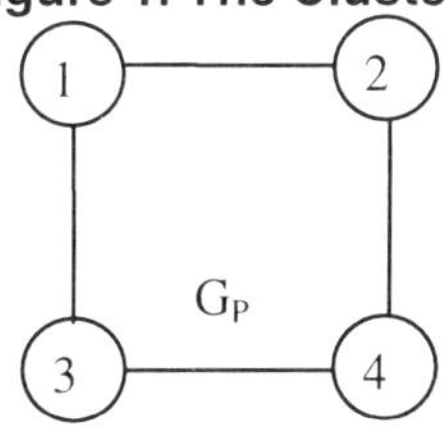

Figure 2 : The target architecture

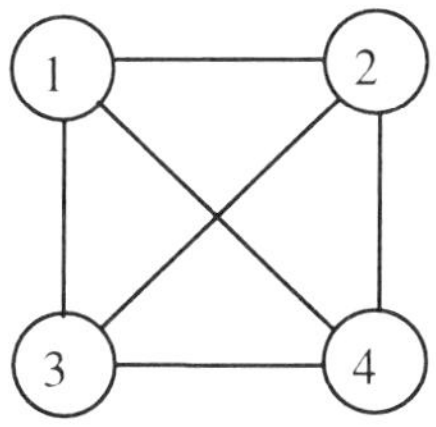

Figure 3: CLIQUE architecture

Obviously there exist 4! alternative mappings which can be found by exhaustive search. For example, consider the following alternative mappings and evaluate the corresponding cost function $CF_m()$:

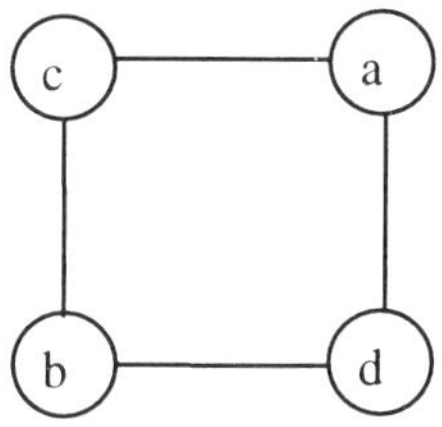

Figure 4: Mapping F_{M1}

$CF_{M1} = 2 + 4X2 + 6 + 3 = 19$

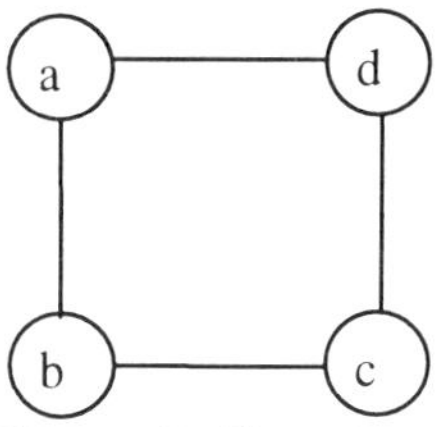

Figure 5: Mapping F_{M2}

$CF_{M2} = 4 + 2X2 + 3 + 6X2 = 21$

Obviously, F_{m1} is better than F_{m2} in terms of total completion time, since it imposes less communication overhead than F_{m2}. The least communication is achieved by mapping F_{m3} shown below:

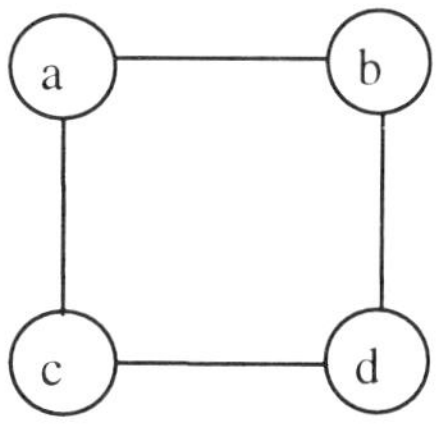

Figure 6: Optimal Mapping F_{M3}

$CF_{m3} = 2 + 4 + 6 + 2x3 = 18$

4. The Physical Mapping Algorithm (PMAP)

This heuristic tries to find the most communication intensive task-nodes and map them and their neighbors into neighboring processing nodes on the processor graph. At the beginning, the processor graph is analyzed and, for each node, the number of adjacent nodes is calculated. Subsequently, the nodes of the task graph are sorted by ascending order of their total communication weight and number of neighbors. The heuristic then places the most demanding task-nodes in terms of total communication links and cost to the respective nodes of the processor graph. Once these core task nodes are placed, there is no backtracking. Next, the heuristic places the adjacent of the core nodes to adjacent cells of the processor graph, by making locally best-fit comparisons.

The algorithm performs the following steps:

4.1. First Phase:

1st step: Adjust the maximum number of neighbors in the task-graph to the maximum number in the processor graph, by removing the less communication cost edges for each task-node.

2nd step: Sort the nodes of the processor graph by ascending order of their neighboring links and the nodes in the cluster graph G_c by the number of communication links they need.

3rd step: Assign the most demanding task-node to the best suitable node of the processor graph and his neighboring nodes to the best suitable neighboring nodes of the processor graph.

4.2. Second Phase:

4th step: Place back the edges removed at the first step.

5th step: From the processors not allocated yet find the one who neighbors with the most processors already assigned.

6th step: Find a task that is distanced by at most i (at the beginning i=1) from all the tasks that are mapped to the neighboring processors of the processor found on the previous step. If found assign this task to the processor of the 5th step.

7th step: Repeat steps 5-6 until no more assignments can be made. If there are more processors to be allocated, increase i by one and go back to the 5th step.

4.3. Details of the algorithm

```
1st Phase:
Adjust_neighbors(G_c);
Adj(v) = {u: (u,v) ∈ E_c}
/* Placement of the most communication costful node */
find v_c ∈ G_c : rank(v_c) = max rank(v)
find v_p ∈ G_p : rank(v_p) = max rank(v)
F_m(v_c) = v_p;
/* Placement of neigbors to neigboring cells */
  while Adj(v_p) ≠ ∅
      begin
            find v_ac : rank(v_ac) = max rank (v_a)
                        Adj(v_c) = Adj(v_c)-{v_ac}
            find v_ap : rank(v_ap) = max rank (v_p)
                        F_m(v_ac) = v_ap
            PROCS_ALLOC = PROCS_ALLOC ∪ {v_ap}
            PROCS_LEFT = PROCS_LEFT-{v_ap}
          TASKS_LEFT = TASKS_LEFT-{v_ac}
      end
2nd phase:
/* Placement of all other nodes */
Place_back_edges;
 i=1
while PROCS_LEFT ≠ ∅
            begin
                  assigning=false
                  for all u ∈ PROCS_LEFT
                     begin
                      find u ∈ |Adj(u)∩ PROCS_ALLOC| = max
                      NEIGH = { v_i: F_m (v_i) ∈ (Adj(u) ∩
                                 PROCS_ALLOC)}
                         /*set of tasks which have already been
                         assigned to neighboring procs*/
                     Adj(1,v_i)=Adj(v_i)
                     Adj(i,v_i)=Adj(i-1, v_i)∪
                                {u:(u,w)∈ E_C,w∈ Adj(i-1,v_i)}
                    let CAND=∩Adj(i,v_i)∩TASKS_LEFT
                  if CAND ≠ ∅
                           begin
                             find v_cand : rank(v_cand) = max rank (v),
                             v∈ CAND
                             F_m(u)=v_cand
                             PROCS_LEFT=PROCS_LEFT-{u};
                            PROCS_ALLOC =
                                   PROCS_ALLOC∪{u};
                            TASKS_LEFT = TASK_LEFT-{v_cand}
                            assigning=true
                           end
            end /* of for*/
            if assigning=false then i=i+1
            /* i increases when during the previous cycle there has been
no assignment */
end
Adjust_neighbors routine:
neigh_card=max |Adj(v)|, v ∈ G_p
For each v ∈ G_c : |Adj(v)| > neigh_card
            repeat
                  find u ∈ Adj(v): comm(v, u) = min comm(v, w) w∈
Adj(v)
                        Adj(v)=Adj(v)-u
            until       |Adj(v)| = neigh_card
end of for;
```

5. Example

Consider the G_c (V_c, E_c) with c_{ij} costs shown in figure 7, and the processor graph $G_p(V_p,E_p)$ in figure 8:

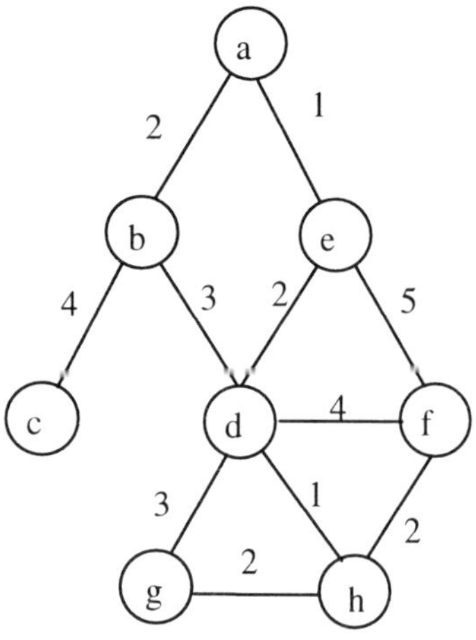

Figure 7: The Cluster Graph for Example

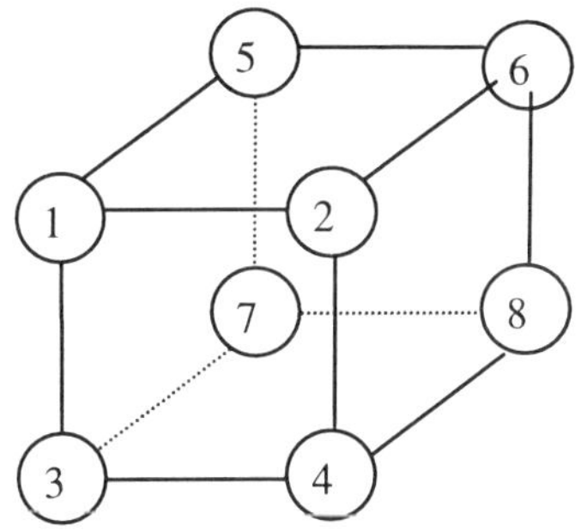

Figure 8: The target architecture for Example

5.1.First Phase

Since # of Neighbors of d > max Neigh we adjust the task graph by deleting edges : (d,h) = 1, (d, e) = 2.

Task	# of Neighbors	Total comm.	ranking
a	2	3	7
b	3	9	3
c	1	4	8
d	3	10	2
e	2	6	4
f	3	11	1
g	2	5	6
h	2	4	5

Table 1: Statsistics for the task graph

$V_p=1, V_c=f$
$F_m(f)=1$
Adj(f)={d, e, h }
$F_m(d)=2$
$F_m(e)=3$
$F_m(h)=5$

TASKS_LEFT={a,b,c,g}

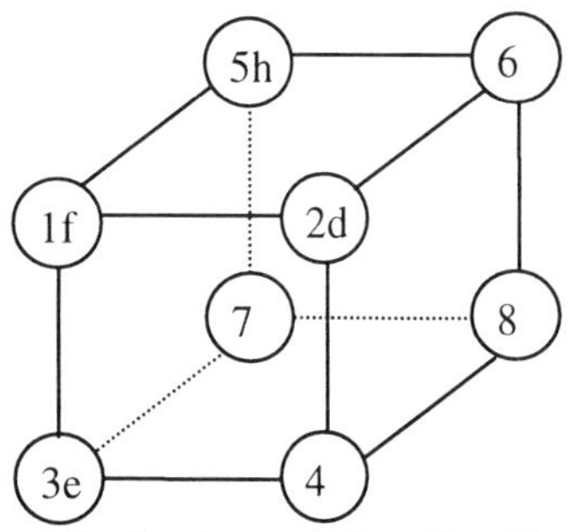

Figure 9: Assignments after the 1st phase

5.2 Second Phase:

insert back edges : (d,h)=1,(d,e)=2
<u>1st cycle i=1</u>
u_1=4, |Adj(4) ∩ *PROCS_ALLOC*|= 2
u_2=6, |Adj(6) ∩ *PROCS_ALLOC*|= 2
u_3=7, |Adj(7) ∩ *PROCS_ALLOC*|= 2
u_4=8, |Adj(8) ∩ *PROCS_ALLOC*|= 0
Let u = 4:
NEIGH = {d,e}
CAND=Adj(d)∩Adj(e)∩TASKS_LEFT=∅

Let u = 6:
NEIGH={d,h}
CAND=Adj(d)∩Adj(h)∩TASKS_LEFT={g}
$F_m(g)=6$
<u>2nd cycle i=1</u>
u_1=4, |Adj(4) ∩ *PROCS_ALLOC*|=2
u_2=7, |Adj(7) ∩ *PROCS_ALLOC*|=2
u_3=8, |Adj(8) ∩ *PROCS_ALLOC*|=1
Let u = 4:
NEIGH = {d,e}
CAND =Adj(d)∩Adj(e)∩TASKS_LEFT=∅
Let u = 7:
NEIGH = {h,e}
CAND=Adj(h)∩Adj(e)∩TASKS_LEFT=∅
Let u = 8:
NEIGH={g}
CAND=Adj(g)∩TASKS_LEFT=∅
No assignment during this cycle: i increases by one

<u>3rd cycle i=2</u>
u_1=4, |Adj(4) ∩ *PROCS_ALLOC*|=2
u_2=7, |Adj(7) ∩ *PROCS_ALLOC*|=2
u_3=8, |Adj(8) ∩ *PROCS_ALLOC*|=1
Let u = 4:
NEIGH = {d,e}
CAND = Adj(2,d) ∩ Adj(2,e) ∩ TASKS_LEFT = {b,a}
$F_m(b)=4$

<u>4th cycle i=2</u>
u_1=7, |Adj(7) ∩ *PROCS_ALLOC*|=2
u_2=8, |Adj(8) ∩ *PROCS_ALLOC*|=2
Let u = 7:
NEIGH = {h,e}
CAND=Adj(2,h)∩Adj(2,e)∩TASKS_LEFT = ∅
Let u = 8:
NEIGH= {b,g}
CAND=Adj(2,b)∩Adj(2,g)∩TASKS_LEFT = ∅
No assignment during this cycle: i increases by one

<u>5th cycle i=3</u>
u_1=7, |Adj(7)∩*PROCS_ALLOC*|=2
u_2=8, |Adj(8)∩*PROCS_ALLOC*|=2

Let u = 7:
NEIGH={h, e}
CAND=Adj(3,h)∩Adj(3,e)∩TASKS_LEFT={a,c}
$F_m(a)=7$
$F_m(c)=8$

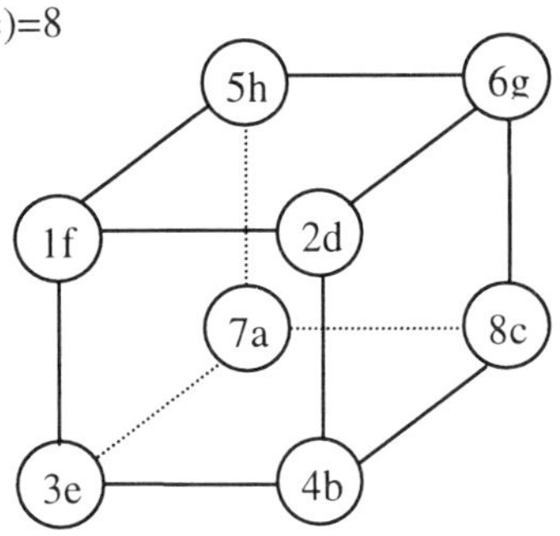

Figure 10: Assignments after the 2nd phase – PMAP result

5.3. NN-Embed algorithm

Sorting of Edges in descending order of their weight:

(e,f)	5	(a,b)	2
(c,b)	4	(d,e)	2
(d,f)	4	(g,h)	2
(b,d)	3	(h,f)	2
(g,d)	3		

Table 2: Weight of edges

Assign (e,f) edge to an arbitrary edge, e.g: $F_m(e)=1$, $F_m(f)=5$
Assign (c,b) edge to an arbitrary edge, e.g: $F_m(c)=2$, $F_m(b)=6$
Assign (d,f) edge: Since f is already assigned, assign d to the closest free neighbor: $F_m(d)=7$
All nodes of (b,d) are assigned.
Assign (g,d) edge: Since d is already assigned, assign g to the closest free neighbor: $F_m(g)=3$
Assign (b,a) edge: Since b is already assigned, assign a to the closest free neighbor: $F_m(a)=8$
All nodes of (e,d) are assigned.
Assign (g,h) edge: Since g is already assigned, assign h to the closest free neighbor: $F_m(h)=4$
All nodes of (h,f) are assigned.

The following table compares the performance of the algorithms for this example:

Algorithm	Cost
NN_embed	39
PMAP	34
Optimal	33

6. Performance Results

We report our experiments on the PMAP algorithm. For the sake of comparisons we have created a program which, given the task and the processor graphs, generates all possible mappings and calculates the total communication time based on the metric of section III. We have also created a random task graph generator with various communication-edge weights and number of tasks-nodes and a graph generator based on fixed topologies. We have also applied the PMAP heuristic and the NN_Embed heuristic on the same graph pairs. The results obtained are shown in the table below. We can see that the PMAP algorithm gives better results than the NN_Embed algorithm, especially when the task and processor graphs have fixed topologies. But even when the graphs have been randomly created PMAP outperforms NN-Embed by more than 10%.

Nodes	Task topology	Processor topology	PMAP vs. NN_Embed	optimal vs. NN_Embed
5-10	Random	Random	13%	26%
10-20	Random	Random	12%	-
20-40	Random	Random	11%	-
32	Ring	Mesh(8x4)	29%	-
32	Mesh(8x4)	Ring	28%	-
32	Mesh(8x4)	Mesh(8x4)	39%	-
32	Mesh(8x4)	Hypercube	10%	-
32	Hypercube	Mesh(8x4)	21%	-
10	Ring	Mesh(5x2)	32%	42%
10	Ring	Binary Tree	10%	20%
10	Mesh(5x2)	Ring	14%	24%
10	Mesh(5x2)	Mesh(5x2)	31%	42%
10	Binary Tree	Ring	20%	30%
10	Binary Tree	Mesh(5x2)	21%	33%

Table 3: Performance results

7. Related Work

There are not many systems which tackle with the problem of task allocation on specific target architectures, thus solving the physical mapping problem. PYRROS, developed by Yang and Gerasoulis, uses the heuristic of Bokhari which is based on simulation annealing. In OREGAMI [6] task allocation is performed in three steps: contraction of the task graph to a smaller graph, assignment of the contracted clusters of tasks to processors and finally routing of messages through the interconnection network to minimize contention. In OREGAMI, there exist canned algorithms for typical interconnection patterns concerning the target parallel architectures, which have been developed *a priori*. If the interconnection pattern is not in the above library, the NN-Embed greedy heuristic is used.

PARALLAX [5], is another scheduling tool which contains a task allocation heuristic assuming a specific interconnection topology for the target architecture.

8. Conclusion

In this paper a new approach was presented for the physical mapping of task graphs into parallel architectures having arbitrary interconnection topologies. It is obvious the general problem is intractable thus allowing only for efficient heuristics. The proposed algorithm has a low complexity and gives very good results for graphs with equilibrated communication loads between adjacent tasks. This new algorithm was implemented and tested, and the outperforming results were reported. Future work includes the introduction of additional criteria which would increase the heuristic's performance as far as non-counterbalanced graphs are concerned.

9. Acknowledgements

This research was supported in part by the Greek Secretariat of Research and Technology (GSRT) under a PENED 99/308 Project.

References

[1] H. Ali et H. El-Rewini. Task Allocation in Distributed Systems: A Split Graph Model. *Journal of Combinatorial Mathematics and Combinatorial Computing*, vol. 14, pp. 15-32, October 1993.

[2] H. El-Rewini, T. G. Lewis and H. Ali. *Task Scheduling in Parallel and Distributed Systems.* Prentice Hall, 1994.

[3] A. Gerasoulis and T. Yang. On the Granularity and Clustering of Directed Acyclic Task Graphs. *IEEE Trans. Parallel Distrib. Syst.*, vol. 4, no. 6, pp. 686-701, Jan. 1993.

[4] N. Koziris, G. Papakonstantinou and P. Tsanakas. Optimal Time and Efficient Space Free Scheduling for Nested Loops. *The Computer Journal, vol. 39, no 5, pp 439-448, 1996.*

[5] T. Lewis and Hesham El-Rewini. Parallax: A Tool for Parallel Program Scheduling. *IEEE Parallel & Distributed Technology*, vol. 1, no. 2, May 1993, pp 62-72.

[6] V. Lo, S. Rajopadhye, S. Gupta, D. Keldsen, M. Mohamed, B. Nitzberg, J. Telle and X. Zhong. OREGAMI: Tools for Mapping Parallel Computations to Parallel Architectures. *Int'l Journal of Parallel Programming*, vol. 20, no. 3, 1991, pp. 237-270.

[7] V. Lo. Heuristic Algorithms for Task Assignment in Distributed Systems. *IEEE Trans. Comput.*, vol. C-37, no. 11, pp. 1384-1397, Nov. 1988.

[8] B. Monien And H. Sudborough. Embedding one Interconnection Network in Another. *Computational Graph Theory, Springer-Verlag, Computing Supplement 7*, pp 257-282, 1990.

[9] C. H. Papadimitriou and M. Yannakakis. Toward an Architecture-Independent Analysis of Parallel Algorithms. *SIAM J. Comput.*, vol. 19, pp. 322-328, 1990.

[10] V. Sarkar. *Partitioning and Scheduling Parallel Programs for Execution on Multiprocessors.* Cambridge, MA: MIT Press, 1989.

[11] H. Stone. Multiprocessor Scheduling with the Aid of Network Flow Algorithms. *IEEE Trans. Soft. Engin.*, vol. SE-3, no. 1, pp. 85-93, Jul. 1977.

[12] T. Yang and A. Gerasoulis. PYRROS: Static Task Scheduling and Code Generation for Message Passing Multiprocessors. *Proc 6th Int'l Conf. Supercomputing (ICS92),* ACM Press, New York, N. Y., 1992, pp. 428-437.

Index of Authors

Allison, C. 77
Andronikos, T. 237
Aversa, R. 368
Baiardi, F. 309
Baraglia, R. 166
Beivide, R. 174
Bobbio, A. 325
Bode, A. 158
Botti, O. 325
Boudouvis, A. 56
Bramley, M. 77
Brégier, F. 275
Brzeziński, J. 220
Cagnard, P. 283
Cano, J. 293
Carmo, M. 376
Cassinari, F. 325
Castellano, J. 383
Cazorla, O. 383
Cérin, C. 357
Chen, Y. 190
Cláudio, A. 376
Cotronis, J. 398
Counilh, M. 275
Cunha, J. 376
Czech, Z. 343
De Florio, V. 325
Deconinck, G. 325
Dembiński, P. 62
Di Martino, B. 368
Di Napoli, C. 391
Doikov, N. 142
Donatelli, S. 325
Feil, M. 351
Ferrini, R. 166
Fink, T. 197
Folino, G. 259
Freund, R. 18
Furnari, M. 391
Gil, J. 293
Giordano, M. 391
Gonzalez, J. 244
Goscinski, A. 110
Gregorio, J. 174
Guerri, D. 309
Guinan, T. 142
Guirado, F. 229
Gurd, J. 101
Hensgen, D. 18
Hluchý, L. 205
Hobbs, M. 110
Hofmann, R. 10
Ibáñez, M. 43
Irvine, C. 18
Izu, C. 174
Jazayeri, M. 126
Justo, G. 28
Kidd, T. 18
Kim, J. 18
Kindermann, S. 197
Klauer, B. 150
Klein, A. 325
Koch, S. 92
Kowalik, S. 38
Koziris, N. 237, 406
Kufner, H. 325
Laforenza, D. 166
Lauwereins, R. 325
Lefèvre, L. 333
Lemmen, F. 10
Leon, C. 244
Leopold, C. 267

Levin, T. 18
Llorente, I. 48
Lugmayr, W. 126
Luque, E. 229
Luz, S. 67
Masoodian, M. 67
Mazzocca, N. 368
McKechan, D. 77
Messer, B. 135
Milazzo, A. 118
Montero, R. 48
Moore, R. 150
Mori, P. 309
Mukherjee, N. 101
Nabrzyski, J. 212
Nachiondo, T. 293
Nguyen, G. 205
O'Hare, G. 142
Palmerini, P. 166
Palyvos, J. 56
Papakonstantinou, G. 237, 406
Perego, R. 166
Piccoli, F. 244
Pont, A. 293, 301
Porter, N. 18
Prasanna, V. 18
Prellezo, J. 174
Prieto, M. 48
Printista, M. 244
Puente, V. 174
Pukacki, J. 212
Puliafito, A. 84
Reymann, O. 333
Ricci, L. 309
Riley, G. 101
Ripoll, A. 229
Rivas, R. 43
Roda, J. 244
Rodriguez, C. 244
Roig, C. 229
Roman, J. 275
Romesis, M. 406
Rowstron, A. 317
Sahuquillo, J. 293, 301
Saleh, A. 28
Sánchez, D. 383
Sande, F. 244
Sandkuhl, K. 135
Schikuta, E. 4
Schneider, G. 92
Senar, M. 229
Serrano, J. 77
Siegel, H. 18
Silcock, J. 110
Spezzano, G. 259
Spyropoulos, A. 56
St. John, D. 18
Stockinger, K. 4
Stroiński, M. 212
Suárez, Á. 383
Sunderam, V. 158
Szczerbiński, Z. 38
Tambouris, E. 182
Thurner, E. 325
Tirado, F. 48
Tomarchio, O. 84
Tran, V. 205
Tsanakas, P. 237, 406
Uhl, A. 351
Van Santen, P. 182
Verhulst, E. 325
Villano, U. 368
Vitobello, F. 391
Waldschmidt, K. 150
Wawrzyniak, D. 220
Zavanella, A. 118
Zoraja, I. 158

Notes

IEEE COMPUTER SOCIETY

Press Activities Board

IEEE Computer Society Publications

The world-renowned IEEE Computer Society publishes, promotes, and distributes a wide variety of authoritative computer science and engineering texts. These books are available from most retail outlets. Visit the Online Catalog, *http://computer.org*, for a list of products.

IEEE Computer Society Proceedings

The IEEE Computer Society also produces and actively promotes the proceedings of more than 141 acclaimed international conferences each year in multimedia formats that include hard and softcover books, CD-ROMs, videos, and on-line publications.

For information on the IEEE Computer Society proceedings, send e-mail to *cs.books@computer.org* or write to Proceedings, IEEE Computer Society, P.O. Box 3014, 10662 Los Vaqueros Circle, Los Alamitos, CA 90720-1314. Telephone +1 714-821-8380. FAX +1 714-761-1784.

Additional information regarding the Computer Society, conferences and proceedings, CD-ROMs, videos, and books can also be accessed from our web site at *http://computer.org/cspress*

Revised 9 November 1999